UNIVERSITY OF ST. THOMAS LIBRARIES

WITHDRAWN
UST
Libraries

The Troublesome Legacy of Commissioner Lin

The Opium Trade and Opium Suppression in Fujian Province, 1820s to 1920s

Harvard East Asian Monographs 227

The Troublesome Legacy of Commissioner Lin

*The Opium Trade and Opium Suppression
in Fujian Province, 1820s to 1920s*

Joyce A. Madancy

Published by the Harvard University Asia Center
and distributed by Harvard University Press
Cambridge (Massachusetts) and London 2003

© 2003 by the President and Fellows of Harvard College

Printed in the United States of America

The Harvard University Asia Center publishes a monograph series and, in coordination with the Fairbank Center for East Asian Research, the Korea Institute, the Reischauer Institute of Japanese Studies, and other faculties and institutes, administers research projects designed to further scholarly understanding of China, Japan, Vietnam, Korea, and other Asian countries. The Center also sponsors projects addressing multidisciplinary and regional issues in Asia.

Library of Congress Cataloging-in-Publication Data

Madancy, Joyce A.

The troublesome legacy of Commissioner Lin : the opium trade and opium suppression in Fujian Province, 1820s to 1920s / Joyce A. Madancy.

    p. cm. -- (Harvard East Asian monographs ; 227)

Includes bibliographical references and index.

ISBN 0-674-01215-1 (cloth : alk. paper)

1. Opium trade--China--Fujian Sheng--History.   2. Opium habit--China--Fujian Sheng--Prevention--History.   3. Narcotics, Control of--China--Fujian Sheng--History.   4. Lin, Zexu, 1785–1850.   I. Title. II. Series.

HV5840.C62M33 2003

362.29'3'095124509033--dc22

2003019710

Index by the author

♾ Printed on acid-free paper

Last figure below indicates year of this printing

13 12 11 10 09 08 07 06 05 04 03

To Jack, Kevin, and Maya,
who endured the good days and the bad
with more patience and love than
I know how to repay

Acknowledgments

This project has been so long in the making and the help that has been rendered so extensive that I hesitate to acknowledge particular individuals for fear of neglecting others. Among the many scholars who have aided my work immeasurably are fellow devotees of the opium question such as Alan Baumler, Carol Benedict, Lucien Bianco, Timothy Brook, Paul Howard, Lin Man-houng, and Bob Wakabayashi. All of them have been extraordinarily generous with time, sources, and advice. Others, such as Steve Averill, Mary Rankin, Vera Schwarz, and Tim Brook, cheerfully read and lent their advice on pieces of the manuscript. My incomparable colleagues and friends at Union College, particularly Ted Gilman, Hyungji Park, Andy Foroughi, Lori Marso, Teresa Meade, Bruce Reynolds, Megan Ferry, Feng Jianping, Bob Wells, Steve Sargent, and Jane Earley, also lent their counsel and encouragement. Paul Halliday, Sarah Henry, and Mark Walker actually read parts of the draft and made valuable suggestions. Jon Sterngass contributed a never-ending stream of valuable references on opium use in the United States and Europe. I found a treasure one summer in Union student Xie Jiandong, whose meticulous translations helped me skim a number of Chinese documents. The librarians at Union's Schaffer Library, especially Mary Cahill, cheerfully and rapidly complied with my many interlibrary loan requests. The Union Humanities Fund for Faculty Development graciously awarded me a grant to cover the cost of reproducing many of the illustrations, and the Union administration and History department allowed me to take a junior sabbatical to travel to China. Deans Christie Sorum and Charlotte Borst have been unfailingly supportive. A grant from the ACLS and the Chiang Ching-kuo Foundation funded dissertation research in Taiwan, France, and England, and a Center for Chinese Studies grant from the University of Michigan enabled a quick trip to Beijing. A post-doctoral research grant funded by the Committee on Scholarly Communication with China and administered by the ACLS supported my research in Fuzhou.

An earlier version of Chapter 8 appeared in an article entitled "Revolution, Religion and the Poppy: Opium and the Rebellion of the 'Sixteenth Emperor' in Early Republican China," published in *Republican China* [now *Twentieth-Century China*], 21, no. 1 (Nov. 1995): 1–41. Portions of Chapters 1, 2, and 8 appeared in an article entitled "Unearthing Popular Attitudes Toward the Opium Trade and Opium Suppression in Late Qing and Early Republican Fujian," published in *Modern China*, 27, no. 4 (Oct. 2001): 436–83. My thanks to those publications and their editors for permission to use that material here.

None of this would have been possible without the guidance and moral support of Ernest P. Young and Albert Feuerwerker at the University of Michigan. The camaraderie and advice of many fellow graduate students from long ago such as Diane Scherer, Tom Buoye, Li Danke, Anne Gorsuch, Wang Jianwei, Bruce Dickson, Benita Wong, Terry Bodenhorn, Scott Wong, Carrie Waara, David Shambaugh, Terre Fisher, David Aiken, and especially Judy Wyman have made a lengthy process more enlightening and enjoyable.

Thanks, too, to the many scholars, librarians, and archivists in the United States, England, France, Hong Kong, Taiwan, Beijing, and Fuzhou who helped locate elusive sources. In Fuzhou, invaluable help was given me by Liu Huiyu and Zhou Yongjun at Fujian Normal University and Lin Yongxiang at the Provincial Library. Grant Alger showed me the ropes at the Provincial Library and helped me retain my sanity in the face of Fuzhou's sweltering temperatures and a particularly vile archives attendant. Ryan Dunch's generous photocopying of opium-related documents and his meticulous notes made my research foray to Fuzhou extremely productive, and his work remains a model of scholarly achievement for me. Edward Rhoads generously shared notes that helped clarify some of the finer points in Chapter 5. Thanks to Milton Gustafson of the National Archives. Dale Patterson and Mark Shenise proffered invaluable support in locating documents and photographs at the Methodist Archives. Thanks also to the two anonymous readers for the Harvard University Asia Center; their comments have made this a much better book. All errors are my responsibility. My mother, R. LaVerne Madancy, took me "behind the scenes" at the Smithsonian storage facility, and she and my father provided consistent encouragement and incentive for me to finish each time they asked: "Isn't that book done yet?"

Finally, this volume could not exist without the unfailing support provided by my long-suffering husband, Jack Kennedy, the only person alive more anxious to have this project completed than myself, and the pleasant distractions offered by our wonderful children, Kevin and Maya. It is to them that all of my work is gratefully dedicated.

J.A.M.

Contents

Tables, Maps, and Figures	xi
Preface	xiii

1 Commerce, Compulsion, and Control   1
State, Society, and a New Public Space 8/ Opium in Rhetoric and Reality: A Historiographical Caveat 17/ Structure of the Volume 23/ "Portable Ecstasies" 28/ Setting the Analytical Stage 37

2 Constructing Fujian's Opium Economy, 1820s–1906   42
The Setting 44/ The Supply Side: Clandestine Commerce and Taxable Vice 48/ "Can You Hear the Poppies Sing?" 62/ Morality, Money, and Demand 78/ Opium in Fujian on the Eve of Suppression 92

3 Ambitious Interlude, 1906–1910   96
The View from Fujian 98/ The Framework of Opium Reform in Fujian 103/ Opium Reform and the Public Sphere, 1906–1910 120/ The Provincial Assembly and the Deliberate Dismantling of the Public Sphere 133/ Opium and Conflicting Loyalties 141

4 Provincial Patterns of Reform Before the Revolution of 1911   144
Opium Suppression in the Northwest 149/ Opium Suppression in the Northeast 154/ Opium Suppression in the Southeast 164/ Opium Suppression in the Southwest 171/ Glimpses of Reform Across the Province 177

5 Tartars, Treaties, and Turmoil — 182
Tartars: Opium and the Fuzhou Banner Garrison 185/ Revolutionary Rumblings 198/ The Treaty: Opium and the British Factor on the Eve of Revolution 202/ Revolution in Fuzhou and the End of Manchu Rule 211/ A Pivotal Year 217

6 Opium Reform Under the Republic, 1912–1914 — 220
Opium and the Military 222/ Opium, the Public Sphere, and Imperialism 226/ Opium Reform Outside Fuzhou 238/ The Joint Inspections 253/ The Closure of Fujian 261/ The Beginning of the End 264

7 Race, Religion, and Reform — 266
Protestant Missionaries and Opium in Fujian 268/ Missionary Motivations 273/ Missionary Involvement in Fujian's Anti-Opium Campaign 288/ The Impact of Missionary Activism 298

8 Huang Lian's Revolt and the Politics of Prohibition — 302
Context for Rebellion 304/ Huang Lian's Revolt 314/ A Rancorous Resolution 329/ The Politics of Reform and Revolution 333

9 The Collapse of the Crusade, 1914–1927 — 339
Opium and China's New Reality 342/ Opium in Fujian, 1914–1917 345/ Civil War, Unification, and Opium 349/ Opium and the Public Sphere, 1914–1927 357/ The Ignominious End of the Crusade 369

Epilogue: The Challenge of Narcotics Control in China — 373

Reference Matter

Character List — 391

Bibliography — 397

Index — 419

Tables, Maps, and Figures

Tables

2.1	Estimated poppy production in China, ca. 1906	64
2.2	Estimated production of domestic opium in South Fujian, 1902 and 1903	74
2.3	Registered smokers in three cities of Funing prefecture, ca. 1910	83
7.1	Missionaries in Fujian, ca. 1905 and 1914	270

Maps

4.1	Northwestern region	150
4.2	Northeastern region	155
4.3	Southeastern region	165
4.4	Southwestern region	172

Figures

1.1	Burning of opium paraphernalia, Fuzhou, ca. 1908	xviii
1.2	Inside a Chinese opium den	35
1.3	Statue of Lin Zexu, New York City	41
2.1	Main road from Fuzhou to Yanping	46
2.2	Early twentieth-century panorama of Fuzhou	47
2.3	Indian opium imports to China, Fuzhou, and Xiamen, 1863–1906	55
3.1	Cartoon from *The Quarterly*	119

4.1	Gutian pipe burning	160
4.2	Missionaries and local dignitaries after a Gutian public pipe burning	161
5.1	Fujian military governor Sun Daoren and Sun Yatsen	212
7.1	Missionaries traveling in style in Fujian	272
7.2	Visit to a Chinese opium den in New York	280
7.3	Etching from the *Police Gazette*	281
7.4	"Opium victims"	285
8.1	Chinese pastor and his flock near Xinghua	307
8.2	Sun Daoren, Bishop Bashford, and other Methodist missionaries	318
8.3	Negotiations with Huang Lian	328
10.1	Statue of Lin Zexu at his birthplace in Fuzhou	384

PREFACE

State and Society in China: A Cautionary Tale

Before embarking on the complex story of opium and opium suppression in late Qing and early Republican China, I preface that analysis with an anecdote designed to remind those of us who seek to analyze the relationship between state and society in China of the pitfalls inherent in that quest.

The setting was Fuzhou, the capital city of Fujian province, in June 1999, a particularly steamy summer evening. I was in the process of sifting archives and libraries for many of the documents that inform this study. As my companions and I approached our favorite restaurant—a small, private establishment nestled along the walled alleys surrounding Fujian Teachers University and distinguishable from so many others like it only by its exceptionally amiable proprietors and consistently delectable cuisine—we noticed unusual activity outside the sliding glass doors that served as the restaurant's storefront. A new regulation had come down from the government sanitation office (whether from Beijing or Fuzhou was unclear from conversations with the owners) mandating the purchase and installation of a heavy curtain of clear plastic blinds through which customers would pass to enter streetside restaurants. The blinds were designed to allow customers inside the restaurants to see the street while being protected from the dust and insects outside.

As we waited outside for the installation to be completed, the restaurant owner grumbled about sanitation inspections, regulations in general, and the cost of this one in particular, while his wife bemoaned the altered appearance of her business. When the curtain had been hung and the inspectors departed, we were politely invited inside and seated. It did not take long to discover that one of the unanticipated side effects of blocking the entrance of a small restaurant without air conditioning was to cut off any hope of air circulation and to trap its inhabitants inside a sauna fueled by the heat of the kitchen and their own bodies. Grasping the situation immediately, the proprietors quickly gathered up the curtain and tied it back, producing a far more pleasant dining experience and totally negating the intended purpose of the curtain. As we strolled the city streets after a satisfying meal, we discovered that every streetside restaurant we passed—small and large—sported the same government-mandated curtain, and every establishment had found a way to tie it back.

Now, was this little incident evidence of the ability of the Chinese state to impose its will on the residents of Fuzhou? Most certainly, since all the restaurants complied by installing the curtains on the designated date, despite their reservations about the effectiveness, cost, and appearance of the measure. But could we not also view it as evidence of the power of China's public sphere to reinterpret those regulations and implement them only to the extent to which they do not detract from the business of making a living? Here, too, the answer must be affirmative, for although the restaurant owners were unable to avoid the monetary outlay required by the government, they saved their businesses by effectively contravening the intention of the state and mitigating the unintended ramifications.

So, was the campaign effective? Again, this depends on one's perspective. Although the desired improvements in restaurant sanitation most certainly were thwarted, it is clear that, first, the state keeps careful records on the vast array of private enterprises; and, second, it wields considerable power over these new entrepreneurs. Obviously, they must conform to certain standards if they wish to remain in business. A more cynical view might be that the state cared more for the revenue generated by this measure than its effect on sanitary conditions. We witnessed no follow-up inspections to correct the sidestepping of the regulation.

Such is the conundrum encountered by historians and social scientists seeking to divine the "truth" of the balance of power between state and society at any point in time in China. This anecdote has particular relevance for the discussion that follows. Like the saga of the restaurant curtains, the attempt of the Chinese state to eliminate China's opium problem also generated a conflict between the ostensible desire of the state to safeguard public health and the considerable cost of this campaign for the public, financially as well as in terms of the increased regulatory presence of the state.

The Troublesome Legacy of Commissioner Lin

The Opium Trade and Opium Suppression

in Fujian Province, 1820s to 1920s

Fig. 1.1 A curious crowd gathers behind barricades at the burning of confiscated opium pipes and other smoking equipment in Fuzhou in 1908 (courtesy United Methodist Archives, Drew University, Madison, New Jersey).

ONE

Commerce, Compulsion, and Control

In the stark black-and-white tableau opposite these words, the men, women, and children of Fuzhou gaze at metal cauldrons overflowing with confiscated opium pipes, opium lamps, and the drug itself, as the reformers who organized the event prepare to incinerate the contraband. It is the spring of 1908, and the bonfires about to be lit will constitute the climax of a noisy parade and mass demonstration, an event full of music and speeches intended to impress, inspire, and educate the crowd. All across China, a very public crusade against opium was in full swing, and in Fujian, the provincial capital and treaty port of Fuzhou was center stage for the rallies and processions that punctuated the campaign. From our vantage point, we can only imagine the curiosity of the crowd as the parade wove through the alleys of Nantai suburb carrying the contraband, the sounds of the drums, gongs, and pipes of the band that accompanied the parade, the calls of the street-side vendors, and the cacophony of everyday life in late Qing China. Then, someone took a photograph, and the celebration was frozen in time.

Also frozen in time and virtually erased from memory in the century that has elapsed since that electrifying moment is what that celebration and others like it represented in the larger context of Chinese history. They were evidence of the most successful attempt undertaken by the Chinese state before 1949 to eliminate opium, the seductive narcotic blamed for despoiling the bodies, families, and economy of the Chinese empire. The Qing took a comprehensive and even modern approach to the challenge of eradicating Chinese dependence—combining the treatment of addicts with a gradual scheme to eliminate the foreign and domestic sources of the drug. The Chinese state presided over a surprisingly successful, nationwide attack on a pervasive problem, yet many historians describe the central state of that era as virtually powerless. This volume attempts to reconcile that apparent contradiction.

Perhaps this striking image provides some clues for solving this puzzle. Photographers capture a moment, it is true, but they also deliberately compose and frame their pictures. In this one, the contraband sits prominently in the foreground, and the crowd is slightly blurred in the background, as though almost an afterthought. For the American missionary who took this picture, the piles of drug paraphernalia probably seemed the most tangible and important evidence that attitudes were changing. However, for the Chinese reformers who organized the event and more politically savvy foreign observers, the presence of the large, diverse crowd illustrated that development even more clearly. In attendance at one such bonfire in Fuzhou in 1908 (perhaps this very event) was a French official who noted astutely that the need to appeal to—and hopefully mold—public opinion was an indication that the nature of political participation in China was changing.[1] Opium reform in the Qing, for example, was galvanized by unofficial, elite-led reform groups that operated outside the official bureaucracy but with explicit state sanction. This deliberate expansion of the political arena by the elite, along with their acquisition of extraordinary police powers, upset the traditional balance between state and society and unfolded in a new and very public space for political activism.

Opium suppression derived much of its momentum from what one scholar has called "the most enduring of China's modern revolutions, the quiet Xinzheng [New Policies] intellectual and institutional revolution."[2] The Qing court presided over a concerted push to reform the military, the legal system, education, and politics, a process that had a particularly profound effect on China's elite, the group that was to carry out and glean the greatest benefits from these changes. Opium reform was but one element of the sweeping attempt by the Qing dynasty to recast itself and Chinese society in a more modern mold. Opium suppression was a very visible manifestation of that spirit of reform and combined anti-imperialist sentiment with a zealous desire to strengthen the Chinese body, physically and metaphorically.

Opium pervaded foreign images of China; indeed the opium trade had in part motivated the imperialist aggression that consumed Chinese territory and sovereignty in the late nineteenth and early twentieth centuries. The

---

1. MAE/Paris, NS 587, Foutcheou to Paris, 3 July 1908, p. 103.
2. Reynolds, *China, 1898–1912*, p. 2.

smuggling of foreign opium, primarily from British India, sparked conflicts that destroyed China's traditional system for dealing with foreign commerce and forcibly opened China to the legal importation of opium and other commodities. The trade that flourished in the aftermath of legalization both revealed and created the enormous market for the drug, inspired Chinese farmers to plant their own poppies, and spawned networks for the importation, preparation, and distribution of opium that involved all levels of Chinese society. By the late nineteenth century, the Chinese government felt compelled to lift official prohibitions on opium cultivation, and tax revenues from the sale and transport of the imported and domestic drug helped prop up the Qing's precarious finances. Casual opium smoking became as common in many areas of China as social drinking in the western world, and opium dependence devastated individual Chinese and their families.

Opium generated strong feelings in China, and it was virtually impossible for opium reformers to approach their task objectively. By the early twentieth century, opium dependence had become synonymous with Qing China, and it seemed impossible that a Chinese crusade against this powerful narcotic would result in anything other than dramatic failure. Eliminating the use and sale of opium in China would require a strong commitment by China's central state and its extensive bureaucracy, the active support of local elites, the compliance—voluntary or coerced—of the country's sprawling population, and the willingness of foreign opium importers to eschew enormous profits.

So it was not surprising that on 20 September 1906, when the Qing government inaugurated a nationwide anti-opium campaign intended to eliminate China's drug problem within ten years, reaction within and outside China ranged from sympathetic skepticism to outright contempt. And yet, by the Revolution of 1911, opium consumption and poppy cultivation had diminished dramatically, and this progress convinced most cynics of the strength of the Qing government's commitment and its authority. During the early years of the new Republic, British opium imports to China ceased entirely, and most Chinese provinces were declared free of poppy cultivation. However, only a few years later, in 1916, the death of the Chinese president brought the end of central government control in China and the collapse of many of the mechanisms and motivations for opium suppression. Poppies flourished throughout the Chinese countryside once again, and the opium trade generated revenues that supported the military campaigns of Chinese warlords, Japanese imperialists, and Chinese patriots in both the Nationalist and Communist armies. Not until a strong central state was re-established under Mao Zedong and the Chinese Communist Party in 1949 was the opium problem attacked again in any systematic or successful fashion.

The significant, albeit temporary, progress achieved by China's late Qing/ early Republican anti-opium campaign is as yet a largely unexplained phenomenon. How these results were achieved, how that progress was squandered so rapidly, and why China's opium problem proved so tenacious are the questions that inspired this volume. The years 1906 to 1917, during which the campaign was conducted, encompassed the collapse of China's imperial order, the new Republic's unsuccessful struggle for legitimacy and control, and the beginnings of warlordism. And yet these were precisely the years during which China's central and provincial authorities, aided by reformist elites and seemingly supported by the bulk of the Chinese population, achieved a tenuous victory over this complex social problem. How was the Chinese government able to guide this systematic attack on a social problem so deeply intertwined with the Chinese economy at a time of political upheaval and instability? And how did the Chinese people, a large number of whom were involved with the drug trade either as cultivators, consumers, or distributors, feel about the drug and attempts to eliminate it? The late Qing/ early Republican anti-opium campaign relied on the control and oversight provided by a multilayered state bureaucracy, the activism and support of unofficial elite-led reform groups, the broad nationalistic and humanitarian appeal of the campaign, and the cooperation of the British government. The extent to which the Chinese state was able to control the pace and direction of the anti-opium campaign and the evolving nature of the political space in which elite reformers who publicized and enforced that campaign operated are the guiding themes of this analysis.

The chapters that follow outline developments affecting the consumption, cultivation, distribution, and suppression of opium throughout China but focus primarily on the opium economy in Fujian, a southeastern coastal province that attracted foreign opium smugglers and merchants and also supported a small domestic poppy crop. Fujian may be unique in the notable leadership role played by reformist elites in implementing the campaign as well as in the materials available to document their role, but it is typical in the way it reveals the strength of the late Qing and early Republican state. And because Fujian was an area in which domestic opium cultivation co-existed with a brisk trade in the foreign product, an analysis of opium reform in Fujian touches on all of the dimensions of the campaign, from local to international.

The appeal of Fujian province as the subject of scholarly scrutiny also derives from the compelling symbolism of Lin Zexu (1785–1850), its renowned native son and China's legendary anti-opium crusader. Despite Lin's role in igniting the Opium War of 1839–42, a conflict that led to a disastrous defeat for China and Lin's demotion and internal exile, continued imperialist aggression and the spread of opium consumption in China resulted in a reappraisal of Lin and his actions in the years following his death in 1850. Lin Zexu became a potent symbol of nascent Chinese nationalism and moral superiority throughout the empire and even among western reformers. In early twentieth-century Fujian, he also came to represent the vitality of elite activism and the complex links between provincial, national, and international interests. Lin Zexu's character and mission embodied the themes and motivations of Fujian's late Qing opium reformers—the righteousness of opium reform, pride in country and province, and a none-too-subtle slap at foreign imperialist greed. During the late Qing/early Republican anti-opium campaign in Fujian, reformist elites and officials presided over the apotheosis of Lin Zexu, whose image loomed, literally and figuratively, over their efforts and shaped the rhetoric and tone of suppression.

The power of Commissioner Lin's legacy was manifested most clearly in the selection of his great-grandson, Lin Bingzhang (ca. 1875–1923), as leader of Fujian's most prominent unofficial, voluntary reform group, the Fujian Anti-Opium Society (Fujian qudu she). The involvement of Lin Zexu's direct descendant in Fujian's battle against opium provided the crusade a sense of inherited mission. But whereas Lin Zexu fought the opium trade as an official with power vested in him by the Daoguang emperor, Lin's descendant operated in a realm where the boundaries were less distinct. Lin Bingzhang's active role in provincial and national opium reform represented continuity with the earlier struggle against both opium and foreign aggression, but his standing as leader of an influential but unofficial reform group made him a more complex example for fellow elites than his famous ancestor.

As activists devoted to reform within and outside the official arena, both Commissioner Lin and his great-grandson exemplified the evolving dilemma of the late Qing elite. Patriotic and altruistic concerns for the transformation of China's traditional society and the salvation of China's international reputation conflicted with more pragmatic elite attempts to shore up their tation conflicted with more pragmatic elite attempts to shore up their bases of power on the local and provincial levels as well as with the Qing strategy for self-preservation. Those conflicts were not always obvious initially. By participating in the anti-opium campaign initiated by the state, Lin Bingzhang and other prominent Fujianese elites found themselves able to regulate local society in ways they had probably never imagined. But they also discovered that as unofficial enforcers of state policy, they were bound by constraints that many of them came to view as unacceptable. Loyalties to province and nation collided with loyalties to the Qing, and by 1911, it was clear that the same international pressures that had made opium reform possible had also restricted the ability of the Qing state to respond to the momentum for further, faster provincial reform. That momentum had been fueled largely by the enthusiasm of elites like Lin Bingzhang.

After the revolution, however, the terms of an agreement with the British and the struggle of the new Republic to re-establish control over both the anti-opium campaign and the country in general worked to erode the influence of the unofficial Anti-Opium Society. At the same time, the heavy-handed but often superficial measures that characterized the postrevolutionary stages of the campaign foretold a slackening of effort after the established deadlines elapsed. As the central state fractured and the nation split into warlord regimes, the insatiable demands of regional military forces virtually erased all but the memory of the campaign's early victories, although elite-led reform groups continued to agitate for opium suppression. The earlier campaign had established a rhetorical norm in which anti-opium sentiment was assumed, but reformers who continued to agitate for suppression now had minimal influence on actual policy and they were increasingly separate from and sometimes in stark opposition to the state.

The dramatic story of China's rocky relationship with opium in the late Qing / early Republican era cannot adequately be explored within the chronological confines of the decade during which the anti-opium campaign unfolded. Construction of Fujian's opium economy began even before the late 1830s, when Lin Zexu's vigorous anti-opium measures in the Guangzhou (Canton) area once again spurred foreign merchants to shift and expand the illicit narcotics trade. Opium smugglers frequently visited northern Guangdong as well as Fujian and Zhejiang provinces as early as the 1820s and perhaps before. After China's defeat in the second Opium War (1856–60, also known as the *Arrow* War), the coastal treaty ports became a favorite destination for the now-legal drug trade. In Fujian, the influx of foreign opium over the next few decades coincided with the decline of the province's lucrative export tea trade, and by 1906, opium was deeply enmeshed with the socioeconomic fabric of the province. The staggering array of vested interests generated by this opium economy made the temporary progress of the anti-opium movement all the more impressive and its rapid demise less surprising.

This volume also follows the story beyond the controversial conclusion of the campaign up to the inauguration of the Nationalist regime in 1927. British opium imports to China ended in the first years of the Republic, and although diplomatic wrangling over the disposal of stocks of the drug in Shanghai and Hong Kong continued for several years, international leverage over Chinese opium policy diminished considerably and with it much of the urgency that propelled the earlier phase of the campaign. When Yuan Shikai (1859–1916), the first president of the Republic, died in 1916, only the semblance of central government control persisted until 1927. Local warlords looked to opium as a ready source of revenue, and Chinese leaders in this era faced the recurring dilemma of whether to enforce prohibitions on poppy cultivation and consumption or to exploit Chinese demand to establish, maintain, or enhance their own power. Some tried to do both by imposing exorbitant taxes on the poppy, ostensibly to eliminate the opium trade even as they profited from it.

This book is part of a small but growing number of works that have recently begun to recast the scholarly dialogue on opium by lifting it out of its long-standing home in the annals of diplomatic history and placing it firmly in the center of sociopolitical and literary analyses of Chinese history from the Opium War to 1949.[3] "In the last few years, the scholarly community has started to see opium as a more complex phenomenon with a multi-stranded history."[4] Opium has now become a lens through which we can examine state building, perceptions of social deviance and mechanisms for its control, and East-West interaction through medicine and religion, among

---

3. See, e.g., Brook and Wakabayashi, *Opium Regimes*; Slack, *Opium, State, and Society*; Zhou Yongming, *Anti-Drug Crusades in Twentieth-Century China*; Baumler, *Modern China and Opium*; McMahon, *The Fall of the God of Money*; Jiang and Shi, *Zhongguo jindu licheng*; Zheng Yangwen, "The Social Life of Opium"; Dikötter et al., "Narcotic Culture"; and Su Zhiliang, *Zhongguo dupin shi*.

4. Brook and Wakabayashi, "Introduction," in idem, *Opium Regimes*, p. 19.

other themes. Such analyses require rereading and reworking classic sources on opium to circumvent historiographical obstacles (see below), incorporate recently discovered materials, and use historical and literary theory to address "a topic that, until recently, most historians assumed was adequately understood and therefore of little interest."[5]

More specifically, the illumination of the long-ignored opium suppression campaign of the late Qing and early Republic offers an opportunity to explore some of the most controversial issues in Chinese history. Because the suppression campaign straddles the traditional divide of the Revolution of 1911, it allows the analysis to focus on the evolution of the state and elite power, as well as peasant dissatisfaction, during critical decades of change. The chapters that follow approach the conduct and course of China's anti-opium campaign as a measure of the strength of China's central state, the extension of elite influence over local society (and changes in that influence), and the evolution of a public space for political activism in which the relationship between the two was altered permanently.

State, Society, and a New Public Space

Understanding the Chinese state's ability to penetrate local society at this time of transition and its methods of doing so are clearly relevant to the analysis of opium reform. I argue that the central Chinese state established and enforced the chronology and content of the suppression campaign through the extension of the state's legal and moral authority inside and outside the formal bureaucracy. This framework specifically encouraged the involvement of reformist elites and initially gave provinces and localities the flexibility to respond to issues specific to their regions. The Chinese state is defined here as the network of officials that extended from the throne in Beijing to the highest provincial administrators in Fuzhou to local county magistrates and their petty functionaries throughout the countryside.[6] It is clear from this study of opium reform that this network remained a viable conduit for central government authority and suppression policies even during the

---

5. Ibid.

6. The term "network" can be somewhat deceiving, in that it can be read to imply a relatively well-defined chain of command. In terms of opium reform, this was often the case, given the confluence of state and local goals in the suppression campaign. In many cases, however, bureaucratic obstacles stymied the state's ability to operate as an effective multilevel network.

final years of the Qing dynasty and the formative years of Yuan Shikai's Republic. Only during the brief period when the Revolution of 1911 swept through China and the new Republican government was constituting itself did the links between localities, provinces, and the center weaken and then temporarily dissolve. From mid-1912 until Yuan Shikai's death, the network once again operated relatively efficiently, although when conflicts between Beijing and Fuzhou disrupted the chain of command, the continuity of the campaign was affected as well. During the warlord era, the campaign and the state itself often existed only in the realm of rhetoric.

A recognition that state power and authority are best measured by the state's ability to regulate local society is crucial to understanding how the opium suppression campaign can serve as a gauge of the strength of the Chinese state during the late Qing and early Republic.[7] The degree of regulation necessitated by the anti-opium campaign cannot be overemphasized. The formal apparatus of the central state was mobilized and augmented to implement opium prohibition, and provincial authorities were commanded to set up systematic means of enforcing the restrictions. In most areas, a census determined the extent of opium smoking and poppy cultivation, and efforts to control both were carefully monitored. Farmers were ordered to plant other crops, and smokers had to register for smoking licenses that rationed and gradually diminished their daily allowance of the drug. Officials and other moral exemplars were the first to submit to examinations and undergo treatment if dependence was discovered. Opium dens were shut down, and shops selling the drug were either closed or forced to purchase short-term licenses. Reform groups and the police had the power to raid private residences and businesses to uncover violations of the opium restrictions, and they used that power.

Measuring the growth and expansion of state power in the late Qing and early Republic by its regulatory reach should not, however, obscure or misconstrue the novelty and power of the role played by unofficial elite-led reform groups. The Fujian Anti-Opium Society and its many branches were not simply updated versions of traditional gentry charitable associations that addressed local needs. Their activities could be construed as taking "private responsibility for public functions," but that deceptively simple description obscures a real shift in the scope of elite power.[8] The actions of elite opium

---

7. Frederic Wakeman, Jr., in "Models of Historical Change," best articulates this theory.
8. Schoppa, *Chinese Elites and Political Change*, p. 4.

reformers differed clearly and fundamentally from the raising of monies to fund public welfare projects and shore up local infrastructure commonly expected of wealthy community leaders.[9] Unofficial reform groups like the Anti-Opium Society were key players in the process of modernization, the conceptualization of the political public, and the reconfiguration of the relationship between the provinces and the central state.

The central Chinese state, as well as provincial and municipal police forces, encouraged and sanctioned the Anti-Opium Society's acquisition of extensive and intrusive police powers. In many cases, it was the members of the Anti-Opium Society and its branches that raided suspected opium dens, staffed opium rationing and treatment centers, harassed foreign opium merchants, and reported officials who attempted to conceal their own consumption. Their participation embodied the clear linking of national, provincial, and local goals in this particular reform, and the state may have been willing to cede the society these extraordinary powers because of this confluence of missions. In fact, "as self-proclaimed representatives of society, the civic organizations [like the Anti-Opium Society] were actually complicit in a process to (re)invent the state."[10] However, that link with the state did not forestall the defection of most reformers from the ranks of Qing supporters in 1911, when many helped overturn the imperial system. Opium reform and the Anti-Opium Society survived the transition, but the irreversible changes that occurred over the next fifteen years in the composition and strength of the state and the hardening of boundaries between the state and society altered the course of opium reform and the nature of Chinese political participation.

What is the best way to view the evolving regulatory space in which the Fujian Anti-Opium Society and its branches performed their duties? Did it constitute what social theorist Jürgen Habermas termed a public sphere, and if it did, to what degree could it or should it be considered autonomous from the state?[11] The debate over the nature and existence of a public sphere in China has generated both a number of theories and heated debates. Some

---

9. The mobilization of native-place merchant groups in Shanghai to forestall resistance to opium suppression—at the request of a local official—is another instance of the state's willingness to permit temporary militarization to fulfill its mission (see Goodman, *Native Place, City, and Nation*, pp. 203–5).

10. Tsin, *Nation, Governance, and Modernity*, p. 32.

11. See Habermas, *The Structural Transformation of the Public Sphere*. William T. Rowe also provides an overview of the applicability of Habermas's ideas to a Chinese context in his seminal article "The Public Sphere in Modern China."

scholars, convinced of the weakness of the late Qing state, have argued that a public sphere emerged after the Taiping Rebellion when the gap left by a weakening state was filled by extra-bureaucratic bourgeois elites (gentry and merchants) who performed many of the functions that previously had been the state's responsibility. This process is said to have increased elite power and authority at the expense of the state. This concept of a public sphere envisions a space that existed in lieu of effective state control and authority.[12] Others have countered that the proliferation of extra-bureaucratic organizations—particularly those set up under the New Policy reforms—must be viewed as evidence of the expanding reach of the state.[13] Still others see no reason why a strong state precludes the emergence of a public sphere and contend that complete autonomy from or opposition to the state is not a necessary element in constituting a public sphere, a possibility that Habermas himself did not firmly exclude.[14] For example, Keith Schoppa posits a strong central state that co-opted elite initiatives because it recognized the benefits of elite-run reform institutions to the financially strapped government.[15] Yet another explanation that straddles these positions claims that the explosion of state-sponsored reform initiatives constituted a process of "state involution" wherein the late imperial and early Republican state successfully penetrated local society but did so through informal networks over which the state had little real control. In this scheme, extra-bureaucratic

---

12. The Taiping Rebellion (1850–64) was a plausible turning point since the Chinese state was compelled to delegate considerable military and administrative power to regional authorities during the conflict. Many scholars believe that the state never fully regained that power after this destructive conflict. For a masterful articulation of this process, see Rankin, *Elite Activism and Political Transformation*. This process was said to have continued into the Republican era; see Strand, *Rickshaw Beijing*.

13. Wakeman ("The Civil Society and Public Sphere Debate"; *Policing Shanghai*) defends this position, although his research focuses more directly on the expansion of the state through official new bureaucracies such as the police force. This is also the guiding theme of most work on Chinese civil society as it evolved after 1949. That literature attempts to situate the Tiananmen Square debacle in the broader process (as articulated by Habermas, *The Structural Transformation of the Public Sphere*) in which the development of true democracy is thwarted by an intrusive government and complicit mass media; see Brook and Frolic, *Civil Society in China*; Frolic, "The Emergence of Civil Society in China"; and White et al., *In Search of Civil Society*.

14. This ambiguity also existed in the European context. See, e.g., the essays in Calhoun, *Habermas and the Public Sphere*.

15. See Schoppa, *Chinese Elites and Political Change*.

elites acted as brokers between the state and ordinary people.[16] And finally, Philip Huang believes that a new space for activism did indeed emerge in China but has urged the use of the term "third realm" to avoid the Eurocentric, Habermasian connotations of the term "public sphere," around which many academic debates on the topic have revolved.[17]

The late Qing / early Republican anti-opium campaign does reveal the existence of a new space or realm in which reformers pursued their mission, ostensibly for the good of society. It was a rather amorphous space with fluid boundaries between state and society that recognized and incorporated the increasing power of both groups. True autonomy from the state at this stage of China's political evolution was impossible, given the strength of the ideological, socioeconomic, and occupational ties binding elites to the government. And in terms of opium reform, autonomy was undesirable. The permeability of this emerging public space allowed for greater participation by a new generation of elites as well as by more traditionally educated reformers who also may have served as officials in another arm of the bureaucracy. From the state's perspective, the participation of the latter did much to justify the granting of considerable power to the Anti-Opium Society. The hardening of the boundaries between government and society that began after 1911 and accelerated with the erosion of state power after 1916 set

---

16. This may well have been the case in Duara's study of *tankuan* collection (*Culture, Power, and the State*), but the opium suppression campaign operated on a different set of assumptions (and motivations) and therefore required extra-bureaucratic elites to remain more closely tied to the state.

17. An important part of the debate over the existence and nature of a Chinese public sphere concerns the feasibility and intellectual integrity of transplanting a concept specifically grounded in a particular historical moment in Europe to a society on a different social and political timeline. In "The Public Sphere in Modern China," the article that began this debate in Chinese studies, William Rowe bases much of his argument supporting the transplantation of this idea on the similar nuances of the Chinese term *gong* and the English word *public*. R. Bin Wong ("Great Expectations") refutes his comparison of those terms in an article that criticizes as Eurocentric the continued attempts of western scholars to view Chinese history through a western template. The publication in *Modern China* (April 1993) of principal papers from a symposium on the subject entitled " 'Public Sphere' / 'Civil Society' in China?" revealed some rethinking on the part of William Rowe ("The Problem of 'Civil Society'") and Mary Backus Rankin ("Some Observations"), the primary proponents of the idea of a relatively autonomous public sphere. In a critique of their work in that same issue, however, Frederic Wakeman, Jr. ("The Civil Society and Public Sphere Debate"), insists that a true public sphere must exist completely outside the regulatory grasp of the state. Philip C. C. Huang ("The Third Realm") concludes with his reasoned compromise terminology.

the stage for the more overtly oppositional politics of the May Fourth era. In some pre-revolutionary initiatives, notably the constitutional and railway recovery movements, the trend toward opposition was evident already, but in the context of opium reform, state and society clearly cooperated toward a common goal until the connection dissolved, along with the cohesion of the Republican state. Opium reformers were expected to turn in corrupt or incompetent officials and often did, but in general, although the two groups remained separate, they did cooperate and the state partially funded the work of the Anti-Opium Society.

I will argue that unofficial elite reform groups in Fujian's opium suppression campaign used the state's authority and support to legitimize their existence and expand their power well beyond that granted elites in traditional public service roles. They did indeed occupy a public space in which they were able to pursue a reformist agenda, even when provincial and national administrations lagged behind. But it was a space initially carved out as much by the force of the central state's moral and legal authority as by a nationalistic movement promoted and led by elites competing with local officials for social and political influence. However, it was a shortage of money and personnel that probably inspired the state's willingness to accept the public expansion of elite power.

To understand the evolution of the public political space, we must trace its changing contours in the crucial transition from imperial to Republican to warlord rule when elite roles and expectations were altered, primarily by changes in the composition and goals of the state and the ranks of the elite.[18] The anti-opium movement allows us to do precisely that. Elite reformers operated with state approval, but in doing so they expanded their traditional social management functions into more overtly political roles.[19] This change has been noted in several books that analyze elite activism and state building under either the Qing *or* the Nationalists but leave readers pondering what

---

18. Many scholarly studies obscure the significance of this period by halting in 1911 or beginning after the revolution. Of course, there are exceptions. For example, in *Party, State, and Local Elites*, Joseph Fewsmith examines the transformation of merchant organizations from the end of the Qing into the Nationalist decade. He clearly acknowledges the growing regulatory functions of extra-bureaucratic elites, but his comparison of these groups with modern special interest groups is not really applicable to those active in the anti-opium movement.

19. This characterization of extra-bureaucratic elite activities as falling under the category of social management prior to the Revolution of 1911 and entering a more political stage in the post–May Fourth period was taken from R. Bin Wong's "Great Expectations."

happened in between to alter the face of public political activism so dramatically.[20] Analyzing the changing roles and identity of Fujian's bureaucratic and unofficial opium reformers from the late Qing through the 1920s allows us to trace one element in the process by which a new space for political involvement was carved out where the Chinese polity met Chinese society. The long-gowned scholars and younger activists who dominated the late Qing public sphere had the implicit approval of the central state and local officials, but after the death of Yuan Shikai, it became an arena where vocal but largely toothless reform groups clashed with warlord governments. The dynamics of reform, revolution, imperialism, and military conflict not only altered the foundations of state power and legitimacy but also transformed Chinese politics and hardened the boundaries between the state and the public space.

A brief discussion of my decision to use the term "campaign" to describe the opium suppression initiative is in order here. The Chinese term *yundong* can be translated as either "campaign" or "movement"; in English, these words carry slightly different connotations (although they can be used interchangeably in some contexts). For example, we speak of political candidates running *campaigns*, but of an anti-war *movement*, with the implication that campaigns are more choreographed and that movements are more spontaneous, tend to have grassroots origins, and protest some element of the status quo. Late Qing documents do not use the term *yundong*, adopted first by the leaders of the May Fourth Movement and later by the Communist Party to designate a mass campaign, but historians writing after the 1950s do.[21] It is not difficult to understand why. The late Qing/early Republican opium suppression campaign mobilized thousands of officials and reformers, generated reams of propaganda from journals to posters, separated patriots and model citizens from traitors, and tapped into a nationalism that seemed strong enough to withstand the serious loss of opium-related revenues by

---

20. The gap is most evident if we examine Rankin, *Elite Activism and Political Transformation*, and Rowe's two volumes on Hankow (1984 and 1989), which deal with the late Qing, on the one hand, and Strand's *Rickshaw Beijing* on Beijing in the 1920s, on the other. R. Bin Wong comments on this gap in "Great Expectations."

21. For a detailed examination of the adoption of this term by Chen Duxiu and other May Fourth activists, see Wagner, "The Canonization of May Fourth." According to Rudolph Wagner, the first Chinese political action consciously construed as a movement was May Fourth, and it is clear from his work that, unlike most Maoist mass campaigns, one of the defining elements of a movement before 1949 was its autonomy and opposition to the state.

the national treasury. However, the term *yundong* obscures the transformation of opium suppression from a campaign initiated by the central state and directed by a coalition of officials and elites to something that resembled a movement during the warlord era. That movement was a highly politicized initiative still organized by elites, not especially populist in nature, but distinctly oppositional.

Because the success of opium suppression depended on a shift in popular attitudes and behavior, elite reformers deliberately worked to mobilize ordinary people. In fact, as Michael Tsin's work has shown, both bureaucrats and elites perceived that social unity was a critical component of a modern state.[22] The most obvious manifestations of this strategy were public gatherings like the one noted at the beginning of this chapter. Fujian's cities became stages for mass meetings and boisterous processions organized to publicize and celebrate any notable milestone in the anti-opium campaign. Enormous, animated crowds watched as confiscated opium and opium paraphernalia were periodically and publicly burned. However, as Tsin points out, "the Qing government, unlike a modern regime, did not consider a mobilized society a legitimating force for its own rule."[23] Granted, the late Qing and early Republican states did not explicitly encourage mass involvement in opium suppression and probably permitted public ceremonies only because they complemented government goals. Elite-led reform groups such as the Anti-Opium Society, on the other hand, grasped the new reality of Chinese politics and recognized that mass involvement not only furthered the goal of changing popular sentiment but also put elite reformers in the forefront of that process. However, although elite reformers mobilized the audiences and carefully choreographed public meetings, parades, and demonstrations, many officials attended and participated in those meetings. What remains unclear is how much, if any, "persuasion" was required to gather and control the crowd. Mobilization was noticeably less successful in the countryside, where the destruction of poppy fields rarely met with enthusiasm. After the death of Yuan Shikai, the tone of public gatherings changed completely, and the more equivocal stance of the state often meant that urban demonstrations took on an air of protest rather than celebration.[24]

---

22. Tsin, *Nation, Governance, and Modernity*, pp. 3–15.
23. Ibid., p. 49.
24. Tsin's research on Canton in the early twentieth century (ibid., chap. 5) emphasizes the difficulty of establishing firm state control over those who were mobilized as well as the

Opium reform cannot be separated from the emergence of nationalism in the late Qing and early Republic, and it was the confluence of provincial and state goals that motivated the high-profile and often emotional anti-opium campaign.[25] The legal and moral authority of the late Qing / early Republican state as well as its regulatory capacities depended in large part on the acceptance of that authority (and the goals to which it was directed) by elite reformers. Acquiescence could have been obtained through a number of means—including coercion—but the voluntary and often enthusiastic acceptance of state authority in the context of opium suppression reveals how the Qing public sphere was constructed by granting extraordinary powers to elite reformers and employing symbolic capital (the image of Lin Zexu, for example) that resonated with state, province, and locality. When the Qing state proved incapable of responding to the momentum of provincial reform, that connection was severed, and many of the elites and officials whose energy had propelled this state-driven policy turned against that same state in the Revolution of 1911. The incorporation of many of these elites into the Republican state left a less reputable, less influential mix of individuals to populate the public sphere after the revolution and a state less willing to sanction extraordinary powers for them.

After 1911, the boundaries between the state and unofficial reform groups began to harden. Early Republican opium reformers played a less important role in the suppression campaign because many of the most admired leaders of the campaign had become part of the new state and because a new agreement with the British necessitated national cooperation that left less room for the local flexibility that had fueled public activism. Once the end of British opium imports had been secured, the Chinese government turned its attention to other pressing domestic problems, and in the years between the death of Yuan Shikai in 1916 and the founding of the Nanjing regime in 1927, the state itself became a casualty of Chinese warlord politics. National and provincial leaders still professed a commitment to opium reform, but the opium trade was too lucrative to remain untapped for long. Elite reformers

---

problematic element of coercion (what he terms the "disciplinary aspects of mobilization") that sometimes characterized public strikes and demonstrations.

25. Several scholars have published work that contributes to a better understanding of the interaction between provincial and national loyalties. For example, Roger R. Thompson's *China's Local Councils* outlines the evolution of nationalism in the context of local self-government, and Bryna Goodman's *Native Place, City, and Nation* shows how native-place associations came to act as channels for the various levels of territorial loyalty.

raged and cajoled, negotiated and investigated, but without genuine state support, the actors in the public sphere were forced to curtail many public gatherings and their own regulatory power diminished. For opium reformers, the highly politicized public space of the 1920s was autonomous from what remained of the state and from the actual business of suppression.

Opium in Rhetoric and Reality: A Historiographical Caveat

Analyzing the opium trade and opium suppression in Fujian requires navigating around some fairly substantive historiographical obstacles. The obvious difficulty of uncovering and interpreting evidence on subjects as controversial (and often illegal) as narcotics use and trafficking is compounded by the political implications of those activities. When I began researching the official opium suppression campaign, I expected to find a wealth of Chinese documentation and secondary analyses. After all, this was a policy initiated by the Chinese themselves and designed to free China from the yoke of narco-imperialism, restore the nation's reputation, and kindle a sense of patriotic pride. Yet, until fairly recently, scholars in the People's Republic of China showed a marked reluctance to deal with the issue of opium outside the confines of the Opium Wars.[26] In the voluminous materials on the Opium Wars, article after article and book after book rail against the immorality of capitalist greed and the self-serving aggression spawned by the imperialist/colonial mentality. But not until the 1980s did the topic of opium suppression in the late Qing and early twentieth centuries become an acceptable avenue for historical exploration. Even then, many of the published works were situated within a rhetorical framework (and political context) that left little room for impartial analysis.[27]

---

26. Historians in Taiwan appear far more willing to delve into the sensitive subject of the opium trade and opium suppression. Lin Man-houng, Zhang Yufa, and Chen Yongfa, among others, have contributed important works. In "Wan Qing de yapian shui" and "Qingmo shehui liuxing xishi yapian yanjiu," Lin looks at the Chinese production and distribution of opium, as well as the lucrative taxation of the drug. Zhang (*Zhongguo xiandaihua de qucheng yanjiu, Shandong sheng*, chap. 5) states quite strongly that opium suppression was a top-down initiative that was not prompted by grassroots activism. Chen ("Hong taiyang xia de yingsu hua") asserts that, its rhetoric to the contrary, the Chinese Communist Party raised much-needed revenue through clandestine involvement in opium trafficking.

27. To be fair, not until the 1990s did western academics take a closer look at opium outside the standard framework of diplomatic relations. The work of Frederic Wakeman, Jr., is an exception to this observation, and his now-classic *Strangers at the Gate* explores the social

That framework, constructed from an amalgam of Marxism–Leninism–Mao Zedong Thought and Chinese nationalism, supported a myth of peasant/mass nobility uncongenial to the reality of China's ambiguous relationship with opium. The story of the opium suppression campaign in the late Qing and early Republic not only illustrates the ability of the central state to play a leading role in condemning and combating the opium trade but also reveals the *need* for it to do so. If the masses, portrayed almost universally by PRC historians as the motive force of progressive revolution in China, had wholeheartedly opposed the importation of foreign opium and felt the sting of imperialist oppression each time they lit up, the market for British opium would not have expanded so rapidly and the social dysfunction associated with widespread smoking would not have been perceived as a national crisis. In fact, foreign involvement in the opium trade essentially ended at the treaty ports, where the imported drug was purchased, conveyed, taxed, distributed, prepared, sold, and consumed by Chinese. And what about the massive domestic production of opium in the latter half of the nineteenth century and the first few decades of the twentieth century? Even a cursory examination reveals a farming population that embraced opium as a cash crop and was sometimes willing to use violence to resist attempts to halt that profitable sideline. Thus, complicity in the opium trade on the part of the Chinese masses often has to be read between the lines of the dominant political discourse.[28] Even the successful Communist anti-drug cam-

---

consequences of the Opium War among the people of Guangdong. A recent conference, "Opium in Chinese History" (Toronto, May 1997), attracted dozens of scholars, several of whom explored the suppression campaigns; others highlighted the complicity of Chinese merchants and officials in establishing, expanding, and sustaining the global narcotics network. Many of the essays presented at the conference later appeared in Brook and Wakabayashi, *Opium Regimes*, and since then, many of those authors have published significant monographs. See, e.g., Baumler, *Modern China and Opium*; Slack, *Opium, State, and Society*; Trocki, *Opium, Empire and the Global Political Economy*; and Zhou Yongming, *Anti-Drug Crusades in Twentieth-Century China*. Valuable work on the social climate of opium consumption also has been published, most notably, Keith McMahon's *The Fall of the God of Money*; John F. Richards's "Opium and the British Empire"; and Zheng Yangwen's "The Social Life of Opium." Other monographs by Baumler and Zheng Yangwen are forthcoming.

28. This generalization excludes the work of historian Lin Renchuan of Xiamen University, who does not hesitate to condemn corrupt Chinese officials, opium dealers, and smugglers who facilitated the trade, along with the despotic clans that strong-armed and cowed the local populations; see, e.g., his "Qingdai Fujian de yapian maoyi." However, even Professor Lin's well-researched and evenhanded article on opium in Fujian did not appear in print until 1985.

paign in 1952 was deliberately erased from the historical record for fear of political fallout.[29]

In addition, a balanced view of opium reform also entails a more positive spin on two regimes vilified by historians in China until quite recently: the "degenerate, backward, and feudal" Qing dynasty[30] and the Republic of the much-maligned Yuan Shikai, both of which guided this far-reaching social reform. Materials on the resurgence of opium consumption and the domestic opium trade in Fujian under warlord rule and Chiang Kaishek's Nanjing regime are understandably more plentiful. Finally, even those mainland historians who laud the suppression campaign almost uniformly portray the policy as an initiative reluctantly adopted by otherwise apathetic or coercive Chinese states in response to powerful mass sentiment against the drug. From this perspective, the weakness of the Qing and Republican states in the face of imperialist pressures, their financial mismanagement, their favoritism toward the wealthy and landholding classes, and so on provoked grass-roots resistance to the suppression policy, a policy the masses allegedly supported in principle.

To be fair, there is ample evidence of popular hostility to opium in Fujian before, during, and after the suppression campaign. Prior to 1906, some Fujianese expressed an aversion to the drug in folk songs and poems and joined groups that espoused an anti-opium philosophy. During the official anti-opium movement, large numbers of ordinary Chinese sought treatment for opium dependence in official refuges ("refuge" was the missionary term for an addiction treatment center), listened to anti-opium propaganda, and participated in events that celebrated the successes of the campaign. Even after the anti-climactic conclusion of the crusade, lyrical and other expressions of hostility toward opium persisted.

But not all Fujianese lamented the damage caused by opium abuse, and many stood to suffer financially and physiologically under the suppression policy. After all, although the British were at fault for supplying opium in

---

29. Zhou Yongming explains that China adopted a secretive policy because of American allegations that China was exporting heroin to Japan; the rulers of the new People's Republic were sensitive to anything that could damage the international image of their young country. According to Zhou, the government "instructed local authorities that the first priority of propaganda should be to reveal the roles of imperialists and the previous Chinese rulers in using drugs to poison the Chinese people" (*Anti-Drug Crusades in Twentieth-Century China*, pp. 101–2).

30. See, e.g., Zhou Ruiguang, "Qing huanghua daoren 'jieyan shi' qianshi," p. 161.

ever-increasing quantities in defiance of Chinese law, many Chinese contributed to the problem by flouting those laws. Fujian's thriving opium economy would not have developed or survived without a vast network of officials, merchants, transporters, distributors, poppy farmers, and opium smokers. Those individuals and any larger interests that they may have represented were the target of various stages of the late Qing / early Republican opium suppression campaign, and they did resist the restrictions on their livelihood.

Admittedly, violent resistance to suppression measures even at their most coercive was minimal in Fujian, considering the scope of the restrictions. When the government limited the amount of opium that could be sold or consumed, opposition tended to occur on an individual level and did not present serious problems for the state. Only when the focus of the campaign shifted to the elimination of the domestic poppy crop did relatively large-scale, organized resistance appear, and even then, the unrest often was sparked by popular resentment toward the coercive and sometimes capricious methods of enforcement. But the flourishing of the opium economy before and almost immediately after the campaign, as well as the problems that stymied certain aspects of the reforms, reveal that popular antipathy toward opium and the opium trade was by no means universal.

In attempting to document grassroots hostility to the drug, recent Chinese chroniclers of Fujian's history have used the district- and provincial-level *wenshi ziliao*[31] to introduce modern Chinese to the anger and sorrow of their ancestors as they shouldered the twin yokes of addiction and foreign oppression. The anti-opium songs and poems featured in these publications testify to the existence of vocal opposition to the opium trade and to popular recognition of the damage wrought by the drug on Chinese bodies, families, and society, although there is no way to determine how representative they

---

31. These collections of historical and literary materials, published from the 1960s on, are the responsibility of *wenshi ziliao* committees in each district in China. They are designed to educate modern Chinese about the past by using oral histories and otherwise obscure materials housed in local historical archives (some of which are closed to foreign researchers). Using a number of indexes, I have located the vast majority of *wenshi ziliao* articles on opium in Fujian. Although they constitute an invaluable means of accessing popular sentiment, they also present problems for researchers today. Many do not contain footnotes, and most are careful to include political and moralistic condemnations of the drug and the pre-1949 regimes under which China suffered its most serious opium problems. For more on this valuable but problematic source, see Cochran, "A Guide to Memoirs in Chinese Periodical Literature."

were of contemporary popular opinion. The folk songs in particular appear to validate the belief of the Chinese Communist Party in the power of popular culture to reflect and shape public opinion. Many folk songs lamented the horrific consequences of poverty, the oppression of women, and the tyranny of the landholding classes; others addressed more specific social ills—among them, the deplorable consequences of opium smoking and dependence.[32] Similar odes devoted to the more pleasing effects of the drug must have existed but were not reproduced for public consumption today because of their dubious pedagogical value.[33]

The work of scholars outside China on opium also has been constrained by politics since many researchers rely primarily on the descriptions of foreign missionaries who lived and worked among the Chinese. It has long been accepted as axiomatic that excessive opium smoking savages the mind, the body, and the spirit of the addict, but such assessments of opium's impact often became mired in the missionaries' own moralistic and political agendas. Those agendas may have obscured the possibility that opium prohibition failed to generate violent resistance because abstinence and withdrawal simply were not that difficult, either because the drug was not as addictive as supposed or because most Chinese were moderate users.

Historian R. K. Newman believes that graphic descriptions of the physical decline and suffering endured by opium addicts may reflect the honest mistake of missionary observers who confused the symptoms of disease, injury, or chronic poverty with the most common local Chinese remedy for those conditions.[34] This thesis provides a useful caveat against

---

32. Hung, *War and Popular Culture*, pp. 256–69.

33. Several such poems do in fact appear in Zheng Yangwen's "The Social Life of Opium," p. 20, and the popularity of opium, first as a luxury and then as a staple of the sex industry and ordinary social interaction, undoubtedly inspired many more. The depiction of opium in late Qing fiction is quite varied, conjuring up both the sensual pleasures of intoxication and the emotional and physical pain of addiction (see McMahon, *The Fall of the God of Money*, chap. 3). I located several opium pipes and other smoking paraphernalia dating from the late Qing that were inscribed with poems rhapsodizing the unearthly delights of opium smoking. The geographical origins of the equipment are unknown. Many thanks to Deborah Hull-Wolski, collections manager for the Department of Anthropology Collections at the Museum Support Center of the Smithsonian Institution in Suitland, Maryland, for permitting me to examine these and other artifacts, and to R. LaVerne Madancy for arranging my visit there on 21 Aug. 2000.

34. Newman, "Opium Smoking in Late Imperial China," p. 776.

excessive scholarly dependence on missionary reports. Foreign missionaries portrayed themselves as operating within a relatively altruistic and impartial framework, but their desire to distinguish themselves from their less noble compatriots and to promote their own good works encouraged them to identify and document serious consequences from opium abuse. However, Newman's provocative research is limited to English-language sources, and his conclusions do not address the genuine Chinese hostility to the drug. After all, Chinese crowds regularly heckled missionaries, whom they perceived as linked with the opium trade, and many Chinese opium addicts freely sought out treatment for their addition in missionary-run refuges. Other non-Chinese sources, such as the dispatches filed by representatives of the British, American, and French governments in China, corroborated many missionary observations while also taking great pains to report instances of Chinese resistance to the official suppression campaign.

What emerges in the sources examined here is the ambivalence of the Fujianese people toward opium, the opium trade, and the suppression campaign.[35] Popular outrage toward the flouting of Chinese laws and social conventions by opium importers and smokers, as well as a grassroots revulsion at the physical, moral, and socioeconomic consequences of opium abuse, existed side by side with considerable resistance to state suppression efforts. Even anti-opium propaganda can be productively mined for evidence of popular resistance. The *Fujian Anti-Opium Society Quarterly*, in trumpeting that group's accomplishments, also outlined the contours of the resistance that confronted reformers. The explanation for such complex popular attitudes lies in a number of factors, including the time frame of these events, socioeconomic conditions, local power structures, geography, ideology, and the evolution of legal responses to opium by the Chinese state. Careful mapping of this volatile historical terrain reveals that the broader narrative of China's troubled relationship with opium has long overshadowed a colorful spectrum of popular sentiment toward a habit simultaneously conceived of as a social vice and an economic windfall. What becomes abundantly clear in these pages is the degree to which that sentiment was embedded in larger social, political, and economic contexts.

---

35. For a more detailed examination of this issue, see Madancy, "Unearthing Popular Attitudes."

Structure of the Volume

Dislodging Fujian's tenacious opium economy was akin to attempting to remove an object from the tentacles of an octopus, and reform efforts stretched in as many directions as the drug trade itself. To accommodate the complexity of that process, several chapters contain case studies intended to highlight the nuances of state-society interaction within the context of opium reform. These case studies and the larger analytical narrative illustrate the continuity of state oversight as well as the complex obstacles to reform presented by political and financial instability, regional and ethnic tensions, international entanglements, popular sentiment, and the extensive network of vested interests involved in the lucrative drug trade.

Chapter 2 outlines the construction of Fujian's opium economy and traces the convoluted path of the province's relationship with the drug from the initial smuggling in the 1820s to the eve of the suppression campaign in 1906. Fujian's opium trade and perceptions of the drug itself were shaped in large part by policies initiated and enforced by the Chinese state, including treaties with foreign governments, a variety of taxation schemes, and restrictions on opium cultivation, sales, and consumption. Beginning with the supply side of the opium equation, the chapter examines the expansion of opium imports and then the growth of domestic poppy cultivation along the coastline. The profile of provincial opium consumption and popular attitudes toward opium and the opium trade that follows allows the analysis to transcend economics and delve into the social and psychological impact of opium use and abuse. The contours of Fujian's opium economy provide the historical context necessary for understanding the popular ambivalence toward opium suppression, the tenacity of the opium problem, and the need for state and elite cooperation during the late Qing/early Republican antiopium campaign.

Chapter 3 examines the first phase of the opium suppression campaign, from its inception in 1906 through 1910. The analysis focuses primarily on developments in and around the provincial capital of Fuzhou, where the New Policies and the large concentration of officials, reformist elites, and foreigners generated the province's most extensive, vibrant public space for political participation. Qing opium suppression policy was among the most visible and most publicly uncontested of the late Qing reforms, and its success hinged on the fluid boundaries that separated the state from the reformers. Implementing and enforcing state-sanctioned opium suppression policy were the official bureaucracy and unofficial reform groups that oversaw the publicizing, implementing, and enforcing of the campaign. The line between these parallel administrative structures prior to the Revolution of 1911 was not always clear, and this blurring of the boundaries between bureaucratic and unofficial opium reform efforts often worked to the benefit of both parties in those early years. Close cooperation between officials and unofficial elite-led reform groups allowed the state to exploit a pool of volunteers with energy, prestige, and talent and to channel the desire of progressive, nationalist elites for change in a direction that meshed with Qing goals. Those groups were given extensive police powers in the context of the state-sanctioned campaign, and although their participation bolstered the prestige of the state, elites also used their power to increase their own status and influence over local society. However, by late 1910, international pressures restricted the ability of the Qing state to respond to the momentum for further and faster reform in the provinces. Even the reformers in the new provincial assembly worried about the financial and political price of such extensive reliance on unofficial reform groups.

Chapter 4 explores the suppression campaign in counties and prefectures outside Fuzhou before the Revolution of 1911. The anti-opium campaign reached even the most remote districts, and state authority remained in evidence even on the verge of the Qing collapse, but the strength and composition of the public space in which the campaign was conducted varied considerably. Available materials indicate a livelier, more public campaign in urban centers; there large clusters of bureaucrats and progressive elites fueled (and documented) the reforms. As we shall see, G. William Skinner's core/periphery approach is of limited value for understanding and characterizing the pattern of opium reform.[36] Geography and population density ultimately proved less significant in determining the quantity, identity, and effectiveness of regional opium reformers than the presence and size of the domestic poppy crop in that locale. Although branches of the Anti-Opium Society played an important role in monitoring all aspects of the campaign, enforcement of the prohibition on poppy cultivation often required the physical uprooting of the plants and was generally left to offi-

---

36. Skinner, "The Structure of Chinese History." For an in-depth exploration of the core/periphery theory and the idea of the public sphere, see Schoppa, *Chinese Elites and Political Change*.

cials. Magistrates and prefects could employ military force if necessary and were less likely than local elites to be enmeshed in local clan politics or have a stake in the poppy harvest. However, the incendiary potential of using troops caused many local authorities to ignore orders to eliminate the poppy harvest. This chapter also highlights the complex response of Fujian's merchant community to a campaign designed to eliminate a very profitable enterprise.

The next chapter explores the suppression campaign within the Fuzhou Manchu Banner garrison, analyzes major developments in the campaign in 1911, and details the simultaneous collapse of opium reform and the Qing dynasty. A serious problem with opium dependence among the Bannermen and their households was part of the well-known decay of military readiness among the Banner garrisons, and despite the rise of the New Army, the Qing court took great pains to monitor opium reform among its dissolute Manchu defenders. The ranking Manchu general in Fuzhou approached this task as a personal mission, enforcing the regulations with a laudable mix of compassion and vigor. But this arm of the campaign did not unfold in public; rather, it took place within the garrison. This chapter also grapples with the relevance of Qing ethnic identity to the campaign. The two most important officials in Fujian during the Qing phase of the anti-opium campaign were Manchus, and their deaths during the revolution left a temporary vacuum that contributed to the illicit revival of the opium economy. Aside from the revolution itself, the other important development in the pivotal year of 1911 was the signing of a new opium agreement with Britain that acknowledged Chinese accomplishments and offered the possibility of early release from treaty obligations, even as it compelled an important change in the focus of the suppression campaign.

Qing rule crumbled in 1911, and with it the imperial system, but the anti-opium campaign revived quickly under the new Republic. Chapter 6 picks up the story of opium reform in 1912 and reveals how the changes imposed by the new agreement with the British and the unsettled landscape of provincial politics affected the tone and methods of opium reform through 1914. The new Chinese state was as committed to opium suppression as the old, and the brief collapse of the administrative mechanisms of reform during the revolution revealed how necessary those mechanisms were. The revival of poppy cultivation and opium smoking that characterized the transitional period also implied that compliance with the campaign before and after 1911 may have been a matter less of spontaneous or voluntary popular support than of state exhortation or coercion.

After the revolution, several developments worked to alter the composition of the Chinese bureaucracy, devalue the role of unofficial reform groups in the reform process, and generate more reliance on military force. This led to the virtual absorption of the public sphere by the state and set the tone for warlord-era politics. The joint British/Chinese inspection team that toured Fujian in 1914 cleared the way for the closing of provincial borders to opium imports. The public celebrations of the demise of Fujian's domestic poppy crop seemed to validate the more heavy-handed Republican approach, but the last-minute crackdown that preceded the inspection implied a somewhat superficial victory. In fact, the triumph of 1914 meant not so much the end of Fujian's opium problem as the end of effective state and international oversight of opium suppression and the marginalization of elite-led reform groups.

The opium suppression campaign highlighted the complex relationship between foreign imperialist aggression and Chinese nationalism, but the only foreigners with whom many Chinese interacted were missionaries. British and American missionaries involved in the suppression campaign encountered hostility and accusations of hypocrisy because of the involvement of their home countries in the opium trade. In many cases, the survival of their broader mission depended on their ability to distinguish themselves in Chinese perceptions from their opium-peddling countrymen. Chapter 7 delves into the role of Protestant missionaries in combating Fujian's opium problem in the medical, educational, and political arenas. British and American missionaries were appalled at what they perceived as the devastating human toll of the opium trade and took a prominent and vocal position against opium. Motivated by a dizzying mix of religious zeal, altruism, guilt, and the desire for converts, as well as the paternalism and arrogance born of imperialism, missionaries pioneered the treatment of opium addiction in China and led efforts to lobby Great Britain and other western nations to end opium exports to China. Within China, they were outside the legal reach of the Chinese state, and their extraterritoriality, familiarity with new forms of association and publicity, and access to modern medical techniques enabled the missionaries to become deeply involved in the reforms.

After the Revolution of 1911, however, popular recognition of the close ties between missionaries and the Chinese state in the context of opium reform in one instance helped spark a violent uprising. In the disturbance in Xinghua prefecture, analyzed in detail in Chapter 8, foreign missionaries and Chinese officials seemed to blend in the public perception into a singular state-controlled mechanism determined to eliminate a much-needed source of income. The Xinghua rebellion reveals that the New Policy reforms look quite different viewed from the perspective of many poor farmers. Instead of appreciating state and elite efforts to eradicate vices such as opium smoking and introduce modern education and electoral politics, the Xinghua farmers were outraged by the excessive taxation that accompanied reform and deeply resentful when ordered to uproot a profitable cash crop. However, Xinghua was an exception to the rule. Despite the addictive quality of the drug, the profitability of the opium trade, and the sheer numbers of Chinese whose livelihoods were intertwined with that commerce, large-scale violent resistance to suppression was unusual in Fujian.

Finally, Chapter 9 outlines the disappointing resurgence of a thriving narcotics trade from 1914 through the early 1920s. The outbreak of World War I, the death of Yuan Shikai in 1916, and the subsequent expiration of the opium agreement with the British meant that the dissolution of a strong central state unfortunately coincided with the waning of British leverage over Chinese opium policy. The drug quickly reappeared as a ready source of revenue for competing warlord regimes, and the admirable efforts initiated by the Qing dynasty and the early Republic were swiftly undone. International pressures for reform persisted but were less influential than the demands of domestic instability. Warlord regimes and even the Guomindang state looked on opium as more amenable to exploitation than eradication. Elite-led reform groups monitored the revival of Fujian's opium trade and vigorously lobbied Chinese and international authorities to reimpose the prohibitions, but as the public space in which their actions took place became increasingly oppositional to and autonomous from the state, it also lost much of the clout it previously had derived from explicit state sanction.

Opium suppression was by no means the only reform movement that swept China in the late Qing and early Republic, nor was it the sole context in which the emergence of a new public space for political activism was situated. But the quest to eliminate opium in China had a tremendous public appeal that tapped into a new sense of nationalism and illuminated the changing relationship between state and society. To explore that process, this volume provides an in-depth analysis of China's late Qing/early

Republican opium suppression campaign in the province of Fujian. By establishing the centrality of state authority and administrative oversight (or their absence) as the hub of reform, investigating the unofficial elite-led reform groups that provided the momentum for suppression, and then examining the impact and reach of state power within more specific constituencies, I hope to present opium reform in all its complexity. The chapters that follow examine how opium became an integral part of Fujian's economy and of the larger perception of Chinese weakness and analyze how the structure of provincial society and administration affected opium trafficking, the relative success of the suppression campaign in the late Qing / early Republic, and the rapidity of its resurgence. But before we begin examining the construction of Fujian's opium economy and the dynamics of opium prohibition in that province, we need to understand that Fujian's opium economy was shaped in part by forces independent of provincial peculiarities. The most obvious of those forces was the drug itself.

"Portable Ecstasies"

Here was a panacea ... for all human woes; here was the secret of happiness, about which philosophers had disputed for so many ages, at once discovered; happiness might now be bought for a penny, and carried in the waistcoat-pocket; portable ecstasies might be had corked up in a pint-bottle; and peace of mind could be sent down by the mail.... O just, subtle and all-conquering opium!

—Thomas De Quincey[37]

Opium ... is an imperious master and treats its subjects like slaves. It first of all comes with gentle touch as though it were full of the tenderest love for man. Then in a few weeks, when it has got its grip upon the man, it shows itself to be the cruelest taskmaster that ever drove men to a lingering death. It knows that no one in the world can allay the intolerable craving that comes over a man's life but itself, and as though it were playing with a man's soul, it demands that before relief is given the dose must be increased. It has no pity or remorse. It will see the home wretched and the girls sold into slavery, and the boys calling another man father, and the wife in the home of a stranger, rather than remit a single pain or give one hour's release from the agony with which the opium tortures both body and soul.

—Proprietor of a Chinese opium den as translated by Rev. J. Macgowan[38]

Opium has been praised as a miraculous healer, celebrated as an avenue to artistic creativity, coveted as a generator of unimaginable wealth, and cursed as a destroyer of morality and health. By the late nineteenth century, opium

---

37. De Quincey, *Confessions of an English Opium-Eater*, pp. 179, 194.
38. Macgowan, *Sidelights on Chinese Life*, pp. 199–200.

also became a potent metaphor for individual and societal somnambulism, depravity, corruption, and weakness. Nowhere did the association between opium and sociopolitical decline seem so obvious as in late Qing China, an empire beset by internal unrest, imperialist threats, and financial crisis. Opium, whether savior or slave master, came to be perceived as a social problem with serious economic and political ramifications, and it was that perception that prompted the Chinese suppression campaign of the early twentieth century.

The juice of the opium poppy (*Papaver somniferum*) is the source not only of raw opium but also, after processing, of refined opium, morphine, codeine, heroin, and other narcotics. Poppy blossoms range in color from white to a spectacular red and wave gracefully atop straight stalks that grow to a height of one to two feet. The poppy reaches full flower within three to four months of sowing and forms a capsule that is ready for harvest within another month or so. The milky latex within the capsule yields raw opium, and its harvesting requires the laborer to determine by touch which capsules are ready and then carefully lance each one in a manner that encourages the greatest flow of latex. The oozing capsules are usually left until the next day, when the hardening, darkened latex is scraped off. This process is repeated until the capsule is completely drained and desiccated.[39] The brownish residue is dried and then shaped into cakes or balls for easy transport.

In nineteenth-century India, raw opium was prepared for export in large factories, where the process began by evaporating the excess liquid from the harvested latex. Then, a lump weighing approximately three pounds was formed into a spherical cake that was covered with thick layers of dried poppy petals and crushed poppy stems and leaves. The cakes were dried for several days, aired, and finally, packed into chests of 40 cakes apiece, weighing approximately 170 pounds per chest. The chests were then shipped to Indian ports and auctioned to merchants, who transported the drug to China and elsewhere.[40]

Although it was possible to eat the drug in this raw form, most Chinese preferred to smoke a more refined version. Raw opium was prepared for smoking by large retailers, by the keepers of opium shops or dens, and even by individuals—usually wealthy Chinese (or their servants)—who purchased the raw drug from a shop and boiled it at home. The preparation of

---

39. Husain and Sharma, *The Opium Poppy*, pp. 10–17.
40. Fay, *The Opium War*, pp. 5, 12–14.

smokable opium, or what Indians call *chandu*, requires little equipment but some degree of skill. The raw opium ball is split open and subjected to a series of boilings and filterings until it attains a paste-like consistency that can be smoked. The raw drug is usually reduced by about one-half during the process.[41]

The physical effects of opium consumption are well documented and have been celebrated in the West since the time of the ancient Greeks. Opium was unsurpassed as an analgesic in premodern times, and the medical world embraced its ability to lessen pain as nothing short of miraculous.[42] In the more tropical regions of East and Southeast Asia, opium was also administered as a prophylactic for malaria, cholera, and other tropical diseases, as well as a treatment for diarrhea, fever, and other ailments.[43] Unfortunately, prolonged consumption, even for medical purposes, can lead to dependence as the body builds up a tolerance for the drug and requires stronger doses to attain the same degree of relief.

Opium is technically a depressant containing alkaloids such as morphine (named for Morpheus, a Greek god of dreams) and codeine, but its ability to kill pain also alters a user's perceptions of the drug:

> The mood effect can make the residual pain more tolerable and generally produce a lessening of emotional distress. The euphoric effect of opium is what was meant by the nineteenth-century term the 'stimulant' use of the drug. . . . Opiates are in present terminology not classified as stimulants, and to apply this word to a class of drugs which produce drowsiness and passivity today seems rather bizarre. The word obviously had a different connotation in the last [nineteenth] century, and may be taken as broadly meaning the pleasure-seeking use of the drug.[44]

This probably explains the popularity of opium among manual laborers in Western Europe and Asia. Missionaries observed that Chinese coolies were almost universally addicted to the drug. Missionary doctors in China confirmed that opium seemed to provide a brief and temporary energy

---

41. Kane, *Opium Smoking in America & China*, pp. 29–30; Park, *Opinions of Over 100 Physicians*, p. 69; and Doolittle, *Social Life of the Chinese*, 2: 349.

42. Owen, *British Opium Policy in China and India*, chap. 1.

43. Rush, *Opium to Java*, p. 554; Spence, "Opium Smoking in Ch'ing China"; Waung, "Introduction of Opium Cultivation to China," pp. 209–10; and Park, *Opinions of Over 100 Physicians*, pp. 37–40.

44. Berridge and Edwards, *Opium and the People*, pp. xvi–xxii. Thanks to Jeannette Sargent for enlightening me on the subject of Morpheus.

boost but warned that physical weakness and deterioration quickly set in.[45] In other parts of Asia, Indian soldiers used opium as a restorative, and in Java, smokers consumed the drug when they needed extra energy, especially to stay awake at night.[46] Thus, for many in the nineteenth century, "pleasure-seeking" was in many cases simply the pursuit of an existence temporarily free from pain or worry. Many of those who initially used the drug as a medicine found the experience enjoyable and continued to use opium either to prolong the relief from pain or for recreational purposes.

For others, particularly the upper classes of Europe and Asia, who had both time and money, opium became the recreational drug of choice for its alleged ability to enhance the powers of the mind. Within British literary circles, for example, opium was touted as a pathway to creativity. Authors such as Samuel Taylor Coleridge and Thomas De Quincey claimed that much of their best work was done under the influence of the drug.[47] De Quincey's autobiographical ode to the joys and pitfalls of opium consumption, *The Confessions of an English Opium-Eater*, attracted a great deal of popular attention on its publication in 1821 and started a debate over the creative powers of opium that continues today.[48] De Quincey rhapsodized that the drug caused a man to feel that "the diviner part of [his] nature was paramount—that is, the moral affections are in a state of cloudless serenity; and high over all the great light of the majestic intellect."[49]

The effects of opium and the motivations for consuming the drug often were tied to the consumer's socioeconomic class. Obviously, medical problems transcended class barriers, but a serious opium dependence tended to have more debilitating consequences for the poor who engaged in heavy

---

45. Park, *Opinions of Over 100 Physicians*, pp. 21–29; and Chang, *Commissioner Lin and the Opium War*, p. 17.

46. Rush, *Opium to Java*, pp. 554–55; and Fay, *The Opium War*, p. 7.

47. M. H. Abrams's *Milk of Paradise* argues that the similarities in works by these authors derive from the nature of the drug itself.

48. A flurry of works on the subject appeared in the 1970s. Schneider (*Coleridge, Opium, and Kubla Khan*) and Lefebure (*Samuel Taylor Coleridge*) conclude that opium did not stimulate creativity, whereas Hayter (*Opium and the Romantic Imagination*) contends that Coleridge did produce at least a draft of "Kubla Khan" in the throes of a laudanum haze. All three scholars, however, deplore the physical toll of opium dependence. Barry Milligan (*Pleasures and Pains*), whose research agenda and conclusions are less judgmental, revisited the controversy in 1995 and focused more on the ways in which opium shaped Orientalist notions in Victorian England.

49. De Quincey, *Confessions of an English Opium-Eater*, p. 182.

manual labor and had less access to adequate nutrition and health care. Laborers were more susceptible to physical injury than the members of the upper classes and thus had more occasions on which to turn to opium for relief. On the other hand, although the wealthy had more leisure in which to indulge in the pleasures of opium consumption, their circumstances ensured that their bodies were better able to handle the strains of even long-term use.

Opium consumption is not synonymous with opium addiction or dependence. Anecdotal evidence from Western Europe as well as from China indicates that moderate and/or occasional consumption do not necessarily transform an individual into an "opium sot" (a term frequently employed by missionaries) or what the Chinese labeled an "opium devil" (*yangui*).[50] Even a missionary-physician admitted, "It is true that cases are frequently met with who have smoked for some years without apparent injury," although he felt it necessary to caution that "he would be a rash man who would argue from this that said smokers could continue to smoke indefinitely without injury!"[51]

By the late nineteenth century, despite its foreign origin and Chinese laws discouraging its consumption, opium smoking had become an integral facilitator of Chinese social interaction, as Zheng Yangwen puts it, "a 'texture' of Chinese life."[52] Many foreigners observed, reproachfully of course, that sharing an opium pipe had become the standard way to begin social and business dealings in China, much the way a cigarette or a cup of tea serves that function now. But before it became so mundane, opium was a luxury good that became fashionable, particularly in the first half of the nineteenth century, when it was still illegal and quite expensive. Opium also appealed to many Chinese because it was imported, although the impact of its foreign origins was affected by political changes. One scholar notes that the popularity of the drug in the early nineteenth century had much to do with a Chinese "craving for foreign stuff," but points out that by the early twentieth century,

---

50. The missionary physicians polled by William Hector Park overwhelmingly concluded that few Chinese smoked opium with no ill effects whatsoever, but several doctors admitted that up to one-half of the smokers they had encountered suffered only minor problems. Most of these individuals were members of the wealthier classes (see Park, *Opinions of Over 100 Physicians*, pp. 9–12, 19–20).

51. Ibid., p. 10.

52. Zheng Yangwen, "The Social Life of Opium," p. 3. Zheng's work on the broader social context in which opium smoking was popularized and the evolving uses of opium provides a much-needed social history of the drug.

"opium defined Chinese people and their culture. What was more, it was not just about misery and tragedy." In the late Qing, the decision to smoke opium may have been a deliberate choice on the part of many Chinese who used it "to remain Chinese while undergoing Westernization."[53]

What was it like to smoke opium? One lyrical, fictional description that seems to jibe with the testimony of opium smokers is contained in *Cat Country*, Chinese writer Lao She's allegorical novel satirizing Chinese society in the 1930s.[54] The story centers around a Chinese explorer who crashes on the planet Mars, where the resident cat-people convince him to try a widely used stimulant they call "reverie leaves." The protagonist's first experience with the drug leaves him reeling:

> My head had began to feel a bit dizzy, and yet it wasn't at all an unpleasant sensation. . . . I was also conscious of an anesthetic effect that it communicated to every part of my body; however, it did not make me very numb at first. My stomach began to feel full and languorous, and my brain too became a bit sluggish as though I should like to doze off but couldn't. It was almost as though I were benumbed and excited at the same time. . . . Then after a very short interval, I shook my head lightly once or twice and the feeling of intoxication was past. And now every last pore in my body felt relaxed and happy enough to laugh, if pores could laugh. I no longer felt the least bit hungry or thirsty, nor did I longer mind the dirt on my body. The mud, blood, and sweat that clung to my flesh all gave me a delicious feeling. . . . "Happiness" is insufficient to describe my state of mind at the time. "Ecstasy" on top of "ecstasy" would be more like it.[55]

Although the novel recognizes the appeal of the drug, it views with outrage the foreigners who introduced the stimulant and is contemptuous of "Martian" society for being so dependent on a foreign narcotic. The allegory is not difficult to decipher, and, as we shall see, the connection between imperialism and the opium trade affected both the rhetoric and the conduct of opium reform in China as a whole as well as in Fujian province.[56]

---

53. Ibid., pp. 17–18, 34–35; McMahon, *The Fall of the God of Money*, p. 176.

54. For another similar but nonfictional testimony, this time from a British physician in the Madras Army who came to China during the first Opium War, see Lubbock, *The Opium Clippers*, pp. 25–26.

55. Lao She, *Cat Country*, pp. 35–37. Lao She is the pseudonym of Shu Qingchun, and the novel was originally published in the 1930s.

56. Keith McMahon's exploration of the fascinating topic of literary representations of opium is an important addition to the discussion of evolving Chinese perceptions of the drug (see McMahon, *The Fall of the God of Money*, esp. chap. 6).

The act of smoking opium in China became a stylized ritual that required practice and some skill, as evidenced by the following description of one man's typical smoking session:

Settling himself comfortably on his side upon a couch, he took up a drop of gum-like opium on the point of a long needle and held it over a spirit lamp. Under the heat of the flame the drop gradually turned pale, softened, swelled, and began to bubble and sputter. Before it could actually turn to vapor, [he] carried it still on the point of the needle to the surface of the pipe bowl, tipped the bowl over the flame, put the stem of the pipe to his lips, and inhaled. The opium passed into his lungs in the form of a heavy white smoke. Two or three puffs entirely consumed the drop.[57]

Smoking opium was obviously not something that usually was done in haste, and true addicts commonly spent a great deal of time at their habit. Heavy users often smoked three to five times per day, often in crowded opium dens (see Fig. 1.2), and even the ashes of the drug were often re-smoked several times by poorer users. Opium also could be adulterated, either to alter the taste or stretch one's supply.[58]

But opium brought suffering as well as relief, and those who derived pleasure from opium did so at their own risk. The undeniable pleasures of opium consumption often were matched or exceeded by the subsequent pain of dependence and withdrawal. De Quincey followed his rapturous odes to opium with descriptions of the horrific consequences of his excessive laudanum consumption. He was haunted by hellish nightmares and hallucinations and incapacitated by suicidal depression and paranoia. Most of those who sought to give up heavy, long-term opium use faced a period of agonizing withdrawal typically characterized by insomnia, intense fatigue, vomiting, diarrhea, and joint pain.[59]

Another worrisome element of opium consumption was the need to control the amount of the drug when it was taken orally. Listen again to Lao She's protagonist: "Reverie leaves were funny things: if you took them in small doses, they would give you a lift, but you wouldn't feel like working; if you took them in large doses, you'd be able to work hard for a short time,

---

57. Fay, *The Opium War*, pp. 8–9.
58. Dudgeon, *Review of the Customs Opium Smoking Returns*, pp. 9–10, 21–23.
59. Park, *Opinions of Over 100 Physicians*, pp. 50–53; De Quincey, *Confessions of an English Opium-Eater*, pp. 210–48.

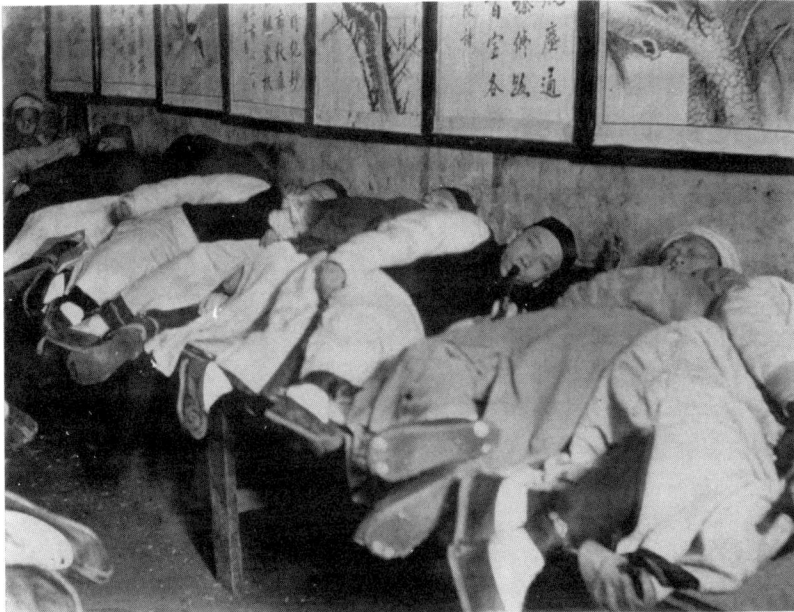

Fig. 1.2 Many Chinese smoked the drug in ubiquitous opium dens. Here a row of reclining opium smokers pack an opium den somewhere in China around the turn of the twentieth century (courtesy United Methodist Archives, Drew University, Madison, New Jersey).

but then you'd die."[60] Lao She was a satirist, but swallowing a large amount of opium was dangerous, and the drug was implicated in many accidental, suicidal, and criminal poisonings in China and abroad. In Great Britain, middle-class outrage over the working-class practice of "infant doping" and the subsequent accidental poisoning of many children provided the impetus for legislation to control access to opium-based remedies.[61] Many progressive Chinese also were alarmed by the frequency of opium suicides, particu-

---

60. Lao She, *Cat Country*, p. 74.

61. The promulgation of opium regulations in Europe reflected the coalescence of a complex set of social developments that included the professionalization of the medical and pharmaceutical fields, as well as fears of class conflict. Several excellent studies analyze these developments in England, although the authors arrive at quite different conclusions. Berridge and Edwards (*Opium and the People*) view the infant-doping scandal and the subsequent Poisons and Pharmacy Act of 1868 as evidence of deliberate attempts at social control by the increasingly dominant middle class; Parssinen (*Secret Passions, Secret Remedies*) argues that the reformers simply were trying to address the deplorable health and working conditions of the working poor.

larly among young women. In the late 1890s, one Chinese Christian estimated that "in such a vast country as China, these suicides must number tens of thousands annually," and missionary physicians were constantly being called to the scene to try to revive the unfortunate victim. Missionaries attributed this phenomenon to the availability of the drug and its low cost,[62] as well as to the miserable lives led by many Chinese women.

Beyond its tangible, physical dangers, the strong link between opium and sexuality generated a titillating blend of fear and fascination. Opium's rumored power as an aphrodisiac generated interest at all levels of society, from the emperor on down, and the pipes and lanterns used to smoke the drug lit up China's urban pleasure quarters. It was a popular form of relaxation that became an essential element of the sex industry, and of the broader lore of sexuality in China.[63] That lore was especially explicit in the pages of nineteenth-century novels; Keith McMahon's analysis of opium in late Qing fiction allows us to glimpse the treacherous ways that opium could allow male and female characters to transgress traditional gender hierarchies. Authors could also use opium in literature to delineate heroes from immoral villains.[64] By the early twentieth century, opium had become synonymous with indolence and vice in literature and in reality, particularly in the teeming city of Shanghai.[65] As the political, temporal, and social context changed, so did the meaning of opium.

In short, opium could represent a conundrum for consumers, physicians, and reformers who wished to avoid opium dependence and its stigma but take full advantage of its palliative properties, especially over an extended period. The lucrative nature of the drug trade also attracted merchants, bandits, and corrupt officials. The demand for opium in China, as abroad, probably originated from both its analgesic and its mood-altering powers. Suppliers of the drug were more than willing to feed that demand, despite the ostensible barriers presented by legal restrictions and moral reservations

---

62. Park, *Opinions of Over 100 Physicians*, pp. 41–43. At least one Chinese Christian, Lian Xianli, agreed with this assessment. He wrote an introduction to Park, *Opinions of Over 100 Physicians*, p. v.
63. Zheng Yangwen, "The Social Life of Opium," pp. 4–14, 20–27.
64. McMahon, *The Fall of the God of Money*, chap. 3.
65. In "Opium/Leisure/Shanghai," Alexander Des Forges nicely accomplishes the two analytical tasks he lays out on p. 168: "examining the role of opium in the construction of Shanghai as a place both of recreation and danger, and investigating the double discursive production of opium as integral to both leisure practices and self-destructive behavior."

about the trade, because of the enormous profits it generated. The drug's addictive powers were only partly responsible for the tenacity of the opium economy when the Chinese state attempted to halt both the supply of and the demand for opium in the early twentieth century.

Setting the Analytical Stage

The early twentieth century marked the first attempt by the Chinese state to eliminate China's opium problem throughout the empire by means of a nationwide campaign, but Beijing had tried to control and eradicate the abuse and sale of the drug through legislation for close to two hundred years. A smaller-scale initiative implemented by Lin Zexu in Guangzhou just before the Opium War had repercussions that shaped the opium economy of Fujian. Many aspects of his comprehensive approach to the opium problem were later replicated during the 1906–17 campaign throughout China and in Fujian—specifically, the focus on eliminating both supply and demand and the use of local elites as the vanguard of reform.

Initial attempts to control opium consumption came directly from the top of China's power structure and were aimed at that same elite group. The Yongzheng emperor was the first to try to end opium smoking and the operation of opium dens by fiat in 1729, apparently in response to growing consumption at court. A British official later speculated that the edict had been ineffective largely because the penalties it imposed were so drastic and because so many officials had become smokers. A similar edict, with even harsher penalties, was issued in 1796, and in 1800 the Jiaqing emperor announced the prohibition of the foreign drug as well as opium cultivation in China.[66] Prior to this point, opium had been imported legally as medicine.[67]

---

66. Yu Ende, *Zhongguo jinyan faling bianqian shi*, pp. 15–24; Spence, "Opium Smoking in Ch'ing China," pp. 148–50, 154–61; Morse, *International Relations of the Chinese Empire*, 1: 174–78; and USDS (1906–10), 774/8–9, Reel 104, Enclosure in Rockhill to Root, 8 Sept. 1906, "Opium in China."

67. In an article published in the *New York Daily Tribune* on 20 Sept. 1858, Karl Marx (*Marx on China*, p. 55) claimed that the timing of Chinese anti-opium legislation was tied directly to British actions and that it was no coincidence that the 1796 edict came only two years after the British East India Company (BEIC) anchored an opium ship at Whampoa Anchorage near the city of Guangzhou. According to Marx, this offshore opium depot facilitated the importation of the drug. Furthermore, in 1798, the BEIC ceased the direct exportation of opium and granted licenses to private traders to purchase Indian opium from the company

Before the 1800 edict, the opium trade was centered in Guangzhou and was conducted openly, although provincial authorities conducted punitive raids on occasion. After 1800, the trade was forced to relocate, first to Macao and Whampoa (Huangpu), and then, after a brief crackdown by local Chinese authorities in 1821, to Lingding (Lintin) Island and eventually to Hong Kong (then still Chinese territory). But the designation of the trade as contraband did not lessen the flow of opium into China. In fact, the trade flourished, and in 1828, when the Lianggung governor-general again began to enforce existing laws in Guangdong and Guangxi, opium merchants simply expanded their market to the southeast China coast, to Fujian and beyond, where this story begins.

In 1836, a heated debate erupted at the highest levels of officialdom over what course of action the Chinese government should pursue. When the state committed itself to prohibition, it created the context from which Lin Zexu would emerge as the symbol of China's determination to fight the opium menace, its foreign conveyers, and its Chinese facilitators. By seeking the moral high ground in the anti-opium initiatives launched by Lin Zexu, the Qing government intentionally reinforced the social stigma and legal sanctions attached to the sale, cultivation, or consumption of opium. It also precipitated the conflict with the British and inadvertently stimulated a thriving black market. The factional disputes over the merits of legalization versus more vigorous enforcement of existing prohibitions have been detailed masterfully by James M. Polachek in *The Inner Opium War* and need not be replicated here. What is relevant is that the memorials exchanged during the debate demonstrated a sophisticated understanding of China's early opium economy and the complex strategy that would be required to dismantle it.

The 1839 anti-opium campaign led by Lin Zexu was largely confined to the port of Guangzhou and its environs, where the geographical isolation of China's foreign trade meant an especially acute opium problem that represented a galling affront to Qing law and sovereignty. Attempts to increase control over opium imports were augmented by draconian restrictions on opium consumption that made smoking a capital offense for Chinese *and* foreigners in certain circumstances. Although the restrictions severely

---

and sell it to willing Chinese buyers. Again, after two years, the Chinese issued another edict outlawing the importation of the foreign drug.

curtailed Chinese demand and the availability of Chinese distributors, foreign merchants responded not by abandoning the smuggling of this illicit commodity but by beginning to move the trade up the coast into northern Guangdong, as well as the provinces of Fujian and Zhejiang.

Lin's campaign began with education against smoking, the registration and treatment of smokers, and the recruitment of a network of informants to discourage smugglers. His admonitions against opium were addressed to all but were particularly concerned with smoking among those expected to act as societal exemplars. For example, he ordered teachers to set up mutual responsibility groups among their students to ensure the elimination of opium smoking in their ranks. According to one American historian, Lin Zexu's attack on opium then expanded to encompass the entire city, as "neighbor spied upon neighbor, houses were entered and searched, quantities of the drug were seized and destroyed, and addicts crowded the Canton jails and the sanitarium outside the wall."[68]

Significantly, Lin devised an innovative plan of attack that used members of Guangzhou's scholar-elite—most of whom were leaders of literary academies in the city—as his foot soldiers.[69] Some of these men used a Guangzhou temple as a clearinghouse for confiscated or abandoned opium and smoking implements, as well as a distribution center for opium remedies. They were ordered by Lin to focus their attention primarily on two categories of offenders. The first were elites much like themselves, and the implementation of a mutual responsibility system was expected to inspire voluntary compliance among these social leaders. The second category—the Chinese merchants and corrupt officials who acted as the middlemen between importers and smokers—required more active, harsher intervention.

According to Polachek, it was Lin's connections with the Spring Purification faction that made this plan possible, since they were "a group fanatically committed to the idea that scholars were fit for—in fact, needed—such responsible social-managerial roles. In effect, Lin was only acting on an assumption that had been latent in the drug crusade idea from the start."[70] But it must be emphasized that Lin's reliance on an existing assumption about

---

68. Fay, *The Opium War*, p. 242. Wakeman (*Strangers at the Gate*, p. 36) adds that heads literally rolled as capital punishment was meted out to some errant smokers.

69. Wakeman (*Strangers at the Gate*, p. 35) also points out that gentry were to oversee the *baojia* system set up in the nearby countryside by Lin for this particular campaign.

70. Polachek, *The Inner Opium War*, pp. 141–44.

the role of elites in no way detracts from the novelty of his decision to put that assumption into practice. The Chinese state's reliance on elites, many of whom were not officials, to enforce state policy, and in fact to oversee and investigate official violations of that policy, set a precedent for the conduct of opium reform that resurfaced in the early twentieth century. By that time, although the symbolic resurrection of Lin Zexu helped to stimulate nationalistic support for opium suppression on a much larger scale, the vastly expanded scope of the opium problem and a financially strapped state meant that elites would have to be granted even more intrusive and coercive powers. In the following chapters, we shall see how those powers expanded with state sanction and began to diminish with the changes that came to Fujianese politics in 1910 and 1911.

The Opium War, provoked in part by Lin Zexu's suppression campaign, now inhabits its rightful place in the ignominious history of foreign imperialism in China. Over the years Lin Zexu has become one of the most recognizable and universally venerated heroes of recent Chinese history. Although he was a tragic figure in his own time, his doomed struggle against a militarily superior power came to symbolize Chinese dignity and righteousness and, by contrast, reveal the greed of the British opium merchants and corrupt Chinese officials he tried in vain to dislodge. The enduring power of his image, as well as its malleability, is evidenced by his resurrection in an epic feature film that commemorated the Opium War on the occasion of the reversion of Hong Kong to Chinese rule and in a statue that now stands in the central square of Chinatown in New York City (see Fig. 1.3).

Although Lin Zexu is not the central subject of this book, his image and influence—both real and imagined—permeated the rhetoric and tone of the late Qing/early Republican anti-opium movement. His legacy was particularly strong in his home province of Fujian among patriotic elites like himself. The ability of that legacy to encompass nationalism, anti-imperialism, and provincial pride made it an especially powerful rallying point when his great-grandson emerged as a leader of the new campaign. But China's relationship with opium was always troublesome, given the drug's physiological, psychological, and financial appeal. As Chinese opium production outstripped foreign imports, rising rates of consumption belied reformist talk of imperialist enslavement through addiction, and as the very bedrock beneath the venerable imperial system began to give way, Lin became an anachronistic reminder of simpler times when China's enemies were more clear-cut.

Commerce, Compulsion, and Control 41

Fig. 1.3 A statue of Lin Zexu gazes into the distance against a New York City backdrop of high-rise apartments and taxicabs (photograph by the author, December 2000).

Like the thick, white smoke that wafted from the pipes of lounging smokers, opium pervaded China's socioeconomic landscape in the late nineteenth and early twentieth centuries and tainted the tumultuous political arena. Airing out an entire nation would require dedication and organization from within and cooperation from abroad. To understand fully the complexity of China's attempts to prohibit opium in the early twentieth century, we must explore that nation's problematic history with the drug. This book traces the process by which opium became intertwined with nationalism, politics, and local socioeconomic conditions, and how prohibition reflected and generated important changes in China's state/society continuum. The conduct of the suppression campaign during the late Qing and early Republic not only revealed the depth of opium-related social disruption in China and the often-ambiguous impact of reform on the Chinese peasantry but also illuminated the shifting and tenuous relationship between the central state and local elites during this exciting but troubled time.

TWO

Constructing Fujian's Opium Economy, 1820s–1906

> How strange it is, that the product of so beautiful a flower should be so misused as to become the bane and curse of a nation.
>
> —Pitcher, *In and About Amoy*

When Lin Zexu was born in Fuzhou in 1784, Chinese law forbid the sale and consumption of opium for other than medical purposes, but neither the drug itself nor the small smuggling trade that brought it into the Qing empire was considered a serious threat to the stability of the Chinese polity or society. The Qing state, then led by the respected Qianlong emperor, appeared strong, in control, and in every sense sovereign of the Middle Kingdom. Within Lin's lifetime, however, the dynasty found itself embroiled in conflicts with increasingly aggressive imperialist nations that did not hesitate to dangle before China the seductive but illicit lure of imported opium to pay for foreign purchases of Chinese tea, silk, and other commodities. A decade after his death, foreign opium had flooded China, all legal obstacles having been removed.

The Indo-Chinese opium trade was shaped by British colonial interests, the inability of the Qing government to fend off either imperialist aggression or the financial allure of the opium trade, and the complicity of a growing network of Chinese merchants, officials, and opium smokers. Although broader forces, such as the conflict between the free trade credo of the West and China's tribute and Canton systems, were at the crux of the mounting tension between China and the West, it was opium that fueled the thriving

East-West smuggling trade and sparked the military confrontations that began the progressive undermining of China's sovereignty and territorial integrity. Those confrontations forced an abrupt change in the nature of Chinese foreign relations and ironically acted as a stimulus for the opium trade.

During the nineteenth century, a complex and multilayered opium economy emerged in Lin's home province of Fujian, shaped by policies enacted by the central Chinese state, their interpretation by provincial and local officials, and, in many cases, the flouting of those policies by eager Chinese opium consumers, distributors, and farmers. Local geography, climate, and the social fabric, as well as the pattern of poppy cultivation, influenced the provincial opium trade, but the most decisive factors in shaping the changing contours of Fujian's opium economy were the variable rates and systems of taxation imposed by the central government in Beijing, treaty port customs houses, and local authorities. Whether those taxes were intended to suppress the drug traffic or simply to profit from it may never be fully proved, but after the mid-nineteenth century, it became clear that the revenue from the opium trade was a prize for which all levels of the state competed. The rapid expansion and flexibility of the social and economic networks that sustained all the components of the provincial opium trade were the primary reasons that Fujian's opium economy flourished in the late nineteenth and early twentieth centuries.

The term "opium economy" should not be understood to imply that opium was the dominant commodity in Fujian's economy. What it does signify is the extent to which this single commodity generated an extensive and entrenched network of individuals who imported, conveyed, distributed, prepared, sold, taxed, and used it. The high price and growing popularity of the drug stimulated that network, but many of its components were closely tied to policies adopted by the Chinese state. The development of foreign and domestic sources of opium as well as Chinese demand were closely tied to early Qing efforts to either eliminate, control, or exploit the growing trade. Before the legalization of foreign and domestic opium, Fujian's underground opium economy was controlled by corrupt officials, as well as powerful local clans, who relied on their familiarity with the province's twisting rivers and mountain paths. After legalization, most of this largely clandestine network came under the control of the government or was exploited by its agents, although some merchants continued to smuggle the drug past tax barriers and expensive ports of entry.

Unlike the major opium-producing provinces of Sichuan and Yunnan, Fujian had a small but increasingly significant domestic poppy crop in addition to a brisk trade in the foreign drug. The sale and distribution of foreign opium added an international dimension that ultimately changed the course and tone of reform and created in Fujian a microcosm of the obstacles and successes that characterized China's empirewide anti-opium campaign. Fujian's lucrative opium economy defrayed provincial- and national-level expenses while spawning expanding networks of merchants, traders, tax brokers, bureaucrats, bearers, smugglers, strongmen, and consumers. When the formal suppression campaign was launched in 1906, reformers faced an opponent with deep and tenacious roots in Fujian.

The Setting

Geography, social and political conflicts, foreign influence, and economic trends shaped Fujian's response to the growing problem of opium in the late Qing and later structured its approach to suppression. Fujian's physical geography, communication and transportation networks, and agricultural patterns provided fertile soil for the sowing of its opium economy, and it was no coincidence that Fujian was the portal through which the habit of opium smoking first entered the Qing empire and became entrenched. Located along China's southeast coast, Fujian is bordered by the provinces of Zhejiang to the north, Jiangxi to the west, and Guangdong to the south and faces the island of Taiwan across the Formosa Strait to the east.[1] Proximity to Taiwan, where the Dutch had established a trading operation in the late Ming / early Qing, and to Guangdong, to which the Qing confined foreign trade in the late eighteenth century, became especially significant in laying the foundation for Fujian's early opium economy. In addition, the many inlets and fishing villages along Fujian's ragged coastline proved irresistible for opium smugglers, who sought to peddle their wares away from Canton (Guangzhou), the locus of foreign trade and Chinese government attempts to control that trade.

---

1. Taiwan was part of Fujian province from 1684 until 1885, when it briefly became a province in its own right. Taiwan's provincial status lasted until Taiwan was awarded to Japan as part of the settlement of the Sino-Japanese war of 1894–95. For the purposes of this volume, which focuses primarily on opium suppression after 1906, Taiwan is treated as a separate entity and will be discussed only when developments there had a significant impact on opium reform in Fujian.

Rich in dramatic scenery, Fujian's jagged coastal cliffs, the rolling hills and mountains of the hinterland, and the river valleys that cross most of the province are not conducive to extensive agriculture or convenient for overland transport.[2] Coastal harbors and the tributaries of Fujian's primary river systems—particularly the Min, but also the Jiulong, Ting, and Jin—are the main avenues of trade and communications within the province, and it was primarily along those inland waterways that the drug was transported.[3] Three mountain passes were the main overland links between Fujian and its three neighboring provinces in the late Qing. Roads were virtually nonexistent outside the major urban areas. Narrow mountain paths were usually passable only on foot, and there was little use for beasts of burden or wheeled vehicles. The light, compact nature of opium as an article of transport made it a perfect commodity for these difficult conditions (see Figs. 2.1–2).

Fujian is among the smallest of China's provinces, with an area of 46,332 square miles, and with the exception of a narrow coastal plain, is not richly endowed in terms of agriculture.[4] With hills or mountains comprising the bulk of the province's terrain, arable land is at a premium, and most crops are grown in small, terraced plots laboriously coaxed from the hillsides and lowlands. The hillsides and foothills of Fujian's many mountains produced the lumber and tea that dominated the province's exports until the late Qing. Only about 8,400 square miles (32.3 million *mu*), primarily along the eastern half of the province, were used as farmland—approximately 15 percent of Fujian's total area.[5] Much of that land was planted in rice. These same regions became the province's primary opium-producing areas in the late Qing. Warm temperatures, high humidity, and mild winters could create ideal growing conditions, but most of Fujian's yearly precipitation tends to occur between April and August. Since the amount of rainfall varies radically from

---

2. The following discussion of Fujian's geography, demography, and agriculture was constructed from information contained in the following sources: Anti-Cobweb Club, *Fukien: A Study of a Province*; Buck, *Land Utilization in China*; Clark, *Community, Trade, and Networks*; Cressey, *China's Geographic Foundations*; Gardella, *Harvesting Mountains* and "Fukien's Tea Industry and Trade"; Hurlbut, *The Fukienese*; and Pitcher, *In and About Amoy*.

3. Lin Renchuan, "Qingdai Fujian de yapian maoyi," pp. 62–71.

4. This is an area approximately the size of Pennsylvania. Only Zhejiang, Taiwan, and Jiangsu are smaller.

5. Cressey (*China's Geographic Foundations*, pp. 95–96) cites figures for 1914 provided by the Chinese Ministry of Agriculture and Commerce and then edited by D. K. Lieu and Chen Chung-min, using the averages for the years 1916–17.

Fig. 2.1 The main road from Fuzhou to the prefectural capital of Yanping (about 100 miles northwest of Fuzhou along the Min River) in the early twentieth century was so narrow that one man had to turn his body sideways so that another could pass. The difficulty of overland transport was one of the reasons why the opium economy sunk such deep roots in Fujian (courtesy United Methodist Archives, Drew University, Madison, New Jersey).

one year to the next, farmers often battled either drought, flood, or typhoon. Poppies can be grown between the rows of other crops or during the winter in some areas; both factors heightened its appeal as a cash crop.

The eastern half of the province comprised Fujian's populous core and encompassed the relatively fertile coastal lowlands, along with the urban commercial zones that grew up around the treaty ports of Xiamen (Amoy) and Fuzhou.[6] The mountainous terrain of Fujian's western half was far less developed and much less populous than the east, although the Min River and its tributaries did allow the emergence of several important commercial centers, particularly in the northwest. This division is particularly relevant to a discussion of opium because the mountain ranges that divide the province

---

6. Each subregion housed a major drainage basin, which in turn was dominated by an urban center. The Min Basin subregion centered on Fuzhou, and the Zhang-Quan subregion contained the Jiulong River basin, which included the treaty port of Xiamen, along with the commercial cities of Zhangzhou and Quanzhou. See Skinner, "The Structure of Chinese History," pp. 273–77; and Benedict, *Bubonic Plague*, chap. 3.

Constructing Fujian's Opium Economy, 1820s–1906   47

Fig. 2.2 An early twentieth-century panorama of the treaty port of Fuzhou, gateway to the Min River (courtesy United Methodist Archives, Drew University, Madison, New Jersey).

east from west also marked the boundary between coastal farmlands, where the domestic poppy crop came to flourish, and the hinterlands, where opium consumption and distribution were the main causes for concern.

Fujian's economy had long relied on coastal trade, and the restrictions on foreign trade imposed by the Ming and Qing dynasties caused economic downturns in the fifteenth century and again from the late seventeenth century until the Opium Wars.[7] The social and economic ramifications of early Qing restrictions, which consisted of a naval blockade of the coast, a decades-long evacuation of the entire coastal population, and the subsequent destruction of towns and villages, were particularly severe. These measures were prompted by the central government's fear of Zheng Chenggong (Koxinga; 1624–62), the defiant Ming loyalist who established bases first in the Xiamen region and then in Taiwan. When the population returned, intense and often violent conflicts broke out over land boundaries and other resources.

---

7. Rawski, *Agricultural Change and the Peasant Economy*; and Falkenheim, "Provincial Administration in Fukien," pp. 18–19. Between these periods of depression, the restrictions were either lightened or removed, and the provincial economy flourished (Skinner, "The Structure of Chinese History," pp. 276–79).

The clan feuds that resulted plagued southeast Fujian throughout the Qing and became entangled with and were exacerbated by the profitable opium-smuggling trade. One source claims that this "resulted in a general suspicion of hostility toward South Fukienese [by the Manchu dynasty] which created an imbalance within the Fukien government in favor of Northern Fukienese which continued into the modern period."[8] It may also have created a reciprocal hostility toward the Qing state among the inhabitants of the southeast, where most of Fujian's domestic poppies were grown.

The Supply Side:
Clandestine Commerce and Taxable Vice

OPIUM FROM OVERSEAS
BEFORE THE *ARROW* WAR

Fujian's opium economy began underground, literally and figuratively, in the 1820s and 1830s, as smugglers brought their goods to the coast and poppy seeds were planted in the fields of the southeast.[9] However, despite increasing domestic cultivation, the backbone of Fujian's opium economy remained the steady influx of opium from abroad and the bustling commercial and bureaucratic networks centered in Xiamen and Fuzhou that worked to document, distribute, and eventually tax the flow.[10]

In Fujian, the means by which the opium trade was established and expanded shaped the provincial opium economy and later attempts to dismantle it. The opium trade helped mold the coastal cities of Fuzhou and Xiamen when they were designated treaty ports as a provision of the Nanjing Treaty of 1842 after the Opium War. Both cities had been visited some years earlier by ambitious traders eager to exploit their proximity to tea-growing regions, as well as the ready market for the drug in those cities. Before foreign opium imports were legalized in 1860 following the *Arrow* War,

---

8. Falkenheim, "Provincial Administration in Fukien," p. 24; Skinner, "The Structure of Chinese History," p. 278.

9. Lin Man-houng ("Qingmo shehui liudong xishi yapian yanjiu," p. 581) cites a memorial from Sun Erzhun, then governor-general of Fujian and Zhejiang, in 1830 that reports a small amount of poppy cultivation in the Quanzhou area.

10. Customs officials at Santu'ao reported that no foreign opium entered China at that treaty port, since consumers in the Funing area were supplied directly from Fuzhou (IMC, *Decennial Reports, Santuao, 1892–1901*, p. 86; and *1902–1911*, p. 83).

the small but growing black-market trade in opium took advantage of the province's coastline, its navigable river systems, and its domination by strong local lineages.

Even in the late nineteenth century, when domestic production in China as a whole caught up to and quickly surpassed imports, the bulk of the opium consumed in Fujian and elsewhere was imported from India, and to a much lesser degree from Persia and Turkey.[11] There were two main varieties of the Indian product: Bengal opium, which included the categories known as Patna and Benares and was produced in the regions controlled by the British colonial government, and Malwa, which was grown in the more or less independent Indian states.[12] Technically the British East India Company (BEIC) did not ship the drug to China itself because it was loath to challenge Chinese restrictions on opium so blatantly, but the company granted licenses to "country traders," the independent transporters who set up a smuggling system in the waters off Macao and Canton.[13]

In Fujian, the foreign drug was initially preferred over the domestic product for a number of reasons, including taste, potency, and availability. Foreigners insisted that the imported drug was stronger and had a more refined flavor.[14] However, the native drug was cheap—in Zhangzhou, prepared domestic opium sold for one-third the price of the imported variety—and, in the early days, went virtually untaxed.[15] The price factor probably explained why Chinese laborers quickly came to prefer the domestic product; one customs official reported in 1887 that Chinese in the Fuzhou region also believed a given amount of the domestic article could be smoked twice as many times as the foreign drug.[16]

---

11. Most of the charts on foreign opium imports compiled by the Maritime Customs list Indian, Persian, and Turkish varieties, but a customs official at Fuzhou noted that what was referred to as "Turkish" was simply another type of Persian opium (IMC, No. 10).

12. Morse, *Trade and Administration of the Chinese Empire*; Richards, "The Indian Empire and Peasant Production of Opium."

13. For an analysis of the BEIC and the trade around Canton, see Owen, *British Opium Policy in China and India*; Fay, *The Opium War*, pp. 11–22; Spence, "Opium Smoking in Ch'ing China," pp. 161–67; and Chang Hsin-pao, *Commissioner Lin and the Opium War*, pp. 18–25, 237–38.

14. Reins, "Reform, Nationalism and Internationalism," p. 116.

15. See ibid., p. 33, for a chart showing the wholesale value of Chinese and foreign opium at Shanghai from 1900 to 1908; and Spence, "Opium Smoking in Ch'ing China," p. 152.

16. Evidently, Indian opium was reduced to ashes after being smoked twice, whereas the domestic drug could be used four or five times (IMC, SS No. 9, Hannen to Hart, 24 May 1887).

The first third of the nineteenth century was marked by an enormous increase in illegal Indian opium imports, from 4,570 chests in 1800 to 23,570 chests in 1832, despite occasional attempts to restrict the illicit trade at Canton.[17] The situation frustrated the Qing court and many reformist elites and was generally believed to have aggravated China's emerging trade deficit by depleting the nation's supply of silver. In fact, the growing opium trade was only one reason for the drain of silver, but the dramatic increase in opium imports made a convenient and compelling scapegoat for opponents of the trade.[18]

Traders carrying Indian opium first discovered the Fujian coastline after the Qing government imposed harsher restrictions on the illegal traffic at Canton in the early 1820s.[19] Their primary goal was direct access to the tea-producing regions of the Fujianese interior, and they hoped to pave the way with opium. According to one source, rather than part with precious silver, western opium traders often tried to pay for Chinese tea at Fuzhou and other locales with imported opium. Ironically, since the early opium market was dominated by a handful of firms from Guangzhou, Chinese tea sellers were not very receptive.[20] However, the official crackdown at Canton came at precisely the time when the BEIC found itself in possession of a large accumulation of opium stocks. James Matheson, of Jardine and Matheson fame, allegedly pioneered the "coast trade" in foreign opium, having made a large profit from selling opium in Xiamen in 1823. But it may have been Fujianese traders, primarily from Quanzhou and Hui'an, who initiated the trade when they sailed south to purchase foreign opium and then urged the foreign vessels to deliver their goods directly. After 1834, when the BEIC monopoly was rescinded, the opium trade became a virtual free-for-all.[21]

---

17. Owen, *British Opium Policy in China and India*, pp. 81–102, 113. Figures on opium imports taken from Morse, *International Relations of the Chinese Empire*, 1: 173, 209; Chang Hsin-pao, *Commissioner Lin and the Opium War*, pp. 48–50, 223; and Spence, *The Search for Modern China*, p. 129.

18. Chang Hsin-pao, *Commissioner Lin and the Opium War*, pp. 36–46; Lin Renchuan, "Qingdai Fujian de yapian maoyi."

19. Lin Renchuan, "Qingdai Fujian de yapian maoyi," pp. 62–63.

20. Gardella, *Harvesting Mountains*, pp. 106–7.

21. Chang Hsin-pao, *Commissioner Lin and the Opium War*, p. 33; Beeching, *The Chinese Opium Wars*, pp. 33–42. See also Lin Renchuan, "Qingdai Fujian de yapian maoyi," pp. 62–63; Collis, *Foreign Mud*, pp. 66–81; and Fay, *The Opium War*, pp. 58–61.

The first center of opium smuggling in Fujian was Zhao'an county, located along the border with Guangdong near the city of Shantou (Swatow). The center of the trade soon shifted north to the jagged coastal regions around the trading ports of Quanzhou and Zhangzhou. The small, isolated fishing villages in these areas, with their easy access to inland waterways, were better situated for distributing the drug throughout the province.[22] For example, the village of Yakou was transformed into a storehouse for the imported drug, with a neat row of warehouses lining the docks.[23] From their primary hubs around Quanzhou and Zhangzhou, smugglers conveyed the foreign opium into Anxi, Nan'an, Yongchun, and Xinghua, primarily along inland waterways. Some was reported in the shops of Nantai, an island suburb of Fuzhou. The opium often was transported to Yanping, where it could then be shipped into Jiangxi and Zhejiang provinces. And in contrast to the distribution network in Canton, where a small number of local firms monopolized the foreign opium trade, the major clans in southeast Fujian competed to import, protect, and sell the drug. In Pucheng county, the Shi, Chen, and Ding clans were among those who cooperated willingly with British traders and set up extensive trafficking networks that moved opium throughout Fujian and into markets in the cities of Ningbo and Shanghai and as far north as Shandong province.[24]

The lucrative nature of the underground opium economy in Fujian often aggravated existing social divisions and contributed to the general deterioration of public order, particularly in the southeast. The escalation of the drug trade inspired a resurgence of piracy along the Fujian coastline,[25] but in many cases local officials accepted bribes to facilitate the landing of the drug.[26] According to one account, the scene along the Fujian coastline was often chaotic, with "thousands upon thousands whistling to sailors on the [foreign opium] boats to make deals."[27] As the opium economy took root in the 1820s and

---

22. Qi Sihe, *Huang Juezi zhoushu, Xu Naiji zouyi hekan*, pp. 103–4.
23. Xu Liangxiao, "Pujiang jindu ji," pp. 137–38; and Lin Renchuan, "Qingdai Fujian de yapian maoyi," pp. 63–65. Both of these authors cite the same source, *Rongma fengtao ji* ('The stormy life of a warhorse' collection), but a search for that volume in library and archival collections in Fuzhou proved fruitless.
24. Xu Liangxiao, "Pujiang jindu ji," p. 137.
25. Beeching, *The Chinese Opium Wars*, pp. 167–68.
26. Lin Renchuan, "Qingdai Fujian de yapian maoyi," pp. 63–65; Chang Hsin-pao, *Commissioner Lin and the Opium War*, p. 33; and Collis, *Foreign Mud*, p. 78.
27. Lin Renchuan, "Qingdai Fujian de yapian maoyi," pp. 63–65.

1830s, clashes erupted among clans in the Zhangzhou-Quanzhou region over the right to dominate local sales of opium. As the violence escalated, many clans hired armed mercenaries for protection, and the ranks of these so-called fighting sticks (*dougun*) harbored many opium smokers and traffickers. The brutality of these private militias often exacerbated clan feuds and created a dangerous climate in the countryside as the mercenaries harassed travelers, searching for and confiscating opium by force.[28]

Despite the expansion of the trade, the ingenious means used to conceal the drug from local authorities indicate that those involved were aware of its illicit nature. Opium was discovered hidden among containers of goods like betel nuts, fish, and cloth. On one occasion, the drug was molded to resemble swallows' nests, which presumably were passed off to customs officials as culinary delicacies.[29] However, much of the trade was carried out openly, and the complicity of many local authorities made a mockery of Qing antiopium laws and implicitly supported the British argument that traders in Indian opium were simply responding to Chinese demand.

In 1834, when the BEIC's monopoly on trade with China was revoked, the opium traffic surged, fueled in part by the need to sell existing stocks of the drug.[30] Private merchants and trading firms rushed to bid for the rights to transport and distribute the lucrative commodity in Canton and all along the Chinese coast. The Qing government felt that the situation had reached a critical point, and after a lengthy and often vitriolic debate in 1836 over whether to legalize or to attack the opium trade, it decided on the latter course.[31] Lin Zexu and others in the prohibition faction favored the vigorous enforcement of existing statutes and the promulgation of more restrictions. The policy necessitated a direct confrontation with the British. The result proved disastrous for the Chinese government, although the Qing state did set an important moral and symbolic precedent on which it was able to draw more successfully in the early twentieth-century campaign.

In March 1839, Lin, by this time a respected and experienced scholar-official, arrived by boat in Guangzhou with an impressive entourage and an

---

28. Ibid., pp. 64–65, 71. For example, in Quanzhou, the Chen, Ya, and Shen clans all specialized in opium trafficking (Qi Sihe, *Huang Juezi zoushu, Xu Naiji zouyi hekan*, juan 13); Lamley, "Lineage Feuding in Southern Fujian and Eastern Guangdong Under Qing Rule," pp. 48–52.
29. Lin Renchuan, "Qingdai Fujian de yapian maoyi," pp. 63–65.
30. Owen, *British Opium Policy in China and India*, chap. 5.
31. Polachek, *The Inner Opium War*, pp. 103–24.

imperial mandate to oversee the dismantling of the flourishing black market in imported opium. His uncompromising rhetoric and forceful seizure and disposal of 20,000 chests of the contraband drug succeeded only in stimulating a military conflict between China and Great Britain that led to defeat for the Qing dynasty. China's humiliating defeat led to the dismantling of the longstanding tribute system that symbolically upheld the cultural superiority of the Qing state. On a more concrete level, the privileges that accrued to the foreign powers in the aftermath of the Opium War of 1839–42 not only increased outside access to valuable Chinese goods but also opened five ports—including Fuzhou and Xiamen—to foreign commerce, a mainstay of which was the still illegal, but rapidly expanding opium trade. The new British acquisition of Hong Kong became the primary entrepôt for Indian opium, and the coastal drug trade flourished as never before. In short, the actions initiated by Lin and other Chinese officials inadvertently stimulated the foundation of the opium economy in Lin's home province.

After the first Opium War, smuggling continued, and in some areas, official complicity made concealment ludicrous and unnecessary. By 1857, the U.S. consul at Fuzhou charged:

There is very little done here in the way of imports, except opium. In this article there is an immense trade, a single firm, selling in one month, more than two hundred thousand dollars worth. Nearly every firm in the port imports opium, and with the full sanction of the Chinese Authorities. . . . There is I believe an understanding between the importers of it, and the officials, that the latter are to receive ten dollars on each chest landed, which amount goes to the Customs House officers and is divided among them, from the Collector down to the Customs House boatmen, each receiving according to his rank.[32]

Ironically, the influx of and open trade in imported opium and the financial demands generated by the Taiping Rebellion apparently compelled Chinese authorities in Fujianese ports and elsewhere to disregard the prohibitions and illegally tax the contraband drug.[33] In summer 1857, Fuzhou prefect Ye Yongyuan discussed this measure with British authorities after clearing it with the governor-general. Ye explained that a similar taxation scheme had

---

32. USDS, Consular Despatches, Foochow, 1849–1906, reel 1, no. 30, Jones to Secy. of State, 1 Jan. 1857.

33. These negotiations are extensively documented in the records of the British Foreign Office, but the Chinese provincial authorities may not have been entirely displeased with the unofficial legalization of foreign opium (Fairbank, "Legalization of the Opium Trade").

been established in Shanghai and elsewhere to raise revenues for the provincial military and justified the proposal as a means by which the Chinese government could monitor and reap some financial benefit from the drug as it was transferred from foreign boats onto Chinese soil. The duty would be factored into the selling price and would be paid by the many Chinese merchants who purchased the drug; consumers would absorb the extra fee. This new scheme would employ the services of several Chinese officials and the police and required the cooperation of British consular officials. A similar conversation took place in Xiamen. A number of complications arose from the new system, and it is unclear how much, if anything, the imperial government knew about these measures.[34] In any case, the settlement of the *Arrow* War soon overrode these de facto taxation arrangements.

AFTER THE *ARROW* WAR: LEGALIZATION AND TAXATION OF OPIUM IMPORTS

Between 1842 and 1860, opium technically remained illegal in China, but the drug's symbolic significance and its potential as a revenue source made further conflict almost inevitable. The *Arrow* War, also known as the second Opium War (as Karl Marx termed it), began in 1856 and ended with the Treaty of Tianjin in 1858 and the Beijing Convention in 1860.[35] Provoked by foreign dissatisfaction with the Treaty of Nanjing, the conflict vastly increased foreign privileges in China, including new protections and freedoms for missionaries, and opened more ports to foreign trade. Most significant for this discussion, Article 26 set a standard tariff of 30 taels per picul of imported opium (one picul weighs 133.33 pounds and was roughly equivalent to a chest of the drug). Finally, the opium trade had been legalized.[36]

---

34. The documentation on the British side is quite extensive and is largely contained in reports from Sir John Bowring to the Foreign Office in FO, PRO 17/271, Bowring no. 340, 4 Aug. 1857.

35. The Treaty of Tianjin (Tientsin) was signed on 26 June 1858, and it was to be ratified a year later. However, when the time for ratification arrived, a diplomatic brouhaha that many felt had been initiated purposely by the British resulted in further military clashes and the sacking of the Summer Palace near Beijing. The ratification and further concessions were finalized in the Beijing [Peking] Convention of 1860. See Beeching, *The Chinese Opium Wars*; and J. Y. Wong, *Deadly Dreams*.

36. J. Y. Wong (*Deadly Dreams*, pp. 413–15) has detailed the process by which opium was included in this article in his superb study of the *Arrow* War. When the treaty was first signed, Article 26 simply stated that the tariff would be revised. No mention of opium was made until an American opium merchant convinced the U.S. minister to lobby his British

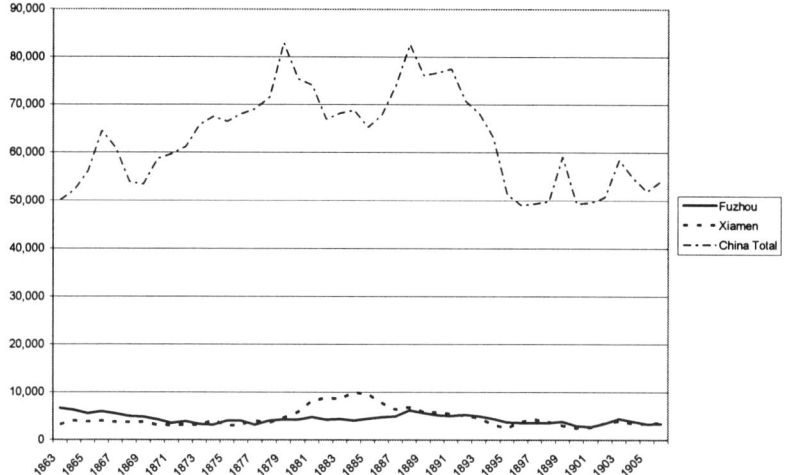

Fig. 2.3 Indian Opium Imports, 1863-1906 (in chests)

The most obvious and immediate impact of the legalization of foreign opium imports was a staggering increase in the amount of Indian drug in China. The peak in Indian opium imports occurred in 1879, when almost 83,000 piculs (more than eleven million pounds) entered China. However, the Chinese market that absorbed this enormous quantity of opium was changing, and the amount of imported opium began to decline steadily after the 1880s until it plateaued in the early 1900s at approximately 50,000 piculs annually. This did not indicate the saturation of the China market or a weakening of Chinese demand for opium. Rather, it signified the growth in domestic production. A similar pattern emerged in Fujian (see Fig. 2.3).

A few years before the *Arrow* War, the costs of fighting the Taiping Rebellion caused Beijing to institute a system of internal transit taxes (likin, or *lijin*) in 1853, a step that greatly affected trade patterns throughout China and increased Qing dependence on the opium trade. Fujian imposed the levy in the seventh year of the Xianfeng era (late 1857 or early 1858).[37] The transit

---

counterpart to add opium to the list of taxable imports. The latter ultimately agreed when presented with evidence that the Chinese authorities at Shanghai were already charging an illegal levy on the imported drug. When the British and the Chinese met to discuss the specifics of the treaty on 13 Oct. 1858, the change was made, apparently with Chinese approval.

37. Beal lists the date as "before November 7, 1858." For a list of the dates when each province began collecting the tax, see Beal, *The Origin of Likin*, preface, and pp. 1, 42–43. See also Luo Yudong, *Zhongguo lijin shi*, 1: 322–33. A detailed study of the evolution of *lijin* structure,

tax provided sizable revenue for both the provincial authorities that collected the tax and the central government; these factors contributed to the decision to retain the tax even after the Taiping defeat in 1864.[38]

The vast discrepancies in transit tax rates at various ports still shaped the opium trade.[39] For example, the decline in foreign opium imported into Fuzhou between 1868 and 1870 was attributed to the lower taxes at the nearby port of Shantou and elsewhere.[40] Importers at Xiamen faced similar obstacles. To dodge the prohibitive taxes at Fuzhou and Xiamen, many Chinese importers and distributors simply purchased the drug at more inexpensive ports and smuggled it into the lucrative Fujian market. In the southeast, for example, a well-traveled smuggling route developed between Hong Kong and the Fujianese city of Zhangzhou.[41] In 1879, one picul of foreign opium was taxed 76 Maritime Customs (*haiguan*) taels if it entered China through the port of Fuzhou and 83 taels if it landed in Xiamen. In contrast, the equivalent rate at Ningbo was 37 taels, at Shantou 38 taels, at Wenzhou 40 taels, and at Shanghai 21 taels.[42]

Despite the clear monetary disadvantages of importing opium legally into Fujian, the Chinese demand for the drug was so strong that opium became one of the principal imports at Xiamen and Fuzhou in the 1860s and 1870s, and a legitimate import and distribution system began to compete with the black market. In 1866, opium constituted one-third of total imports through

---

the ideology that spawned it, and the distribution of revenues can also be found in Mann, *Local Merchants and the Chinese Bureaucracy*, esp. chaps. 6-8.

38. Beal, *The Origin of Likin*, p. 43.

39. Rule of Trade number 5 (Subsection 1) under Article 26 of the Tianjin Treaty set a tariff of 30 taels per picul on foreign opium imported into China, in effect legalizing foreign imports of the drug. However, the same treaty stipulated that foreign opium had to be sold at the port of entry and that only Chinese could convey the drug to the interior, where it was then considered a Chinese good and subject to whatever transit taxes Chinese authorities wished to levy. See Reins, "China and the International Politics of Opium," pp. 32-34; Morse, *Trade and Administration of the Chinese Empire*, pp. 338-40; Spence, "Opium Smoking in Ch'ing China," p. 169; USDS, Consular Despatches, Amoy, 1844-1906, reel 2, no. 13, Hyatt to Secy. of State, 1 Oct. 1859; Beattie, "Protestant Missions and Opium in China," p. 105.

40. The U.S. consul at Fuzhou also believed that the beginnings of domestic cultivation contributed to the decline (USDS, Consular Despatches, Foochow, 1849-1906, reel 4, DeLano to Secy. of State, 15 Nov. 1870).

41. USDS, Consular Despatches, Amoy, 1844-1906, reel 3, no. 42, LeGendre to Dept. of State, 30 Sept. 1867, and map in no. 45, LeGendre to Dept. of State, 28 May 1868.

42. For opium tax rates at a number of treaty ports, see Lin Man-houng, "Wan Qing de yapian shui," p. 15.

Xiamen.[43] From 1869 to 1879, the value of foreign goods imported into Fuzhou averaged five million dollars annually, almost half of which came from Indian opium.[44] These two ports came to house an extensive array of retail establishments, many of which boiled the raw drug on the premises to prepare it for smoking. There were also separate boiling firms, and larger retailers belonged to an opium merchants' guild.[45]

In addition, Fujianese authorities took advantage of what they felt was a loophole in the provisions of the Treaty of Tianjin to extract more profit from the legal trade. The agreement stipulated that foreign goods were to pay the transit tax (as well as the import duty) only at the point of entry, after which they circulated freely throughout the empire without being subject to additional transit fees. However, the U.S. consul at Fuzhou complained in 1870 that once in Chinese hands, foreign goods had to pay the likin at every tax barrier they encountered. Local authorities absorbed the resulting revenue, and smugglers continued to do a booming business ferrying foreign opium past treaty port customs houses.[46]

Transit tax collections on foreign opium imports became an important source of revenue to defray provincial military expenses, charitable projects, and some of Fujian's obligations to the throne.[47] From its inception in 1858 to 1899, transit taxes and surtaxes on foreign opium in Fujian constituted an average of 20 percent of the total transit tax revenues for the province.[48] In 1902, the governor-general of Fujian and Zhejiang claimed that the transit

---

43. USDS, Consular Despatches, Amoy, 1844–1906, reel 3, no. 29, Jones to Secy. of State, 13 Dec. 1866.

44. USDS, Consular Despatches, Foochow, 1849–1906, reel 5, no. 245, DeLano to Secy. of State, 29 Sept. 1879.

45. The guild is referred to in ZZGB 37, a memorial from the Ministry of Revenue, endorsed 26 Sept. 1910, pp. 27–29. For a general description of the opium import-retail system, see Spence, "Opium Smoking in Ch'ing China," pp. 166–67; and IMC, SS No. 10.

46. USDS, Consular Despatches, Foochow, 1840–1906, reel 4, Delano to Secy. of State, 15 Nov. 1870.

47. From 1857 to 1870, an average of 94 percent of all *lijin* revenues collected in Fujian went toward provincial military expenses each year. That percentage fell to an average of 50 percent for the next 30 years (Luo Yudong, *Zhongguo lijin shi*, 2: 575–76 [table 87]). From 1875 to 1880, the British consul at Xiamen reported that 10 percent of the *lijin* collected on foreign opium imports in his consular district was used to fund a local foundling hospital, supplement the local salt gabelle, and purchase edible birds' nests for the emperor (PRO, FO 228/645, no. 54, enclosure 1 in Giles to Wade, 20 Dec, 1880, and PRO, FO 233/92).

48. Luo Yudong, *Zhongguo lijin shi*, 2: 562–63 (table 77).

tax essentially funded the operations of the Fuzhou city government and paid for the soldiers stationed there.[49]

The central state also benefited from the taxes on foreign opium imported into Fujian, although Beijing's initial enthusiasm for the transit tax—and its share of the provincial take—diminished as authorities in Fuzhou moved to channel less of the revenue to the central government and to reduce private involvement in opium tax collection.[50] According to the U.S. consul at Fuzhou in 1870, the transit tax quickly became "a means of maintaining a numerous and ever-increasing class of officials who receive little or no compensation from the general government"[51]—in other words, a self-supporting and self-perpetuating provincial tax system essentially beyond the reach of Beijing. By contrast, an entirely extra-bureaucratic system persisted for many years in southeastern Fujian until the provincial government stepped in.[52]

The implementation of the Additional Article of the Chefoo Convention of 1 February 1887, caused a decisive shift in the pattern of foreign opium importation in Fujian, simultaneously rerouting more opium-related taxes to

---

49. U.S. consul Samuel L. Gracey at Fuzhou reported that Governor-General Xu Yingkui admitted this in the Peking Gazette (USDS, Consular Despatches, Foochow, 1849–1906, reel 10, no. 123, Gracey to Dept. of State, 24 June 1902). In 1909, an imperial edict also noted the strong connection between army expenditures and opium tax revenue (including *lijin*). The edict was dated 15 March 1909 and was cited in ZZGB 20, a memorial by Governor-General Songshou, endorsed 19 May 1909, pp. 104–8.

50. According to Susan Mann (*Local Merchants and the Chinese Bureaucracy*, pp. 111–16), between 1870 and 1909, over half of the empire's *lijin* revenues came from four provinces: Jiangsu, Fujian, Zhejiang, and Guangdong. From 1867 to 1902, the Board of Finance (Hu bu) appropriated an average of about 18.7 percent of Fujian's total transit tax revenue, or an average of two million taels yearly. Beijing's exactions began at 4.46 percent in 1862 and peaked at 33 percent in 1875 (Luo Yudong, *Zhongguo lijin shi*, 2: 575–76 [Table 87]). For charts detailing the state's use of these fees, see Luo, 2: 565–70.

51. USDS, Consular Despatches, Foochow, 1849–1906, reel 5, no. 217, DeLano to Secy. of State, 20 Oct. 1878.

52. Changes in the system by which the transit tax on opium was collected in Xiamen illustrate that the transition from "protective brokerage" to "entrepreneurial brokerage" that characterizes Duara's thesis in *Culture, Power, and the State* on the growing intrusiveness of the late Qing state in north China corresponded with a similar phenomenon in the south. This would seem to contradict Mann's (*Local Merchants and the Chinese Bureaucracy*, pp. 155–160, 201) contention that there was a general expansion of the defensive "liturgical" tax collection method after the turn of the twentieth century—a development that she contends is a function of the weakness of bureaucratic control in local commerce.

central government coffers and enriching provincial treasuries. The article, signed on 18 July 1885, established a fixed, one-time charge of 110 taels per picul for imported opium—80 taels for transit tax and 30 to cover the import duty—both of which were to be collected by the Imperial Maritime Customs.[53] This action was designed to eliminate excessive taxes and allow the foreign drug to remain competitive with domestic opium, but in fact it resulted in a burgeoning of domestic cultivation. As Thomas Reins explains, "Even with a ceiling on taxes for foreign opium, a levy of 110 taels per picul went a long way toward making the British opium non-competitive in China."[54] In other words, the domestic article was still taxed at a much lower rate than its foreign counterpart.

This move to standardize taxes on foreign opium also presented provincial authorities in Fuzhou with an unexpected windfall and Chinese opium merchants with much-needed tax relief. The circuit intendant (*daotai*) of Fuzhou had indicated at a meeting with the British consul in 1881 that a levy of anywhere from 80 to 100 taels would benefit the provincial government enormously.[55] The new system shifted the transit tax burden from the shoulders of Chinese merchants who handled the drug after it landed in China onto those of foreign importers.[56] However, despite the conspicuous labeling required for foreign opium after 1887, both domestic and foreign supplies were still subject to local extortion and harassment on occasion.[57]

Foreign observers had predicted that with the standardization of import duties, foreign opium that had previously been routed through less expensive ports would be imported directly through Fuzhou, with its easy access to the Min River. The increase was actually a bit less than 20 percent—significant, but far less than expected. And beginning in 1889, imports to Fuzhou began to decline (see Fig. 2.3).[58] In Xiamen, foreign customs officials reported that imports of the foreign drug fell from a high of over 9,000 piculs in 1884–85 to just over 5,000 piculs in 1891.[59] Apparently, most of the Malwa and Patna

---

53. Morse, *Trade and Administration of the Chinese Empire*, p. 340.
54. Reins, "China and the International Politics of Opium," p. 34.
55. PRO, FO 233/92, no. 27, Hillier to Wade, 8 Sept. 1881.
56. Lin Man-houng, "Wan Qing de yapian shui," p. 17.
57. IMC, *Decennial Reports, Santuao, 1892–1901*, p. 86.
58. IMC, *Decennial Reports, Foochow, 1882–1891*, pp. 409, 412–13; IMC, SS No. 14.
59. In 1881, opium tax rates at Shantou exceeded even those at Xiamen, causing imports to the latter port to soar; they declined only when Shantou tax rates did the same (IMC, *China Opium Trade, 1889–1894*, "Amoy" [1889], pp. 15–16).

varieties of Indian opium previously imported into Xiamen were diverted to Shantou, where it was more popular, although Xiamen's imports of Benares opium remained virtually the same throughout the 1880s.[60]

This did not, however, indicate a lessening of Fujianese demand for the drug. The U.S. consul at Fuzhou noted that after 1887, "The new regulations have been followed by a manifest increase in the number of opium dens, and I have been told by officials that the number of smokers has also increased."[61] Decreasing imports of the foreign drug, coupled with a visible surge in the number of consumers, meant either an expansion of domestic cultivation, a surge in smuggling, or most likely, a combination of both. A customs report in 1888 speculated that the older generation of smokers who had preferred the Indian drug was dying off and being replaced by younger consumers accustomed to cheaper Chinese varieties.[62]

Foreign opium imports into Fujian continued to drop dramatically in the 1890s. Persian opium imports at Xiamen and Shantou fell from 2,060 piculs in 1882 to 550 piculs in 1890, due largely to the improved quality and increased quantity of the domestic drug.[63] Indian opium was apparently less in demand as well, and one foreign observer speculated that adulteration may have been partly responsible, noting that, "a man smoking Foreign drug would at one time perfume the whole room, whilst now there is little or no aroma perceptible."[64] Fuzhou customs officials reported a drop in foreign opium imports of almost 50 percent, from 5,256 piculs in 1892 to 2,702 piculs in 1901. They speculated that the decline was partly due to the increased importation of Chinese opium and expanding domestic cultivation, but noted

---

60. The opium smokers of Shantou favored Patna and Malwa. The price of Benares opium, preferred by smokers in Xiamen, also fell during this decade, from $564 per picul in 1884 to $418 in 1891 (IMC, *Decennial Reports, Amoy, 1882–1901*, pp. 502–3). The Shantou connection was easy to access because many Shantou opium hongs had opened in Xiamen when the opium tax there was farmed out to a Shantou man (IMC, *China Opium Trade, 1889–1894*, "Amoy" [1889], pp. 15–16).

61. USDS, Consular Despatches, Foochow, 1849–1906, reel 7, no. 203, Wingate to Secy. of State, 29 Mar. 1888.

62. IMC, SS No. 14, pp. 6–7.

63. IMC, *Decennial Reports, Amoy, 1882–1891*, p. 502–5.

64. IMC, *Decennial Reports, Foochow, 1892–1901*, p. 101. A customs report from Xiamen implied an alternative explanation. Since domestic opium in Fujian, particularly in the south, was almost always used in combination with the foreign drug, it is possible that an increased proportion of Chinese opium in the mixture may have weakened the distinctive odor referred to above (see IMC, SS No. 14, pp. 40–41).

that even after these two sources were added to foreign imports, consumption still appeared to have fallen 1,500 piculs over the decade. The decline in the tea trade may have reduced the income of the people to such an extent that they could no longer afford a "luxury" item such as opium, but the continued population increase convinced these officials that the number of Chinese opium smokers had probably not decreased. Smuggling, either from Singapore or Hong Kong, was blamed.[65]

At Xiamen, the customs reported a similar decline in foreign opium imports over the decade—from 5,044 piculs in 1892 to 2,556 piculs in 1901. Much like their counterparts at Fuzhou, customs officials at Xiamen insisted that the number of Chinese consumers of opium had soared during this same time period and reported a surge in domestic poppy cultivation as well as a growing taste for the much-improved Chinese product.[66] Rumors reached the Xiamen customs office that a great deal of domestic opium was being transported from Taizhou—in Zhejiang near Wenzhou—by junk to Quanzhou, thereby reducing the demand in the latter city for the foreign drug.[67] No imports of Chinese opium at Xiamen were recorded for either 1892 or 1893, but by 1901, 1,407 piculs were entering that port.[68]

The continuing difference in price between the foreign and the Chinese drug was also a significant element in the decline of Fujian's foreign opium imports. In Xiamen, a picul of foreign opium that cost about 400 Maritime Customs taels in 1892 was worth 600–700 taels in 1901. The same amount of the native drug could be purchased for between 360 and 380 Maritime Customs taels throughout the decade. In addition, morphine imports at Xiamen increased dramatically from 460 ounces in 1891 to 16,776 ounces in 1900, indicating to foreign customs officials that morphine was probably serving as a substitute for opium.[69] In 1906, China imported just over 54,000 piculs of Indian opium, 7,000 of which entered through Xiamen or Fuzhou.[70]

---

65. IMC, *Decennial Reports, Foochow, 1892–1901*, pp. 100–101; and *1882–1901*, p. 413; IMC, SS No. 14, p. 37.
66. IMC, *Decennial Reports, Amoy, 1892–1901*, pp. 125–26, 128.
67. IMC, SS No. 14, p. 40.
68. IMC, *Decennial Reports, Amoy, 1892–1901*, p. 128.
69. The same officials blamed this development on misinformed but well-meaning western missionary physicians who initially believed that morphine was an excellent drug to be used in the treatment of opium addiction. Unfortunately, their Chinese pupils also adopted this method, even after the Christian church took a definitive stand against morphine in 1900 (IMC, *Decennial Reports, Amoy, 1892–1901*, pp. 127–28).
70. Lin Man-houng, "Qingmo benguo yapian zhi tidai jinkou yapian," table 2, pp. 402–4.

The steady decline in opium imports did not mean that Fuzhou and Xiamen were beginning to wean themselves from opium-related revenue. In fact, taxes on foreign opium imports (customs duties and the transit tax) constituted an increasingly substantial proportion of customs revenue at those treaty ports. Taxes on imported opium as a percentage of total customs duties at Fuzhou went from an average of 6.7 percent for the years 1867–86 to an average of 30 percent for 1887–99 to almost 40 percent in 1900–1906. At Xiamen, the importance of the revenue from taxes on imported opium peaked in the late 1890s, but the percentages in relation to the port's total customs take were at times even higher than in Fuzhou, averaging 25 percent in 1867–86, 53.5 percent in 1887–99, and 45 percent in 1900–1906.[71]

Competition between foreign opium and its domestic counterpart not only inspired foreign calls for Chinese regulation but also dictated the ebb and flow of the trade itself. As a foreign consular official at Zhenjiang, in Jiangxi province, put it:

A regular see-saw has been established in the [opium] trade.... If Chinese opium is cheap and abundant, the import of Indian opium must be diminished or its price fall. If, on the other hand, the price of native opium is artificially raised by prohibition or taxation, or naturally by a poor crop, the void is instantly supplied by Indian opium.[72]

Although the seesaw analogy was essentially accurate, demand for the drug continued to grow, and the supply expanded to meet it. Increasingly, that supply was grown and prepared in China.

"Can You Hear the Poppies Sing?"

One day I saw an attractive scarlet flower growing on your uncle's land. I said to him, "Laoxin, you better stick to growing vegetables; what are you doing growing flowers?" Laoxin said, "Those aren't flowers, those are the best damned vegetables of all; eat them and you won't want to eat any other vegetables.... Opium. Opium is what you get from the flowers." His eyes brightening, Dad said, "When I walked into that field of opium poppies and felt those big follicles, I heard those damned flowers singing to me; it's true! I heard them singing, and I was captivated."

---

71. Lin Man-houng, "Wan Qing de yapian shui," tables 8 and 10, and appendix; IMC, *Decennial Reports, Amoy, 1902–1911*, pp. 101–2.

72. Report by E. L. Oxenham in 1883, cited in Waung, "Introduction of Opium Cultivation to China," p. 218.

> The distinction between intelligence and stupidity was right there beside that field of opium poppies—can you hear the opium poppies sing?
>
> —Su Tong, "Opium Family"[73]

After the Opium Wars, the tune of the poppies became increasingly tempting, inspiring more and more Chinese farmers to adopt opium as a cash crop. Poppy fields began to spring up in Fujian in the nineteenth century and blanketed other parts of the Chinese countryside.[74] The improved quality and low price of the homegrown article, relative to that of its foreign competition, ensured a vast domestic market, especially among the lower classes.

As the amount of Chinese land devoted to cultivation of the poppy expanded after the legalization of foreign opium imports, particularly in the provinces of Sichuan, Yunnan, and Guizhou, imports began to decline. In fact, by 1904, Sichuan province alone was producing four times the total amount of opium imported into China from India.[75] Table 2.1 gives a sense of how much opium was being produced domestically on the eve of the suppression campaign, although the figure for Fujian is a gross underestimate, as noted in subsequent tables.

The burgeoning domestic harvest had a profound impact on strategies employed by opium reformers after 1906 and contributed disproportionately to the intractability of Fujian's opium problem. That problem would have been sufficiently complex without domestic cultivation, but as the amount of land devoted to poppies increased during the final decades of the Qing, so did the investment of many Fujianese farmers in the continuation of the province's opium economy. The role of the Chinese state in determining and implementing opium-related policies, often as demanded by western powers, was as important in shaping the domestic side of Fujian's opium supply as it was in regulating the flow and pattern of foreign imports into the province.

The poppy was generally planted in the late fall in Fujian. It reached full flower in February or March and was harvested (drained) in the spring—a profitable use of the winter months.[76] A variety of poppies were cultivated

---

73. Su Tong, "Opium Family," *Raise the Red Lantern*, pp. 211–12. The story from which this citation was taken is situated during the rise of the Chinese Communist Party in the 1930s–40s.

74. Waung, "Introduction of Opium Cultivation to China," pp. 210–11; Turner, *British Opium Policy*, pp. 135–37; and USDS, 1906–1910, reel 104, 774/8, Rockhill to Root, 8 Sept. 1906.

75. Wyman, "Opium and the State in Late-Qing Sichuan," pp. 214–15.

76. PRO, FO 228/2457, Opium (January-March, 1914), note from E.C.W. at British Legation, 16 Jan. 1914 and attached to no. 91; IMC, *Decennial Reports, Amoy, 1882–1891*, pp. 503–4.

Table 2.1
Estimated Poppy Production in China, Circa 1906
(in piculs)

Province	Opium production	Province	Opium production
Guangdong	500	Anhui	3,000
Fujian	2,000	Henan	5,000
Zhejiang	5,000	Shanxi	5,000
Jiangsu	5,000	Shaanxi	10,000
Shandong	10,000	Gansu	5,000
Zhili	5,000	Sichuan	250,000
Manchuria	15,000	Yunnan	30,000
Hunan	3,000	Guizhou	15,000
Hubei	4,000	Guangxi	3,000
Jiangxi	500	TOTAL ESTIMATE	376,000

SOURCE: Morse, *Trade and Administration*, pp. 345–50. Morse claims to have cited the most conservative figures available and states that the figure for Fujian is clearly an underestimate.

in the province, providing passersby with what one foreign customs official described as "quite a charming view from the medley of white, yellow, red, and pink poppy flowers."[77] Opium could be cultivated alone or alongside potatoes, beans, and other crops.[78] The plants thrived in relatively sandy soil and took well to hills and terraces unsuitable for other crops. Poppies did, however, require a good deal of fertilizer—sometimes manure, but more frequently beancake (*doufu*)—and a harvest could easily be destroyed by excessive wind or rainfall.[79] In addition, the harvesting process was very labor intensive. Once harvested, whether "raw" or in prepared form,[80] the drug was light and easy to

---

77. IMC, SS No. 9, Van Aalst to Hart, 6 June 1887.

78. Ibid.; Buck, *Land Utilization in China*, pp. 206–7, shows a photograph of poppies growing between rows of tobacco in Gansu.

79. According to an assistant to the customs commissioner in Amoy, poppy farmers in Tongan county were reported to have spent up to $3 worth of beancake to fertilize a crop that yielded $15 of opium (IMC, SS No. 9, Van Aalst, 6 June 1887). Another customs official once pointed out that by gauging the pattern of beancake imports, one could at least determine if the domestic poppy crop had increased or decreased over a particular period of time (IMC, *Decennial Reports, Santuao, 1892–1901*, p. 85; IMC, *Decennial Reports, Amoy, 1882–1891*, p. 504).

80. Prepared domestic opium was known locally as opium paste (*tu jiang*) or local paste (*bendi jiang*) (IMC, SS No. 9, Brown to Hart, 31 May 1887). Domestic opium was also sold as *xiao tu* or "small opium," a category that included Persian imports (IMC, SS No. 9, Van Aalst, 6 June 1887).

carry or conceal. In short, it was a commodity unlikely to be hindered by the difficult conditions for cultivation and transportation in Fujian.

Tongan county, located about twenty miles north of Xiamen, had the dubious distinction of being the center of opium cultivation in Fujian's southeast throughout much of the late Qing / early Republic. Opium cultivation had been reported there since the 1830s.[81] Foreign customs officials described Tongan as a "turbulent district over which the [Chinese] authorities have but little control" and reported some 500 piculs of opium produced in Tongan in 1863, a tenfold increase over production there just two years earlier.[82] Tongan was also known for clan feuding so violent that its landscape was marred by hundreds of gun towers.[83] Opium production, smuggling, and sales became entangled with clan rivalries, and officials hesitated to attempt to enforce the law.

The British consul at Xiamen offered an intriguing but unsubstantiated explanation for Tongan's ability to bypass longstanding government restrictions on opium cultivation:

The prohibition affects little beyond providing a convenient excuse for the underlings attached to the Magistrate's yamen to make every attempt to extort as much as possible from those who openly violate the law. The genius of the T'ung-an opium proprietors has, however, proved almost too much for their rapacious enemies. The entire management of the crop from seedtime to its enclosure in hermetically-sealed cylinders is entrusted to women, who oppose any hostile movement on the part of official underlings by such feminine demonstrations as invariably result in their being left mistresses of the situation.[84]

---

81. Lin Man-houng, "Qingmo shehui liuxing xishi yapian yanjiu," pp. 581–82. Lin cites a memorial dated 1830 from Sun Erzhun, then governor-general of Fujian and Zhejiang. British estimates are slightly more conservative. In 1880, the British consul at Amoy claimed that the poppy had been grown in Tongan for no less than 30 years, despite the annual posting of a proclamation prohibiting cultivation (PRO, FO 228/644, Giles to Wade, 7 June 1880).

82. Customs officials also noted that the domestic drug was sold in a prepared state. As noted in Chapter 1, preparation of the drug usually entailed boiling it down to about one-half its original weight/volume (Appendix to IMC, SS No. 9, Hughes to Hart, 16 Mar. 1864; USDS, Consular Despatches, Amoy, 1844–1906, reel 3, no. 2, Bradford to Secy. of State, 30 June 1864).

83. Lamley, "Lineage Feuding in Southern Fujian," p. 49.

84. PRO, FO 228/644, Giles to Wade, 7 June 1880; USDS, Consular Despatches, 1844–1906, Amoy, reel 7, no. 85, Henderson to Secy. of State, 8 Nov. 1875.

Unfortunately, there are no further references to or descriptions of these "feminine demonstrations" in this or any other source that I have encountered. However, the U.S. consul at Amoy noted in 1875 that in his district, which included Tongan, it was the job of women and girls to pick the tea leaves. It is possible that when the tea industry declined, those workers may have become involved in opium production.

A decade later, a foreign official speculated that Tongan's large poppy harvest was less a question of poor government control than a general lack of knowledge about correct cultivation methods elsewhere.[85] The same official also commented on the alleged character of the people of Tongan:

> [They] have a very bad reputation among Chinese: they are daring, and they descend from a race of pirates. Yet I have found the T'unganese as quiet, as good-natured, and as well disposed toward Foreigners as anyone could wish. They plant Opium just as they would plant potatoes—without suspecting they are doing wrong. They plant Opium because it brings them one or two strings of cash more than other crops [about double the return of a similarly-sized crop of rice]; and like all the peasants in the world, they like cash because cash buys land.[86]

Some Chinese may have seen the cultivation of poppies as indicative of a serious flaw in these farmers' characters, probably because such an action was not only illegal but also profitable. More likely, however, is that the bad reputation referred to above had less to do with a violation of Confucian ethics than jealousy on the part of other struggling farmers or frustration on the part of officials seeking to quell the endemic violence in that area.

It was reported that west of Tongan city, "every farmer has his plot of ground devoted to the cultivation of poppy during the winter months," an estimated total of 10 square *li*.[87] By 1887, Tongan was said to be producing anywhere from 100 to 500 piculs, and Anxi (about 40 miles north of Xiamen) about 200 piculs,[88] although accurate figures were hard to come by

---

85. That official noted that poppy cultivation was being attempted in several areas without notable success (IMC, SS No, 9, Van Aalst, 6 June 1887).

86. Ibid.

87. One square *li* is approximately 4 million square feet, according to this source (ibid.). However, that source assumes that one *li* is 2,000 feet long. Current conversion rates assume that it was about half that length.

88. IMC, SS No. 9, Brown to Hart, 31 May 1887. It should be noted, however, that Brown's assistant stated that no opium was being cultivated in Anxi.

since poppy cultivation was still technically illegal.[89] Much of Tongan's bounty was distributed throughout the region.[90] As early as 1863, about 200 piculs of Tongan's total estimated production of 500 piculs was consumed in and around Xiamen, with the rest shipped to the districts of Anxi, Zhangzhou, and Quanzhou, as well as to Taiwan and even Tianjin.[91] As for the rest of the southeast region, one missionary observed that farmers had begun to plant poppies in the immediate vicinity of Xiamen by 1871.[92] And in 1874, Xiamen customs claimed that "the poppy has replaced wheat as this area's winter crop, and one-third of the hillside plots are planted in poppy."[93]

Poppies also were cultivated in other parts of the province, particularly in the northeastern prefecture of Funing. One foreign customs official claimed that "tradition credits Fu-an [Fu'an], in this prefecture, with having produced the first crop of poppies, 150 years ago [circa 1750], from seed brought from India," although the accuracy of that statement cannot be confirmed independently.[94] In 1879, customs reports indicated that the Fujian-Zhejiang border region produced about 1,000 piculs of opium, and Fu'an county and the surrounding prefecture of Funing remained the center of northeastern domestic poppy cultivation throughout the late Qing.[95] There is no evidence that the poppy was cultivated in Fujian outside the coastal regions before the late nineteenth century. At this point in time, the *amount* of opium in Fujian did not concern the authorities as much as its illegal existence and the fact that the amount of land planted in poppies was increasing steadily.

---

89. For the same reason, customs officials in Fuzhou could not even arrive at an estimate for their area in that year (IMC, SS No. 9, pp. 32–52, and chart facing p. 52).

90. IMC, *Decennial Reports, Amoy, 1882–1891*, p. 504.

91. Appendix to IMC, SS No. 9, Hughes to Hart, 16 Mar. 1864.

92. LMS, China—Fukien, Incoming Correspondence (1845–1927), box 1 (Fukien, 1845–71), folder 5, jacket B, Macgowan to Mullens, 9 May 1871.

93. 1874 customs report for Xiamen cited in Lin Man-houng, "Qingmo shehui liuxing xishi yapian yanjiu," p. 582.

94. IMC, *Decennial Reports, Santuao, 1892–1901*, p. 86. This may have been true with regard to the province of Fujian, but not for China as a whole. In a report derived from earlier customs documents, an American official stated unequivocally that "the cultivation of the opium poppy in the province of Yunnan was already an important industry in 1736" (FRUS, 1906, pt. 1, pp. 354–55).

95. 1879 customs report cited in Lin Man-houng, "Qingmo shehui liuxing xishi yapian yanjiu," p. 582.

DOMESTIC OPIUM AND THE TEA TRADE

One historian claims: "The importation of narcotics to offset the export of Chinese tea and silk of course became *the* great moral issue of nineteenth-century Sino-Western commerce."[96] Unsurprisingly, then, the collapse of the tea trade in Fujian revealed the degree to which it had become intertwined in the provincial economy with the spread of foreign opium and the expansion of domestic poppy cultivation. The cultivation of tea, a longtime tradition in the Bohea Hills (Wuyi shan) of northwest Fujian, spread to the southeast and even into the northeast in response to rising foreign demand. From the 1850s to the 1880s, Fujian experienced a "tea export boom."[97] By the 1880s, however, a combination of local negligence, heavy state taxation, and competition from the tea plantations of India and Ceylon caused the export market for Fujianese tea to collapse.[98] Furthermore, the occupation of Taiwan by Japan in 1895 soon resulted in direct trade between Taiwanese tea producers and other markets, virtually eliminating the once-thriving re-export trade in Xiamen. As a result of all these elements, the export of black tea from Fujian fell by 50 percent between 1892 and 1901, and by 1901, a foreign customs official at Xiamen pronounced the once-popular Amoy oolongs "vile."[99]

Tea exports remained a crucial prop for the provincial economy, largely because of the healthy trade in brick and green tea to Chinese emigrants in Southeast Asia, but the "tea bust" took an especially severe toll on Fujian's southeast. Many farmers searching for an equally lucrative crop turned to opium. Others may have turned to it for solace. As early as 1874, the U.S. consul at Xiamen reported the early signs of the impending downturn, blaming the poor quality of recent tea crops on opium addiction: "Lately, the ravages of English opium have been fast reducing many of [the tea bearers and cultivators] to bankruptcy, starvation and death. In some localities, whole mountains once occupied and highly cultivated are now deserted and the people themselves say opium is impoverishing and depopulating the

---

96. Gardella, *Harvesting Mountains*, p. 105.
97. Gardella, *Harvesting Mountains*, chap. 2.
98. IMC, *Decennial Reports, Amoy, 1882–1891*, pp. 497–99; IMC, *Decennial Reports, Foochow, 1892–1901*, p. 99; IMC, *Decennial Reports, Santuao, 1892–1901*, p. 84. Customs officials at the treaty port of Santu'ao blamed the decline less on price than on changing foreign palates and the failure of the Chinese to advertise their product.
99. Gardella, "Fukien's Tea Industry and Trade," pp. 191–207; IMC, *Decennial Reports, Amoy, 1892–1901*, p. 124.

country."[100] By 1901, another official offered this gloomy assessment of Xiamen's trade prospects: "Tea has practically disappeared, and nothing has taken its place. Native opium has, as we have seen, advanced by leaps and bounds, and probably a large quantity of this drug is grown on the ground which at one time produced tea; I understand, however, that the greater part of this land is now waste."[101]

Fuzhou and the northeast suffered far less, since that area retained access to many internal tea markets and also boasted a robust export trade in timber and paper, but many tea merchants in the traditional tea-growing regions of the northwest and far northeast were ruined.[102] The last decades of the nineteenth century thus brought economic disaster for the Fujianese tea industry, and as farmers searched for a substitute that was profitable and compatible with local growing conditions, some turned to poppies to salvage their losses.

TAXING THE DOMESTIC POPPY

As the need for revenue by farmers and officials became urgent, the Qing state came under pressure to legalize poppy cultivation. Like its foreign counterpart, domestic opium was not systematically taxed until it became legal, and in Fujian legalization was preceded by irregular and often arbitrary policies. The confusion reflected the Qing court's indecision and its attempts to reconcile its longstanding moral and legal objections to opium with its desperate financial situation. The taxation of domestic opium began at different times in different provinces, but by 1891, poppy cultivation was legalized throughout China.[103] The Qing government had on numerous occasions reiterated its strict prohibition of domestic poppy cultivation, but to little avail in Fujian.[104] In Xiamen, the circuit intendant was said to have farmed out the collection of the transit tax on domestic opium around 1877, although his successor revoked the license shortly thereafter. In 1887, a customs official complained that although the prohibition on domestic cultivation was well known in the Xiamen region, and the drug therefore subject to

---

100. USDS, Consular Despatches, Amoy, 1844–1906, reel 7, Henderson to Dept. of State, Annual Trade Report, 30 Sept. 1874.
101. IMC, *Decennial Reports*, Amoy, 1892–1901, p. 147.
102. Gardella, "Fukien's Tea Industry and Trade," pp. 214–16.
103. Jiang and Shi, *Zhongguo jindu licheng*, pp. 89–90.
104. Yu Ende, *Zhongguo jinyan faling bianqian shi*, pp. 94–95, 103.

confiscation if discovered in transit, the trade had "not as a matter of fact been much interfered with."[105]

After implementation of the Additional Article to the Chefoo Convention in 1887, opium harvests in Fujian increased significantly, and the poppy began to appear in districts where it had previously been absent.[106] Central authorities claimed that the new policy would reduce poppy acreage in China, but in fact, the newly regularized and more efficient collection of taxes on imported opium stimulated domestic poppy cultivation. In effect, the measure constituted official recognition and legalization of poppy cultivation.[107]

The Qing government formally permitted Chinese farmers to plant opium poppies in 1891 by announcing the inauguration of a nationwide policy of taxing the domestic drug "in a straightforward bid to improve central government finances by drawing tax proceeds on opium away from the provincial authorities."[108] This was a major decision by the Chinese state, and it had an enormous impact on the development of Fujian's opium economy. In Fujian, some confusion apparently surrounded the new system. The British consul at Xiamen reported that the central government directive was issued and posted by Fujian's Head Transit Tax Office (Huashui zongju) in early January 1891 but was dated November 10, 1890. After the harvest, each opium farmer was to remit 42 taels per picul of raw opium as transit tax, after which the drug was to be free of all further charges. According to foreign customs officials at Fuzhou, the tax rate was close to one-third of the going price.[109] For a very brief period, an additional fee was also charged for each

---

105. Raw domestic opium apparently was assessed at half the rate for the foreign drug (IMC, SS No. 10, p. 53, Brown to Hart, 31 May 1887).

106. Waung believes that commercial cultivation of opium in China can be divided into four stages: "Phase I: from the beginning of cultivation to 1860, the year foreign opium became a legal import to China; Phase II: from 1860 to 1877, the year that north China was struck by a devastating famine which heralded a series of governmental moves to prohibit the growth of the drug; Phase III: from 1877 to 1891, the year in which poppy cultivation in China was legalized; and Phase IV: from 1891" (Waung, "Introduction of Opium Cultivation to China," p. 210). This division is quite reasonable, when considering the history of opium cultivation in China as a whole, but in Fujian, the prohibitions of the late 1870s had virtually no effect.

107. Beattie, "Protestant Missions and Opium," p. 121; Waung, "Introduction of Opium Cultivation to China," pp. 219–20.

108. Beattie, "Protestant Missions and Opium," p. 121.

109. Chinese opium imported from other provinces also was charged a 42 tael per picul fee (IMC, *Decennial Reports, Foochow, 1882–1891*, p. 414; IMC, *China Opium Trade, 1889–1894*, "Amoy" [1890], pp. 14–15).

mu planted in poppies.[110] Provincial authorities were enjoined to levy a tax on domestic opium sold in local opium shops, but in a controversial move the circuit intendant at Xiamen in effect established an extra transit fee on foreign opium sold in those shops. In response, all the opium establishments in the city closed their doors for five days.[111] The new system was part of the central government's attempt to gain some control over the flourishing provincial opium economy, but it met with opposition again. When the Maritime Affairs Office (Haifang ting) and transit tax officials imposed a tax on house rentals and opium shops in May 1898, business in Xiamen shut down for part of a day in protest, and within days, the emperor rescinded the tax.[112]

Many Chinese historians have interpreted China's legalization of poppy cultivation as a clear case of Qing greed and weakness, and as Chinese opium began to outcompete the Indian drug, the Chinese state indeed had little choice. Any attempt to eliminate the domestic poppy crop probably would have resulted in a surge in Indian imports, left the Qing government looking even more vulnerable to foreigners, and might have sparked internal unrest. After poppy farming became legal, the amount of domestic opium soared, and Indian imports plummeted from a peak of over 80,000 chests to 50,000–60,000 chests per year from the mid-1880s to 1906.[113] However, taxing the Chinese product, just as foreign imports were taxed, not only helped eliminate the black market but also brought in much-needed cash. To some degree this did constitute capitulation on the part of the Qing state, but legalization gave the government the opportunity to monitor the domestic opium trade and put the state in a better position to control that trade.

Despite the efforts at regularization by Chinese authorities at the provincial and national levels, the rates and methods of opium taxation varied considerably by region during the 1890s. The often-arbitrary taxation of domes-

---

110. Apparently this levy lasted less than one year, largely because it was so unpopular and hard to enforce (IMC, *Decennial Reports, Foochow, 1882–1891*, p. 414; Lin Man-houng, "Wan Qing de yapian shui," pp. 18–19).

111. According to British diplomats at Xiamen, the scheme laid out by the original edict would have charged each shop a fixed rate based on the amount of domestic opium sold each month. However, the circuit intendant decided that for every picul of foreign opium sold, the shopkeepers would be charged transit tax on half that amount of the domestic drug, whether or not the shop even sold the domestic product. The strike evidently was unsuccessful in bringing about a change in this policy (PRO, FO 228/1063, From Amoy and Canton, 1891; memo by Bourne, enclosure 1 in no. 2, Forrest to Walsham, 28 Jan. 1891).

112. IMC, *Decennial Reports, Amoy, 1892–1901*, pp. 121–22.

113. Lin Man-houng, "Qingmo benguo yapian zhi tidai jinkou yapian," table 2, pp. 402–4.

tic opium remained a serious problem, not the least because it encouraged smuggling, which led to a concomitant loss of official revenue.[114] In Funing prefecture, for example, domestic opium was not taxed until 1901, when the governor-general appointed a special deputy to collect a transit fee of 60 taels per picul. The official set up his headquarters in the city of Fu'an and established branch offices throughout the prefecture, but that year's harvest had already been sold. Customs authorities in Funing also noted that a well-traveled smuggling route in northern Fujian managed to bypass transit tax barriers to convey domestic opium to Fuzhou, Xiamen, and other cities.[115]

In 1893, the estimated yield for Fujian province was 1,460 piculs of domestic opium; by 1900, the figure was 7,784 piculs, and by 1901, approximately 8,000 piculs from northern Fujian alone, much of it from the Tongan region.[116] Farmers there had refined their product until it was said to be "not much inferior to the Persian,"[117] and some harvested two poppy crops in one year.[118] The poppy even appeared on Gulangyu island by 1896, three years after the Xiamen suburb became an international settlement.[119] By 1902, the Xiamen Chamber of Commerce (Shangzheng ju) reported, "There are numerous areas in the hinterlands that five years ago did not know the planting of opium, and now attempt to use opium poppies to substitute for the second rice crop of the year."[120]

The situation in Fujian's northeastern region was similar. The Fuzhou customs commissioner received reports in 1887 that the poppy was being cultivated in the counties of Fu'an, Ningde, and Fuding (Funing prefecture),

---

114. The situation tended to make British opium more competitive with the Chinese product (Reins, "Reform, Nationalism, and Internationalism," p. 123; *FRUS*, 1906, pt. 1, p. 357).

115. Miao, "Fu'an renmin fankang yapianjuan douzheng jishu," p. 54 (many thanks to Steve Averill for alerting me to this source); IMC, *Decennial Reports, Santuao, 1892–1901*, p. 87.

116. Many sources cite an upsurge in poppy cultivation following this measure, but estimates for provincial poppy production varied widely. See, e.g., *The China Review* 22, no. 6 (1896), in Presbyterian Church of England archives [hereafter PCE], FMC box 96 (Home, Print); Waung, "Introduction of Opium Cultivation to China," pp. 219–20; IMC, *Decennial Reports, Amoy, 1892–1901*, p. 129; and Pitcher, *In and About Amoy*, p. 127. Pitcher claims that the Xiamen region alone (including Tongan) produced an estimated 6,000 piculs in 1899 and 8,000 piculs in 1901.

117. *The China Review* 21, no. 4 (1893), in PCE archives, FMC box 96 (Home, Print), p. 270; and IMC, *China Opium Trade, 1889–1894*, "Amoy" (1893), p. 11.

118. IMC, *Decennial Reports, Amoy, 1892–1901*, p. 129.

119. Yearly customs report for Xiamen, 1896, cited in Lin Man-houng, "Qingmo shehui liuxing xishi yapian yanjiu," p. 583.

120. Ibid., pp. 583–85.

and in the counties of Gutian and Yongfu (Fuzhou prefecture).[121] Opium production in the far northeast continued to increase during the 1890s. In 1891, a customs officer remarked: "Whereas a few years ago it was difficult to find Native Opium offered for sale in the retail shops, it is now easy to procure it in almost any quantity," and relayed rumors that "several tea planters were giving up tea and turning to the more promising Opium industry instead."[122] Foreign customs officials at the port of Santu'ao reported the importation of great amounts of bone and beancake, which served as fertilizer for poppy fields, and observed that "the quality [of the native drug in that region] is said to have greatly improved."[123]

By the turn of the twentieth century, a contemporary observer wrote, "poppy fields may now be seen everywhere, the restriction against the cultivation of the flower being evidently a dead letter, as far as this province is concerned."[124] The poppy was cultivated throughout Fujian's populous coastal plain.[125] Prices for domestic opium were approximately $360 per picul for the Fuzhou product, $560 per picul for Sichuan opium, and $620 for the Yunnan drug,[126] and one customs official estimated that the province as a whole produced about 20,000 piculs of opium in 1901.[127] In the area surrounding Quanzhou, poppy growing was especially profitable after the turn of the century. Estimated opium production in southeast Fujian in 1902 and 1903 is shown in Table 2.2, and although the figures may not be precise, they do reflect a substantial increase within one year's time.

Negligible amounts of poppy were grown in the northwest and southwest of Fujian, and the crop had all but disappeared in those areas by 1900. If some tea farmers here switched to opium, the trend evidently did not catch on.[128] In 1887, foreign customs officials reported some poppy cultivation in the northwest, primarily in the counties of Zhenghe and Pucheng in

---

121. The official explained that what little domestic opium existed was considered private property and not charged *lijin* (IMC, SS No. 9, Hannen to Hart, 24 May 1887; SS No. 10, p. 43).
122. IMC, *Decennial Reports, Foochow, 1882–1891*, p. 413.
123. IMC, *Decennial Reports, Santuao, 1892–1901*, p. 85.
124. IMC, *Decennial Reports, Foochow, 1892–1901*, p. 109.
125. ZZGB 20, Memorial from Songshou, endorsed 19 May 1909, pp. 104–8; ZZGB 32, endorsed 11 May 1910, pp. 159–60.
126. IMC, *Decennial Reports, Foochow, 1892–1901*, p. 101.
127. IMC, *Decennial Reports, Santuao, 1892–1901*, p. 86.
128. Gardella, "Fukien's Tea Industry and Trade," p. 215.

Table 2.2
Estimated Production of Domestic Opium
in South Fujian, 1902 and 1903
(in piculs)

Location	Guangxu 28 (1902)	Guangxu 29 (1903)
Anxi	318	540
Changtai	780	1,520
Huian	186	430
Jinjiang	300	620
Nanxi	294	520
Tongan	2,130	4,008
Yongchun	462	810
Zhangpu	300	730
TOTAL	4,771	9,178

NOTE: With the exception of Yongchun, all locations listed are counties.
SOURCE: Chinese merchants reported these figures to the Chamber of Commerce in south Fujian, which in turn believed that the statistics were underestimates. "Xiamen shangzhengju baogao," cited in Li Wenzhi, ed., *Zhongguo jindai nongye shi ziliao*, vol. 1, pp. 461–62. The contrast with Table 2.1 is striking.

Jianning prefecture.[129] But in 1908, a British missionary reported that no opium was grown in Jianning, possibly because the climate was too chilly.[130] In the southwest, Longyan subprefecture was reported to have produced a small amount of opium in 1887—well under 200 piculs—all of which was consumed in that area.[131]

The interprovincial commerce in domestic opium was another dimension of the supply side of Fujian's opium economy, and although the clandestine nature of the trade meant that reliable figures before the 1890s are all but impossible to unearth, it is clear that before 1887, the pattern of that trade was dictated primarily by the manipulation of duties and fees by local authorities. Collection of the duty on opium was often farmed out to local agents, who could, and often did, raise or lower the charge at will to compete with other provinces or localities. The customs commissioner at Fuzhou noted that the first instance of the importation of Chinese opium into that

---

129. There was no information whatsoever as to the extent of that cultivation (IMC, SS No. 9, Hannen to Hart, 24 May 1887).

130. Dr. H. M. Churchill, "Progress of Opium Reform in Kien-ning," *Mercy and Truth* 12, no. 140 (Aug. 1908): 245–49, in Church Missionary Society archives (hereafter CMS).

131. IMC, SS No. 9, Brown to Hart, 31 May 1887.

port—one chest from Hankou—occurred in 1861. During the last half of the nineteenth century, domestic opium was primarily imported from Wenzhou and Taizhou (both in Zhejiang province) as well as from Yunnan, Jiangxi, and Sichuan provinces into Fuding county and Funing prefecture.[132]

In the southeast, quantifiable imports from other provinces apparently began much later. In 1887, the Xiamen customs commissioner stated that he knew nothing of domestic opium from outside Fujian, although he had heard that earlier attempts to introduce the Sichuanese product had failed.[133] However, by 1891, some 200 carriers per month, each bearing 30 catties (a catty, or *jin*, weighed about 1.33 pounds) or so of opium from Sichuan, entered Zhangzhou via a longstanding, well-traveled route from Sichuan through Hunan and into Jiangxi. Opium from Wenzhou was also transported overland into northeast Fujian and by junk to the southeastern city of Quanzhou.[134] Domestic opium imports arriving in Xiamen by steamer from Shanghai rose from 57 piculs in 1894 to 1,466 piculs in 1900. In 1901, the 1,407 piculs arriving in Xiamen from Shanghai were augmented by an estimated 4,000 piculs arriving overland from Sichuan, as well as 500 piculs transported by junk from Wenzhou.[135]

Despite the growing number of tax-collection stations and opium-related fees, domestic opium was still taxed at a rate far below that of its foreign counterpart, and as Chinese-grown poppies began to overwhelm the foreign competition, Chinese authorities tried several times around the turn of the twentieth century to raise and regularize taxes on the domestic drug.[136] The competition between Beijing and provincial authorities for

---

132. In 1887, 200–250 piculs of the estimated total of 3,000 piculs of opium produced in Wenzhou prefecture made its way into Fujian (IMC, SS No. 9, p. 30). In 1891, according to information from the Fujian guild at Wenzhou, about 700 piculs from Wenzhou were imported into Fuzhou that year (IMC, *Decennial Reports, Wenchow, 1882–1891*, p. 399; IMC, *Decennial Reports, Foochow, 1882–1891*, p. 413; *The China Review* 22, no. 6 [1896], in PCE, FMC, box 96 [Home, Print]; IMC, *Decennial Reports, Foochow, 1892–1901*, pp. 100–101).

133. According to this official, "The flavour and strength [of opium from Sichuan] did not satisfy smokers" (IMC, SS No. 9, Brown to Hart, 31 May 1887).

134. IMC, *Decennial Reports, Amoy, 1882–1891*, pp. 503–5.

135. The domestic opium was grown in Jiangsu, Sichuan, and Yunnan (IMC, *Decennial Reports, Amoy, 1892–1901*), p. 128.

136. In 1897, the Board of Finance ordered the establishment of a domestic opium tax system that essentially mirrored that used to collect levies on the foreign product, but provincial leaders balked. The very next year, an attempt to tax opium shops by dividing them into three categories based on their "prosperity" was rescinded for the same reason. In 1901, the need to raise funds for the Boxer indemnity evidently allowed Beijing to raise

this lucrative revenue source stymied these efforts until Zhang Zhidong, then serving as governor-general of Hunan and Hubei, helped devise a scheme whereby Chinese opium was required to pay only a single, fixed tax (including transit taxes and customs duties), after which no further levies could be collected. By 1905, this consolidated tax on opium (*tongshui*) was adopted in several provinces, including Fujian, and in May 1906, only a few months before the start of the anti-opium campaign, the Qing government extended the consolidated tax (now set at 115 *kuping* taels per picul) throughout the empire.[137]

The consolidated tax meant a significant restructuring of the existing opium tax bureaucracy in the provinces and yet another rerouting of opium tax revenues. The new tax explicitly replaced provincial taxes on domestic opium, including the levy on poppy fields,[138] and dictated that each year, after the treasury in each province had retained an amount equivalent to whatever it had collected in domestic opium taxes in 1904, the remaining revenue would go directly to Beijing to fund the continuing reorganization of the military.[139] This step reversed previous practice wherein the central government retained a fixed sum and the provinces kept the excess, possibly to prevent provincial officials from encouraging the planting of more poppies. The consolidated tax was collected at the first tax office or barrier encountered, and a special label was affixed to prevent further levies.[140] To supervise collection, nine Branch Offices for the Collection of Excise on Native Opium (Tuyao tongshui fenju) were established, including one for the provinces of Fujian and Zhejiang; the Head Office (Tuyao tongshui zongju) was located

---

the tax on domestic opium about 30 percent (Yu Ende, *Zhongguo jinyan faling bianqian shi*, pp. 103–5; see also Reins, "Reform, Nationalism, and Internationalism," p. 123; and *FRUS*, 1906, pt. 1, p. 357).

137. According to U.S. government officials, "The tax thus provided for is that to be levied on raw opium. Prepared opium will pay at double the rate, and opium dross at one-half the rate. Travelers, however, are allowed to carry 10 *liang* (ounces) of prepared opium free, and 20 *liang* of opium dross." The total amount, 100 *kuping* taels for the duty and an additional 15 taels to cover administrative costs, was equivalent to 114.08 *haiguan* taels per picul. Before 1906, the charge varied from 72 to 134.79 taels per picul. For a concise but detailed sketch of the evolution of the consolidated tax, see *FRUS*, 1906, pt. 1, pp. 357–59.

138. The regulations did, however, permit the collection of a "lamp tax" levied on the proprietors of opium dens to continue (*FRUS*, 1906, pt. 1, p. 358).

139. Ibid., pp. 358–59; Reins, "China and the International Politics of Opium," pp. 38–39.

140. A certificate to that effect was also issued (*FRUS*, 1906, pt. 1, p. 358).

in Wuchang, Hubei.[141] "As a step toward the centralization of power in Peking, and the adoption of a single policy throughout the country with regard to trade, finance, and taxation, the importance of this innovation cannot be exaggerated," insisted a British consular official.[142]

This new system ostensibly was intended to discourage both the cultivation and the smuggling of domestic opium,[143] but the guarantee of a substantial sum for imperial coffers,[144] as well as the elimination of additional provincial taxes, caused some foreign observers to view the measure with skepticism.[145] With the new tax, levies on the domestic drug exceeded the taxes on foreign opium, but the considerably higher price of the latter still ensured a large market for the homegrown drug, which remained cheaper.[146] In addition, the collection of the consolidated tax was often inefficient.[147]

Despite British qualms, the new system could be viewed as useful in a number of ways from the Chinese perspective. The central state benefited financially in the short term, and the consolidated tax served simultaneously as an important stage in Qing state-building and as a reasonable first step toward the ultimate prohibition of opium. If provincial governments could be weaned from their dependence on opium-related revenues, which were already being siphoned off by the central state, then a nationwide suppression scheme might face less opposition in the future.

---

141. Ibid., pp. 358–59; Brunnert and Hagelstrom, *Present Day Political Organization of China*, pp. 194–95. For a further discussion of the *tongshui*, see USDS (1906–10), 774/8–9, reel 104, Cloud to Root, 8 Sept. 1906.

142. PRO, FO 228/2414 (Opium Taxation 1905 and 1906), Ottewill to Satow, 6 July 1905.

143. This was specifically stated in Article 30 of the new regulations (*FRUS*, 1906, pt. 1, p. 358).

144. Reins ("Reform, Nationalism, and Internationalism," p. 123) cites a variety of sources that estimate the central government would receive anywhere from 17 to 67 million taels annually, but U.S. officials guessed that about 8 million would reach the imperial treasury each year (*FRUS*, 1906, pt. 1, pp. 358–59). In any case, the sum was substantial.

145. As Reins ("Reform, Nationalism, and Internationalism," pp. 122, 125) explains it, the British feared that the *tongshui* system would either drive the Indian product out of the China market by encouraging more domestic cultivation (since the new system meant the end of frequent and arbitrary levies in transit) or that it indicated Beijing's intention to gain control over the domestic opium trade in order to eliminate it completely. If the latter were true, this would also place strong pressure on the British to eliminate their end of the trade (*FRUS*, 1906, pt. 1, p. 359).

146. *FRUS*, 1906, pt. 1, p. 359.

147. USDS (1906–10), 774/110, reel 104, Gracey to Secy. of State, 28 May 1907.

In sum, the growth and structure of the supply side of Fujian's opium economy were largely the results of government action (or inaction), in the form of laws that restricted or taxed the foreign and domestic drug, and foreign pressure to keep the domestic product from pushing imported opium out of the Chinese market. Before 1860, arrogant foreign traders ignored Chinese law, and the indifference of local authorities to violations of the longstanding prohibition on domestic cultivation created a booming smuggling industry while keeping the untaxed domestic product far cheaper than its foreign competition. Legalization of foreign imports in 1860 undermined the black market but allowed the opium economy to grow without fear of state reprisal. The adoption of the transit tax to defray military and administrative expenses at the central and provincial levels gave the Chinese authorities an important stake in the continuation of the opium trade. Finally, the legalization of domestic opium cultivation, the revision of transit tax regulations, and the implementation of a nationwide consolidated tax on domestic opium indicated a trend toward centralization by extending state control over provincial tax revenues.[148]

The result of China's growing market for affordable opium, foreign pressure to regularize levies on their product, and Beijing's desire to claim as much opium-related revenue as possible was a substantial surge in poppy cultivation in Fujian province. The amount of domestic and foreign opium available in Fujian, however, is a somewhat deceptive measure of the depth and significance of the province's opium economy. Although steadily increasing, the amount of opium produced in Fujian on the eve of reform was far less than that cultivated in the great opium-growing provinces of Sichuan, Yunnan, and Guizhou, and even in Fujian, the poppy occupied only a fraction of the province's limited arable land. But by 1906, opium had become a crucial cash crop, particularly along the coastline, for farmers reeling from the loss of lucrative tea revenues, not to mention the tens of thousands of individuals involved in its preparation, distribution, and consumption.

Morality, Money, and Demand

The Qing state, in its traditional role as arbiter of social mores and formulator of the legal criterion for social deviance, enacted a series of harsh legal restrictions beginning in 1729 on the sale, consumption, importation, and cul-

---

148. See the chart in Lin Man-houng, "Wan Qing de yapian shui," p. 13.

tivation of opium in an attempt to control the trade and stigmatize those involved in it.[149] Thus, in the eighteenth century, long before Western Europeans became concerned about narcotic dependence, the Qing court believed that opium had harmful effects on individuals and society in general. But even in China, opium consumption did not raise alarms until the drug began to be smoked, first blended with tobacco and then on its own.[150] From 1729 to 1858, Chinese government concern over the spread of opium smoking and the expansion of the illegal drug trade prompted edict after edict in a futile attempt to control the supply of and demand for the drug. Despite its increasing popularity even among the members of the imperial court, however, opium acquired a degree of social stigma at an early date. Whether legal constraints reflected or determined broader social attitudes is difficult to know; what is certain is that the growing severity and scope of punishment for opium-related offenses indicated a perception at the highest levels of government that the opium trade had become a serious problem, with social, political, and economic ramifications. The growth of both the illegal trade in opium and the demand for it not only indicated the power of foreign imperialists to circumvent Chinese law but also highlighted Qing inability to enforce those laws.

After the opium trade and domestic opium cultivation were legalized, the strategy of controlling the flow and consumption of the drug through heavy taxation reinforced the official stance of moral condemnation, even as opium became an important element of the provincial and national economies. The history of opium taxation in Fujian ostensibly demonstrated the commitment of the state to the policy of "prohibition through excessive taxation" (*yujin yuzheng*), but it also highlighted conflicts between authorities in Beijing and those in Fujian as they vied for the sizable revenues that accumulated.[151] The rapidity with which those revenues became a crucial prop for the provincial economy attracted the attention of a deficit-ridden central government increasingly concerned about post-Taiping trends toward provincial autonomy and militarization.

---

149. For a detailed discussion of these edicts, see Yu Ende, *Zhongguo jinyan faling bianqian shi*. For an abbreviated list of Chinese anti-opium edicts in English, see Chang Hsin-pao, *Commissioner Lin and the Opium War*, app. A.

150. Fu, *A Documentary Chronicle of Sino-Western Relations*, 1: 162–64.

151. Lin Man-houng, "Qingmo benguo yapian zhi tidai jinkou yapian," pp. 427–28; Reins, "Reform, Nationalism, and Internationalism," p. 102.

The habit of opium smoking entered China through Fujian during the seventeenth century and may have evolved from the smoking of a mixture of tobacco, hemp, and opium in tobacco pipes by Chinese in Southeast Asia. From Southeast Asia, Dutch and Portuguese traders probably brought the practice to Fujian via Taiwan or Manila. Tobacco smoking had arrived in China along the same routes—probably during the late sixteenth or early seventeenth century—and quickly became extremely popular.[152] Fujian's dubious distinction as the first province in which the practice of opium smoking appeared and flourished meant an especially entrenched demand.[153]

Why the consumption of opium soared in China from the mid-nineteenth century remains one of the most intriguing mysteries of the late Qing era. Some point to British increases in the supply and the addictive nature of opium. Others believe that the widespread opium smoking was symptomatic of serious social problems, including poverty, the humiliation of foreign imperialism, the decay of the Chinese military, and a fatally overcrowded "ladder of success."[154] Other scholars focus on the more pleasurable aspects of opium, tracing its popularity to its use as a stimulant, aphrodisiac, and status symbol.[155] We may never fully understand why the Chinese consumed the drug in ever-increasing quantities, but we can analyze how state-initiated legal restrictions and Confucian moral imperatives contributed to the perception of opium as a vice.

Confucian social mores mitigated against opium abuse. The frequently cited first line of the *Classic of Filial Piety* (*Xiao jing*) explicitly condemns any act that harms the body one inherits from the ancestors. Furthermore, in an ideal Confucian world where society was an extended family with a fatherly emperor at its apex, a decline in an individual's health or morality was evaluated in terms of its impact on that person's family and on society as a whole. One western source notes a Chinese belief that chronic opium abuse re-

---

152. Waung, "Introduction of Opium Cultivation to China," pp. 209–10; Spence, "Opium Smoking in Ch'ing China," pp. 146–47, 161–62.

153. According to a memorial submitted in 1729, shortly after the first imperial edict against opium, by an advocate of opium prohibition named Lan Dingyuan, opium smokers were particularly numerous in Taiwan and Xiamen (Fu, *A Documentary Chronicle of Sino-Western Relations*, 1: 162, 2: 518–19n84).

154. Those familiar with Chinese history will recognize the reference to Ho Ping-ti's classic work on the examination system and social advancement. An example of this phenomenon is Hong Xiuquan, who failed the civil service examinations several times and led the Taiping Rebellion of 1850–64. The rebel platform included a strong stance against opium smoking.

155. Zheng Yangwen, "The Social Life of Opium."

sulted in childlessness by the third generation—the ultimate unfilial consequence.[156] Of particular concern to China's rulers was the high rate of addiction among China's educated population, who were expected to serve as moral exemplars for the rest of society. Wealthy young men were among the country's first opium smokers, and the habit quickly spread to lower-level bureaucrats, the military, and on down the social ladder, where it was perceived as generating corruption and moral turpitude.[157]

A PROFILE OF OPIUM
CONSUMPTION IN FUJIAN

Who were the opium smokers of Fujian and what impact did their habit have on themselves and those around them? Precise statistics are hard to come by, given the illegality and stigma of opium smoking, the desire of local officials to downplay the problem in their jurisdictions, and the difficulty of determining whether individuals were addicts or casual smokers. Formulas that extrapolate from the amount of the drug grown or imported into an area and the average amount consumed by a heavy smoker over a set period of time are of limited use. One missionary opponent of the trade pointed out that many estimates mistakenly assume that only pure opium was smoked and then discarded. In fact, opium was often adulterated and its ashes were resmoked as many as three times by poorer smokers.[158] For example, manual laborers in Xiamen commonly chewed the opium husk—the skin of the opium ball—which contained only about 10 percent opium, but was very cheap.[159]

The only official estimate of the extent of opium consumption in Fujian province appears in a memorial to the Chinese throne in 1909 from Songshou, then governor-general of Fujian and Zhejiang. He claimed that over 230,000 people in Fujian, approximately 1.5 percent of the province's total population at that time, had been regular opium smokers at the outset of the anti-opium campaign.[160] However, regional figures indicated that the rate of

---

156. Turner, *British Opium Policy*, p. 19.
157. Hsin-pao Chang, *Commissioner Lin and the Opium War*, p. 34; Spence, "Opium Smoking in Ch'ing China."
158. Dudgeon, *Review of the Customs Opium Smoking Returns*.
159. IMC, *Decennial Reports, Amoy, 1902–1911*, p. 103.
160. ZZGB 20, memorial from Songshou, endorsed 19 May 1909, pp. 104–8. For estimates of Fujian's population and discussions of the difficulties presented by demographic statistics for the province, see Ho, *Studies on the Population of China*; Chen Hanguang, "Minguo yilai Fu-

addiction in some areas far exceeded that of the province as a whole; this implies either that Songshou's numbers are gross underestimates or that consumption was particularly common in urban centers situated near pockets of domestic cultivation. Table 2.3 shows the number of officially registered opium addicts in the prefectural capital of Funing as well as in the county seats of Fu'an and Ningde around the outset of the anti-opium campaign. Funing did produce a small poppy crop.

The extent of opium smoking in any given town or village varied widely, and only the broadest of generalizations can be derived from the anecdotal evidence. On a visit to Shaowu, in northwest Fujian, one missionary was informed that two-thirds of the residents smoked opium. That same individual estimated that 30 percent of adult males in Fuzhou city were addicts, and an additional 15 percent smoked infrequently. He also added that he knew of a village just outside the provincial capital that was entirely free of the drug.[161]

Attempts to discern an occupational pattern of dependence or consumption in Fujian may be skewed by the biases of observers and the stigma of opium smoking then and now. Addiction often became a powerful metaphor for the debilitating effects of political oppression (from either China's dynastic system or foreign imperialism) as well as for the moral weakness of the smokers themselves. Foreign diplomats and missionaries reported that the vice was particularly serious among sedan-chair bearers, laborers, and merchants, not coincidentally the groups with whom these westerners were most likely to have frequent contact and conflict. For the same reasons, local officials and the notoriously corrupt yamen runners also were subject to accusations of addiction by foreigners. A recent Chinese discussion of the opium problem in the late Qing also equated opium smoking with social deviance, noting high rates of addiction among such unsavory elements as "local tyrants and evil gentry, hooligans, actors, Buddhist monks, and chair bearers."[162] Another modern Chinese author takes a more sympathetic stance, arguing that in the northeastern county of Youxi (Yanping prefecture), "it was the lower-class working people who above all suffered [opium's]

---

jian sheng difang xingzhengqu hua," pp. 22–27; and Chen Hanguang, "Fujian renkou jianjie," pp. 12–14.

161. *FMMH* (1877), pp. 2–5.

162. Lin Wenji, "Jiefang qian de Shima 'san hai,'" p. 61.

Table 2.3
Registered Smokers in Three Cities of Funing Prefecture, Circa 1910

City	Registered smokers	City population	Addicts/ population (%)
Funing	2,150	20,848	10.3%
Fu'an	1,950	31,000	6.3
Ningde	1,793	25,340	7.0

SOURCES: The population figures were taken from an official Chinese census in 1910, and the number of addicts was taken from "the first lists of registered smokers," which probably were recorded in 1907 or 1908 (IMC, *Decennial Reports, Santuao, 1902–1911*, pp. 83–84).

damage . . . [including] boatmen and sailors, shoemakers, prison guards, chair bearers, sojourners (*liumin*), small shopkeepers, and doctors."[163]

Although the opium habit attracted Fujianese regardless of social class, profession, or gender, the high cost of the Indian drug meant that opium consumption probably began with officials and the upper classes and descended the social ladder over time. Yamen secretaries may have introduced the habit to the Fujianese administrative apparatus, but magistrates were among the earliest documented smokers.[164] Smoking among officers and soldiers throughout the provincial armed forces was common as well. Jonathan Spence asserts that the last to take up the habit were the Chinese peasants who cultivated the poppy, and although there is no way to determine how many of Fujian's farmers smoked their own harvest, a foreign customs official claimed in 1887 that even in the opium-producing county of Tongan, the number of heavy smokers was still quite small.[165]

Male smokers in Fujian apparently far outnumbered their female counterparts, although significant numbers of women, especially prostitutes or members of wealthy families, did indulge in the habit.[166] Missionaries in Funing prefecture claimed that many shopkeepers' wives were addicts, and a high-ranking provincial military official complained to Beijing of the harmful

---

163. Pan, "'Zhenkong jiao' liuxing zai Youqi," p. 51.
164. Lin Renchuan, "Qingdai Fujian de yapian maoyi," pp. 68–71.
165. Spence, "Opium Smoking in Ch'ing China," p. 146; IMC, SS No. 9, Van Aalst, 6 June 1887.
166. Lin Wenji, "Jiefang qian de Shima 'san hai,'" p. 61; Park, *Opinions of Over 100 Physicians*, pp. 12–18.

influence of female smokers in the homes of Fuzhou's Banner troops.[167] Although underrepresented in the ranks of opium smokers, Fujianese women often suffered not only the poverty that often accompanied a husband or father's dependence on the drug but also the pain and humiliation of being sold to pay off the addict's debts or feed his habit. Historian Zheng Yangwen takes a different view, noting that many upper-class women probably enjoyed the drug and other women in the sex industry made a living by preparing it for their customers.[168]

A more detailed profile of a small pool of so-called addicts can be constructed from the reports of the Fuzhou Opium Asylum from 1880 to 1883. Missionary physicians there conducted annual surveys that documented the age, occupation, and motivation of the opium patients, as well as the length and severity of their habit. Over 50 percent of the respondents stated that they had begun smoking between the ages of 20 and 30, and close to half were between 31 and 40 years old when they stopped. Approximately one-third of the sample listed their occupation as storekeepers, and another third claimed to be farmers. Thirteen percent worked as artisans, 12 percent as soldiers, and the rest of the group consisted of a handful of boatmen, literati, yamen attendants, and military officers. Close to 60 percent of those surveyed indicated that they began smoking out of temptation or a desire for pleasure; the remaining 40 percent first took the drug for medicinal purposes.[169]

The extent of opium consumption in Fujian can also be measured in the thousands of opium shops and dens found throughout the province, although many Chinese were either too rich or too poor to frequent these es-

---

167. CMS Fuhkien [Fujian] Mission-Original Incoming, Report by Dr. Mackenzie, 20 Jan. 1905, no. 62; ZZGB 11, memorial from Pushou, endorsed 13 Sept. 1908, pp. 410–12.

168. Zheng Yangwen, "The Social Life of Opium," pp. 24–31.

169. The data chart the habits of approximately 2,000 smokers admitted to the asylum. Founded in 1872, the asylum was an offshoot of the Fuzhou Medical Missionary Hospital that was itself established by the American Board of Commissioners for Foreign Missions (ABCFM) in 1872. American missionary physicians supervised the asylum until February 1883, when Dr. Henry T. Whitney allowed his Chinese assistant—listed only as Dr. Chang—to run the asylum independently of the mission. Dr. Chang either did not keep or did not publish detailed records of his patients. The number of opium patients at the asylum began to drop in 1882 because enforcement of anti-opium laws became more lax and also because several Chinese-run asylums were established ([*Annual*] *Report of the Foochow Medical Missionary Hospital in Connection with the A.B.C.F.M. Mission, 1880–1883*). For more detailed tables compiled from these data, see Madancy, "Ambitious Interlude," pp. 134–35.

tablishments. One missionary based in Fuzhou in the 1890s noted that at that time, "in a certain neighborhood, three or four years ago, there were twelve shops where opium was retailed, and seven shops where rice, which is the 'staff of life' in this part of China, was sold."[170] In the coastal city of Zhangzhou, "there is a long street, near the south gate, occupied solely by Opium shops and dens."[171] Just south of Zhangzhou, in Shima township, one account claims that in the Guangxu years almost 100 opium dens served the 20,000 residents.[172] In the remote northwestern county of Guangze (Shaowu prefecture) and the surrounding towns, it was said that "a forest of opium dens were established."[173] In Jianning, too, "opium dens abounded within the city walls, and indeed, in very many private houses and places of business one could also find the opium pipe."[174] Opium smoking also occurred in the brothels, teahouses, and bars of Fujian, where smoking equipment often was available, and numerous establishments throughout the province sold and manufactured smoking tools and accessories.[175] Pawnshops thrived on the business generated by needy smokers.[176]

The easy availability of the drug throughout Fujian province also created many casual smokers. The offering of a pipe of opium became an established social ritual in the homes of the well-to-do, as well as in some businesses and even in some official yamens.[177] In Xiamen, U.S. consul Fesler claimed that "there are now practically no houses in this locality where opium is not procurable. . . . If the inmates do not smoke it themselves they keep it for their friends to smoke when calling."[178] In Shima, "the social intercourse of polite society no doubt could not do without opium to entertain guests."[179] Much like modern American attitudes toward alcoholism and social drinking, in

---

170. Doolittle, *Social Life of the Chinese*, 2: 355. This comparison may be rhetorical, since I have encountered the opium den / rice shop ratio in many missionary sources as a measure of the seriousness of the opium problem.

171. IMC, SS No. 9, Van Aalst, 6 June 1887.

172. Lin Wenji, "Jiefang qian de Shima 'san hai,'" p. 61.

173. Zheng Bangning, "Minqu xianling Su Shouqiao," p. 61.

174. Churchill, "Progress of Opium Reform in Kien-ning," *Mercy and Truth* 12, no. 140 (Aug. 1908): 245–49.

175. Lin Wenji, "Jiefang qian de Shima 'san hai,'" p. 61; ZZGB 20, memorial from Songshou, endorsed 19 May 1909, pp. 104–8.

176. Dudgeon, *Review of the Customs Opium Smoking Returns*, p. 17.

177. Doolittle, *Social Life of the Chinese*, 2: 351–52.

178. Pitcher, *In and About Amoy*, pp. 129–30.

179. Lin Wenji, "Jiefang qian de Shima 'san hai,'" p. 61.

late Qing China opium addiction was deplored, even though an occasional pipe was part of the acceptable social landscape.

ANTI-OPIUM SENTIMENT BEFORE THE SUPPRESSION CAMPAIGN

The construction and growth of Fujian's opium economy from the 1820s to 1906 indicates not only the physical and financial attraction of opium but also the growing number of individuals with a stake in the opium trade. Until the foreign drug was legalized and during the decades when the status of the domestic poppy was somewhat uncertain, the burgeoning supply of and demand for opium attested to the willingness of many of those individuals to flout the law in pursuit of profit or pleasure. Other Fujianese, however, were strongly opposed to opium. The evolution and expression of that sentiment indicate the degree to which opium had become enmeshed with Chinese politics and society, and how objections to the opium trade and opium smoking became an integral aspect of Chinese nationalism directed against both foreign imperialism and the Qing state.[180]

In many cases hostility toward the opium trade from the 1830s to 1906 reflected an overtly political anger directed either at foreign merchants or at a dynasty considered weak and hopelessly corrupt. The Opium Wars may have demonstrated the sincerity of Chinese government opposition to Indian opium imports, but the drug's subsequent legalization through the aptly named "unequal treaties" engendered a reservoir of ill will toward a Qing state too weak to enforce its laws on foreign purveyors of the drug, despite the growing Chinese demand for opium. Opium was but one symptom (or cause) of the internal strife that characterized the second half of the nineteenth century in China.

The events surrounding the first Opium War generated angry responses from educated Chinese such as the anonymous priest who called himself the "Chrysanthemum Daoist." He composed an intriguing lyrical expression of hostility to opium in Fujian in the early 1840s; the twenty-stanza poem was elegantly carved into a rectangular wooden tray. Firmly embedded in its specific historical context, the poem is punctuated by literary allusions and tied together by an undercurrent of sarcasm condemning all strata of Chinese

---

180. For an in-depth examination of opium smoking as cultural encounter, see McMahon, *The Fall of the God of Money*.

society for their complicity in the flourishing opium trade. Within the small sample of anti-opium songs and poems discovered in the course of researching this volume, this poem stands out as unusual for its author's explicit condemnation of Chinese complicity in the trade and his frank acknowledgment of the drug's powerful allure.[181]

In a tone often savage and mocking, the poet worked his way through each stratum of Chinese society, from the imperial court to the common farmer. He skewered Chinese peasants for planting poppies and then claiming to the government that the land lay fallow. He indicted officials for their hypocritical condemnation of the trade although they themselves smoked the drug and their corruption allowed it to bypass legal restrictions. Chinese soldiers came in for particularly intense criticism because they allowed addiction to destroy their capacity to fight. One compelling stanza asks the military how it expects to defeat the enemy using only opium pipes as weapons. Smokers among the literati were said to have diluted their intellect, and addiction was blamed for destroying the livelihoods of artists and craftspeople by making them listless and dispirited. Toward the end of the poem, the author rose to a more global condemnation of the drug, decrying the sins of smokers against their ancestors and illustrating the pitiful consequences for families of these unfilial men. Then his readers were hit with a jarringly crude description of the appalling physical damage suffered by individual addicts. The conclusion warned readers to avoid "sinking in the opium sea," which could cause more damage than excessive drinking and gambling—a sea whose seductive powers were compared to the charms of a beautiful woman.

Another poet writing around the time of the Opium War, this time from Zhenghe county in the northwestern prefecture of Jianning, included the following poem, titled simply "Opium," in his book *Songs from Central Fujian*:

> *Materia Medica* records the *yangfu* plant,
>   *Afurong* is another name, they say;
> Sown beneath the springtime moon,
>   Harvested till the first winter's day;
> Foreigners gather the flower's sap,
>   Mix the poison and boil away;

---

181. The following discussion was derived from Zhou Ruiguang, "Qing Huanghua daoren 'Jieyan shi' qianshi." Since the numerous allusions and slang make it extremely difficult to reproduce an elegant translation, the discussion of the poem does not include the verses themselves.

> Smoking the drug brings suffering,
>> But fragrance like an orchid, so they say;
> The ignorant folk develop a need,
>> Like worms in smartweed, for more and more each day;
> For years the sickness was concealed,
>> So it isn't easy to push away;
> Foreigners each day grow more and more rich,
>> While Chinese grow poorer by the day.[182]

This author acknowledged the lengthy history of the poppy in China, but opium is clearly presented as a commodity prepared and imported by foreigners to seduce Chinese into giving up their wealth.

Quanzhou scholar Wu Zeng, writing at around the same time, included another poem in his book *A Stimulating Piece About Quanzhou Customs*. The lyrics excerpted below bemoaned the dehumanizing consequences of opium smoking:

> People consume opium,
>> The drug consumes them whole,
>> Melts away one's fat and blood,
>> Devours the very soul.
> To the marrow of the bone the craving goes,
>> Smokers are living devils, everybody knows.
> New devils crave a little,
>> Old ones need much more,
>> Scorched black is the color of a new devil's face,
>> Of human color, an old devil has no trace.[183]

Eschewing the need to assign blame for China's opium problem, Wu's piece focused on human suffering and the social stigma attached to longtime addicts, commonly referred to as opium devils (*yapian gui*) for their allegedly inhuman appearance and behavior.

Another compelling testament to popular recognition and disapproval of the social ravages of opium addiction in Fujian was passed down orally from the late eighteenth or early nineteenth century in the following "Anti-Opium Song." The villagers of Xiamao, located in Yanping prefecture, were said to have composed the lyrics:

---

182. Song Kuai'an as cited in Qi Sihe et al., *Yapian zhanzheng*, 1: 335.
183. Wu as cited in Lin Renchuan, "Qingdai Fujian de yapian maoyi," p. 68.

The opium pipe is made of *zihua* bamboo;
 I lie on the mat in a shrimp-like curlicue.
Smoking a pipe, I see a light;
 the fire on the stove burns red and bright.
I gulp hot tea, purse my lips and start;
 in a hundred ways the taste invades my liver and heart.
Yama himself runs the opium den;[184]
 good men and women need not go in.
When first you smoke, the blood runs hot;
 but smoke more, need more, and soon you are a sot.
Skin and bones, the fat became lean;
 everyone calls me an opium fiend.
An opium addict cannot sit still;
 sells his wife, his kids, and the land they till.
Wife and daughter, the fields he tends;
 all go up in smoke in the opium den.
Evil merchants make money for the West;
 disaster for the nation—it can't be for the best.[185]

The song vividly describes the power of addiction, the terrible toll the drug exacts on both the body and the family of the smoker, and the amoral greed exhibited by opium merchants. The anti-foreign sentiment with which the undated song concludes leads me to believe that it was composed before the boom in domestic cultivation, although the lyrics could also reflect the absence of a domestic poppy crop in this inland prefecture after the boom had begun. Folk songs such as this were and are viewed by the current Chinese government as expressions of longstanding, class-based antagonisms that can be used to foster class consciousness and embroider the historical tapestry of peasant revolution with rich, emotional hues.

Anti-opium sentiment was not confined to poetry and song in the second half of the nineteenth century. Discontented individuals in Fujian increasingly turned to heterodox religious groups in search of spiritual renewal in those troubled times, and many such groups required that members abstain from opium smoking. Spirit-writing societies and the Emptiness sect (Zhenkong jiao) were examples of organized expressions of popular opposition to opium in Fujian before the suppression campaign was inaugurated. Known by a variety of names, the spirit-writing societies originated in

---

184. Yama was the King of Hell in Chinese cosmology.
185. Xiao et al., "Jin yapian ge."

coastal Fujian (in the Quanzhou region) and Guangdong provinces in the mid-Qing, and their influence spread to the island of Taiwan in the 1850s. Members believed that the spirits communicated with them through mediums who waited with planchettes ready to transcribe messages from the supernatural world onto sand tables. The messages usually related to specific prayers offered by the society, and in the mid- to late nineteenth century, those prayers often requested cures for opium smoking. In Taiwan, one such cure involved consuming a concoction containing the ashes of incense burned to summon the spirits mixed with the water used to clear the sand table. This allegedly efficacious combination often led to abdominal pain and vomiting. Smokers were also asked to burn their smoking equipment in front of the sand table to demonstrate their sincerity.[186]

The Emptiness sect apparently was a similar type of spiritual brotherhood. One of the primary requirements for membership was abstention from opium smoking, and a Chinese account credited the widespread appeal of the group to its position on the drug. This well-organized sect was headquartered in Youxi county, Yanping prefecture, an important commercial center that served as a hub for opium importers from the coastal areas who wished to transport their goods into Jiangxi province. The sect attracted followers primarily from lower-class workers.[187] The popularity of these groups indicated a strong tendency among some non-elites to support anti-opium initiatives, but their role in the official anti-opium campaign is unknown and likely problematic, given the anti-state bias implicit in such heterodox organizations.

Knowledgeable readers will wonder at the omission of the Taiping Rebellion here, since abstention from opium was a key pillar of Hong Xiuquan's social agenda. There is very little documentation regarding the impact of specific elements of Taiping ideology on the masses of Fujian. The province generally fell outside the area of Taiping occupation and became a battlefield primarily during the frantic, bloody Taiping retreat from Nanjing. Ironically, the most significant impact of the Taiping Rebellion on Fujianese attitudes

---

186. See Wang Shiqing, "Riju chuqi Taiwan zhi Jiangbihui yu jieyan yundong." Evidently, the Taiwanese incarnation of this society launched a well-organized and very popular anti-opium movement at the turn of the twentieth century, but the anti-Japanese undercurrent caused the Japanese occupation authorities to crack down. Many thanks to Professor Philip Clart of the University of Missouri-Columbia for making this article available to me.

187. Pan, "'Zhenkong jiao' liuxing zai Youqi," pp. 51–53.

regarding opium may have been not a broadening of support for suppression but rather resentment toward the Qing state for violently suppressing the rebellion and imposing the despised transit tax to cover the astronomical cost of battling the Taipings.[188]

Anti-opium sentiment in Fujian also surfaced, paradoxically, as part of a more generalized mistrust of foreign missionaries, even as it inspired other Chinese to join the Christian church. Vocal skepticism and pointed heckling greeted many British and American missionaries, as some members of the Chinese audience questioned their motives in the face of the prominent role played by their home nations in the Sino-Indian opium trade.[189] Such reactions were particularly common during the mid-nineteenth century, and remained prevalent in areas free of poppy cultivation. In Fujian, however, there was virtually no violence directed at missionaries solely as representatives of opium-importing nations, despite the predominance of imported opium in the province.

Anti-opium sentiment was not necessarily accompanied by blanket hostility to foreigners. Many Chinese joined Christian churches in Fujian precisely because of the missionaries' anti-opium stance and their "modern" opium treatment facilities. Some of the most devoted Chinese converts were former opium smokers rehabilitated in missionary hospitals and clinics.[190] A healthy dose of anti-opium propaganda was part of the broader moral curriculum advanced in missionary schools and churches. Villagers outside Fuzhou heard of the anti-opium work of mission hospitals in the city and, in several cases, sent representatives to bring missionaries to the villages to administer the "cure."[191]

The opium problem generated a significant degree of popular antipathy in late Qing Fujian well before the suppression campaign began in late 1906. Without further documentation, it is difficult to link that sentiment directly to grassroots support for that campaign, but available evidence does indicate

---

188. For more on the Taipings in Fujian, see Ma, "Qiantan Taiping tianguo de jinyan zhengce," pp. 50–51; Cai Rujin, "Taiping jun zhuanzhan Zhangzhou"; Michael, *The Taiping Rebellion*; and Shih, *The Taiping Ideology*. Some discussion of the Taipings also appears in various mission sources.

189. Macgowan, *Sidelights on Chinese Life*, pp. 200, 340–41.

190. Missionary publications are full of anecdotes to support this statement. See also Latourette, *A History of Christian Missions in China*, pp. 480–45; and Gewurtz, "Do Numbers Count?," pp. 21–24.

191. *Mercy and Truth* 11, no. 125 (May 1907): 147–53.

that expressions of hostility toward opium could be found in all strata of society, as well as outside the major urban centers, and was as multifaceted as the problem itself.

Opium in Fujian on the Eve of Suppression

Although Lin Zexu was resurrected in the opium suppression campaign that began in 1906 as a symbol of China's resolute opposition to foreign imperialism and the opium trade, his role in Fujian's opium economy was not that simple. Lin's actions in the first Opium War helped set the stage for the expansion of that trade into his native province, and the Qing state eventually presided over the legalization of the drug. It would not be remotely fair or accurate, of course, to lay the blame for the expansion of Fujian's opium economy on the shoulders of one man, even one who has grown larger than life over time. In the end, it was Lin's intentions that led to his canonization.

The steady growth of that economy was closely linked to policies determined and implemented by China's central state, often under pressure from aggressive foreign powers. Its expansion was closely related to developments in the importation and taxation of foreign opium and efforts by the central government to control the domestic trade, as well as Fujian's social and economic structure. The reopening of the province to foreign trade, the institution of an internal transit tax, and the rise and decline of the tea industry were closely tied to the emergence and growth of the Fujianese opium economy. Natural factors, such as poor land transportation and the scarcity of arable land, undoubtedly shaped the pattern of opium cultivation, consumption, and distribution in Fujian, but for the most part lineage feuds, official corruption, and even popular attitudes toward the drug were reactions to state policies and laws.

The construction of an opium economy in China and Fujian was at its heart a matter of supply and demand. Some poppies had been grown in China for medicinal or decorative purposes since antiquity, but the supply side of the Chinese opium equation really began in India, where merchants from Great Britain, the United States, and elsewhere saw an ideal opportunity to recoup the silver they spent so freely on Chinese goods like tea and silk. The British initially controlled the supply and tried to gear the importation of Indian opium to what they perceived as a growing Chinese demand. That demand in turn fed the desire of Chinese farmers to contribute to the lucrative supply and even compelled the Chinese state to legalize the trade in its entirety and adopt taxation schemes that enhanced provincial and national revenues. And still the demand seemed to grow, as ever-larger quantities of opium were conveyed, distributed, prepared, and consumed throughout the Qing empire. By the 1890s, the bulk of that opium was grown in China. By 1906, when the Qing government announced its ambitious plan to eliminate the consumption, sale, and production of opium within its borders, the opium trade had ceased to be a simple matter of foreign exchange and had spawned an immense economy that absorbed Chinese land, labor, and lucre.

In Fujian, the provincial opium economy followed essentially the same pattern as that in the rest of the Qing empire, although relatively speaking, it was more dependent on foreign opium imports than the homegrown drug. When the Indian drug was first landed at various ports along the Fujianese coast, probably in the 1820s, smuggling networks dominated by local clan organizations quickly materialized to convey the opium to markets beyond the coast. By the time the importation of foreign opium was legalized in 1858, the demand was already well established. That demand, and the price of the foreign drug, soared when freed from the stigma and judicial constraints of illegality, tempting some of Fujian's farmers to enter the market with homegrown poppies. However, only after the Chinese state stepped in to legalize domestic cultivation did Fujian's poppy crop increase substantially. Consumption increased correspondingly among the lower classes that could afford only the cheaper domestic opium or an adulterated compound.

In Fujian, the size of the opium economy paled in comparison to those that emerged in the big opium-growing provinces of Sichuan or Yunnan, but the dimensions of that economy were not as significant as its social impact and the degree to which opium became intertwined with other issues of politics, ideology, and economics. Opium was not just a vice, it was a symbol and a commodity. Unchecked, it symbolized Chinese weakness vis-à-vis the western powers; eliminated, it represented the victory of Chinese nationalism, the strength of the Chinese state, and the willpower of the Chinese people. More than a century of prohibition had done little to stem opium trafficking or opium smoking, and the Chinese state felt compelled to try to control the trade by legalizing and taxing it. However, the control through taxation strategy was a double-edged sword that pitted the government's strong anti-opium rhetoric against the reality of the enormous benefits to a desperate Qing treasury.

If the institution of official taxes was truly intended to discourage domestic cultivation in Fujian, then the measure must be considered a dismal failure. On the other hand, if those policies are interpreted as an attempt to undermine the smuggling trade by establishing government control or to raise revenue while maintaining the appearance of propriety, it must be assessed quite differently. Rivalries for opium revenues among Chinese authorities at the local, provincial, and central levels began with the imposition of the transit tax in the mid-nineteenth century, but by 1906 the central state had taken important steps to assert its control over opium-related revenues. Aside from the obvious financial benefits for Beijing, it can also be argued that the move toward centralization of opium taxation was indeed a logical step toward state control and eventual suppression of the domestic trade. In addition, the channeling of opium revenues away from provincial coffers—however painful—may have made provincial officials more receptive to a nationwide scheme to do away with the trade altogether. Smuggling continued even after the legalization of the foreign drug, but a legitimate system of opium importation and distribution quickly grew up alongside the black market, and the state was able to establish control over much of the opium trade in Fujian by 1906.

The opium economy of Fujian was a complex and multilevel framework of supply and demand that rapidly became an integral part of the society, economy, and politics of the province. Fujian was never a major opium-producing province, but the timing and expansion of domestic cultivation in that province throws some light on the social networks that fueled the opium economy in Fujian and in China as a whole. By 1905, those networks included multitudes of farmers, merchants, laborers, boatmen, boilers, bureaucrats, strongmen, and manufacturers of opium-smoking paraphernalia, not to mention the owners and patrons of pawnshops, brothels, wine shops, and opium dens, all of whom depended on either the financial or physiological returns of the opium trade in late Qing Fujian. One account estimates that at least 100,000 people in Fujian were involved just on the supply side of that province's opium economy in the mid-nineteenth century, and that number undoubtedly increased substantially with the expansion of domestic poppy cultivation along the Fujianese coast.[192] Presumably, many of these individuals did not wish to see their livelihoods eliminated. And yet, within the next few years, much of the provincial opium economy was shut down.

---

192. Lin Renchuan, "Qingdai Fujian de yapian maoyi," p. 68.

The contours of Fujian's opium economy were carved out in large part by state policies that alternatively prohibited the drug or imposed heavy taxes on it. In the following chapters, we will see what happened when the Chinese state decided to forgo much of the revenue generated by these policies and turn its still considerable authority toward ending the opium economy it had been so instrumental in shaping.

THREE
Ambitious Interlude, 1906–1910

By 1906, the dramatic whites, purples, and scarlets of poppy blossoms blazed in the fields of eastern Fujian, merchants in treaty ports along the Chinese coast hustled to sell and distribute thousands of chests of Indian opium, and revenue from taxes on domestic and foreign opium helped prop up a precarious Qing economy. Well-intentioned allusions to Lin Zexu's mission and the righteous fervor that had compelled the Chinese state to order it seemed more mockery than homage as the state attempted to balance its noble rhetoric with an alarming financial reality. And yet, within five years, a central state described by many as teetering on the brink of collapse galvanized the nation into undertaking a massive campaign to eliminate the cultivation, importation, sale, and consumption of opium. Incredulity and scorn on the part of foreign observers were transformed into admiration and fervent support, and by the final year of the Qing dynasty, China's anti-opium movement had attained considerable success.

Resurrected along with China's sense of purpose was the image of Lin Zexu. As an icon representing a powerful amalgam of pride in province and nation, as well as a renewed determination to eliminate the opium plague, nowhere was that image more resonant than in Lin's home province of Fujian. For officials, elite reformers, and the general population, the memory of Lin's doomed mission provided historical context for Fujian's anti-opium campaign and the righteous indignation that fueled it. Images of Lin adorned the walls of provincial opium refuges and were carried at the heads of parades celebrating milestones in the crusade; his recipe for medicinal tea was used to treat addiction, and his words inspired the new reformers. In a dramatic coup for the province's anti-opium activists, the new movement's connection with Lin was solidified by the election of his great-grandson as head of Fujian's leading unofficial reform group. As state-sponsored reform, imperialist pressure, and revolutionary rumblings altered traditional political relationships and opened a space for activism outside the formal bureaucracy, Lin Zexu's image became an important part of a larger ideological drawbridge by which elite nationalism could either be joined to or separated from the Chinese state.

During the first stage of Fujian's anti-opium campaign, from 1906 to 1910, the goals of the state and those of elite reformers meshed. Manpower shortages in the formal bureaucracy and abundant enthusiasm and nationalism among reformist elites led to a state-sanctioned public space that incorporated a broader spectrum of elites outside the formal bureaucracy than would have been permitted before the Boxer debacle. The New Policy reforms that provided the context for the emergence of this nascent public sphere sought to remold Chinese political, military, and educational systems, as well as cultural values, while repulsing foreign intrusions and avoiding dynastic collapse. In between the officials trying to implement this far-reaching reform scheme and the general public, who often were expected to pay for it, a vast array of unofficial, elite-led reform societies emerged to support both the general trend and specific reform initiatives. These groups were encouraged and sometimes even financially supported by the state, which saw in them the means of pursuing its own agenda at very little cost while simultaneously directing potentially revolutionary sentiment toward a more positive, state-endorsed overhaul of imperial government.

In return, this space, contoured in large part by the still commanding legal and moral authority of the state, had much to offer reform-minded, energetic elites searching for access to a rapidly changing political process, particularly in urban areas like Fuzhou. In the arena of opium reform, reformers who dominated this public space amassed unparalleled powers, markedly different in scope and content from their traditional philanthropic and public service roles. They employed these new powers to regulate the population—in the name of public welfare (*gongyi*)—but they did so in a way designed to control as well as to exhort and educate. These men recognized the power of public opinion and their own power to shape it, and they mobilized the populace, incorporating it into both the physical and political meanings of the new space. A new China required new citizens, new forms of expression, and new goals that transcended private needs. The nation came first, and at the outset of the suppression campaign, its needs meshed with the goals of the state.

As this public space evolved, bound to the state and yet apart from it, the Qing government made the electrifying decision to transform itself gradually into a constitutional monarchy. The organization of provincial assemblies gave progressive elites a license to engage in substantive political activism as part of a state-to-be. Ironically, from the vantage point of this new semiofficial forum, the public space in which the opium suppression campaign was being conducted looked superfluous and a bit threatening, even to those elites whose first forays into politics had been staged within that space. As the elites involved with the Provincial Assembly began to envision themselves as more than advisors to a new kind of state and to identify with it, they moved to absorb many of the functions, members, and funds of the Anti-Opium Society.

These were heady days for reform-minded officials and elites. Reformist sentiment was trumpeted in a flurry of newspapers and journals dedicated to the expression and the molding of public opinion. Practices such as footbinding and the old education system were decried as fettering minds and bodies. New schools were established to train the men and women who would be the citizens of a new and reinvigorated China, and the New Army, trained in modern techniques and armed with modern weapons, was created to protect Chinese territory. Ridding China of opium would reinvigorate Chinese pride by eliminating a source of moral and physical decay within China and by demonstrating to the world that China would no longer accept subordinate status in global politics. By 1911, it looked to the entire world as though these ambitious goals might be attained.

The View from Fujian

The late Qing strategy for eliminating opium consisted of complementing the enforcement powers of the official bureaucracy, from the national to the local level, with the voluntary efforts of unofficial reform groups. The anti-opium campaign endowed officials with new titles and new duties, but from the streets and alleyways of Fuzhou and Fujian's lesser towns and cities, the boundaries between official and unofficial efforts must have been difficult to perceive. In some areas, officials took the lead in managing the campaign and may have organized and spoken at mass meetings to denounce opium smoking, but in many areas the most visible enforcers were the members of the local branches of the Anti-Opium Society, whose powers were augmented by and often almost indistinguishable from those exercised by the new police forces.

It became a point of great pride for local elites that Fujian's anti-opium campaign began several months before the issuance of the September 1906 edict, with the inaugural meeting of the Fujian Anti-Opium Society (Fujian qudu zongshe, literally "the headquarters of the Fujian Society to Eliminate Poison") on 22 June 1906. Ten prestigious local literati/officials from the ranks of the gentry-merchant elite (*shenshang*) founded the Anti-Opium Society, which served as the vanguard of the province's unofficial reform efforts throughout the campaign.[1] Outrage generated in large part by the anti-American boycott of 1905 galvanized these men into forming an outlet for their patriotic fervor.[2] The society's influence derived initially from the reputation, wealth, and clan connections of its prominent founders, but its activities remained confined to publicizing the new initiative until the group was empowered by and simultaneously subsumed under the official arm of the suppression campaign when that materialized in 1907.[3] Once it became part of a state-sanctioned campaign, although still outside the opium reform bureaucracy, the society was granted extraordinary powers of search and seizure.

From its inception, the society proved itself a savvy manipulator of nationalistic symbolism, cognizant of the need not only to appeal to provincial loyalties but also to cement the approval of the central state and co-opt its symbolic and legal authority. Perhaps the society's most deliberate move in that direction was the selection of founding member Lin Bingzhang (1875–1923) as its first leader. It would be difficult to imagine a more suitable leader, given Lin's bureaucratic experience, family connections, and personal background. Lin brought an impressive array of professional accomplishments to the job, having studied at the renowned Hanlin Academy and earned the coveted *jinshi* degree. In 1906, Lin was serving as president of Fuzhou Provincial College.[4] On a more personal note, through his marriage to the

---

1. The organizers were Chen Baochen, Lin Bingzhang, Lin Shaonian, Shao Zhicheng, Liu Xuexun, Luo Jincheng, Zhang Zanting, Li Funan, Chen Maoding, and Lin Zhixuan (Wu Jiayu and Lin Jiazhen, "Fujian jinyan yundong 'Qudu she,'" pp. 15–17).

2. *The Quarterly* 1 (1907), history (*lishi*) section, p. 1.

3. According to British diplomats, the society seized on the inaction of the acting governor-general, who hesitated to publicize the edict announcing the campaign, to become the city's first anti-opium organization. The society printed copies of the announcement and distributed them throughout the greater Fuzhou area (PRO, FO 228/2415, doc. 66, enclosure in Playfair to Jordan, 25 Feb. 1907).

4. Liu Decheng and Zhou Xianying, *Fujian mingren cidian*, p. 207; Xu Youchun, *Minguo renwu da cidian*, p. 469; and Tahara, *Shinmatsu minsho Chūgoku kanshin jimmeiroku*, pp. 240–41.

daughter of fellow Anti-Opium Society founder and local notable Chen Baochen (1848–1935), Lin represented the combined social and financial weight of the influential Chen and Lin clans. Lin's wedding to Chen's eldest daughter symbolized the power of that union. The elaborate ceremony evidently generated a good deal of curiosity among the general public as they lined the streets to view the lavish bridal procession troop past.[5] More to the point for the purposes of this study, however, was that Lin Bingzhang also happened to be the great-grandson of Lin Zexu.[6]

If the society had been devoted to combating any vice other than opium, the older and more experienced of the society's founders undoubtedly would have overshadowed Lin Bingzhang. Among the most prominent of those men was Lin's father-in-law, Chen Baochen, also a *jinshi* and Hanlin scholar. Chen was a prominent educator who had held offices in the Grand Secretariat and the Board of Rites. He was also deeply involved in reform in his home province of Fujian. He was active in the chamber of commerce, was appointed to run the new Fujian Normal College, and eventually became provincial director of education.[7] From Chen's generation also came Lin Shaonian (1849–1916), another Hanlin graduate and *jinshi*, who had amassed an extremely impressive résumé that included stints as a grand councillor and governor of several provinces.[8] Chen Maoding (b. 1871) was a *jinshi* of the same generation as Lin Bingzhang and had served in several provincial and national-level posts.[9] These and other society founders used their clout to impress local officials with the urgency and importance of their mission, but for public appeal Lin Bingzhang's genealogy was unsurpassed.

The symbolic impact of selecting Lin's descendant to play a leading role in Fujian's contemporary anti-opium crusade cannot be overstated. It was as though Lin Zexu himself had a hand in the society's activities. Lin

---

5. Wu Jiaqiong, "Lin Bingzhang shengping gaishu," pp. 98–99.

6. In fact, according to a relatively recent biographical essay, the Qing throne granted Lin Bingzhang the *jinshi* degree in recognition of the accomplishments of his illustrious ancestor, and his subsequent success was largely the result of his father-in-law's influence. Many similar allegations that cast aspersions on Lin's talents and character are contained in Wu Jiaqiong's often snide account; however, the essay contains no footnotes against which the author's opinions can be corroborated. See Wu Jiaqiong, "Lin Bingzhang shengping gaishu," pp. 98–99; and Liu Decheng and Zhou Xianying, *Fujian mingren cidian*, p. 207.

7. Liu Decheng and Zhou Xianying, *Fujian mingren cidian*, p. 180.

8. Ibid., p. 181.

9. Ibid., p. 202.

Bingzhang clearly understood the power of his lineage and stressed the link between his mission and that of his venerable ancestor at every possible opportunity. According to the Min county gazetteer, he marked his election as head of the Anti-Opium Society with a speech that read in part: "My ancestor Lin Zexu took great pains to get rid of opium, but he did not fulfill his wish. This bad habit took hold and spread. The nation grew poorer each day, and [poppy] cultivation made it grow weaker by the day. Today, this election has fulfilled the desire that Lin Zexu could not. All of Fujian is very blessed."[10] A Chinese historian writing today concurs: "Lin Bingzhang acted in accordance with the solemn behest [of his ancestor] to carry out the prohibition of opium."[11] In short, the late Qing opium reformers in Fujian had taken up the standard of reform from their fallen native son, and Lin Zexu's Fujianese origin was as important an element in the rhetoric of reform as his uncompromising opposition to the opium trade. As we shall see, the memory of Lin Zexu was invoked in a variety of contexts to exhort reformers and the general population. His image was flexible enough to encompass beneath its symbolic umbrella both the patriotic support of a national suppression policy designed to restore China's strength and pride and the turn toward a more provincially oriented perspective that eventually became hostile to the state.

Lin Bingzhang's leadership brought a sense of inherited mission to the campaign and reinforced the link between the goals and policies of elites and those of the province and central state. Perhaps that link was too explicit for the central authorities, because, in 1908 or 1909, as Fujian's anti-opium crusade gathered momentum, Lin Bingzhang was given an appointment in Beijing.[12] This position may have been a reward for Lin's leadership in the provincial suppression campaign or a simple case of his father-in-law pulling strings, but Beijing may have wished either to exploit his symbolic power itself and/or to ensure that that power did not get out of hand in Fujian. Even after departing his native province, however, Lin remained active in the unofficial side of the movement as a prominent member of a national anti-

---

10. *Minxian xiang tuzhi* (1906), p. 349.
11. Lin Honghuan, "'Qudu she' shimo," p. 48.
12. Lin served briefly as an assistant secretary (*chengcan*) in the Ministry of Posts and Communications (Youzhuan bu). He also served on the Qing government's Committee for Drawing up Regulations for Constitutional Government (Xianfa bianchaguan), but the dates of those appointments are unclear. One source states that he went to the capital sometime after Chen Baochen left Fujian in 1909, because Chen had secured his son-in-law a good position (Wu Jiaqiong, "Lin Bingzhang shengping gaishu," p. 99).

opium association and kept himself informed about and involved in the situation at home.[13] However, he became increasingly entangled in provincial politics and played no significant leadership role in Fujian's opium crusade after the Revolution of 1911.

During this first phase of reform, the Fujian Anti-Opium Society threw itself into its mission with a fervor fueled by nationalist convictions. Ordinary Fujianese, however, found themselves subjected to increasingly intrusive measures. Accustomed to the ubiquitous presence of opium smokers and the many opium dens (*yanguan*), shops, and brothels in which the drug was readily available, Fujian's urban dwellers now found their lives regulated to an unprecedented degree in the name of opium reform, as well as of other New Policy measures. The residents of many cities and towns were subjected to a census designed not only to identify opium smokers and record their age and occupation but also to ascertain the severity and length of their habit.[14] This information was used to set deadlines for smokers to give up their habit and, in many cases, to determine precisely the amount of their opium ration as they gradually weaned themselves from the drug. Those identified as addicts and registered for the rationing program were photographed and issued smoking licenses. The opium shops and dens that dotted the alleyways were either shut down, converted to more reputable pursuits, or carefully regulated by the local authorities. Violators of the restrictions were subject to fines, prison terms, or public humiliation. Society members carried out much of the monitoring, documentation, and enforcement of the campaign in the cities.

Those living in rural areas were not exempt from the campaign. Farmers in the province's opium-growing regions often faced increased regulation. Local officials ordered cultivators to cease sowing poppy seeds immediately, and the Anti-Opium Society branches scattered across the province reported back to Fuzhou on the status of the domestic poppy crop. Soldiers could be deployed to uproot the crop of any farmer who proved unwilling to do so himself.

---

13. The American consulate in Xiamen reported that Lin visited that city in 1910 as ex-president of the provincial Anti-Opium Society (USDS [1910–29], 893.114, reel 113, report from Charles Brissel, enclosure in Xiamen to Secy. of State, 20 July 1911).

14. The Qing plan for self-government also required a census, and the panoply of New Policies were funded by a barrage of new taxes and surtaxes that took a heavy financial toll on many poor Chinese farmers (Prazniak, *Of Camel Kings and Other Things*, pp. 30–35).

Opium reform clearly involved considerable coercion on the part of the state and unofficial reform groups, but because the Anti-Opium Society also relied on raising the level of collective nationalism and provincial pride to sustain the campaign, some aspects of the crusade—mainly public demonstrations and mass meetings—were designed to teach the general public about the evils of opium through more attention-grabbing methods. Eloquent speakers, some of whom were foreign, held forth on the moral and social toll of opium smoking. Pamphlets were handed to those who could read. Noisy parades wound their way through city streets to announce important achievements in the campaign and culminated in ceremonial bonfires. In addition, compassion and concern were extended to addicts through in-patient clinics and a vast array of medications for those who preferred to treat themselves.

Despite the intrusive elements of the campaign, opium reform tapped into a strong popular antipathy toward the drug. Besides officials and elite reformers, many not directly involved in the mechanisms of reform also supported the initiative. Numerous smokers and their families took advantage of increased opportunities for treatment; in addition, the public celebrations attracted enormous audiences. Many undoubtedly were drawn by the spectacle, but some must have come away influenced by the fiery oratory and the dramatic pipe burnings. Since, however, popular hostility to opium during the campaign generally was expressed through and interpreted as support for state policy, it is admittedly difficult to discern if such cooperation and interest were purely voluntary.

Although it is unclear how much ordinary individuals understood about the structure of the campaign that was unfolding around them, local officials and the unofficial reform groups that publicized, implemented, and enforced the opium restrictions were well aware of their own positions in a network of organizations and a chain of command that extended to Beijing and beyond to Great Britain. The plan to dismantle Fujian's web-like opium economy required an equally extensive bureaucratic and legal network. It is to that network that we now turn.

The Framework of Opium Reform in Fujian

Fujian's opium suppression campaign took place within a policy framework constructed by the central Chinese state under strong pressure from the British and Indian governments. Control over foreign opium imports was only one of a long list of prerogatives taken from the Qing state by increasingly aggressive imperialist powers in the second half of the nineteenth century. After the defeat of the Boxer Rebellion in 1900, however, growing Chinese dissatisfaction generated a wave of nationalism that threatened to become as critical of the Manchu dynasty that had succumbed to western pressure as it was of the imperialists. Many of the Qing state's early twentieth-century reforms can be included under the Rights Recovery Movement that sought to regain for China the control over its internal affairs that had been eroded by the unequal treaties. China's right to close its borders to the importation of a harmful narcotic was among the most emotionally charged of the movement's goals.

In reality, it is unlikely that the Qing state would or could have initiated the opium suppression campaign unless it could, with a reasonable degree of certainty, count on the cooperation of the British in ending Indian opium imports. History had proved that focusing on domestic suppression simply spawned a thriving black market in the foreign drug. However, by signing an agreement with the British to diminish Indian imports over the course of the campaign, the Qing government not only guaranteed that its own efforts would be matched by the gradual elimination of the foreign opium trade but also created a situation in which local and provincial interests had to be subsumed under a broader national effort. China's central state *had* to establish guidelines for all provinces and monitor the implementation and enforcement of the plan lest foreign merchants use evidence of excessive poppy cultivation or interprovincial smuggling as an excuse to resume the Sino-Indian opium trade. The lucrative nature of the trade led to suspicion among traffickers in the Indian drug that China simply wished to eliminate foreign competition for the domestic poppy. However, the provisions of the agreement also compelled the Qing government to limit the flexibility of the provinces to set priorities and timetables for reform within their own jurisdictions.

THE OFFICIAL STRUCTURE OF OPIUM REFORM

On 20 September 1906, an imperial edict condemned opium and announced the inauguration of a nationwide push to eliminate the drug over the next ten years. "Though the government is in straitened circumstances, it will neither seek to satisfy its hunger nor quench its thirst at the expense of this harmful poison, so that it may rid its people of this great bane."[15] The throne

---

15. Cited in a memorial from the Anti-Opium Commission, ZZGB 18, endorsed 15 Mar. 1909, pp. 469–71; trans. from *IWCD* 29, no. 278 (Aug. 1909): 120.

deplored the social and economic devastation wrought by the widespread sale, cultivation, and consumption of opium and charged the Office of Government Affairs (Zhengwu chu) with designing a plan to implement the prohibition.[16]

The September edict simply expressed the indignation of the Qing court, but supplemental edicts spelled out the campaign's specific structural and chronological contours. In November 1906, the state outlined its strategy for the elimination of opium in eleven articles that mandated the following measures: a ten-year timetable for the gradual eradication of poppy cultivation; a registration and licensing scheme to wean smokers from their habits and discourage new smokers; orders to courtiers, officials, and other social exemplars commanding them to cease smoking by certain deadlines; a six-month deadline for the closure of all opium dens; a plan for inspecting and licensing opium shops; and a call for the widespread manufacture of opium remedies. Provincial and local officials were to lead the campaign, and although one article specifically encouraged unofficial, elite-led anti-opium societies, it warned these groups against the discussion of political topics. And finally, the Qing government pledged to initiate negotiations with foreign governments to cut off opium imports from abroad.[17]

The crusade needed a national headquarters, and in accordance with another edict dated 7 April 1908, the Opium Prohibition Commission (Jinyan zongju) was formed in Beijing and charged with the design and oversight of the campaign. The four opium prohibition commissioners (jinyan dachen) who led the commission—two Chinese and two Manchus—were, according to one source, "given great power with reference to the examination of officials and populace."[18] The commission served as the titular head of the na-

---

16. The decision was not entirely unexpected. CMS missionaries cited rumors from allegedly reliable sources six months earlier that an opium reform plan soon would be presented to the nation's officials and literati. Yuan Shikai, then serving as governor-general of Zhili, was said to have conceived that plan. See Mercy and Truth 10, no. 115 (July 1906): 196.

17. The original edict is reprinted in Yu Ende, Zhongguo jinyan faling bianqian shi, pp. 124–30. Numerous English translations exist, including one in China No. 1 (1908): 4–8, which appears to be the version on which the British government based its diplomatic response.

18. The first four commissioners were Prince Gong, Assistant Grand Secretary Lu Zhuanlin, and two members of the Board for the Organization of the Deliberative Assembly (Associate Directors of the Senate), Jing Xing and Ding Zhenduo. Later, three or four proctors (tidiao) joined the commissioners (Brunnert and Hagelstrom, Present Day Political Organization of China, pp. 68–70; Qian Shifu, Qingji xinshe zhiguan nianbiao, p. 66; and USDS [1906–10], reel 105, 774/198–99, Fletcher to Root, 8 Apr. 1908).

tional anti-opium bureaucracy, but its primary function outside Beijing was to serve as an administrative clearinghouse for memorials between provincial authorities and the other central bureaucratic organs involved in opium reform. The commission was intimately involved in documenting the progress of opium suppression in and around Beijing, but its duties in the provinces tended toward the mundane, such as providing standard registration forms for opium smokers.[19] The commission did issue edicts to clarify or alter suppression regulations, but the multilayered opium economy was not easily dismantled, and the state could not leave management of the campaign to this tiny new bureaucracy. Since opium suppression touched on matters of taxation, police administration, public health, and transportation, the Ministries of Revenue (Duzhi bu), Interior (Minzheng bu), and War (Lujun bu) also had jurisdiction over various aspects of the initiative.[20]

The commission was to focus its energies on three main tasks—inspection, treatment, and enforcement—and its first duty was to draw up regulations and delegate responsibility to the provinces. Each province was charged with establishing an opium prohibition bureau (*jinyan gongsuo*) in its capital. High-ranking provincial officials were to staff the bureau, under a bureau chief (*zongban*) appointed by the governor-general. In other cities and towns, local authorities or elite reformers were to set up smoking cessation clinics (*jieyan ju*), also known as opium treatment centers or opium refuges (the missionary's preferred term).[21] Operating funds for the commission were provided by taxes on domestic opium, and it was envisioned that the reduction of imports, opium smokers, and land devoted to poppy cultivation would result in the tapering off of opium tax revenues. The new opium bureaucracy would gradually die a natural death along with China's opium problem.

However, opium reform caused a number of problems. The campaign's economic impact was initially cushioned by taxes levied on the drug, but as reform progressed, the gradual cessation of the trade threatened to bring economic privation to many levels of the Chinese economy. Some highly

---

19. Records of the commission at the Number One Historical Archives of China in Beijing; and more specifically, ZZGB 20, memorial from Songshou, endorsed 19 May 1909, pp. 104–8.

20. Another edict endorsed 23 May 1908 laid out the regulations and timetable for opium suppression throughout China, based on recommendations by the Ministries of Finance and Interior. That edict stated clearly that the campaign fell under the jurisdiction of these two bureaucratic entities (*China No. 2* [1908]: 14–17).

21. Brunnert and Hagelstrom, *Present Day Political Organization of China*, pp. 68–70.

touted late Qing reform initiatives—most notably the Hubei Arsenal—relied heavily on opium tax revenues.[22] As the opium supply dwindled, the high prices fetched by what remained served as a powerful incentive for smugglers and for some poppy farmers to resist government attempts to uproot the valuable cash crop. Finally, many ordinary Chinese, who bore the burden of tax hikes intended to substitute for opium-related tax revenues, saw opium suppression as yet another expensive, intrusive reform that further strengthened the power of allegedly progressive elites. The effect, especially in many rural locales, was to generate hostility toward the state.[23]

Further unexpected ramifications emerged when it quickly became clear that China's drug problem was not confined to opium. As the suppression campaign progressed, the continuing Chinese demand for narcotics was sated in part by the importation of increasing amounts of morphine and cocaine.[24] On 1 January 1909, Beijing forbade the importation of morphine, although smuggling continued. Cocaine, which was openly imported into Xiamen for the first time in 1908, was not yet considered dangerous, and importers of that drug paid a tariff of only 5 percent *ad valorem*. Less than 2,000 ounces of cocaine flowed into Xiamen legally in 1908, but that amount rose to 27,578 ounces by the first half of 1910. China prohibited its importation in June 1910.[25]

The blueprint for Qing opium reform was rational, comprehensive, and relatively humane; it also was intended to strengthen the authority of the state under the banner of a highly nationalistic crusade. The central government dictated that the official anti-opium bureaucracy encourage and embrace unofficial opium prohibition societies (*jieyan huishe*) and set few limits on their powers.[26] These groups not only provided a relatively regulated avenue for elite anti-opium sentiment but also served state goals by reporting opium vio-

---

22. This modern munitions facility, championed by Zhang Zhidong in the early twentieth century, received close to 50 percent of its income from opium taxes in 1903–5, but the consolidated tax in 1906 channeled most of that revenue directly to Beijing. The arsenal's ordnance production plummeted, and the situation promised to worsen under the new campaign (Kennedy, "Mausers and the Opium Trade," pp. 118–23).

23. This was true of many New Policy reforms (Prazniak, *Of Camel Kings and Other Things*).

24. The growth and development of the supply and demand for these opium derivatives is not explored in this volume, except to note when this relatively new problem complicated the conduct of the anti-opium crusade.

25. IMC, *Decennial Reports, Amoy, 1902–1911*, p. 102.

26. Brunnert and Hagelstrom, *Present Day Political Organization of China*, pp. 68–70.

lations among local officials as well as common folk. However, although the central authorities encouraged elite activism and cooperation with local officials, they also encouraged local bureaucrats to take the lead in the anti-opium campaign. Paradoxically, then, by allowing unofficial groups to pursue their reformist objectives within the framework constructed by Beijing, the central government was able to further extend its control over local authorities in pursuit of its own policy agenda. This strategy was only effective, however, as long as provincial officials, the central states, and the reform groups saw themselves as working toward the same goals.

At the same time, the regulations that reflected the state's desire and ability to establish the pace, priorities, and broad contours of the campaign also demonstrated the central government's recognition that successful suppression had to reflect local conditions. Beijing's opium-related edicts provided a template for provincial reform, but provincial authorities sometimes were granted permission to impose tougher restrictions and shorter deadlines for suppression within their jurisdictions. However, the 1908 agreement with the British—perceived by both sides as crucial to the success of the campaign—constrained the pace of reform, and the inability of the Chinese state to comply with many provincial requests to accelerate reforms contributed to anti-Qing nationalist sentiment among reformist officials and elites in 1911.

THE BRITISH FACTOR BEFORE THE REVOLUTION

The Qing government's decision to issue the 1906 edict was a result not only of a domestic climate receptive to reform but also of a series of political and economic circumstances that affected British attitudes and policies toward the opium trade. In 1906, a newly elected Liberal majority in the British House of Commons signaled that change in attitude by proposing a resolution on 30 May 1906 condemning the trade as "morally indefensible."[27] An increasingly vocal anti-opium lobby, primarily fueled by Protestant missionaries and influential Quakers, helped mold public opinion against British involvement in the trade with China. Most important, however, was the steady decrease in Indian revenues from the Chinese opium trade, a development precipitated by increased Chinese poppy cultivation and the comparatively high price of the Indian drug. In 1905, the colonial Indian gov-

---

27. IWCD 28, no. 265 (July 1908): 106.

ernment allegedly hinted to Chinese diplomat Tang Shaoyi, who was in India on an unrelated diplomatic mission, that India might be willing to forgo the revenue from the sales of opium to China.[28] The Qing government jumped at the unexpected chance.

That China was compelled to depend on a voluntary change in official British attitudes and policies was necessitated by the terms of the aptly named "unequal treaties." This series of agreements began after the Opium War and substantially eroded Chinese sovereignty and territorial integrity. Several of the treaties, particularly the Treaty of Tianjin and the Additional Article to the Chefoo Convention, had important impacts on the Sino-British opium trade and China's efforts to eliminate the drug. These two treaties limited the amount of revenue the Chinese could squeeze from the foreign arm of the trade and prevented China from banning opium imports.[29] Without the ability to cut off the flow of opium from abroad, domestic prohibition was bound to fail.

Securing British cooperation required a series of diplomatic negotiations. The British wanted clear evidence of Chinese sincerity, since some skeptical British officials (most notably India's secretary of state) feared that India would be giving up a declining but still profitable trade only to see the Chinese opium market flooded by the homegrown product. After a good deal of diplomatic squabbling, Great Britain and China signed an agreement that went into effect on 1 January 1908 and stipulated that Indian opium imports to China would be reduced by 5,100 chests per year.[30] The agreement was to be reviewed and renegotiated after three years on the basis of China's progress in its domestic suppression drive.[31] The provisional nature of the agreement meant that British officials would be keeping close track of China's suppression campaign, and the Chinese government had to contend with the implicit threat of the agreement's collapse should it lose control of provincial reform efforts. Although the prospect of ending Indian imports

---

28. *China No. 1* (1908): 1–2; *Friend of China* 26, no. 2 (Apr. 1909): 38–39; and Owen, *British Opium Policy in China and India*, pp. 329–33.

29. Ironically, as discussed in Chapter 2, the opium-related provisions of these treaties eventually worked to the disadvantage of foreign opium merchants by virtually guaranteeing that the price of imported opium would greatly exceed that of the Chinese drug.

30. This number was approximately one-tenth the average number of chests of opium imported annually to China from India from 1901 to 1905. Negotiations had bogged down over this figure (Owen, *British Opium Policy in China and India*, pp. 335–37).

31. *China No. 1* (1908): 45–46; Owen, *British Opium Policy in China and India*, p. 337.

gave tremendous impetus to the campaign, the terms of the agreement ultimately complicated the relationship between the Qing state and local reformers. That the state was to oversee a campaign with international ramifications empowered Beijing, but forged a link to British interests that eventually undermined its leadership.

THE MECHANICS OF OPIUM REFORM IN FUJIAN

The agreements discussed above and Beijing's blueprint for reform established the chronological confines and the basic template for Fujian's suppression campaign. However, scrambling to comply with the state mandate meant that authorities in Fuzhou had to rely on manpower and money from unofficial reformers. This was not unusual in late imperial China, since local elites had long been expected to provide for the public good when state coffers were low. What was unusual was the scope of the powers the Anti-Opium Society acquired, and the degree to which those powers enabled it to regulate and coerce the local population with state approval. This organization worked side by side with local police and officials to publicize, implement, and enforce opium prohibition. The powers of the society conformed to the guidelines for opium suppression established in Beijing; the only difference was that those guidelines spelled out a leading role for officials. During the first stage of the campaign, however, Beijing and Fuzhou saw the activism of unofficial reform groups as an advantage, given the tenacity of the provincial opium economy, the problem of official corruption, and the pressures imposed by the British. Elite reformers seemed to grasp that the success of a policy like opium suppression rested in conducting a true campaign, which meant attempting to change popular attitudes not only about opium smoking but also about the nature of political activism.

Heading up the official arm of Fujian's campaign was Songshou (d. 1911), governor-general of Fujian and Zhejiang (*Min-Zhe zongdu*) from 1907 to November 1911 and a Manchu bannerman with a lengthy civil service career. From his Fuzhou yamen, Songshou oversaw the suppression campaign within Fujian's civilian bureaucracy and among its general population. Opium suppression among the military became the responsibility of Pushou (d. 1911), the provincial Manchu general (*jiangjun*).

Songshou's job was to assess the nature and extent of Fujian's opium problem and then devise and implement a scheme to attack it, all the while working within the legal and temporal boundaries drawn up by Beijing and Great Britain. His early reform efforts were directed at eliminating demand for the drug, particularly among officials. His memorials to Beijing delineate the scope of dependence in Fujian and the amount of land devoted to poppy cultivation and detail his accomplishments—setting up addiction treatment centers, closing opium dens, and reducing the number of opium shops. He also supervised the reduction of poppy cultivation and increased salt taxes to make up for the loss of opium tax revenues.[32] Songshou communicated regularly with Beijing to keep the central state apprised of progress in his jurisdiction, and several of his memorials are cited below.

Opium suppression required a new bureaucratic network, and under Songshou's oversight, local and provincial officials implemented and enforced national and provincial regulations. Songshou delegated joint authority for the supervision of provincial opium prohibition and investigative offices (*jinyan diaocha ju*) to five existing provincial administrative organs: the Department of the Commissioner of Education (Tixueshi si), the Department of the Provincial Judge (Anchashi si), the Department of Civil Administration (Chengxuan shizhengshi si), the salt intendant (*yanfa dao*), and the grain intendant (*liang dao*). These organs were to set up provincial suppression mechanisms, prosecute violators, publicize the campaign, impose taxes to fund the reforms, and help farmers locate substitute crops for poppies, respectively. In reality, however, county magistrates and prefects were in charge of the crusade in most localities, and yamen runners helped monitor and enforce the anti-opium regulations.[33] Those who were declared opium smokers had to register with the government by filling out several forms issued by the Anti-Opium Commission in Beijing, and Beijing was to be kept informed of local developments.

Much of the footwork of opium reform became the duty of the provincial police force. Police reform began in the provinces as early as 1902 as part of the New Policies, and although the Qing state attempted to incorporate provincial variations into a standard framework of regulations in 1908, the task was still in progress when the revolution erupted.[34] It was not until 1909 that a Police Department (Jingwu bu) was constituted in Fuzhou. A police intendant (*daotai*) directed the department and presided over a force of 700–

---

32. ZZGB 20, memorial from Songshou, endorsed 19 May 1909, pp. 104–6.
33. Ibid.
34. Stapleton, "The Rule of Avoidance Reaffirmed," p. 4.

800 men. The police officers patrolled each of the city's eighteen wards (*chu*). In Xiamen, a police force was established in 1906 and consisted of 208 officers who worked out of six police stations.[35] Judging from the descriptions of the Anti-Opium Society's nightly raids, it appears that the force provided muscle when the Opium Prohibition Bureau or the society wished to arrest suspected violators or raid their premises.[36] In addition, beginning in 1909 or 1910, the Fuzhou police intendant also served concurrently as head of the Opium Prohibition Bureau. The close relationship between the new police department, the anti-opium bureaucracy, and the Anti-Opium Society reinforced state control over the campaign and was indicative of an initial atmosphere of cooperation between officials and unofficial reform groups.[37]

In many cases, however, opium suppression simply was added to the administrative duties of overextended, underfunded local officials. This often left a gap that was quickly filled by the Anti-Opium Society. By 1911, the society had branches in virtually every county in the province, including six in Fuzhou alone.[38] Beijing had placed few restrictions on the activities that unofficial reform societies could undertake—except political discussions—and the Anti-Opium Society took full advantage of that leeway. The society investigated illegal opium smokers and opium dens and compiled the official census of smokers used to issue opium-smoking licenses. Society members were even known to have physically uprooted poppy plants.[39] In this way, they amassed great powers with explicit state approval and commandeered the symbolic authority of the state to legitimize and publicize their activities, as well as to enhance their ability to regulate local society.

As the suppression campaign gathered momentum, the society's roster expanded to include men occupying the entire spectrum of late Qing politi-

---

35. IMC, *Decennial Reports, Foochow, 1902–1911*, p. 95; *Decennial Reports, Amoy, 1902–1911*, p. 107.

36. *The Quarterly* 1 (1907), report (*baogao*) section, pp. 21–29.

37. In the city of Shanghai, "gentry-led police initiatives preceded bureaucratic reforms." These initiatives, which included merchant guilds and fire brigades, also existed in Fuzhou, although their connection to the new police force is not clear (Wakeman, *Policing Shanghai*, p. 18).

38. Customs officials and French diplomats report that the society had 112 branches, but *The Quarterly* in 1914 lists only 75, although this may reflect a reduction in society influence after the revolution. In any case, branches were established in most counties, and some counties had more than one. See IMC, *Decennial Reports, Foochow, 1902–1911*, p. 91; MAE/Nantes: translation from *Minbao*, Aug. 1908, in Foutcheou, carton 71; *The Quarterly* 12 (1912–14), *tubiao* section, pp. 3–6.

39. *IWCD* 28, no. 265 (July 1908): 106.

cal activism. In 1907, the first issue of *The Quarterly*, the society's periodical, published a roster of the society's officers during the group's first two years of operation. The publication also included names and brief descriptions of the education and/or employment status of the men in the society's two inspection departments.[40] These inspectors included men with traditional degrees as well as those with backgrounds forged by the late Qing reforms. (Not noted in *The Quarterly* was that several prominent society members were Chinese Christians.)[41] However, 22 of the 30 inspectors in the municipal office had graduated from the new schools that had emerged after the abolition of the civil service examinations in 1905. The rest had acquired lower degrees in the old system.[42]

A number of individuals affiliated with the suburban Nantai office, however, were simply listed as members of other reform societies, evidence that opium suppression took place within a much broader context of reform. Sixteen out of the 42 inspectors in the Nantai office were listed as members of the Speak the News Society (Shuobao she).[43] A surviving set of that society's regulations contains the rather vague mission statement that the group was an outlet for "progressive individuals to use their intelligence to weigh and consider local public welfare issues." Members were forbidden to smoke opium and strongly opposed opium smoking, among other vices. The group was also deeply involved in spreading revolutionary propaganda.[44] Seven others on the Anti-Opium Society roster listed only their membership in the local chamber of commerce. A handful more belonged to other public welfare groups, and a few had obtained official degrees and either were serving or had served as officials.[45] The lack of any other educational or occupational information implies that the New Policy reforms and the anti-opium campaign created and attracted a new kind of progressive and potentially revolutionary coalition to Fuzhou's emerging public political space; among

---

40. One of these offices was located within the Fuzhou city walls, and the other on the island suburb of Nantai. By 1911, the number of offices had grown to six.

41. See Dunch, *Fuzhou Protestants and the Making of a Modern China*. Dunch argues persuasively that Chinese Protestants made important contributions to late Qing reforms and that their faith augmented rather than competed with their nationalist sentiments.

42. *The Quarterly* 1 (1907), regulations (*zhangcheng*) section, pp. 8–11.

43. Ibid.

44. *Fuzhou shuobao she zhangcheng*, pp. 1, 4–5; Zheng Zuyin et al., *Fujian xinhai guangfu shiliao*, pp. 19–20.

45. *The Quarterly* 1 (1907), regulations (*zhangcheng*) section, pp. 8–11.

them were many men whose lack of a traditional education cemented their commitment to change and would have disqualified them from political participation a few years earlier.

One of those men was Chen Nengguang (also known as Ding Nengguang), a reform-minded Christian who became prominent in the unofficial and official arms of the opium suppression campaign after 1911. Born in approximately 1876 to a Chinese Methodist preacher, Chen converted to Christianity and graduated in 1896 from the Anglo-Chinese College run by the American Methodist mission in Fuzhou. The year after his graduation, he joined the provincial postal service and worked his way up to the position of senior clerk. In 1907, he took a job as an interpreter at the American consulate in Fuzhou, where he worked until the revolution.[46]

At the time he was retained by the U.S. consulate, Chen was widely recognized as an active reformer who had helped found several progressive groups, a circumstance that brought him close to losing his job in 1909. His political activism, especially with a group called the Society to Benefit the Hearer (Yiwen she), began to antagonize several prominent foreigners, most notably the British consul at Fuzhou. The society evidently was another vehicle of Fuzhou's radical student element, whose complaints included foreign control of the provincial customs and postal services. The British were further incensed by Chen's vocal opposition to cigarettes, a cause he pursued "to such an extent as to threaten the peace and quiet of the entire city, and about which the British and American Ministers at Pekin [sic] had to telegraph their Consuls here [Fuzhou]."[47]

With this background, it is clear that the zeal of opium reformers was not confined to that single issue, and it seems natural that Chen Nengguang took up the banner of opium suppression. Chen became an officer in the Fuzhou headquarters of the Anti-Opium Society and used his linguistic skills to translate the speeches of foreign reformers. He himself also addressed anti-opium meetings on occasion. The U.S. consul admired Chen's reformist sentiment but deplored his arrogance and the implied association

---

46. He was also a member and officer of the YMCA before and after 1911; see Dunch, *Fuzhou Protestants and the Making of a Modern China*, pp. 62, 70, 150; and *Fuzhou Meiyimei nianhui shi*, p. 90. I thank Ryan Dunch for sharing the latter source with me.

47. USDS (1906–10), reel 351, no. 3823/23, Gracey to Dept. of State, 27 Aug. 1907, no. 3823/110–11, Gracey to Cheshire, 29 July 1909, and no. 3823/114–16, Gracey to Dept. of State, 27 Aug. 1909; Zheng Zuyin et al., *Fujian xinhai guangfu shiliao*, pp. 3–5; MEC Annual Report (1908), p. 138; and Dunch, *Fuzhou Protestants and the Making of a Modern China*, pp. 61–62.

of the U.S. government with Chen's actions and politics; at one point he complained that Chen "has become so puffed up with his importance as to be almost unbearable." The consul also grumbled that Chen's commitments to myriad reform organizations took valuable time away from his job. When confronted with the charges, Chen quickly apologized and pledged to curtail his involvement in politics, a promise he broke almost immediately.[48] Chen's prominence in local reform groups enhanced not only his visibility but also his influence. After the revolution, he would continue his involvement in opium suppression and other aspects of provincial politics as a high-ranking official of the Republican government.

But before 1911, and after the departure of Lin Bingzhang, it was Yang Tinglun and then Chen Peikun (1877–1964), not Chen Nengguang, who assumed the mantle of leadership in the Anti-Opium Society. About Yang, little is known, but Chen Peikun (no relation to the other Chen) was a classically educated reformer in his thirties whose decision to study abroad in Japan even after having earned the prestigious *jinshi* degree can be interpreted as an indication of his progressive inclinations and his recognition of the changing political landscape. His traditional pedigree may have prompted his selection as Lin's replacement over other possible candidates with more modern résumés, but Chen Peikun was deeply involved in progressive causes in the late Qing. Chen remained a key player in the anti-opium campaign during the early Republic and served in several important provincial posts.[49]

The Anti-Opium Society apparently was open to all, but since much of the funding for the society had to be raised privately, the ability to pay monthly dues and contribute to special donation drives was the fundamental qualification for membership. Those who wished to participate could do so as a society member (*sheyuan*), staff person or officer (*zhiyuan*), or "friend of the society" (*sheyou*). According to the society regulations, "Any gentleman who can donate or raise funds to glorify the cause can join," and "those willing to sign a pledge to prevent or give up opium and to observe the society's regulations can be a friend to the group." Friends were encouraged, but not required, to donate. Staff were members who either volunteered or were se-

---

48. USDS (1906–10), reel 351, no. 3823/110-11, Gracey to Cheshire, 29 July 1909.
49. Chen served as head of the Provincial College in Fujian in the late Qing / early Republic. On Chen, see Xu Youchun, *Minguo renmin da cidian*, p. 1045; Dunch, *Fuzhou Protestants and the Making of a Modern China*, p. 108; Liu Decheng and Zhou Xianying, *Fujian mingren cidian*, pp. 212–13; and Wu Jiayu and Lin Jiazhen, "Fujian jinyan yundong 'Qudu she,'" p. 18.

lected to perform official society functions. Society officers were elected by and from the roster of members and friends.[50]

As society members and friends sought to energize and mobilize the city to eradicate the evils of opium, they did not have to look far for an inspiration that could be used to connect the local mission of these elite reformers to the goals of the province and the nation. The society was keenly aware of the power implicit in its geographical and genealogical links to the legendary Commissioner Lin, and over the next decade it presided over his iconization. The founding of the society was marked by a lively parade through Fuzhou punctuated by the cacophony of gongs and drums and featuring a large portrait of Lin Zexu held high.[51] Each summer mass celebrations marked the anniversary of the founding, and society officers, preferably Lin Bingzhang, would publicly invoke Lin Zexu's name and mission.[52] To further emphasize the link, the society headquarters was housed in a shrine dedicated to Lin Zexu's memory. In addition, at least one Fuzhou opium refuge required that smokers who completed the treatment regimen be photographed and lectured on the evils of opium while standing in front of a portrait of the venerable Lin Zexu.[53]

Like many other political activists, the members of the Anti-Opium Society also spread their message in the pages of their own periodical. *The Quarterly* lays out not only the organizational structure of the society but also the extensive scope of its activities. Society members were elected or assigned to the following positions and duties: administrative officers, who supervised the operations and the all-important fundraising activities of the society; medical staff, who specialized in concocting and administering Chinese and western remedies for addiction administered in society treatment centers; investigators, who conducted daily raids on suspected violators; auditors, who supervised the society's finances; clerks, who handled correspondence; and "exhorters" (*quandao yuan*), who performed propaganda work. The society was in charge of registering opium smokers and distributing the licenses with which smokers could legally purchase decreasing rations of the drug.[54]

---

50. *The Quarterly* 1 (1907), regulations (*zhangcheng*) section, p. 1.
51. *The Quarterly* 3 (1908), miscellaneous (*zazhi*) section, p. 10.
52. Lin Honghuan, "'Qudu she' shimo," p. 48; Wu Jiaqiong, "Lin Bingzhang shengping gaishu."
53. *Mercy and Truth* 11, no. 126 (June 1907): 184–85.
54. *The Quarterly* 1 (1907), regulations (*zhangcheng*) section, pp. 4–13.

As branch societies popped up in rural locales, members were also assigned to monitor the eradication of poppy cultivation.[55]

Society members were expected not only to pledge to commit themselves to opium reform but also to adhere to a strict personal code of conduct to ensure their integrity and the society's reputation. All staff, members, and friends of the society signed a pledge not to smoke opium and were prohibited from displaying opium-smoking equipment in their homes and businesses or using that equipment to entertain. Opium smokers were not to be invited into the homes of society staff, members, or friends or even to loiter outside the businesses of those connected with the society. However, the society did believe in rehabilitation, and opium smokers could join if they pledged to give up the habit within six months.[56] Those affiliated with the society could not accept rent money from those who bought or sold opium and were forbidden to allow their tenants or family members to plant poppies. Violators were dismissed or fined on a sliding scale appropriate to the gravity of their offense and were threatened with the publication of their names and offenses should they resist punishment.[57] The regulations embodied the society's mission to mold upright, committed reformers and to build public confidence and respect. However, these intentions did not completely mask the vigilante style of the reformers or the potential for popular resentment.

Unlike the public meetings and celebrations designed to shape public opinion and encourage public support for the campaign, the society's nightly raids highlighted the ways in which the new public political space could be used to coerce the masses. Most notable was the seemingly arbitrary nature of the investigations, as well as the public humiliation that awaited the guilty parties. A regular feature in *The Quarterly* described the daily activities of society investigators. A small group of four or five investigators, together with several police patrolmen, sallied forth each night (barring inclement weather) to raid homes and businesses suspected of harboring illicit opium smokers or smoking equipment. Each foray was briefly outlined, along with a pipe-by-pipe accounting of contraband confiscated that night. The squads visited

---

55. *Fan nietai lilin Qudu zongshe kai huiyi an* (1909), p. 6.
56. Quitting was optional for those over 60 years of age, out of a concern that withdrawal might cause serious health problems or even death. The same rules applied for opium smokers in the families of society members, staff, and friends.
57. *The Quarterly* 1 (1907), regulations (*zhangcheng*) section.

all manner of locations where groups of people might gather to smoke opium, including temples, military barracks, former opium dens and shops, and sedan chair rental companies. These teams organized at the nearest society office and then returned after the raids to write up their report. Names and addresses of violators were publicized in *The Quarterly*.[58]

The function of *The Quarterly* as an organ of publicity that trumpeted the progress of the campaign as well as the dedication of society members embodied the new vision of the new public political space held by many elite reformers. The dissemination of anti-opium propaganda was among the first tasks to which the society turned its considerable energies.[59] The society recognized the power of both polemic and satire in garnering attention to and support for their crusade. Toward that end, some issues of *The Quarterly* contained cautionary essays, as well as illustrations or political cartoons that lampooned opium smoking and lauded elite-official cooperation. One illustration portrayed a group of gowned scholars and officials bowing down to an altar on which a tablet bearing the emperor's order to "eliminate the poison" (*qudu*) rests. Those two characters, not coincidentally, are the same as those in the name of the Anti-Opium Society. Two flags are attached to the tablet: one is the dragon flag of the Qing; on the other is written "officials and gentry joyfully celebrate" (*guanshen huanzhu*). Another three-panel cartoon (see Fig. 3.1) employed simple but graphic imagery to trace how addiction warped the body, destroyed the family, and consumed the smoker. *The Quarterly* also featured a commentary section with arguments in favor of opium suppression.[60] Since, however, the circulation of and audience for the periodical are unknown, it is difficult to analyze its impact.[61]

Fujian's implementation and enforcement of Beijing's opium suppression campaign mobilized a virtual army of bureaucrats, investigators, medical personnel, police, and reformist orators and educators. They operated within official and unofficial reform organizations that theoretically were

---

58. The examples used in this paragraph were drawn from the daily activities section (*riji*) of *The Quarterly*, 1 (1907), but the daily activities and report (*baogao*) sections of any issue give similar anecdotes.

59. Wu Jiayu and Lin Jiazhen, "Fujian jinyan yundong 'Qudu she,'" p. 16.

60. *The Quarterly* 1 (1907), *lunshuo* and *xiaoshuo lei* sections. The quality of the first illustration mentioned was too poor to allow it to be reproduced here.

61. The *North China Herald* of 6 Feb. 1909 states that *The Quarterly* was "distributed widely" but does not elaborate (cited in MAE/Paris, NS 588, 6 Feb. 1909, pp. 43–48).

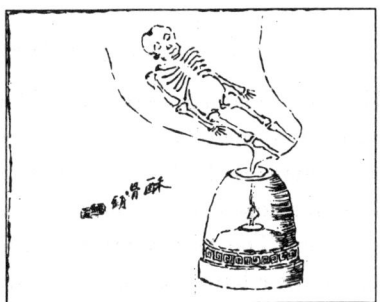

Fig. 3.1 Three-panel cartoon from *The Quarterly* (1907) illustrating the toll opium smoking could take on the body and the family.

linked by a chain of command originating in Beijing and extending into Fujian through the local and provincial administrations. Within this framework, which penetrated every county in Fujian, opium smokers, poppy farmers, and purveyors of opium and opium-smoking paraphernalia were subject to restrictions designed to count, register, control, and eventually eliminate their ties to the drug. The mechanisms of opium reform extended the regulatory powers of the state beyond officialdom and deep into a new group of progressive advocates energized by nationalism, provincialism, and a willingness to act out their commitment to reform in a new public space. By allowing unofficial reform groups unprecedented control over local society in the name of furthering a state-initiated policy, the Qing state believed that it could retain the loyalty of these activists, fulfill its obligations to the Chinese people and the British government, and reduce official corruption, all with a limited financial investment. But what happened when these activists interacted with the official arm of reform during the first stage of the suppression campaign?

Opium Reform and the Public Sphere, 1906–1910

The Anti-Opium Society plunged into the promotion of opium suppression even before the official campaign, but not until the state called for opium prohibition, established a timetable and a clear set of administrative guidelines, and concluded an agreement with the British did the campaign begin in earnest. The dismantling of Fujian's opium economy required that all factors in the relatively complex supply/demand equation outlined in Chapter 2 be addressed, but the reformers of the Anti-Opium Society were best situated and equipped to focus their energies and new powers on limiting demand for the drug in urban areas. As the campaign gained momentum, branch societies also monitored and publicized the campaign's progress against domestic poppy cultivation, but they generally were not involved in enforcing this part of the crusade.

A brief delay in the implementation of Fujian's campaign caused by a vacancy in the important post of governor-general and the inaction of the acting provincial leader allowed the society time to take the lead. When that situation was remedied by Songshou's promotion in 1907, the province began to attack the opium problem in accordance with the central government's regulations. In early February 1907, the British consul at Fuzhou reported that although no smoking licenses or restrictions on poppy cultivation had yet been issued, a deadline had been set for closing all opium dens, officials appeared to have ceased smoking, popular opium remedies were on sale everywhere, and anti-opium societies were being encouraged and supported by local authorities and the public.[62]

Once the formal campaign was announced, the Anti-Opium Society took charge of eliminating opium smoking by assessing the extent of consumption and establishing treatment centers. As a result of the society's inaugural meeting in June 1906, four smoking cessation clinics were opened in Fuzhou. The foreign missionaries who visited one in early 1907 were favorably impressed.[63] The facility accepted smokers in groups of 25 and had already treated about a hundred when the missionaries arrived. By the fall of 1907, *The Quarterly* reported that the four clinics had cured a total of 2,465 smokers. A small fee of one *jiao* per day was charged to defray boarding costs, with the society footing the bill for medications and medical care. All "cured"

---

62. PRO, FO 228/2415, doc. 66, enclosure in Playfair to Jordan, 25 Feb. 1907.
63. *Mercy and Truth* 11, no. 126 (June 1907): 184–85.

smokers were to be lauded in print for their accomplishment, but they also were subject to continued surveillance outside the refuge. Each had to find a guarantor who took responsibility for assuring that they did not resume smoking. Furthermore, the society required them to attach a sign on the doors of their home as proof they had undergone treatment. This requirement probably was also intended to make it easier for society investigators to keep an eye on likely recidivists.[64]

Those who wished to quit smoking were examined, and some who were determined to be truly addicted were granted opium-smoking licenses (*jieyan pai*, literally "cease smoking licenses") that allowed them to legally purchase a ration of opium at a licensed shop. According to a 1907 issue of *The Quarterly*, 108 licensed shops distributed opium rations in Fuzhou and 104 in Nantai.[65] Numbered smoking licenses were issued on a monthly basis; the depth of dependence determined the daily amount of opium each licensee was allowed to purchase. State regulations describe the licenses as a type of identification card with a series of squares that were stamped each day by a licensed opium paste dealer. A photograph of the smoker was affixed to the license; the name and address of the licensee and the ration amount were also printed on the card. Those who left town had to purchase a temporary traveler's license, and visiting smokers had to request a temporary license during their stay. The rules even mandated how licenses were to be placed on the counters of opium shops and the means by which the ration was to be measured out and spread on a leaf. Smokers had to smoke their ration in designated places. The society issued the smoking licenses, kept records of registered smokers and their opium rations, and made this information available to provincial authorities. Violations brought a hefty fine.[66]

The society was not without its enemies. Just as the campaign got under way in 1906, malicious slander by a group of men associated with the trade almost resulted in the death of Lin Bingzhang and the demise of the society. One source described the conspirators as "compradors, foreign flunkies, and traitorous merchants" in alliance with "'sons of the banners' [Manchus] and opium devils." They apparently spread a rumor that Lin was associated

---

64. *The Quarterly* 1 (1907), regulations (*zhangcheng*) section, pp. 5–8.
65. Ibid., *gongdu* section, pp. 7–16.
66. *Fujian xianding jianyan xinzhang* (1911). By early 1909, more than 6,000 licenses were being used (*North China Herald*, cited in MAE/Paris, NS 588, 6 Feb. 1909, pp. 43–48).

with the supporters of the Hundred Days reform in 1898 and that the society was working to drive out the Empress Dowager. The foundation of the accusation rested on the character *du* 毒, "poison," which was used in the society's name (*qudu she* 去毒社). They pointed out that if the two radicals used to make the character *du* were separated, then the name of the society would read *qu zhumu she* 去主母社, or the "eliminate the 'head mother' society." Evidently the rumor sent Cixi into a rage. She telegraphed the governor-general of Fujian and Zhejiang to execute Lin on the spot and to round up the other members of the society and raze their meeting place if the rumor proved correct. Fortunately, Lin's father-in-law, Chen Baochen, was in Beijing on other business. Chen got wind of the danger and warned Lin and his colleagues, who subsequently straightened out the situation by writing an explanatory memorial to Cixi.[67] As the campaign accelerated and became more and more visible and intrusive, the potential for resentment also increased, although violent resistance in Fujian before 1911 was minimal.

Despite the general consensus among foreign and Chinese observers that opium abuse and the opium trade constituted a serious socioeconomic problem in Fujian, the lucrative nature of the trade, the addictive quality of the drug, and the legal consequences of admitting a role in the provincial opium economy meant that an accurate census of the acreage devoted to poppy cultivation and of the number of smokers was difficult. Figures collected on Songshou's orders claimed that 37,000 *mu* of poppies were planted in Fujian in 1908. He also reported that an Anti-Opium Society survey in 1907 found that some 230,000 smokers had been registered since the outset of the campaign, about one-quarter (54,200) of whom had been able to give up the habit during the first two years of the policy.[68] In a provincial population estimated at 14–15 million, just under 2 percent of Fujianese admitted to habitual opium smoking.

Other statistics, however, call that figure into question. Fuzhou was divided into counties, each of which was patrolled by teams of police and society investigators as they compiled smoking registries. In September 1908, the

---

67. Unfortunately, I have been unable to locate this memorial, which allegedly was signed by Chen, Chen Bi, Lin Shaonian, Wang Renkan, and others. On this incident, see Lin Honghuan, "'Qudu she' shimo," pp. 48–49; and Wu Jiayu and Lin Jiazhen, "Fujian jinyan yundong 'Qudu she,'" p. 18.

68. ZZGB 20, memorial by Songshou, endorsed 19 May 1909, pp. 106–7.

French consulate in Fuzhou acquired a list of opium smokers for every street in the city. The statistics are of limited use because many sections are incomplete or missing. However, what remains of the survey lists the number of resident families and the number of opium smokers among those families for several parts of the city. The data are remarkably consistent and indicate that an average of one out of every ten families in the areas surveyed contained an opium smoker.[69] The acquisition of accurate statistics on the extent of opium use and cultivation, a fundamental precondition for the accurate assessment of the progress of the campaign, was problematic for opium reformers, not only because provincial averages obscured the seriousness of the problem in some areas, but also because the stigma of addiction paired with the intrusive nature of the campaign, undoubtedly discouraged many smokers and many farmers from coming forward.

The most visible success of the cooperation between officials and unofficial reformers was the closing of all of Fuzhou's opium dens by 12 May 1907, as ordered by Songshou. The ban extended to teahouses, bars, and other places that provided opium pipes for their customers.[70] An estimated total of 3,000 dens were shut down in Fuzhou, and although this figure may have been exaggerated, foreign observers agreed that the campaign had eliminated the vast majority of local dens within a matter of months. One leader of those who opposed opium restrictions failed to sway officials with petitions or bribes and was "cast into prison." The shutters on the shops were closed, and doors were sealed with an official stamp.[71] Celebrations took place on 12 May in Nantai: "I remember the excitement there was. The young fellows at the college at Foochow City went up and down with flags through the different villages, so pleased were they that the opium dens were really closed."[72] Another foreign observer added that students from government and mission schools participated in the processions "shouting their hatred of the opium vice" and were led by the president of the Board of Education and many of the city's leading gentry. The missionary also noted that the police who closed the dens were particularly resented by den owners, several of

---

69. MAE/Nantes, carton 71-72, "Enquête sur le nombre des fumeurs d'opium dans la cité," Sept. 1908.

70. ZZGB 20, memorial from Songshou, endorsed 19 May 1909, p. 106.

71. An article in the *North China Herald* (cited in MAE/Paris, NS 588, 6 Feb. 1909, pp. 43-48) puts the total number of dens at 820, but the figure of 3,000 appears in *Mercy and Truth* 11, no. 131.

72. *IWCD* 28, no. 264 (June 1908).

whom were imprisoned for opposing the measure.[73] A few owners attempted to evade the prohibition by shifting their operations to boats that traveled slowly along Fuzhou's rivers and canals or by transforming smokers' homes into impromptu dens, but many of these violations were discovered and dealt with swiftly.[74] On a less positive note, a CEZMS missionary lamented the deaths that resulted from the crackdown: "When the opium dens were first closed the mortality among the poorer people was dreadful, for the opium smokers lived from hand to mouth, and, as they could not work without their usual opium, they died, partly of starvation, and partly from sudden deprivation of the drug."[75]

Songshou ordered provincial officials to establish smoking cessation offices (*jieyan suo*) to examine all of Fujian's civil officials for evidence of opium use. These apparently were distinct from the clinics for ordinary individuals run by the Anti-Opium Society and/or missionaries. Officials were first required to sign a pledge stating either that they had never smoked opium or that they had conquered the habit, and then they had to attach several verifying signatures. These claims were doublechecked through a rigorous regimen detailed in an excerpt from one of Songshou's memorials to Beijing:

All those officials who come to the office for examination are not allowed to bring anything. First, those in charge of the office assign a special official for examination. Facing that official, the examinees are ordered to change into clothes provided by the office. Then they must eat and stay with the examiner for one week. After fulfilling the terms of the examination, if they have not smoked opium up to then, they receive the signed verification of the examiner that they are truly not addicted. Those who previously ceased smoking or who have adhered to the deadline and quit will receive the signed verification of the examiner that they have already truly quit. These examinees will be permitted to leave the office to resume their duties. If examiners dare to conceal violations, they will be fired and punished together with the smoker. Those undergoing treatment/examination are not permitted to smoke anything. They can only drink medicinal tea and take [anti-opium] pills. After leaving the office, although [these officials] have received the signed verification, a sample must still be chosen to be examined again in six months to guard against their falling into the same old rut.[76]

---

73. CMS, Fuhkien, Incoming Originals, 1900–1934 (1907), no. 182, letter from Wolfe, 15 May 1907; USDS (1906–10), reel 104, Gracey to Bacon, 28 May 1907.
74. USDS (1906–10), reel 104, 774/113–14, enclosure in Paddock to Rockhill, 24 July 1907.
75. Faithfull-Davies, *The Banyan City*, pp. 17–18.
76. ZZGB 20, memorial from Songshou, endorsed 23 May 1909, pp. 106–7.

Songshou also ordered the establishment of six hospitals (probably large treatment centers) for smokers regardless of wealth or employment status. The poor had to bring their own food but were charged no other fees. In early 1909, statistics from two-thirds of the hospitals indicated that more than 3,200 smokers had been treated and released.[77]

Several of Songshou's reports to Beijing dealt exclusively with smokers who were either officials or expectant officials, reflecting the strict attention that was given to (or was expected to be given to) investigating and eliminating opium smoking among officials. Smoking was not uncommon among Fujian's current and future bureaucrats. For example, Songshou dutifully reported that when expectant county magistrate Cui Zhaoxiang was subjected to a body search before entering a refuge, the inspector discovered "a parcel of opium paste and pills attached to Cui's body." Ye Xindi, the magistrate of Min county (which encompassed the city of Fuzhou), underwent the examination to confirm that he had quit; "The period for examination had not yet been fulfilled when he asked to leave because of illness. Obviously, his longstanding addiction had not yet been eliminated." Songshou unceremoniously fired these and other opium-smoking officials, including a county jail warden and a county education director, after receiving permission from Beijing.[78] This attention to reducing demand among officials reinforced the Confucian ideal of administrators as social exemplars, but the flow of memorials of this sort from the provinces to Beijing (where copies were sent to the Anti-Opium Commission and the other three ministries involved) also reflected the degree to which the central state supervised and was kept informed about developments in the provinces.

From the perspective of local reformers, however, the more immediate concern was drumming up popular support and enthusiasm for the campaign. The Anti-Opium Society apparently felt that the new political space in which their activities took place had to incorporate public opinion and public participation if opium suppression was to succeed. By making a conscious effort to involve the public in the campaign, the society guaranteed that Fujian's nascent public sphere was a physical as well as a political entity. The society's most dramatic and probably most successful efforts toward that end were the public incinerations of confiscated opium and smoking

---

77. *North China Herald* cited in MAE/Paris, NS 588, 6 Feb. 1909, pp. 43–48.

78. ZZGB 22, memorial from Songshou, endorsed 8 Aug. 1909, pp. 412–13, and another in ZZGB 30, endorsed 17 March 1910, p. 173.

implements that often climaxed mass meetings and celebrations. *The Quarterly* describes such events in vivid detail, and the provincial and local administrations apparently approved of the gatherings. Two public pipe burnings staged in 1908, one in Fuzhou proper and the other in Nantai, attracted large and enthusiastic crowds that cheered the long processions of carrying poles on which the contraband materials were hung. The parades often featured the Qing dragon flag as well as the society's flag and included noisy marching bands. Police and society staff burned the contraband as an offering to the God of Fire as they prayed for his intervention to halt opium smoking.[79] By 1909, in eight separate ceremonies, the bonfires reportedly consumed 4,433 opium pipes, 4,482 pipe bowls, 3,693 lamps, 3,497 boxes, 3,620 plates, 8,971 needles, hundreds of cooking vessels, 3,138 ounces of opium, and an additional 577 ounces of opium residue.[80]

Fuzhou became the provincial showplace of public opposition to opium, and although it was largely the society that orchestrated mass demonstrations in support of opium reform, local officials often not only attended but spoke. Some skeptical observers claimed that these dramatic public activities were more spectacle than substance. But even pure spectacle had its role in a campaign like this. The parades, pipe burnings, and mass meetings illustrated the immediacy and vigor of opium reform and clearly laid out the geography of modern citizenship and demonstrated the implicit approval of the state.

The Fujian Anti-Opium Society was not the only unofficial reform group that grappled with opium reform, and membership in the society did not require or imply an exclusive commitment to that cause. For example, The South-of-the-Bridge Public Welfare Society (Qiaonan gongyi she) sponsored a branch of the Anti-Opium Society, and maintaining that organization constituted the single largest expenditure of the welfare society's budget. Some individuals were members of both groups.[81]

College students from Christian and non-Christian institutions were among the most enthusiastic participants in public anti-opium activities and periodically conducted parades of their own. These same students some-

---

79. *The Quarterly* 3 (1908), miscellaneous (*zazhi*) section, p. 10.
80. IOC, 2: 117; and MAE/Paris, NS 588, 6 Feb. 1909, pp. 43–48. For a detailed description of one such public pipe burning, see MAE/Paris, NS 587, Foutcheou to Paris, 3 July 1908, pp. 101–13.
81. *Qiaonan gongyi she zhengxin lu* (1908–9).

times patrolled Fuzhou's streets and on occasion roughed up offenders. An American diplomat personally observed a group of students beating an opium smoker who held a high literary degree.[82] Missionaries also noted that the new western-style schools in the city signed a petition forbidding the hiring of teachers who smoked.[83]

At the outset of Fujian's anti-opium campaign, particularly with regard to anti-consumption measures, the line between official and unofficial reform was intentionally blurry. The participation of Lin Bingzhang and other reformers not only allowed the state to extend its control over a public space with the potential to erode or usurp state power but also provided authorities with an army of committed reformers to work alongside police to document, implement, and enforce the campaign. Songshou noted that officials helped to raise funds to defray some of the society's expenses and had conferred with society members on the selection of the group's financial officer. In a memorial to Beijing, Songshou praised "Lin Bingzhang, Chen Baochen, and others who established a series of anti-opium societies." However, although Songshou claimed "the officials and gentry are united as one" in terms of opium suppression, he went on to discuss the advantages of using each group to monitor the other, with the aim of cleansing officialdom of corruption and maintaining state control over unofficial reform groups. "The gentry are enthusiastically for the public good. They fix their eyes and ears on petty officials and eliminate the officials' selfish use of public office to seek profit. By giving the local gentry authority, what is seen and heard in the community is particularly reliable. They investigate and examine more closely than the officials." Songshou also claimed that on his orders, any important meeting held at the society's headquarters in Fuzhou was attended and *supervised* by high-ranking local officials, and at least one magistrate was present at every regular meeting of the group.[84]

The society did not seem to discourage this attention, nor was it really in a position to do so, since state approval and financial help strengthened the reformers' power and prestige. Local and provincial officials were included in society events, and the Fuzhou prefect spoke at the society's inaugural meet-

---

82. USDS (1906–10), reel 104, Gracey to Bacon, 28 May 1907. Missionary testimony confirmed this; see *Mercy and Truth* 11, no. 132 (Dec. 1907): 402.
83. *Mercy and Truth* 11, no. 129 (Sept. 1907): 268–72.
84. ZZGB 20, memorial by Songshou, endorsed 19 May 1909, pp. 104–8.

ing. Other officials frequently attended other meetings and celebrations.[85] In addition, the society was cognizant of the attention imperialist governments were giving to their efforts, and they courted missionary reformers who might influence British policy. Lin Bingzhang, for example, received many missionary supporters in a refurbished, westernized wing of his home.[86]

By the beginning of 1909, foreign missionaries reported that opium reform was in full swing in Fuzhou. One source claimed that all opium dens had been closed, all opium shops licensed, all smokers registered, and cultivation near the city entirely eliminated. Clearly, the campaign had made visible progress, even if that progress may not have been as comprehensive as that source indicated. However, the missionaries cautioned that the campaign was not nearly so thorough outside the provincial capital, in the areas where Fujian's poppy crop grew.[87]

The society played a lesser role in the effort to reduce poppy cultivation. A number of possible reasons suggest themselves: the reluctance of society investigators to take on powerful clans in poppy-growing regions; the increased likelihood of violent resistance to the elimination of this cash crop, particularly if it became necessary to forcibly uproot the plants; the need for military reinforcements if the latter course were required; and state reluctance to allow unofficial reformers to wield military power. Or perhaps, despite Songshou's claims, local and provincial authorities did little to halt poppy cultivation until after the revolution. In any case, available documentation indicates that local officials generally took charge of this aspect of the campaign.

Eliminating opium smoking was difficult enough, but provincial authorities also had to deal with a small but tenacious domestic poppy crop and the farmers who had a lucrative stake in its continuation. In 1908, Songshou acknowledged that domestic poppies grew along the coast in Fuzhou, Zhangzhou, and Quanzhou prefectures, and despite the unimpressive dimensions of Fujian's poppy crop, its elimination was proving to be one of the most troublesome aspects of the campaign. That September, Songshou ordered all tillers of land currently under poppy cultivation to sow cereal grains or

---

85. Wu Jiayu and Lin Jiazhen, "Fujian jinyan yundong 'Qudu she,'" p. 15; *Mercy and Truth* 11, no. 129 (Sept. 1907), pp. 268–72; PRO, FO 228/2415, no. 66, enclosure in Playfair to Jordan, 25 Feb. 1907.
86. Faithfull-Davies, *The Banyan City*, pp. 23–24.
87. *The Foochow Messenger* 6, no. 2 (Apr. 1909): 1.

risk the confiscation of that land.[88] However, the success of the measure relied in part on accurate statistics regarding the size of the provincial poppy harvest.

Because poppy farming was illegal, estimates had to take the place of more accurate figures. In 1905, a missionary claimed that the area around Xiamen produced 7,270 piculs of domestic opium, about half of which was cultivated in Tongan.[89] However, after conducting its own investigation, the Ministry of Revenue concluded that the entire province produced only 1,500 piculs that year.[90] Historian Lin Man-houng estimates Fujian's opium production at over 9,000 piculs in 1903,[91] and the U.S. government, which derived its figures from an Imperial Maritime Customs report, estimated that the province produced 13,270 piculs in 1905.[92] According to my own calculations, which are based on Songshou's figures for the number of opium smokers in the province on the eve of the suppression campaign, Fujian had to produce a minimum of 8,700 piculs (about 1,160,000 pounds) of raw opium, which required approximately 290,000 mu of land.[93] It was likely, then, that poppy cultivation was more widespread than Songshou realized or wished to admit.

---

88. ZZGB 20, memorial from Songshou, endorsed 19 May 1909, pp. 104–8.

89. Pitcher, *In and About Amoy*, p. 136.

90. ZZGB 12, memorial from Ministry of Revenue, endorsed 4 Oct. 1908, pp. 464, 466. The larger number may have included the sale of domestic opium imported from other provinces.

91. Lin Man-houng, "Qingmo shehui liuxing xishi yapian yanjiu," p. 585.

92. FRUS (1906), pt. I, p. 356. This was the highest of the many estimates that were bandied about at this time. A report from the American legation in 1908 cites a Chinese newspaper as listing the production of domestic opium in Fujian in 1906 as approximately 200 piculs, which the U.S. official noted "seems to be entirely too low" (USDS [1906–10], 774/239–40, reel 105, Rockhill to Secy. of State, 8 June 1908).

93. To estimate the amount produced in Fujian, we must first calculate the total amount of opium consumed there and then subtract imports. In 1907, Songshou reported 230,000 smokers resided in Fujian at the outset of the campaign, probably an underestimate. In 1905, Fujian imported a total of 11,600 piculs of opium from abroad and from other Chinese provinces. It was generally agreed that the average habitual smoker used three *qian* of prepared opium per day, or about twelve pounds of raw opium per year. Multiply this figure by 230,000 regular smokers, subtract imports, and we are still left with 8,700 piculs. One *mu* (about 1/6 of an acre) of poppy produced an average of four pounds of raw opium (ZZGB 20, memorial from Songshou, endorsed 19 May 1909, pp. 107–8; USDS [1906–10], 774/73–74, reel 104, Cloud to Rodgers, 8 May 1907, 774/8–9, reel 104, Rockhill to Secy. of State, 8 Sept. 1906). This estimate does not take into account the frequent resmoking of opium and opium ashes.

Songshou was one of several provincial leaders who became convinced that the central government should change its gradualist approach to eliminating poppy cultivation over the full ten years of the agreement.[94] These officials feared that farmers who were compelled to change crops or uproot their poppies first would resent not only their counterparts lucky enough to be given extended deadlines but also the officials in charge. Songshou ordered all farmers in Fujian to cease planting the poppy in the fall of 1908, and he reported his progress the next spring.

Now, according to the continuous reports of my subordinates, there are areas in which the prohibition has been carried out completely, and the people have switched to planting grain. But there are also areas that are not yet reported clear of poppies. I sent strict orders to the officials in charge of these areas and selected and dispatched a very capable deputy (*ganbu*) to each place. They were issued supplies and traveling expenses and rushed to secretly investigate. If there are those savages who openly hesitate to obey the prohibition, then local officials (*difang guan*) are ordered to rush with the militia to uproot the poppies. Those who dare to disobey are strictly punished. After the poppies have been completely uprooted, the offenders must switch to planting edible grains. Destitute households will be carefully investigated and given money for seed to show our sympathy. Proper use must be made of kindness and harshness in dealing with those below so that they know the order must be carried out and do not harbor reckless hopes of trying to plant again.... Additionally, in the future, land planted in poppies will be confiscated as public property. Landlords will be punished accordingly.... Summon the elders and persuade them in various ways that this poisonous flower must be wiped out.[95]

The memorial reveals a philosophy of suppression that took into account the lucrative nature of opium cultivation and the possibility of peasant suffering and resistance.[96] The central government approved the immediate and

---

94. In an edict received by Songshou on 15 March 1909 and cited at length in one of his memorials, Beijing acknowledged that the leaders of Yunnan, Sichuan, Shanxi, Zhili, and Heilongjiang, among others, had asked permission to impose a total ban on poppy cultivation within one year (ZZGB 20, memorial by Songshou, endorsed 19 May 1909, p. 104-8).

95. Ibid., p. 108.

96. Foreign missionaries and diplomats attempted, on occasion, to help former opium farmers fill the vacuum created by the prohibition. In one case, the U.S. consul at Xiamen responded to missionary pleas and requested cottonseed from the U.S. Department of Agriculture to distribute to interested farmers. In the northeast, cotton was something of a success in Fu'an county, mainly due to the efforts of the local agricultural society, although most poppy farmers in Funing prefecture planted wheat, beans, and sugarcane to replace their poppy crop

complete prohibition of domestic poppy cultivation, but not until 1910.[97] Beijing probably belatedly acquiesced to provincial requests because those requests furthered national suppression goals and did not contravene the agreement with the British. Songshou and the others apparently chose to view Beijing's silence in the interim as an affirmative.

Since the widespread custom of double-cropping in Fujian meant a greater possibility of secret planting, Songshou reportedly dispatched 60 to 70 special investigators across the province to exhort local reformers, reiterate restrictions, and monitor poppy prohibition.

> The investigators meet with officials and gentry, make speeches wherever they go, and are stationed in a particular locale to aid in the investigations. . . . If, in the course of investigation it is discovered that some people are stealthily planting a little opium, they are ordered to plow it up and destroy the crop and switch to planting beneficial grains. . . . As for investigating and prohibiting the planting of opium sprouts, those specially assigned officials personally walk among the fields. They suffer, and the situation is dangerous.

To confirm the positive reports he received from those investigators, Songshou in 1910 informed "the officials in charge of each circuit, prefecture, and subprefecture to investigate and obtain the verifying signatures of the headmen of the villages, households, and clans." By spring 1910, he reported to Beijing that Fujian no longer cultivated the opium poppy and humbly requested rewards for those responsible.[98]

Beijing was not so easily convinced, however, and central authorities demurred on the issue of rewards. Accordingly, on 19 April 1910, the Grand Council (Junji chu) called on the Ministry of Revenue to investigate the claims of provincial officials in Fujian and elsewhere. The skepticism was justified. Secret inspections revealed that Songshou's assertions were false, and in its subsequent report on the progress of the campaign, dated 26 September 1910, the ministry singled out Xinghua prefecture as Fujian's most conspicuous violator.[99] Clearly, the Qing government was not about to sacri-

---

(USDS [1906–10], reel 1103, no. 21091, Arnold to Secy. of State, 11 Apr. 1910; and IMC, *Decennial Reports, Santuao, 1902–1911*, pp. 85–86).

97. ZZGB 20, memorial by Songshou, endorsed 19 May 1909, p. 104; ZZGB 35, memorial from the Ministry of Revenue, endorsed 11 Aug. 1910, pp. 262–63; ZZGB 37, memorial from the Ministry of Revenue, endorsed 26 Sept. 1910, pp. 27–29.

98. ZZGB 32, memorial from Songshou, endorsed 11 May 1910, pp. 159–60.

99. ZZGB 36, memorial from Ministry of Revenue (n.d.), pp. 473–77; ZZGB 37, memorial from Ministry of Revenue, endorsed 26 Sept. 1910, pp. 27–29.

fice progress toward the elimination of China's national opium problem for lack of provincial compliance, and it made certain that provincial reports were strictly monitored.

The elimination of poppy cultivation and opium smoking in Fujian was continually hampered by the influx of opium from other provinces as well as from abroad, a problem Songshou blamed in part on unethical Chinese merchants. According to Songshou, poor households used to harvest small poppy crops for their own use, but the campaign eliminated that practice. Now, many smokers purchased the drug that flowed in from Yunnan, Sichuan, Jiangsu, and Shaanxi, and Songshou wanted the power to halt this traffic.[100] While waiting for a response, he imposed a unilateral prohibition on the importation of opium from neighboring provinces.

This time, however, the Ministry of Revenue refused to grant his request on a number of grounds. First, it advised Songhou that if he wanted to eliminate the importation of domestic opium into Fujian, he should focus his attention on eliminating demand for the drug within his own borders. The ministry noted that similar requests from other provinces had been turned down, and there was no compelling need to make an exception for Fujian. Songshou evidently complied with the ministry's order to lift the ban, but only after initially sending two telegrams in which he respectfully refused, claiming that he had implicit permission from the emperor and that if the restrictions were even "slightly relaxed, then they would dissolve." He asserted that it would be wrong to contradict the sovereign and pointed out that there was talk in Fujian about organizing a provincial boycott of opium from other provinces. Even the opium merchants' guild had pledged to cooperate. The timing of this exchange also exacerbated Songshou's concern. Fall was poppy-sowing time, and he feared the resentment of farmers forbidden to plant poppies when farmers in other provinces were profiting from opium sales in Fujian.[101]

Despite his defiance, the ministry initially acknowledged Songshou's righteous motivations. Justification for refusing Songshou's request was muted by the ministry's praise for the work of elites and officials in Fujian and an assurance that once opium smoking had been eliminated, the demand for the imported drug would evaporate on its own.[102] However, Song-

---

100. ZZGB 32, memorial from Songshou, endorsed 11 May 1910, pp. 159–60.
101. ZZGB 37, memorial from the Ministry of Revenue, endorsed 26 Sept. 1910, pp. 27–29.
102. ZZGB 35, memorial from the Ministry of Revenue, endorsed 11 Aug. 1910, pp. 262–63.

shou's position was undercut when Beijing's secret investigation uncovered illicit poppy cultivation in Fujian. More to the point, perhaps, a prohibition of domestic imports would have damaged the ministry's collection of excise taxes on opium transported between provinces.[103] The Ministry of Revenue apparently was not willing to discuss forgoing that revenue until Fujian had eliminated poppy cultivation and, presumably, the tax revenue it generated for Fujian. This intriguing exchange demonstrates the hands-on, supervisory role played by the central Chinese state and the manner in which opium reform may have exacerbated existing tensions and the competition for revenue between Beijing and the provinces.

Curiously, Songshou did not dwell at length in his official communications on the financial repercussions of the campaign. Only one memorial mentioned the issue at all and then only in passing.

As for the substitution of funds for opium taxes, although the price of a catty of salt was increased . . . it is not enough for Fujian province. I have already ordered high provincial officials (*si dao*) to quickly confer and find a way [to deal with this issue]. In the future, if this substitution is still insufficient, we will again memorialize, begging Your Majesty to order the Ministry of Revenue to appropriate [funds].[104]

Raising salt taxes to make up for lost opium-related revenues tended to dissolve in the popular mind the distinction between the allegedly altruistic suppression campaign and other extractive or intrusive New Policy reforms, if the coercive actions of the Anti-Opium Society and local officials had not done so already. Despite Songshou's seeming nonchalance, this problem of revenue substitution was to inspire in 1912 the only large-scale, organized popular resistance to the campaign in Fujian, an incident detailed in Chapter 8.

The Provincial Assembly and the Deliberate Dismantling of the Public Sphere

The Provincial Assembly (Ziyi ju) became another important actor in Fujian's anti-opium crusade and reflected a significant change in elite conceptions of political activism as the Qing state struggled to forestall revolution. A coalition of progressive-minded officials and reformist elites dominated the assembly. Their wholehearted approval of the majority of the New Poli-

---

103. ZZGB 37, memorial from the Ministry of Revenue, endorsed 26 Sept. 1910, pp. 27–29.
104. ZZGB 20, memorial from Songshou, endorsed 19 May 1909, p. 108.

cies was not surprising, given that they stood to benefit considerably from the proposed transformation of the Chinese imperial state into a constitutional monarchy. However, in the context of opium reform, to which the assembly lent its vocal support, Fujian's assemblymen devised a comprehensive plan that officially recognized the functions and powers of the Anti-Opium Society and subordinated them more explicitly to the state and its local bureaucratic representative. Minutes of assembly sessions in 1909 and 1910 preserved in the Fujian Provincial Library allow a fascinating glimpse into the often-heated debate over the fate of the Anti-Opium Society. These debates marked a turning point in the conduct of opium reform in Fujian and the nature of provincial politics. The result was a deliberate attempt to absorb the powers of the public space by some of the same men who had first become involved in politics through the public sphere. That process extended beyond opium reform and encompassed unofficial reform groups combating footbinding, gambling, and prostitution.[105] Whether this decision was tied more to ideological or financial motivations remains debatable.

The provincial assemblies were among the most contested of the New Policies because in many ways, they pleased neither the Qing state nor the small minority of Chinese elites who constituted the electorate.[106] The assemblies were intended to serve as advisory bodies to the provincial administration and as the first stage in the eventual establishment of a national assembly. Despite the rigid requirements for the vote, Fujian's assembly became a lively forum for progressive reformers who seemed to view themselves as policymakers for a provincial state-in-waiting. They chafed at the incremental progress toward a national assembly and urged the Qing court to accelerate the process. The assemblymen debated a variety of issues that

---

105. Dunch states that "having discovered the power of voluntary societies to effect social reform, the assembly members sought to make voluntary societies *involuntary*—and thus to formalize, with modern tools such as written constitutions, the traditionally flexible relationship between magistrates and local elites, to the advantage of the latter" (*Fuzhou Protestants and the Making of a Modern China*, p. 86). However, I see the process as imposing a framework of state control that could and did infringe on and restructure elite activism, but to their disadvantage. It must be noted, however, that opium suppression was different from the campaign against footbinding and other social ills, because the opium question had international implications that made the retention of state control seem more imperative.

106. For specific voting qualifications, see IMC, *Decennial Reports, Foochow, 1902–1911*, p. 94. Generally speaking, only those men who were educated or wealthy could expect to be enfranchised, although the qualifications did extend the vote to those who had been involved in public service for at least three years. Opium smokers were specifically disenfranchised.

touched on every aspect of the New Policies as well as problems peculiar to Fujian, and in the case of the opium suppression campaign, the provincial government seemed willing to listen.

The newly constituted Fujian Provincial Assembly met for the first time during the fall of 1909 and consisted of 72 elected members, including the president (*yizhang*) and vice-president (*fu yizhang*); another three members were appointed from the banner garrison. A roster of assemblymen with a handwritten date of 1910 lists each member's name, occupation or rank, age, educational status, address, and the county he represented. Most were quite young, with 29 under the age of 40. Twenty-five possessed the *juren* (provincial degree) and 48 more had earned the rank of tribute student (*gongsheng*) or licentiate (*shengyuan*), but "the other striking fact about the list is the near-total absence of really high-ranking men."[107]

Many assemblymen were vocal supporters of opium reform in general and the Anti-Opium Society in particular. At least six assemblymen were active in the society or its branches. Most notably, Gao Dengli, the assembly president and a reformer who had served as subprefect of Yanping and a director of a government school, was an active member of the Fuzhou Anti-Opium Society.[108] Li Funan, one of the original founders of the society, was also elected. One of the older delegates, Wu Tingchang (AKA Wu Guangchen), from Lianjiang county in Fuzhou prefecture, was a physician who founded and led a branch of the society in his county seat. Wu was so well respected for his work in this arena that local children apparently used to sing this ditty:

> Wu Guangchen, Wu Guangchen
> Not for profit, and not for fame,
> Calls for prohibition for the people's own good
> Like a god he is worshipped by the hundred surnames.[109]

Two representatives from Jianning county, Meng Sipei and Li Dihu, belonged to the society. A U.S. consular official claimed that Lin Zikeng, head

---

107. Dunch, *Fuzhou Protestants and the Making of a Modern China*, p. 84; *Fujian ziyi ju diyi jie quanti yiyuan yilan biao* (1910), pp. 1–6.

108. MAE/Nantes, Foutcheou, carton 9, Reynaud's undated report; MAE/Paris, NS 19, Fuzhou to Pichon, 26 Oct. 1909, pp. 93–110; MAE/Paris, NS 18, Foutcheou to Pichon, 10 May 1909, pp. 26–35; *Fujian ziyi ju diyi jie quanti yiyuan yilan bia*, pp. 1–6.

109. Wu Tianchang, "Wu Tingchang xiansheng chuangban Qudu she," pp. 27–28. The "hundred surnames" (*laobaixing*) is a colloquial name for the common folk.

of the Xiamen branch society, also served as an assemblyman, but his name does not appear on the roster. However, Lin Lucun, who took the helm of that branch in 1911, was listed.[110] Other delegates may have belonged to county or prefectural branches, but without local rosters, it is impossible to be certain. The minutes of the assembly sessions in 1909 reveal a body that not only was quick to take up the issue of opium reform but also returned to that topic many times over the course of its deliberations.[111]

Despite the presence of these men and the generally progressive slant of the assembly, the debate over a plan to reorganize the suppression campaign concluded in a consensus that intentionally diminished the role of the society. The goal was to devise a strategy to expedite reform that could be presented to and eventually implemented by Songshou. Financing the campaign proved a serious concern. The discussion began with a suggestion to attack the opium problem by dividing the province into five districts (north, south, east, west, and center), a strategy similar to one suggested in the Guangxi Provincial Assembly.[112] This scheme ignored traditional administrative boundaries and was somewhat controversial. Later sessions altered the plan and proposed four divisions. Under the new scheme, which addressed opium cultivation and smoking, each region was assigned a different deadline according to the severity of its opium problem. Officials, gentry, and self-government organizations were to work together to investigate the extent of the opium problem in their particular section and to eliminate it by the deadline. The treaty ports were left till last, until after the inland was clean, so as not to upset the British.[113]

All smokers were to be registered during the first three months of Xuantong 3 (approximately February, March, and April 1911) and given temporary smoking permits. Smoking was to cease within six months of the general deadline for opium suppression in each region. Monthly audits of opium

---

110. USDS (1910–29), 893.114, reel 113, enclosure in Xiamen to Secy. of State, 20 July 1911; *Fujian ziyi ju diyi jie quanti yiyuan yilan biao* (1910), pp. 1–6.

111. *Fujian ziyi ju diyi jie yi an zhaiyao*, handwritten date of 1909. Foreign diplomats also were intensely interested in the assembly and kept records of its members and their qualifications, debates, and decisions. See, e.g., IMC, *Decennial Reports, Foochow, 1902–1911*, p. 94; MAE/Nantes, Foutecheou, carton 9, Reynaud's undated report; MAE/Paris, NS 19, Fuzhou to Pichon, 26 Oct. 1909, pp. 93–110; and MAE/Paris, NS 18, Foutcheou to Pichon, 10 May 1909, pp. 26–35.

112. *Dierci Fujian ziyi ju yi shi suji lu* 1.6 (14 Oct. 1910), p. 13.

113. *Dierci Fujian ziyi ju yi shi suji lu* 3.12 (31 Oct. 1910), pp. 13–14.

shops would be conducted, and all shops closed on or before the regional deadline. Increased regional and provincial taxes on prepared opium were to fund the entire scheme. The assembly also favored a profitable provincial monopoly on opium paste modeled on the Japanese system in Taiwan, but start-up costs were prohibitive and the plan was tabled.[114]

In addition to restructuring the timetable and administrative structure of opium reform, part of the assembly's plan involved establishing another level of the official bureaucracy modeled on the pattern suggested by the Anti-Opium Commission at the outset of the campaign. Early on, however, the assembly also appeared to be searching for a way to strengthen the clout and scope of the society while simultaneously bringing it more explicitly under the control of local authorities. Several assemblymen expressed concern about the progress of the fight against opium smoking and speculated that the society may have spread itself too thin. One suggestion was to divide every county into sections, mirroring the provincial divisions, and mandate the establishment of a branch society in each. The heads of each branch would work with county authorities to monitor the situation and devise ways of setting up more refuges.[115]

The proposal set before the delegates for open debate began with a strong statement that officials could not tackle this immense problem on their own without the cooperation of the gentry (*yishen* or "advisory gentry") and called for an opium prohibition bureau in every administrative division of the province. Officials appointed by the governor-general, in cooperation with the gentry and police, would manage those offices. The new offices would be responsible for licensing addicts, running treatment facilities, monitoring the campaign, and investigating violations. The governor-general was responsible for punishing those who disobeyed. The provincial tax on prepared opium paste would be raised 10 percent to support the bureau headquarters, and the taxes on prepared opium in each division would be raised a whopping 33.33 percent to pay for the local bureau's upkeep. Fines levied on violators would also fund the bureaus.[116]

---

114. *Fujian ziyi ju diyi jie yi an zhaiyao* (handwritten date 1909), pp. 11–12.
115. Ibid.
116. *Dierci Fujian ziyi ju yi shi suji lu* 3.12 (31 Oct. 1910), pp. 13–16. British diplomats (PRO, FO 228/1800, enclosure in Foochow Intelligence Report for December Quarter 1910) reported that the bureau's budget would be supplemented by an annual government allowance of 4,000 taels for the bureau headquarters in Fuzhou and 400 taels per year for each county

The debate began with a pointed question from Wang Ziyi, a 33-year-old *juren* from Jianyang county: "After the opium prohibition bureaus have been established, what will be the distinction between them and the Anti-Opium Society?" Zheng Zuyin, who had designed the new regulations with Huang Naishang (1849-1924), defended the proposal, which they apparently intended to strengthen the society's authority.[117] Zheng claimed that under this new plan, officials sent by the provincial authorities to run the bureaus would be able to employ more forceful measures to ensure compliance. Wang replied that the duties of the two groups appeared almost identical to him, and Zheng countered that opium was a serious problem and the more people and groups that were involved in suppression, the more likely the campaign would succeed. The debate then revealed that authorities in Fuzhou had been giving the society a substantial subsidy of more than 10,000 *yuan* per year. Wang wanted to earmark these funds in advance and then deal with financing the new plan. The assemblymen decided to investigate further.[118]

When the subject was raised again a few weeks later, the investigators' report sparked a lively and sometimes heated debate on the difficulty of stretching the province's meager finances to pay for the new program. The plan originally called for a bureau in each of Fujian's 60-odd administrative divisions. Each branch bureau would be run by a manager/inspector who drew a salary of 40 taels per month. The expense was deemed excessive. The assemblymen proposed instead that these duties be handled by existing local officials *and* suggested that the society and its branches be reduced in size and merged with the new bureaus. Zheng Zuyin vigorously objected, noting that these amendments totally undermined the plan's original intent. Lu Chuhuang and Chen Xipeng focused on the budgetary incompatibility of both groups, and Lu made the point that this would not be an issue if it were not for the large government subsidy paid the society. Zheng replied, "The Anti-Opium Society must always exist" (*Qudu she zongzhishe zong bu ke cai*). He also added that since opium smoking was ubiquitous, every location needed a branch of the society. Chen replied that no law forbade the public from doing precisely that. At that point, Gao Dengli ended the discussion and tabled it until the vote.[119]

---

branch as well as by an additional tax on prepared opium, but these figures do not appear in the published transcripts of the assembly debates.

117. Both men belonged to the Tongmenghui, and Zheng led the provincial branch.
118. *Dierci Fujian ziyi ju yi shi suji lu* 3.12 (31 Oct. 1910), pp. 16–18.
119. *Dierci Fujian ziyi ju yi shi suji lu* 6.21 (18 Nov. 1910), pp. 9–11.

Two days later, an amended proposal was approved after a final burst of debate. In its ultimate incarnation, the new plan called for elite/official cooperation, but the language of the regulations marked a desire to differentiate the two groups and to subordinate the unofficial society. The new bureaus, led by officials but with a mandate to work closely with local reformist elites, were to be issued government seals to distinguish them from the unofficial group. The description of the duties and responsibilities of the bureaus was virtually identical to those performed by the society, and it was recommended that the society be diminished and possibly merge with this new bureaucracy. There were only a few other specific references to the society in the proposal. One vague allusion urged self-government organizations and "public welfare societies" (*gongyi she*) to set up addiction treatment centers. When it came to financing the bureaus, however, Article 28 clearly recommended that half of the annual allocation for the Anti-Opium Society should be directed to the new bureaus instead.

Zheng Zuyin made a last attempt to forestall the reduction in size and power of the society by making the rather disingenuous claim that the bureaus were organs of policy and the societies were organizations of exhortation and therefore could not and should not be combined. Gao Dengli called for a vote, and Zheng's position was defeated, 42 to 8. The discussion ended with a few sarcastic remarks by Zheng and a rather ambiguous position for the society, since the jurisdictions and duties of the two groups still overlapped considerably and the assembly did not have the power to order the two groups to merge, except through its budgetary recommendations.[120]

Toward the end of 1910, perhaps in response to Beijing's criticism of Fujian's lack of progress in stamping out poppy cultivation in Xinghua and elsewhere, Songshou approved the restructuring of the provincial suppression campaign along the lines of the assembly plan. The measures for eliminating smoking and poppy cultivation, as well as the scheme for funding the new plan, closely resembled those in the assembly proposal. The province was divided into four districts, although Songshou apparently considered the treaty ports separate entities, and deadlines for opium prohibition were set for each. The northwest was to be free of the drug by mid-January 1912, followed, at six-month intervals, by the northeast, the southeast, and finally, the southwest. Deadlines for the treaty ports of Fuzhou, Santu'ao, and Xiamen were to be established after consultations with the British.

---

120. *Dierci Fujian ziyi ju yi shi suji lu* 7.23 (20 Nov. 1910), pp. 19–24.

The opium prohibition bureaus that had been such a point of contention in the assembly were to oversee the plan, and each was to be run by a high official personally appointed by Songshou. Local authorities in each subprefectural district were to set up and run the branch bureaus. Under each branch director was an assistant director and a committee of local elites. Songshou had to approve the appointment of each of the assistant directors and would dispatch other officials to supervise the final stages of suppression in each region. Once constituted, however, the branch bureaus were allowed to take whatever measures they deemed necessary to enforce the regulations in their area. Local police and military troops were to be at the bureaus' disposal.[121]

The new regulations can be interpreted in many ways. First, since the content of much of the plan was similar to many earlier proclamations, the new strategy indicates that Fujian's suppression campaign still had a long way to go. They also illustrate the assembly's steadfast commitment to opium reform. Songshou's adoption of this new plan affirmed the recognition on the part of Beijing, the assembly, and himself that the continued involvement of elite reformers was a crucial component in the success of opium suppression, particularly since the central government had allocated no specific funds for provincial opium reform. But the plan also emphasized the realization by the state and the new assembly that state support of the Anti-Opium Society had to be tempered by reality. Unofficial reform groups were welcome to contribute their time and effort, but in an age of budgetary constraints and revolutionary rumblings, the state could no longer afford to fund or to delegate such extensive powers to those outside the formal bureaucracy. That progressive reformers who knew the power of the public sphere suggested this plan is illustrative of how the perceptions of the assemblymen changed once they viewed themselves as an integral element of a constitutional state-in-the-making. Their actions also seemed to mark the beginning of the end for one sector of the flourishing public political space. But implementation of the new plan and the realization of its ramifications were postponed by the cataclysmic events of 1911.

---

121. This description of the new plan was taken from an enclosure in the Foochow Intelligence Report for the December Quarter 1910 in PRO, FO 228/1800. A Chinese version of the plan, excerpted from *Minbao*, is enclosed along with the English translation.

Opium and Conflicting Loyalties

Despite the prominent role of unofficial reform groups in Fujian's battle against opium before 1911, China's central state was the guiding force behind the late Qing phase of the suppression campaign. It was the central state that signed the agreement with the British, and it was the central state that ultimately remained accountable for provincial progress. The agreement with the British allowed the Qing state to assure its subjects that China's opium suppression campaign would not be sabotaged by imperialist greed. Beijing also established the legal and temporal guidelines for provincial reform that encouraged unofficial elite involvement, although reform groups were to be subsumed under the mantle of state control at the provincial and state levels. Within this broad template, provincial officials were given some freedom to formulate their own schemes for opium prohibition as long as their innovations did not contravene the agreement with the British or hinder national goals.

It is difficult to believe that Beijing anticipated the power of the public political space carved out in part by its anti-opium policies, and equally difficult to imagine that the campaign could have achieved the rapid progress it did without the elite activism that unfolded in that space. The Fujian Anti-Opium Society used its extraordinary powers to publicize, implement, and enforce the suppression campaign. Part of the society's ability to transform itself from a fairly traditional, small-scale, unofficial reform group into an organization with extensive coercive powers and dozens of branches scattered throughout the province was due to its influential leaders, but its actions were conducted within a framework established by the state, and its power was sanctioned by that state.

Opium reform was an important part of the reworking of Chinese society under the New Policies. Officials and elite reformers recognized the need for strict regulations and enforcement if the campaign were to succeed in eliminating this particular source of Chinese weakness, and they knew that the campaign was intertwined with Chinese nationalism. Elite reformers also recognized that the campaign's success relied on the revamping of customary attitudes toward political participation; the people of Fujian had to be brought into the campaign, into the new public political space.

The staging of ritualized ceremonies in which the public could learn about the evils of opium, observe the consequences of violating the campaign, and lend their support illustrated how the permeable borders of the new political space allowed its manipulation by reformist elites and the state. The gatherings represented a transitional stage in the reworking of the traditional relationship between rulers and ruled, elites and masses. Elite reformers encouraged ordinary Chinese to occupy the public political space long enough to absorb anti-opium oratory, accompany processions bearing confiscated opium and smoking equipment, and cheer the consumption of the contraband by the God of Fire instead of their friends, family, or neighbors. But the masses remained in a supporting role. They were not empowered to confiscate drugs, issue licenses to smoke or sell opium, or light the flames of the bonfires that signaled each ceremony's climax. That was the still the job of elite reformers or officials.[122] The demonstrations could not help but impress upon ordinary Fujianese the police powers appropriated by the society, as well as the close relationship between the Qing state and unofficial reformers.

The public also seemed to know that this was not yet the space or time for debate. Those who might have opposed the suppression campaign were not welcome to present their side of the argument. In the new Republic, Henrietta Harrison argues that observance of new and modern customs and rituals marked a "national community."[123] The same can be said of those who attended public meetings that marked stages in Fujian's anti-opium campaign, but it was still a hierarchical community. Elite reformers choreographed the celebrations and the state approved them as long as the state reform agenda remained at the forefront.

Elite activism in the context of opium reform was a sign of the central state's ability to co-opt elite nationalism and desire for power into the state's own functional and ideological framework. At the outset, the porous boundaries of the public political space allowed a degree of mutual exploitation by the state and reformers, but reformers became emboldened by their victories in the suppression campaign and by their ability to influence policy through the Fujian Provincial Assembly.

Ironically, it was the assembly, a body that included reformers directly involved in opium suppression, which set out the most concrete plan for fold-

---

122. Henrietta Harrison's intriguing *The Making of the Republican Citizen* has analyzed how the new Republic devised or co-opted a number of rituals and customs, from handshaking to queue-cutting to the adoption of the solar calendar, to establish a new set of modern Chinese norms and a modern Chinese identity. She also notes that those who rejected the new rituals and behaviors were explicitly excluded from power.

123. Ibid., p. 76.

ing the new public space into the state. The assembly wanted not to halt or slow opium reform but to conduct it more efficiently. Many assemblymen recognized that the permeability of the public space in which many of them began their political careers was a volatile and often unorganized place that had the potential to undermine state power. The assembly was intended to function as an advisory body to the provincial administration, but the assemblymen clearly saw themselves as playing a more significant role in a constitutional monarchy and did not want unofficial reformers to diminish that role. The efficiency and cost of reform were also concerns, since the formal absorption of the Anti-Opium Society might enable a strengthening of the chain of command for opium suppression and state subsidies could then be transferred to the official reform bureaucracy.

Nationalism did fuel enthusiasm for opium prohibition among officials and unofficial reform groups and within at least some of the general public, but it also created tensions among reformers and officials whose loyalties were torn between nation, state, and province. Opium reform made balancing those loyalties even more difficult. The agreement with the British imposed constraints on provincial reform that helped focus Chinese anger on the Qing state and redirect the mainstream of elite nationalism from enthusiasm for reform into revolutionary action. It became abundantly clear to many reformers that the concept and goals of the Chinese nation transcended the more narrow aims of the Qing state. But the powerful combination of provincial and racial pride cannot be discounted as a major motivation for revolution as well. As anti-Qing grumbling grew louder, so did the refrain "Fujian for the Fujianese."

FOUR

Provincial Patterns of Reform Before the Revolution of 1911

Thus far, this analysis of Fujian's opium suppression campaign has concentrated on Fuzhou, the bustling treaty port where the provincial administration and the Fujian Anti-Opium Society were headquartered. Fuzhou boasted a high concentration of educated Chinese, many of whom joined or supported reform groups, as well as foreign diplomats and missionaries who observed and participated in the anti-opium campaign. Members of each of these groups left detailed records of their activities. The focus on Fuzhou has highlighted the permeable nature of the public sphere in the context of opium reform and foreshadowed the hardening of the boundaries separating private, public, and governmental activities and interests in the early Republic. The conduct of the campaign in Fuzhou also implies a good deal of popular support for the anti-opium crusade, or at least acquiescence to it. But the suppression campaign affected every prefecture and county in the province, and the dynamics of reform in the towns and villages outside Fuzhou, particularly in the coastal trouble spots where poppy farmers clung to their profitable sideline, provide revealing insights on the structure of the public sphere, the strength of official-elite cooperation, the role of the merchant community, and the nature of local sentiment toward opium suppression in the rest of Fujian.

The basic framework of the suppression campaign in Fuzhou was reproduced throughout Fujian. The importance of the central Chinese state in determining both the pace and the content of reform efforts is reinforced here, as is the active role of branches of the Fujian Anti-Opium Society.

Chinese authorities, unofficial reform groups, and missionaries in all regions of Fujian publicized, monitored, implemented, and/or enforced comprehensive reforms that addressed both the demand and the supply side of the opium problem. Anti-opium measures adopted in almost every county and region in Fujian were implemented only after the official suppression campaign was initiated by the imperial edict of 1906. In addition, the measures themselves—the closing of opium dens, the issuing of licenses to smoke and distribute opium, the banning of poppy cultivation, and even the organizing of unofficial anti-opium societies—were precisely those outlined by the central state in its regulations for opium reform.

The anti-opium campaign was well known in even the most remote districts of Fujian, but the intensity and efficiency of enforcement varied considerably from county to county. Official and unofficial reform efforts began in the capital city of Fuzhou and spread to the surrounding counties, other treaty ports, and outlying regions, roughly in that order. Within each county, the campaign almost always began in the local administrative seat and was more actively implemented in towns and cities than in rural villages. By the time the campaign trickled down to rural market towns and villages, the energy and the funding available for reforms were often greatly diminished despite extensive opium smoking and poppy cultivation.

The development of a public space for political activism in which much of the drama of opium reform unfolded in Fuzhou depended on factors such as elite leadership, the active cooperation of local officials, and the availability of funding that were often absent in other parts of the province. The engagement of Anti-Opium Society members in virtually all aspects of the campaign throughout Fujian was especially significant in areas where local authorities were corrupt or ineffective. The society headquarters in Fuzhou attempted to extend its regulatory reach over a loose network of branch societies, occasionally conducting investigations in more remote regions of the province. However, because the power of the society's branches appears to have been directly related to the reputation, energy, and affluence of individual reformers, more remote and impoverished counties tended to host less active branches. The public ceremonies that were such a crucial tactic of reformist elites in Fuzhou were replicated in some areas surrounding the capital but were noticeably absent in more isolated regions. What is particularly striking in the accounts that follow is the foot-dragging of many county magistrates, despite the clear wishes of the central and provincial authorities. Whether that hesitation reflected the difficulties of enforcement—either due to a lack of funds or popular support for the campaign—or more personal issues is not always clear.

In general, the pace of the campaign in the southeast, with its more numerous poppy fields, independent mercantile tradition, local clan rivalries, and distance from the seat of provincial administration, tended to lag behind the northern half of the province. Skinner's core/periphery distinction is relevant here, but the issue is complicated by Fujian's political and economic geography and the relative dearth of documentation on the campaign outside Fuzhou. The division between Fujian's core and peripheral regions corresponded almost exactly with the separation between the opium-growing regions of the east and the opium-smoking areas in the west.[1] The mountain ranges that divide the province east from west marked the boundary between the densely populated coastal farmlands, where the domestic poppy flourished, and the hinterlands, where opium consumption and trafficking remained the primary concerns for those involved in opium suppression. As we might expect, better-educated and more reform-minded individuals tended to cluster in the core regions, but the size, strength, and shape of reform efforts hinged to a large degree on the presence or absence of poppy cultivation. Unofficial reform groups tended to assume more police powers and conduct a more public campaign in areas that imported opium (from abroad or from other parts of the province or nation); in contrast, the responsibility for eliminating poppy cultivation rested in the hands of local officials and the troops under their command.

At the same time, in the treaty port of Xiamen and in other commercial centers, the involvement of merchants tended to temper enthusiasm and generate obstacles to opium reform, and the activism of men Keith Schoppa terms "nongentry elites" diminished the prestige and clout of local Anti-Opium Society branches.[2] The involvement of merchants in the regulation of the opium trade meant less incentive for rapid suppression. Chinese distributors of the drug also were quick to spot loopholes in the new regula-

---

1. Governor-General Songshou stated that very little opium was grown in the western prefectures of Tingzhou, Jianning, and Shaowu but admitted that the poppy thrived in the coastal prefectures of Fuzhou, Xinghua, Quanzhou, and Zhangzhou (ZZGB 32, memorial from Songshou, endorsed 11 May 1910, pp. 159–60).

2. Schoppa, *Chinese Elites and Political Change*, pp. 4–5.

tions and presented a serious challenge to local administrators, unofficial elite-led reform groups, and even the national mission.

One of the most glaring differences between the conduct of the suppression campaign in Fuzhou and in the rest of the province was the dearth of funding outside the capital. The state subsidies for the Anti-Opium Society that became the object of such heated debate in the Provincial Assembly simply did not exist elsewhere. Most branches of the society relied on the generosity of members and supporters (although the society headquarters occasionally doled out small grants), and the funding problems in less prosperous regions affected not only the ranks of the branch societies but also the scope and the nature of their activities.

Always lurking in the background of Fujian's opium suppression campaign were the British, not necessarily in the shape of individual opium merchants or interfering diplomats, but more often as an intangible but undeniable obstacle to an unfettered attack on the opium trade. The central Chinese state was willing to allow provincial officials and reformers some degree of flexibility in pursuing the state-directed framework for reform, but only if local initiatives did not contravene the Sino-British agreement. In general, the provincial government was more likely to side with local officials as they struggled to support the reform efforts with concrete plans to eliminate the temptation of the imported drug. The central state, however, remained bound to its agreement with the British and was responsible for the compliance of the entire empire. Any local challenges to the treaty, however well intentioned, could derail the campaign by provoking British anger. By 1911, some reformers perceived Qing support for the international agreement necessary to eliminate Indian opium imports as unpatriotic.

Finally, despite the undeniably positive connotation of reform in western thinking and in the minds of many Chinese reformers, the New Policies had distinctly repressive aspects that belied the nationalistic rhetoric that surrounded and justified them. The more extractive and intrusive elements of opium reform provoked popular resistance—passive and violent—throughout Fujian and seriously compromised the campaign's goals. Magistrates and members of the Anti-Opium Society sometimes faced considerable personal danger as they attempted to convince and coerce local residents to stop smoking, selling, or harvesting the drug.

This chapter follows the lead of the Provincial Assembly by dividing the province into four regions and tracking the campaign as the assemblymen believed it should progress.³ The assembly chose to depart from the standard division of the province into circuits (*dao*), which did not reflect the geography of Fujian's opium problem. Instead, the fourfold division grouped prefectures and subprefectures with opium problems of similar types and degrees. As Skinner has noted, the eastern half of the province consisted of Fujian's populous core, encompassing the relatively fertile coastal lowlands, along with the urban commercial zones that grew up around the treaty ports of Xiamen and Fuzhou.⁴ The mountainous western half was far less developed and populated than the east, although the Min River and its tributaries did give rise to several important commercial centers, particularly in the northwest. In 1900, there were fourteen cities with populations at or above ten thousand in Fujian, and although these cities were distributed evenly between the east and the west, it is clear that the urban core of the province lay along the coastline.⁵ The treaty ports of Fuzhou and Xiamen were considered separate entities, and it was assumed that their opium problem would evaporate after the sale, consumption, and cultivation of the drug had been eliminated around them. By leaving the treaty ports as the last targets for the campaign, the assembly also hoped to forestall foreign complaints.⁶ The regional approach allows an analysis of Fujian's struggle against opium that in-

---

3. *Dierci Fujian ziyi ju yi shi suji lu*, 31 Oct. 1910, p. 13. This contradicts the arrangement translated by the British consul in Fuzhou, in which the deadlines were staggered as follows: the northwest region (Yanping, Jianning, and Shaowu prefectures) was to achieve suppression first, then the southwest (Tingzhou prefecture and Longyan subprefecture), then the northeast (Fuzhou, Funing, and Xinghua prefectures), and finally the southeast (Quanzhou and Zhangzhou prefectures and Yongchun subprefecture). Both arrangements have advantages and disadvantages, but it is unclear which was actually implemented, given the events that overtook Fujian and the rest of China in 1911 (see PRO, FO 228/1800, enclosure in Foochow Intelligence Report, December Quarter, 1910).

4. Each subregion housed a major drainage basin, which in turn was dominated by an urban center. The Min Basin subregion centered on Fuzhou, and the Zhang-Quan subregion contained the Jiulong River basin, which included the treaty port of Xiamen, along with the commercial cities of Zhangzhou and Quanzhou. See Skinner, "The Structure of Chinese History," pp. 275–80.

5. The cities and their population, listed by region, are as follows: southwest: Zhangzhou (138,000), Tingzhou (11,000), Longyan (11,000); northwest: Zhenghe (24,000), Nanping (26,000), Shuiji (34,000), Pucheng (11,000), Jianning (32,000); southeast: Hui'an (10,000), Quanzhou (220,000), Xiamen (114,000); and northeast: Xinghua (10,000), Xianyou (25,000), Fuzhou (350,000) (Li Guoqi, "Qingmo Minchu Min-Zhe diqu renkou liudong yu dushihua," pp. 512–13).

6. *Dierci Fujian ziyiju yi shi suji lu* 12, 31 Oct. 1910, p. 14.

corporates not only the flow of policy from core to periphery but also the ways in which regional economic, social, and geographical differences affected policy implementation. Although the documentation is not evenly distributed, some information about the conduct of the opium suppression campaign in each of Fujian's nine prefectures and two subprefectures survives and enables us to develop a montage of opium reform throughout Fujian.

An examination of the progress of suppression throughout the province also clarifies the rationale behind the new opium reform plan drawn up by the Provincial Assembly in late 1910. In many ways, that plan's reiteration of the basic framework for suppression laid out by earlier edicts indicates that opium reform had not been progressing as quickly or effectively as desired by local authorities and elites. Since progress within the city of Fuzhou was impressive, the backsliding and resistance must have occurred outside the provincial capital, in the counties and prefectures we will visit below. It should be noted, however, that a new agreement with the British and the outbreak of revolution (both in 1911) meant that the regional framework for reform had to be completely reworked.

Opium Suppression in the Northwest

The northwest region comprises Jianning, Shaowu, and Yanping prefectures, and although the natural geography of the region made possible an enormous traffic in opium, the assembly believed that by August 1911, this region could be the first to report a victory over opium, presumably because it lacked a large domestic poppy crop.[7] The waterways that flowed through Yanping branched off westward into Shaowu and eastward into Jianning, providing convenient routes for opium importers (particularly from Fuzhou) into the neighboring provinces of Jiangxi and Zhejiang. The prefectural cities of Jianning and Yanping were large commercial centers located on the upper reaches of the Min River, one of the few areas in the province where waterways were navigable by relatively large ships.[8] Very little poppy had ever been cultivated in the northwest, but the ready availability of both the

---

7. The deadline for this region, as listed in the assembly minutes, was the seventh month of the third year of the Xuantong emperor's reign (ibid., p. 13).

8. Benedict, *Bubonic Plague*, chap. 3. Tea, from the renowned Bohea hills (Wuyi shan), was exported from this region to Fuzhou and beyond, along with camphor, mushrooms, bamboo shoots, rice, indigo, and timber (*Mercy and Truth* 12, no. 140 [Aug. 1908]: 245–49).

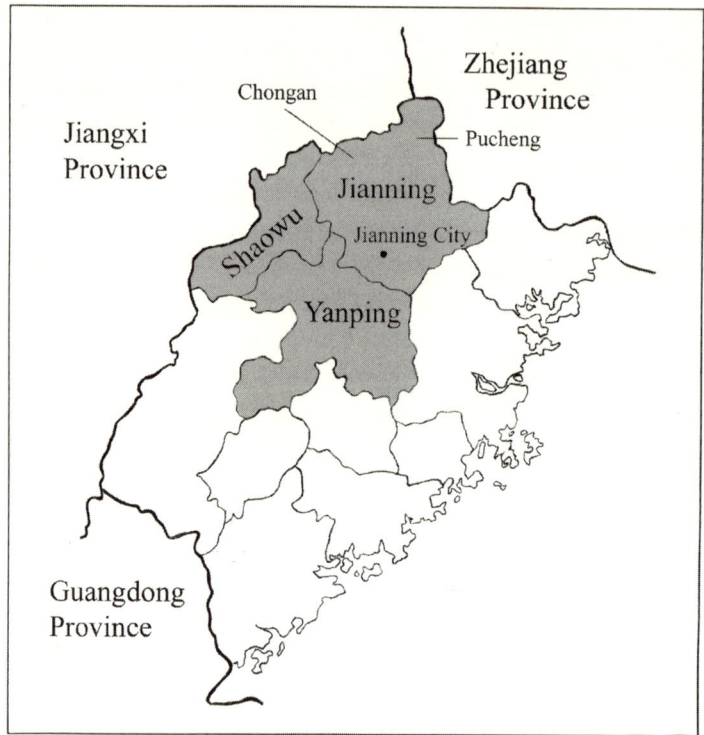

Map 4.1 Northwestern Region

domestic and the foreign drug created serious social and economic problems in the area.

The opium suppression campaign in this region was led largely by local elites, even in the more remote districts. With the exception of Yanping, the region stood out for the notable lack of cooperation between foreign missionaries and Chinese elites in the context of the suppression campaign. The antagonism was probably a result of the longstanding anti-imperialist, anti-Christian sentiments evinced by local officials since the early days of the missionary "occupation" of Jianning.[9] The hostility may also be related to the dearth of domestic poppy cultivation. Since much of the locally consumed drug was grown elsewhere, Chinese reformers may have resented the advice and intrusion of missionaries with links to opium-importing countries.

---

9. *IWCD* 19 (July–Nov. 1899); Latourette, *A History of Christian Missions in China*, pp. 468, 501; Lin Wenhui, *Qingji Fujian jiao'an zhi yanjiu*, pp. 189, 200.

JIANNING PREFECTURE

Opium consumption in the prefectural seat and trading city of Jianning was quite widespread. A large number of manual laborers, particularly chair bearers, were dependent on opium, and upper-class smokers were not uncommon. Numerous opium dens crowded the city streets, and opium was also consumed in private homes and places of business.[10]

The anti-opium movement in Jianning was conducted jointly and very publicly by local officials and unofficial elite-led reform groups. The results, according to foreign observers, were unimpressive. In mid-1907, the Jianning prefect presided over the closing of all opium dens in the city. Outside the large cities, however, dens apparently remained open well into 1908.[11] Later, local magistrates and other officials, as well as members of the literati, cooperated to open and staff an Opium Prohibition Bureau (*jinyan gongsuo*) and refuge in Jianning City. Located in a large temple, which a CMS missionary complained was dark, damp, and dirty, the refuge had an intimidating array of rules for inmates, and its walls were hung with frightening illustrations of the punishments that awaited those who relapsed.[12]

According to the CMS missionaries, the shoddy condition of the refuge was representative of a generally lackluster attitude toward the anti-opium campaign, even in the prefectural seat. The refuge treated only a handful of smokers, and although the price of the drug had risen considerably, opium suicides were still frequent. In addition, many of the opium dens closed with such fanfare in mid-1907 continued to do business through less conspicuous side doors. Missionaries complained that no one seemed to know who was responsible for the enforcement of the anti-opium regulations, a development that may have resulted because the boundaries between the responsibilities of officials and elite reformers were unclear. One CMS missionary also alleged:

It is not that the Central Government is insincere in its efforts, or that the people are not anxious to be done with the hateful drug, but that our city officials are unwilling to lead the way, are insincere in carrying into effect the orders from Peking,

---

10. *Mercy and Truth* 12, no. 140 (Aug. 1908): 245–46.
11. CMS, Fuhkien Mission, Original Incoming, 1900–34 (1908), no. 148, letter from H. S. Phillips, 29 Mar. 1908.
12. *Mercy and Truth* 12, no. 140 (Aug. 1908): 245–49.

are, in fact, too selfish and sordid either to stop the habit themselves or to encourage the people to do so.[13]

However, the fact that many of these same local officials had harassed the missionaries when they first came to Jianning may have colored their impressions.

Local authorities and elite reformers discouraged direct cooperation with missionary groups in the Jianning prefectural seat by acknowledging the missionaries' contribution to the suppression campaign and their goodwill but limiting the foreigners' involvement to exhortation. For example, the Chinese doctor and the pastor from the CMS hospital were seated prominently at the opening of the Chinese refuge in Jianning City and were asked to address the crowd. However, CMS efforts to convince local elites to join with them in opening a refuge outside the mission hospital were in vain.[14]

Results in Pucheng county, well to the north of Jianning City, were more inspiring, as a result of a more active group of local elites. In June or July of 1907, seven local notables and others responded to the call of their compatriot Chen Peikun in Fuzhou to establish and sponsor the Pucheng branch of the Anti-Opium Society.[15] Two of the founders, Meng Sipei and Li Dihu, later became Pucheng's representatives in the Provincial Assembly.[16] The society was housed in a temple on a back street in the county seat of Pucheng; there it doled out funding for anti-opium medications and other treatment for addiction. The temple also served as a treatment center where smokers could kick their habit without having to pay for food or medicine. During its first six months of operation, 525 people were said to have given up opium there. Later, gentry and officials cooperated to establish an opium prohibition bureau as required by the central state.[17]

The exclusion of missionaries from a hands-on role in the official Chinese reform effort in Jianning City may have reflected the resentment of local officials and elites at being hamstrung in their attempts to combat the local opium problem by the 1908 agreement with the British or a fear that missionaries would report local contraventions of that agreement. The treaty

---

13. Ibid.
14. Ibid.
15. The seven were Zhan Xianba, Meng Sipei, Xu Peihua, Li Dihu, Su Wukai, Zhu Huanpo, and Zeng Fengyuan (Zhang Xingsheng, "'Jinyan' zaji," p. 31).
16. *Fujian ziyiju diyi jie quanti yiyuan yilan biao* (n.p., n.d.—probably 1910), pp. 3–4.
17. Zhang Xingsheng, "'Jinyan' zaji," p. 31.

forbade Chinese opium monopolies and the obstruction of the wholesale drug trade, but local authorities in some Jianning locales attempted to use precisely these methods to control the drug trade in their area. In the fall of 1910, for example, the Chongan county magistrate established a monopoly on raw opium and forbade merchants to transport opium from Chongan without a permit from the local Anti-Opium Society. Since Chongan lay along a major tributary of the Min River that flowed into Jiangxi province, the disruption of the trade could have had a major impact on imports to the Chinese interior. Fujian's Bureau of Foreign Affairs (Waijiao bu) defended the actions of the Chongan magistrate, but pressure from Beijing carried the day, and the Jianning prefect was commanded to instruct the Chongan magistrate to cease interfering with the wholesale trade. However, merchants dealing in Indian opium insisted that the monopoly persisted, and the incident became the subject of voluminous and often contentious diplomatic correspondence between the British and the Chinese.[18]

YANPING PREFECTURE

In Yanping, in central Fujian, available evidence suggests that elite reformers were far more active than local officials in combating opium smoking, and elite activism was channeled through branches of the Anti-Opium Society. French consular officials obtained and translated the regulations for a branch society in Yanping in 1908, and the document echoed the regulations of the society headquarters in Fuzhou. However, no government subsidies aided this group; members of the branch society were expected to contribute funds for its operations, and a list of donors was published each winter as an incentive. Monthly meetings to review the status of the local campaign and discuss solutions were scheduled, and speeches against opium smoking were to be a feature of every local wedding. The group also strongly cautioned friends of the society to abstain from opium smoking and from patronizing any business that served opium smokers.[19]

Unlike Jianning, Christians in Yanping were involved in treating opium smokers as well as in prompting the anti-opium activities of local students. The Methodist Alden Speare Memorial Hospital in the Yanping prefectural

---

18. PRO, FO 228/1800, enclosure in Foochow Intelligence Report for December Quarter 1910; and numerous dispatches in PRO, FO 228/2444 and 2445.

19. MAE/Nantes, Foutcheou, Opium, carton 71, translations from *Fujian xinwen*, 12 and 15 Aug. 1908, respectively.

seat treated 170 opium patients in 1907, although James E. Skinner, the physician in charge, lamented that much of his work was in vain because greedy local officials conspired to make the ban on opium shops a travesty.[20] In 1908, a group of missionary-educated Chinese youth in Yanping organized The Resolution Society. They pledged "to abstain from opium, tobacco, liquors, swearing, lying, stealing and gambling."[21]

SHAOWU PREFECTURE

Jianning county (not to be confused with the prefecture of the same name) in Shaowu was littered with opium dens in the late Qing, and it was said that opium smokers could be found among each of the "four classes" (*shi nong gong shang*, or the literati, farmers, artisans, and merchants). One source states that although local elites were enthusiastic reformers, their attempts were thwarted by corrupt administrators. Supposedly, the county branch office of the Anti-Opium Society did not begin to experience significant successes until the 1920s, around the time the Fuzhou headquarters closed its doors in despair and disgust. In the absence of a strong branch of the society, some local residents joined an alternative group called the Brother-in-Law Society (Dabai hui) that offered a cure for opium addiction.[22]

Opium Suppression in the Northeast

The Provincial Assembly set mid-February 1912 as the deadline for suppression in the northeast—six months after the deadline for the northwest. Fuzhou City was excluded from the deadline to avoid conflict with the British.[23] The northeast region consisted of Funing and Fuzhou prefectures, areas in which reformers had to deal with foreign imports as well as domestically grown opium. By September 1908, poppy cultivation surrounding the capital was said to have been reduced by 80 percent, although planting continued in the more remote areas of both prefectures.[24] The northeast was home to some of Fujian's most enthusiastic reformers, many of whom found an outlet for their activism in the branches of the Anti-Opium Society.

---

20. MEC *Annual Report*, 1907, p. 165.
21. *Foochow Messenger* 6, no. 1 (Jan. 1909): 9.
22. Chen Guansan and Zou Xiutong, "Yapian yandu zai Jianning de fanlan yu chajin," pp. 43–44.
23. *Dierci Fujian ziyiju yi shi suji lu* 12, 31 Oct. 1910, pp. 13–14.
24. *IWCD* 29, no. 271 (Jan. 1909): 9.

Map 4.2 Northeastern Region

FUZHOU PREFECTURE
(EXCLUDING FUZHOU)

As headquarters for both the official anti-opium bureaucracy and the Fujian Anti-Opium Society, Fuzhou served as the center for opium reform throughout the province. Developments within the city had a strong impact on surrounding counties and, to a large degree, on the province as a whole. The energy and efficiency of the campaign beyond the capital depended on the motivation and leadership of either elite reformers or local officials and the extent to which those groups were willing and able to cooperate with each other.

Just northeast of Fuzhou lay Lianjiang county, the center of a vigorous anti-opium effort led by local elites. On 5 October 1907, a grand public festival was staged to celebrate the launching of the Lianjiang branch of the Anti-Opium Society. Speakers included city elders and local officials, representatives of local schools, Chinese Christians, and foreign missionaries. The speaking platform was set up outside a large temple, and the festivities began with a solemn ceremony that included a dramatic public offering to an effigy of Lin Zexu. Attendance apparently was enormous. According to William C. White, of the Church Missionary Society (CMS), who lived and worked in the area:

> This Chinese Anti-opium League is entirely non-Christian; a patriotic movement that seeks to remove the opium not by force, but by methods of persuasion, and especially by creating public opinion against it. Amongst other things, they (1) *got the officials of each district to carry out the commands of the Imperial Edict with regard to the local growth and sale of opium*; (2) send deputations throughout the country to preach against opium; (3) establish refuges where opium patients can be cured. One of the latter is to be opened almost immediately, next door to the temple where the demonstration was held. [Italics added]

White downplayed the role of local officials in Lianjiang's anti-opium campaign and claimed that the unenthusiastic county magistrate felt compelled to support the actions of the Lianjiang Anti-Opium Society because of the high status of the local elites involved, an echo of the situation in Fuzhou. The branch society opened subbranches in smaller towns in the county, and its uniformed members planned house-to-house investigations. They also expressed their desire to work with the magistrate to set up an opium monopoly to better regulate the trade. The elite reformers who ran the Lianjiang Society were also committed to a variety of other progressive reforms, including popular representative government.[25]

The most prominent of those elites was Wu Tingchang, the founder of the Lianjiang Anti-Opium Society and, as we saw in Chapter 3, a member of the Fujian Provincial Assembly, an affiliation that undoubtedly influenced the society's opinion of constitutional reform.[26] One source states that Wu was a well-respected physician with much influence among elites in his county. Apparently, simply at his request, three gentry closed an opium shop and handed over their stock for incineration. His integrity even spawned the popular children's song reproduced in Chapter 3. The society was headquartered in the Wu family's ancestral temple, which also doubled as an addiction treatment center.[27]

---

25. CMS, Fuhkien Mission, Incoming Originals, 1900–1934 (1907 and 1908), nos. 266 and 99, letters from White, 21 Nov. and 10 Dec. 1907, respectively.
26. *Fujian ziyi ju diyi jie quanti yiyuan yilan biao*, p. 2.
27. Wu Tianchang, "Wu Tingchang xiansheng chuangban Qudu she," pp. 27–28.

As the year progressed, the Lianjiang Anti-Opium Society sustained popular interest in the anti-opium movement by printing and distributing literature (utilizing CMS printing presses), sponsoring mass meetings, and maintaining a successful treatment center. Only licensed opium shops remained open in the city of Lianjiang, and smokers were subject to a monthly registration and rationing scheme organized and administered by the society. White observed that every house in the prefectural seat flew a dragon flag with characters declaring "Glad to put away OPIUM." He also noted that the society's members were usually degree-holding local elites who served as an informal city council. White was deeply impressed by the society's commitment "to clear out the opium to save our children and our country."

The Lianjiang Society also formed a de facto police force in the county seat. Each member of the society, with a staff of volunteers, took total responsibility for enforcing opium restrictions in one ward of the city. The society's strategy included unannounced searches for opium and smoking utensils. White believed that the Lianjiang Society was notable for two reasons: "First, their generous and almost prodigal use of money.... The members themselves were personally responsible for all expenses.... Second, the way these long-gowned Confucian scholars themselves turned to and did the work."[28] Another source noted that the group "observed publicly and investigated privately" (*mingcha anfang*), a phrase that refers to the branch society's exhortations in the streets of Lianjiang and its nightly raids on suspected violators of the opium restrictions.[29] The danger of associating the society so intimately with a single individual, however, became apparent when Wu Tingchang died.[30] No one of the same caliber or reputation (or possibly financial worth) emerged to take up his work, and the vigorous Lianjiang Anti-Opium Society apparently died with him.[31]

White contrasted the situation in Lianjiang with that in Luoyuan county, only a short distance away, where local officials were far more active in the campaign than elite reformers:

---

28. CMS, Fuhkien Mission, Incoming Originals, 1900–1934 (1907 and 1908), nos. 266 and 99, letters from White, 21 Nov. and 10 Dec. 1907, respectively.

29. Wu Tianchang, "Wu Tingchang xiansheng chuangban Qudu she," p. 27.

30. The date of Wu's death is unknown, but he was sixty years old in 1910 when he served as a provincial assemblyman. *Fujian ziyi ju diyi jie quanti yiyuan yilan biao*.

31. Wu Tianchang, "Wu Tingchang xiansheng chuangban Qudu she," p. 28.

The [Luoyuan] mandarin has shown himself particularly eager to suppress opium, and has gone to considerable expense himself in starting an opium refuge; but because the city elders, though they have nominally a league [a branch of the Anti-Opium Society], have not taken the matter up heartily, no very material results have been affected. It is true that the local production of opium has considerably decreased, but this is altogether due to the mandarin's strict prohibition of the growth of the poppy, while the consumption of opium is little if any less than last year.[32]

According to one account, in the late Qing / early Republic, eight opium shops and over 50 opium dens were located in the county seat, and poppies grew in nearby villages.[33] By April 1908, however, the members of the local branch of the Anti-Opium Society appear to have warmed to their task.[34] Like society members, White seems to have believed that even where local officials were vigorous champions of opium reform, elite activism was necessary for the ultimate success of the campaign.

In northwestern Fuzhou prefecture, on the border with Jianning and Yanping prefectures, lay isolated and mountainous Gutian county, where British missionaries and Chinese reformers reported extensive opium smoking and extraordinarily active elite involvement in the suppression campaign. Opium smoking had apparently reached epidemic proportions in the towns and cities of Gutian before the campaign and was only slightly less serious in rural villages. Smokers could be found among all social classes, and the drug was said to have depleted the local economy, weakened smokers' bodies, and destroyed their families. Farmers in Gutian harvested a small poppy crop, but the bulk of the opium consumed in the area was from abroad; four local firms specialized in the importation of British opium.[35]

The local branch of the Anti-Opium Society led the campaign in Gutian. The group was founded in May 1908 by Chen Weilin, a student of law and politics. Opium dens in the county seat had been closed, most likely by local officials, but some had reopened illegally. Opium shops also conspired to foil the efforts of opium reformers by selling a form of the drug that could be smoked inconspicuously in ordinary bamboo tobacco pipes rather than the

---

32. CMS, Fuhkien Mission, Incoming Originals, 1900–1934 (1908), no. 99, letter from White, 10 Dec. 1907.

33. "Luoyuan yanhai yu jinyan jishi," p. 19.

34. USDS (1906–10), (no case no.) reel 105, Gracey to Secy. of State, 30 Apr. 1908.

35. *The Quarterly* 3 (1908), official documents (*gongdu*) section, pp. 1–2; Yu Zuliu, "Gutian lishishang de jinyan yundong," p. 81.

more distinctive opium pipes.[36] Local officials expressed a willingness to combat the opium problem but blamed their inactivity on a lack of funding. The Anti-Opium Society claimed that the magistrate was corrupt. Inspired by his compatriots in Fuzhou, Chen called a meeting of local public welfare societies, and the reformers decided to tackle Gutian's opium problem.[37]

The Gutian branch of the Anti-Opium Society was actively involved in the three areas of opium suppression laid out by the Qing state—the prohibition of consumption, cultivation, and distribution—and elite reformers in Gutian were determined to make the crusade a very public one. Large processions wound through the county seat to the county magistrate's yamen, where public burnings of opium pipes took place. In one parade, on 1 April 1910, the marchers held aloft yellow banners proclaiming the abolition of opium by the emperor, and the procession featured "a miserable man, just sodden with opium and reduced to skin and bone, who was led around in the wake of the opium pipes, between two soldiers, as a warning to onlookers, and had two small yellow flags—miniature duplicates of the big banners—stuck in his tousled hair, giving a comical effect."[38]

After some urging from the branch society and the appointment of a new magistrate, the magistrate and local elites worked closely to enforce the opium restrictions and investigate suspected violators. Policemen and society investigators traveled to rural villages to inform local literati about the prohibition on poppy cultivation and request their assistance. Even the magistrate occasionally supervised raids on possible offenders. Local authorities and reformers cooperated to compile a list of known opium smokers and used each person's history to determine a reasonable deadline for a cure. They also worked together to open opium treatment centers, arrest illicit drug dealers, and monitor the prohibition on the use of opium lamps in private homes.[39] The society branch set up a smoking cessation clinic (*jieyan ju*) in Gutian City; demand proved so overwhelming that the group quickly established two more. These treatment centers accepted even those smokers too poor to pay for the cure and were funded by the fees paid by wealthier patients and donations from society members.[40]

---

36. This form of opium was called *xiao gui*, but the meaning is unclear.
37. *The Quarterly* 3 (1908), official documents (*gongdu*) section, pp. 1–2.
38. *IWCD* 30, no. 286 (Apr. 1910): 106.
39. Ibid., pp. 106–7; *The Quarterly* 3 (1908), official documents (*gongdu*) section, pp. 1–2; Yu Zuliu, "Gutian lishishang de jinyan yundong."
40. Yu Zuliu, "Gutian lishishang de jinyan yundong," p. 82.

Fig. 4.1 Many spectators, including several American missionaries, crowd around a single smoking cauldron in Gutian overflowing with confiscated opium pipes and other smoking paraphernalia some time between 1907 and 1911 (courtesy United Methodist Archives, Drew University, Madison, New Jersey).

Gutian's most notable accomplishment in its campaign against opium was its bold and innovative approach to getting rid of opium shops, which was seen as the key to effective suppression. Because counties were compelled to pay the provincial government taxes collected from licensed opium shops, the Gutian branch society feared that local authorities had no incentive to close the shops before the established deadline. At Chen's urging, a meeting of the county elite resulted in a pledge by three hundred men to donate seven yuan apiece annually for the next three years. The money was to be given to the county magistrate to defray the provincial tax and enable him to shut down the shops immediately with no financial loss.[41] A report on the Gutian situation was delivered to Lin Bingzhang in Fuzhou, and he pledged the financial and moral support of the Anti-Opium Society headquarters.[42] A British missionary publication also reported this extraordinary development, although they attributed the proposal rather vaguely to "the people":

---

41. Ibid.; *The Quarterly* 3 (1908), official documents (*gongdu*) section, p. 1.
42. *The Quarterly* 3 (1908), official documents (*gongdu*) section, p. 1.

Provincial Patterns of Reform Before the Revolution of 1911

Fig. 4.2 British and American missionaries and local dignitaries pose for a photograph after a public pipe burning in Gutian in the first years of the campaign. The missionary in the foreground to the right holds an opium pipe, presumably to commemorate the occasion for the formal gathering. Another missionary, on the left, holds an ax that may have been used to destroy the contraband before it was burned (courtesy United Methodist Archives, Drew University, Madison, New Jersey).

The people . . . have been unanimous in their desire to put an end to the opium trade in their city. In three years they raised the sum of 5,280 dollars by voluntary contributions to help the Central Government in keeping out the drug. At the request of the magistrate, permission was granted by the Foochow Viceroy [Governor-General Songshou] to close all the opium dens in Kutien [Gutian], and also the Government opium warehouse which formed the chief distributing centre for the county. The reform was carried out with public rejoicing on July 6, 1909, all the opium shops being closed.[43]

The Provincial Assembly specifically noted this accomplishment in September 1910 and, as a reward, exempted Gutian from the tax.[44]

The local opium importers did not take kindly to what amounted to a prohibition on the importation of foreign opium, however, and the Chinese

---

43. *IWCD* 30, no. 284 (Feb. 1910): 24–25. It is unclear if the figure of 5,280 dollars was the 6,000 *yuan* noted by the Fujian Anti-Opium Society.
44. Yu Zuliu, "Gutian lishishang de jinyan yundong," p. 84.

companies complained to their British counterparts. British merchants then protested to the authorities in Fuzhou that "treaty rights had been contravened, and that opium was a recognized legitimate article of commerce until the ten years stipulated for had expired." Several days after Gutian City's opium shops and dens were closed by popular demand, the vocal protests of British traders at Fuzhou forced several to reopen. Missionaries reported that "the whole city was indignant, and all of the shops have been closed again by the magistrate in spite of the protest."[45] In response, Chen Weilin delivered a petition to Fuzhou stating that the people in Gutian approved of the blockage of the foreign drug and would pay the tax. Impressed, Songshou ordered Gutian authorities to support the branch society's initiative.[46]

In the midst of this controversy, a serious violation of the order to close Gutian's opium dens presented another opportunity for provincial and local authorities to demonstrate their commitment to the campaign and their ability to enforce it. The gentry manager of Gutian City's largest opium warehouse resisted attempts to close him down until Songshou ordered his arrest and punishment. The man was stripped of his degrees and sent to Fuzhou for sentencing. After this, proprietors of local opium shops and dens did not dare to resist orders to close.[47] The incident also served as a clear reminder that local opium reformers were an unofficial arm of a larger, more powerful bureaucratic web that possessed the capacity to intervene locally when necessary.

On occasion, however, violence was directed at Chinese reformers. Chen Weilin found that his well-intentioned crusading did not come without risk. In one case, when Chen's investigators discovered and shut down several illegal opium dens, the two women who ran them pretended to poison themselves in despair. Local residents responded with outrage, publicly beating the investigators.[48] On another occasion, irate opium dealers torched the home of a reformer prominent in the suppression campaign.[49] After leading another successful raid that resulted in the public exposure of opium dealers and some of their literati customers, as well as the confiscation of the dealers' equipment, Chen himself was ambushed on a back street by several dozen people from one dealer's family (including seven women). A missionary reported that he

---

45. *IWCD* 30, no. 284 (Feb. 1910): 24–25.
46. Yu Zuliu, "Gutian lishishang de jinyan yundong," pp. 83–84.
47. *IWCD* 30, no. 286 (Apr. 1910): 60.
48. Yu Zuliu, "Gutian lishishang de jinyan yundong," p. 83.
49. *IWCD* 30, no. 286 (Apr. 1910): 106.

was badly beaten and refused to fight back because "I want to do my people good and help them, not fight them." However, a Chinese account claims that Chen knew enough martial arts (*gongfu*) to defend himself.[50]

Thirty miles east of Gutian, the headman of the crowded market town of Xiyang (Sa-Iong in the local dialect) was said to have independently opened an opium refuge in spring 1906. He declared that anyone caught smoking or selling the drug in his town would be fined. He was also concerned with finding work for recovering addicts and contemplated an assault on other vices such as gambling. The Church of England Zenana Missionary Society (CEZMS) had a small mission in Xiyang and stressed that he was a regular churchgoer. Two British missionaries who resided there in the late 1890s had begun treating opium addicts in makeshift sheds erected alongside their residence,[51] and by 1910, a CEZMS missionary reported: "Now I am glad to say that there is a mutual benefit society established in Sa Yong with the object of doing away with the opium and the many opium dens as well as the gambling and other evils. The eight leading men in it are coming to church."[52]

The headman of the village of Cheu-dau (Chinese characters unavailable), nine miles from Xiyang, requested the help of the CEZMS mission in Xiyang in 1906 in curing himself and about a dozen other village smokers. During the course of a meeting to welcome the Christians, the village's opium den proprietors voluntarily offered to shut down their businesses and apparently did so. The headman suffered a great deal during his withdrawal, but later wrote an article condemning the drug that was printed in a Chinese newspaper published by the CMS. He evidently was an educated man who had placed first in the local examinations at Gutian, and his experience resulted in eloquent testimony to the ravages of opium and the possibility of a cure.[53]

FUNING PREFECTURE

Bordering Fuzhou prefecture to the north, this coastal region contained the lackluster trading port of Santu'ao, a fairly sizable poppy crop, and considerable variety in local approaches to the region's opium problem. Poppy fields

---

50. Apparently, the attackers also attempted to cut off Chen's queue. Chen is referred to as "Ding," the local pronunciation, in some missionary reports (ibid., p. 83; *IWCD* 30, no. 286 [Apr. 1910]: 60).

51. *IWCD* 26, no. 239 (May 1906): 72–73, and 26, no. 241 (July 1906): 108–10.

52. *IWCD* 30, no. 292 (Oct. 1910): 158–59.

53. *IWCD* 26, no. 244 (Oct. 1906): 154–55.

grew throughout Funing, particularly in the county of Fu'an, but local officials responded energetically to the announcement of a national anti-opium campaign and Songshou's call in 1908 for the total prohibition of domestic poppy cultivation. The poppy all but disappeared from Funing within a few years. However, according to foreign customs officials, the retail trade in opium was more intransigent. Part of the reason for this was that the sale of opium was handled very differently in various districts of Funing. "At Funing prepared opium continued to be sold by the Lung Chi [Longxi] firm, which held a monopoly; at Fu'an it was still purveyed by an official establishment (*guan'gao ju*); and at Ningteh [Ningde] the trade remained in the hands of various licensed shops."[54] The opium dens of Funing were ordered shut down by 12 May 1907, but the deadline was extended in the more remote areas in the prefecture, and on the eve of the Revolution of 1911, a few dens were still in operation. A branch of the Anti-Opium Society operated in Fu'an and was responsible for registering and treating smokers, as well as investigating violators.[55]

Opium Suppression in the Southeast

Opium reform efforts in the southeast region were complicated and delayed by the combination of a more extensive poppy crop than in the northeast and a lively trade in foreign opium. The Provincial Assembly recognized these issues and gave the region until the summer of 1912 to complete its suppression campaign.[56] Many of the most notorious centers of poppy cultivation in Fujian province were located in the southeastern prefectures of Xinghua and Quanzhou and the subprefecture of Yongchun. Because Chapter 8 is devoted to a detailed analysis of the suppression campaign in Xinghua, that prefecture is omitted from this discussion. The major urban centers in the southeast—the treaty port of Xiamen and the large prefectural city of Quanzhou—were less administrative than commercial hubs, and the corps of bureaucrats and would-be bureaucrats who fueled the campaign in Fuzhou was smaller and less active here. Opium suppression in Xiamen, with its strong tradition of merchant associations and independent

---

54. IMC, *Decennial Reports, Santuao, 1902–1911*, p. 83.
55. Miao Xiaoning, "Fu'an renmin fankang yapian," pp. 54–55. I thank Steve Averill for making this source available to me. See also IMC, *Decennial Reports, Santuao, 1902–1911*, p. 83.
56. *Dierci Fujian ziyiju yi shi suji lu*, 12, 31 Oct. 1910, p. 13.

Map 4.3 Southeastern Region

tax farmers, makes an intriguing comparison with Fuzhou.[57] In general, the entire region lagged well behind the northeast in its implementation of opium suppression measures, and responsibility for dealing with belligerent poppy farmers fell on local officials as elite reformers concentrated their efforts on combating opium consumption.

QUANZHOU PREFECTURE
(EXCLUDING XIAMEN)

Outside Xiamen, the primary target of Quanzhou's local officials and opium reformers was poppy cultivation. Provincial authorities were deeply concerned about the trouble spots of Hui'an and Tongan, since these counties

---

57. The strong Japanese presence along the southeast coast also hindered the enforcement of opium restrictions.

were infamous for the tenacity of their poppy farmers and the truculence of the local population. Resistance in these areas endangered the success of the suppression campaign at the provincial and national levels.

In the notorious county of Tongan, the center of Fujian's prerevolutionary poppy cultivation, the amount of land planted in opium had soared by the late nineteenth century. According to an observer from the Presbyterian Church of England (PCE) mission: "I passed thro' [sic] the Tong-an region in January 1894 and patches of the poppy were to be seen here and there. I passed thro' the same region again in January of this year [1895] and save for an occasional small patch of sugar cane, nothing but the poppy was to be seen." The missionary noted that land often was held jointly by three or four families, and crops were chosen either by consensus or by the majority. This, he worried, could produce a profound dilemma if, for example, one of the shareholders was a Christian (and thus forbidden to smoke, sell, or cultivate opium) and the others decided to plant poppies.[58] For opium reformers, the situation had the potential to generate considerable popular resistance, since the efforts and expectations of a relatively large number of people were invested in any single plot.

During the late Qing suppression campaign, the strength of the violence-prone Tongan area clans meant that officials attempting to enforce the prohibition on poppy cultivation risked their lives. In early 1909, one particularly powerful clan staged a riot when the local magistrate ordered them to uproot their poppy crop; in another instance, a yamen runner was killed in a tense confrontation between magistrate and clan members. The magistrate in the first case responded by implementing a draconian strategy that resulted in the complete destruction of several villages.[59]

Hui'an, another poppy-growing county in Quanzhou, was in a general state of unrest as the anti-opium campaign began. Clan fights were commonplace, and resident missionaries complained of persecution and "gross misgovernment" by local officials.[60] By the fall of 1909, banditry and clan battles raged, and the local authorities were helpless. Stray bullets frequently fell

---

58. PCE, box 9 (S. Fukien, General Correspondence, pre-1900–1907), folder 3, Bates to Matheson, 30 May 1895.

59. USDS (1906–10), Reel 107, 775/585, Arnold to Secy. of State, 28 Jan. 1909; USDS, Reel 108, 774/690.

60. CWM/LMS, box 8 (Incoming Correspondence, China-Fukien, 1904–7), folder 4, Reynolds-Turner to Cousins, 28 Apr. 1907.

into London Missionary Society (LMS) compounds.⁶¹ The atmosphere was not conducive to venturing into the countryside to punish violators of the restrictions on opium cultivation.

OPIUM SUPPRESSION IN XIAMEN:
PROFIT AND PATRIOTISM

The anti-opium campaign in Xiamen reveals the ambiguous role of merchants and the merchant culture in opium reform. Like Fuzhou, Xiamen was a treaty port with a lively cosmopolitan population, but Xiamen was primarily a commercial town with far less of an administrative presence than the provincial capital. Although Xiamen's opium suppression campaign followed the general template laid out in Beijing and Fuzhou, the dominance of the commercial culture in Xiamen can be seen in the men who occupied the public space in which opium suppression and other reforms were carried out.

Well before the advent of opium reform, the opium trade was handled differently in Xiamen, because of its long tradition of tax farming. During the 1870s, collection of the transit tax on opium in Xiamen was farmed to a Chinese syndicate that guaranteed the circuit intendant a certain sum from a fixed number of chests per month, leaving a sizable profit from the surplus for the tax farmers.⁶² The Xiamen syndicate manipulated fees by charging lower tax rates on chests of foreign opium bound for Taiwan or locations in Fujian's interior, probably to encourage the expansion of the market.⁶³ To assure the continuation of their monopoly and to diminish the stigma attached to their business, the tax farmers were said to have contributed some of their profits to the local foundling home. Since they also were keenly interested in maintaining their lucrative trade, they also contributed funds to the circuit intendant for his personal use, as well as to the compradors of opium firms like Elles & Co. and Tait & Co. for useful intelligence on opium shipments.⁶⁴ By 1902, however, the Xiamen Chamber of Commerce

---

61. CWM/LMS, box 9 (China Correspondence, Fukien, 1908–9), folder 2, Joseland to Currie Martin, 4 Oct. 1909.
62. For the years 1872–78, the tax farmers at Xiamen took home about one-third of the taxes they collected each year.
63. According to the acting British consul at Xiamen, a chest of foreign opium bound for Xiamen was charged an average of $127.35 for the years 1875–78 inclusive, and a chest headed for the following locations paid the amount in parentheses: Huafeng ($118), Anxi ($105.93), Quanzhou ($102), Xianyou ($98.30), Longyan ($68.31), and Taiwan ($41.00).
64. PRO, FO 233/92, no. 6, Giles to Wade, 30 Oct. 1879.

noted that although merchants had previously managed the collection of taxes on domestic opium, the provincial government had recently dispatched a special official to take over those duties and was now receiving double the amount of revenue as it had under the old system.[65] This tradition of private tax farming had important ramifications during the subsequent opium suppression campaign.

Xiamen had a mixed record regarding the campaign itself. The city was the administrative headquarters of the Xing(hua)-Quan(zhou)-Yong(chun) circuit, but by March 1907, the British consul knew of only one anti-opium proclamation that had been issued in the entire jurisdiction—one posted by the Jinjiang county magistrate in the city of Quanzhou.[66] According to the consul, "No steps whatsoever have yet been taken by the Chinese authorities at this port [Xiamen] to check the use of opium."[67] However, as soon as the circuit intendant at Fuzhou dispatched investigators to Xiamen, his counterpart in Xiamen called for the closure of all opium dens by 20 July 1907 (several months after it was accomplished in Fuzhou).[68] Apparently, however, minimal efforts were expended on this task. It is unclear how many of Xiamen's dens were shut down at this point; not until 1908, when elite reformers plunged into the task of opium suppression, were the opium dens truly shut down. In any case, their closure did not eliminate the public sale and consumption of opium. Many opium dens in Xiamen simply purchased a license and reopened legally as shops selling the prepared drug. By 1911, the number of licensed opium shops had been almost halved, from 125 to 65, and demand obviously continued.[69]

The Anti-Opium Society branch in Xiamen was founded two years after the headquarters in Fuzhou, and from the outset it was plagued by unstable leadership.[70] The group elected a new president each year, and the unique stature and symbolism that Lin Bingzhang's presidency lent the Fuzhou

---

65. Lin Man-houng, "Qingmo shehui liuxing yapian yanjiu," pp. 583–85.
66. PRO, FO 228/2415, doc. 76, Amoy to Jordan, 13 Mar. 1907.
67. PRO, FO 228/2415, doc. 75, Amoy to Jordan, 5 Mar. 1907, and doc. 76, 13 Mar. 1907.
68. USDS (1906–10), reel 104, no. 774/113–14, Paddock to Rockhill, 24 July 1907.
69. There were twelve opium dens in the International Settlement of Gulangyu, and they were not permanently shut down until March 1910 (IMC, *Decennial Reports, Amoy, 1902–1911*, p. 103).
70. The information in the following section on the Xiamen Anti-Opium Society before 1911 is derived from a lengthy report from Charles Brissel, American vice consul at Xiamen, USDS (1910–29), 893.114, reel 113, enclosure in Xiamen to Secy. of State, 20 July 1911. Brissel also enclosed a translation of the Xiamen Anti-Opium Society's regulations.

headquarters eluded the Xiamen branch. In Xiamen, the first president of the association was Yang Jingwen, a graduate of the Fuzhou Normal School. Yang was succeeded by Huang Tingyuan, a dentist by trade, and in 1910 Lin Zikeng took over. However, Lin was absent for most of his term, and his temporary replacement, Shi Shiji, was implicated in a scandal concerning the farming of the prepared opium tax in Xiamen. The Xiamen Anti-Opium Society then elected Lin Lucun as its leader in 1911. Lin also served as one of the three Provincial Assembly representatives from Xiamen, and a trip abroad resulted in his replacement by Vice President Chen Bingzhang. The society's next president resigned for unknown reasons shortly after his election. In general, then, the leaders of the Xiamen society were not from the same social strata as their counterparts in Fuzhou, whose considerable prestige lent so much weight to their initial reform efforts. Most of the leaders of the Xiamen branch were dedicated reformers, but their many commitments and interests apparently diminished the amount of time they could devote to the society, and this instability diminished the stature of the Xiamen branch.

Funding for the Xiamen Anti-Opium Society initially was provided by the license fees paid by prepared opium shops and dealers. In September 1910, however, the subprefect of Xiamen imposed a tax on prepared opium, and the collection of that tax was farmed out to a yamen runner. The monthly fee paid by the tax farmer was divided among the Anti-Opium Society in Xiamen City (30 percent), the society's branches in the countryside (26 percent), and the police department and schools of Xiamen (22 percent each). Former Anti-Opium Society President Shi Shiji was discovered to have influenced the tax farmer, and the scandal reflected poorly on the perceived integrity of the society.

In May 1910, the Xiamen Association was embarrassed by another scandal during the visit of Lin Bingzhang in his capacity as ex-president of the Fuzhou Anti-Opium Society and de facto leader of the unofficial wing of the provincial campaign. Apparently, Guo Daozhi, the Xiamen circuit intendant, requested that the entire anti-opium campaign in Xiamen be suspended because of difficulties in enforcement. Lin reported Guo Daozhi's comments to Beijing, and Guo was fired. Later that year, Chen Peikun, one of Lin's successors as head of the Fuzhou Anti-Opium Society, also visited Xiamen to lend moral support to his counterparts in the southeast.

After its slow start, however, the Xiamen Anti-Opium Society took an active and effective role in opium suppression until the outbreak of the

Revolution of 1911. The licensing and registration schemes it set up were quite similar to those instituted in Fuzhou. By 1911, the Xiamen Anti-Opium Society boasted 340 members and was divided into a number of departments, the most active of which were the departments for detection and lecturing. The detection department consisted of 31 men who were charged with ferreting out and investigating violations of the opium restrictions; the 21 members of the lecture department specialized in public education.

From the outset, the society operated a special hospital devoted to the cure of opium dependence. The 50-bed facility admitted smokers for a twenty-day treatment regimen, and each patient was responsible for paying for his or her own food and medicine. Fines collected by the society's detectives were used to defray the cost of treating impoverished smokers. Initially underused, the hospital treated about 200 smokers in 1908, double that number in 1909, and approximately 600 in 1910.

In sum, the commercial culture of Xiamen generated an anti-opium society with less prestige and more opportunities for corruption than the more public-service-oriented reformers in Fuzhou. Not only were the leaders of the society of a lesser stature than those in Fuzhou, but they also confronted a population with a tradition of resisting government intrusion or profiting from it by a system of tax farming.

YONGCHUN SUBPREFECTURE

Unlike the coastal prefectures of Quanzhou and Zhangzhou to the south, local officials and elites in inland Yongchun did not have to contend with the problem of poppy cultivation. The sale and consumption of opium, however, had reached enormous proportions by 1906, and American missionaries lamented that although some smokers sought cures, opium abuse was a serious social problem that had not been cured by taxation. According to Rev. Harry G. Dildine, a member of the Methodist Episcopal Church (MEC) residing in Yongchun in 1908, "The increase of the price of the article is tending thus far rather to impoverish the consumers than to reduce their number or the amount of the drug used. So far officialdom has shown itself too weak and the zeal of the reform societies too easily smothered to bring any real relief from this plague."[71]

---

71. MEC *Annual Report*, 1908, p. 162.

By the end of 1910, the progress of the opium suppression campaign in Yongchun was apparently still lackluster at best. One British missionary wrote:

In regard to the anti-opium movement I'm afraid it is pretty much a dead letter here [in Yongchun City]. Mr. Chin [presumably the local magistrate] issued proclamations, but I heard that tho [sic] he had forbidden the use of opium, he was issuing as many licenses to sell it as usual. I called on the secretary of the Salt Mandarin the other day, I found him with all the appliances for smoking opium on his bed. In the country . . . I asked if proclamations forbidding the smoking of opium had been posted up. The answer I got in both places was the same—not one had been seen. In both places, quite small villages, there were several opium shops. No opium is grown in this district, I believe: it is all imported.

The same missionary observer noted that the only evidence he saw of the New Policy reforms in that area was increased respect for foreigners and Christianity, the formation of a Yongchun City police force, and disappearance of a few queues.[72] The mountainous terrain, which isolated villages and encouraged banditry, may have adversely affected enforcement of opium restrictions. Why the local anti-opium society was ineffective is not clear.

Opium Suppression in the Southwest

The southwest region contained the coastal prefecture of Zhangzhou as well as Tingzhou prefecture and Longyan subprefecture, both of which were mountainous, remote regions. The Provincial Assembly gave this region until February 1913 to eliminate opium, a deadline that probably reflected the assembly's pessimism about the possibility of success and the difficulties of monitoring the campaign in this isolated area. The coastal regions and commercial city of Zhangzhou were the source of most of this area's domestic poppy crop, although Tingzhou, a sprawling prefecture with an area of over 22,000 square miles and a population of approximately two million, dominated this region geographically. The Tingzhou region borders Guangdong province to the south and the Wuyi Mountains separate Tingzhou from Jiangxi province to the west, although a pass led directly to Huichang county in Jiangxi. Most of Tingzhou's inhabitants resided in rural villages,

---

72. PCE/FMC, box 10 (S. Fukien, General Correspondence, 1910–19), file 1, Thompson to Dale, 22 Dec. 1910.

Map. 4.4 Southwestern Region

and large towns were scarce. Unlike the coastal areas of the region, farmers in the southwest usually managed to coax only one crop per year from the hilly, inhospitable terrain.[73] In this region, local elites, often serving as educators, took the lead in establishing branches of the Anti-Opium Society, although in many counties, there was little activism of any sort. Most of the campaign-related activity took place in the seats of the county and prefectural administration, and it is quite likely that only minimal attempts to enforce opium suppression were made in the outlying villages before 1911.

---

73. LMS, Box 8 (Incoming Correspondence, China—Fukien, 1904–7), folder 3, Wasson to Cousins, Amoy, 6 June 1906.

ZHANGZHOU PREFECTURE

This coastal prefecture was plagued by a serious opium problem in the late Qing. For example, in the township of Shima, in Longxi county just southeast of Zhangzhou city, several firms specialized in imported opium, and nearly 100 opium dens were said to have served the estimated 20,000 adult male residents. One Chinese account noted that government inspectors insisted on a pipe before setting down to work, and the author lamented that those who ran the opium shops and dens were often as captive to the drug's appeal as their customers. Over time, "local ruffians and hooligans not only smoked or ate opium but also bought and sold it, eventually seizing a monopoly [on the trade in Shima]."[74] The Longxi magistrate, who had jurisdiction over Zhangzhou City, issued a strong proclamation against opium smoking but failed to specify measures to achieve that goal.[75] Unfortunately, as the anti-opium campaign gained momentum in much of the southeast, a huge typhoon-driven flood hit the city of Zhangzhou in October 1908, and opium and other reforms were forgotten for a time as officials and residents struggled to repair the damage and defend themselves against an epidemic of banditry.[76]

Just north of Zhangzhou city, in Changtai county, a branch of the Anti-Opium Society was established in 1907. Under its leadership, opium dens were shut down, and opium shops were licensed or closed. The only available account of the suppression campaign in Changtai expresses serious misgivings about the effectiveness of the society, however, claiming that what appeared to be progress was simply the transformation of an open trade in opium into an underground commerce. The author also states that the loss in opium tax revenue was countered by a hike in the tax on rationed opium paste, a practice that presumably penalized those trying to quit smoking.[77]

LONGYAN SUBPREFECTURE

According to the limited information available, opium reform efforts in Longyan were spearheaded by local elites before 1911 but fell under the control of the state after the revolution. Chen Yi, the principal of the subprefec-

---

74. Lin Wenji, "Jiefang qian de Shima 'san hai,'" pp. 60–62.
75. PRO, 228/2415, doc. 75, Amoy to Jordan, 13 Mar. 1907.
76. CWM/LMS, box 9 (China Correspondence, Fukien, 1908–9), folder 1, Fahmy and Hutchinson to Cousins, 19 Oct. 1908, and Hutchinson to Cousins, 25 Oct. 1908.
77. "Yapian dui Changtai renmin de huohai," pp. 100–101.

tural school, founded a branch of the Anti-Opium Society in the administrative seat in 1907. Under his guidance, the group moved to shut down opium dens in Longyan City and its outskirts and prohibited the sale and cultivation of opium. Longyan did not produce much poppy, and the amount that was grown was greatly diminished before the Revolution of 1911. Unlike many other urban areas, the crusade in Longyan against opium smoking was not as successful as its prohibition on poppy cultivation, probably due to the minuscule size of the local poppy harvest and the limited scale of suppression efforts.[78]

TINGZHOU PREFECTURE

Even this remote and impoverished region could avoid neither the opium problem nor the reach of the anti-opium campaign. According to Chinese and western observers, the campaign hit a number of significant obstacles in Tingzhou, most notably the lack of cooperation between local elites and officials and a dearth of funds. Western reports are more optimistic than the Chinese, however, probably because Tingzhou was known among foreign missionaries for the exceptional friendliness of the local officials. The resident members of the LMS were quite involved in the region's anti-opium campaign.

Tingzhou's opium economy was extensive and entrenched. According to one member of the LMS who visited the city of Tingzhou in 1906, "Opium smoking and gambling are very prevalent—more than in the Amoy [Xiamen] region." Representatives of the Fuzhou headquarters of the Anti-Opium Society who arrived on an inspection tour in 1908 observed public smoking in every district they visited.[79] Investigators either saw or heard of opium-smoking policemen, teachers, laborers, and businessmen, and in many towns and villages, opium dens publicly carried on their forbidden commerce. Opium cultivation was concentrated in the northern county of Guihua—where one-third of the county was alleged to have been planted in poppies, and a number of opium dens peddled the local product[80]—and Liancheng

---

78. Li Hanzhou, "Longyan jianyan shihua," p. 102.
79. The lengthy report filed by the investigators and published in *The Quarterly* discusses the progress of the campaign in almost every county of the prefecture; see *The Quarterly* 4 (1908), report (*baogao*) section, pp. 1–5.
80. According to this source, villagers often hired people from nearby Jiangxi province to plant the poppies. The reason is unknown (ibid., p. 1).

county (in the center of the prefecture). Society investigators estimated that poppies bloomed in close to half of the fields in Liancheng and noted disparagingly that the lazy inhabitants there grew opium as a living, rather than a sideline. Although poppy farming was very labor intensive, the remark implied that indolence was defined by the absence of any labor deemed beneficial to society. In addition, the number of opium dens in Liancheng's urban areas were said to be beyond counting.[81]

Officials and reformist elites in Tingzhou attempted to address the serious opium problem during the suppression campaign, with mixed success. At the time of the Anti-Opium Society investigation in 1908, close to a year after the closure of virtually all of Fuzhou's opium dens, many counties in Tingzhou had not yet begun this first step in the campaign. In some counties the local administration was corrupt, and in others popular resistance was such that the suppression campaign stalled completely. In Wuping, for example, local residents were extremely belligerent and were even said to have insulted and beaten local officials who sought to enforce the ban on opium smoking.[82]

The treatment of opium addiction was a high priority for the Anti-Opium Society, and as its investigators moved through the prefecture, they attempted to raise money for medicine by addressing local officials and literati and soliciting funds from local companies. In Tingzhou City, the poverty of both residents and the local administration may have encouraged close cooperation between officials and foreign missionaries in the battle against addiction. Local authorities asked LMS physician C. E. Blair if the mission hospital would serve as an official opium refuge, and despite rumors that the foreign doctors would mutilate Chinese patients, dozens of smokers responded to an official proclamation encouraging them to check in at the "Gospel Hospital." Evidently, local elites provided funds to feed patients too poor to do so themselves.[83]

Of great concern to the society's investigators was the total absence of branches of the Anti-Opium Society in several counties and the scandalous incompetence or corruption of other branches. Guihua county lacked a branch allegedly because local elites were unable to forge a connection with

---

81. Ibid., pp. 2–3.
82. Ibid., pp. 1–5.
83. CWM/LMS, box 8 (Incoming Correspondence, China-Fukien, 1904–7), folder 3, Wasson to Cousins, 6 June 1906; box 10 (China Correspondence—Fukien, 1910–12), folder 2, Blair to Martin, 20 Apr. 1911 and 6 May 1911.

local authorities, who were profiting from the illegal operation of opium dens.[84] Other counties claimed to have branch societies, but in one case, the inspectors arrived to find that every member of the branch had mysteriously left. In Xixiang, the local branch society claimed to have staged one public pipe burning and sent 52 smokers to a smoking cessation clinic, but the inspection team visit found all but one member out on sick leave. This society apparently changed the location of its headquarters constantly, and the list of registered members did not jibe with the situation that confronted the inspectors. In several other areas, the inspectors gathered local elites, usually at schools, and urged them to donate enough money to establish a branch society. In areas where local elites were uninterested in the campaign, the society representatives urged officials to fund branch societies by increasing the taxes on opium. The latter approach apparently was not well received.[85] Eliminating the cultivation of poppies was also a major concern of the inspectors, but they realized that this step could be undertaken only by the local military.

Although enthusiasm for the campaign obviously was not universal, the inspectors did find some praiseworthy individuals and developments. Even Tingzhou prefecture boasted several active branches of the society that had staged bonfires of confiscated opium and smoking equipment, taken action to close opium dens and opium shops, and opened treatment centers. Some proprietors of opium dens resisted the campaign by secretly relocating their businesses, but the report lauds local society members for their successful pursuit and arrest of these men.[86] However, as the Provincial Assembly's deadline presumed, the campaign was far from over in Tingzhou when the Qing dynasty fell. One British missionary estimated that at the time of the Revolution of 1911, thousands of smokers still resided in Tingzhou City alone.[87]

The report of the Anti-Opium Society inspection team report not only highlighted the depth of Tingzhou's opium problem in 1908 but also clearly spelled out the leadership role the Fuzhou headquarters of the society at-

---

84. *The Quarterly* 4 (1908), report (*baogao*) section, p. 1.
85. Ibid., p. 3.
86. *The Quarterly* 4 (1908), report (*baogao*) section.
87. He claimed that 7,000–9,000 smokers resided in Tingzhou (PRO, FO 228/2454, doc. 7, Letter from Blair, 13 Apr. 1913). However, that figure seems grossly inflated, given that the population of Tingzhou in 1900 was estimated at only 11,000 (Li Guoqi, "Qingmo Minchu Min-Zhe diqu renkou liudong yu dushihua," pp. 512–13).

tempted to assume. Society branches may have operated autonomously on a day-to-day basis, but they were expected to conform to certain standards and timetables, and it was the job of the headquarters to monitor, exhort, and reprimand each branch. The report also revealed a strong belief on the part of the inspectors that only elite activism could bring success in the campaign against opium. Areas with less than stellar compliance were always characterized as lacking in elite enthusiasm. Despite the good intentions of the inspection team, their visit to Tingzhou illustrated the difficulties of enforcing the campaign so far from the provincial administrative headquarters in Fuzhou. Aside from threats and inspiring oratory, the inspectors could only register their frustration and dismay.

Glimpses of Reform Across the Province

Once the analytical gaze shifts from the city of Fuzhou to the rest of Fujian, the landscape of provincial opium reform becomes more varied and less defined. The chronology and the basic content of the campaign were determined and monitored in large part by Beijing and Fuzhou, but the particular contours of the opium economy in each county and prefecture of Fujian reflected the physical and socioeconomic geography of each locality. More specifically, the presence of a domestic poppy crop, strong clan organizations, and poverty, as well as distance from local authorities and access to water transport tended to contribute to a more deeply entrenched opium problem. Eliminating those factors required competent local officials, motivated elite reformers, reliable sources of revenue, and a cooperative populace.

The rhythm of opium reform throughout Fujian moved to the beat hammered out by the Qing state in Beijing and Fuzhou. When the state ordered the eradication of opium consumption, sales, and cultivation, local officials acknowledged the call, and many made concerted efforts to enforce the new restrictions. When the state set deadlines, they became goals for the entire province. And when the state sanctioned unofficial elite-led reform groups to work alongside the official bureaucracy, reformers emerged from the ranks of local progressive elites to spearhead the campaign. None of the extraordinary powers acquired by the branches of the Fujian Anti-Opium Society deviated from the original guidelines laid out in a number of edicts from Beijing. Only when the state called for an end to opium cultivation did the campaign falter.

Despite the variety of ways in which the opium campaign unfolded across Fujian, some basic patterns did emerge. The clustering of officials and other reformist elites in Fuzhou meant that the campaign was most effective and most extensive in that prefecture, and surrounding areas were affected by the progress and the methods of the campaign in the capital.[88] There also was a clear distinction between the conduct of the campaign in the poppy-growing regions of the east and the poppy-free regions of the west. For the most part, cooperation between reformist elites and local officials was the hallmark of successful opium suppression. This was particularly the case in cities, where the elimination of opium consumption was the primary focus of the campaign. Suppression measures in areas with little poppy cultivation were more frequently initiated and enforced by non-official elite reform groups, although often with the active support (and sometimes under the strong leadership) of the local authorities. In poppy-growing regions, however, the burden of opium suppression tended to fall more heavily on the shoulders of local officials, who presumably were able to draw on their official authority and the power of provincial military forces, if necessary. Many of Fujian's most infamous poppy-growing regions were also located in areas of the southeast notorious for clan feuding, and perhaps only an impartial official could attempt to implement reforms that affected the clans involved in the local opium economy. It also is possible that rural elites in these areas were concerned more with the business of owning (and profiting from) the land on which profitable poppy crops were grown than with eliminating this source of income.

Within each region, the targets of the campaign and the focus of reformers and local officials were essentially the same. In general, the closing of opium dens and shops was the first, and apparently the easiest, stage of the campaign. This measure brought quick and visible results and seemed to elicit more accolades than protests. Opium dens were notorious as havens of vice, particularly for the lower classes, and their closure generally was perceived as a public service. Eliminating opium smoking among individuals in their own homes and ridding the province of poppy cultivation were lengthier, more difficult tasks with more potential to stir up public resentment. Significantly, in commercial centers such as Funing and Xiamen, the elimination of the importation, distribution, and sale of opium proceeded less

---

88. The fact that documentation for this region is unusually rich may skew this chapter, however.

rapidly than in areas closer to Fuzhou. The elimination of poppy cultivation generally was the most contentious element of the campaign, and it was largely the responsibility of local officials, although the Anti-Opium Society often monitored local opium fields and reported violations.

As the campaign spread throughout the province, so did a network of branches of the Fujian Anti-Opium Society. Although the symbolic predominance and financial strength of the Fuzhou headquarters was well established, the chain of command was tenuous at best. The Fuzhou headquarters supposedly established the basic rules and organization to be adopted by all its branches. It claimed responsibility for monitoring, encouraging (morally and with small cash grants), and reprimanding branch societies, but these were voluntary groups that had little incentive beyond their own altruism, nationalism, or desire for power to motivate them. The leaders of the society were unable to force local elites to establish or maintain active branch societies, and headquarters was often reduced to little more than hand-wringing and publicizing particularly egregious violations of society rules or ethics. The power of reformist elites to regulate local society that was so striking in Fuzhou and in several surrounding counties diminished or disappeared in areas where the stature and wealth of local reformers were unexceptional and provincial oversight was minimal. Branch societies, denied the luxury of the sizable government subsidy enjoyed by the society headquarters, had to rely on other means of financing their efforts, many of which compromised their integrity and influence.

Despite the prominent role played by the headquarters and many branches of the Anti-Opium Society, that group did not have a monopoly on anti-opium sentiment. In areas with weak or nonexistent branch societies, reformers formed other organizations to combat the opium problem or joined existing groups that incorporated opium suppression into their agenda. The crusade against opium smoking often was combined with opposition to other vices, most notably gambling and prostitution. Not coincidentally, all three activities often took place in the same facilities.

Outside Fuzhou, the opium suppression campaign still tended to unfold in an emerging public space that could be found in cities and towns all over Fujian. Most of the reformers in the province came from local elites involved in the New Policies, a number of whom were key players in the new Provincial Assembly. However, the very public nature of the anti-opium campaign in Fuzhou was not always replicated in the rest of the province. The large ceremonies and processions that punctuated the Fuzhou campaign and also took place in the nearby counties of Lianjiang and Gutian did not seem to have occurred in regions further away from the capital. In remote Tingzhou, for example, the local branch of the Anti-Opium Society focused on treating addiction and raising money from wealthy elites and other reform-minded individuals. The absence of elaborate public ceremonies and processions could have been more of a reflection of local poverty than a lack of enthusiasm for the campaign. However, it could be argued plausibly that public processions also were less likely to occur in localities where popular and state support for the campaign was less palpable. A focus on eliminating cultivation was more conducive to resentment and resistance than public celebration. A less pervasive foreign presence in more remote areas may also have convinced local elites and officials that without the opportunity to impress the British with their progress, large spectacles might not be as important an investment of scarce resources.

In light of the complexity and depth of Fujian's opium economy, the relative absence of large-scale violence or organized popular resistance to the campaign throughout the province is intriguing. The gradual, relatively humanitarian approach to weaning smokers from their habit, along with the various licensing and rationing schemes, probably tempered resistance among smokers. Many operators of opium shops were able to purchase licenses to sell opium, and many were allowed time to change their line of work. However, small-scale resistance by smokers and owners of opium shops and dens required constant vigilance.

Resistance was more likely from poppy farmers whose livelihood depended on the maintenance of the provincial opium economy, as Lucien Bianco astutely points out.[89] However, even in Fujian's most productive opium-producing districts in the southeast, many of which were also the sites of endemic clan violence, violent confrontations over the suppression policy were minimal. The relatively peaceful response with which many poppy farmers in the southeast greeted the new prohibitions may have been less an indication of popular support for the campaign than the failure of the restrictions to affect many of Fujian's poppy-growing hot spots significantly. It appears that the inhabitants of opium-producing districts were well aware of the campaign, but although progress against poppy cultivation in some areas was impressive, others were virtually untouched by the restrictions

---

89. Bianco, "Rural Tax Resistance," pp. 27–28.

prior to 1911. Only when intrepid magistrates decided to prohibit opium cultivation forcibly did resistance become violent. Administrative incompetence or fear of violence undoubtedly prevented many other officials from actively pursuing opium reform. Clearly, the progress of the campaign in much of Fujian on the eve of the Revolution of 1911 was not as rosy as it appeared to be in Fuzhou.

Foreign missionaries and their converts remained deeply involved in opium suppression throughout the province, although this impression is undoubtedly somewhat source-driven. Missionaries and Chinese Christians provided extensive testimony on the progress of opium reform throughout Fujian, but they sometimes emphasized their own contributions and either obscured or belittled the role of elite reformers or officials hostile to Christians. In rare cases, foreigners aided in the enforcement of opium restrictions, but their work generally was limited to the medical treatment of smokers, the sponsorship of lobbying groups, and the distribution of anti-opium literature. They also were alternatively lauded and resented for their monitoring of the campaign for foreign governments, especially the British. However, missionary hospitals, although few in number (a dozen or so in Fujian during the late Qing), often had a disproportionately large impact on reform-minded Chinese, and Chinese physicians seeking to treat opium smokers sometimes copied western medical techniques. Missionary schools also produced many enthusiastic, reform-minded students of a variety of ages.

The anti-opium campaign outside Fuzhou was dynamic and comprehensive, relied on guidance from the Chinese state in Fuzhou and Beijing, and was complemented by a network of branches of the Fujian Anti-Opium Society. By 1911, the campaign had made considerable progress toward achieving its goals, especially in eliminating opium dens and distributing licenses for smokers and opium shops. The reduction in the amount of land planted in poppies had begun but was far from complete. On the eve of the revolution, reformers in Fujian were optimistic about the possibility of dismantling its multifaceted opium economy in the near future. But revolution brought unanticipated setbacks, and the new agreement with the British further altered the relationship between the state and elite-led reform groups. When the state collapsed, so did the official and unofficial mechanisms for opium reform; when it revived, having reconstituted itself as a republic with a renewed focus on eliminating poppy cultivation, strategies all over Fujian had to change too.

FIVE

Tartars, Treaties, and Turmoil

In the spring of 1908, the anti-opium campaign was in full swing in Fuzhou, and if those in violation of the restrictions were on edge, the Banner community garrisoned in the provincial capital was particularly jittery. Their commanding officer, a Manchu named Pushou, had adopted the suppression campaign as his own crusade. According to one American missionary, Pushou

> has made quite a stir in the city by his modern methods of investigation. He goes out on the street or to the soldiers' barracks or out to the forts on the river in citizen's clothes and often they don't know who he is until he has seen all that he cares to. His prosecution of those in his office, and those under his care is no less drastic. This past week he capped the climax by having all his petty officials locked up, and he is going to keep them under guard for three months so as to find out for sure who of them smoke, and make them get cured.[1]

However, the vigor with which Pushou and other high-ranking officials pursued opium suppression and other reforms was no match for the momentum of revolutionary change that swept through China in 1911. The revolution that toppled the Qing dynasty and dissolved China's ancient system of imperial governance pushed even reform-minded Manchus out of the political arena. For Pushou and several other Manchu officials in Fujian, the expulsion was more than political. Pushou's leading role in organizing a futile Manchu resistance that some termed valiant and others needlessly stubborn cost him his life. He was preceded in death by his superior and fellow Man-

---

1. Newell Papers, American Board Mission, Foochow, China, folder 2, letter from George Newell, 7 Apr. 1908.

chu, Min-Zhe Governor-General Songshou, who chose to commit suicide rather than to risk capture.

Pushed to the brink of destruction by financial weakness, imperialist pressure, and internal rebellions, the Qing dynasty in its final years instituted the New Policies, a comprehensive series of reforms designed to rework both the form and substance of the Chinese state. One characteristic of that state that the Qing court had neither the ability nor the inclination to change, however, was its own Manchu heritage, a factor that became increasingly relevant and inflammatory as Chinese nationalist sentiment coalesced against foreign imperialism. By the first years of the twentieth century, the concept of what was foreign came to include the Manchu dynasty that had proven itself too weak to prevent violations of Chinese sovereignty by Japan and the western powers. Those incursions were precipitated in several cases by diplomatic and military confrontations over opium. In addition, the inability of the Qing state to lead China out of the broader socioeconomic morass generated in part by widespread dependence on the drug challenged its legitimacy at home and abroad. Eliminating opium would not only force a re-evaluation of the strength of the Chinese state on an international level but also prove within Chinese borders that the Qing government was devoted to the salvation of a nation in which the ruling Manchus constituted only a tiny ethnic minority.

The year 1911 brought profound change to the landscape of Fujianese opium reform, as well as to Chinese politics in general. The erosion of the public sphere that had begun in 1910 continued in 1911 with the issuance of a new set of provincial regulations for opium reform. These guidelines established a new distribution of power and responsibility that favored the official bureaucracy over the Anti-Opium Society. At the same time, the pace and conduct of reform were further altered by the renegotiation of the agreement with the British just months before the revolution. The new agreement diminished the role of the society and other unofficial reform groups and generated new strategies and priorities that ultimately hardened the boundaries around the public space in which Republican opium reform took place.

The revolution did not reach Fujian until the late fall of 1911, and in the interim, the momentum of the anti-opium campaign accelerated to the point that the British merchants and authorities feared that Chinese progress would outrun the more leisurely pace of the mandated ten-year grace period. Of intense interest and concern to British observers was the tendency of local elites and officials in some areas to use their considerable—and often unwritten—powers to halt or hinder the trade in foreign opium. British complaints had to be addressed because the Qing government recognized that the agreement with the British was an unprecedented opportunity to secure international cooperation in the fight against opium. The central Chinese state was torn between the desire to eliminate the drug within its borders as quickly as possible (a goal that seemed to require provincial flexibility), and the knowledge that long-term victory over opium was impossible without cutting off the Indian trade on the terms offered by the British. In the context of a growing spirit of anti-imperialism among many progressive officials and elites, this Qing tie to British interests was enough to test the loyalty of many reformers. That loyalty was further frayed by a revived resentment of the ethnic background of China's ruling dynasty.

Ethnic considerations clearly guided the content of some of the New Policies, several of which were designed to eliminate the ethnic preferences and legal barriers that fueled Manchu separatism and generated anti-Manchu discrimination.[2] In other cases, the highest levels of the imperial court seemed oblivious to the growing depth of Han hostility. In 1911 for example, Zaifeng, Manchu regent for the young Xuantong emperor, appointed what derisively came to be known as the "imperial kinsmen's cabinet" to oversee the shift to constitutional government. The Manchu-dominated group infuriated many reformers.[3] When it came to opium reform, restrictions on the cultivation, consumption, and distribution of the drug applied to all strata of Chinese society, but cleansing Banner ranks of opium addiction appeared to be a dynastic priority. The emphasis was understandable, given the notoriety of the role opium had allegedly played in sapping the military readiness and morale of Banner troops. Even as the Banners were phased out in favor of the New Army, the Qing court evinced a marked determination to rehabilitate its fellow Manchus and former protectors in Beijing as well as in provincial garrisons such as Fuzhou and transform them into useful citizens of what was to be a new China under a constitutional Qing monarchy.

---

2. For example, in 1902, Empress Dowager Cixi issued an edict permitting Han-Manchu intermarriage and soon moved to eliminate the status of the northeast as an exclusively Manchu preserve. However, according to Edward Rhoads (*Manchus & Han*, pp. 73–80), these and other measures were often ignored because of continuing ethnic prejudice or simply put the state seal of approval on measures that were already in effect.

3. Ibid., pp. 167–70.

Tartars: Opium and the Fuzhou Banner Garrison

The substance of opium reform within the Fuzhou Banner garrison differed little from the campaign among the city's other residents; however, in the context of the broader discussion of the public sphere, the opium suppression campaign within the Banner forces was distinctly less public than the same process among the largely civilian population outside the garrison. Unofficial elite-led reform groups occasionally discovered and informed on violators of the opium restrictions among garrison dwellers, but no Manchu opium reform groups emerged from or operated within the garrison itself. Manchu opium smokers were examined, treated, and monitored by the commander of the Banner forces. This constituted a Manchu arm of the suppression campaign more segregated from the rest of Fuzhou than the garrison itself. The Qing state, on the national and provincial levels, was deeply concerned with ridding the Fuzhou Bannermen and their families of opium addiction, and the limited size of the garrison community enabled a more personal touch, just as ethnic considerations seemed to demand it.

Most of the Manchu voices heard in this chapter are those of men who served in the Fuzhou Banner garrison during the opium suppression campaign or had friends who did—from Fujian's most prominent Manchu officials to ordinary soldiers. Among the materials consulted here are memorials that were sent to Beijing during the heyday of the suppression campaign in 1908–9 by Pushou, who was also the highest-ranking military officer in Fujian. The memorials paint a picture of a frustrated but obedient official with a sincere desire to address the opium problem among the Manchu military population of Fuzhou. The measures he proposed sometimes clashed with the content and time frame of reform as set by the Qing court, but as a loyal Manchu, he naturally eschewed the revolutionary option chosen by many equally discouraged Han Chinese reformist officials. In addition, the minutiae contained in the memorials, including lengthy justifications for individual personnel decisions, reveal the degree to which the Qing state micromanaged the campaign within the Banner communities.[4]

---

4. Whether this indicated Qing determination to maintain a clear chain of command or simply reflected the smaller dimensions of the Banner communities is unclear. Songshou also sometimes reported individual infractions among civilian officials and gentry who were not Manchus.

Oral histories in the recently compiled *wenshi ziliao* series supplement these official sources. In particular, the recollections of Yi Tongfu, a former resident of the Fuzhou garrison who was eighteen years old when the Revolution of 1911 broke out, and Guo Gongmu, a Han educator with many Bannermen friends, have proved especially useful not only in fleshing out the size and organization of the Manchu community but also in reconstructing the lifestyle and sentiments within the Manchu quarter before, during, and after the revolution.[5] The publications and reports of the Anti-Opium Society, local Chinese authorities, and western diplomats and missionaries also touch on opium reform within the Manchu quarter.

A quick word about Manchu ethnicity and the Banner garrisons is in order at the outset. The work of Pamela Crossley, Mark Elliott, Evelyn Rawski, and others has cast serious doubt on notions of the ethnic purity of the Manchus and the Banner communities. That debate will not be revisited here.[6] What matters here is not how many garrison residents were in fact Manchu, but how public and official perceptions of them as ethnically distinct not only guided the conduct of the suppression campaign but also determined their fate in the chaotic days during and after the revolution.

OPIUM AND THE DECLINE OF THE FUZHOU BANNER GARRISON

The final years of the Qing dynasty saw the acceleration of the already precipitous economic and psychological decline of the Manchu Bannermen. A serious problem with opium abuse was but one manifestation of that decline. Manchu military readiness decayed further after the Taiping Rebellion, largely due to a depleted Qing treasury.[7] Increasingly irrelevant after the formation of the New Army and legally prohibited from engaging in com-

---

5. Yi Tongfu, "Xinhai geming qianhou Fuzhou Manzu qiying neiqing shilu." However, the compiler of this oral history notes that on occasion, Yi became confused about the sequence of events, especially when describing the unfolding of the Revolution of 1911 in Fuzhou. The interview was originally recorded in 1963 when Yi Tongfu was 70 years old. Guo Gongmu's account, "Xinhai geming Fuzhou chuli baqi guanbing jingguo," is more systematic and is corroborated by other, more scholarly studies.

6. See Crossley, "Thinking About Ethnicity in Early Modern China"; Elliott, "Bannerman and Townsman"; Rawski, "Reenvisioning the Qing"; and Ho Ping-ti, "In Defense of Sinicization." Even the ethnic composition of the Hanjun, or Chinese-Martial Banner, was questionable.

7. Crossley, *Orphan Warriors*, pp. 138–39, 146–47.

merce, many Bannermen in urban garrisons barely subsisted on meager government pensions.[8] Some foreign observers reported a palpable increase in anti-Manchu sentiment among ethnic Chinese and noted that the tension appeared to be particularly high in garrison cities like Fuzhou, where Manchu troops and their dependents lived in a mostly segregated quarter of the town.[9]

The most salient characteristics of the Fuzhou Banner garrison at the end of the Qing were its physical isolation from rest of the city and its small size relative to the rest of the capital's population. According to one source, the Manchu enclave was located in the southeastern corner of Fuzhou, within the city walls, and could be entered only through its own gate.[10] Another source argues that the Fuzhou Manchu garrison was one of the few that was not walled off from the rest of the city.[11] Whether or not a gate separated the Manchu quarter from the rest of the city, legal and historical boundaries kept its residents geographically, financially, and occupationally distinct from their civilian counterparts.[12] Pushou's yamen was located within this quarter, and he lived and worked with the Bannermen and their families under his command.[13] The total Manchu population of Fuzhou is unknown, but they probably numbered between 40,000 and 50,000, including approximately 2,500 soldiers and their dependents.[14] This made the

---

8. Bannermen were allowed to work only as officials, soldiers, or farmers (Rhoads, *Manchus & Han*, p. 36).

9. USDS (1906–10), reel 171, enclosure 3 in no. 1518/77–80, "Racial Antagonism," in *North-China Daily News*, 23 Sept. 1907.

10. Guo Gongmu, "Xinhai geming Fuzhou chuli baqi guanbing jingguo," pp. 50–51.

11. Rhoads, *Manchus & Han*, p. 38.

12. One account states that the segregation of the Manchu quarter eased after the Opium War, when some Han families were allowed to relocate there and do business (Guo Gongmu, "Xinhai geming Fuzhou chuli baqi guanbing jingguo," p. 51).

13. Li Guoqi, *Zhongguo xiandaihua de quyu yanjiu*, pp. 15–16.

14. Yi Tongfu ("Xinhai geming qianhou Fuzhou Manzu qiying neiqing shilu," p. 1) recalls no more than 2,000 soldiers, but then says that each of the Eight Banners contained about 300 troops. He also says that the entire Manchu population numbered only 4,000, half of whom were soldiers. This seems unlikely. Guo Gongmu ("Xinhai geming Fuzhou chuli baqi guanbing jingguo," p. 51) states that when the Manchu presence was established in Fuzhou in the mid-seventeenth century, the garrison boasted about 3,000 soldiers and the Manchu community numbered between 40,000 and 50,000. Rhoads (*Manchus & Han*, p. 34) makes no estimate for the Fuzhou garrison specifically but states that the size of most garrisons was twenty times the number of active soldiers. The figure used here adopts that formula and assumes that approximately 2,500 men served as Banner soldiers at the time of the Revolution of 1911. It is unknown how many of these individuals lived within the Manchu quarter of Fuzhou and how many resided in the teeming suburbs.

Manchus a visible minority in a city of over 350,000.[15] Over the years, their segregation reinforced a strong sense of ethnic identity among the residents, despite the steady decline in the standard of living within the garrison and a futile attempt in 1865 by the Tongzhi emperor to force an end to ethnic segregation.[16]

Tensions between Han and Manchu in Fuzhou had existed since the bloody Qing takeover in the mid-seventeenth century, and the forcible claiming of a Manchu quarter within Fuzhou's walls. The mutual contempt intensified in the late Qing as the growing poverty of the Banner community became more apparent. The privileges granted to the Manchus, including their regular stipends and less arduous path to government service, continued despite their increasing irrelevance, and according to one account, idle Bannermen and their families often initiated confrontations with any Han Chinese who entered the Manchu quarter on business.[17] Over time, the physical isolation (compounded by cultural and linguistic differences),[18] the atmosphere of racial antagonism, and the occupational vacuum in which many of the Bannermen and their families existed proved the perfect breeding ground for opium smoking and addiction.[19]

The two Manchus who headed the province's civil and military bureaucracies led the opium suppression campaign in Fuzhou and the rest of the province. Songshou became governor-general of Fujian and Zhejiang provinces in 1907 and presided over the province's anti-opium campaign until his death in the Revolution of 1911. Songshou belonged to the Manchu Plain

---

15. That estimate of Fuzhou's total population was compiled in 1900 (Li Guoqi, "Qingmo Minchu Min-Zhe diqu renkou liudong yu dushihua," pp. 512–13).

16. Comprehensive reform of the Banner system was proposed at that time and again in 1898 but never seriously implemented (Rhoads, *Manchus & Han*, pp. 35–42, 63–67).

17. Guo Gongmu, "Xinhai geming Fuzhou quli baqi guanbing jingguo," pp. 51–52. Yi Tongfu ("Xinhai geming qianhou Fuzhou Manzu qiying neiqing shilu," p. 15) also claimed that a group of Han Chinese who lived near the garrison organized a small group to defend themselves against any Manchu aggression. These Han Chinese contemptuously referred to their Manchu neighbors as "the Banner burdens" (*qixia zi*), and the Bannermen responded by calling them "defeated burdens" (*pozi*). An alternative translation for *zi* in these expressions, "young animal" or "whelp," makes the epithets even more insulting.

18. Many Manchus did not speak Chinese fluently, and most dressed in a distinctive fashion. Manchu women's clothing and hairstyles were noticeable cultural markers (Rhoads, *Manchus & Han*, pp. 54–62; Guo Gongmu, "Xinhai geming Fuzhou quli baqi guanbing jingguo," pp. 51–52).

19. For a detailed analysis of the decline of the Banner forces, see Crossley, *Orphan Warriors*.

White Banner and served the Qing dynasty for over twenty years in a number of positions, both civilian and military.[20] Pushou was Manchu general (*jiangjun*) in charge of military operations for the entire province. He belonged to the Manchu Bordered Yellow Banner, was awarded the *juren* degree in 1894, and served the Banner forces in several capacities before he stepped into the vacancy left by Songshou's promotion to governor-general. Pushou was responsible for the opium suppression campaign within the Manchu quarter of Fuzhou. His brief biography in the *Draft History of the Qing Dynasty* (*Qingshi gao*) emphasizes Pushou's bravery and integrity and specifically praises his strict enforcement of opium restrictions.[21]

The perception was that opium addiction had weakened both the morale and the military prowess of the Banner troops in Fuzhou. By the advent of the suppression campaign, opium smoking had reached epidemic levels within the garrison, particularly among the lower ranks.[22] Pushou claimed that 60–70 percent of the soldiers (*ding*) smoked opium and noted in a memorial to the throne that at least thirteen high-level or expectant officers were "infected" by the habit. As he described it, the impact of this situation on the soldiers was devastating: "Their spirits are weakened. Their lives are difficult. Defense work has been neglected, and the connection [between all of this and the smoking of opium] is particularly strong."[23] Thus, in seeking to rehabilitate the Bannermen, the suppression campaign also called attention to the deprivation and malaise that characterized the Fuzhou Banner community. In the city local officials, unofficial reform groups, and the city's fledgling police force worked to stamp out unlicensed opium consumption and sales, and in rural districts the soldiers of the New Army were called on to enforce the prohibition against poppy cultivation. In contrast, the former vanguard of the mighty Qing military sat idle, targeted by Beijing for special attention during the campaign.

---

20. Zhao Erxun, *Qingshi gao*, 41: 12787. Apparently, Songshou entered the bureaucracy as a Manchu-language scribe after passing a fairly simple examination open only to Manchus (Rhoads, *Manchus & Han*, p. 44).

21. Zhao Erxun, *Qingshi gao*, 41: 12805. Zhao was a respected scholar and also a Manchu.

22. The Manchu Bannermen had been plagued by opium addiction since the early nineteenth century, and the problem fed upon their growing poverty and demoralization during the final years of the Qing dynasty; see Crossley, *Orphan Warriors*, pp. 4, 92–93, 100–102, 117, 176, 195. Also informative on the decline of the Manchu troops is Im, "The Rise and Decline of the Eight Banner Garrisons."

23. ZZGB 11, memorial from Pushou, endorsed 13 Sept. 1908, pp. 410–12.

Opium smoking was particularly virulent among those whose immune systems were already compromised. Pushou tended to place most of the blame for the "infection" on the environment surrounding his officers and soldiers. Evidently, the popular local explanation for the proliferation of opium use and abuse was the topography and tropical climate. "The province of Fujian is a coastal area that backs onto mountains, and this brings poisonous and pestilential miasmas," Pushou explained. "The populace recognized that opium could be used to get rid of these poisonous vapors and so smoking increased accordingly." He noted that domestic poppies were harvested in the Fuzhou area, as well as in the nearby coastal prefectures of Zhangzhou and Quanzhou, and "since the price of [domestic] opium was cheap, this poison spread." Pushou was cognizant of social factors as well: he also attributed the extensive smoking to the fact that his men "live together with the populace," among whom opium smoking was a longstanding habit.[24] Given the segregation of the Banner community, the charge is either disingenuous or indicative of a greater degree of Manchu-Han interaction than most accounts describe.

At the same time that the anti-opium campaign and other late Qing reforms disrupted life within and surrounding the garrison, ethnic tensions in Fuzhou came to a head and life within the small Banner community must have felt more and more claustrophobic. Some of the same reform groups and progressive schools that spearheaded and supported the New Policies under Songshou's direction also nursed revolutionary sentiments with a distinctly racist tinge.[25] Other, more blatantly racist groups were organized secretly.[26] In addition, the same New Army that was busy uprooting poppies was also a hotbed of anti-Manchu sentiment in Fuzhou, a situation that became especially significant during the revolution, when officers in the New Army emerged as local revolutionary leaders. Many of the members of the Fujian branch of the New Army were Hunanese and were strongly influ-

---

24. Ibid., p. 410. It is unclear whether the opium smoked by the Banner community was domestic or imported, although the cheaper price of the domestic drug might have appealed to impoverished Bannermen.

25. See Dunch, *Fuzhou Protestants and the Making of a Modern China*, pp. 61–62; and Zou Lu, "Fujian guangfu," pp. 277–78. Also, Zheng Zuyin, a man who was said to harbor anti-Manchu sentiments, founded one of Fuzhou's foremost reform groups, the Society to Benefit the Hearer, in 1902; see Zheng Zuyin et al., *Fujian xinghai guangfu shiliao*, p. 3.

26. See, e.g., Zheng Zuyin et al., *Fujian xinghai guangfu shiliao*, pp. 7–9.

enced by the anti-Manchu ideas of the Tongmenghui.[27] So, although overt hostility toward the Manchus was of necessity muted before the revolution, ethnic tension seethed just under the surface.

THE SUPPRESSION CAMPAIGN IN THE BANNER GARRISON

The opium problem Pushou confronted and the manner in which he attempted to solve it reveal the tenuous nature of Manchu existence in late Qing Fujian and the ways in which the drug served as both cause and symptom of the decline of Manchu military strength and social significance. It also highlights the strength of state oversight in this small provincial enclave. The memorials cited below document how the desperate straits into which many Manchu Bannermen and their families had fallen by the late Qing hindered state-initiated reform efforts. The detailed supervision of the situation by the Qing state in Beijing and Fuzhou seemed to reinforce Manchu isolation by establishing a separate suppression apparatus for the Banner community. This strategy and its outcome were ironic, in light of the Qing attempt to use the anti-opium campaign to rehabilitate the Banner garrison and ease its integration into Chinese society.

Pushou was solely responsible for the conduct of the campaign among the Bannermen and their dependents, and he was either unwilling or unable to take advantage of the assistance offered by unofficial reform groups or the civilian police.[28] The exception was his handling of the suppression campaign among the Han naval squadron that fell under his jurisdiction but was stationed outside the city walls in Mawei, a port at the eastern end of Nantai Island. The distance of these troops from the smoking cessation clinic in the Manchu quarter—and perhaps their ethnicity—evidently made limited civilian oversight acceptable. Pushou reported that when he transmitted the regulations for opium prohibition to Mawei, he also selected and assigned officials and gentry to set up smoking cessation clinic(s) there.[29]

---

27. In fact, virtually all of the officers joined the Tongmenghui before 1911 (Zou Lu, "Fujian guangfu," pp. 277–80).

28. His actions were not remarkable, given the separate judicial and administrative mechanisms that military forces around the world have adopted, but in the case of the Bannermen, the continuation of ethnic segregation during the suppression campaign highlighted the tenuous position of the Banner community at the end of the Qing.

29. ZZGB 11, memorial from Pushou, endorsed 13 Sept. 1908, p. 410.

Within the Manchu quarter, the orders to eliminate opium consumption required the establishment of a reform mechanism that resembled its civilian counterpart, albeit far more limited in scope and size. Those orders originated in Beijing with the Anti-Opium Commission (Jinyan ju) and were transmitted to Pushou through the Board of War (Lujun bu). Pushou was to investigate and count opium smokers within Fujian's military, enroll violators in a treatment program, implement a scheme of rewards and punishments to encourage compliance with the regulations, and devise a system of post-treatment oversight.

As with the civilian population, opium suppression among the Bannermen began with a census, and some of this work was begun even before Pushou became Manchu General in early spring 1907. Former Manchu General Suishan and then–Acting Manchu General Songshou had initiated the campaign by ordering the colonels of each regiment (*xieling*) to investigate their subordinates and determine the extent of opium smoking in the ranks.[30] Pushou reported that some 341 men pledged to stop smoking as a result. However, upon taking office, he insisted on conducting follow-up examinations of those men and discovered that some had resumed their old habits. He also found that several regimental colonels and company commanders (*zuoling*) were still smoking, and that the prohibitions were enforced with varying degrees of ardor from Banner to Banner. Thus, his first priority was standardizing enforcement procedures and designing more effective investigation and treatment facilities. Much like the effort within the civilian population, the central state ordered that special attention and harsh punishment be directed at violators who were social exemplars, in this case, military officials. After all, agreed Pushou, "Officers are models. How can we forgive them?"[31]

Pushou lived and worked among the Bannermen, and his yamen in the Manchu quarter became the nerve center for his part of the anti-opium campaign.[32] The smoking cessation clinic he set up to the west of the yamen served as part police station and part clinic:

---

30. Translations of all Banner garrison titles follow those established by Brunnert and Hagelstrom, *Present Day Political Organization of China*, pp. 323–36.

31. ZZGB 11, memorial from Pushou, endorsed 17 Sept. 1908, pp. 410–12.

32. CMS Fuhkien Mission, Original Incoming, 1900–1934 (1906), no. 318, 1906. Circular letter by Miss M. I. Bennett, Fuzhou, 11 Sept. 1906.

The office was separated into two offices—one for officers and one for soldiers—and I can personally inspect [their operations]. All the officers beneath the rank of regimental colonel, as well as degree holders (*juren, gongsheng, shengyuan, jiansheng*), soldiers, porters, those who used to be addicted, and those whose situation is still under suspicion were ordered to enter an office to cease [smoking and have their behavior] examined. If this caused job vacancies, other officers were appointed to temporarily substitute. After their smoking ceases, they should be permitted to serve in their old positions.

Regulations have been set for the offices, and strict deadlines have been established. Pills [to wean smokers from the drug] are issued by the offices, and illnesses [that occur during treatment] are treated.[33]

First, each man was carefully searched for concealed opium. "Smoking implements and opium paste are noted and burned. . . . Clothing and other things that inmates are sent are inspected." Those who had to undergo treatment were kept at the clinic. "The time limit for the cessation of smoking is two months, with an additional month [reserved for post-treatment] examination. A public notice announced this, and rewards and punishments will be used to carry it out. If they are really able to stop using the pills, then they will be permitted to leave the clinic."[34]

Special steps were undertaken to implement reform among the members of the provincial navy, many of whom apparently were Han Chinese. The sailors were examined several times and split into three levels: the top-level designation was for those who had conquered their addiction; the middle was for those who had quit but had not yet recovered their previous strength and appearance; those who found themselves incapable of quitting were assigned to the lowest level. Those in the bottom level were to be fired and the Bannermen among them stripped of their hereditary status.[35]

Pushou was keenly aware of the need for continual vigilance when attacking the opium problem. In addition to clandestine personal investigations, Pushou indicated that he made daily trips to the officers' smoking cessation clinic to check on their progress. By the spring of 1909, he reported to the throne that 392 soldiers (including thirteen officers) had successfully undergone examinations and treatment.[36] In order to prevent relapses, Pushou

---

33. ZZGB 11, memorial from Pushou, endorsed 13 Sept. 1908, pp. 410–11.
34. Ibid.
35. ZZGB 20, memorial from Pushou, endorsed 19 May 1909, pp. 108–10.
36. Ibid., pp. 108–9.

demanded mandatory, monthly re-examinations in each Banner, and ordered the colonels of each regiment to conduct secret investigations among their men. Severe punishment was to be meted out to recidivists. Repeat offenders among the officers were reported directly to Beijing, and any officer who dared to conceal violations among his friends or family was to be punished along with the smoker.[37]

The Qing state meticulously monitored the progress of opium reform among the Manchu forces in Fuzhou, requiring, among other evidence, the regular submission of the memorials that are liberally cited here. In addition to a careful accounting of his suppression methods, Pushou evidently was deluged with opium-related edicts from Beijing, and the national anti-opium commissioner issued reminders that officers should submit the proper paperwork for each individual treated under their jurisdiction. Pushou replied that he would comply with the regulations, which compelled him to submit forms to the anti-opium commissioner, the Committee of Ministers (Huiyi zhengwu chu), the Board of War, and the Ministry of Interior.[38]

Judging from his memorials, Pushou approached the task of opium suppression with vigor, diligence, imagination, and a steadfast loyalty to Beijing, but the anti-opium campaign among the garrison residents encountered a number of obstacles. The most serious included insufficient time to treat those with longstanding addictions and a shortage of qualified permanent or temporary replacements for officers undergoing treatment. Recidivism, addiction among Banner dependents, and the ubiquitous temptation of foreign opium in the shops outside the Banner quarter also hindered suppression efforts. Furthermore, foreign diplomats and missionaries alleged that both Pushou and Songshou were or had been addicted to opium themselves, although in each case, the accusation appears in only one source and cannot be independently confirmed.[39]

One of Pushou's most frustrating obstacles was the lack of time and the seriousness of the problem in the small Manchu enclave, but his pleas to deviate from the schedule set by the central state usually were rejected.

---

37. ZZGB 11, memorial from Pushou, endorsed 13 Sept. 1908, pp. 411–12.

38. ZZGB 20, memorial from Pushou, endorsed 19 May 1909, p. 110.

39. Pushou's alleged addiction is discussed in a letter from George Newell dated 7 Apr. 1908 (Newell Papers, American Board Mission, Foochow, China, folder 2). French diplomats claimed that Songshou was a habitual opium smoker (MAE/Paris, NS 13, Bourgeois to Bapst, 17 Jan. 1908, pp. 15–23).

There is no good method for rehabilitation.... So, once [opium smokers] are fired, they wander around with no job. There is no way to encourage them, and they inevitably become self-indulgent.... The opium problem in the Fuzhou Manchu garrison has been around a long time and has resulted in a great disaster.... Since opium addiction cannot be eliminated in one day, it is naturally difficult to complete [the prohibition order] in time. This is truly a situation that I have heard with my own ears and seen with my own eyes.[40]

As early as the fall of 1908, Pushou begged the throne for permission to delay or even rescind the dismissal and punishment of several officers and soldiers. His sympathy was directed at those who had quit smoking but would still be on medication past the government-set deadlines, as well as those in whom he saw the potential for reform. "Several hundred people have already been punished and fired. Among them are those who are young and vigorous and who diligently did their duties and military exercises. They have the potential to be good soldiers. If all of them are discarded, I fear that they will have no way to make a living." The central government, however, generally viewed such requests as weak excuses for not having completed the assigned task on time and refused to give its sanction.[41]

Pushou apparently recognized that this sort of request was unlikely to be granted. A subsequent memorial reads: "There are those among them who became addicted because of illness, and those who find it difficult to stop because of their age. Their situation could be forgiven, but this is connected to Your Majesty's prohibition order so I do not dare to indulge their behavior."[42] In some cases, the throne was more forgiving. For example, Pushou successfully pleaded for permission to pardon longtime smokers Shanchun and Yiteheng'e, both high-ranking Banner officers. According to Pushou, the two men were the first to volunteer to undergo treatment and, despite advanced age and ill health, had continued to serve as exemplars for their underlings.[43]

Of particular worry to Pushou were the thirteen high-ranking officers who were treated for addiction and subsequently released, since he felt that their reform was key to the inspiration of those beneath them: "In the last several months, it has been very hard to distinguish whether or not those who have

---

40. ZZGB 20, memorial from Pushou, endorsed 19 May 1909, p. 110.
41. ZZGB 11, supplementary memorial from Pushou, endorsed 14 Sept. 1908, pp. 395–96.
42. ZZGB 11, memorial from Pushou, endorsed 13 Sept. 1908, pp. 410–12.
43. ZZGB 20, memorial from Pushou, endorsed 19 May 1909, pp. 108–10.

stopped smoking and ceased taking the anti-opium medicine have again been infected by this weakness, and whether or not those whose appearance and behavior is suspicious are concealing their evasion [of the restrictions]."[44] To allay his suspicions, Pushou ordered these men to meet with him and to undergo personal examinations. He compelled some to proffer public testimony as to the permanence of their cure and others to re-enter the anti-opium clinic for another investigation. In the case of one officer, he was outraged to discover blatant evidence of continuing dependence on the drug. "During the inspection, traces of opium paste were discovered on Lieutenant Yuqi of the Bordered White Banner . . . this is truly audacious!"[45] And on one occasion that revealed the extent of opium smoking among Manchu officers, Pushou was forced to admit to the throne that he could not appoint the designated substitutes for two officers currently being treated for addiction because the substitutes had not yet completed the cure.[46]

Pushou was also concerned about the potential for serious social ramifications when unreformed addicts were dismissed and their families no longer had the grain and monetary allowances allotted to Bannermen. He recognized that this harsh punishment ignored the limited employment opportunities for Bannermen and could exacerbate existing social tensions:

> If we only fire [those offenders] and don't establish a plan to encourage them, their future will be sunk and there will be no way for self-renewal. The damage from opium will still be difficult to cut off. Moreover, most of the soldiers in the Eight Banners use one share of money and grain to nourish and supply an entire family [or household]. If one person's [stipend or allowance] of money and grain is eliminated, the entire family's cold and hunger immediately will become apparent. Hunger and cold produce urgency. What won't they do [to obtain relief]? For the Banner battalions, if just one useless soldier is fired, the locality will gain one trouble-making bandit. We must prepare a plan to address this situation. Punishment and encouragement must be employed simultaneously.[47]

His comments revealed considerable discontent among a Banner community with few ties to the Han world that surrounded it.[48]

---

44. Ibid. p. 108.
45. Ibid., p. 110.
46. ZZGB 11, memorial from Pushou, endorsed 14 Sept. 1908, p. 394.
47. ZZGB 20, memorial from Pushou, endorsed 19 May 1909, p. 110.
48. The memorial also clearly indicates the irrelevance of the 1865 reforms intended to eliminate Manchu privileges and constraints; see Rhoads, *Manchus & Han*, chap. 1, on these reforms.

When his request for leniency was refused, the resourceful Pushou followed the lead of other Manchu officials and suggested building factories to keep otherwise idle Bannermen busy at something besides opium smoking.[49] Later, he also proposed the construction of handicrafts workshops (*gongyisuo*) to utilize the talents of those who otherwise would have been abandoned:

Already, I have ordered all of the posts and regimental colonels to quickly procure funds to establish handicrafts shops. From all those soldiers who have been fired for not quitting smoking and for other things, those who are strong and can build should be selected and ordered to enter the shops and study handicrafts. In the future, they will attain skills that will enable them to become self-supporting. In this way, included within the plan to set things in order [through opium prohibition] will be the intention to care for all.

His plan was endorsed by the central government in the spring of 1909, but whether it was implemented is unknown.[50]

Pushou also recognized that when the Bannermen were released from the smoking cessation clinic with a clean bill of health, they often returned to an environment full of temptations. Ensuring an opium-free soldiery also required addressing drug use among their dependents, particularly the women. Unlike his rigorous attack on opium abuse among his men, General Pushou approached the problem of addiction among Manchu women with a scheme that was gentler in tone and method:

Although the men have already stopped, many women still smoke. After the men leave the treatment offices and return home, it is difficult to guard against falling again into the same old rut.... Each regimental colonel should be ordered to carefully select an old, pure, honest woman to persuade female offenders to surrender smoking implements for burning. After they achieve some success, they will be given encouragement through rewards.

Pushou encouraged the Emperor and the Empress Dowager to instruct the anti-opium commissioner to order provincial officials to pursue the issue of female smoking. The memorial in which this suggestion appears bears a note

---

49. ZZGB 20, memorial from Pushou, endorsed 19 May 1909, pp. 110. According to Rhoads (*Manchus & Han*, pp. 124–25), this was not Pushou's innovation. Several garrisons had established similar institutions after the Boxer debacle, and the court officially encouraged the workshops after General Yigu in the Suiyuan garrison found them particularly effective.

50. ZZGB 20, memorial from Pushou, endorsed 19 May 1909, p. 110.

from the throne directing the idea to the attention of the anti-opium commissioner and the Ministry of Interior.[51]

Continued abstinence hinged on the elimination of temptation outside the home as well, and Pushou's lack of personal control over the supply of opium hampered his efforts. Like Songshou, Pushou found it difficult to enforce the ban on smoking when processed, smokable foreign opium was available.[52] "Opium paste," lamented Pushou, "is displayed and sold in every store, and those who sell it rely on it for their living."[53] His frustrations, however, were expressed in terms of his loyalty to the dynasty and the emperor: "If there is no hope of eliminating [the source of the drug], how can we comfort His Majesty in his late-night worries? How can we fulfill our promises to foreign nations?" However, the rules concerning opium shops came directly from Beijing, and in their memorials, Songshou and Pushou could only emphasize to the throne the difficulties posed by the ten-year plan for gradual prohibition.[54]

It appears, then, that the elimination of opium consumption even among the residents of Fuzhou's relatively small Banner quarter presented Fujian's highest-level officials with a number of challenges. Those challenges were illustrative of the pervasiveness of Fujian's opium economy and its penetration deep into the supposedly insular Manchu Banner community. By 1911, considerable progress had been made in the campaign, but it was tempered by the knowledge that ridding the garrison of opium addiction was only the first step in transforming this increasingly superfluous community into useful citizens of a reformed Qing empire.

Revolutionary Rumblings

Meanwhile, outside the Manchu quarter, revolutionary rumblings were shaking Fujian. By 1911, although the province could claim measurable progress in the suppression of the domestic and foreign opium trade within its

---

51. Again, the impact of this decision is unknown. ZZGB 11, memorial from Pushou, endorsed 13 Sept. 1908, pp. 411–12.

52. At this point, foreign opium should only have been distributed to licensed smokers by licensed shops. Pushou's memorials imply either that he favors the immediate closure of all licensed opium shops, that the licensed shops were numerous, or that he has evidence of the continuation of a black market in the drug.

53. ZZGB 11, memorial from Pushou, endorsed 13 Sept. 1908, pp. 411–12.

54. ZZGB 20, memorial from Pushou, endorsed 19 May 1909, p. 110.

borders, the anti-opium campaign and other late Qing reform initiatives took place within (and indeed, probably helped foment) a larger context of dissatisfaction that threatened the continuation both of reform and of Manchu rule. Fuzhou was the primary stage on which Fujian's revolutionary drama was played out, but developments throughout the province contributed to the growing tension that set Fuzhou on edge and created popular expectations for the revolution to come.

Southeast Fujian was particularly prone to revolutionary incidents, due in part to its history of clan violence and its geographic location. For example, in February 1910, riots broke out in Pinghe county, located on the Guangdong border. The violence was rumored to have originated in anti-Qing sentiment and popular objections to the opium suppression campaign. The 1,000 troops dispatched from Fuzhou to the scene quickly defeated the rioters, and although the reasons for the outbreak were never fully ascertained, the incidents contributed to the growing political and social tension.[55]

Fujian's proximity to turbulent Guangdong province made it a natural target for sympathizers of Sun Yatsen. The Tongmenghui established several branches in the Fujianese cities of Fuzhou, Putian (Xinghua prefecture), Quanzhou and Xiamen (both in Quanzhou prefecture), and Jian'an (Jianning prefecture). Students educated abroad or in progressive missionary schools in China, and Fujian's Provincial Assembly had also agitated for change before 1911.[56]

In addition, Fujian's New Army, which had been formed in 1908 and placed under the command of Sun Daoren, was dominated by troops from outside Fujian with strong revolutionary tendencies. The officers and soldiers from Hunan, who had originally come to Fujian under the command of Zuo Zongtang during the Taiping Rebellion, were firmly opposed to Manchu rule. Many were rumored to belong to the Gelaohui, a secret society with distinctly anti-Qing leanings. In 1909, Sun Daoren (a Hunanese) appointed a Cantonese named Xu Chongzhi (1887–1965) to head the provincial army training school. Xu was a Japanese-trained officer who joined the Tongmenghui and later the Guomindang, and he exerted a strong personal influence on Fujian's New Army before and after 1911.[57] Another im-

---

55. USDS (1906–10), reel 1162, nos. 24403 and 24403/1, Arnold to State Dept., 19 Feb. 1910 and 2 Mar. 1910, respectively.
56. Zou Lu, "Fujian guangfu," pp. 277–79.
57. Xu was the grandson of Xu Yingkui, former governor-general of Fujian and Zhejiang. The younger Xu had served as military aide to Sun Yatsen ally Chen Jiongming (1878–

portant and highly controversial leader of the revolution in Fujian was Peng Shousong (1869–1918), a Hunanese military man with Japanese training who became the leader of Fujian's Tongmenghui and was an important (and ruthless) player in Fujian's early Republican politics.[58]

Not all of the upheaval was due to popular opposition to or disillusionment with the Manchu dynasty, however. Anti-imperialist sentiment, directed particularly at Japan, also sparked Chinese hostilities and added to the general tension.[59] To make matters worse, Fujian was hit by a serious famine in the months preceding the revolution. Missionary groups in a variety of locations reported starvation and panic in the countryside. The famine appeared to take its harshest toll on the coastal regions of Xinghua and southern Fuzhou prefectures and continued into the first year of the Republic.[60] Frustration with the pace and scope of the New Policies also pushed many reformers to seek or at least support a more radical solution to China's ills.

Political tensions and economic duress, however, did not seem to slow the pace of opium reform. After the establishment in 1910 of a new strategy for opium suppression, the momentum of the suppression campaign actually accelerated. The plan hotly debated by the Provincial Assembly in 1910 and adopted later that same year by the provincial government went into effect in early 1911. Details can be derived from a surviving set of regulations. The role of the Anti-Opium Society was openly acknowledged and appreciated, and although the group retained its control over the registration and licensing process for opium smokers and prepared opium shops, offices for the collection of taxes on the drug were set up and run by gov-

---

1933). Although he commanded only one brigade at the time of the revolution, he became one of the leaders of the revolution in Fujian. See Zou Lu, "Fukien guangfu," pp. 277–79; Falkenheim, "Provincial Administration in Fukien," pp. 29–30; Boorman, *Biographical Dictionary of Republican China*, 2: 124–26; *Minguo renwu da cidian*, pp. 791, 839; CMS, Fuhkien Mission, Original Incoming 1900–1934 (1911), no. 241, letter from Taylor, 8 Dec. 1911; and Tahara, *Shinmatsu minsho Chūgoku kanshin jimmeiroku*, p. 353.

58. Peng opposed Yuan Shikai's attempts to re-establish the monarchy and, after 1915, served under Sun Yatsen in the Hunan-Hubei army. He was assassinated in 1918 (*Minguo renmin da cidian*, p. 1093).

59. USDS (1906–10), reel 826, enclosure in case no. 12705/2, Canton to Dept. of State, 10 Apr. 1908.

60. MEC *Annual Report* (1911), pp. 75, 102–3. Fortunately, the scarcity was temporary, and in August 1913, another missionary reported a bountiful harvest in Xinghua (MEC Archives, 73-43, 1043-3-2: 41, Carson to North, 7 Aug. 1913).

ernment officials, possibly to siphon off some of the traditional sources of the society's funding.[61]

The details of the new regulations also implied the existence of widespread evasion of the restrictions on opium smoking and validated Pushou's worries about the temptations that lurked outside the Manchu garrison. Special fines were set for brothels, teahouses, soup kitchens, taverns, and sedan chair depots that kept opium smoking lamps and equipment on their premises. Temples and monasteries were also warned to buy a license to light lamps or risk being accused of running a clandestine opium den. Small transport boats and sampans also had to purchase licenses to light lamps.[62] At the same time, the regulations also highlighted the local authorities' awareness of the campaign's weak spots and their determination to monitor and compel compliance.

Most reformers involved in the opium suppression campaign were intimately involved with other facets of the New Policy reform agenda, and many were radicalized by continued state control over the pace of reform and attracted to more revolutionary groups and goals. For example, despite his promise to his American employers, Chen Nengguang became involved in the revolutionary and anti-Manchu activities of the Society to Benefit the Hearer, "the mobilization headquarters of the revolution in Fujian," and joined the Tongmenghui.[63] A number of Anti-Opium Society inspectors also belonged to the Speak the News Society. Apparently, the news spread by this innocuous-sounding group actually was intended to promote revolution, and the members of the organization disseminated political literature and gave regular streetside speeches to inspire the public.[64] At the same time, as Peng Shousong lay the groundwork for revolution within the Fuzhou branch of the Tongmenghui, he recruited many members of Fuzhou's fledgling police force, whom we know were intimately involved in enforcing the restrictions on opium sales and consumption.[65]

---

61. *Fujian xianding jinyan xinzhang*, pp. 1–3.
62. Ibid., pp. 4–5.
63. Dunch, *Fuzhou Protestants and the Making of a Modern China*, p. 62; Zheng Zuyin et al., *Fujian xinhai guangfu shiliao*, p. 3.
64. Ibid., pp. 19–20.
65. Peng's branch of the Tongmenghui had so many soldiers and policemen that it was named the Revolutionary Alliance of Fujianese Military and Police (Fujian junjing tongmenghui) (Zou Lu, "Fujian guangfu," p. 278).

Progressive reform groups with agendas broader than that of the Anti-Opium Society often evolved into hotbeds of revolutionary action and anti-Manchu rhetoric; other groups emerged with specific revolutionary objectives. The South-of-the-Bridge Public Welfare Society, which sponsored a branch of the Anti-Opium Society, became one of the centers of provincial revolutionary activism.[66] A very clandestine and short-lived organization called the Han Independence Union (Hanzu duli hui) had a more explicitly racist revolutionary agenda. Its members, some of whom also belonged to the Tongmenghui, conducted military drills, stockpiled weapons, and ritually consumed a boiled concoction of beef, mutton, and pork to symbolize their desire to rid China of the hated Northern barbarians.[67] The anti-Manchu sentiment that festered within an increasingly radicalized political environment in Fujian affected local reactions to Chinese-British negotiations on opium suppression that might earlier have been welcomed.

The Treaty: Opium and the British Factor on the Eve of Revolution

Caving in to imperialist pressure was one of the most damning charges leveled at the Qing dynasty by reformers and revolutionaries alike, but in the case of opium suppression, the British promise to gradually cut off the importation of opium from India was widely (although often grudgingly) recognized as key to China's success. The three-year trial period mandated by the British was one of the more controversial aspects of the original Anglo-Chinese opium agreement of 1908. From the outset, skeptical British negotiators and anxious Indian opium traders suspected that the Chinese anti-opium initiative was nothing more than an attempt to substitute Chinese opium (and the tax revenue it generated) for the foreign drug. The trial period gave the British an opportunity to invalidate the agreement if the Chinese government could not demonstrate significant progress within three years. But when the agreement came up for renegotiation in 1911, even the most vocal foreign critics could not deny China's accomplishments. That progress empowered Chinese negotiators with enough moral leverage to wrest important concessions from the British, and the

---

66. Zheng Zuyin et al., *Fujian xinhai guangfu shiliao*, p. 5; Dunch, *Fuzhou Protestants and the Making of a Modern China*, pp. 104–6.

67. Zheng Zuyin et al., *Fujian xinhai guangfu shiliao*, pp. 7–8.

new treaty had a profound impact on the course of the suppression campaign.

On 8 May 1911, only a few months before the Revolution of 1911, the British and Chinese signed a revised agreement that marked a new and important stage in China's attempts to eliminate opium. The new agreement retained the original ten-year schedule for the total elimination of Indian opium imports, but with several important provisions that gave the Chinese government the chance to end the trade well before 1917. Article II praised China's progress and pledged to support the Qing government's efforts by making a tantalizing offer: "With a view to facilitating the continuance of this work, His Majesty's Government agree that the export of opium from India to China shall cease *in less than seven years* [my italics] if clear proof is given of the complete absence of production of native opium in China." Article III explained that "Indian opium shall not be conveyed into any province in China which can establish by clear evidence that it has effectively suppressed the cultivation and import of native opium." That "clear evidence" was to be obtained by joint Sino-British investigation teams that would tour each province claiming to be free of the domestic drug. As each province was declared poppy-free, larger and larger chunks of Chinese territory would be closed to foreign opium imports. In giving the Qing government this opportunity, the British were not only responding to the growing public sentiment in China and at home against the opium trade, but also addressing the fear of Indian opium producers and merchants that ending opium exports would simply abandon the lucrative Chinese market to their Chinese competitors. The agreement tried to establish conditions that would extricate the British from an increasingly unpopular position *and* ensure the destruction of Chinese poppy fields. Significantly, a timetable for the elimination of consumption was not included in the agreement, since negotiators on both sides probably felt that once the supply evaporated, demand would quickly follow suit.[68]

There were other concessions as well. The Chinese government was given the authority to raise the import duty on Indian opium from 110 to 350 taels per picul. In addition, all opium chests legally exported from India were to be sealed in the presence of a Chinese official and given numbered export certificates. The number of certificates was to be reduced by 10 percent annually, in accordance with the 1908 agreement. The British also agreed to

---

68. PRO, FO 233/134, "Opium Agreement, 1911" (in English and Chinese).

decrease the number of certificates for 1912–14 by an additional one-third of the number of chests of Indian opium without certificates in Hong Kong and in bond in Chinese treaty ports on 8 May, and by one-third the number of chests without certificates imported into Shanghai and Guangzhou for two months after 8 May.[69]

However, the agreement still guaranteed a high degree of British influence over both the structure and timetable of China's anti-opium campaign. The increase in the duty on imported Indian opium was to be matched by a rise in the excise tax on Chinese opium to 230 taels per picul. Article III also contained the stipulation that the important depots of Shanghai and Guangzhou would remain open to opium imports until prohibition was complete in the rest of China. In addition, British inspectors ultimately were the final judges of whether a Chinese province had indeed successfully prohibited domestic opium.

The renegotiated agreement of 8 May 1911 made explicit the need for all Chinese provinces to work toward a national goal. Indeed, it offered an extremely attractive incentive for unified action and forced the Chinese state to re-evaluate its opium suppression strategy. The possibility of ending Indian opium imports before the original deadline in 1917 now hinged entirely on eliminating domestic poppy cultivation. An imperial edict on the subject, dated 9 May 1911 (just one day after the signing of the agreement), explicitly endorsed this new policy: "The prohibition of the import of foreign opium depends on the prohibition of the cultivation of native opium and so it has been decided to proceed province by province. The earlier native opium is suppressed the earlier will the import of foreign opium come to an end."[70] In practice, this meant less attention to the demand side of the opium equation, where unofficial reform groups had performed such important roles. Treatment of opium smokers and control over sales presumably would become less crucial and, in fact, increasingly unnecessary as the supply of the domestic and foreign drug tapered off. It was this new strategy that Yuan Shikai adopted after the Revolution of 1911. Unfortunately, the demand for opium did not dry up, and the new approach met with many obstacles.

---

69. In Fuzhou, 329 chests of Indian opium—278 with certificates, 25 without, and another 26 doubtful—were housed in bond at that port on 8 May 1911. PRO, FO 228/2443, no. 22, draft of Jordan to Werner, 8 Aug. 1911.

70. PRO, FO 233/134, Addendum to the "Opium Agreement, 1911" (in English and Chinese).

In Fujian, news of the agreement was not greeted with the enthusiasm that the Qing government might have expected. Emboldened by the momentum of the campaign and encouraged by the concessions wrested from the British, opium reformers felt that this was the time to push for even more provincial autonomy in the conduct of the suppression campaign. Led by members of the Provincial Assembly, hundreds of individuals from districts all over the province, including several officers of the Anti-Opium Society (among them its new leader, Chen Peikun) signed a petition calling on Songshou to halt imports of the foreign drug immediately.

A strong sense of provincial pride pervades the document. The petitioners noted the progressive nature of opium reform in Fujian, pointing with satisfaction to the early establishment of the Fujian Anti-Opium Society. They also claimed that the damage wrought by foreign opium had been more serious in Fujian than elsewhere because the drug had entered Fujian so early. They implored Songshou to take this serious and important step immediately, so as to save the province from bankrupting itself through the purchase of foreign opium:

> Every year the money that flows out [of the province] and into foreign [hands] amounts to twelve million taels. Is it any wonder that Fujian is commonly called a poor and barren land? Unknowingly, it has squandered an enormous sum.... The wealth and the blood of the people have already been sucked dry.... This is one reason why we cannot delay the prohibition on imports.[71]

The petitioners also worried that the announcement of the new agreement had generated a frenzy among opium merchants, who were rushing to get stocks into Fujianese ports before the mandated tax hike took place.

The fundamental unfairness of the new agreement and, by implication, China's position vis-à-vis Great Britain drew objections as well. The petition warned, "If domestic opium has already been prohibited, but foreign opium monopolizes the profits, this will certainly cause ordinary people to feel the inequity in their hearts."[72] Furthermore, since provincial deadlines for the closure of all opium paste shops and the end of all opium smoking were set for later that year, they felt that the continued importation of foreign opium would constitute an inexcusable temptation for the masses.

---

71. "Lieming kenqing Min-Zhe zongdu Song." There is no date marked on this document, but its contents seem to indicate that it was written in 1911 just after the new agreement was signed.

72. Ibid.

The document also pleaded with Songshou to quickly appoint an investigative team so that the province could prove that it had eliminated domestic poppy cultivation. They recognized the setback caused by the previous attempt to have Fujian declared poppy-free but insisted that this time around they had amassed a "mountain" of proof in the form of affidavits signed by foreign missionaries and local gentry. They asked Songshou to memorialize the Ministry of Foreign Affairs to contact the British minister to halt British imports in accordance with the provisions of the treaty.[73] The signs of tension between provincial and national goals had begun to emerge, and it must have seemed to the activists that neither level of the Chinese state was able to move fast enough to take advantage of the pace of reform.

The new agreement generated a number of international incidents that dominated British diplomatic communications, kept the Chinese state on edge, and continued to remind reformers that the Qing state's hands were tied by its bargain with the British. Before the signing of the revised agreement, the Opium Prohibition Bureau and the headquarters of the Anti-Opium Society had taken the lead in jointly devising measures to govern situations not specifically mentioned in the new provincial regulations. Although their actions addressed issues of local concern, on occasion they antagonized foreign interests. The most notorious incident began on 12 March 1911, when the two offices drew up regulations requiring purchasers of foreign opium to possess passes from the Anti-Opium Society or risk the confiscation of the drug. That same month, Lü Chenghan, the police intendant of Fuzhou and president of the provincial Opium Prohibition Bureau, had announced that all prepared opium shops in the province were to be closed by 18 March. A howl went up from the British opium traders who imported much of the raw opium sold to those shops. British diplomats also claimed that officials and local elites in Sha county and Shangyang subprefecture (both in Yanping prefecture) had independently and illegally set dates for closing their jurisdictions to all opium imports.[74] The British protested vigorously that distribution of the foreign drug was not to be hindered until the province was declared closed to its importation, but the issue remained a point of contention up to the revolution. Despite

---

73. Ibid.
74. PRO, FO 228/2444, no. 19, Jordan to Waiwu bu, 18 Sept. 1911.

reassurances from Beijing and Fuzhou, the British were never satisfied that the restrictions had been totally removed.[75]

The renegotiation of the agreement with the British was in part intended to discourage such unilateral ultimatums by the provinces, but the momentum of the campaign proved difficult to halt. The central Qing state and provincial authorities in Fuzhou seemed unwilling to dampen the ardor of a crusade that had galvanized officials and elite reformers into working together toward a goal that would not only satisfy their nationalistic sentiment but also shore up the authority and legitimacy of the Qing state. When confronted with alleged treaty violations in Fujian, Chinese authorities in Beijing and Fuzhou often had little choice but to investigate or order compliance in the most blatant cases, but in reality, there was little attempt to forestall most of these actions unless they constituted an imminent threat to the agreement. Correspondence between the British Foreign Office and the Chinese Ministry of Foreign Affairs (Waiwu bu) has a patronizing, conciliatory tone but often sidesteps the real issue. In this way, "the Court neatly balanced off the explosive mixture of foreign and provincial confrontations over the opium issue,"[76] but it was unable to openly approve of actions that furthered its ultimate goal for the campaign but violated the treaty. Up to the outbreak of revolution, many local authorities and elite reformers in Fujian continued to place obstacles in the way of the foreign opium trade. British consul E. T. C. Werner threatened to abrogate the new opium agreement if Songshou did not order the removal of all restrictions on the flow of foreign opium in Fujian, but even after the governor-general agreed to do so, Werner confessed, "I left with the impression that the Viceroy [Songshou] was fully convinced that the instructions he had issued were inadequate."[77] For the Chinese authorities, however, the danger was that even such transparently insincere gestures could be interpreted by reformers as pandering to foreign interests.

During the last few years of the Qing dynasty, Songshou and other provincial officials continued to alter the regulations concerning opium suppression in an attempt to regain more official control. According to a local news-

---

75. PRO, FO 228/2444, no. 27, Prince Qing to Jordan, 20 Sept. 1911; numerous dispatches in PRO, FO 228/2444 and 228/2445.
76. Reins, "China and the International Politics of Opium," p. 79.
77. PRO, FO 228/2445, Werner to Jordan, 30 June 1911. Werner also insisted that Songshou was "largely in the hands of the anti-opium society" (PRO, FO 228/2445, Werner to Jordan, 16 June 1911).

paper in July 1911, the anti-opium societies were still responsible for counting and registering smokers, but the Opium Prohibition Bureau was to conduct the main business of suppression and coordinate reform efforts in each county and subprefecture. Fuzhou would appoint a local official as director of the bureau in each locality, and the assistant director would be a member of the gentry. In reality, overworked officials often served only as figureheads, thus ensuring that the gentry still ran the bureau's day-to-day operations in many areas. Official addiction treatment centers were to be established, and the Anti-Opium Society was expected to contribute, but the new bureaus would decide what medicines could be used and handle the licensing of opium shops.[78]

As always, the most controversial measure had significant financial implications. Before July 1911, taxes on prepared opium were collected by the Anti-Opium Society in Fuzhou, as well as by local self-government societies in surrounding villages, and the revenue was applied to the upkeep of those groups. However, provincial authorities decided to shift that responsibility to deputies dispatched by the provincial Committee of Finance (Caizheng chu), a move that would presumably funnel more revenue to provincial coffers. According to a local newspaper, however, the proprietors of prepared opium shops objected to the new rule, and expressed concerns about higher taxes and more abusive collectors.[79] Eventually, it was agreed that the shops would pay the tax to the Prepared Opium Tax Bureau (Gaojuan ju), but in early August Lü Chenghan and the head of the Anti-Opium Society again set deadlines for the closure of all prepared opium shops within the following months. The British, who claimed that the tax contravened the new opium agreement, contested all these measures. The Opium Prohibition Bureau and the Finance Office (Duzhi gongsuo) then declared a monthly tax on opium smoking licenses, ostensibly to encourage more smokers to quit but also perhaps to ensure themselves adequate revenue.[80] The incident revealed a degree of competition between officials and unofficial reform

---

78. PRO, FO 228/1800, Werner to Jordan, Foochow Intelligence Report for September Quarter 1911, 2 Oct. 1911, translation from *Minbao*, 28 July 1911. Since the date of the regulations cited earlier was simply listed as 1911, it is unclear whether they were published to reflect these changes or whether the changes occurred despite the existence of the regulations.

79. Ibid.

80. The deadlines called for the smaller, less successful shops to shut down first, thus allowing the larger stores to become even more profitable in the short term (ibid.; translation from *Minbao*, 12 Aug. 1911).

groups for the revenue generated by opium prohibition as the success of the suppression campaign (and the end of those funds) seemed within reach. Here again, we catch a glimpse of the tug-of-war that threatened to solidify the boundaries between the state and the still amorphous public space in which much of the opium suppression campaign was being played out.

Ironically, profits from the opium trade did not diminish as much as predicted because China's internal campaign and India's willingness to reduce the amount of opium it exported to China each year caused a steep rise in the price of Indian opium. This development was particularly evident along the Chinese coastline, where most provinces relied heavily on the foreign drug. According to one source, India's opium revenue from China totaled 3,867,700 pounds sterling in 1908–9. The next year, those receipts fell slightly to 3,637,200 pounds, but in 1910–11, India's opium trade with China brought in 5,697,000 pounds sterling.[81] At the port of Xiamen, prices peaked in 1910–11, just before the imposition of the increased duty on imported opium mandated by the new agreement.[82]

The price increase, along with widespread rumors that Indian opium imports would cease in 1913, fostered fears among British merchants and diplomats that domestic opium smuggling would soon flourish again.[83] The southeastern coast of Fujian seemed especially susceptible to the resurgence of the underground opium economy because of its many coves and inlets, the history of piracy and lowlessness among some of its people, and its proximity to Taiwan, where Japanese and Chinese merchants operated under the privilege of extraterritoriality. In fact, customs officials made several seizures of illegal opium, as well as contraband morphine, cocaine, and weaponry in that area. Officials also discovered the importation of large amounts of a powerful opium extract that was able to remain legal for a time by using the name "foreign medicine" (*yang yao*), a term that used to be the generic Chinese reference for the imported drug.[84] Another head-

---

81. Cantlie and Jones, *Sun Yat Sen and the Awakening of China*, p. 210.

82. IMC, *Decennial Reports, Amoy, 1902–1911*, pp. 102–3.

83. In March 1911, British authorities at Fuzhou complained that aggressive enforcement of opium restrictions by overzealous local authorities had caused the price of the Indian drug to fall slightly (although it was still quite high compared to previous years) (PRO, FO 228/1800, Werner to Jordan, Foochow Intelligence Report for March Quarter 1911, 23 Apr. 1911).

84. PRO, FO 228/1797, Sundius to Jordan, Amoy Intelligence Report, September Quarter 1911, 10 Oct. 1911.

ache for officials and elites in Fujian involved in the anti-opium movement was the private—and therefore, illegal—manufacture and sale of medicinal opium preparations that combined opium with a variety of extracts from wine, pigskin, and the like. In July 1911, Lü Chenghan formally outlawed these practices.[85]

In Fuzhou, the Revolution of 1911 was immediately preceded by a city-wide strike of sedan chair bearers in September, which erupted when a monthly tax was imposed on the laborers. The bearers refused to work, and officials seen on the streets in private chairs were often attacked and their chairs destroyed. After several days of chaos, in which the strikers closed down all business in the city, fought with soldiers, and wrecked not only the new court building but also all of the city's police stations and the offices of Lü Chenghan, the tax was rescinded and order returned to the city until the outbreak of the revolution. Foreign customs officials reported that the tax had been levied by the city's Anti-Opium Society to fund its work, but the British consul at Fuzhou countered that the tax was intended to fund the hiring of more police. Because Lü Chenghan was not only the city's top police official, but also president of the official Anti-Opium Bureau, the confusion was understandable and indicative of popular indignation at the broad powers (extractive and coercive) perceived to have been granted to those enforcing opium restrictions. Both organizations were products of New Policy reforms that increased the state's regulatory power over ordinary Fujianese, a situation that acted as both a source of revolutionary anger and post-revolutionary dissatisfaction.[86] As the political tension grew in late 1911, it became clear to reformers and revolutionaries alike that the Chinese state itself was the source of many of China's problems.

---

85. PRO, FO 228/1800, Werner to Jordan, Foochow Intelligence Report for September Quarter 1911, 2 Oct. 1911, translation from *Minbao*, 28 July 1911.

86. PRO, FO 228/1800, Werner to Jordan, 19 Sept. 1911, and enclosures to Foochow Intelligence Report for September Quarter 1911, 2 Oct. 1911 (including translation of *Minbao*, 28 July 1911); IMC, *Decennial Reports, Fuzhou, 1902–1911*, p. 91; and MEC Archives, 74-11, 1259-6-2:08, Main to Stuntz, 20 Sept. 1911. Consul Werner asserted, "The chair-coolie strike above-referred to is directly connected to the opium question, since this class is the largest consumer of the drug, and was made discontented by deprivation of the solace of the pipe and by the large additional taxes suddenly imposed last week on all chairs and chair-bearers in the City and Prefecture." However, in his handwritten marginalia, Sir John Jordan commented, "this seems rather farfetched" (PRO, FO 228/2444, doc. 43, Werner to Jordan, 13 Sept. 1911). Werner's credibility was compromised by his reputation for being irascible and increasingly combative (Coates, *The China Consuls*, pp. 440–41).

Revolution in Fuzhou and the End of Manchu Rule

For the Manchus of the Fuzhou Banner garrison, the upheaval generated by opium reform and the myriad other changes wrought by the New Policy reforms were entirely eclipsed by the overthrow of the Qing dynasty and the collapse of China's imperial system in 1911. Not only did the revolution halt the separate suppression campaign conducted within the garrison and claim the lives of the two Manchus who had directed Fujian's anti-opium efforts, but it also resulted in the violent death of close to 300 other Manchus, the disintegration of the Manchu quarter, and the end of a way of life in the Banner garrisons.

The New Army brought the revolution to Fuzhou, and the old Manchu military marshaled a defiant but ultimately futile resistance. Sun Daoren (b. 1867), Xu Chongzhi (1887–1965), and Peng Shousong (1869–1918) initiated the revolution in Fuzhou, and it was this shaky triumvirate that led Fujian into the Republican era. On 7 November, the Provincial Assembly declared the province independent of Qing rule. Evidently, Xu tried to negotiate a peaceful turnover of power with high-ranking provincial officials and members of the Provincial Assembly, pleading that the Manchus in the city surrender and "assist in a revised system of government" and threatening to attack only if resistance to the transition were offered. The demands were clear but somewhat compassionate. Manchus were ordered to obey the new government, turn over all weapons and ammunition, and abolish the Manchu quarter; in return, the new Republic would continue to give them their allotted stipends. Although Xu apparently found Songshou and many others in the Manchu community receptive to this approach, Pushou refused to cooperate.[87]

Even before hostilities broke out in Fujian, Pushou had tried to use his authority to disarm Chinese soldiers in Fuzhou and give their arms to Manchus, but the plan was thwarted by Sun Daoren. Pushou then emptied the city's six arsenals and consolidated the city's ammunition in the Manchu quarter, where all able-bodied Manchu males—somewhere between 2,000 and 3,000 "men" over the age of thirteen—were armed, usually with guns,

---

87. Zou Lu, "Fukien Guangfu," pp. 280–82; and CMS Fuhkien Mission, Original Incoming, 1900–1934 (1911), no. 255, 1911, excerpts from *The Foochow Daily Echo* (*Fuzhou meiri huisheng bao*) of 7 Nov. 1911.

Fig. 5.1 Fujian's military governor, Sun Daoren, in a postrevolutionary (1912) photo-op with Sun Yatsen, then acting president of the new Chinese republic (courtesy United Methodist Archives, Drew University, Madison, New Jersey).

and then posted to strategic points around Fuzhou's city walls.[88] Manchu women were given knives. In addition, he ordered Captain Wenkai to organize a "Kill Han Regiment" (Sha Han tuan), but the group seemed to generate more fear and antipathy among Han Chinese, most likely because of its inflammatory name, than actual violence.[89] However, Pushou himself was later accused by revolutionary forces of ordering the gruesome murder and mutilation of two young members of the revolutionary army and was blamed for the many acts of arson that Manchu soldiers committed during the brief but fierce battles.[90]

---

88. Zou Lu, "Fukien Guangfu," pp. 280–82; and CMS Fuhkien Mission, Original Incoming, 1900–1934 (1911), no. 255, 1911, excerpts from *The Foochow Daily Echo* of 7 Nov. 1911; MEC Archives, 74-11, 1259-6-2:08, Main to Stuntz, 27 Oct. 1911. This account and the following descriptions of the revolution in Fuzhou were verified by numerous other missionary letters, as well as by the reports of French, British, and American consular officials. There is some discrepancy between estimates of the size of the able-bodied Manchu population, which some missionaries put as high as 3,000 men (*Mercy and Truth* 16, no. 181 [Jan. 1912]: 9–11).

89. Allegedly, 500 men were members of the squad (Guo Gongmu, "Xinhai geming Fuzhou chuli baqi guanbing jingguo," p. 54).

90. Zheng Zuyin et al., *Fujian xinhai guangfu shiliao*, pp. 55–56.

The revolution arrived in Fuzhou literally with a bang, as the city awoke to the din of cannon fire in the early morning hours of 9 November. Manchu sentries on guard at several of the city gates were shot, and chaos descended on the city along with the shells lobbed by revolutionary troops. The explosions rattled the homes and the nerves of local residents, and within two days, one American missionary testified, "the dead and wounded were numbered by the hundreds."[91] Some of the casualties were suicides, usually Manchu women who took their own lives in anticipation of rape or capture by the Chinese. Ironically, Pushou's inability to eradicate the opium problem among his people may have facilitated some of these desperate actions:

Back in the [Manchu] Quarter the Manchu mothers, crouched in the darkest corners of their houses, hushed the cries of their little ones, while struggling with their suffocating fears, and waiting for they knew not what horror. *Not a few took opium;* others jumped into their court-yard wells; or threw themselves on the pyre of their burning possessions.[92] (Italics added)

Manchus fought back in vain, and wild rumors about the status of Pushou circulated through the foreign missionary community.[93]

The revolution had devastating consequences for the Manchus who occupied the top ranks of Fujian's provincial administration—the same men who had overseen the province's opium suppression campaign. Several days after the violence began, Songshou took his own life in an art shop near the West Gate where he had fled to escape retribution. Accounts of his death and assessments of his tenure varied considerably. One British missionary reported that Songshou hung himself and that "he was an old man and is said to have been well liked."[94] A recent Chinese account claims that Songshou was "a mediocre, cowardly bureaucrat," although acknowledging that his actions in office had been neither laudable nor objectionable. The new military leader of the province, Sun Daoren, evidently thought enough of his former superior to organize a well-attended funeral, personally make sacri-

---

91. MEC *Annual Report*, 1911, p. 73.
92. *The Foochow Messenger*, Sept. 1912, p. 23.
93. Some heard he had died, others that he had been seriously wounded, and still others that he had holed up somewhere in the city with several hundred of his most loyal soldiers (CMS Fuhkien Mission, Original Incoming, 1900–1934 [1911], no. 255, excerpts from *The Foochow Daily Echo*, Nov. 1911).
94. CMS Fuhkien Mission, Original Incoming, 1900–1934 (1911), no. 255, including excerpts from *The Foochow Daily Echo*, 11 and 18 Nov. 1911.

fices to Songshou's spirit, and arrange for the body to be transported back to the Manchu ancestral homeland.[95]

Pushou, in contrast, was unambiguously classed as a counterrevolutionary. Although some foreign observers confessed to a degree of admiration for his staunch resistance, Pushou posthumously shouldered much of the collective blame for the brief bloodiness of the revolution in Fuzhou. According to one missionary:

> The Tartar garrison here was men who had always lived here, many of them were the descendants of families who had been living here for several generations. They had no personal quarrel with their Chinese neighbors, and did not want to expose their families to danger of massacre by fighting with a force so largely outnumbering them. However they were forced to fight by the Tartar General [Pushou].[96]

Another missionary concurred, describing below the reluctance with which many Manchus joined the battle:

> The revolutionists visited the Manchu quarter and found that at the door of every family a sign of surrender was erected; with tears streaming down their cheeks, [the Manchus], with one accord, declared that the Tartar General has been the cause of their misery and that he has been the only person whom they feared, etc. They then led the revolutionists to arrest the Tartar General.[97]

These accounts may be colored, however, by missionary sympathy for the Manchus as well as the missionaries' desire to breach the physical and cultural barriers that the Banner community had erected around itself. Those barriers, originally intended to limit Han influence, served to prevent missionary attempts at conversion as well.

Whatever the reason, a good deal of confusion surrounds the circumstances of Pushou's arrest and subsequent death. Some Chinese reports claim that he fell in battle or was killed while trying to escape the revolutionary army. Zheng Zuyin, a historian who at the time of the revolution was a member of the Provincial Assembly and a leader of the Tongmenghui,

---

95. Guo Gongmu, "Xinhai Fuzhou guangfu jige wenti de diaocha yanjiu," pp. 90–91. On Songshou's suicide, see also Zheng Zuyin et al., *Fujian xinhai guangfu shiliao*, p. 54. Zheng (ibid., p. 294) also claims that when the Kill Han Regiment targeted Sun, Songshou stepped in to prevent them, thus Sun's obligation to Songshou.

96. *The Foochow Messenger*, Jan. 1912, p. 19.

97. CMS Fuhkien Mission, Original Incoming, 1900–1934, No. 255, 1911, excerpts from "Foochow Surrendered," in the *Foochow Daily Echo* of 13 Nov. 1911.

claimed that the revolutionary forces arrested Pushou, held him under extremely generous conditions, and had no intention of harming him until the troops were infuriated by a surprise attack by several hundred Manchu soldiers.[98] Missionary eyewitnesses tell yet another story. An American Methodist wrote of rumors that Pushou, tenacious to the end, initially refused to surrender to the revolutionaries and for a few tense hours threatened to blow up the magazine where he had consolidated all the ammunition he could get his hands on. Thousands of Fuzhou residents fled the city to avoid the possibility of a devastating explosion.[99] A British missionary reported that Pushou and approximately a thousand of his men then surrendered on the morning of 10 November.[100]

Chinese historian Guo Gongmu has examined the controversy in detail and has reconstructed a chronology that appears to corroborate the western reports.[101] Evidently, Pushou advocated violent resistance to the revolution against the wishes of several representatives of the small core of Banner gentry/officials who led Fuzhou's Manchu community (several of whom surrendered voluntarily to Sun Daoren). It appears that Pushou was seized at the home of a friend (Mongol Bannerman Ming Yu) and unceremoniously marched or carried into imprisonment under the orders of Sun Daoren, his former colleague and now head of the revolutionary army, whom Pushou evidently had angered by calling a traitor. Accused of having been responsible for the burning of much of the city, attacking revolutionaries under the guise of surrender several times, and neglecting the welfare of his people by stinting on their rations of food and arms and then forcing them to fight, Pushou was declared guilty of capital crimes by a hastily assembled, private revolutionary tribunal.[102] Despite Sun's promises to foreign missionaries that Pushou would be kept as a prisoner of war, the defiant Manchu was summarily and secretly beheaded the night of his ar-

---

98. Zheng Zuyin et al., *Fujian xinhai guangfu shiliao*, p. 55.

99. MEC *Annual Report*, 1911, p. 73; USDS (1910–29), reel 8, no. 893.00/720, Thompson to Dept. of State, 2 Nov. 1911.

100. CMS Fuhkien Mission, Original Incoming, 1900–1934, 1911, no. 239, letter from Muller in Fuzhou on 9 Nov. 1911 (he was able to insert this news because the mail did not go out on 9 Nov.).

101. Guo Gongmu, "Xinhai Fuzhou guangfu jige wenti de diaocha yanjiu."

102. CMS Fuhkien Mission, Original Incoming, 1900–1934 (1911), no. 255, excerpts from *The Foochow Daily Echo*, 18 Nov. 1911; Guo Gongmu, "Xinhai geming Fuzhou chuli baqi guanbing jingguo," p. 55.

rest.[103] Another account, this one provided by his nephew, claims that Pushou died fighting his guards and his body was "hacked into four pieces."[104] He was the only Manchu executed by the Republican forces. Even Wenkai, allegedly the head of the Kill Han Regiment, was spared, although he did serve two years in prison for his role in the violence.[105]

Despite reports from the Church Missionary Society hospital in Fuzhou that 135 wounded Manchus had been treated there for injuries,[106] and confirmation of several hundred dead, most foreign observers felt that the violence was limited, and that for the most part, Manchu civilians were unmolested. Guo Gongmu writes that even Manchu soldiers who surrendered were given a small amount of food and rice, and those who had fled the area were urged to return lest they starve to death.[107] Many of the Manchu noncombatants who were killed were accidentally caught in the line of fire or committed suicide.[108] According to one British missionary, violence was virtually unheard of outside Fuzhou, "except in one or two places near Foochow where some trouble was caused by Manchus who had fled from the city."[109] Sun Daoren briefly confined the city's Manchus to a section of

---

103. PRO, FO 228/1800, Werner to Jordan, 20 Nov. 1911; CMS Fuhkien Mission, Original Incoming, 1900–1934, no 241 (1911), lengthy letter from Taylor on 8 Dec. 1911; and PRO, FO 228/1838, Foochow Intelligence Report, December Quarter 1911.

104. Rhoads, *Manchu & Han*, p. 195.

105. Guo Gongmu, "Xinhai geming Fuzhou chuli baqi guanbing jingguo," p. 54. Yi Tongfu ("Xinhai geming qianhou Fuzhou Manzu qiying neiqing shilu," pp. 31–32) implies that Wenkai may have been falsely accused by a Han Chinese member of the Tongmenghui who lived in or near the Banner quarter and had a grudge against Wenkai.

106. *Mercy and Truth* 16, no. 188 (Aug. 1912): 276–80. The author notes, however, that he is unclear as to whether this number reflects all of the casualties being tended to in the hospital or just the Manchu wounded.

107. Guo Gongmu, "Xinhai geming Fuzhou chuli baqi guanbing jingguo," pp. 55–56.

108. Dr. B. van Someren Taylor of the CMS visited Pushou's yamen and found evidence that it had been struck by a single shell. He was told that the shock had killed Pushou's wife (CMS Fuhkien Mission, Original Incoming, 1900–1934 [1911], no. 255, excerpts from *The Foochow Daily Echo* of 11 Nov. 1911; no 241 [1911], letter from Taylor, 8 Dec. 1911).

109. CMS Fuhkien Mission, Original Incoming, 1900–1934 (1911), no. 149, letter from Muller in Fuzhou, 15 Nov. 1911. However, in the remote southwestern prefecture of Tingzhou, although the Manchu prefect peacefully handed over the reins of government to the revolutionary troops, he then killed his son and poisoned himself. The head military official, also a Manchu, fled the city disguised as a priest (LMS Archives, box 10, folder 2, Blair to Martin, 20 Nov. 1911 and 3 Dec. 1911). In addition, Qingfan, the Manchu circuit intendant and ranking civil official in Xiamen, went into hiding, but apparently was unharmed (PRO, FO 228/1797, Sundius to Jordan, 17 Nov. 1911).

town that one missionary referred to as a Manchu "colony," but they were later allowed to live and work where they pleased.[110] Minor ethnic tensions lingered in the months after the revolution, however, and on one occasion, the police were compelled to issue orders forbidding the spreading of malicious rumors that Manchu homes would be torched.[111]

The Revolution of 1911 brought terror, humiliation, and death for some Manchus in Fuzhou, and although the turbulence was brief, the change was momentous. In the aftermath, Manchu privilege dissolved, and the Bannermen were left largely to fend for themselves. Songshou, Pushou, and others were dead, and the Manchu quarter ceased to exist as an enclave of ethnic segregation. The revolution did not usher in the new era that many of its supporters envisioned, but for the Manchu garrison community in Fuzhou, the transition was traumatic and profound. The revolution also had tremendous implications for the conduct of the opium suppression campaign outside the garrison.

A Pivotal Year

By 1911, the opium suppression campaign, implemented and overseen by provincial authorities, often using unofficial elite-led reform groups and the new police force as its foot soldiers, had made considerable progress in Fuzhou. Many opium dens were shut down; opium shops were closed or licensed; the smoking population was counted, registered, and given a ration of the drug to wean them from their habits; and the acreage devoted to poppies was beginning to diminish. At the same time, other reforms, most notably the Qing empire's first steps toward constitutional government, created a state-in-waiting, in the form of the Provincial Assembly. The many progressive men who served in this ostensibly advisory body in Fujian gained a new perspective on the conduct of Chinese politics that was critical of the Qing dynasty yet were anxious to consolidate central power when it came their turn to rule. Clearly, something happened to change the attitudes of many Chinese elites who had staked out a place for themselves in the new and exciting space for political activism and reform that had emerged in the final years of Qing rule. In and around 1911, even many of those who had whole-

---

110. CMS Fuhkien Mission, Original Incoming, 1900–1934 (1912), no. 73, letter from Lloyd in Fuzhou, 16 Jan. 1912.
111. Zheng Zuyin et al., *Fujian xinhai guangfu shiliao*, p. 177.

heartedly supported state reform policies turned against the state. Much of that antagonism had its roots in nationalism and racism.

Unfortunately for the Qing government, support for opium prohibition was not the only sentiment aroused among the Chinese people in the early twentieth century. Nationalism in its many incarnations, the growing disenchantment of elites and some officials with the pace of government-driven reform, burgeoning dissatisfaction in the countryside with the extractive, intrusive elements of some of the New Policies, and the rumblings of a loosely bound coalition of revolutionaries generated tremendous pressure on the beleaguered Manchu dynasty. Ironically, many Manchus were strong supporters of reform, believing that the only way to sustain Qing rule was to strengthen the central state and respond to popular pressure by transforming the dynasty into a constitutional monarchy.[112] In 1911, however, the metaphorical dam broke and when the floodwaters of revolution receded, China's venerable imperial system had been washed away with the remnants of the Qing dynasty. Also temporarily overwhelmed by that current of change were the official and unofficial mechanisms for opium suppression.

The role of ethnic loyalties and tensions in shaping the opium suppression campaign in the Fuzhou Banner garrison remains somewhat ambiguous. On the one hand, the campaign not only clearly emphasized the isolation of the Banner community from the rest of Fuzhou's population but also called attention to the depths of poverty and the lack of morale that characterized the Manchu quarter by the late Qing era. This may have exacerbated the anti-Manchu sentiment that brewed beneath the surface of the New Policies. At the same time, surviving documents indicate that the Qing state did not attempt to exempt Manchus from the restrictions on opium consumption and, in fact, exerted a great deal of effort in overseeing the rehabilitation or punishment of those Bannermen and their dependents who smoked.

Opium and the opium trade played an important part in stimulating anti-Manchu sentiment during the late Qing. By the end of the nineteenth century, China's opium problem constituted a real crisis for the already embattled Qing dynasty. Not only had conflicts over the drug trade sparked military hostilities with the western powers that eroded Chinese sovereignty and territorial integrity, but Manchu capitulation to British pressure to legalize opium imports exacerbated China's drug problem and reminded many

---

112. Rhoads, *Manchus & Han*, pp. 96–101.

Qing subjects that their overlords were foreign. Chinese reformers and revolutionaries who evinced anti-Manchu attitudes could not openly fault the Qing for attempting to eliminate the opium problem, but reformers often were frustrated by what appeared to be the attempts of the central and provincial governments to slow the pace of reform. The Qing state was blamed for tying the progress of Chinese opium reform to a timetable that benefited British economic interests, even as Chinese authorities attempted to deflect British demands to squelch local violations of the new opium agreement.

The opium suppression campaign in Fuzhou's Banner garrison was intentionally set apart from the elite activism generated within that city's fledgling public sphere, for reasons that may or may not have had to do with ethnic considerations. However, the emergence of elite-led reform groups outside the formal bureaucracy and the implementation of the first stages of constitutional reform gave Han Chinese who harbored anti-Manchu attitudes a space in which those ideas could germinate into support for outright revolution. Ethnicity did not seem to affect the conduct of opium suppression significantly, but this did not mean that the residents of Fuzhou were unaware of racial differences between themselves and the Manchu Bannermen. When the revolution arrived in Fuzhou, it was the residents of the Manchu quarter who were targeted for revenge by Chinese mobs, the soldiers of the New Army, and even progressive reformers.[113] Perhaps the most significant difference between the general opium suppression campaign and the campaign as it was conducted among Fuzhou's Banner garrison was that the former continued into the early Republic whereas the latter disappeared along with the Qing dynasty itself.

---

113. The British consul at Fuzhou witnessed young students affiliated with the American Presbyterian mission executing captured Manchu prisoners with bayonets (PRO, FO 228/1800, no. 35, Werner to Jordan, 20 Nov. 1911).

SIX

Opium Reform Under the Republic, 1912–1914

> Enfeebled and corrupt China may have been. Not so now. She has crushed the poppy beneath her feet and at last she is aroused.
>
> — James Cantlie and C. Sheraton Jones, 1912

International, national, provincial, and local politics had a strong impact on the anti-opium campaign in early Republican Fujian, just as it had in the late Qing years. As word of the revolution spread, local administrations shut down, and local officials fled or simply retired to their yamen to await the revolutionaries. Taking advantage of the lack of formal state authority and perhaps believing that the dearth of officials, taxes, and other restrictions was indeed the fulfillment of the promise of the revolution, some farmers responded by planting poppies. The enforcement of restrictions on opium consumption also broke down, and there was a general resurgence of opium smoking throughout the province.

The reins of government and control of opium reform efforts in Fujian changed hands after the revolution, but the new Republic quickly endorsed the anti-opium campaign initiated by its Qing predecessor. As governor of Zhili province, Yuan Shikai had demonstrated his own personal commitment to opium reform even before the Qing campaign, and there was every reason to believe that as president he could lead China to victory against opium. He pledged to honor the terms of the international agreements that so strongly influenced the pace and conduct of opium suppression under the

---

EPIGRAPH: Cantlie and Jones, *Sun Yat Sen and the Awakening of China*, p. 213.

Qing.[1] This meant that the Republican state committed itself to the *second* Sino-British agreement on opium, which linked the end of Indian opium imports to the elimination of domestic poppy cultivation in every province in China. In Fujian, the urgency of eradicating poppy cultivation further reduced the clout of the Anti-Opium Society, a process already begun by the Provincial Assembly.

The careers of reformers like Chen Nengguang, Chen Peikun, and Lin Bingzhang revealed the implications of the lingering permeability of the public sphere in the early Republic and illustrated how deeply opium reform was imbedded in the broader spectrum of provincial and national politics. The two Chens shifted easily from unofficial activism to officialdom after the revolution. Chen Nengguang, a son of the "New China," with no traditional qualifications for office, quickly ascended to high provincial office and dominated the formal anti-opium bureaucracy after 1911. Chen Peikun assumed roles in both official and unofficial suppression organizations, among other positions. And Lin Bingzhang, Fujian's living link to the mission of his venerable ancestor, temporarily found himself hostage to the machinations of the new revolutionary clique, his symbolic significance to the anti-opium campaign seemingly irrelevant.

When the revolutionary government restored order, the battle against opium was again enforced in each prefecture and county, often with renewed vigor. That vigor was sometimes excessive and often resented, because the new Republic based much of its authority on military force. After the revolution, cooperation between reform-minded officials and elite-led reform groups continued. However, officials like Chen Peikun and Chen Nengguang were well aware of the power that elite reformers like themselves had derived from the anti-opium campaign and were careful to clarify the supervisory role of the provincial Opium Prohibition Bureau (Jinyan ju) over the unofficial Anti-Opium Society. For opium reformers, the public space in which much of their work had taken place during the Qing seemed on the verge of absorption by the new Republic largely because of the need to em-

---

1. Sun Yatsen reissued anti-opium proclamations during his brief term as provisional president, and Yuan Shikai announced mandates on 11 June and 28 Oct. 1912 confirming that the old opium regulations were still in effect (PRO, FO 228/2446, Jordan to FO, 18 Mar. 1912; *China Year Book*, 1914, pp. 513, 532–33). For more on the influential document that came to be known as Sun's "Anti-opium Will," see Chapter 9, p. 368, in this book; and Slack, *Opium, State, and Society*, pp. 71, 86–89, 91.

ploy the state's military strength and the convergence of state interests with those of reformist elites.

The new Republic wasted no time in declaring its intention to honor the Sino-British opium agreement that had been renegotiated in 1911, and the new regime recognized the ramifications of that policy for the conduct of the suppression campaign. The Republican government now had to intervene in poppy-growing regions that the Qing had skirted because of official incompetence, clan disputes, or fear of peasant resistance. The decision was not popular with opium farmers, nor did it present as much opportunity for the Fujian Anti-Opium Society and its branches to regulate local society. At the same time, the new provincial government found itself embroiled in a series of conflicts within its own military that hampered its plan to eradicate poppy cultivation quickly and endangered national goals.

Opium and the Military

In the early Republic, tensions within Fujian's military had a strong impact on the course of provincial and national politics and slowed the progress of opium suppression. After the revolution, the state's first and most important task was to restore and maintain order so that the new government could pursue its policy agenda. Beijing was committed to the re-establishment of order within provincial armies so as to better extend central government control over a potentially dangerous group and, among other things, to enable the nation as a whole to meet the conditions necessary to end Indian opium imports.[2] The paradox that confounded and frustrated the British in Fujian immediately following the revolution—strict Chinese enforcement of restrictions on smoking, sale, and transport of opium and a relatively lax approach to illicit poppy cultivation—was not an intentional favoring of Chinese interests by the provincial authorities but a reflection of an upheaval in the provincial military. A strong military was often needed to uproot illegal poppies. This problem was only temporary, however, and by mid-1913, the provincial government was able to concentrate the bulk of its efforts on eliminating the supply side of Fujian's opium problem.

---

2. The British, in order to justify their financial sacrifices in India, were particularly interested in compelling China to continue the fight, and the British Foreign Office privately advocated withholding recognition of the Republic until China proved its sincerity by continuing the suppression campaign (PRO, FO 228/2451, doc. 94, Jordan to Foreign Office, 12 Dec. 1912).

The trio of officers heading up the new Republican government—Sun Daoren, Peng Shousong, and Xu Chongzhi—was never particularly stable, and a strong rivalry between Military Governor Sun and the ruthless revolutionary leader Peng apparently arose from a longstanding antagonism between Fujianese soldiers and the Hunanese troops who dominated the provincial army.[3] These tensions almost exploded into open warfare in February 1912.[4] Peng was accused of engineering a political assassination in April 1912, and rumors of an impending mutiny by approximately 4,000 Hunanese soldiers loyal to Peng caused many Fuzhou residents to flee the city in May. Sun Daoren was able to defuse the situation, but Peng assumed the post of chief of the provincial police and was said to exercise almost dictatorial powers.[5]

Somewhat incongruously, Peng seemed serious about enforcing the restrictions on opium—or perhaps profiting from them—even in the midst of these conflicts. The British consul at Fuzhou reported that Peng ordered the execution of a police officer on 20 July 1912 for taking a bribe during an investigation of opium violations.[6] The same diplomat claimed that Peng had also been appointed head of the Anti-Opium Society around that time, but that assertion is not corroborated by the society's *Quarterly*.[7]

By fall 1912, the situation was heading for a confrontation, and when Peng began to summon Hunanese troops from Shaowu prefecture and elsewhere in Fujian to Fuzhou, Beijing stepped in. Peng attempted to forestall any punishment from the center through a series of negotiations, but Yuan Shikai appointed Cen Chunxuan (1861–1933) as Fujian's pacification commissioner and sent him to Fuzhou.[8] Cen and his troops arrived in October and

---

3. Shen Laiqiu, "Xinhai qianhou de Peng Shousong."
4. PRO, FO 228/1838, Werner to Jordan, 20 Feb. 1912.
5. Multiple dispatches in PRO, FO 228/1838. For more on Peng's perfidy, see Dunch, *Fuzhou Protestants and the Making of a Modern China*, p. 181.
6. Ibid., Werner to Jordan, 9 Aug. 1912.
7. Ibid., Werner to Jordan, 30 Sept. 1912, enclosure in Foochow Intelligence Report for Sept. 1912. It is likely that Werner's assumption derived either from his familiarity with the Qing pattern of appointing the same official to head up the police force and the official opium prohibition bureaucracy or from his consistent criticism of the powers exercised by the society.
8. Cen Chunxuan was born in Guangxi, earned the *juren* degree, and served in a number of high-level offices under the Qing. A strong supporter of the imperial family, he was offered the job of governor-general of Sichuan after 1911, which he was unable to accept because of the revolution. He was also a longtime rival of Yuan Shikai, and it was during a brief reconciliation that Cen was sent to Fujian. British documents allege that Cen had become Peng Shousong's enemy at the time of the revolution. According to one foreign report that cannot be verified, Peng was rumored to have cut off Cen's queue during the revolution (PRO, FO

supervised Peng's departure, negotiated in part by members of the South-of-the-Bridge Public Welfare Society and aided by a large sum of money raised by the Fuzhou Chamber of Commerce.[9] But by early February 1913, the political and economic situation in Fuzhou had reached a crisis point, exacerbated by acts of political terrorism allegedly committed by the Fujian Protection Society (Humin she), which was dedicated to returning control of Fujian to Fujianese.[10]

On the economic front, British officials reported that the province was on the verge of bankruptcy and that Beijing was either unwilling or unable to provide a loan to Sun Daoren. Lin Bingzhang, in his new capacity as provincial salt commissioner (*yanyun shi*), proposed a further surtax on salt to raise funds for the military. Ironically, the taxes he imposed in his new role contributed mightily to popular dissatisfaction over, among other things, the continuation of opium reform.

Several uprisings in Fujian's poppy-growing regions broke out during the post-revolutionary chaos, and the roller-coaster of provincial politics meant that local officials could not count on reliable military backup. The most serious revolt occurred in Xinghua prefecture in the summer of 1912, led by a man named Huang Lian, who opposed high taxes (especially salt taxes), the influence of local missionaries, and the order to uproot poppies. The revolt cost hundreds of lives, caused considerable property damage, and consumed a great deal of diplomatic and military energy before it was finally squelched in 1914.[11]

With the political situation in Fujian bordering on anarchy in mid-1913, the so-called Second Revolution, a multiprovince rebellion against Yuan Shikai, erupted. On 20 July 1913, Fujian declared its independence from Beijing and cast its lot with the neighboring province of Jiangxi.[12] Xu Chongzhi engineered the move, and although Sun Daoren was apparently not in favor

---

228/1838, Werner to Jordan, 10 Oct. 1912; Boorman, *Biographical Dictionary of Republican China*, 3: 305–8).

9. Wu Jiaqiong, "Lin Bingzhang shenping gaishu," p. 99.

10. Shen Laiqiu, "Xinhai qianhou de Peng Shousong"; MAE, Paris, NS 48, no. 1, Doire to Conty, 8 Feb. 1913.

11. For more on this incident, see Chapter 8. See also Madancy, "Revolution, Religion and the Poppy."

12. USDS (1910–29), 893.00/1765, telegram from Fowler to Secy. of State, 10 July 1913. For more on this episode, see Young, "Politics in the Aftermath of Revolution," pp. 228–36; and multiple dispatches in PRO, FO 228/1838.

of the declaration, Xu and the 7,000–8,000 Hunanese soldiers in Fujian's New Army carried the day.[13] Support for the Second Revolution among most officials and the general population was lukewarm at best, however, and the uprising was quickly crushed. On 4 August 1913, Fujian rescinded its declaration of independence. Xu fled to Japan, and Sun Daoren regained control.[14]

Determined to eliminate any further threat from Fujian's volatile New Army, Yuan Shikai dispatched Liu Guanxiong (1858–1927), a Fujianese who had served as minister of the navy during Sun Yatsen's brief presidency, to Fuzhou to oversee the disbanding of the rebellious Hunanese troops and to settle the Xinghua revolt. An Anhui officer by the name of Li Houji (1869–1942) commanded the soldiers accompanying Liu. Li assumed the new position of Fujian defense commissioner (*Fujian zhenshoushi*) in November 1913[15] and soon became the most powerful man in Fujian, a position he retained for the next decade. His regime is generally recognized as the beginning of warlordism in Fujian. By mid-December 1913, Liu had overseen Sun Daoren's dismissal and the peaceful disbandment and repatriation of the Hunanese troops. Some 4,000 soldiers primarily from Shandong and Zhili provinces, approximately half of the province's previous military strength, replaced them.[16] The shortage of troops hindered the forcible uprooting of poppies in the countryside, and the general volatility of the military situation in Fujian and elsewhere made Yuan Shikai increasingly wary of the possibility for dissent in the public political space and in the provincial assemblies. The unpredictable provincial military politics, dominated by men from outside the province, also probably intimidated many Fujianese activists who

---

13. Sun Daoren's family was Hunanese, but his father had served in Fujian for years and was immensely popular there. U.S. consul Fowler and Beijing were convinced that Sun's loyalties were with Fujian, not Hunan. The French concurred (USDS [1910–29], 893.00/1795, enclosure in no. 51, Fowler to Secy. of State, 21 June 1913; MAE/Paris, NS 50, no. 8, Knight to Paris, 1 July 1913).

14. USDS (1910–29), 893.00/1912, Fowler to Secy. of State, 6 Aug. 1913; USDS, 893.00/1803, telegram from Fowler to Secy. of State, 4 Aug. 1913; MAE/Paris, NS 50, nos. 9 and 10, Knight to Pichon, 8 and 9 July 1913, and NS 51, nos. 11 and 13, Knight to Pichon, 2 and 4 Aug. 1913.

15. Liu Shoulin, *Xinhai yihou shiqinian shiguan nianbiao*, p. 342.

16. Wen Gongzhi, *Zuijin sanshinian Zhongguo junshi shi*, 1: 233–34; Falkenheim, "Provincial Administration in Fukien," p. 34; USDS (1910–29), 893.00/2012, no. 1063, Williams to Secy. of State, 20 Oct. 1913; MAE/Paris, NS 53, nos. 22, 47, and Asie no. 30, Danjou to Conty, 3 and 22 Nov. 1913 and 12 Dec. 1913.

were loath to make themselves vulnerable to the violence that characterized the times.

Opium, the Public Sphere, and Imperialism

The new government in Nanjing moved quickly to restart the opium suppression campaign by establishing a national Opium Prohibition Office (Jinyan gongsuo) to assist the minister of civil affairs. However, that organization apparently did not perform especially well, and on 21 March 1914, the Opium Prohibition Supervisory Department (Jinyan ducha chu) was set up to bring the campaign more firmly under central control. This organization was affiliated with the Police Department of the Internal Administration Bureau (Neizheng bu, Jingzheng si). Its investigators and examiners were to fan out and make secret investigations to determine the progress of suppression in every province, and in theory, every county. In some provinces, this new organ was effective, but despite historian Wang Hongbin's assertion that the department was extremely powerful and had considerable impact on the campaign in the early Republic, it does not seem to have played much of a role in Fujian.[17] There are occasional references to government-appointed deputies overseeing the uprooting of poppies in the province, but no indication of whether they came from Beijing or Fuzhou. In any case, in 1915, Yuan Shikai "approved a government-managed opium monopoly in the Jiangsu, Guangdong, and Jiangxi provinces, effectively acknowledging the legalization of opium again."[18]

After the revolution, several developments revived the suppression campaign but eroded the influence of the Anti-Opium Society vis-à-vis the official reform bureaucracy: the loss of some of the society's most experienced and energetic leaders; a shift in central government policy that signaled a new emphasis on curtailing the cultivation of opium rather than its consumption; the eventual elimination of legal foreign opium imports into China; and finally, the rise of the warlords. As a result, the powers that had accrued to the Anti-Opium Society in the public sphere began to dissipate or be absorbed by the state even before British imports ended.

The society survived the political transition, but not without sacrificing much of its reputation, independence, and authority largely due to the ab-

---

17. Wang Hongbin, *Jindu shijian*, p. 349.
18. Zhou Yongming, *Anti-Drug Crusades in Twentieth-Century China*, p. 40.

sorption of its leaders by the new Republican bureaucracy. Of the seven men who served as its directors and vice-directors from the group's inception until 1911, only one remained to run the society after the revolution.[19] One left the province for another position, Chen Peikun and Lin Bingzhang remained in Fujian in high-level positions, and three simply resigned or retired.[20] Other prominent members also took positions in the new provincial government. Most notably, Gao Dengli, head of the Provincial Assembly before the revolution, briefly directed the Fujian Ministry of Civil Affairs (Minzheng bu), the apex of civilian administration under the new Republic, and then served as acting head of the provincial Department of Education (Jiaoyu sizhang) for a few months.[21] Immediately following the revolution, the Anti-Opium Society elected Lin Yushi and Yang Zhanyun to head up the group. Lin, who had apparently served as society director or vice director before the revolution, was a prominent member of the Tongmenghui and a founder of the South-of-the-Bridge Public Welfare Society in the late Qing. Under the auspices of the Public Welfare Society, he had also organized the Minnan Fire Department (Minnan jiuhuo hui), which also became involved with the revolution. He remained in charge of the Anti-Opium Society from 1912 until at least 1914, after which there is no consistent record of the group's leadership.[22] Lin Yushi's political experience and revolutionary credentials before 1911 certainly seemed to match that of Chen Nengguang and Chen Peikun, but his post-revolutionary clout was unimpressive.

The fate of Lin Bingzhang, the most high-profile of the society's leaders, was another clear indication of how deeply opium reform was enmeshed in local politics. After stepping down as leader of the society in 1908, Lin pursued an official career in Beijing and continued to lend his name and efforts to the unofficial arm of the anti-opium crusade until the revolution.[23] After 1911, Lin returned to his home province, where he was suspected of harboring anti-Republican sentiments. He was placed under house arrest at the provincial Ministry of Civil Affairs. However, his longstanding connections

---

19. The identities of several of these men are unknown, because the issues of *The Quarterly* that cover the last three years of the Qing are unavailable.
20. Zheng Zuyin et al., *Fujian xinhai guangfu shiliao*, p. 157.
21. Ibid., p. 143.
22. Ibid., pp. 25–26; *The Quarterly* 12 (1914), *tubiao* section, pp. 1–2. Chen Nengguang was also affiliated with the Fire Department (Dunch, *Fuzhou Protestants and the Making of a Modern China*, p. 66).
23. MAE/Paris, NS 587, Lecomte to Paris, 3 July 1908.

with the infamous Peng Shousong, then head of that ministry, proved advantageous. After the marriage of Peng's daughter and Lin's son, Lin was not only set free but also given the important job of commissioner of the provincial Salt Gabelle, as well as a position in the ministry. This development apparently triggered popular outrage, and to address that dissatisfaction and lingering suspicions regarding his politics, Lin felt it necessary to assert his pro-Republican sentiments publicly in a letter to the *Heart of Fujian Daily* (*Minxin ribao*).[24] When Peng fell from grace, Lin once again came under suspicion. By 1914, the tide had turned in Lin's favor again, and he was resurrected as salt commissioner.[25] Lin's impressive genealogy and previous service in the anti-opium campaign could carry him only so far in the new reality of Republican politics. What ultimately saved his career was not his link to Lin Zexu but his skill in money management, a talent in great demand at this time of financial crisis.

Lin's successor and friend, fellow Hanlin scholar Chen Peikun, stepped into officialdom as director (*zongban, suozhang*) of the Fujian Opium Prohibition Bureau (Fujian jinyan ju or Jinyan gongsuo) after the revolution. However, he kept his feet in both realms by retaining his membership in the Anti-Opium Society. The *Quarterly* lists him as an officer in the group's 1913 roster.[26] During his tenure as director, Chen also served as director (*tingzhang*) of Fujian's Provincial Police Department (Fujian quansheng jingwuting) until he was reassigned in early 1913 to serve as intendant (*guancha shi*) of the Eastern Circuit (Donglu).[27] After Chen Peikun's departure, Chen Xiurong served briefly as interim director of the Opium Prohibition Bureau, and shortly thereafter, the job was given (again briefly) to Wu Wei'ao before it passed to Chen Nengguang. Chen initially refused the job, purportedly because provincial authorities would not give him virtually unlimited powers, but he ultimately agreed and assumed office in June 1913.[28]

---

24. Zheng Zuyin et al., *Fujian xinhai guangfu shiliao*, pp. 291–92; MAE/Paris, NS 587, Foutcheou to Paris, 3 July 1908, pp. 101–13.

25. Wu Jiaqiong, "Lin Bingzhang shenping gaishu," p. 99; Li Guoqi, *Zhongguo xiandaihua de quyu yanjiu*, pp. 558–59.

26. *The Quarterly* 12 (1914), *tubiao* section, p. 1.

27. Liu Shoulin, *Xinhai yihou shiqinian zhiguan nianbiao*, pp. 342–43. Chen served successively as circuit intendant (*daoyin*) for the Tingzhanglong, Minhai, and Xiamen circuits from 1912 to 1919 (Liu Decheng and Zhai Xianying, *Fujian minren cidian*, pp. 212–13).

28. PRO, FO 228/2453, doc. 12, Werner to Jordan, 25 Feb. 1913. However, Werner's analysis of Chen's motivations may reflect the former's intense dislike of Chen.

Even more than Chen Peikun, the trajectory of Chen Nengguang's career from unofficial opium reformer to leader of the official arm of the suppression campaign embodied the permeability of the public sphere as well as its pitfalls. Chen Nengguang's upbringing marked him as a citizen of the new China, and he was one of many reformers in Fujian who benefited immensely from the Revolution of 1911. His dogged devotion to opium suppression even during the political upheaval caused the British consul E. T. C. Werner at Fuzhou to condemn him as "one of the worst scoundrels in the place."[29] He became director of the Provincial Department of Foreign Relations (Min zhengfu waijiaosi) after the revolution, and two years later, he became head of Fujian's Opium Prohibition Bureau. He also was instrumental in eroding the power of the Anti-Opium Society, although his name appears as an officer of that group in its 1914 roster.[30] Under Chen's leadership, the Opium Prohibition Bureau worked closely with the society and its branches but firmly extended state control over the unofficial group.

The last extant issue of *The Quarterly* was published in 1914 but covered the events of the preceding few years. It included the latest version of the society's regulations, which highlighted how dramatically the independence and integrity of the group had been reduced, at least on paper. With 75 branches across the province, the society was still a presence in the continuing battle to eliminate the sale and smoking of opium, and it still exercised considerable power, but only under the constant supervision of the Opium Prohibition Bureau. Part of the bureau's oversight was justified by the abuse of the society's powers by disreputable individuals and a decline in discipline among society members. The bureau sought to keep track of the society by requiring the head of each branch to compile a registry of members; it then issued each member an identification certificate. That certificate was to be held at the branch headquarters for safekeeping, but it had to be carried on investigations and raids, in part to distinguish genuine members of the Society from "ruffians of evil character [who] have impersonated the searches of various departments of the Anti-Opium Society . . .

---

29. PRO, FO 228/1800, doc. 35, Werner to Jordan, 20 Nov. 1911. Werner alleged that until his appointment with the Opium Prohibition Bureau, Chen had led a group of Chinese Christians in plotting to assassinate Sun Daoren (PRO, FO 228/1872, Werner to Jordon, Intelligence Report for December Quarter 1912, 25 Jan. 1913).

30. *The Quarterly* 12 (1914), *tubiao* section, p. 2.

in the hope of extorting money."[31] In one such case, Werner alleged that the society had violently harassed a prominent Chinese opium merchant by the name of Yang Zhengqun after Yang failed to offer a bribe.[32] Society investigators now had to be accompanied by policemen on their nightly rounds, and each branch was instructed to work only within its own geographical jurisdiction. The regulations ordered investigators to report poppy plantings to local officials so that the officials could arrest and prosecute the culprits.[33] Confiscated contraband had to be brought to the bureau or one of its branches for storage and disposal.[34] China's emergent public sphere had always moved to the rhythms of state policy, but now the state began to use its authority to supervise and/or absorb many of the society's powers and functions.[35]

Opium restrictions were hastily reimposed when provincial authorities regained control, and the official and unofficial arms of the campaign continued their work. The Opium Prohibition Bureau was revived and reorganized under the provincial Ministry of Civil Affairs after 1911 and continued to consolidate its control over the suppression campaign. It published new regulations and issued a monthly publication that resembled *The Quarterly*. This new journal included relevant proclamations, changes in regulations, brief reports on the progress of reform in various localities, and statistics compiled by the Anti-Opium Society. The three extant copies housed in the Fujian provincial library (from the third, fourth, and fifth months of the new Republic's first year)[36] clearly spell out the continued close relationship between the official and unofficial arms of the campaign but reiterate the prominence of the bureau over the groups that it subsidized. Local branches

---

31. This quotation is taken from an Opium Prohibition Bureau proclamation of March 1912 condemning such impersonators (PRO, FO 228/2447, enclosure no. 8 in Werner to Jordan, 26 Mar. 1912).

32. PRO, FO, 228/2447, Werner to Jordan, 28 Apr. 1912.

33. *The Quarterly* 12 (1914), *zhangcheng* section, pp. 1–4.

34. *Min dudufu Minzhengsi Jinyan gongsuo*, no. 1 (Apr./May 1912): 4.

35. Other reform groups also dissolved after the revolution. The South-of-the-Bridge Public Welfare Society shut down in 1912, citing lack of funds and the fact that its duties were taken over by the new government (Zheng Zuyin et al., *Fujian xinhai guangfu shiliao*, pp. 279–80).

36. This corresponds to the period between mid-April and early August 1912 in the western calendar. *Min Dudufu Minzhengsi Jinyan gongsuo*, nos. 1–3 (1912). Heartfelt thanks to Grant Alger who rescued these from oblivion in the Provincial Library copy room and sent me a copy.

of the bureau and the society were the only such groups mentioned by name in official regulations.[37]

The bureau's structure reflected the importance of opium suppression in the eyes of the local administration, as well as a recognition that reformist assistance was necessary but had to be kept under tight control. Ten men managed the bureau's seven departments,[38] and the bureau was expected to work closely with the police and judiciary. The regulations clearly state that the bureau director controlled the opium suppression campaign and all officials and unofficial elite reformers involved with that policy. Each local administrative unit was ordered to set up a branch, and each branch was directed by a local official, who was charged with selecting a vice director from the most upright and impartial gentry. The bureau headquarters apparently expected that the bulk of the work of directing the branch bureaus would fall to these gentry vice directors and explicitly ordered them to compile detailed reports of their activities for the official in charge.[39]

The bureau issued comprehensive anti-opium regulations in spring 1912 that established the priorities of the new regime. Opium dens, opium poppies, and the sale of opium substitutes were strictly forbidden. Opium shops had to be licensed monthly, and shops that sold the prepared drug were given a deadline for closure. Only foreign imports of the drug that had already been paid for and certified could be transported. Opium smoking was permitted for those with licenses, and smokers were ordered to report to the nearest branch bureau immediately to be examined, registered, and licensed.[40] The crackdown on the domestic drug, despite the continuation of a relatively small traffic in the imported variety, set the stage for considerable Chinese resentment and sparked the confrontations with the British discussed below.

By the summer of 1912, Sun Daoren reported that 176 shops dealing in certificated Indian opium were in operation throughout the province and that the number of registered smokers was approximately 67,000. Officials established 69 opium treatment centers, and the Anti-Opium Society opened 109 more.[41] The new government took especially active measures to

---

37. *Min dudufu Minzhengsi Jinyan gongsuo*, no. 1 (Apr./May 1912): 4.
38. There were separate departments for documentation, general affairs, accounts, examination, and smoking cessation, as well as two departments for investigation.
39. *Min dudufu Minzhengsi Jinyan gongsuo*, no. 1 (Apr./May 1912): 10-11
40. Ibid., pp. 4-9.
41. *Republican Advocate*, 10 Aug. 1912, pp. 751-52. A British consular officer was suspicious of those statistics: "I am informed that when the registration system was in force only two out

enforce anti-opium restrictions in and around Fuzhou by threatening to remove all officials who dared to smoke. The bureau dispatched an inspector to tour Minhou county, which included Fuzhou, to demand that local elites hand over opium-smoking implements and to obtain written commitments that no poppy would be planted.[42]

At the port of Fuzhou, the final stages of the anti-opium campaign were not marked by a dramatic decline in the amount of Indian opium imports. In fact, according to British figures supplied by Jardine Matheson & Company, "a net import . . . of foreign opium into Foochow in 1913 was 983 chests as compared with 974 in 1912." However, total sales, including unsold chests left in stock from the previous year, fell from 1,069 chests in 1912 to 1,013 chests in 1913. According to British observers, these figures illustrated that China's success at restricting opium consumption and domestic opium sales had temporarily enabled foreign merchants to maintain a fairly steady business. Profits were also considerable, since the scarcity of Chinese opium caused the wholesale price of the Indian article to double from 1912 to 1913. In addition, British diplomats noted an increase in the appropriation of foreign names and nationalities by Chinese opium traffickers forbidden by their own government to participate in the trade.[43] Chinese merchants operating under Japanese protection were especially problematic, given the proximity of Taiwan, with its thriving colonial opium monopoly.

Despite the bureau's efforts and a steady stream of proclamations, not until the spring and summer of 1913 was Fujian's anti-opium campaign able to regain the momentum it had lost after the revolution, probably due to the political and military obstacles discussed above. That spring, Chen Weilin, Gan Huangtao, Chen Zongshu, and Liao Shangqing of the Provincial Assembly introduced bills to bolster the anti-opium campaign. The provincial minister of governmental affairs approved a sweeping new set of opium suppression laws in June 1913 that commanded the end of opium sales by mid-July. Dealers of foreign raw opium in Fuzhou were compelled to relinquish their licenses, retail shops were to close down, and all Chinese-owned opium was to be seized and burned. The bureau published new regulations on 17 July that included an outright ban on all opium smok-

---

of ten smokers registered themselves" (PRO, FO 228/2453, doc. 12, Werner to Jordan, 25 Feb. 1913).

42. *Republican Advocate*, 20 July 1912, p. 619.

43. PRO, FO 228/2457, doc. 71, Wilkinson to Jordan, 26 Jan. 1914.

ing.[44] On 8 August 1913, Minister of Civil Affairs (often referred to as "civil governor") Jiang Yujing renewed the existing prohibition on poppy cultivation in Fujian, and in September, he appointed Huang Peisong as Fujian's pacification commissioner (*hujun shi*).[45] A native of Quanzhou, Huang had led the official effort to prohibit poppy cultivation in south Fujian since the revolution. Along with the circuit intendant of Zhangzhou and Xiamen, Huang issued a strongly worded proclamation threatening the confiscation of land and harsh physical punishment for violators of the prohibition. That summer and fall, provincial officials in Fujian began to implement these and other measures designed to accelerate the campaign and win Fujian a place on the list of provinces closed to Indian opium imports.

Provincial newspapers reported that the anti-smoking part of the campaign faced some obstacles during the summer of 1913. There were insinuations that opium investigators from the society or the bureau sometimes delayed investigations to allow violators to flee (presumably for a price).[46] A lack of manpower as the campaign regained its momentum also resulted in a call for scholars and students residing in areas outside Fuzhou to become investigators when they returned home for summer vacation. Chen Nengguang evidently was plagued by complaints that wealthy offenders could bribe their way out of a jail sentence and by a lack of prison space for opium offenders. British consul Werner noted that more than a dozen of the 300 suspected smokers in Fuzhou jailed by mid-August 1913 had died from the heat and other unhealthy conditions.[47]

The reinvigorated campaign spawned a number of petty diplomatic crises surrounding Chinese interference with the still legitimate British opium trade, incidents that allow a glimpse at the ability of the new Chinese state to control the campaign.[48] However, one reason that diplomatic controversy

---

44. *Fujian jinyan jishu*, p. 49; PRO, FO 228/2455, doc. 85, Werner to Alston, 31 July 1913.

45. PRO, FO 228/2455, multiple enclosures in doc. 40, Werner to Alston, 31 July 1913, and doc. 89, Werner to Beijing, 23 Aug. 1913.

46. *Fujian jinyan jishu*, p. 49.

47. PRO/FO 228/2455, doc. 89, Werner to Alston, 23 Aug. 1913.

48. Werner and Chen Nengguang also clashed over the veracity of reports on the eradication of poppies in the countryside. Werner refused to accept evidence provided by Chinese officials, stating that photographs of soldiers and local officials uprooting poppies did not prove widespread enforcement or indicate whether the poppy pods had been tapped. Werner acknowledged Chen's sincerity, but insisted that real progress could not be proved until next year's planting season (PRO, FO 228/2455, doc. 84, Werner to Alston, 29 July 1913). Despite his argumentative nature, Werner had a point.

characterized the last stage of opium reform in Fujian was Werner himself, a man whose devotion to the letter of the law ignored the success of the campaign in delegitimizing the entire trade. In fact, Werner's fixation on violations of the opium restrictions and his antipathy toward Chen Nengguang in particular were only the latest manifestations of what his colleagues and superiors felt was increasingly unacceptable and irrational behavior. By the early Republic, states one source, "Werner was a byword throughout China for maniacal quarrelsomeness," and in 1914 he was relieved of his duties for a bizarre and violent outburst.[49] F. E. Wilkinson, who replaced Werner as consul in 1914, was far less interventionist and reactionary and conceded that the British were "conniving at a trade that is being carried on by means which are discreditable and demoralizing to all concerned."[50]

Wilkinson reflected the new tenor of a British government distracted by the start of World War I and embarrassed by public opinion in China and at home that cast the British as greedy and immoral traders whose lust for money was all that stood in the way of the triumph of the new Republic. These cases did not concern enormous amounts of money, but they challenged the British to renounce their mercenary intentions and revealed the commitment and ability of China's central and provincial governments to accomplish the genuine suppression of opium. However, provincial authorities in Fujian were also concerned about Chen Nengguang's considerable powers, in other words, his ability to derail the national campaign, and the new regulations ordered him to clear any changes in the restrictions with the minister of governmental affairs.

In the most notorious case, opium purchased by Chinese traders Kun Ji, Yu Maolong, and Yu Ji from the Indian firm of Messrs. Petigura & Co. (known by the Chinese name Fuji yanghang) was seized in July 1913 at the Shuikou transit tax barrier (*lijin guan*) just outside Fuzhou. The drug was headed upriver to Jianning prefecture, and the goods were returned only when Chen Nengguang forced the dealers to promise to ship the opium to Shanghai, which had become a national storehouse for unsold imports. However, customs officials then refused to allow the reshipment and confiscated the drug. Shortly thereafter, officials of the Opium Prohibition Bureau also confiscated several chests of Petigura's opium at the Zhuqi transit

---

49. Coates, *The China Consuls*, pp. 438–41.
50. PRO, FO 228/2457, doc. 71, Wilkinson to Jordan, 26 Jan. 1914.

tax barrier (about forty miles from Fuzhou) and arrested the three Chinese boatmen conveying the opium inland. Chen and several deputies took charge of the contraband and the prisoners and brought them back to Fuzhou, where the boatmen were confined at bureau headquarters. The Minhou magistrate then took custody of the men.[51]

Werner lashed out at Chen and then complained to Sun Daoren, who referred the matter back to the bureau. Since the bureau was the subject of Werner's objections in the first place, the irate consul took his protests directly to Beijing. British Minister John Jordan took up Werner's protests and informed the national Ministry of Foreign Affairs. Despite high-level negotiations, Chen held on to the prisoners until 16 October 1913, when they were finally released after paying a large fine. As for the opium, Beijing's instructions to Fuzhou that the chests *not be burned* inspired a flurry of anxious letters from Werner and Petigura, who apparently had not considered this possibility. Ultimately, Beijing defended Chen's actions despite British threats, even as an indignant Jordan asked the Ministry of Foreign Affairs if Fujian's "Civil Governor's idea of the opinion of the common people is to override the solemn obligations entered into between our two countries?"[52] The chests were finally returned to Petigura on 10 March 1914.

The Petigura affair stirred more than the passions of a few diplomats and officials. Local newspapers in Fujian expressed outrage at British conduct, and a leaflet outlining the controversy urged Chinese authorities to resist British pressure.[53] Clearly, the conflict between central and provincial interests had not disappeared, and it remained in Beijing's interest to avoid the appearance of siding with the British.

Another less contentious case arose in Fuzhou in November 1913 between the British and opium reformers. Local police and society investigators apparently ambushed and arrested Li Jiang, a clerk from the Indian opium firm of Mehta & Co., carrying cash and samples of Malwa opium. Mehta complained that the society had disrupted his business by patrolling in front of

---

51. Numerous dispatches in PRO, FO 228/2455 and FO 228/2456. In 1913, Min and Houguan counties became Minhou county (Chen Hanguang, "Minguo yilai Fujian sheng difang xingzheng quhua," pp. 22–23).

52. PRO, FO 228/2457, doc. 134, Jordan to Ministry of Foreign Affairs, 16 Feb. 1914.

53. PRO, FO 228/1872, Werner to Jordan, 31 Dec. 1913, December Quarter Intelligence Report; translated excerpts from *Qiushi bao*, in PRO, FO 228/2456, doc. 18, Werner to Alston, 23 Sept. 1913.

his firm to intimidate potential Chinese customers. He also alleged that the society had searched and harassed those who emerged from the firm.[54]

Werner insisted that the problem lay entirely with Chen Nengguang and "the unchecked aggression of the Anti-Opium [Bureau]," which was acting in defiance of orders from Beijing.[55] Available documents do not support his assertions, however. In fact, Beijing appears to have recognized the issues at stake in this case and generally supported Chen and Sun Daoren. There may, however, have been a brief weakening of Beijing's resolve in the fall of 1913. According to local newspapers, in September of that year, British protests appeared to have finally swayed the opinion of high Republican officials, who sent a telegram to Sun Daoren ordering the suspension of funding for the Anti-Opium Society. Sun protested, and in response, the national Ministry of Revenue amended its order by commanding only a reduction in the society's subsidy.[56] This less than resolute action on the part of the central government indicated that the new Republic did not wish to cave in to foreign demands and seemed to highlight the Chinese state's precarious position vis-à-vis the provinces immediately following the abortive Second Revolution. It also clearly indicates that the society and the state were still closely linked.

Wang Shouchang, head of Fujian's Department of Foreign Relations, defended Chen's actions as Werner complained that Chinese dealers would no longer buy from Indian merchants if the Indian drug was likely to be confiscated and destroyed. He also questioned the genuineness of a petition allegedly submitted on 7 July 1913 by He Chun and other Chinese opium merchants from ten firms in the Yunjitang Merchants Association (Fuzhou yunjitang tushang). Werner claimed that Chen Nengguang and others had coerced the association's "voluntary" offer to retire from their current occupation.[57] That accusation was confirmed in part by a report in a local newspaper in December 1913 that the largest firm in the guild had opened a large

---

54. PRO, FO 228/2456, doc. 85, Werner to Jordan, 17 Dec. 1913.

55. Werner's assigning blame for society actions to Chen implies that the official bureau was charged with supervising the unofficial society.

56. PRO, FO 228/2456, doc. 18, Werner to Beijing, 23 Sept. 1913.

57. In that petition, the merchants express a strong patriotic motivation, asserting that "opium merchants are also Chinese citizens." They pledged to give up their occupation because of pride and popular outrage but also applied for government financial help to pay back the debts that would accrue because of their action (*Fujian jinyan jishu*, pp. 53–54).

opium shop under a different name.⁵⁸ Chen informed Werner that authorities in Beijing had reassured Chen that his actions had the support and approval of the central government. Privately, Werner conceded that the trade had come to a standstill by the end of July 1913.⁵⁹

The British were not the only foreign government that came into conflict with the Chinese over the renewed push for opium suppression. Part of the plan to impose a "cold turkey" strategy on the entire province included the push to shut down all commerce in unauthorized anti-opium medicines, a measure that generated a brief conflict with the Japanese. In the summer of 1913, the Opium Prohibition Bureau accused the Japanese Dragon Company (Rilong gongsi) of selling anti-opium pills laced with narcotics. The bureau reached this conclusion after subjecting the pills to a chemical analysis. The Japanese consulate pointed out the difficulty of accurately assigning blame, noting that hundreds of stores in the province peddled this type of medicine and explaining that this particular company's products were so much in demand that they inspired many Chinese counterfeiters. The consul also complained that despite their treaty rights, Chinese harassment impaired the Rilong merchants' ability to conduct trade. He accused Chinese officials of banging on company doors late at night, pestering would-be customers on the street, and writing insulting letters to the company. The controversy apparently ended amicably when the Chinese Foreign Affairs Department (Waijiao si) agreed to order an investigation into what it termed incorrect Chinese behavior and thanked the Japanese for halting sales of the pills in question.⁶⁰ However, the Japanese were well on their way to displacing the British as the main source of illicit narcotics in Fujian, and the case illustrated that Chinese anti-opium efforts, even in the cities, still faced serious obstacles.

These diplomatic controversies and the publication of new regulations by the Anti-Opium Society and the Opium Prohibition Bureau reflect the tensions involved in redrawing the boundaries of the public political space and in balancing the renewed momentum of Fujian's campaign with British concern for the letter of the agreement. Chen Nengguang's energetic leadership of the bureau and his continued role in the society implied the endurance of

---

58. PRO, FO 228/1872, Werner to Jordan, 31 Dec. 1913, December Quarter Intelligence Report.
59. PRO, FO 228/2455, doc. 85, Werner to Alston, 31 July 1913.
60. *Fujian jinyan jishu*, pp. 45–49.

the fluid boundaries between the state and the public political space, but his emphasis on his official duties and his deliberate attempt to supervise and absorb the society's activities indicated his desire to curtail or diminish the power of the public political space. That desire seemed reasonable, given the decline in the society's reputation and power and the oversight of a state bureaucracy staffed by reform-minded officials like Chen. In the meantime, the state's ongoing subsidy of the society and allegations of corruption point to continuing problems with funding and staffing the opium reform bureaucracy. Public ceremonies continued but apparently not on as large a scale as before 1911. As an official, Chen seemed less concerned with public participation, but popular resentment at the intrusive nature of opium reform, especially in rural venues, may mean that the public was less receptive.

Opium Reform Outside Fuzhou

Fujian's battle against illicit poppy cultivation was joined in earnest in 1913, when the tantalizing prospect of cutting off the flow of Indian opium inspired Chen Nengguang to take the suppression campaign deeper into the countryside than it had probably penetrated before. There he found a pervasive flouting of the restrictions, and with a joint inspection looming, he acted forcefully. The most comprehensive source on the extent of poppy cultivation in early Republican Fujian and the response of the provincial government is a lengthy, handwritten report, *Objective Account of Opium Prohibition in Fujian (Fujian jinyan jishu)*. The report is undated but all the events it describes appear to date from the spring or summer of 1913, and it seems to have been compiled either by the Opium Prohibition Bureau or the provincial Ministry of Civil Affairs.[61] It probably was intended to serve as proof that the province was prepared to undergo the joint inspection. Almost thirty pages are devoted to county inspections, and although the document provides compelling evidence of Republican success in the revived anti-opium campaign, the findings reveal a startling degree of popular resistance to the prohibition of poppy farming. In many areas, the acreage of poppy

---

61. No author or publisher is listed. The report can be divided into three sections. The first is a collection of dated proclamations from various provincial officials, including the civil governor and Chen Nengguang, in his capacity as head of the Opium Prohibition Bureau. The second is a county-by-county report on the progress of opium prohibition, and the final part is a collection of correspondence regarding the incident, described above, involving the Japanese government during the campaign.

cultivation was minimal, but out of the 57 counties and departments visited, only nine were declared to have been free of poppies since the revolution.

The report is striking not only for its meticulous accounting—in one county where the total area cultivated in poppies was less than two *mu*, each uprooted plant was counted and each violator's name listed—but also for the almost total absence of any mention of the Anti-Opium Society.[62] This appears to support the contention that the society's hands-on activism was largely confined to the cities.[63] Other sources, particularly foreign diplomatic dispatches, indicate that members of the Anti-Opium Society may have been involved in investigating and monitoring illegal poppy cultivation in and around urban areas. However, in most cases, the leaders of this stage of the suppression campaign in the countryside were county magistrates, the soldiers at their disposal, local councils (*zizhi hui*), local gentry (*shendong*), and heads of the local mutual security organizations (*baojia*), as well as the officers and inspectors of Chen Nengguang's Opium Prohibition Bureau.[64] The state, clearly and understandably, was unwilling to allow unofficial reformers to become involved in policing or military operations in the villages.

Early Republican authorities in Fujian sought to avoid violence in the countryside, and despite their frequent reliance on military force to compel compliance with the restrictions, they did attempt to use a carrot-and-stick approach. In many areas, the arrival of troops was preceded by meetings with local gentry and village leaders to convince them of the need to cooperate and to publicize the regulations. For those reporting illegal poppies, the provincial regulations offered monetary rewards commensurate with the amount of land planted in the drug.[65] Proclamations announced the imminent arrival of the investigators and urged poppy farmers to destroy their illegal crops voluntarily; presumably the intent was to give fair warning of what was to come and to allow a peaceful resolution. In fact, many farmers

---

62. The one explicit reference, in the entry for Guihua county in Tingzhou, indicates that the local branch of the Anti-Opium Society (founded in 1908) was in charge of investigating poppy cultivation before 1911, but after the revolution, the Opium Prohibition Bureau took over those duties (*Fujian jinyan jishu*, p. 41).

63. Another possible explanation is that the report was produced by a state entity, most likely the Opium Prohibition Bureau, that may have viewed the Anti-Opium Society as a rival.

64. In some cases, it may be that local gentry were members of branches of the Anti-Opium Society, but in the absence of any specific references, I hesitate to make that assumption.

65. *Fujian jinyan jishu*, p. 9.

who did uproot their own poppies received monetary compensation or government forgiveness of their crimes. Chinese authorities labeled violators lawless or greedy, and punishment ranged from arrest and imprisonment to large fines and severe beatings, to the outright confiscation of their land. Their lucrative cash crop was destroyed, as soldiers, policemen, members of the Opium Prohibition Bureau, village leaders, and hired laborers worked to uproot each and every poppy plant. Mindful of the significance of their actions, investigators sometimes photographed the poppy fields, before and after destruction, or took sample plants to contradict the claims of local officials. In this tense milieu, the colorful celebrations that marked victories over opium smoking in the cities were absent.

The focus on eradicating poppies should not obscure the resurgence of opium smoking or continuing elite/official efforts to combat it. The Anti-Opium Society remained actively involved in efforts to address opium smoking in Fujian's urban centers. Its members moved decisively to shut down opium dens, issue temporary smoking licenses, fund and staff addiction treatment centers, and intimidate unauthorized traffickers and shop owners.

OPIUM PROHIBITION IN THE NORTHWEST

The breakdown of government control that accompanied the revolution inspired many in northwest Fujian to resume smoking or selling opium, and some poppies were planted as well. The opium economy was especially difficult to dislodge in Jianning, which had served as a major entrepôt for opium shipments from the coast of Fujian to Jiangxi. Local political tensions seriously complicated the concluding stages of the anti-opium campaign in Jianning and Shaowu prefectures, but as noted above, this region was not suited for poppy cultivation, a circumstance unaffected by the Revolution of 1911. Seven of the nine counties reporting no poppy cultivation were located here. The total amount of land devoted to poppy cultivation by "lawless villages/villagers" (wuzhi xiang) in the northwest amounted to only about twenty mu, and all plants were said to have been uprooted in spring 1913.[66]

Reports on Pucheng county in Jianning, where British merchants in Fuzhou insisted that the poppy was being grown, were mixed.[67] A Chinese source counters that the people of Pucheng were so opposed to opium that

---

66. Ibid., pp. 30–36.
67. PRO, FO 228/2447, Werner to Jordan, 26 Mar. 1912.

in 1912 a number of residents in a patriotic rage spontaneously seized and burned an unspecified amount of the drug.[68] However, as late as January 1914, an English businessman informed the British consul at Fuzhou that he had seen a fair number of poppies growing along the border between Jianning and Yanping prefectures.[69] This was especially disturbing because Jianning had never known significant poppy cultivation.

Opium smoking reappeared after 1911 as well, and toward the end of 1912, an American missionary wrote that he himself had witnessed the brazen smoking of the drug in Jianning prefecture. He reported a long conversation with two men as they puffed away, and he was deeply disturbed that they seemed absolutely unconcerned, which was in marked contrast to the secrecy with which the drug was used before the revolution.[70] However, as government pressure to enforce the campaign increased, more residents of Jianning sought help for addiction. The CMS hospital in the prefectural seat reported an increase in the number of middle- and upper-class smokers seeking treatment in 1913. Several of the city's reform societies joined with the CMS to help impoverished smokers in the summer of 1914:

> The third-class opium patients, or street-coolie class, are greatly to be pitied, and our workers at Kienningfu [Jianning City] are now combining with the city gentry and others in order to attempt really to rid the city at least of this 'sore': villages would have to be dealt with afterwards. It will be a difficult matter, but we understand that many of the gentry and leaders in the city are most favourable.[71]

The Chinese donated money for food, and the missionaries took care of medicines and the treatment. Smokers initially were housed in the CMS hospital in Jianning City, but were eventually shifted to a nearby temple.[72] About 150 patients were treated during the first months of operation.[73]

In Shaowu, the former magistrate was said to have profited from the licensing of opium shops and opium imports, but his replacement, Zhang Zuhan, vigorously enforced the government prohibitions. Zhang opened an anti-opium treatment center and funded many reforms from his own sal-

---

68. Zhang Xingsheng, "'Jinyan' zaji," pp. 31–32.
69. PRO, FO 228/2457, doc. 139, Wilkinson to Jordan, 27 Feb. 1914.
70. USDS (1910–29), 893.114, reel 113, enclosure in Fuzhou to Secy. of State, 9 Jan. 1913.
71. Mercy and Truth 18, no. 211 (July 1914): 246.
72. Mercy and Truth 19, no. 223 (July 1915): 244.
73. CMS, Fuhkien Mission, Original Incoming, 1900–1934 (1914), no. 176, letter from Phillips, 24 Aug. 1914.

ary.[74] In July 1913, a local newspaper reported that the Shaowu magistrate actively enforced opium restrictions in his jurisdiction. Just a month earlier, he evidently toured the fourteen local opium shops with members of the society and officials from the bureau. He stamped each of the 800 packages of opium that were discovered and ordered that they be disposed of by a certain deadline, after which no further opium would be sold in Shaowu. However, he was then notified by the civil governor of the decision that all shops were to be closed immediately and any inventory returned to its port of origin. The magistrate complied and announced his intent to shoot offenders and burn any remaining opium.[75]

OPIUM PROHIBITION
IN THE NORTHEAST

In Fuzhou prefecture, arguably the best-monitored region of the province, poppies blanketed 30,000 *mu* in Lianjiang county alone in the spring of 1913. It took county troops and police more than two months to wipe out the crop that was spread over almost 400 villages.[76] In many other counties, such as Changle, Fuding, Minhou, Luoyuan, Pingnan, and Yongfu, magistrates and opium inspectors found minuscule plots of poppies and dealt accordingly with the culprits. It took military force in Minqing and Gutian, with 300 and 50 *mu* apiece, respectively, to oversee the uprooting of the plants.[77] In October 1913, however, opium inspector Zhang Zhijun (presumably from Fuzhou) made a careful examination and discovered clandestine cultivation in the counties of Lianjiang, Luoyuan (both in Fuzhou prefecture), and Ningde (Funing prefecture).[78]

Local officials and elites also combated the return of opium smoking. The first Republican magistrate in Luoyuan strictly prohibited the drug and

---

74. PRO, FO 228/1872, Werner, Intelligence Report for Dec. 1912. He also organized an anti-footbinding society among local women (*Foochow Messenger*, Mar. 1913, pp. 12–13).

75. It is not clear if these two accounts describe the same energetic magistrate (PRO, FO 228/2456, Werner to Beijing, 23 Sept. 1913).

76. *Fujian jinyan jishu*, pp. 17–18. However, another source claims that the anti-opium work was conducted by the county magistrate and the local branch of the Anti-Opium Society (PRO, FO 228/2454, doc. 70, letter from Curtis, 24 Apr. 1913).

77. To put things in perspective, reports claimed that about 320,000 poppy plants grew on Gutian's 50 *mu* (*Fujian jinyan jishu*, pp. 16–20).

78. PRO, FO 228/1872, Werner to Jordan, 31 Dec. 1913, December Quarter Intelligence Report, excerpts from *Qiushi bao*.

founded a branch of the Anti-Opium Society.[79] Opium smoking was reported on the rise in Gutian county late in 1912. A British missionary added, however, "There is a real determination, not only among the officials, but among the better class of citizens, to stamp out the evil by uprooting the crops and meting out punishment."[80] One source notes a possible explanation for the enthusiasm of local officials; in the early Republic, the Gutian magistrate was Lin Binghua, yet another great-grandson of Lin Zexu.[81]

Further north in Funing prefecture, farmers in the countryside near the treaty port of Santu'ao took advantage of the uncertainty that lingered as late as the fall of 1912 and planted and harvested a sizable poppy crop.[82] Those poppies were gone by spring 1913.[83] Most of the planting violations occurred in Fu'an and Xiapu counties. Chinese investigators sent to Fu'an in early 1913 reported that a raid timed during seeding meant that it was impossible to determine how many poppies would blossom. Not until spring did the magistrate and dozens of soldiers and workers uproot approximately 4,500 *mu* of poppies.[84] However, British observers claimed that the Fu'an magistrate merely snipped off a few capsules and left the rest for the upcoming harvest. In mid-1913, British missionaries also spotted considerable amounts of poppy in Ningde county.[85] The magistrate and Opium Prohibition Bureau were aware of the violations, but with no troops to spare, the local councilmen (*yiyuan*) ripped out the plants themselves.[86]

British missionaries also reported that opium smoking was "quite prevalent amongst loadmen and chairmen" and complained that reformers used their powers recklessly to cheat and harass smokers.

Opium smokers are having an intolerable time of it; for the various reform societies extort all the money they can from the purses of the opium habitues, who, fearing imprisonment—and even, it may be, the death sentence—are forced to buy off their accusers. Though in dread of being fleeced, opium smokers come to the [CMS] hospital as to a city of refuge. A great change has come over the country since the

---

79. "Luoyuan yanhai yu jinyan jishi," p. 21.
80. *IWCD* 33, no. 327 (Sept. 1913): 176–77.
81. Yu Zuliu, "Gutian lishishang de jinyan yundong," p. 84. It is odd that this is not mentioned in missionary publications or other sources.
82. PRO, FO 228/2455, doc. 84, Werner to Alston, 29 July 1913.
83. *Fujian jinyan jishu*, p. 23.
84. Ibid., pp. 28–29.
85. PRO, FO 228/2455, doc. 84, Werner to Alston, 29 July 1913.
86. *Fujian jinyan jishu*, p. 28.

prohibition; only the very well to do can afford to use the drug, and that in the form of opium or morphia pills.[87]

This particular report also suggests that the high-minded reformers of the late Qing Anti-Opium Society may have been replaced by men attracted to opium reform more by the opportunites it presented for graft than by altruism or nationalism.

OPIUM PROHIBITION IN THE SOUTHWEST

In Zhangzhou prefecture, social tensions in some of the areas notorious for poppy cultivation before the revolution hampered the campaign. Clan feuding erupted in southern Zhao'an county in the spring and summer of 1913, and similar unrest, exacerbated by banditry, broke out in the nearby counties of Anxi, Jinjiang, and Changtai.[88] Significantly, there were no reports from Zhao'an, Anxi, or Jinjiang in the *Fujian jinyan jishu*, and it is possible that the violence prevented a thorough investigation of these trouble spots. The same source noted that illegal poppies were destroyed in Changtai, Longxi, and Nanjing counties in the spring of 1913, but British reports in October that same year claimed that poppy cultivation was proceeding without harassment.[89]

Changtai was especially volatile, a situation attributed to the draconian enforcement strategy of local officials. When the circuit intendant of Tingzhou, Zhangzhou, and Longyan found poppies growing less than five *li* from the county yamen at Changtai in 1913, he apparently became enraged and arrested and then executed the clan elder in the offending village. The following year, peasant farmers organized a branch of the Eight Trigrams Society and attacked and killed a number of soldiers and members of the local suppression bureaucracy, allegedly in retaliation for their brutal enforcement of opium restrictions in Changtai and Anxi.[90]

A missionary reported large poppy fields in Zhao'an, Haicheng, and Zhangpu counties in November 1913, but by the time of the joint inspection

---

87. *Mercy and Truth* 19, no. 223 (July 1915): 239.

88. PRO, FO 228/1869, Little to Jordan, 4 July 1913, June Quarter Intelligence Report for Amoy.

89. *Fujian jinyan jishu*, pp. 31, 34, 37; PRO, FO 228/2456, doc. 29, Little to Alston, 22 Oct. 1913; "Yapian dui Changtai renmin de huohai," p. 101.

90. "Yapian dui Changtai renmin de huohai," p. 101.

in January 1914, the plants were gone.[91] In Zhangpu, some farmers fought with troops dispatched by Chen Nengguang to dig up their poppy plants. In a situation similar to that which arose in Xinghua, the arrival of the troops generated strong anti-missionary sentiments (local farmers often blamed missionaries for summoning the soldiers), and the soldiers were compelled to spend the first part of their stay guarding local British missionaries.[92]

Shortly after the formation of the new Republic, a branch of the Opium Prohibition Bureau was established in Longyan subprefecture and set about energetically fulfilling the goals of the campaign. The bureau evidently was especially vigorous in its attempts to close down opium paste shops (*tugao dian*).[93] It also assisted local magistrates in their search for poppy plants. Investigators reported just over 100 *mu* planted in poppies, all of which was eliminated without resistance. Police sent to enforce the prohibition in Ningyang county found that all the guilty farmers had fled.[94]

In remote Tingzhou prefecture, local officials discovered about 4,000 *mu* of poppy, most of it in Shanghang county, nearly all of which was eliminated by police, soldiers, and the farmers themselves without resistance.[95] However, farmers in Ninghua county violently fought attempts to destroy their small but lucrative crop.[96] By April 1913, a CMS missionary reported that poppies could be found only in a small area in Liancheng county,[97] but Chinese reports were less positive.[98] In the spring of 1913, the Tingzhou City magistrate apparently instructed local opium shops to sell off their inventory and cease the purchase of additional stock.[99] Reports to British authorities by October 1913 indicated that the opium restrictions were being vigorously enforced in Tingzhou.[100]

---

91. PRO, FO 228/2457, doc. 67, Little to Jordan, 19 Jan. 1914.
92. PRO, FO 228/2457, doc. 59, Little to Beijing, 27 Dec. 1913; and USDS (1910–29), 894.114/104, reel 113, Maynard to Secy. of State, 15 Dec. 1913.
93. Li Hanzhou, "Longyan jianyan shihua," p. 102.
94. *Fujian jinyan jishu*, pp. 39–40.
95. Investigators in Shanghang reported the destruction of 3,610 *mu* of poppies (ibid., pp. 37–38).
96. Ibid., pp. 32–33.
97. PRO, FO 228/2454, doc. 71, letter from Blair, 13 Apr. 1913.
98. Several investigators noted poppy cultivation and implied some degree of resistance but stated that they would report on their progress at a later date (*Fujian jinyan jishu*, pp. 32–33, 41).
99. PRO, FO 228/2454, doc. 71, letter from Blair, 13 Apr. 1913.
100. PRO, FO 228/2456, doc. 29, Little to Alston, 22 Oct. 1913.

OPIUM PROHIBITION IN THE SOUTHEAST

The center of illicit poppy cultivation before 1911, the southeast retained that dubious distinction after the revolution, a situation exacerbated by the link between poppy cultivation, clan violence, and the temporary loosening of state control. Many farmers in the southeastern prefectures of Xinghua and Quanzhou and the subprefecture of Yongchun, where most of Fujian's opium had been grown prior to the revolution, were quick to take advantage of the governmental vacuum to plant poppies. Local and provincial officials, and the soldiers at their disposal, attacked the problem of renewed poppy cultivation and widespread opium smoking from 1912 to 1914. Poppy farmers and opium dealers were given no quarter in many areas, and the increased military muscle was a result of an influx of troops from Fuzhou that had been dispatched not only to oversee the destruction of poppies but also to quell clan violence. They were headquartered in Xiamen and evidently carried out their task thoroughly.[101]

The poppy farmers of Xinghua presented the greatest challenge to provincial authorities. The enormous poppy crop there (more than 150,000 *mu*) and the violent, organized, extended resistance to its uprooting resulted in bloody battles. This uprising is analyzed in detail in Chapter 8 and will not be explored further here.

Quanzhou was home to some of the most recalcitrant poppy farmers in the province, and the resurgence of poppy cultivation in the trouble areas of Tongan, Anxi, and Hui'an counties was reported as early as October 1911.[102] Vicious clan fighting and anti-government sentiment complicated enforcement of the restrictions. The Hui'an magistrate died in the fighting, and the provincial authorities were said to fear the "turbulent and well-armed brigands of Tongan."[103] By March 1912, large amounts of good-quality opium had been harvested in Anxi and Tongan, and it was selling for well below the price of the highly taxed foreign drug.[104] One foreign observer reported that officials in Tongan arrived at a compromise designed to ward off imme-

---

101. PRO, FO 228/2456, doc. 18, Werner to Beijing, excerpt from *Minbao*, 23 Sept. 1913.
102. USDS (1910–29), 893.00/836, reel 9, Arnold to Williams, 4 Nov. 1911.
103. USDS (1910–29), 893.00/857, docs. 14 and 16, Arnold to Secy. of State, 17 Nov. 1911; PRO, FO 228/2447, Struch to Jordan, 31 Mar. 1912 and 2 Apr. 1912.
104. PRO, FO 228/2447, doc. 14, Struch to Jordan, 31 Mar. 1912.

diate violence. They had decided to allow one last crop of opium to be harvested in 1912 but threatened harsh measures if poppies were planted again.[105] In Quanzhou and Anxi, the same policy was announced, although restrictions on opium smokers and the sale of the drug appeared effective and relatively well enforced.[106] However, the Anxi magistrate's yamen and the transit tax office had been destroyed in a riot in 1911, presumably to protest Qing policies, and in June 1912, quelling another anti-government uprising required hundreds of soldiers and two cannons from Fuzhou.[107] The violence may explain why the Chinese inspectors who compiled the *Fujian jinyan jishu* did not visit this county.

By spring 1913, Chinese sources reported that in Tongan, troops uprooted over 4,000 *mu* of poppies, and farmers cleared other land themselves.[108] Several hundred soldiers were posted to the area that fall to forestall further violence.[109] That November, a local newspaper reported that fields in Tongan were checked for traces of poppy seedlings. In one case, a violator's home was torched and his land confiscated.[110]

Similar struggles erupted in other poppy-growing counties. More than 6,500 *mu* of poppies were uprooted in Hui'an, and the local magistrate tried to prevent further violations by sending police to make daily investigations.[111] The poppy problem in Majiaxiang required cooperation between the county magistrate, village councils, local gentry, and government soldiers. The strategy seemed to work, and the poppies were destroyed quickly and easily.[112] In Nan'an, forcible uprooting was reported in the fall of 1913 after exhortations of the local gentry failed to produce results. The poppy farmers of Nan'an presented a particularly ingenious challenge; large clans in some of the wealthier villages that dared not openly resist instead used their women to obstruct the troops. The report does not detail the methods employed by

---

105. USDS (1910–29), doc. 390, Amoy to Secy. of State, 1 July 1912.
106. PRO, FO 228/2455, doc. 44, Little to Beijing, 21 July 1913.
107. USDS (1910–29), 893.00/848, reel 9, Arnold to Secy. of State, 13 Nov. 1911; PRO, FO 228/1838, Werner to Jordan, 26 June 1912.
108. *Fujian jinyan jishu*, p. 24.
109. PRO, FO 228/2456, doc. 29, Little to Alston, 22 Oct. 1913.
110. The same paper reported that numerous plots had been seized in the nearby county of Jinjiang (PRO, FO 228/1872, Werner to Jordan, 31 Dec. 1913, excerpt from *Qiushi bao*, December Quarter Intelligence Report).
111. *Fujian jinyan jishu*, pp. 25–26.
112. Ibid., pp. 26–27.

the women, but whatever they did forced the troops to spend ten full days in the area.[113]

Even the cities of Quanzhou were not immune to the scourge of illicit poppy cultivation. Anxiety gripped Quanzhou City in December 1913, when soldiers arrived to crack down on violations of the opium restrictions. Some poppy farmers decided to resist, and many townspeople fled in anticipation of violence. The prefect requested more soldiers, but by the time they arrived, most of the offenders had disappeared.[114]

The spring of 1912 also heralded the return of opium harvesting to the treaty port of Xiamen, a stunning development in light of the large number of officials and foreign diplomats who lived and worked there. A consular official at Xiamen stated that the Chinese in his county "recommenced planting as soon as the Imperial executive collapsed."[115] According to the British consul at that port:

> Two of the Foreign residents walked round Amoy island. As soon as they were clear of Amoy City [Xiamen] on the side of the Island away from Kulangsoo [Gulangyu], they encountered field upon field of poppies stretching in all directions, some still in flower, but the greater part ready for lancing: a good proportion of the heads were in the process of being tapped. This industry was being carried on by the local farmers without let or hindrance on the part of the Authorities, who must have been fully aware of what was going on almost within sight of their yamens. . . . It is said that the Authorities at Foochow are doing their best to carry out the terms of the Opium Agreement of last year, but as far as Amoy is concerned one can safely say that it is a dead letter.[116]

The American vice consul at Xiamen observed a similar scene the following spring. He remarked that soldiers were in evidence everywhere but appeared to be taking no action. And he hoped that the recent appointment of a new circuit intendant—who had already led troops to uproot poppies in Tongan—would make a significant difference.[117] That promising new offi-

---

113. Ibid., pp. 24–25. Nan'an was not far from Tongan, where women had been in charge of opium growing in the late nineteenth century (see Chapter 2, pp. 65–66).
114. PCE-Second Series, Box 28–*Our Sisters in Other Lands*, 1906–29, OSOL, Apr. 1914, p. 24.
115. PRO, FO 228/2447, doc. 14, Struch to Jordan, 31 Mar. 1912.
116. PRO, FO 228/2447, doc. 16, unsigned to Jordan, 2 Apr. 1912.
117. USDS (1910–29), 893.114/81–82, reel 113, Brissel to Secy. of State, 7 Apr. and 23 Apr. 1913.

cial was none other than seasoned reformer Chen Peikun, former head of the Anti-Opium Society.[118]

Opium smoking also returned to Xiamen during the chaos of the revolution. According to foreign customs officials:

In December 1911 the new police authorities issued a proclamation requiring the recently and illegally opened opium shops [of which there were about 220] to close their doors, and the authorized shops to take out new licenses; but apparently no serious effort was made to enforce obedience to this order, for the boiled opium shops have multiplied exceedingly and, at the time of writing, opium smoking proceeds unchecked and apparently unheeded.[119]

A conference on this problem in July 1912 attended by 50 members of the Xiamen Anti-Opium Society, a representative from the Fuzhou society headquarters, the circuit intendant at Xiamen, and other local officials determined that about 800 opium shops had operated in Xiamen before the inauguration of the suppression campaign. On the eve of the revolution, that number had fallen to just over 100, but the lack of enforcement during the revolutionary transition had emboldened about 200 additional shops to open.

Officials and elite reformers took quick and decisive action. The Anti-Opium Society compiled a roster of shops in the city's eighteen wards that were to be closed immediately and categorized the remaining shops by the amount of business they conducted. All shops had to procure licenses, and those paying the lowest monthly fees (presumably because they did the least business) were to be shut down first. The rest would follow at intervals. But once again, Xiamen's tradition of mercantile independence surfaced. The operators of opium shops formed a guild and paid a fee scaled to the amount of business conducted by each, thus taking control of the suppression process themselves. Each time a percentage of shops were to be closed by orders from Fuzhou, the guild members drew lots at the offices of the Xiamen Anti-Opium Society. Those who had to close down were then able to draw some income from the pool of fees. But even this attempt by merchants to create a buffer between themselves and the regulatory powers of the state-sanctioned reform group did not forestall the eventual closure of the shops.

---

118. Liu Shoulin, *Xinhai yihou shiqinian shiguan nianbiao*, p. 342.
119. IMC, *Decennial Reports, Amoy, 1902–1911*, p. 103.

The Xiamen Anti-Opium Society reinstituted the policy of distributing inexpensive smoking licenses in July 1912. A photograph of the smoker (provided by the society's photographer) was attached to each license, and a catalogue of those photographs was kept at the society's offices. Most of the licenses allowed smokers ten months to quit their habits. Visitors had to obtain a special license if they wished to consume opium in the city. An American consular official commented on the enthusiasm for the opium reform evinced by Republican officials in Xiamen, a development that he felt was a welcome difference from the late Qing phase of the campaign. He estimated that 3,000 smokers resided in Xiamen in mid-1912 and reported several public pipe burnings and anti-opium processions.[120]

In the spring of 1913, a joint proclamation by the Anti-Opium Society and the circuit intendant of Xiamen (Chen Peikun) announced the closure of all prepared opium shops and pledged to enforce the prohibition on smoking. Ironically, during a subsequent search, a high official involved in the campaign was himself discovered to be an opium smoker, but it was hoped that his dismissal and punishment would serve as an example.[121] The guilty party may have been the head of the local branch of the Opium Prohibition Bureau, whom the British reported was caught smoking and fined heavily. If so, the report also indicated that the official was able to avoid punishment.[122] At the same time, a concerted effort to uproot the poppies around Xiamen was implemented. By April 1913, British diplomats reported that the poppy was gone and that "the work of destruction appears to have been carried out by the peasants themselves without the direct compulsion of military force."[123]

Yongchun prefecture also experienced renewed poppy cultivation, but its proximity to and the efficiency of the local authorities affected the degree of enforcement in the area. Few poppies had ever been grown in the subprefectural seat of Yongchun, where the prefect actively enforced the restrictions. In Dehua, an energetic magistrate led efforts to ferret out and uproot poppies.[124] Minuscule amounts of poppy were scattered across Datian, but the magistrate, an Opium Prohibition Bureau representative,

---

120. USDS (1910–29), 893.114/43, reel 113, Brissel to Secy. of State, 13 July 1912.
121. USDS (1910–29), 893.114, reel 113, Amoy to Secy. of State, 22 May 1913.
122. PRO, FO 228/2454, doc. 99, Little to Beijing, 11 June 1913.
123. PRO, FO 228/2453, doc. 101, Amoy to Jordan, 16 Apr. 1913.
124. *Fujian jinyan jishu*, p. 32.

and several policemen eradicated them.[125] In contrast, "field after field of waving white poppies flaunt themselves in the most prominent places all along the roadside" in more distant counties, and at least one county magistrate delayed his plan to uproot poppies after farmers promised that this would be their last crop.[126]

Local authorities also stressed anti-consumption measures, with tangible results. In the year 1911–12, the English Presbyterian mission hospital in Yongchun was designated the official opium refuge for Yongchun, Datian, and Dehua counties, and patients were admitted only with a government certificate issued by the magistrate. Over 150 opium smokers were treated there that year, 167 in the year 1912–13, and over 200 in 1913–14, but the problem seemed to have peaked that year, according to the missionary physician in charge:[127]

The crusade against smoking still continues, and there has been a vast diminution in the number of opium smokers. The hospital has been the official anti-opium refuge, and sometimes we have had our hands full. As this report is being written we are using one of our anti-opium "lock-ups" for the first time as a general ward, there having been a considerable diminution of opium patients in the last two months. Although we shall have a number for some years to come, owing to hidden stores and smuggling; yet, as far as one can see, there will never be the same demand as before on our opium wards. For this God be praised![128]

Despite the visible decline in opium smoking, the craving for narcotics persisted, and the hospital was treating more morphine addicts than opium smokers. The morphine they injected was evidently smuggled into the area from Japan, a disturbing omen that the elimination of opium might not mean the end of China's narcotics consumption.[129]

---

125. Ibid., pp. 43–44.
126. PCE-Second Series, Box 28–*Our Sisters in Other Lands*, 1906–29, OSOL, July 1913. However, *Fujian jinyan jishu* (p. 37) reported only 30 *mu* of poppies in Yongchun, all of which were uprooted by spring 1913.
127. PCE/FMC, box 10 (S. Fukien, General Correspondence, 1910–19), Amoy Council Meeting Notes, July 17–21, 1912; and folder 12, Yungchun Hospital Report for the years 1911–12, 1912–13, 1913–14.
128. PCE/FMC, box 10 (S. Fukien, General Correspondence, 1910–19), folder 12, Yungchun Hospital Report for the year 1913–14.
129. PCE/FMC, box 10 (S. Fukien, General Correspondence, 1910–19), folder 12, Yungchun Hospital Report for the year 1914–15.

Officials and elites in southeast Fujian in general found enforcement particularly difficult because of the heavy maritime traffic and the Japanese influence. According to a letter from Chen Nengguang to local Chinese officials, the entire southeast region of Fujian was plagued by the blatant disregard of opium-smoking restrictions by the crews and passengers of boats plying that area's many waterways. In addition, many Taiwanese with Japanese citizenship intervened to prevent the investigation or arrest of their Chinese friends or customers.[130]

The growing popularity of morphine and the willing connivance of the Japanese were not the only warning signs for Fujian's opium reformers. Insufficient troops hindered the investigation and destruction of poppy fields, and provincial investigators skipped some infamous trouble spots altogether. At the same time, the surprising extent of poppy cultivation on the eve of the inspection and the haste with which Chinese authorities conducted the final push for suppression hinted at the tenacity of Fujian's opium economy and the unrepentant attitude of some farmers. Many apparently stored their poppy seeds, hoping that the next planting season would bring less oversight, and others were willing to resist the uprooting of their lucrative crop at the cost of their lives. Despite these omens of future problems, the authorities in Fujian had quickly overcome widespread opposition to the opium restrictions.

The most important and most immediate goal for Fujian's early Republican authorities was to achieve the coveted status of a province closed to the importation of Indian opium. Achieving a place on that list not only constituted a crucial step in eliminating the supply side of the opium trade but also represented an important victory over imperialism and symbolized the degree to which the central state was able to control the conduct of the suppression campaign in the provinces. Once the most serious disturbances in the Xinghua region had been quelled and other provincial political crises resolved, the way was clear for provincial authorities to call for the joint Chinese-British inspection to certify that Fujian was free of poppy cultivation.

---

130. USDS (1910–29), 893.114/104, reel 113, enclosures in Maynard to Secy. of State, 15 Dec. 1913.

The Joint Inspections

By the end of 1913, China had made such rapid progress in ridding itself of domestic opium cultivation that Britain had no choice but to end the export of Indian opium to *all* Chinese provinces, although opium still held in stocks could continue to be sold in provinces like Fujian that had not yet undergone the requisite inspections. It was a tremendous moral victory for the Chinese, especially in light of the chaos of two years earlier. For authorities and reformers in Fujian, however, the delay in closing their province was profoundly embarrassing, given their pride in being the birthplace of Lin Zexu and the early leadership of the Anti-Opium Society.

In January 1914, provincial officials in Fujian felt confident enough of their progress against domestic poppy cultivation to request the joint inspection. The inspection took place in February and March, since these were the months in which Fujian's poppies would be in full bloom and thus easier to locate. The British representative in the northeast was A. D. Blackburn and in the southeast, W. P. Turner. Blackburn and Turner were assistants at the British consulates in Fuzhou and Xiamen, respectively. Chen Nengguang, in his capacity as head of the Fujian Opium Prohibition Bureau, was to be one of the Chinese officials, but his aggressive actions against British and Chinese opium merchants had infuriated British diplomats, and his name was dropped after vehement British objections. Chen Peikun served in his place. Ironically, this left Chen Nengguang free to troubleshoot along the inspection route, and the inspectors were to encounter him several times. Each of the inspections lasted approximately one month.[131]

In order to measure Chinese progress and guide the expeditions to provincial hotspots, British Consul Wilkinson in Fuzhou contacted CMS Bishop Horace Mc. E. Price and asked him to solicit reports from British missionaries in the field on the status of opium reform throughout the province.[132] The reports were generally encouraging. The bishop himself reported that on a recent, lengthy tour of the north and northwest regions, he had seen no poppies, although he did meet some troops on their way to suppress illegal cultivation in Ningde county in Funing prefecture. Price also

---

131. The negotiations over locations, dates, and personnel are documented in PRO, FO 228/2457, docs. 91–105, all of which were written in Jan. and Feb. 1914. For exact itineraries and dates, see PRO, FO 228/2457, doc. 106, enclosure in Little to Beijing, 24 Feb. 1914.

132. PRO, FO 228/2457, doc. 71, Wilkinson to Jordan, 26 Jan. 1914.

noted that despite his observation that popular consumption had dropped considerably, his chair-bearers did not find it difficult to purchase the foreign drug wherever they traveled.[133] Other British missionaries were similarly impressed by government suppression efforts elsewhere in the province, although some expressed dissatisfaction that the crackdown on the supply side of the opium equation did not seem to be matched by an effort to eliminate opium consumption.[134]

Blackburn's account of the anti-opium bureaucracy in the northern half of Fujian described a model of organization and efficiency. He also remarked on the active role played by elite reformers, possibly members of the Anti-Opium Society, affiliated with the official opium prohibition bureaucracy:

In every town and village there is an Anti-opium Office or Sub-office, to which as a rule the majority of the gentry belong. In each Hsien [xian or county] there is an Inspector and a number of Hsien are grouped under an Inspector-General, of whom there are four in North Fukien. Most of the Inspectors are gentlemen and well educated, who are devoting their time entirely and without remuneration to the eradication of opium. They claim to have personally examined, not once but frequently, every portion of their respective counties and from their intimate knowledge of even the minutest features of the landscape, I am of the opinion that their claim is well founded.

However, he also noted that some deputy inspectors had to be impressed into service, possibly against their will: "In some districts every household is bound to supply one person to assist in the general search . . . failing which a fine . . . is imposed." The inspections, which departed in late February, set off an additional flurry of activity in areas rumored to harbor illegal poppy fields.[135]

Back in Fuzhou, as the two deputations of inspectors scoured the countryside for illicit poppy cultivation, the Petigura case had not yet been resolved to the satisfaction of the British, and it became apparent that these separate developments were connected. Throughout the inspection tours, British officials continued to wrangle about the case with Chen Nengguang

---

133. PRO, FO 228/2457, doc. 72, Wilkinson to Jordan, 25 Jan. 1914.

134. PRO, FO 228/2457, doc. 72, Wilkinson to Jordan, 25 Jan. 1914 and 28 Jan. 1914; doc. 106, Little to Beijing, 24 Feb. 1914.

135. Unless otherwise noted, the following description of the northern inspections was taken from PRO, FO 228/2457, doc. 122, Blackburn to Jordan, 11 Mar. 1914. The southern inspection is described in detail in PRO, FO 228/2458, doc. 51, Little to Jordan, 2 Apr. 1914.

and Chen Peikun, the latter of whom insisted that the release of the confiscated opium before the completion of the investigations would send the wrong message to the people of Fujian. Chen Peikun also asserted that since the opium had been sold to Chinese dealers—who had earlier voluntarily signed an oath to abandon their occupation—the matter did not involve the British, and the dealers deserved punishment. Evidently, however, the dealer had not yet paid Mr. Petigura, and British Consul Wilkinson refused to drop the matter.

Despite Wilkinson's general inclination to support Chinese suppression efforts, he sometimes became irritated at the transparency of Chinese attempts to use the incident to force Britain's hand. At one point during the inspections, Wilkinson reported:

[Chen Peikun] made the somewhat surprising admission to me that the smoking of opium in Fukien had not diminished during the past year, his explanation being that, owing to lack of funds, all the opium refuges had been closed. It was, however, amongst the poorer classes only that the habit was still prevalent, especially amongst the chair coolies most of whom could not work without opium. He also gave me the impression that he was not at all confident that the Province would be found free from opium; in fact, I believe that one reason why the chests seized [in the Petigura case] have not been returned is that the Authorities have a ridiculous idea that they may prove a useful lever on their side should we be in any doubt whether to declare the Province free from opium or not.

Beijing stepped in and the five chests were released in March 1914.[136] Provincial authorities tried to manipulate the controversy to their own advantage, but in the end, intervention from Beijing made certain that the case did not derail the larger suppression effort.

In any case, the inspectors were satisfied with their findings. For the most part, the fields that earlier blazed with poppy flowers were now planted in rice, barley, sweet potatoes, sugarcane, and tobacco. Blackburn, accompanied on his tour of the northern half of Fujian by Ye Keliang, from Fujian's Office of Foreign Affairs (Waiwu bu), and Zheng Shouxing, a provincial assemblyman, reported satisfaction with Chinese prohibition efforts in that part of the province. Despite the intention of the inspectors to visit all the locations where poppy cultivation had been recently reported, difficult weather and traveling conditions sometimes forced changes in the itinerary.

---

136. PRO, FO 228/2457, doc. 139, Wilkinson to Jordan, 27 Feb. 1914; PRO, FO 228/2457, doc. 143, Wilkinson to Jordan, 11 Mar. 1914.

It is important to note, however, that the inspectors apparently were allowed to go anywhere they wished. In fact, when they were forced to skip several counties, some magistrates wrote Blackburn and begged him to visit, "as it would be a disappointment for those who had laboured so hard to eradicate the poppy if their work was not so much as looked at."

In north Fujian, most county magistrates reported few attempts by their constituents to skirt the prohibition on poppy cultivation. Blackburn concentrated on areas known for poppy growth, particularly Lianjiang county in Fuzhou prefecture, and Ningde, Fu'an, and Shouning counties in Funing prefecture. Blackburn "found not so much as a single poppy" and was deeply impressed by the thoroughness of Chinese officials and local elites. He was surprised to note that the gentry were active in opium reform—in his opinion, because opium smoking was no longer socially acceptable—and that only members of the working class were resisting prohibition measures. Blackburn pointed out how well the official bureau worked with the unofficial society, noting however, that in many areas, "the brunt of the field work is borne by the latter." (By "field work," he meant the monitoring of violations, not the uprooting of crops.)

The suppression campaign was well advertised along Blackburn's route, and local authorities seemed to recognize that decisive action and continued vigilance were necessary to attain and to maintain the success of the crusade. The magistrate of Fu'an county, Funing prefecture, was noted as being particularly vigorous, having assigned over 1,000 people to enforce the prohibition, and he had spent months personally supervising the destruction of local poppy fields. Rewards for information on the location of illegal poppy fields were posted in many areas in north Fujian, and violators were threatened with—and occasionally subjected to—capital punishment. Blackburn was also assured that the threat of this especially severe punishment would continue for one more year, after which any concealed poppy seeds would be useless, although local authorities would be on the lookout for poppies for three more years. During Turner's tour of the southern half of the province, however, he was told that poppy seeds were good for four years.

In many cases, the inspections themselves were powerful incentives for reform. News of the inspectors' approach was often enough to inspire local magistrates to conduct large-scale sweeps of their counties. Blackburn traveled with an impressive retinue of about 40 soldiers, and many county magistrates welcomed him as a foreign dignitary, hoping perhaps to impress the people of the importance accorded the anti-opium crusade. Both groups of inspectors also met often with foreign missionaries and their Chinese converts, whom the British inspectors viewed as the most reliable witnesses of Fujian's progress.

In Zhangzhou prefecture, Turner and his entourage—Shao Jiquan from the Ministry of the Interior in Beijing, the ubiquitous Chen Peikun (having just concluded his tour with the northern inspectors), then serving as president of Fuzhou City's Opium Prohibition Bureau and circuit intendant of Fuzhou, and a British interpreter of the Xiamen dialect—reported progress in virtually every county, with the exception of rumors concerning a few isolated poppy patches in remote areas. In Changtai, the magistrate was Shao Jiquan's brother, and he appeared to approach the task of suppression with vigor.

Resistance and enforcement problems in Zhangzhou prefecture were largely confined to two counties. In Zhao'an, on the border with Guangdong province, Magistrate Zhang Zengjue was forced to arrest several local elites for encouraging poppy cultivation for profit. Zhang's predecessor had been removed in part for his apathetic approach to opium suppression. In Longxi county, corrupt and greedy opium inspectors who used their office to extort money, often from the innocent, and others who conducted similar scams while masquerading as opium officials plagued opium reform in Longxi county. The head inspector in Longxi, confirmed Chen Peikun, even tried to sell his office for a large sum.

Turner's group headed north from Zhangzhou to the adjoining prefecture of Quanzhou, in which lay the notorious opium-growing counties of Tongan and Hui'an. The observations of the inspectors in these two counties testify to the ability of the Chinese authorities to enforce the prohibitions by force when necessary. However, the hurried manner in which uprooting was conducted indicated a lack of cooperation by local officials or farmers that did not bode well for the future. And finally, the decision of the inspectors to forgo personal visits to some of the more contested areas in these and other counties implied a conscious policy on the part of the British to give Chinese officials more latitude in their attempts to end British opium imports.

Just south of Tongan, an official in Mahang claimed that the people of his region had earned about two million yuan annually from opium. Turner commented that, if this were true, the lack of violent resistance to opium suppression was suspicious and recommended close observation of the area after the inspection. Chinese authorities recognized the potential for trouble and assigned six opium inspectors to Tongan and another three to Mahang. In addition, the ranking official at Mahang was given the title of magistrate (*zhishi*), presumably to increase his standing and his authority while conducting the anti-opium campaign.

In Hui'an, a county known for opium cultivation and endemic clan feuding, the situation was even more troubling, and the inspectors discovered that Chen Nengguang himself was conducting an inspection when Turner and his group arrived. The Hui'an magistrate had apparently reported falsely to the Opium Prohibition Bureau in Fuzhou that his region was free of poppy cultivation. Turner's Chinese companions railed against the magistrate's obvious corruption and promised that he would be tried and punished; Turner felt that the official in question "appeared rather mentally deficient and incompetent rather than corrupt." Chen Nengguang had raced Turner's team to the site and brought soldiers to enforce the opium prohibition. Turner himself, however, was told that no roads existed in the contested region (Toubei) and felt compelled to skirt the area. What little he did see convinced him that considerable uprooting had occurred within the past week, and that most residents had locked themselves inside their homes to avoid punishment. Turner also skipped Anxi county, an area well known for poppy cultivation and popular belligerence.

Apparently, local authorities were given a great deal of leeway in implementing opium suppression measures, probably to forestall violence. For example, in the area between Anhai county and the city of Quanzhou, the authorities made a not uncommon bargain with local farmers that allowed the harvesting of the opium crop in 1913 on the promise that no more poppy would be sown. Both parties evidently were true to their word. Nearby, however, soldiers were called in to Nan'an county to uproot poppies by force in December 1913.

In the end, Turner pronounced himself satisfied with southeast Fujian's opium suppression efforts. Most of the poppies had disappeared, and there was no evidence of opium imports from other Chinese provinces. Although he remained skeptical about the prospects for enduring success, Turner reported that Chinese authorities had pledged to continue the campaign even after the flow of Indian opium dried up completely. Chen Peikun informed Turner that provincial regulations designed to maintain the ban on opium cultivation were being drafted and that while addressing a meeting of the Anti-Opium Society at Fuzhou, the civil governor of Fujian had recently "announced amidst great applause that there would be plenty of executions in the future for breaches of the anti-opium laws."

The absence of poppy cultivation did not end opium smoking, and Turner noted that smokers were not subject to the severe penalties that descended on violators of the ban on cultivation. Opium apparently was not difficult to obtain in many remote areas of the province, but according to Turner, "the present scarcity of the drug has so inflated the price that it is now almost beyond the reach of all save the wealthy classes, and the authorities have doubtless realized that the cessation of smoking follows automatically the cessation of cultivation and are devoting all their attention to the latter office."

This last comment stands in stark contrast with Blackburn's observations that foreign opium was readily available in the north but was generally smoked only by members of the lower and working classes. The difference probably lay in the composition of each region's opium economy and the nature of suppression in each region. The elimination of poppy cultivation in the northeast was evidently quite thorough and left only the foreign drug available for consumption. However, since the port of Fuzhou and other marketing centers in the north remained open for foreign opium imports, opium merchants had little trouble finding a market for their goods, especially among the lower-class laborers who were so dependent on the drug (and were receptive to the lower prices). The active involvement of prominent local elites in the suppression campaign in the northeast also meant that there may have been an added stigma regarding opium smoking among the upper classes not found in the southeast.

For the most part, sales of the drug had dropped precipitously, and ironically the very success of the campaign also sometimes meant that enforcement had to become less rigorous. A British diplomat reported that local anti-opium societies in some areas were forced to relax their vigilance against illicit opium sales because of a lack of revenue from opium taxes and licenses.

But in many former opium-growing counties, British investigators commented that the coercion and violence that characterized this last stage of the campaign had created a climate of terror. Blackburn wrote that in Shouning county, in northern Funing prefecture, peasants had uprooted any plant "which in leaf or flower in the remotest degree resembled the poppy," presumably in order to avoid any possibility of punishment. In Zhangzhou prefecture, Turner reported widespread rumors that if the inspectors found any poppies, a heavy fine would be imposed and the cultivator and the county magistrate would be executed. Violators in the Mahang area of Quanzhou prefecture had their homes burned down, their land seized, and heavy fines imposed. Any resistance to those measures could, and often did, bring beheading.

Turner and Blackburn had significant reservations concerning the long-term success of Fujian's opium suppression measures, but the accomplishments of the provincial and local authorities and non-official elites were undeniable. Domestic cultivation of the opium poppy had been virtually eliminated in Fujian province, at least for the duration of the inspections. The British government agreed with the assessments of the inspectors, and Fujian was officially closed to Indian opium imports. A few residual conflicts kept British officials busy over the next year or so,[137] but for the most part, direct British government involvement in Fujian's anti-opium movement was over. Now, oversight, as well as enforcement, was primarily in the hands of the Chinese.

The inspections revealed how much the new Republic's suppression strategy differed from that of its imperial predecessor and how the same international agreements that had hampered the late Qing phase of the campaign could also serve as a powerful incentive. However, the comprehensive, measured steps that had characterized the Qing suppression campaign gave way to a more hurried, slash-and-burn approach that stressed military force, harsh punishment, and less support for addiction treatment. There was less emphasis on mobilization because in the countryside, those mobilized might not gather for reasons their organizers intended. The British inspectors cautioned that although poppy cultivation had indeed been severely curtailed in Fujian, the prohibitions had often been enforced by coercive means that "in some cases preceded the investigating party's visit by a few days or by even a few hours."

---

137. British opium importers in Fujian tried to make the case that they should be permitted to sell any opium stocks imported before May 1, but the British government replied that warnings had been issued and as of 1 May, all Indian opium in Fujian was illegal and would have to be re-exported. See the numerous dispatches on the subject in PRO, FO 228/2458 and 2459.

The Closure of Fujian

None of that seemed to matter in the short run. In Fuzhou, euphoric reformers greeted the announcement of the official closing of the province on 1 May 1914 with a massive celebration symbolically led by Lin Zexu and reminiscent of the early days of the campaign. One British missionary described the festivities in detail:

> Friday, May 2nd was a great day here in Foochow.... All the opium that was stored in the Customs here was burned that day; over $100,000 (10,000 British pounds) worth was destroyed. The city was *en fete*, we all went to see it. We did not see the opium burned, as that was done at the Customs House, but we went to the headquarters of the Anti-Opium Association [the Anti-Opium Society] where there was a great demonstration.... In the centre of the hall was a life-sized image of the gentleman, Mr. Lin [Lin Zexu], who threw all the opium into the sea at Canton, which was the cause of the great Opium War. They carried this effigy in procession through the city, with the band playing, etc., etc.[138]

Lin Zexu was symbolic of so many of the victories that the celebration represented, and his presence was particularly poignant because Lin himself had failed to keep the foreign drug out of China. Lin's image linked provincial pride and strength with a larger national goal, but without foreign opium as its foil, that icon lost much of its symbolic power and virtually disappeared from provincial anti-opium rhetoric. The ostensible conclusion of Fujian's suppression campaign also meant fewer occasions on which to feature Lin.

The Anti-Opium Society took great pains to make this a public triumph. *The Quarterly* described the celebration in great detail and reprinted the lyrics from the stirring anti-opium songs offered by student groups. Penned by supporters of opium suppression (possibly foreign missionary teachers at the schools), the lyrics were intended not only to *reflect* popular exultation but also to *produce* it. The songs signal a clear shift from anger and antiforeignism to pride in nation and province. All the songs contain references to the western origins of the commerce in opium, but they also stress the current confluence of Chinese and foreign sentiment against that trade.[139]

---

138. IWCD 34, no. 336 (July 1914): 130.

139. The songs (and *The Quarterly* contained many more than are translated here) have a decidedly formulaic quality; their marked similarity in meter and phrasing implies commonal-

Students from a YMCA school sung the song translated below. The lyrics were representative of other tunes at the gathering.[140]

> This terrible thing—who can trace?
> Disaster it brought to our native place.
> The once-closed ocean was opened wide,
> And allowed the poison to come inside.
> A thousand ships, ten thousand again,
> Continued to arrive without an end.
> So many years, no one can say,
> Our country weakened by the day.
> The people drank that poisoned wine,
> Drank till they lost their presence of mind.
> Now East and West, hearts beat as one,
> From today begins the prohibition!
> By sealing off the river's source,
> We can stop the poison's course.
> From Fujian's rivers and mountains high,
> Our country's flag waves in the sky.
> And so, then, from this day on,
> The people's illness is all gone!

Society member Wang Junwen contributed a brief poem to express his enthusiasm:

> How can poppies blight our blessed land?
> We wailed for help for many a year.
> Now the filthy flow has finally ceased,
> Today the Min River flows clean and clear.

Finally, a single verse from a longer song presented by the Xiehe School "joyfully celebrated the prohibition of opium imports" and reiterated the same themes:

> Taut in the wind our national flag flaps,
> As the pipes are destroyed, the crowd all claps,
> Flap, clap, flap, clap.
> There are ten thousand ways to right this wrong,

---

ities in the background of the composers. If the authors were not foreign missionaries, then they most probably were Chinese Christian students in missionary schools.

140. All the songs that appear here were taken from *The Quarterly* 12 (1914), *zazhi* section, pp. 6–7.

And change our country from weak to strong,
The masses celebrate them in a song.

How accurately these children represented the sentiment of those "masses" is unclear.

During the anti-opium campaign, it became difficult to distinguish genuine popular antipathy toward opium from a general tolerance of official policy or fear of state repression. In Fujian's cities, the restrictions that closed down numerous opium shops and dens apparently met with relatively little resistance, and throngs of townspeople attended mass meetings, thousands enrolled in the state-controlled opium-rationing scheme, and others sought treatment for addiction. The relative ease with which these anti-consumption measures were implemented may have reflected the strength of progressive urban reformism present long before 1911 or even 1906. However, the sheer number of those who responded to or were targeted by the campaign indicated the severity of the opium problem, and once the state-mandated opium reforms began, open hostility to the reforms became a crime.

The closing of Fujian and all of China to Indian opium did not mean the end of the opium trade in either the province or the nation. What it did mean was that the incentive for continued compliance with opium suppression measures was considerably diminished at the provincial, national, and international levels. With Indian opium imports eliminated, the central Chinese state became far less concerned with the opium situation in the provinces, and the overarching policy framework through which it had guided and coordinated provincial suppression campaigns began to teeter. The weakening of central oversight was felt in the provinces almost immediately.

The joint inspections also signaled official British readiness to abandon connections with the opium trade. With imports to China halted, the British found themselves with much less leverage in the campaign, since the deliberate revival of the opium trade (the likely consequence for a province that failed an inspection) would not be warmly received in a global environment that had begun to organize against drug trafficking. Unsubstantiated reports from Wilkinson at Fuzhou that some British firms were clandestinely importing and selling opium after 1 May 1914 brought a response from the British government that reflected the hands-off approach. Wilkinson's superiors commented that smuggling was now the Chinese customs' problem and that "it would be . . . quixotic to go out of our way to assist the Foochow anti-opium bureau after its behaviour in the Petigura case—and it does not seem to be any part of Wilkinson's duty to spy on the contents of British premises, or to receive information from the anti-opium bureau."[141] Given their doubts about Fujian's commitment to continued suppression, the British did not seem to regard the closure of the province as a genuine Chinese accomplishment. The rapid resurgence of the opium economy seemed to bear out that pessimism.

The Beginning of the End

After the renegotiated agreement with the British was signed in May 1911, the Qing state and later its Republican successor made the decision to focus state resources on stamping out domestic poppy cultivation as quickly as possible. If that goal were achieved, foreign opium imports would cease, the supply of opium in China would be eliminated, and in due course, the demand side of the opium equation was expected to follow suit. Many provincial officials also were undoubtedly in favor of eliminating domestic poppy cultivation on its own merits as well as to obtain the relief from foreign opium imports that would follow. But the ultimate effectiveness of suppression in any individual province was directly tied to the success of its neighbors and the Chinese nation as a whole. This conjunction of provincial and national interests was responsible to a large extent for the ability and the desire of the central Chinese state to assert its control over the official and unofficial arms of the campaign and to intervene in provincial affairs should they appear to threaten the national effort.

The Anti-Opium Society was still assisting the state despite the diminution of its role. The shifting and porous boundaries between local society and officialdom had allowed the Anti-Opium Society to appropriate the symbolic and legal authority of the state to increase its own prestige and power. After the revolution, society members moved easily into officialdom, where many of them continued the process of limiting the power of unofficial reform groups begun in 1910 by the Provincial Assembly. The Provincial Assembly was weak, a victim of Yuan Shikai's growing authoritarianism, but by sapping the society of some of its revenue and many of its most energetic leaders, it had presided over the beginning of the shift in the balance of power in the suppression campaign from the unofficial society to the new

---

141. PRO, FO 228/2458, doc. 73, note from Tours to Jordan in Jordan to Wilkinson, 1 June 1914.

state. However, the Republic faced many pressing issues, and when the terms of the agreement with the British were fulfilled, the task of suppression fell to a fatally weakened society that found it difficult to continue its mission without state support or venerable, wealthy leaders. At the same time, the Second Revolution had convinced Yuan Shikai to stifle dissenting political voices, inside and outside the state, that might further erode his hold on power. By 1915, the foundations of warlord government were already in place in Fujian.

Before the revolution, anti-opium activists throughout the province were as concerned (if not more concerned) with treating opium smokers and controlling opium consumption as they were with reducing and eliminating the amount of land planted in poppies. This approach to the opium problem adopted by the late Qing government contrasted with the more draconian enforcement methods implemented by their Republican successors, particularly with regard to stamping out poppy cultivation. The latter, however, was key to fulfilling the requirements of the *second* Anglo-Chinese agreement that promised an end to British opium imports if domestic cultivation ceased.

When the campaign targeted illicit poppy cultivation, the popular reception was much different from the curiosity and enthusiasm evinced by urban audiences to the public burning of confiscated opium paraphernalia. The status of the entire campaign now rested on the ability of the state to wipe out domestic cultivation, and the benign tolerance or incompetence of late Qing officials in Fujian's more notorious opium-growing regions could not continue. The campaign began to affect and anger many farmers who had never been touched by it before 1911, but the size and spirit of the public political space was very different in the countryside. Unofficial reformers and officials did work together in rural areas to pursue the goals of suppression, although less consistently than in the cities, but it is hard to imagine enormous celebratory rallies to mark the destruction and confiscation of fields belonging to a relative, neighbor, or landlord. Even Lin Zexu was less relevant, since his mission had to do with cutting off foreign imports. The temporary success of the new measures, often brutally enforced, was testimony to the commitment and diligence of many local officials, but it also implied the need for continued surveillance and oversight. After 1914, however, the pressing need for money to finance the military incursions and regimes that devastated the province revived the provincial opium economy.

SEVEN

Race, Religion, and Reform

The great anti-opium, anti-footbinding and educational reforms of the present are largely, if not entirely, the result of missionary efforts.

—Frederick Barckhardt, Methodist Episcopal Church in Yanping, Fujian

Is it not true that opium was brought to China by you English? How cruel of your people to bring such wretchedness upon a nation that never did them any wrong!

—Owner of a south China opium den to Rev. John Macgowan

If only you could relieve us of missionaries and opium, all might be well!

—Prince Kung [Gong] to Sir Rutherford Alcock

Opium reform constituted a delicate problem for the Chinese state because it fell under the categories of both domestic and foreign policy. The success of the suppression campaign hinged not only on enforcing restrictions among the Chinese but also on adhering to international treaty provisions and controlling the actions of foreigners who existed outside the reach of Chinese law. Many of those foreigners were merchants who came to China with the express intention of contravening these and earlier Chinese prohibitions on the sale and consumption of opium. Ironically, the settlement of the Opium War of 1839–42, which marked the end of China's restrictive Canton System and opened the way for the further expansion of the opium trade, also attracted a small but growing number of foreign missionaries appalled at

---

EPIGRAPHS: (1) MEC Archives, 74-11, folder 1259-5-3: 20, Barckhardt, Yanping, 12 Jan. 1909; (2) Macgowan, *Sidelights on Chinese Life*, p. 200; (3) this legendary, and possibly apocryphal, quotation appears in Alcock, "France, China and the Vatican," *Nineteenth Century* (Nov. 1886), p. 620, cited in Wolferstan, *The Catholic Church in China*, p. 267. Authentic or not, the frequency with which this exchange was cited by missionaries indicates that the sentiment it expressed struck a nerve with many missionaries and western diplomats.

what they saw as the immoral actions of their profit-hungry countrymen. Subsequent conflicts between China and the West simultaneously extended the rights of missionaries to live and work throughout the Chinese empire and compelled the legalization of opium imports. The missionaries who flocked to China in ever-increasing numbers roundly condemned the Sino-British opium trade but found that their intentions and actions were often misinterpreted. Many Chinese had understandable difficulty reconciling the benevolence of the missionary message with the involvement of their imperialist governments in the opium trade.

Opium complicated the already tangled relationship between the Chinese state and foreign missionaries, but in some cases it completely reversed the traditional antagonism between Chinese elites and foreign missionaries. Many Chinese elites and officials opposed Christian initiatives and agitated grassroots antiforeign sentiment, in part because Christianity seemed the theological corollary to western imperialism. At the same time, Christian teachings about social justice and the leveling power of divine love threatened many elites because these doctrines were directed at the lower classes, whose acceptance of their debased status in China's social hierarchy was seen as the key to social stability and gentry domination. Opium prohibition, however, seemed to offer missionaries an unusual opportunity to work *with* Chinese elites inside and outside the formal bureaucracy. In this arena at least, the goals of Christian morality and incipient Chinese nationalism coincided.

In Fujian, as in many provinces, Protestant missionaries became deeply involved in the opium suppression campaign from the local to the international level and exercised an influence that far outweighed their numbers.[1] Their ideas and observations helped construct perceptions of opium abuse in China and affected the rhetoric of suppression in China and abroad. Missionary propaganda disingenuously promoted missionaries to a

---

1. Roman Catholics also worked in Fujian province, but on the whole their influence in the opium suppression campaign was greatly overshadowed by that of their Protestant counterparts, and I confine my focus to the latter. For a detailed discussion of this point, see MAE/Paris, NS 342 (Chine/Missions Protestantes, 1907-1917), Danjou to Doumergue, Asie no. 8, 24 Mar. 1914. For more on the history of the Catholic church in Fujian, see Latourette, *A History of Christian Missions in China*, pp. 100-101, 108-9, 238-39, 328, 542-43, 706, 719; *New Catholic Encyclopedia*, 3: 999 and 5: 594-95; and Wolferstan, *The Catholic Church in China*, app., tables A and C, pp. 444-45, 450.

leading role in the campaign, although they were, at best, supporting actors.[2] The missionaries' opposition to the opium trade and their attempts to treat opium addiction predated the suppression campaign, but their actions and influence worked to promote and legitimize the state-driven prohibition policy. However, in one notable instance in the early years of the Republic, the relationship between the Chinese state and foreign missionaries fueled a violent uprising, when Chinese farmers perceived ostensibly noble missionary motivations as furthering the broader extractive and regulatory goals of the state.

Protestant Missionaries and Opium in Fujian

The success of what John King Fairbank termed the "missionary enterprise" relied largely on the ability of missionaries to promote their message of Christian salvation, but that message often was obscured by smoke from the gunboats and opium pipes that literally and figuratively accompanied missionary expansion into the Chinese hinterland. Missionaries found their inability to extricate themselves from the shadow of military and diplomatic imperialism particularly frustrating with regard to the opium trade. China's humiliating defeat in the Opium War set the stage for the incorporation of both the opium trade and the expansion of missionary rights and privileges into the unequal treaty structure. Under the terms of the Tianjin Treaty of 1858, ratified in 1860 after the *Arrow* War of 1856–60, Indian opium was no longer considered contraband, and foreign missionaries were no longer confined to the treaty ports. Although access to the hinterlands exposed missionaries to the full extent of China's opium problem and strengthened their resolve to combat the drug, many Chinese registered only that the influx of both missionaries and Indian opium occurred under the protection of western gunboats. The popular association of these two foreign "imports" often surfaced in the recriminations that greeted many missionaries entering Chinese villages. One British missionary complained, "God knows how often and often is our message of peace and salvation contemptuously thrown back in our face with the scornful remark, 'You destroy us

---

2. One Chinese historian does credit missionaries with laying the groundwork for the suppression campaign by convincing Europeans of Chinese antipathy toward the drug, as well as providing modern medical evidence of the harm of opium; see Lin Zhiping, "Jidujiao chuanjiaoshi yu Zhongguo jinyan yundong."

with your opium, and now you insult us with your offer of peace and salvation.'"³

In Fujian, the link between missionaries and the opium trade went beyond simple chronology. Fujian's proximity to Taiwan, Hong Kong, and Guangzhou as well as its jagged coastline tempted traders and smugglers from the West and Japan.⁴ Even before missionaries set up shop in the province, the soon-to-be renowned merchants Jardine and Matheson sailed north from Guangzhou to test other markets for foreign opium. When they came ashore somewhere near Nanri Island off the coast of Xinghua prefecture in the early 1830s, they not only assessed the potential demand for their illicit wares but distributed books by missionary-scholar Robert Morrison.⁵ And in 1846, the first Protestant missionary in Fuzhou arrived aboard an opium clipper, albeit with regret. Missionaries, diplomats, and opium merchants were often the only foreigners resident in the treaty ports, and in the early days, missionaries frequently found themselves working with or for their commercial and diplomatic counterparts.⁶ For some time, the missionaries were even compelled by circumstance to use opium ships as informal banking houses.⁷ Shaking off the stigma of association with what they felt was an odious and amoral trade became a missionary priority, despite the obvious difficulties.

Fujian was "generally regarded, as far as missionary work is concerned, as the best occupied province in China."⁸ Table 7.1 reveals that even so, Fujian

---

3. John R. Wolfe of the CMS, cited in Carlson, *The Foochow Missionaries*, p. 70. See also Macgowan, *Sidelights on Chinese Life*, pp. 200, 340–41.

4. Falkenheim, "Provincial Administration in Fukien," p. 21.

5. At this time, however, foreign merchants were concerned primarily with greater access to the tea-growing regions of Fujian; the market for opium was secondary (Collis, *Foreign Mud*, pp. 77–78; J. Y. Wong, *Deadly Dreams*, esp. pp. 312–13).

6. For example, Justus Doolittle, a well-known ABCFM missionary in Fuzhou frustrated with the penury of the home office and relations with his fellow missionaries, was successfully recruited as a well-paid interpreter for Augustine Heard and Co., a firm that dealt in the sale and distribution of opium (Blatt, "Problems of a China Missionary," p. 43). Dr. Carstairs Douglas, one of the pioneers of the PCE, wrote of his first view of Quanzhou in 1859 that the city's "sole specimen of Christianity consists of two opium ships moored at the mouth of the harbour" (cited in PCE—Foreign Missions Committee, box 21 [Fukien, South—Individuals, later T-W & Notes], file 9; and *Foochow Messenger* 7 [Sept. 1928]: 5).

7. Carlson, *The Foochow Missionaries*, pp. 5–7, 35, 69–70.

8. According to this source, Protestant missionaries were laboring in almost every county in the province by the 1920s (Stauffer, *The Christian Occupation of China*, p. 69).

Table 7.1
Missionaries in Fujian, ca. 1905 and 1914

Missionary group	No. of missionaries 1905	No. of missionaries 1914
ABCFM	39	50
MEC (and WFM)	69	105
RCA[a]	21	22
LMS	13	20
CMS/CEZMS[b]	86	149
PCE	36	37
Dominicans[c]	78	50
TOTAL	342	433

SOURCES: For 1905, see MacGillivray, *A Century of Protestant Missions*. For 1914 figures, *The Foochow Messenger*, June 1915, n.p.
[a]The 1905 figure is actually for 1904 (MacGillivray, *A Century of Protestant Missions*, p. 378).
[b]It is unclear whether the 1905 figure includes the 43 members of the CEZMS (ibid., pp. 37–38, 62).
[c]These figures are for 1907 and 1913, respectively (Wolferstan, *The Catholic Church in China*, app. tables A and C, pp. 444–45, 450; Bitton, *The Regeneration of New China*, app. III, p. 264).

boasted only a tiny missionary community. The members of that community, however, exerted an influence on Fujianese society and politics that far exceeded their numbers. The Fujian missions, particularly those established by Protestants, built a network of educational, religious, and medical facilities that extended Christian institutions and influence into remote rural villages and often altered the Chinese political and social landscape.[9]

By the end of the nineteenth century, Fujian was home to six main Protestant missionary groups, half from the United States and half from Great Britain. Of the British groups, the largest was the Church Missionary Society (CMS)[10] and its women's affiliate, the Church of England Zenana Missionary Society (CEZMS).[11] By 1914 the two boasted 149 missionaries in

---

9. The bulk of Fujian's foreign community, as in other Chinese provinces, tended to cluster around the treaty ports, although a sizable minority was thinly scattered at outlying missionary stations and smaller commercial cities along the coastline and in the hinterlands.
10. The CMS began its work in Fujian in 1845 (CMS Handlist—China, in CMS archives).
11. The CEZMS was established in 1880, when it disconnected itself from the interdenominational Indian Female Normal School Society (founded in 1852). The CEZMS began its work in Fujian in 1883 or 1884 (CMS Handlist—Zenana Missionary Society, in CMS archives; MacGillivray, *A Century of Protestant Missions in China*, p. 51).

Fujian.[12] The CMS and CEZMS concentrated their labors in the northwest and northeast regions. They began by setting up operations in Fuzhou (1850)[13] and gradually spread into the prefectures of Xinghua, Jianning, and Funing. The Presbyterian Church of England (PCE) operated primarily in the southeastern region, focusing on the city of Xiamen (1847), as well as Quanzhou (1866), Yongchun (1890), and Zhangpu (1880). The London Missionary Society (LMS) confined its work to southern Fujian, developing centers in the southeastern cities of Xiamen (1844), Zhangzhou (1862), and Hui'an (1866), as well as in the remote southwestern region, particularly Tingzhou prefecture (1870).[14]

On the American side, the American Methodist Episcopal Church (MEC) mission began its work in Fuzhou in 1847,[15] where it opened a small dispensary the next year. Beginning in the 1860s, the MEC expanded its mission into Fujian's interior and, by 1880, had established six districts in the Fuzhou Conference: Fuzhou, Xinghua, Fuding, Yongchun, Gutian, and Yanping.[16] It was aided by the Woman's Foreign Missionary Society (WFM). The (Dutch) Reformed Church of America (RCA) mission operated in southeast Fujian, primarily in Xiamen (1842), Zhangzhou (1861), Tongan, and Xiaoxi.[17] The American Board of Commissioners for Foreign Missions (ABCFM) concentrated its efforts in the northeast, in Fuzhou city (where its first missionary had arrived in 1846)[18] and the counties of Changle and Yongfu in the surrounding prefecture of Fuzhou, as well as in the northwestern prefectures of Jianning, Shaowu, and Yanping.[19]

Despite their enthusiasm and claims of altruistic motivations, foreign missionaries and their converts in Fujian often encountered hostile responses from the Chinese, and the last half of the nineteenth century was

---

12. It is unclear whether or not this figure includes the wives of CMS missionaries (*Foochow Messenger*, June 1915, p. 20).

13. The dates in parentheses indicate the year in which a particular missionary society began work in a specific region.

14. MacGillivray, *A Century of Protestant Missions in China*, pp. 1–62, 175–77.

15. Harmon, *Encyclopedia of World Methodism*, 1: 475; Barclay, *Widening Horizons*, p. 367.

16. Barclay, *Widening Horizons*, pp. 370, 380, 387–88, 390. In 1896, the Xinghua group became a separate annual conference (Copplestone, *Twentieth-Century Perspectives*, p. 673).

17. MacGillivray, *A Century of Protestant Missions in China*, pp. 366–70.

18. Stephen Johnson arrived in Fuzhou on 2 June of that year (Barclay, *Widening Horizons*, p. 368).

19. MacGillivray, *A Century of Protestant Missions in China*, pp. 253–65.

Fig. 7.1 Although one missionary is walking in this photograph from around the turn of the twentieth century, the other is being carried by sedan chair along a narrow Fujian path. Missionary attempts to blend in with the local population sometimes clashed with their de facto elite status (courtesy United Methodist Archives, Drew University, Madison, New Jersey).

punctuated by a series of missionary-related conflicts.[20] Although most incidents amounted to little more than petty persecutions, there were several notable outbreaks of violence. Virtually all were attributable either to property disputes or cultural miscommunication, such as the apparent inability or unwillingness of missionaries to appreciate the importance of geomancy (*fengshui*) when constructing churches or residences. In addition, fear of western medical practices often meant that missionary hospitals were the targets of particularly inflammatory antiforeign rhetoric, especially in the early days. On one occasion in 1895 in Yongchun, Hope Moncrieff of the PCE reported a placard warning the public that the foreigners wished to rip open the bodies of the sick.[21]

---

20. Lin Wenhui, *Qingji Fujian jiao'an zhi yanjiu*.
21. PCE—FMC, box 9 (Fukien, South—General Correspondence, Hospitals, pre-1900 to 1910), file 2. See also Barclay, *Widening Horizons*, p. 433, for further examples.

Establishing a clear-cut relationship between anti-Christian violence and the opium trade was more difficult, despite missionary hand-wringing over their guilt by association. One British missionary lamented:

> Oh! To think that our nation should have been guilty of insisting on the opium trade, for the sake of filthy lucre! . . . We could hardly blame the Chinese if they rose up against us, on account of it, and wished to turn us all out. Oh, that we could only bring our rulers to see the misery in every home in China, through this awful sin![22]

In reality, although missionaries were often heckled about the role of their home countries in importing opium, I have located only one instance in which an anti-missionary attack in Fujian was sparked by popular hostility against the opium trade or against missionaries as the representatives of opium-trading governments. Just before the initiation of the suppression campaign, when members of the ABCFM were in the process of relocating one of their schools for girls, missionaries reported hearing a rumor that the children were being kidnapped to be made into opium.[23] The apparent lack of violence linked to anti-opium sentiment may have been the result of the difficulty of isolating opium from China's myriad social and political ills, but it may also have been due to the high visibility of Christian efforts to combat addiction and end the opium trade.

Missionary Motivations

Why were Protestant missionaries in Fujian and elsewhere so adamantly and vocally opposed to opium consumption and the opium trade? On the surface, the answer to this question may seem obvious. After all, missionaries were involved in a number of moralistic crusades during the nineteenth and early twentieth centuries, including the temperance movement. Opium fit quite neatly into the Christian rhetoric condemning alcohol. China missionary Rev. Griffith John asserted that "opium smoking cannot be compared with moderate drinking, but with drunkenness itself."[24] Many missionaries, however, felt that a somnolent, supine opium smoker did not pose the same danger to social order as did a raging drunk.[25] In fact, missionary

---

22. IWCD, Oct. 1906, p. 155.
23. Foochow Messenger 2, no. 2 (Apr. 1905): 30–32.
24. Cited in Turner, British Opium Policy, p. 25.
25. See Park, Opinions of Over 100 Physicians, pp. 32–33. The comparison between opium smoking and drinking was a significant theme in at least one novel in the United States in the

hostility to the sale and consumption of opium derived from a complex mix of cultural, moral, and practical motivations. China, Great Britain, and the United States responded differently to opium, and each society constructed its own attitudes toward the "problem" of narcotics. Chinese emperors had moved rapidly to halt the consumption and sale of the drug in the first half of the eighteenth century, and the perception of recreational opium use as social or moral deviance persisted. The concept of addiction as a treatable disease was a relatively new development in Great Britain and the United States a century later, when opium was just beginning to be viewed as a commodity that ought to be controlled and regulated.[26] Missionaries in China had to reject many of their assumptions about opium smoking in order to treat Chinese smokers with compassion, lobby effectively against the opium trade, and participate enthusiastically in China's opium suppression campaign.

Protestant missionaries in Fujian and elsewhere in China operated in a broader sociopolitical environment not entirely sympathetic to their diatribes against opium. Many powerful members of the western merchant and diplomatic community, particularly in England, regarded the missionaries as moral extremists who misunderstood and exaggerated the potential and actual harm presented by the opium trade and opium consumption. This was the heyday of free trade, and many of these individuals asserted that the market for opium in China was driven primarily by the enormous demand and was implicitly encouraged by the inability or unwillingness of the Chinese government to enforce its own laws against opium.[27] Those in favor of continuing the opium trade argued that China not only profited from cus-

---

late nineteenth century. T. Fulton Gantt's *Breaking the Chains* featured a villain whose opium-induced debauchery was concealed from the public because his pallor and abstinence from alcohol marked him as a temperate man; see esp. pp. 48–49. Thanks to Jon Sterngass for this and many other references to opium smoking in nineteenth-century American literature cited in this volume.

26. See Yu Ende, *Zhongguo jinyan faling bianqian shi*, for a good history of Chinese legal restrictions on opium.

27. Lodwick, *Crusaders Against Opium*, pp. 78–85. Two exceptions were an American merchant named D. W. C. Olyphant and his nephew Charles W. King who refused out of Christian principle to involve their firm in the opium trade. King and another man were the only foreigners permitted to witness the actual destruction by Lin Zexu of the 20,000 chests of foreign opium forfeited in 1839. During the 1820s and 1830s, Olyphant & Company of New York offered their services as untainted transportation for missionaries of the ABCFM (Charles, "Olyphant and Opium," pp. 66–69).

toms revenues but also had begun to nourish a domestic poppy crop. Furthermore, they added, to deprive the Chinese working man of opium was to remove from his reach an efficacious prophylactic or remedy for a number of debilitating diseases.[28]

This often-heated difference of opinion came to a head in 1893, when agitation from the missionary community in China and the West prompted the appointment of a Royal Commission on Opium in London. The commission was to study the nature of opium use and the impact of ending the trade on the Indian government, but its failure to examine China's opium problem and its refusal to condemn opium consumption infuriated missionaries and other western anti-opium activists. Despite the concerted effort of missionaries stationed in China to gather information that refuted the commission's conclusions, the political environment in England cooled toward the idea of opium reform until a new investigation a decade later.[29] This subsequent investigation, again prompted by missionary activism, was undertaken in 1904–5 by the U.S. government to explore the impact of the opium trade on the Philippines. The report contained the testimony of a number of missionaries stationed in China and elsewhere, and its resounding condemnation of the drug revitalized the anti-opium lobby in China and abroad.[30]

The cultural motivations for missionary hostility to opium in China stemmed not only from the colonialist/imperialist mentality but also from western attitudes regarding narcotics control and the social implications of that control, as well as the association between the dangers of opium and the Chinese people. Ironically, the western missionaries who deplored the widespread dependence on opium in China and associated opium smoking with individual and social depravity came from societies in which the casual consumption of opiates had long been an accepted part of everyday life. In early nineteenth-century Great Britain and the United States, opium was an integral part of popular medicine, and habitual consumption was usually noted

---

28. Lodwick, *Crusaders Against Opium*, pp. 79–82. In India, the British tried to eliminate only the *abuse* of opium through a government monopoly (Owen, *British Opium Policy in China and India*, pp. 103–4). The Japanese colonial government on Taiwan used the same argument to justify the establishment of a profitable opium monopoly on the island while strictly prohibiting it at home (Wang Shiqing, "Ri-ju chuqi Taiwan zhi jiangbihui yu jieyan yundong," p. 111).

29. Richards, "Opium and the British Empire."

30. Great Britain, Royal Commission on Opium; U.S. War Department, *Report of the ... Philippine Commission*; Lodwick *Crusaders Against Opium*, pp. 85–115.

without condemnation.[31] Doctors were too expensive for most of the population, and opium became a popular home remedy for all classes. As one modern scholar explains, "Opium was the Victorian's aspirin, Lomotil, Valium, and Nyquil, which could be bought at the local chemist's for as little as a penny."[32]

In Great Britain, opium did not become a major societal concern until the mid-nineteenth century when increasing self-medication among the working classes clashed with a broad public health campaign and the professionalization of medicine and pharmacy.[33] In addition to concern over the use of opium as a stimulant, the practice of ingesting opium made it difficult to control the effects of a drug that could poison a person if consumed in too great a quantity. It was in this context that the British government ultimately attempted to bring the drug under its control with the Poisons and Pharmacy Act of 1868.[34] The new science of statistics had revealed what the public viewed as an unacceptable rate of criminal and accidental poisoning, particularly among children of the working class, who were often given opium-based syrups to quiet their cries.[35] At the same time, the growing popularity of injectable morphine in England and the United States increased public alarm over the danger of this and other opium derivatives.[36]

---

31. Courtwright, *Dark Paradise*, chaps. 1–3; Berridge and Edwards, *Opium and the People*, pt. II; Parssinen, *Secret Passions, Secret Remedies*, chap. 1; and Harding, *Opium Addiction, Morality and Medicine*, pp. 1–2.

32. Parssinen, *Secret Passions, Secret Remedies*, pp. 25–28, 36; Whitaker, *The Global Connection*, pp. 10–11. Self-medication with opium was also common in parts of China (Park, *Opinions of Over 100 Physicians*, p. 61).

33. Berridge and Edwards (*Opium and the People*) argue that since the physicians, pharmacists, and statisticians who served as the vanguard of the ascendant middle class throughout the nineteenth-century public health campaigns were major beneficiaries of the legislative restrictions, the anti-opium movement must be viewed as part of a larger attempt to control lower-class deviance. Harding (*Opium Addiction, Morality and Medicine*, pp. 83–86) counters that although this was indeed the case in some instances, the public health campaign was also a sincere attempt by public-minded activists to cure what they viewed as a serious social ill.

34. The rising number of poisoning cases may reflect a concomitant increase in the amount of opium imported into Great Britain. Annual opium consumption rose precipitously from 17,000 pounds in 1827 to 61,000 pounds in 1859 (Whitaker, *The Global Connection*, p. 11).

35. Ironically, it may have been "the very act of keeping statistics [that] drew attention to certain causes of death . . . that could seemingly be altered by government action. The poisons agitation of 1860s, then, was . . . an outgrowth of a more general public health concern of which mortality statistics were both cause and effect" (Parssinen, *Secret Passions, Secret Remedies*, chap. 6).

36. Ibid., chap. 7.

The manner in which the drug was consumed also had powerful cultural connotations and racial overtones that strongly affected the opium debate in the early twentieth century. In the United States, Western Europe, and even in British India, opium usually was swallowed in liquid form, ostensibly for its therapeutic properties. Opium was the primary ingredient in a number of popular remedies in those regions, including laudanum and paregoric, as well as in children's syrups such as Godfrey's Cordial and tonics like Chlorodyne.[37] The fact that virtually everyone consumed opium-based medications in the privacy of their own home lent the drug an air of respectability in western societies.[38] Many individuals may have tipped the laudanum bottle more for ailments of the spirit than for diseases of the body, but usually only those in the less respectable classes did so in a manner that generated public condemnation. Bohemians, artists, and writers seemed to have been given more license to experiment with mind-altering substances, but for the most part the British and American publics deplored the non-medicinal use of opium as immoral.[39] The Chinese themselves did not act to control or prohibit opium consumption until the habit of opium smoking—derived from tobacco smoking—became popular.[40]

Indeed, it was the *smoking* of opium that brought swift disapproval from non-Chinese moralists.[41] Unlike most others, the Chinese took their opium, for medicinal and recreational purposes, in this form and in places that reeked of pleasure seeking. During the nineteenth century, British and Americans came to link opium smoking with negative Orientalist images, and the enormous population of China began to blend in the popular imagination with the handful of Chinese and whites who mingled in the opium dens of the American West, New York's infant Chinatown, or London's

---

37. Berridge and Edwards, *Opium and the People*, p. xix.

38. Harding, *Opiate Addiction, Morality and Medicine*, pp. 31–32.

39. That did not mean the drug had no allure for respectable citizens. Even celebrated reformer Jane Addams (*Twenty Years at Hull House*, pp. 28–29) confessed to attempting to attain DeQuincey-like heights through opium consumption. The incident occurred at boarding school when Addams was seventeen, and she and four friends sought to alleviate their boredom during a holiday. They were discovered and reprimanded but not punished severely.

40. Berridge and Edwards, *Opium and the People*, chap. 5; Yu Ende, *Zhongguo jinyan faling bianqian shi*.

41. The Chinese are said to have originated the habit of smoking opium, and they carried their pipes and opium dens with them to Southeast Asia, the United States, and Europe. The oral consumption of medicinal opium predated the practice of opium smoking in China.

East End.[42] In England, those images generated fears that the opium trade would spread from China to England in an ironic reverse-colonialism that undoubtedly reflected guilt combined with a fear of the exotic Other.[43] The noble imperialistic impulse sought to civilize the heathen Oriental, but that process of incorporation held the danger that it might backfire.[44] Popular authors such as Charles Dickens, Arthur Conan Doyle, and Wilkie Collins contributed to and reinforced that perceptual shift by incorporating into their widely read works references to the insidious nature of opium consumption and the vulnerability of innocent whites.[45]

In the United States, physicians and legislators raised the alarm when opium smoking began to spread outside the emigrant Chinese communities and the white criminal element and threatened upper-class white society.[46] Particularly threatening was the specter of innocent, young white women being seduced into drug-induced immorality by Asian men, the denizens of China's so-called bachelor community in the United States.[47] Popular attitudes were reflected and sustained by late nineteenth-century American fiction. The final scene of T. Fulton Gantt's novel Breaking the Chains, written in the 1880s, uses opium smoking to depict the true nature of the indolent upper class. When the villain returns home from a night of carousing, he surprises his wife and his Chinese manservant indulging in the pleasures of the opium pipe in a secret room set aside for that purpose.

The drunken warrior was suddenly sobered and petrified by the sight that met his gaze. Li Hung was there, but stretched out unconscious on the divan for the first time in his life, helpless in the firm grip of the deadly drug. The pipe had fallen from his nerveless fingers. The fashionable and fascinating young bride of a few months was enjoying with reckless abandon the strange dissipation as she lay by his side, the dead whiteness of the skin contrasting strangely with the glittering jewels, dressed as she left the brilliant reception a few hours before—décolleté.[48]

---

42. The Police Gazette, 1883, p. 42; Parssinen, Secret Passions, Secret Remedies, chap. 8.

43. Milligan, Pleasures and Pains, p. 13 and chaps. 5–6.

44. China missionary Rev. George Piercy cautioned his fellow countrymen about the perils of the opium trade, warning that "it begins with the Chinese, but it does not end with them!" (Friend of China 6 [1883]; cited in Milligan, Pleasures and Pains, chaps. 6–7).

45. Berridge and Edwards, Opium and the People, chap. 5; Milligan, Pleasures and Pains, chaps. 2–4.

46. Courtwright, Dark Paradise, pp. 63–64.

47. Parssinen, Secret Passions, Secret Remedies, chap. 8.

48. Gantt, Breaking the Chains, p. 133.

The dangers of opium were entangled with the apparition of interracial sex and, more explicitly, with anti-Chinese biases. In this novel, that prejudice was further tied to the prevailing hostility within the American labor movement toward Chinese immigration.[49] The working class was not immune to the narcotic's allure either, although in Philander Deming's moving story "Ike's Wife," the protagonist is driven to cruelty and suicide during withdrawal from a legitimately prescribed dose of opium.[50]

Opium could be consumed anywhere, and was, but it was the image of the darkened, squalid opium den, shrouded in white, pungent smoke and owned and patronized by mysterious Chinese, that captured the imagination and horror of westerners inside and outside China.[51] The opium den became synonymous with the Chinese and with what westerners perceived as the more unsavory elements of the predominantly male Chinese diaspora. Americans and the British tended to view opium dens as the Asian counterparts of the bars and public houses in which disreputable members of white society pursued drunkenness. During the first quarter of the twentieth century, the emergence of small Chinatowns, replete with opium dens, inspired fear, contempt, and curiosity.[52] Tabloids often featured stories and etchings that reflected white fears of this seductive vice and its ramifications. For Western Europeans and Americans, China was mysterious and strange, and the fascination and fear with which its people and their customs and habits were viewed were highlighted by firsthand encounters with the nineteenth-century Chinese diaspora. Those encounters generated a wide range of cultural misunderstandings and cemented in western minds the close relationship between the Chinese and opium.

The missionaries who confronted China's opium problem in Fujian and throughout the Qing empire thus brought with them a confusion of western-based assumptions concerning gender, race, class, and the drug itself

---

49. *Breaking the Chains* is dedicated to the cause of labor organizing, and earlier in the book, the author describes in contemptuous, unambiguously racist terms the servant alluded to in the earlier quotation. "[He was] . . . among the most intelligent of the Chinamen immigrating to this country when Asia first turned loose upon us her horde of filthy, festering degradation" (Gantt, *Breaking the Chains*, p. 47).

50. Deming, *Adirondack Stories*, pp. 26–39.

51. For example, see Macgowan, *Sidelights on Chinese Life*, pp. 196–200; McMahon, *The Fall of the God of Money*, chap. 4.

52. Berridge and Edwards, *Opium and the People*, chap 15.

Fig. 7.2 Caucasian women visit a Chinese opium den in New York City's Chinatown in the early twentieth century (courtesy United Methodist Archives, Drew University, Madison, New Jersey).

that quickly collided with Chinese reality. The medical arm of the Protestant missionary enterprise had to accept the fact that in China, opium smoking had been and continued to be an acceptable means of consuming the drug for medicinal as well as recreational purposes. A survey of 100 missionary physicians in China revealed that virtually all had encountered the prescribing of opium for a variety of physical ailments, and most attested that the drug brought temporary relief.[53] This evidence was probably intended to address foreign misconceptions of opium smoking, elicit sympathy for Chinese smokers, and generate antipathy toward the opium trade.

Race- and gender-based assumptions could not be shaken off quite so easily, however, and some missionaries were not entirely sympathetic to the plight of all Chinese opium smokers. British and American missionaries were the products of imperialist nations whose forceful acquisition of Chinese territory, trading privileges, and legal immunity underlined the weakness of the current Chinese state. Despite their guilt over their nations' role

---

53. Park, *Opinions of Over 100 Physicians*, pp. 37–40.

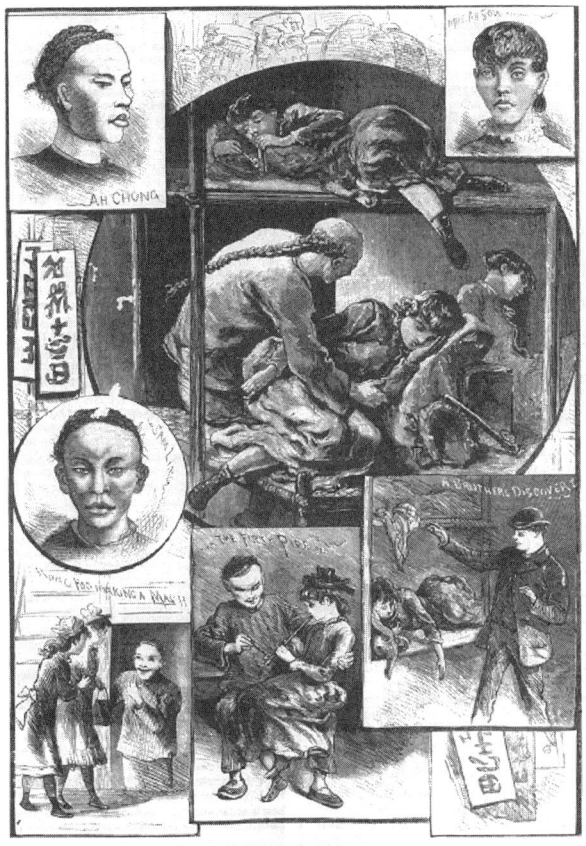

Fig. 7.3 This etching from from the *Police Gazette* (2 June 1883) is an artist's rendition of the scene like that depicted in Fig. 7.2.

in introducing and providing the drug to China, many missionaries viewed widespread opium addiction as both cause and symptom of political instability and the enormous class divisions, and as evidence of the moral weakness of the Chinese race and the Confucian social framework in which it existed.[54] One missionary physician even voiced the opinion that narcotics abuse was "the judgment of God on a dishonest race."[55]

---

54. Ibid., pp. 1–8.
55. Ibid., p. 65; McMahon, *The Fall of the God of Money*, chaps. 3–4.

Foreign assumptions concerning gender also played a prominent role in the construction of missionary attitudes toward China's relationship with opium. As in virtually all aspects of missionary life, opium work in China was divided into male and female spheres, and female missionaries were particularly sensitive to the plight of their unfortunate Chinese sisters. Although a wealth of anecdotal evidence indicates that most Chinese opium smokers—approximately 90 percent—were male, female smokers were not uncommon. Chinese women who smoked opium usually were found either in the leisure class or among prostitutes and other "fallen women." But the wives of shopkeepers and soldiers and any women with a little extra time or money were also vulnerable. Poor women evidently were less susceptible to addiction because in impoverished households men usually controlled the limited resources.[56]

Chinese women were profoundly affected by opium not only as smokers themselves but also and more often as the unfortunate relatives of male smokers. Missionaries reported that, in addition to enduring the poverty and unemployment that often plagued an opium smoker's household, many wives and daughters were sold—sometimes into prostitution—to satisfy the craving of an addicted husband or father.[57] Missionaries deeply mourned the loss of some of their students in this manner. One British missionary lamented:

One young promising woman who had been with us was sold, while I was away, to a heathen house, just that her miserable husband might indulge himself to his own destruction in that dreadful drug. He has died since and the poor wife is in the hands of the heathen husband to whom she was sold; she is only one out of many.[58]

In addition, missionary writings often graphically described addicted mothers blowing opium smoke into their crying infants' mouths or recounted the tragic consequences of accidental poisonings among young children.[59] The

---

56. Park, *Opinions of Over 100 Physicians*, pp. 12–18; Wang Shuhuai, "Yapian duhai," p. 193. However, these answers may reflect Chinese expectations that respectable women remain in their homes, out of sight of the foreigners; see also Pruitt, *Daughter of Han*.

57. Park, *Opinions of Over 100 Physicians*, pp. 6–8, 63–75, 87; Crafts et al., *Protection of Native Races*, pp. 117, 123–26.

58. *IWCD*, Oct. 1906, p. 155.

59. Appendix to "Hearing Before Secretary Hay on Release of China from Opium," USDS, 1906–10, 774/475–76; Park, *Opinions of Over 100 Physicians*, pp. 12–18, 62.

horror of these images recalled the indignation of anti-opium activists in Great Britain toward lower-class "infant doping."

Most missionaries, regardless of gender, expressed compassion for Chinese opium addicts and indignation at the profit motive that fueled the opium trade, but a few were contemptuous of wealthy male Chinese smokers who took up the habit for pleasure.[60] Opium was seen as sapping an individual's manhood and passion for life, and there was something inherently disturbing to a missionary steeped in the Protestant work ethic about the indolent pose of a reclining Chinese opium smoker.[61] One American author agreed, sneering that opium was "the most luxurious vice on earth."[62] Ironically, although racism fueled western fears of Chinese opium smokers abroad, in China, the passivity that characterized many male Chinese opium smokers was sometimes viewed by western missionaries as not only scandalous but downright emasculating. "It tends on the whole to repress the fighting passions of a man," claimed one missionary.[63] In contrast, opium smoking (and footbinding) came to symbolize the enslavement of Chinese women by the dual bonds of imperialist greed and Chinese patriarchy.[64] Chinese authorities and social reformers appeared to have been concerned most about the negative impact of opium smoking on the family and, by extension, on society as a whole. Chinese officials castigated male and female smokers for indulging in a habit that could impoverish their households and cause a breakdown of social order. Individual suffering was recognized, but the health of the family and society was China's first priority.

Missionaries took pains to point out that the toxic effects of opium, which became the focus of legislative and popular concern in Great Britain and the United States, also plagued the Chinese. According to Protestant missionary physicians whose Christian morality and medical ethics deplored such acts, opium was the most prevalent method of suicide among the Chinese. This,

---

60. Among the more critical was the venerable Rev. Griffin John, who stated that the majority of Chinese smokers took up the habit out of a "love of pleasure and vice" and that "the phlegmatic temperament and indolent habit of the Asiatic [made] him more liable to contract the habit" (*Chinese Recorder* 25 [Apr. 1894]: 198).

61. Macgowan, *Sidelights on Chinese Life*, pp. 197, 342–45; Park, *Opinions of Over 100 Physicians*, pp. 1–8; McMahon, *The Fall of the God of Money*, pp. 56–57, 72, 75.

62. Gantt, *Breaking the Chains*, p. 52.

63. Macgowan, *Sidelights on Chinese Life*, p. 345.

64. Ironically, what was seen as emasculating in China was perceived as mysterious and powerful abroad, as noted in the earlier discussions of opium dens in the United States and England.

too, was a gendered phenomenon, since missionaries observed that most Chinese who attempted suicide were young women.[65] The missionaries attributed this phenomenon to the ready availability and low cost of the drug, but the popularity of opium as a means of suicide might also be interpreted as a powerful, and very intentional, indictment of the vice that brought despair to so many Chinese women. Suicide in China carried with it a strong connotation of blame, and women suffering from some form of abuse often employed self-destruction as a protest of last resort. Chinese women were traditionally more prone to suicide than men, largely because of their marginal position in the Confucian social universe, and this bolstered the foreign image of Chinese women as victims of opium and patriarchy.[66] However, the suffering of Chinese women was but one element in a larger process of social decay that missionaries attributed to opium and that confirmed missionary opposition to the consumption and importation of the drug.

Above all, their encounters with Chinese opium smokers and their families convinced missionaries of the dire moral, physical, social, and economic consequences of opium consumption and reinforced their commitment to opium suppression. The racist and imperialist assumptions that were part of the cultural baggage carried by most missionaries did not preclude a genuine sense of compassion for Chinese opium smokers. Many missionaries were deeply moved and genuinely horrified by the damage apparently wrought by opium abuse, and some claimed that they could recognize hard-core opium addicts or "opium devils" (*yapian gui*) simply by their appearance.[67]

Missionary compassion was particularly forthcoming for impoverished Chinese laborers whose dependence was clearly prompted by physical injury or illness. Many missionaries employed servants or utilized the services of workers like rickshaw pullers and had the opportunity to see firsthand the suffering endured by those individuals. Evidently, this bias was well known to the Chinese. One British missionary at a CMS women's hospital in

---

65. Park, *Opinions of Over 100 Physicians*, pp. 41–43; Crafts et al., *Protection of Native Races*, pp. 123–26.

66. Wolf, "Women and Suicide in China."

67. Harding, *Opiate Addiction, Morality and Medicine*, pp. 32–33; Park, *Opinions of Over 100 Physicians*, pp. 5, 85; FMMH, 1877, pp. 2–5; Doolittle, *Social Life of the Chinese*, pp. 353–55; Owen, *British Opium Policy in China and India*, pp. 236–37. We should keep in mind, however, that the missionaries may have been confusing the symptoms of hunger and disease with the opium taken to "cure" those conditions (Newman, "Opium Smoking: A Reconsideration," p. 776).

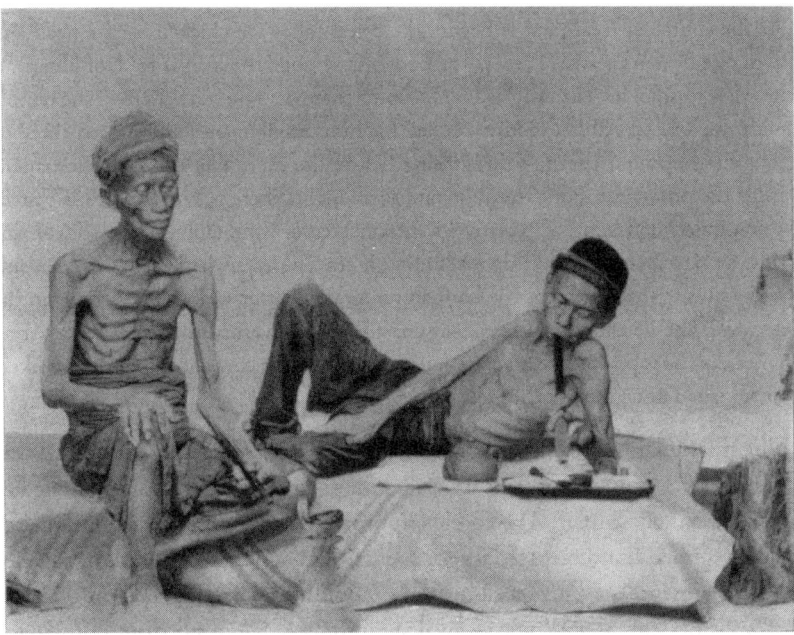

Fig. 7.4 As horrifying as this early twentieth-century missionary photograph entitled "Opium Victims" is, it is not clear if opium smoking caused the emaciated appearance of these two smokers or if they sought solace in opium because of poverty or physical ailments (courtesy United Methodist Archives, Drew University, Madison, New Jersey).

Fuzhou reported that "sometimes . . . rich women come dressed in rags to excite more sympathy and get better medicine."[68] The wealthy classes also were susceptible to illness, of course, but missionary sympathies often rested with the poor. Most elite opium smokers were perceived as consuming the drug for social purposes or, as one British opium reformer put it disdainfully, for "animal indulgence."[69]

Missionary physicians were often horrified and amused at the various folk methods by which their non-Christian Chinese counterparts attempted to cure opium addiction and believed that they had a duty to introduce the wonders of modern medicine and Christian faith to suffering Chinese addicts. One American missionary was told that opium smokers seeking cures in the Yongchun area were instructed to go to a nearby temple with rice and a live chicken where the following ritual unfolded:

---

68. *Mercy and Truth* 10, no. 120 (Dec. 1906): 357.
69. Dyer, *Word-Pictures of Chinese Life*, p. 13.

As the course of treatment is begun, the priest takes the chicken by the head and with one dexterous stroke severs the body—a symbol, the man is told, of himself if he takes to smoking the drug again. Then for three days he stays there in the temple with the priests. All his food is cooked for him, brought out, and passed three or four times around the incense burning before the idol. The chicken, the patient helps the priests eat. For three days and three nights there is kept up for his benefit a continual mumbling of priestly incantations before the idol. At the end of this time he is said to be cured. He is told that if any one asks whether he has been suffering during the treatment (he has had no medicine, they say), he is to reply in the negative; else he is likely to smoke again. Then he is warned that he is to say at all times that he is positively and completely cured; else the curse of the chicken is likely to be visited upon him by the idol.[70]

The missionary narrator obviously was skeptical of the superstitious aspects of the ritual, but animal sacrifice aside, the Chinese and missionary remedies were strikingly similar. The foreign approach often employed a similarly holistic regimen that consisted of good nutrition, supervised isolation, psychological pressure, and abstention from opium. Both groups relied on a variety of ways of dealing with withdrawal symptoms that ranged from homemade medicines to entertainment such as lantern shows to distract patients.[71] Of course, Christian education and propaganda were an integral element of missionary opium treatment because recovery was believed to be contingent on the establishment of spiritual as well as physical well-being. Missionaries disparaged non-Christian treatment centers for ignoring the necessity of prayer. One CMS missionary, for example, criticized a refuge run by the official Opium Prohibition Bureau in the prefectural seat of Jianning as dark, damp, and dirty, as well as intimidating. Inmates allegedly were confronted by an enormous list of rules, and the walls of the refuge were hung with frightening illustrations of the punishments awaiting those who returned to the habit.[72]

Missionary zeal in the battle against opium may not have been based entirely on altruism or remorse for the sins of their commercial compatriots. Clearly, the opium trade constituted an obstacle to evangelism by debauching potential converts and calling into question the sincerity of missionaries whose home governments profited from the sale of opium in China. By in-

---

70. Dildine to "Dear Friends," in MEC Archives, 74-11, 1259-5-3, 24 Mar. 1910, p. 51.
71. *Chinese Recorder* 37, no. 11 (Nov. 1906): 596; Beattie, "Protestant Missions and Opium in China," p. 110.
72. *Mercy and Truth* 12, no. 140 (Aug. 1908): 245–49.

creasing social and physical distress among the general Chinese population, however, opium may have had the ironic consequence of sending many of those affected by opium addiction into the welcoming arms of missionary physicians, ministers, and educators. Opium treatment proved especially rich soil for conversions. Opium refuges and dispensaries provided the ideal environment for all the major aspects of nineteenth-century missionary work in China—education, evangelization, and relief. In testimony after testimony, missionaries and Chinese Christians told of ardent converts who gratefully joined the church after they or a family member had been cured in a missionary hospital or after they had witnessed the rescue of a friend or relative (or themselves) by mission doctors from an opium-induced suicide attempt.[73] The MEC mission in Fujian reported that fourteen of the first seventeen converts in Gutian had previously smoked opium.[74] Chinese women affected by opium were particularly inclined to seek solace in Christianity.[75] In addition, opium users, like bigamists, idol worshippers, and other undesirables, were forbidden to join Christian churches, a missionary-imposed restriction that was intended not only to inspire Chinese to eschew opium smoking but also to ensure the purity of the flock and deflect any opium-related criticisms from the church.

However, another circumstance may have further inclined the foreign missionary community toward compassion. In a book condemning the opium trade, one British missionary noted sadly: "Nor have Asiatics alone been thus snared. I could name, among others, a young woman, a once promising missionary in China, who has had to return to her native land, a wrecked life, a pitiable, hopeless slave to opium which she says she first took under medical advice." Another non-Chinese victim was a British missionary with some medical knowledge who injected himself with morphine to relieve the pain of a medical condition, "until he became so en-

---

73. For some examples, see Latourette, *A History of Christian Missions in China*, pp. 480–85; *Chinese Recorder* 37, no. 11 (Nov. 1906): 596–99; and *Chronicle of the London Missionary Society*, Sept. 1906, p. 213. One scholar specifically notes that cure of opium addiction was one of the primary paths through which Chinese were converted to Christianity in the Canadian Protestant missions of northern Henan (Gewurtz, "Do Numbers Count?" pp. 21–24). However, some missionary physicians disputed this conclusion and argued that many of the few one-time addicts who did join the church quickly relapsed (Park, *Opinions of Over 100 Physicians*, pp. 53–57).

74. Barclay, *Widening Horizons*, p. 443.

75. The testimony is voluminous, but for some examples, see virtually any issue of *IWCD* from 1906 to 1911 in CEZMS—Publications.

slaved that he was unable to end its use." His career and his marriage collapsed, he was compelled to leave China, and many years later, his family testified that he remained in the grip of morphine addiction.[76] Of course, the tragic element of both these stories rests on the involuntary nature of the addiction. The stories clearly imply that missionaries would never indulge in opium consumption for pleasure.

In sum, the missionary's unwavering hostility toward the Indo-Chinese opium trade and the simultaneous sympathy and contempt for the Chinese smokers were shaped as much by prejudices concerning race, class, gender, and narcotics consumption formed at home as by their experiences in China. The imperialist-colonialist mentality ensured that race and class considerations colored missionary perspectives on Chinese opium smoking. Sympathy could be extended to a hard-working laborer who resorted to opium to ease his aches, pains, and minor ailments, whereas contempt greeted the indolent upper-class smoker who took up the habit out of boredom, a desire for status, or, worst of all, sheer pleasure. Opium abuse also was a gendered problem that deeply affected the predominantly female missionary cohort and highlighted for them the tyranny of the Confucian family system and their own sexual vulnerability. On the other hand, the evolution in nineteenth-century Europe and the United States of a concept of addiction as a medically treatable ailment elicited from missionaries a considerable degree of compassion for Chinese opium smokers. All these sentiments contributed to missionary determination to battle China's narcotics problem at its source—the Indo-Chinese opium trade—and at its destination in Chinese society.

Missionary Involvement in Fujian's Anti-Opium Campaign

> Well may we fast and pray and be humbled on account of the untold misery that our race has brought on China. We must pray, but we must work.[77]

And work they did. Western missionaries and their converts not only were vocal and visible supporters of the Qing anti-opium campaign but also pioneered unofficial efforts to deal with China's opium problem in the period between the end of the first Opium War in 1842 and the inauguration of the

---

76. Dyer, *Word-Pictures of Chinese Life*, pp. 13–14.
77. *Chinese Recorder*, Aug. 1906, p. 433.

prohibition policy in 1906.[78] Missionary efforts focused on the medical, educational, and political arenas, each of which is discussed below. Their activities included the establishment of addiction-treatment centers known as opium refuges, the distribution of numerous publications warning of the dangers of opium, and the organization of anti-opium committees and societies among themselves and in conjunction with Chinese elites that lobbied the British and Chinese governments to end the drug trade. In addition, all missionary groups in China prohibited opium smoking, cultivation, or sale by current or prospective church members, and many Chinese Christians assumed prominent roles in grassroots opium reform. However, before the suppression campaign, opium was still legal, and all these activities occurred within a context of state tolerance of opium consumption and cultivation.

After the launching of the official campaign, however, missionaries found their position both elevated and complicated as they allied with the Chinese state and unofficial reformers. For the most part, the campaign created an opportunity for missionaries in Fujian to join forces with elites, who traditionally opposed missionary work. Missionaries sought the kind of reaction they obtained from local elites attending the Anglican church on Christmas 1907 in Lianjiang county (Fuzhou prefecture), who declared: "Before we would not listen to anyone from England, the country that forced opium on us, but now if you help us to get rid of it we honour your church."[79] In some areas, missionaries seemed to feel that they acted de facto as agents of state policy when their medical facilities were designated government opium refuges. On one notable occasion, detailed in Chapter 8, however, by associating themselves with the Chinese state during this chaotic time, missionaries found their noble aspirations pitted against the survival instincts of Chinese poppy farmers with a large stake in the continuation of Fujian's opium economy.

MEDICAL INVOLVEMENT

The most visible and welcome contribution of foreign missionaries to the suppression campaign in Fujian came in the medical arena, where they were able to address the ravages of opium on an immediate and individual level. Missionaries pioneered the treatment of opium addiction in Fujian and

---

78. For detailed discussion of this topic, see Lodwick, "Chinese, Missionary, and International Efforts"; Lodwick, *Crusaders Against Opium*; and Beattie, "Protestant Missions and Opium in China."

79. *IWCD* 28, no. 267 (Sept. 1908): 138.

throughout China, and Protestant mission hospitals and dispensaries reported a constant trickle of Chinese patients seeking cures for addiction, and a veritable flood of those requiring treatment for opium-related maladies and disorders, as well as suicide attempts. On the eve of the anti-opium campaign, they had established a number of medical institutions throughout the province and claimed to have treated hundreds of thousands of Chinese patients.[80] Records kept by one American missionary clinic, the Fuzhou Opium Asylum, indicate that this facility alone treated more than 2,000 opium smokers from 1880 to 1883, well before the cessation of smoking was mandated by the Chinese state.[81] By 1921, Fujian boasted 41 Protestant hospitals and nine separate dispensaries.[82] Many mission groups ran opium refuges within their hospitals,[83] and most medical missionaries longed for a special building or wing to house those trying to overcome addiction.

British and American missionary physicians also introduced the Chinese to the questionable practice of administering morphine to affect a cure for the opium habit, and this and other missionary methods of treating addiction were adopted and adapted by the Chinese. As late as 1890, renowned anti-opium physician and missionary John Dudgeon seemed to ignore the irony when he wrote that the ideal opium pill, such as the eponymous Dudgeon's Pills, should contain some form of opium so as to ease the suffering of the patient.[84] It is no wonder that these medications came to be known as "Jesus opium" among many Chinese. The use of a narcotic substitute for opium quickly caught on among Chinese, perhaps, as one missionary postulated, because "the Chinese entertain the opinion that since the drug comes from a foreign land, foreigners must know some infallible remedy." A foreign customs official theorized that this practice created a heavy demand for morphine among Chinese students of western doctors and may have explained why, by 1900, the port of Xiamen was second only to Shang-

---

80. Medical work was a part of Protestant mission work in Fujian from the very outset, but it was not until after 1870 that missionary physicians began to arrive with the intention of undertaking permanent, full-time medical work (Carlson, *The Foochow Missionaries*, pp. 62–63).

81. *Annual Report of the Foochow Medical Missionary Hospital in Connection with the A.B.C.F.M. Mission* (1880–84).

82. Stauffer, *Christian Occupation of China*, p. 74.

83. The CMS reported in the early twentieth century that "Opium Refuges are adjuncts of most of the hospitals" (MacGillivray, *A Century of Protestant Missions*, p. 36).

84. Letter to the Editor by Dudgeon in *Chinese Recorder* 21 (Nov. 1890): 517.

hai in the amount of morphine it imported annually.[85] The proximity of smugglers on Taiwan, with Japanese citizenship and immunity from Chinese legal penalties, also may have contributed to the problem. By the late 1880s and 1890s, however, many missionaries recognized the addictive properties of morphine and condemned Chinese purveyors of morphine-laced opium remedies.[86]

Word of missionary success in treating opium addiction spread, and occasionally desperate Chinese villagers even requested missionaries to take the refuge "on the road." In one instance, a few months before the promulgation of the initial suppression edict, representatives from one small village outside Fuzhou came to the CMS mission station and escorted a missionary medical crew into the countryside. The missionaries were greeted with great fanfare, and all the village's male smokers—80 in all—were ensconced in the village ancestral hall and its attached temple. Nine women were treated separately in the nearby home of one of the patients.[87] Two female missionaries and several Chinese aides attended to the patients. All were subjected to the typical mission regimen, which consisted of equal parts of commonsense nutrition and of religious teaching and prayer. The very elderly or particularly inveterate smokers were weaned off the drug more slowly than the others. The proprietors of the village's opium shops agreed to close their doors, and the village itself raised the funds to pay for the medicines used in treating the smokers.

The missionaries were granted permission to take whatever steps they felt necessary to ensure the cure of all the smokers in the village. At one point, Rev. W. C. White and Dr. G. Wilkinson personally raided the opium shops and confiscated a considerable amount of opium paraphernalia that had not yet been destroyed. The local authorities' approval of the missionaries' actions is evidenced by the request of the village elders that the local magistrate post a proclamation prohibiting opium shops in the village. He complied. When the missionaries left triumphantly in late March, they were laden with gifts from the grateful villagers and apparently left behind a cadre of enthusiastic converts, most from the ranks of the re-

---

85. IMC, *Decennial Reports, Amoy, 1892–1901*, p. 127.

86. Lodwick, "Chinese, Missionaries, and International Efforts," pp. 205-8; Howard, "Ministers of Health," p. 14.

87. The total population of the village was about 1,000, and so the ninety addicts constituted almost 10 percent of the population (*Chinese Recorder*, Nov. 1906, pp. 591, 593).

cently cured.[88] Missionary publications indicate that this scene was repeated numerous times in Fuzhou prefecture during the first few years of the campaign.[89]

In some areas, local Chinese officials and activists strengthened the link between the Chinese state and the missionaries by requesting the use of missionary opium treatment facilities as the official opium refuges mandated by provincial and national authorities. This probably resulted as much from financial constraints as from a shared hostility to opium addiction or respect for western medical skills. Missionaries in Fuzhou, Xinghua, and remote Tingzhou eagerly consented to this proposal. In Xinghua prefecture, the CMS asserted that "we are in charge of the official refuge," an approximately 30-bed facility located inside the missionary hospital. The responsibility for conducting the suppression campaign in Xinghua, as elsewhere in Fujian, was split between the officials and gentry. The officials apparently took charge of shutting down opium dens, licensing opium shops, and monitoring poppy cultivation, and the gentry oversaw the investigating, capturing, and treating of smokers. It was under gentry auspices that the CMS refuge became an official part of the campaign, and the pride of the British missionaries may also have been linked to the fact that a refuge run by American Methodists apparently was not granted the same status.[90]

Not all Chinese reformers welcomed foreign participation, however, and missionaries resented exclusion from a cause they had adopted as their own. In northwest Jianning prefecture, where longstanding anti-Christian sentiment undoubtedly contributed to a notable lack of cooperation between missionaries and Chinese elites, missionaries were contemptuous of Chinese reform efforts. Chinese activists duly acknowledged missionary contributions, but the missionaries were dismayed to find themselves confined to exhortatory roles. Upon inspection of the Chinese-run opium treatment center, which had been whitewashed in apparent imitation of the foreign practice, one evangelist noted caustically that the paint was "somewhat emblematic of the superficial method in which the whole attempt at reform is being conducted."[91] Even in Fuzhou, one missionary physician complained

---

88. *Mercy and Truth* 10, no. 116 (Aug. 1906): 242–49; *IWCD* 26, no. 245 (Nov. 1906), p. 171; *Chinese Recorder* 37, no. 11 (Nov. 1906): 591–600.

89. See, e.g., *IWCD* 26, no. 239 (May 1906): 72–73; and 30, no. 290 (Aug. 1910): 121.

90. *Mercy and Truth* 15, no. 179 (Nov. 1911): 377–79.

91. Zhang Xingsheng, "'Jinyan' zaji," pp. 31–32; *Mercy and Truth* 12, no. 140 (Aug. 1908): 245–49; Lin Wenhui, *Qingji Fujian jiao'an zhi yanjiu*, pp. 174–88.

that "the opium habitue is not eager at present to enter the mission hospital" and theorized that this phenomenon probably resulted from a desire to confine foreign help in the battle against opium to more superficial activities, such as speechmaking.[92]

EDUCATIONAL/POLITICAL INVOLVEMENT

However, missionary oratory could be a powerful tool in the fight against opium. Before and during the suppression campaign, Protestant missionaries in Fujian not only continued to treat opium addiction but also worked to publicize the dangers of opium and lobby against the opium trade in China and in their home countries.[93] Lobbying was conducted by individual missionaries, who gave graphic testimony on the ravages of opium among the Chinese, as well as by organized mission reform groups, such as the regional and denominational missionary conferences, ecumenical organizations like the China Medical Missionary Association, and societies dedicated to opium suppression. In addition, a number of missionaries penned passionate books on the subject.

In Fujian, various missionary groups organized conferences and set up societies to publicize the dangers of opium smoking. The MEC organized an anti-opium society in Fujian as early as 1877.[94] International societies, such as the International Reform Bureau (IRB) based in the United States, the British Society for the Suppression of the Opium Trade (SSOT), and the International Opium Commission, actively encouraged Chinese reformers. For example, in late 1906, SSOT dispatched its secretary, Joseph Alexander, to Fuzhou on an inspection tour where he was welcomed by foreign and Chinese anti-opium societies and honored by Lin Bingzhang at a banquet.[95] Later, the IRB and the SSOT wrote to provincial authorities in Fuzhou to address the issue of poppy planting during the Revolution of 1911.[96] The SSOT's publicity organ, *The Friend of China*, helped fan the anti-opium flame from its inception in 1901 and throughout the suppression campaign. During the early twentieth century, missionaries also supported

---

92. Dr. Marcus Mackenzie as cited in the *Chinese Recorder* 39, no. 3 (Mar. 1908): 152.

93. Lodwick, "Chinese, Missionary, and International Efforts"; Beattie, "Protestant Missions and Opium in China," p. 111.

94. Barclay, *Widening Horizons*, p. 443.

95. PRO, FO 228/2415, doc. 53, enclosure in Playfair to Jordan, 30 Jan. 1907.

96. *Republican Advocate* 1, no. 2 (13 Apr. 1912): 70–72.

and often attended a number of international meetings designed to address global narcotics issues.[97]

Missionary periodicals such as the *Chinese Recorder*, *Mercy and Truth*, and *India's Women and China's Daughters*, gave prominent exposure to editorials, features, photographs, and essay contests supporting opium suppression. Reports on the progress of suppression measures implemented by missionaries as well as by the Chinese state were publicized and lauded in a concerted effort to agitate for the end of the Sino-British opium trade and the reworking of the 1908 agreement with the British. Evidence of the Chinese commitment to opium reform was necessary to silence the suspicions of some British merchants and diplomats that the Chinese sought an end to the trade simply to monopolize the huge Chinese market for opium. Missionaries in Fujian also toured Chinese-run opium refuges and attended public anti-opium meetings and celebrations organized by the Chinese. The facilities and events that met with their approval were trumpeted as Chinese accomplishments in missionary publications.[98] Missionaries also fed their diplomatic representatives a constant stream of information about China's progress against opium outside the treaty ports that housed all foreign consulates and embassies.

Just as important, the anti-opium message was conveyed to thousands of Chinese Christians and other Chinese students enrolled in the missionary schools of Fujian. Missionary literature is full of descriptions of the anti-opium activities of these students, who established opium refuges, joined anti-opium societies, signed petitions, organized mass meetings and spoke publicly against the drug, participated in celebrations, and on occasion even roughed up violators of the prohibition against opium smoking. Mission schools often encouraged processions of younger students in support of various opium reform measures and sponsored essay contests on China's opium problem.[99] One group of missionary-educated boys in Yanping prefecture organized The Resolution Society; the members pledged to abstain from smoking opium and tobacco, drinking liquor, swearing, lying, stealing,

---

97. The first International Opium Commission met in Shanghai in 1909, the second and third at The Hague in 1911–12 and 1913, respectively, and later conferences were organized under the auspices of the League of Nations.

98. See, e.g., *Mercy and Truth* 11, no. 126 (June 1907): 184–85; and *IWCD* 27, no. 252 (Sept. 1907): 137 and 28, no. 264 (June 1908): n.p.

99. *Foochow Messenger* 5, no. 2 (Apr. 1908): 3, 34.

and gambling.[100] In Xinghua, American Methodists reported that non-Christians specifically requested students and instructors at the Christian schools to participate in the local anti-opium movement.[101]

Many Chinese Christians became involved in the whole range of late Qing reforms, and when some assumed pivotal positions in the new Republican regime, they brought their commitment to opium suppression with them.[102] Examples include Chen Nengguang, who assumed the leadership of the province's suppression movement not long after the Revolution of 1911. Several other prominent members of the Fuzhou Anti-Opium Society were Chinese Christians, and foreign missionaries strongly supported the society's activities. Chinese Christians organized a number of the Anti-Opium Society branches, and missionaries were featured speakers at many public meetings and celebrations organized by various Chinese opium reform groups.[103] Missionary propaganda and opium treatment strategies also inspired Christian and non-Christian Chinese to establish their own anti-opium groups and treatment centers.[104] However, although the missionaries might take credit for the reformist attitudes of their students and converts, the Chinese had a long tradition of elite-led reform societies, and some groups simply added opium smoking to a long list of social evils, such as gambling, drinking, prostitution, footbinding, and tobacco smoking. It also has been persuasively argued that young Chinese reformers were attracted to Christianity as a means of expressing their patriotism through progressive reform.[105]

In the cities and villages of Fujian, missionaries worked closely with Chinese officials and elite reform groups, apparently with the approval and encouragement of reformers inside and outside the Chinese state. Chinese acceptance stemmed not only from respect for the missionaries' oratorical and

---

100. Ibid., 6, no. 1 (Jan. 1909): 9.
101. MEC *Annual Report*, 1907, p. 186.
102. For excellent discussions of Chinese Christian activism in the late Qing reform effort, see Dunch, "Piety, Patriotism, Progress"; and idem, *Fuzhou Protestants and the Making of a Modern China*. I am extremely grateful to Dr. Dunch for sharing with me many documents on the Qudu she that he obtained in Fuzhou and his careful research notes, which enabled an unusually productive visit of my own.
103. A Pastor Lao, for example, organized the branch in Baojia (Pagoda Anchorage) just outside Fuzhou City; references to missionary speakers are too numerous to list. See *Foochow Messenger* 5, no. 2 (Apr. 1908): 28; and virtually any issue of *Mercy and Truth* or *IWCD* from 1906 to 1911.
104. Beattie, "Protestant Missions and Opium in China," pp. 110, 113.
105. Dunch, *Fuzhou Protestants and the Making of a Modern China*.

medical skills but also from a recognition that missionary testimony was taken seriously by the foreign governments (especially Great Britain) monitoring Chinese progress. In 1908, *The Fujian Anti-Opium Society Quarterly* noted with approval that missionaries attending a public incineration of confiscated opium and smoking equipment not only approved of the proceedings but also took photographs, presumably to document the gathering.[106] Missionaries often spoke at the mass meetings and demonstrations organized by that society and its branches, and many had close relationships with the Chinese reformers. One member of the CEZMS recalled frequent visits to the home of Lin Bingzhang. Lin apparently took great care to express his gratitude for the support of foreign missionaries and Chinese Christians; he received foreign guests in a gracious, western-style wing of his home and corresponded with church leaders in China and abroad.[107]

The revolution brought unprecedented prestige and opportunities to missionaries and their converts in Fujian and elsewhere in China. The new Republic, anxious to forestall western intervention and eager to incorporate progressive policies like those advocated by reformist missionaries, protected the missionaries during the revolutionary transition and patronized Christianity in its early statements of purpose and philosophy. Missionaries were heartened by the sympathetic attitude of Sun Yatsen, who had been educated in missionary schools, and called on Christians inside and outside China to support the new Republic.[108] Yuan Shikai's call for a national day of prayer shortly after he assumed office elated Christians. Missionary hospitals and opium refuges experienced a surge of interest from an opium-smoking population anxious to comply with the increasingly strident demands of the new state. However, even as the old regime shattered and the new Republic struggled to constitute itself and establish control over the countryside, the administrative mechanisms that implemented and enforced the opium suppression campaign temporarily broke down.

Many farmers in Fujian's opium-growing regions responded to the brief political vacuum by planting poppies, a move that reflected either an attempt to take advantage of the temporary political chaos or perhaps the misconception that an end to government intervention was a goal of the revolution. Either way, the resumption of poppy cultivation meant that Republican opium

---

106. *The Quarterly* 3 (1908), *zazhi* section, pp. 9–10.
107. Faithfull-Davies, *The Banyan City*, pp. 19, 23.
108. Gray and Sherman, *The Story of the Church in China*, p. 335.

reformers now faced farmers who felt that they had been given a second chance to profit from this previously prohibited crop. Missionaries naturally supported the continuation of the anti-opium campaign under the new Republic. But this time, the atmosphere in the countryside was far more volatile, and the central state was far more motivated to extend the prohibition on cultivation deep into the Fujianese countryside.

After the renegotiation in 1911 of the agreement with the British, the elimination of opium imports into a province hinged on its ability to rid itself of poppies. Teams of Chinese and British officials were to evaluate the success of this effort. The small size of the British diplomatic corps in Fujian and its location in the coastal treaty ports necessitated a more extensive and reliable source of information—from the British perspective, one that was not Chinese—on the progress of the campaign in the poppy-growing regions. Despite suspicions that missionaries might be inclined to favor the Chinese, British consular officers relied heavily on missionary observations, as they had before 1911. The role of missionaries in reporting violations of the prohibition of domestic poppy cultivation evidently was well known in the Fujianese countryside. In one missionary publication from the early 1920s, a report on opium violations in central China declined to list the names of the offending villages, since "the missionary is always suspected of giving the information we publish, and is not infrequently subjected to annoyance for so doing."[109] After the revolution, this practice not only cemented the missionary/state alliance in the minds of villagers but also threatened local offenders with the coercive power of that state. The 1912–13 uprising in Xinghua prefecture illustrates how popular outrage over the extractive, coercive enforcement of the suppression campaign could backfire on well-meaning missionaries. (See Chapter 8 for a detailed examination of this incident and its implications for the politics of opium suppression.)

Another instance in which missionary zeal and official goals were pitted against vested interests in Fujian's opium economy took place in Gutian county, where missionaries and Chinese clergy were asked to perform police functions in conjunction with the suppression campaign. As the Rev. James H. Worley (MEC) reported:

Local authorities requested our preachers to serve as heads of vigilance committees for the suppression of illicit sale and use of opium. Some of them have met with thrilling experiences and all have aroused the ill will of the baser element, but they

---

109. *Chinese Recorder* 53, no. 10 (Oct. 1922): 656–57.

have gained the gratitude of all good citizens. For several years our church has received consistent praise for its leadership in the fight against this great evil.[110]

Exactly who constituted this "baser element" is not explained, nor is it clear if anything other than compliance with opium restrictions and approval of missionary actions qualified a person as a "good citizen." Clearly, missionary attitudes toward opium were inseparable from their problematic relationship with the Chinese state and the survival strategies of Fujian's poppy farmers and opium consumers. At the same time, Chinese politics at the national and international levels significantly altered the framework that structured missionary activism.

The Impact of Missionary Activism

> The wonderful modern movement against Opium in China was born of . . . Christianity, introduced by Christian nations: 'it was directly from the Christian Church in China that the Anti-Opium movement sprang.' All efforts hitherto made by the heathen Chinese alone had failed to accomplish what has now been done by the efforts of the Christian Chinese helped by their Christian brethren in Western nations, whose united effort by God's blessing has freed England's escutcheon from this foul blot which has defaced it for so many years, and freed China of a body and soul destroying vice.[111]
>
> —J. Dyer Ball, editor of *The Friend of China*

The overall impact of missionary activism on Fujian's opium suppression campaign was colored by racial and cultural prejudice and inflated by missionary-generated rhetoric that tended to downplay the efforts of non-Christian Chinese. Missionaries were not impartial observers, and non-Christian reform efforts often were described unfairly as inadequate or improperly motivated. The hyperbole that characterized many missionary publications often obscured the complex mix of factors responsible for the success of opium reform in one area and its failure in another. Many missionaries echoed their colleague who claimed: "In general the anti-opium movement has been strongest and most successful in the places where the Christian church is strong and active."[112] In truth, although missionaries and their converts were deeply involved in China's campaign, the strength of the movement in any particular area had more to do with the support of local officials and non-Christian reformist elites, the area's proximity to a large

---

110. *MEC Annual Report*, 1912, p. 67.
111. *Friend of China* 31, no. 2 (May 1915): 28.
112. *Foochow Messenger* 5, no. 2 (Apr. 1908): 2.

urban center, and the amount of poppy cultivation than with the number of Christians active there.

Only by eschewing Christian propaganda and examining just how close missionaries came to fulfilling their own goals can we come to an impartial and comprehensive assessment of the impact of Protestant missionary activism on Fujian's opium suppression campaign. The missionaries of Fujian wanted to alleviate the suffering of Chinese opium smokers, to manufacture and manipulate popular opinion against the opium trade in China and in their home countries, to support the Chinese state in its campaign to suppress the drug, and to disassociate themselves from their opium-peddling compatriots. All these measures were intended to contribute to the ultimate purpose of converting as many Chinese as possible to Christianity.

Missionary activism did have a direct impact on Fujian's opium suppression movement. The rescue of would-be opium suicides and the treatment of opium addiction undoubtedly contributed to the amelioration of suffering. The publication and distribution of anti-opium tracts, the preaching of anti-opium sentiment in missionary churches and schools, the organization of anti-opium societies, and missionary attendance at mass meetings and other public spectacles supporting the campaign helped to sustain the momentum of reform in China and at home. Missionary lobbying efforts kept the issue of the opium trade in the public eye in China and abroad, publicized the commitment of the Chinese state to stamping out the opium problem within its borders, pressured the British government to end the opium trade, and stimulated global efforts to control narcotics. In addition, many Chinese who converted to Christianity or received their education in missionary schools vigorously pursued the cause of opium suppression.

In many ways, however, missionaries were still relegated to the sidelines of reform. Missionary efforts such as those noted above affected only a fraction of Fujian's population and were in many cases the result of developments outside the control of missionaries. In the medical arena, political, ideological, and financial constraints confined missionaries to individual treatment and salvation, a strategy that created a small cohort of loyal converts (and a larger group of grateful patients) but was inadequate to affect far-reaching change at the grassroots level. Missionary education about the harmful nature of opium won over many Chinese students, but in many cases, this approach owed much of its success to the rise of Chinese nationalism that was both cause and effect of the official suppression campaign.

Politically, missionary lobbying for an end to the Indian side of the opium trade was vocal and insistent, but real change came only when necessitated by transformations in British politics and the economics of colonialism. The rise to power of the Liberal Party coincided with a realization on the part of the Indian government that the market share of Indian imports in China was being steadily and irrevocably reduced by Chinese poppy production. The decision to enter into a ten-year agreement to eliminate the trade was less a response to the sentiment stoked by missionaries than a practical reaction by the British government to economic realities, although missionary rhetoric certainly made the decision more politically palatable.

The Chinese reactions to missionary participation in opium reform implied a growing willingness and ability on the part of Chinese elites and the Chinese public to distinguish between the evangelical and the mercantile arms of western imperialism in Fujian. Missionaries never failed to express their hostility toward opium in their publications, classrooms, churches, and clinics. These actions were responsible in large part for this shift in attitude by many Chinese, but the enormous increase in the amount of opium grown in China during the first decade of the twentieth century also helped correct the popular impression that China's opium problem was a foreign import. In fact, the changing Chinese perception of opium from foreign to domestic commodity may have been the factor most responsible for the success of missionary activism. In a province such as Fujian, where the domestic drug constituted only a small part of the provincial opium trade, appeals to anti-imperialism had to be somewhat muted.

The opium trade presented a practical and moral conundrum for missionaries in Fujian and elsewhere in China. Their ability to work, travel, and reside in China was won by the same gunboats that forced the Chinese to accept the importation and legalization of foreign opium. Although missionaries did not hesitate to call on those gunboats for protection in times of need, they resented their mercenary countrymen and blamed Chinese opium addiction on the merchants' amoral greed. Missionaries occupied an ambiguous space in China, between and somehow apart from both state and society. Their methods influenced elite reformers in the new public space, and missionaries themselves played a role in mobilizing the audience and the orators in many public ceremonies. However, as the boundaries between the state and the public space hardened, the missionaries of Fujian discovered that by rejecting their opium-peddling compatriots, they had aligned themselves with the opium suppression campaign of the Chinese state. When that campaign became unpopular, especially in the countryside, so did its missionary supporters. Once again, activists involved in attempts to address China's opium problem found that the problem could not be isolated from the larger sociopolitical issues of the time. Those issues became especially relevant in the Xinghua rebellion.

EIGHT

Huang Lian's Revolt and the
Politics of Prohibition

As we have seen, the suppression campaign apparently enjoyed a good deal of success and popular support in Fujian's cities, largely because of the cooperation between officials and elite-led reform groups, an alliance forged by the nationalistic goals of Chinese elites and both the Qing and the Republican states. At the same time, however, it trampled powerful vested interests and revealed deep popular dissatisfaction with the content and conduct of reform, particularly in opium-growing regions. Despite the commitment of foreign missionaries and the diligence of Republican officials and elite reformers throughout Fujian—and in the case studied in this chapter, *because* of those efforts—popular opposition to opium suppression erupted in large-scale violence shortly after the revolution. Chapter 6 discussed numerous instances of violent resistance to the restrictions on poppy cultivation; Huang Lian's revolt was exceptional not only for its scale and duration but also for the voluminous correspondence on the incident documenting the intertwining of opium reform and Republican era politics.

When the first reports of the "opium rebellion" in Xinghua prefecture reached the American consulate in Xiamen in June 1912, foreign diplomats did not view the situation as serious. However, by the time the conflict sputtered to a conclusion in the spring of 1914, the uprising had cost hundreds of lives and resulted in the burning and looting of numerous properties, most of them owned by Christian churches and church members. The political cost was also significant: the sackings of Fujian's governor, a host of lesser Chinese officials, and the American consul in Fuzhou were attributed in part to the revolt. Huang Lian, a local hero also known as the Sixteenth

Emperor or Number Sixteen, led the insurgents. Huang's alleged imperial pretensions, as well as his protection of local opium fields and his anti-Christian bent, convinced foreign observers and Chinese officials that the rebellion deserved national-level attention and intervention.

Beyond its status as an international incident, Huang Lian's uprising revealed how deeply opium had become enmeshed with popular hostility toward the late Qing and early Republican reforms. The elimination of the poppy crop and opium smoking required what many peasant farmers viewed as intolerable government intrusion, excessive taxation, and the continued oppression of the poor. The success of opium reform hinged in large part on the ability of the Chinese state to locate substitute revenue sources, but popular resistance to taxes levied for that purpose endangered that success. From the farmers' perspective, the state was not only eliminating a profitable crop but compounding peasant financial difficulties by imposing taxes on necessities such as salt. The poor quality of local administration and antimissionary sentiment also generated considerable anger.

The revolt exposed the transience of grassroots support for the postrevolutionary regime. Many Chinese across the economic spectrum embraced the revolution, largely because it promised a change in the status quo. That status quo often included corrupt local government, exorbitant taxation, the threat of imperialist aggression, and disruptive reforms. Discontent with each and all of these factors spawned rural unrest during the final decade of the Qing era; disappointment with the reality of the early Republic would spark more.

The recent work of Roxann Prazniak highlights the ways in which new taxes, census taking, and other methods of funding the late Qing New Policy reforms alienated many Chinese farmers by extending the reach of the state and further empowering local elites. In terms of opium suppression, the extent of resistance to anti-consumption measures, the persistence of poppy cultivation, and the use of military force to uproot crops seem to confirm her contention that rural dwellers were far less receptive to the call for reform than their urban counterparts.[1] However, because the suppression campaign persisted across the revolutionary divide, the chronological boundaries of Prazniak's study obscure the persistence of the trends she discusses. The basic patterns and motivations for resistance accompanied opium reform into the Republican era, and their endurance speaks to the

---

1. Prazniak, *Of Camel Kings and Other Things*.

failure of the revolution to address the needs and desires of much of the Chinese population. Analyzing the causes, course, and resolution of Huang Lian's revolt allows an in-depth exploration of the instability of the new Republic, reveals the complex implications of resistance to opium reform, and illustrates how closely the two were linked.

Context for Rebellion

Huang Lian's uprising, ostensibly sparked by popular opposition to opium suppression, cannot be understood outside the larger context. Popular dissatisfaction with state-initiated reform before and after 1911 had its roots in Xinghua's geography and climate, its history of contentious relations with foreign missionaries, strong provincial loyalties, anti-military sentiments, poor local administration, tax resistance, and endemic clan violence. All these factors contributed to the pressures that fueled the revolt and guided its course.

In the Qing and early Republican periods, Xinghua prefecture consisted of Putian and Xianyou counties, located on Fujian's fertile coastal plain, midway between the treaty ports of Xiamen and Fuzhou.[2] The prefectural city of Xinghua and the county seat of Xianyou served as the administrative centers of Xinghua.[3] Although eastern Fujian constitutes the province's core region, the Xinghua area is somewhat isolated from the two main urban zones. Xinghua's western regions are crisscrossed by mountain ranges and river valleys, and its craggy coastline is dotted with inlets and islands that were, for much of the early modern period, infested with pirates. The Xinghua region was among the most densely populated in the province, and the vast majority of the population made their living from agriculture.[4] Tenancy abounded, and each person in Xianyou county cultivated an average of just two *mu*, although Xinghua farmers could often coax three crops per year (two of rice, plus another winter crop) from the coastal plain and surround-

---

2. Chen Hanguang, "Minguo yilai Fujian sheng difang xingzhengqu hua," pp. 22–24.
3. Li Kuo-chi, "Qingmo Minchu Min-Zhe diqu renkou liudong yu dushihua," pp. 512–13; MEC *Annual Report*, 1914, p. 125; USDS (1910–29), 893.00/1754, reel 12, Fowler, 23 May 1913.
4. Anti-Cobweb Club, *Fukien: A Study of a Province*, chap. 1; Stauffer, *The Christian Occupation of China*, p. viii; and Chen Hanguang, "Fujian renkou jianjie," pp. 12–13. For more on Fujian's population and the problematic nature of available figures, see Ho, *Studies on the Population of China*, pp. 283–88.

ing hills.⁵ Huang and his followers, however, hailed from a particularly barren and impoverished area.

The final years of the Qing dynasty were characterized by violent clan fights in Xinghua, and the revolution itself brought considerable social and economic dislocation to the region. Membership in local secret societies increased, banditry became commonplace, commerce slowed considerably, and a general sense of anxiety gripped the region. In addition, a devastating combination of drought, typhoons, and flooding in August and September 1911 brought famine to Xinghua. After the revolution, local unrest and lawlessness persisted, and American Methodist church officials in Xianyou complained that the new county government was dominated by members of the Gelaohui—perhaps an indication of the influence of Hunanese troops stationed in the city. This secret society apparently conducted a campaign of persecution against local Christians.⁶

Most of the missionaries discussed in Chapter 7 focused their labors on treating addiction and stemming opium consumption in Fujian's cities and towns, but their role was less defined and far more constrained in the countryside. Xinghua prefecture was one of Fujian's opium-growing regions, and it quickly became a notorious violator of the new restrictions on poppy planting. Several inspections initiated by Beijing in 1910 and 1911 resulted in strong criticism of Xinghua authorities for lax enforcement of the ban on poppy cultivation.⁷ This situation became even more of a concern following the negotiations with the British in 1911. The new agreement held out the possibility of ending the opium trade with India well before 1917 if each province was certified poppy-free. After 1911, then, Xinghua's thriving poppy crop presented obstacles not only to regional compliance with the campaign but also to the provincial goal of obtaining a coveted place on the list of provinces closed to British opium and to the national mission to end the Sino-Indian opium trade. Missionaries were as anxious for that to happen as

---

5. Chen Kan, "Wusi qianhou de Xianyou shehui," pp. 73–74; Anti-Cobweb Club, *Fukien: A Study of a Province*, p. 46; IMC *Decennial Reports, Foochow, 1892–1901*, pp. 95–116; IMC, *Decennial Reports, Amoy, 1892–1901*, p. 140. See also Rawski, *Agricultural Change and the Peasant Economy*, chap. 3.

6. MEC Archives, 74-11, 1259-5-3: 38; MEC *Annual Reports*, 1907, pp. 178–79, 1911, pp. 93–97, and 1912, pp. 93–95.

7. ZZGB 32, memorial from Songshou, endorsed 11 May 1910, pp. 159–60; 36, memorial from Ministry of Revenue (no endorsement date), pp. 473–77; and 37, memorial from Ministry of Revenue, endorsed 14 Oct. 1910, pp. 339–41; *Mercy and Truth* 15, no. 179 (Nov. 1911): 377–79.

Chinese reformers, but the foreigners soon found that their zeal was not always appreciated by local residents, who equated missionary support for suppression with approval of the government's heavy-handed strategies for attaining that goal.

Xinghua's foreign community resided primarily in the cities of Xinghua and Xianyou and consisted of missionaries from several groups who had preached in the region since the 1860s and resided there since 1890. By 1911, the prefecture was "occupied" by the CMS and CEZMS, as well as the MEC and its Women's Board. English Presbyterians worked in the neighboring subprefecture of Yongchun. Several Spanish Dominican priests in the area suffered from the general anarchy, but they do not seem to have been targeted specifically by the rebels.[8] The exact number of Chinese Christians in the Xinghua area at the time of the rebellion is uncertain, but they could have constituted only a fraction of the total local population. However, small churches and "outstations" dotted the countryside, and the influence of the missionaries and their converts far outweighed their numbers. That influence derived in large part from their ties to England and the United States. Xinghua housed two mission hospitals, several educational institutions, and the MEC press.[9] All these facilities played a role in publicizing and supporting the opium suppression campaign before and after 1911.

Protestant missionaries and their Chinese converts encountered petty persecutions, waves of intolerance, and even some serious violence before the revolution.[10] According to one Chinese historian, missionaries in Xinghua repeatedly antagonized local elites by cowing yamen officials into influencing lawsuits in favor of Christian converts. Methodists complained that their flock had been persecuted by frequent lawsuits. In addition, the refusal of Chinese Christians to contribute money to public festivals and projects they termed "ungodly" generated popular resentment and the impression that the

---

8. MAE/Paris, NS 342, no. 4, from Danjou, 31 Jan. 1914. On the Protestants, see MEC *Annual Report*, 1911.

9. "Kaoding yu buchong," p. 71. The anonymous author of this account was an eyewitness to the revolt and, despite living in a remote, mountainous region of Xianyou, recalled that he had to walk only three or four *li* to run into a Methodist branch chapel. See also MEC *Annual Report*, 1910, pp. 95–100.

10. For more details, see any issue of MEC *Annual Report*; *Jiaowu jiao'an dang*, vols. 6–7; Lin Wenhui, *Qingmo Fujian jiao'an zhi yanjiu*, pp. 95–99; and Carlson, *The Foochow Missionaries*, chap. 2.

Huang Lian's Revolt and the Politics of Prohibition 307

Fig. 8.1 This Chinese pastor, pictured with some of his flock near Xinghua, would have been in great danger during Huang Lian's revolt (courtesy United Methodist Archives, Drew University, Madison, New Jersey).

converts viewed themselves as being outside the local community.[11] But in general, the most brutal anti-foreign movements of the late nineteenth century bypassed Xinghua.

Unlike many other instances of violence against missionaries, the anti-Christian component of Huang Lian's rebellion had its roots in popular opposition to the intrusive and coercive policies of the Chinese state. Many scholars have described the range of cultural and legal offenses committed, intentionally or unwittingly, by foreign missionaries and their converts before the revolution.[12] But in this case, although missionary interference in local lawsuits created a reservoir of anti-Christian sentiment, foreign missionaries and their Chinese converts were not attacked primarily for espousing a strange dogma, violating Chinese social norms, importing foreign goods, appropriating Chinese territory, or their foreign-ness.[13] Instead, the Christians

---

11. MEC *Annual Report*, 1906, pp. 139–40, 146.
12. See, e.g., Cohen, *China and Christianity*; and Esherick, *The Origins of the Boxer Rebellion*.
13. For detailed analysis of the wide range of interpretations assigned to the term foreign (*yang*), see Esherick, *The Origins of the Boxer Rebellion*; Wyman, "Social Change, Anti-

of Xinghua were condemned for acting as agents of the new but already unpopular Chinese Republic.

Another source of tension in Xinghua came from a different set of outsiders—the Hunanese officers and soldiers who had dominated the provincial army since their arrival in the 1870s under the command of Zuo Zongtang. The Hunanese troops were staunchly opposed to the Manchu government, and many were said to have joined the Gelaohui. When the New Army was organized in Fujian under then-general Sun Daoren, Xu Chongzhi headed the provincial military training school. Xu's strong influence on Fujian's New Army was colored by his revolutionary politics. In 1913, during Sun's term as military governor, Xu led Fujian in opposition to Yuan Shikai, evidently against Sun's will. Even before the Second Revolution, then, the loyalty of Fujian's New Army to Yuan and Sun was highly questionable.[14] From the popular perspective, however, the gross misconduct of those troops during Huang Lian's uprising reflected unfavorably on the provincial and national administrations.

In Xinghua, anti-Hunan sentiment was expressed in a "Fujian for the Fujianese" movement. During the revolution, these gentry who opposed the Hunanese presence formed a branch of the Freedom Party (Ziyou dang) and, according to MEC missionaries, successfully connived to have their candidates elected to the Provincial Assembly. One of those assemblymen, Lin Shizhao, was to play an important role in revealing the antipathy between the state-controlled military and the local population. The Freedom Party, organized in 1912, was a national progressive alliance that included many members of the Tongmenghui and chose Sun Yatsen as its leader. It opposed Yuan Shikai's authoritarian tendencies and was suppressed in the summer of 1913.[15] Many of the local elites who supported Huang Lian apparently belonged to this party, and missionaries believed that a number of Huang's rebels came from the bands of village fighters organized during the revolution by men who later joined the Freedom

---

Foreignism and Revolution in China"; and idem, "The Ambiguities of Chinese Antiforeignism."

14. Zou Lu, "Fujian guangfu," pp. 278–79; Falkenheim, "Provincial Administration in Fukien," pp. 29–30; Boorman, *Biographical Dictionary of Republican China*, 2: 124–26; Xu Youchun, *Minguo renwu da cidian*, pp. 791, 839. For more on the connection of the Hunan Army with the Gelaohui, see Cai Shaoqing, "On the Origin of the Gelaohui."

15. Tan Zongying and Zhou Linmei, *Zhongguo jindaishi cidian*, p. 218.

Party.[16] This appears to have been the only identifiable organization that may have been incorporated into the ranks of the rebels and is perhaps the ideological link between the rebels' local and national grievances.

At least part of the blame for Huang Lian's revolt and its lengthy duration must be assigned to the rapid turnover of local officials after 1911. If brevity of service and frequency of personnel changes are an indication of administrative instability and/or incompetence, then Xianyou county would have to be declared a disaster area. From 1911 to mid-1914, the period encompassing Huang Lian's uprising, eight men held the office of county magistrate (including Pan Mu, appointed by Huang Lian during the brief rebel occupation of Xianyou city), each serving an average term of approximately 3.5 months. This was far below the average tenure of magistrates in other districts of Fujian.[17] In fact, although discontent with local government was but one aspect of the rebellion, Fujian's Provincial Assembly specifically blamed the rapaciousness of Xinghua prefect Yu Wenzao for driving the people to rebellion.[18]

Resistance to new or exorbitant taxation sparked violence in Xinghua before the fall of the Qing. Most notably, in the summer of 1902, Xianyou City was the scene of a mass demonstration against the levying of new business and transit taxes. The tax rate apparently was extremely high, and merchants and common people together protested against this joint action of local officials and elites. The damage was confined to the property of those responsible for the new taxes, but soldiers from Fuzhou and Xinghua brutalized several villages in response, and anti-government, anti-military sentiment ran high. Significantly, the fact that the new levies were assessed to defray the cost of the Boxer Indemnity did not provoke any obvious anti-foreign sentiment. In fact, a missionary was asked by both sides to act as mediator. Some Chinese Christians were among those arrested during the crackdown, however, and foreign diplomats and missionaries remained

---

16. USDS (1910–29), 893.00/1780, reel 12, enclosure no. 1, no. 50, Fowler to Secy. of State, 16 June 1913; and 893.00/1795, reel 12, enclosure in no. 51, Fowler to Secy. of State, 21 June 1913.

17. During the last decade of the Qing dynasty, the average tenure of all magistrates in fifteen Fujianese counties was over one year. From 1912 to 1926, the average magistrate's tenure in over half of eighteen Fujianese counties (not including Putian and Xianyou) fell to less than one year, but none served less than six months (Li Guoqi, *Minguo shilun ji*, pp. 82–86; Lin Zongtang, "Minguo shiqi Xianyou xianzhang qunxiang," pp. 58–60; and "Kaoding yu buchong," p. 67).

18. PRO, FO 228/1869, no. 15, Little to Jordan, 19 June 1913.

wary.[19] Huang Lian was said to have been arrested for involvement in tax protests before the revolution, but the dates and specific offense are unknown.

The opium suppression campaign also generated popular hostility. Opium consumption was ubiquitous in Xinghua, especially among the lower classes. In Xianyou City, a CEZMS missionary noted that most of the chair-bearers in that town were regular opium smokers, and although they earned a good income, most of the money went toward feeding their drug habit. Several of these men claimed that "if we do not eat opium, we could not carry the chairs."[20] Xinghua City's streets were crowded with opium dens, and the rural countryside concealed a small but thriving poppy crop.

Initially, Xinghua reported some success toward the goal of opium suppression, despite the tenacity of poppy farmers. In late 1907, a British diplomat noted, "At Hsing-hua [Xinghua] all the dens are closed, six proprietors having been cangued for refusing. A meeting has been held by the officials and gentry, when it was decided to open refuges."[21] In 1907, Liang Guandeng, the Xinghua prefect, established an official opium prohibition bureau.[22] The British physician in charge of the CMS hospital in Xinghua City at that time reported an increase in patients seeking cures for addiction and noted that many Chinese-run asylums had also been recently established. However, the same doctor condemned his competitors for allegedly offering medications laced with opium or morphine and revealed that after a brief closure the owners of the city's opium shops had convinced the magistrate to grant them a three-month reprieve.[23]

Xinghua's anti-opium campaign picked up momentum in its second year, but according to a questionnaire circulated by the French consul at Fuzhou, progress was limited and confined largely to the county and prefectural cities. In the city of Xinghua, local officials posted an anti-opium proclamation, but only at the prefect's yamen. After initially throwing down their pipes, the zeal of many officials apparently ebbed, and they continued to smoke.

---

19. USDS, Consular Despatches, Foochow, 1849–1906, reel 10, no. 124, Gracey to Secy. of State, 22 July 1902.

20. *IWCD*, August 1899, pp. 177–78.

21. Great Britain, Parliamentary Papers, *China No. 1* (1908), report by Mr. Leech, in no. 28, Jordan to Grey, 27 Nov. 1907.

22. Wang Yiwei, "Xianyou dashi ji," p. 25.

23. Dr. B. Van S. Taylor, untitled article dated 17 May 1907, *Mercy and Truth*, 11, no. 129 (Sept. 1907): 262–63.

Opium dens remained in the city, although surveillance (evidently by officials and the local anti-opium league) became more rigorous. Many dens were able to stay in business by becoming much smaller—some subsisted on one pipe and one lamp—and therefore less conspicuous. There was no interference at all with dens in outlying villages, and the poppy still grew in the rural valleys.[24] According to the French consul, students attending classes in the provincial capital formed the core of the anti-opium societies that dotted the region during the late Qing phase of the campaign. When some students from Xianyou returned home for summer vacation in 1908, they yanked out poppies in nearby fields, and farmers did nothing to stop them.[25]

British and American missionaries in Xinghua were highly visible advocates of opium prohibition before the advent of the suppression campaign, and they remained vocal supporters of the campaign after 1906. The CMS hospital in Xinghua City doubled as the official, government opium refuge for the area, and missionaries seemed to recognize this alliance with state interests.[26] A Chinese convert affiliated with the MEC also ran a refuge, and non-Christian Chinese established a number of treatment centers in the region.[27] American Methodists reported that non-Christian reformers specifically requested the participation of students and instructors at Christian schools in the anti-opium movement.[28] In 1909, a Christian evangelical revival became an occasion on which Methodists and their converts preached publicly about the evils of opium. Much to the missionaries' delight, twenty opium smokers spontaneously requested help breaking the habit, and the public donated enough money to treat several hundred more.[29]

In 1910, violence directed in part at opium reform broke out in the county seat of Putian. Evidently, new graduates of the local police school banned roadside stalls and impromptu markets and charged vendors ten coppers to sleep unmolested by the side of the road, where presumably they awaited the

---

24. MAE/Nantes, Foutcheou, no. 71 (Opium, 1904–1935). There is no date on this questionnaire, but since it was grouped with many other documents dated 1908 and specifically refers to the Imperial Edict issued in November 1906, it is likely that the document was probably produced in 1907 or 1908.

25. MAE/Paris, NS 587, Lecomte to Paris, 3 July 1908.

26. Dr. Ronald Walker, "Anti-Opium Work in Hinghwafu," *Mercy and Truth*, 15, no. 179 (Nov. 1911): 377–79.

27. Ibid.

28. MEC *Annual Report*, 1907, p. 186.

29. Ibid., 1909, pp. 103, 106.

next morning's business. An irate mob, indignant at these heavy-handed and seemingly arbitrary actions, burned down the police sentry boxes and the police school, and then torched the residences of Chen Qiao and Wu Hongbin, the two men responsible for local enforcement of opium prohibition.[30] The incident reveals yet another example of the link in public perceptions between these two costly and intrusive Qing reforms. After the revolution, that popular resentment reappeared along with opium reform.

Before 1911, Xinghua poppy farmers' ability to defy, apparently with impunity, the restrictions on opium cultivation angered provincial officials and obstructed national goals for eliminating the crop. In May 1910, Governor-General Songshou submitted a memorial stating that the cultivation of domestic opium had been completely halted in Fujian. However, the central authorities called for an investigation to determine the veracity of the claims of provincial officials in Fujian and other provinces. Beijing's skepticism was justified when inspectors clandestinely traveled to Fujian and discovered that Songshou's testimony was false. In its subsequent report on the progress of the campaign, dated 27 September 1910, the Ministry of Revenue singled out Xinghua prefecture as Fujian's most conspicuous violator.[31] Fujian's comprehensive new opium prohibition regulations, issued in late 1910, mandated that the region in which Xinghua was situated was to eliminate the use and cultivation of opium by mid-August 1912.[32] The intransigence of the Xinghua farmers had to be overcome in less than two years.

Reports on the progress of prohibition in Xinghua continued to be unreliable through the next year, indicating the persistence of popular resistance, as well as incompetence, apathy, or connivance on the part of local authorities. Xinghua officials soon declared the county free of opium cultivation once again, but when a Chinese investigator from Fuzhou arrived in early 1911, he uncovered many violations. According to a British missionary, the inspector closed down 22 opium dens in Xinghua City, paraded several smokers through the streets in cangues, and attended a public meeting on the opium problem. That meeting demonstrated the diligence of the inspec-

---

30. Chen Zhangcheng, "Xinhai qianxi Putian qunzhong zifa kangguan douzheng," p. 113.

31. ZZGB 32, memorial from Songshou, endorsed 11 May 1910, pp. 159–60; 36, memorial from the Ministry of Revenue (no endorsement date), pp. 473–77; and 37, memorial from the Ministry of Revenue, endorsed 14 Oct. 1910, pp. 339–41.

32. PRO, FO 228/1811, enclosure in no. 5, from Werner, 20 Feb. 1911. For an English translation, see PRO, FO 228/1800, "Foochow Intelligence Report, December Quarter, 1910."

tor and his elite allies, but their laudable goals were thwarted by an even more determined group of poppy farmers.

> There was a 'mass meeting,' and the gentry of the town who are very anti-opium spoke most strongly against the city magistrate and the district official, and the Foochow official blamed them in public—a most extraordinary thing for China, where 'face' is everything, and this was a large 'loss of face.'
>
> After this the official went to the country to look for the growing opium he had heard about and it was conspicuous by its entire absence! This was because the chair men and attendants had been carefully 'squared' by the opium growers to carry him elsewhere.[33]

Out of frustration, and in an unusual instance where an elite reformer (and a Christian) was permitted to wield military force, a Chinese Methodist pharmacist and former pupil at the MEC school "obtained some soldiers from the official and went to look for the planted opium which the Foochow official failed to see. They cut down in one month many thousands of dollars worth of nearly ripe poppy plant. It was all growing in out-of-the-way places. . . . He did not meet with a very warm welcome from the owners."[34] Aside from this report, virtually nothing is known of the situation in the Xinghua countryside, where most of the region's poppies were grown, and it is likely that some cultivation persisted before the revolution. This became a pressing problem for the new Republic, which had to eradicate domestic poppy cultivation to end the Sino-Indian opium trade. The absence of voluntary cooperation pushed the state to resort to force, especially when missionaries and Chinese Christians continued to publicly expose violators.

In addition to the coercive measures imposed by many officials in the name of opium suppression, opium-related taxes also sparked Huang Lian's revolt and revived longstanding local anti-tax sentiment. A primary concern of Chinese authorities at all levels was the need to replace the revenue obtained by taxes on the sale, cultivation, and distribution of the drug. Fujian was one of many provinces to opt for an increase in the salt tax during the first years of the campaign. The salt tax was raised again in the summer of 1912, just prior to the outbreak of the revolt. One Chinese account states that as Huang Lian and his troops marched to attack Xianyou later that year, the masses spontaneously rose up in support and destroyed salt storehouses and

---

33. *Mercy and Truth*, 15, no. 179 (Nov. 1911): 377–79.
34. Ibid.

other properties.³⁵ Since Xinghua was known for its large salt deposits, the crackdown on salt smuggling that often accompanied the tax increase may also have generated strong resentment.³⁶

In general, then, although the province of Fujian had made rapid strides in opium prohibition by 1911, Xinghua lagged noticeably behind. In the confusion that accompanied the revolution, the poppy was planted in great profusion, particularly in the coastal prefectures where it had grown under Qing rule.³⁷ But only in Xinghua did large-scale, protracted resistance occur. The Republic had achieved—with relatively little bloodshed—at least the appearance of political control in Fujian's treaty ports and prefectural and county cities, only to be faced with a revolt that tested its practical control over provincial and local authorities, its commitment to reform, and its popular support.

Huang Lian's Revolt

THE REBELS AND THEIR LEADER

Who was Huang Lian, the Xinghua rebel leader who supposedly declared himself the sixteenth emperor of the Ming Dynasty, and what motivated his rebellion? The answer varies considerably depending on the source. American and British sources tend to highlight those aspects of the uprising that affected their people and their interests. Rebel opposition to opium suppression, asserted foreign diplomats (particularly U.S. consul John Fowler and British consul E. T. C. Werner, both at Fuzhou), missionaries, and Chinese Christians, was aided and abetted by local elites (termed "old-school literati" by missionaries) who, not coincidentally, had historically opposed the Christian missions. Fowler's dispatches usually stress Huang's illegal behavior, referring to him contentiously as an opponent of the Republic, and "a notorious bandit and robber," as well as an ex-convict who escaped from a Putian prison as the Qing fell in 1911.³⁸ British sources, concerned largely with the

---

35. ZZGB 20, memorial from Songshou, endorsed 19 May 1909, pp. 104–8; MAE/Paris, NS 40, no. 24, Doire to Margarie, 17 Apr. 1912; "Kaoding yu buchong," pp. 68–69.
36. This is what occurred in Waichow, located in nearby Guangdong province (Hsieh, "Triads, Salt Smugglers, and Local Uprisings").
37. PRO, FO 228/2452, no. 92, Werner to Jordan, 31 Jan. 1913.
38. USDS (1910–29), 893.00/1992, reel 13, enclosure in Fowler to Williams, 13 Sept. 1913; MEC *Annual Report*, 1913, p. 230.

safety of their own missionaries as well as the conduct of the opium suppression campaign, demonstrate similar biases. Both British and American documents highlight unsubstantiated rumors that Huang Lian may have been trained in Japan, a reflection of their concern that the uprising transcended local tensions and had national or even international implications.[39]

By contrast, mainland Chinese histories focus heavily on the background and motivations of Huang Lian, stressing his populist roots, as well as his heroic opposition to both the Qing dynasty and the revolutionary usurper Yuan Shikai. Hailing from the impoverished village of Yangmian in Putian county, Huang was born in 1862 and acquired a limited education in the Classics at a local private school. He served as the village leader of a local religious sect, and it was rumored that he had joined the Gun and Knife Society (Qiangdao hui). He is described as a chivalrous and generous champion of the people, who was arrested for leading a local tax revolt in the late Qing. Just before the revolution, Huang augmented his legend by allegedly feigning death and escaping from prison in a casket.[40] At the time of the Wuchang uprising, he was said to have been recruited into the Putian branch of the Tongmenghui by Lin Shizhao, a member of the local elite who supported Huang Lian throughout the revolt to come. This is plausible, given Huang's anti-Qing tendencies.[41]

The variety of interpretations of Huang Lian's pseudonym reveal a great deal about foreign and Chinese biases, then and now. Initially, the American and British consuls, taking their cue from missionaries residing in Xinghua, referred to Huang as "Emperor Sixteen" and assumed that he was a self-styled Ming pretender to the throne. This interpretation jibed with Huang's supposedly anti-Republican, anti-foreign bent, although later his title was presumed to refer to the Qing dynasty, for reasons that remain unclear.[42] American missionaries and diplomats apparently chose to play up Huang's alleged imperial pretensions in the hope of convincing Chinese authorities that the uprising deserved a swift and decisive response.

In contrast, a recent Chinese analysis convincingly dismisses the imperial moniker, since no definitive evidence exists of any such pretensions on

---

39. USDS (1910–29), 893.00/1887, reel 12, no. 974, Williams to Secy. of State, 15 Aug. 1913; PRO, FO 228/1872, no. 21, Werner to Jordan, 18 May 1913.
40. "Kaoding yu buchong," p. 63.
41. Zou Lu, "Fujian guangfu," p. 277; Yu Qiqiang, "Huang Lian qiyi," p. 45.
42. USDS (1910–29), 893.00/1754, reel 12, Fowler to Secy. of State, 23 May 1913; PRO, FO 228/1838, Werner to Jordan, no. 38, 15 Sept. 1912.

Huang's part. Those aspirations would not have jibed with the mainland Chinese portrayal of Huang as a true populist hero. The Chinese account contends that Huang was often called "Brother Sixteen" or "Uncle Sixteen" because of his position in the Huang clan and was given the grander title by ignorant local peasants in awe of his leadership abilities. "Emperor" is simply taken to mean "leader." The historian admits that Huang and his troops used "feudal" titles and retained their queues but denies that this indicates a restorationist bent. The titles, he asserts, were those historically used in peasant uprisings and would thus more readily appeal to the masses. He also claims that foreign missionaries and the reactionary government of Yuan Shikai originally gave Huang this title to discredit the rebel's noble intentions, but this is unsubstantiated.[43] The queues were attributed to habit and the newness of the revolution, which is plausible, given Huang's apparent support of the Revolution of 1911 before the rise of Yuan Shikai, and the fact that queues were not uncommon outside the walls of Xinghua City before the revolt. The queues could also signify active rejection of the new Republic.

Initially, foreigners may indeed have believed that Huang had imperial aspirations, but their discovery of the truth did not stop them from perpetuating this myth. British consul Werner conceded that the number sixteen did indeed represent Huang's clan ranking, and there is no evidence that Huang ever referred to himself as emperor. When Huang and his men occupied the city of Xianyou, they installed one of their own as magistrate, but Huang did not assume any title himself.[44] In fact, one of Huang's own proclamations in mid-1913 bears the date Xuantong 5, an indication that he rejected the Republic in favor of the deposed Qing monarch.[45] In short, available evidence suggests that Huang Lian did not harbor imperial ambitions and that his impressive title derived from his clan standing and the respect of local residents. His apparent loyalty to the Qing regime is more difficult to understand, since the targets of Huang's rebellion originated in the reign of the Xuantong emperor. The rebels probably were reacting in anger against the more coercive approach of a new Republic that had promised change.

Huang Lian's troops were known as the Black Tiger Righteousness Society (Heihu zhongyi tang), and their identity is even more obscure. The Brit-

---

43. Yu Qiqiang, "Huang Lian qiyi," pp. 48–49.
44. Ibid., pp. 45, 48–49; PRO, FO 228/1872, no. 8, Werner to Jordan, 28 Feb. 1913.
45. USDS (1910–29), 893.00/1797, reel 12, enclosure in Fowler to Secy. of State, 27 June 1913.

ish minister in Beijing referred to the rebels as "a force of brigands and smugglers which probably amounted to some 2,000 men."[46] There seems to have been a core of approximately 500 insurgents at the outset, although local supporters often joined the rebels during battles against government troops. One British missionary asserted that Huang had no regular troops and simply paid local villagers to fight when the occasion arose.[47] Mainland Chinese sources describe the rebels as peasants who took up arms to protest exorbitant taxes. American missionaries called the rebels "bandits, secretly encouraged by old-school literati [who] told the [opium] farmers that they would protect them in breaking the law."[48] Little more is known about Huang's troops, but there is no evidence of widespread ties to local religious sects, secret societies, or revolutionary organizations.

THE UPRISING

The Revolution of 1911 changed the tone and content of opium reform, as well as the composition of the Chinese state, and resulted in the popular perception of a strong link between the MEC and the new Republic. American missionaries in Xinghua, probably influenced by the number of Chinese Christians opposing the Manchus, as well as the hostility and corruption of local officials, openly supported the revolution. In 1911, as a show of support for the revolution and solidarity with the people, the male missionaries of the MEC remained at their stations in Xinghua City despite evacuation orders from the U.S. consul at Fuzhou.[49] Bishop James Whitford Bashford (1848–1919), a leader of the MEC mission in China, personally favored a gradual transition to a constitutional monarchy and claimed to have tried in vain to maintain the neutrality of Fujian's Methodists during the revolution. But the bishop himself participated in two meetings in Fuzhou in December 1911 at which Methodists publicly demonstrated their support for Military Governor Sun Daoren, Fujian's post-revolutionary leader. This stance

---

46. PRO, FO 228/2454, no. 49, Jordan to Grey, 26 May 1913.
47. PRO, FO 228/1872, no. 8, Werner to Jordan, 28 Feb. 1913.
48. MEC *Annual Report*, 1913, p. 230; USDS (1910–29), 893.00/1868, reel 12, Williams to Secy. of State, 8 Aug. 1913; and "Kaoding yu buchong," pp. 62–63.
49. The British also remained but seem to have successfully maintained their neutrality in the conflict (*IWCD* 32, no. 309 [Mar. 1912]: 57–59). See MEC Archives, 74-11, 1259-6-2: 08 and 1259-5-2: 36 for missionary attitudes toward the revolution.

Fig. 8.2 This photograph of Sun Daoren posing next to Bishop Bashford and many Methodist missionaries in 1911 or 1912 indicates that the church's claim that it remained apart from politics was somewhat disingenuous. The banner reads "Photograph of the Republican military government welcoming a mass meeting of the Methodist Episcopal Church" (courtesy United Methodist Archives, Drew University, Madison, New Jersey).

became a severe liability in Xinghua, where the new regime quickly lost its popularity, due in large part to its aggressive assault on illegal poppy fields.[50]

Minor disturbances were reported in the Xinghua area as early as June 1912, when Huang Lian gathered a crowd at Putian's Hugong Mountain on the day of the Dragon Boat Festival and called for an uprising. He allegedly condemned the ascension of Yuan Shikai, criticized Sun Yatsen for his abdication, called for an end to the land tax, denounced local officials for their exploitation and their fear of foreigners (especially local missionaries), and criticized the MEC by name. On 6 July, the rebels thwarted the prefectural magistrate's attack on Hugong Mountain, and Sun Daoren dispatched Commander Sun Baorong to put down the rebellion.[51]

---

50. MEC Archives, 74-II, 1259-5-2: 36; MAE/Paris, NS 33, no. 43, Fuzhou to Beijing, 20 Dec. 1911; PRO, FO 228/1872, no. 8, Werner to Jordan, 28 Feb. 1913; and CMS Fuhkien Mission, Original Incoming (1911), no. 253.

51. USDS (1910–29), 893.00/1401, reel 11, no. 389, Brissel to Secy. of State, 1 July 1912; Yu Qiqiang, "Huang Lian qiyi," p. 45; "Kaoding yu buchong," p. 63.

The first major outbreak of violence occurred in August 1912. Huang Lian led peasants from a particularly impoverished region known as the Thirty-Six Villages in an uprising, demanding the abolition of the land tax and the right to plant opium poppies.[52] The rebel leader reportedly protected poppy fields for a fee.[53] The rebels waged several inconclusive battles in fall 1912, but Sun Baorong's soldiers soundly defeated Huang Lian during an unsuccessful rebel assault on Xinghua City on 25 September 1912. A missionary source claims that Huang ordered local farmers to plant poppies so that he could tax them, and Chinese Methodists angered him when they cited religious convictions and loyalty to the Republican suppression policy as grounds for refusing.[54] Rumors that MEC missionary William N. Brewster had requested the troops evidently intensified the anti-Christian rumblings in the countryside.[55]

That fall, Yuan Shikai took the Xinghua situation into his own hands, allegedly reprimanding local officials with the admonition, "The whole country is of more importance than any one part; the poppy must be destroyed."[56] He appointed Cen Chunxuan Fujian's pacification commissioner and sent him to Fuzhou.[57] Cen appointed Jiang Chunlin (1855–1918), a censor under the Qing dynasty, then residing in his Xinghua home, to negotiate with the insurgents.[58] Jiang was instructed to offer amnesty to the rebels and enlistment in the army or a petty administrative position to Huang in exchange for ending the uprising. He met with all the parties involved, including Huang Lian and various members of the Christian church, and soon reported to Cen that the trouble was over. But foreign missionaries and their leading converts distrusted Jiang, who was rumored to be an old enemy of Yuan Shikai, and felt that the settlement was too lenient and bore the im-

---

52. Yu Qiqiang, "Huang Lian qiyi," p. 45.
53. USDS (1910–29), 893.114/57, reel 113, Shanghai to Secy. of State, 15 Jan. 1913; and PRO, FO 228/2454, Jordan to Grey, 26 May 1913.
54. Copplestone, *Twentieth-Century Perspectives*, p. 712.
55. PRO, FO 228/1838, no. 38, Werner to Jordan, 15 Sept. 1912; USDS (1910–29), 893.114/57, reel 113, Shanghai to Secy. of State, 15 Jan. 1913; "Kaoding yu buchong," p. 63; Wang Yiwei, "Xianyou dashi ji," pp. 26–27.
56. MEC *Annual Report*, 1913, p. 230.
57. See Chapter 6, pp. 223–24.
58. USDS (1910–29), 893.00/1815, reel 12, enclosure in no. 54, Fowler to Secy. of State, 8 July 1913.

print of the Freedom Party.[59] In fact, the suppression of bandits by incorporating them into the local military was a longstanding Chinese government strategy.[60]

In any case, the rebels did not accept the offer. The rebellion escalated with an unsuccessful rebel attack on the city of Xianyou in mid-December 1912, but five days later the city fell briefly to the insurgents. Cen Chunxian decided to eschew negotiation for a more forceful approach. Government troops stationed within the city quickly regained control but failed to pursue the retreating rebels.[61] Rebel strength peaked over the next six months, but the tone of the uprising changed dramatically after bloody government victories in February and May.

In January 1913, in a letter published by *The China Republican*, MEC missionary Brewster made the astonishing claim that 200,000 *mu* of poppy (over 33,000 acres) had been planted in Xinghua prefecture. British Consul Werner initially scoffed that the amount was "greatly exaggerated," but in subsequent letters to the British minister in Beijing, he conceded that the latest reports indicated that "the amount is enormous; all south of city and in Hsien-yu [Xianyou] is solid in poppy; no one has ever seen so much under cultivation."[62] Chinese accounts agree that the harvest was huge.[63] Missionaries claimed that the rebels were paid for guarding the crop, and local officials allowed the planting because of the money to be gained by confiscating the illicit crop or fining the farmers.[64] The potential profit of approximately

---

59. "Kaoding yu buchong," p. 63; USDS (1910–29), 893.00/1795, reel 12, enclosure in no. 51, Fowler to Secy. of State, 21 June 1913; USDS (1910–29), 893.00/1815, reel 12, enclosure in no. 54, Fowler to Secy. of State, 8 July 1913.

60. Billingsley, "Bandits, Bosses, and Bare Sticks," pp. 249, 251–56.

61. PRO, FO 228/1872, Intelligence Report for December Quarter 1912; USDS (1910–29), 894.114/57, reel no. 113, Shanghai to Secy. of State, 15 Jan. 1913; Yu Qiqiang, "Huang Lian qiyi," pp. 46–47; "Kaoding yu buchong," p. 65; Huang Shangyuan, "Nongmin douzheng shihuo si ze," pp. 39–40. According to Huang Shangyuan, the government troops at that time were vagrants, newly recruited to fight, and thus very poorly trained.

62. USDS (1910–29), 893.114/57, reel 113, Shanghai to Secy. of State, 15 Jan. 1913; PRO, FO 228/2452, doc. 34, Werner to Jordan, telegram 1, 11 Jan. 1913; PRO, FO 228/2452, doc. 44, Werner to Jordan, telegram 2, 16 Jan. 1913.

63. *Fujian jinyan jishu*, pp. 21–22. This report claimed that 130,000 *mu* of poppies were destroyed in Xinghua in 1913.

64. MEC *Annual Report*, 1913, p. 230.

20 million *yuan* would have constituted a powerful incentive for the rebels to continue their fight.[65]

Brewster's letter constituted direct disobedience of Bishop Bashford's wishes that the affair be handled without undue publicity. Bashford preferred to negotiate with the authorities in Beijing and Fuzhou behind the scenes, and according to one source, "at one point, he even intercepted a telegram of William N. Brewster's and kept the Hsinghua missionary's protest from reaching the press."[66] By "exposing" the Xinghua opium situation to the national press, Brewster and others hoped to pressure the Beijing government to take direct action. Missionary publications justified this action with the reminder that intransigence in a single locality could derail the agreement with the British and possibly endanger the entire suppression campaign.[67] Bashford felt that this sort of tactic would result in humiliation for provincial officials and lead to accusations of foreign intervention in domestic Chinese affairs. He was right on both accounts.[68]

In late January 1913, Zhang Yuanqi, Fujian's minister of civil affairs (*minzheng zhang*; often referred to as the "civil governor"), informed Werner that the 1,000 soldiers he had dispatched to Xinghua to uproot the poppy had arrived and were busy at their task.[69] But hostilities erupted again, and several fierce battles were fought in February. The rhythm of the hostilities may not have been accidental. The sowing season for opium poppies in that region was September or October, the poppies were in full flower in February, and harvesting was to begin shortly. An MEC missionary pointed out that as harvest time drew near, the opium farmers and those protecting them were more motivated to fight.[70] Huang Lian and his followers not only op-

---

65. Each *mu* was said to yield 100 *yuan* worth of opium; thus 20 million *yuan* could be expected from 200,000 *mu*. Huang Shangyuan, "Ershi nian huo Xian zhi yanmiao," p. 41.

66. Copplestone, *Twentieth-Century Perspectives*, pp. 712–13.

67. MEC *Annual Report*, 1913, p. 230; MEC Archives, 73-43, 1043-3-2: 41, Carson to North, 26 Feb. 1913. Apparently Bashford had prevented Brewster's earlier reports from being published (Copplestone, *Twentieth-Century Perspectives*, pp. 712–13).

68. MEC *Annual Report*, 1913, pp. 240–41; Copplestone, *Twentieth-Century Perspectives*, pp. 712–13.

69. PRO, FO 228/2452, no. 92, Werner to Jordan, 31 Jan. 1913; PRO, FO 228/2453, no. 56, Werner to Jordan, 19 Mar. 1913.

70. USDS (1910–29), 893.00/1589, reel 11, enclosure in no. 31, Fowler to Secy. of State, 12 Feb. 1913. Consul Fowler also noted that the rebels could use their profits to bribe or buy the services of poorly paid provincial troops.

posed taxes on opium but even more strongly resisted attempts to uproot existing poppies.[71]

Government soldiers engaged the rebels in mid-February, about eleven miles from Xinghua City. In the ensuing rout, the insurgents were pushed southward toward Pinghai and eleven villages were torched, with no government casualties.[72] Several days later, an even bloodier confrontation occurred about 24 miles from Xinghua City. Dr. Ronald Walker, a British missionary working in the city, reported that hundreds of rebels were killed in the second battle, and Huang Lian himself barely escaped by boat.[73] After this, things seemed to quiet considerably. Troops cut down poppies growing within a ten-mile radius of the city, and Walker reported no resistance and noted that in some cases the farmers pulled up the plants themselves.[74] American missionaries returned to Xinghua against Sun Daoren's orders and wrote that virtually all the poppy had been torn out and the countryside was quiet. Poppies remained standing in Xianyou, however, where the soldiers were to head next.[75] In April, two British missionaries reported 300 or so poppy fields being harvested a short distance away from Xianyou City, and rumor had it that the authorities could be bought in some areas.[76]

The corruption and depredations of government troops and local officials as they moved to destroy the prefecture's opium crop created, or at least bolstered, the reservoir of popular support for the rebels. Werner reported that opium cultivators requested permission to harvest one final crop; according to Walker, they instead were given two days to uproot the poppies. Soldiers threatened to torch the homes of those who did not. Opium that had already been harvested was burned along with the house in which it was discovered. Walker also reported that government troops storming a rebel fortress in early March forced many local people into boats to serve as floating shields against the rebel guns, an understandably unpopular tactic.[77] One

---

71. Opposition to destruction of the poppy crop did not technically constitute tax resistance. I am grateful to Lucien Bianco for pointing out this crucial difference (Bianco, "Rural Tax Resistance," p. 28; and pers. comm.).

72. PRO, FO 228/1872, no. 8, Werner to Jordan, 28 Feb. 1912.

73. USDS (1910–29), 893.00/1618, reel 11, no. 34, Fowler to Secy. of State, 27 Feb. 1913.

74. PRO, FO 228/1872, no. 8, Werner to Jordan, 28 Feb. 1913.

75. USDS (1910–29), 893.114, reel 113, enclosure in no. 41, Fowler to Secy. of State, 22 Apr. 1913; Copplestone, *Twentieth-Century Perspectives*, p. 714; MEC *Annual Report* (1913), p. 241.

76. PRO, FO 228/2453, no. 106, Werner to Jordan, 12 Apr. 1913.

77. PRO, FO 228/2453, telegram no. 7, Werner to Jordan, 11 Mar. 1913, and no. 56, Werner to Jordan, 19 Mar. 1913.

Chinese account states that the troops harassed the villagers and stole or extorted money and food.[78]

Many Xinghua residents echoed Huang Lian's opposition to excessive taxation, bad government, and the meddling of the Christian church; some of them viewed Huang and his men as folk heroes. Some evidently saw the well-disciplined, well-behaved rebels as a welcome respite from the hostility and brutality of local and provincial troops. According to one eyewitness description of the rebels as they marched toward Xianyou City in May 1913, the 500 or so insurgents were armed with primitive weapons such as knives, spears, old-style firearms, and a few locally made machine guns and wore uniforms printed with the characters Black Tiger Righteousness Society. Following the men was a sturdy young woman said to be the younger sister of Huang Lian, who was rumored to be able to fire two guns simultaneously. Leading the group was Huang Lian himself, sitting tall in a sedan chair, dressed unpretentiously in an old, blue unlined gown.[79]

Support for the rebels crossed class lines at times. According to Rev. Stanley F. Carson, head of the MEC mission in Xinghua City, "Many of the literati and the coolie class even here in the city are in sympathy with the rebels but the merchant and business class are not as the present situation seriously affects their trade."[80] Provincial assemblyman Lin Shizhao claimed that the depredations of "our troops forced people to follow the rebels."[81] However, most of the Xinghua gentry withdrew their support and called for government troops when they learned that the prefect intended to levy a costly penalty on local residents for opium cultivation.[82] Huang even seemed to garner respect from the soldiers sent to defeat him. A letter allegedly written by Xinghua Brigade Commander Sun Baorong at the outset of the revolt praised Huang's goals of "eliminating taxes and strengthening the foundation of the nation," although this was probably a conciliatory gesture designed to allow Huang to surrender without losing face.[83]

---

78. Huang Shangyuan, "Nongmin douzheng shihuo si ze," pp. 39–40.
79. Yu Qiqiang, "Huang Lian qiyi," pp. 45–49.
80. USDS (1910–29), 893/1590, reel 11, enclosures 3 and 4, Fowler to Secy. of State, 18 Feb. 1913.
81. Zhongguo dier lishi dang'anguan, *Zhonghua minguoshi dang'an ziliao huibian*, pp. 940–41. Many thanks to Steve Averill for making this source available to me.
82. USDS (1910–29), 893/1590, reel 11, enclosures 3 and 4, Fowler to Secy. of State, 18 Feb. 1913.
83. Yu Qiqiang, "Huang Lian qiyi," p. 48.

Unrest in the Xinghua countryside coincided with political trouble in Fuzhou. A dramatic attempt by the Fujian Protection Society in February to assassinate Fujian's civil governor, Zhang Yuanqi, left the provincial administration intact but cowed.[84] The society's animosity was directed at the Hunanese soldiers who exerted a great deal of influence in Fujian through the New Army. Fowler reported that the society, also known as the Second Revolutionary Party, was rumored to have Japanese backing and to have joined forces with the Xinghua rebels.[85] This does not appear to have been true, but the implication enhanced the potential significance of the Xinghua situation.

In early May 1913, after most of the soldiers had departed, the rebels attacked and again captured the walled city of Xianyou. The magistrate's yamen was burned down, and Lin Qigan, the county magistrate whose mismanagement was blamed for outbreaks of famine and banditry in the region before the rebellion, fled.[86] The five resident foreign missionaries also escaped, and although the Anglican hospital and mission compound within the city walls were ransacked, the MEC compound, located outside the west gate of the city, was untouched, allegedly because Huang wished to spare the locals a costly indemnity.[87] Rebel forces, now rumored to have swelled to almost 1,500, moved east, threatening the more strongly fortified prefectural seat of Xinghua. Fowler demanded action from provincial authorities, and Sun Daoren responded by dispatching Huang Peisong and his soldiers to the scene. Huang Peisong had been given the job of enforcing opium restrictions in southern Fujian and was stationed in Quanzhou. Well-armed and

---

84. *China Year Book*, 1914, p. 539; PRO, FO 228/1872, no. 4, Werner to Jordan, 5 Feb. 1913, no. 8, Werner to Jordan, 28 Feb. 1913, no. 20, Werner to Jordan, 12 May 1913, and Werner to Jordan, March Quarter Intelligence Report, 1913.

85. MAE/Paris, NS 48, no. 1, Doire to Conty, 8 Feb. 1913; USDS (1910–29), 893.00/1618, reel 11, no. 34, Fowler to Secy. of State, 27 Feb. 1913.

86. Lin is portrayed in one Chinese account as a well-meaning but overly pedantic official who tended to deal with practical problems by citing the Confucian classics (Lin Zongtang, "Minguo shiqi Xianyou xianzhang qunxiang," pp. 42–43).

87. Werner noted that this last statement was unverified. The British Consul at Xiamen also stated that Huang held a celebration to which the U.S. missionaries were invited. They declined. This is not mentioned in U.S. mission accounts. See PRO, FO 228/1872, no. 21, Werner to Jordan, 18 May 1913; PRO 228/1869, Little to Jordan, 19 June 1913; USDS (1910–29), 893/1740, reel 11, Maynard to Secy. of State, 17 May 1913; USDS (1910–29), 893/1807, reel 12, no. 924, Williams to Secy. of State, 9 July 1913; and USDS (1910–29), 893.00/1754, reel 12, no. 46, Fowler to Secy. of State, 23 May 1913.

well-trained, Huang Peisong's soldiers and the local garrison troops laid siege to Xianyou and drove the rebels out of the city.[88]

Accounts of the conduct of Huang Lian and his troops during their two-week occupation of Xianyou City vary wildly. Chinese historians insist that with the exception of one death during the burning of the yamen, Huang Lian's troops behaved impeccably, and business inside the city walls was conducted as usual throughout the occupation.[89] One popular anecdote recalled that Huang summoned a local scholar and opium addict and had him publicly consume large amounts of the drug to assure residents that opium was no longer illegal. Huang Lian then apparently issued a proclamation pledging that opium fields would not be taxed.[90] But according to British diplomats, the rebels levied high taxes on everyone, looted numerous properties, beat queueless men, took prisoners (including some Christians), and brutally tortured and murdered those who were police runners.[91] American diplomats or missionaries reported no such atrocities.

All accounts agree on the abominable behavior of government troops who recaptured Xianyou City. In May 1913, after most of the rebels had escaped from the city, Huang Peisong's soldiers indulged in large-scale looting and killed an unknown number of people, especially men with queues, assumed to be a symbol of antipathy toward the Republic. A British missionary reported that "the soldiers paraded the town carrying a ladder, to the rungs of which were attached the heads of rebels swinging by their pigtails."[92] One Chinese account blamed the soldiers for only eight deaths but contended that most were innocent merchants; it noted that the brutality of the murders infuriated the masses.[93] The incendiary effects of the soldiers' rampage were profound, and many now turned their anger on the Christians,

---

88. USDS (1910–29), 893.00/1502, reel 11, Amoy to Secy. of State, 4 Nov. 1912; USDS (1910–29), 893.00/1754, reel 12, no. 46, Fowler to Secy. of State, 23 May 1913; Yu Qiqiang, "Huang Lian qiyi," p. 47.

89. Yu Qiqiang, "Huang Lian qiyi," p. 47.

90. Huang Shangyuan, "Nongmin douzheng shihuo si ze," p. 39. However, "Kaoding yu buchong," p. 67, implies that the story may have been legend.

91. PRO, FO 228/1872, no. 21, Werner to Jordan, 18 May 1913; PRO 228/1869, Little to Jordan, 19 June 1913.

92. CMS, *Mercy and Truth* 19, no. 217 (Jan. 1915): 24–26; USDS (1910–29), 893.00/1754, reel 12, enclosure no. 26 in no. 46, Fowler to Secy. of State, 23 May 1913; PRO, FO 228/1869, no. 15, Little to Jordan, 19 June 1913.

93. One casualty was allegedly the visibly pregnant wife of a shopkeeper (Yu Qiqiang, "Huang Lian qiyi," p. 47).

whom they held responsible for summoning the troops. The link was not imaginary, since Werner reported that Bishop Bashford, ostensibly to enhance the status and influence of local Methodists, had apparently told a large public meeting in Xinghua City in February that troops were coming from Fuzhou at his request. The soldiers actually had been dispatched by Governor Sun on the orders of Yuan Shikai, but locally the damage was done.[94] Published transcripts of a series of telegrams between Sun Daoren and Xinghua officials, Sun Daoren and Yuan Shikai, and Provincial Assemblyman Lin Shizhao and Civil Governor Wang Shengling indicate that the provincial and national administrations were fully involved in the suppression of the rebellion.[95]

The actions of the various branches of Fujian's military establishment were not unusual in the context of early Republican rural unrest, nor was grassroots hostility toward the troops. Banditry in the early Republic often met with apathy or outright complicity on the part of locally based troops, and both the insurgents and local residents endured brutal repression by the regular army. The latter were often mobilized only after the "violation of some foreigner's treaty rights or by a change of civil/military command," since local officials knew full well that "to request suppression troops from outside was to invite more trouble than the bandits themselves caused."[96] In Xinghua, anti-military sentiment became linked with early Republican anti-tax, anti-opium protest.[97]

Somewhat incongruously, the new civil governor of Fujian, Jiang Yujing, chose this moment to issue a proclamation (dated 24 May 1913) announcing that opium cultivation in Xinghua had been completely suppressed. On 6 June 1913, the Ministry of Foreign Affairs wrote to the British minister in Beijing that Fujian wished to be placed on the list of provinces into which the importation of Indian opium was forbidden. Citing telegrams from Sun Daoren and Jiang Yujing as proof, the letter specifically pointed out that Pu-

---

94. Bashford must have abandoned his earlier, less inflammatory approach. PRO, FO 228/1872, no. 8, Werner to Jordan, 28 Feb. 1913. The coexistence of British and American missions in Xinghua was complicated by the fact that Werner and Fowler detested one another and constantly contradicted each other's interpretation of the events surrounding the uprising (Coates, *The China Consuls*, p. 440).

95. Zhongguo dier lishi dang'anguan, *Zhonghua minguoshi dang'an ziliao huibian*.

96. Billingsley, "Bandits, Bosses, and Bare Sticks," pp. 250–56, 280.

97. See Bianco, "Rural Tax Resistance," pp. 34–35, for a discussion of how several types of tax resistance could intersect in a single uprising.

tian and Xianyou counties were clear of the poppy. However, as the British minister pointed out to the Ministry of Foreign Affairs, the poppy would not be in full flower until February in the disputed region, and any investigation launched before that time next year would be pointless.[98]

By June 1913, the poppy season was over, and the revolt appeared to become decidedly anti-Christian, targeting primarily the property and members of the MEC. Huang Lian issued a proclamation vowing to destroy Christians, and the American missionaries were recalled to Fuzhou again, where they remained until early 1914.[99] The rebels terrorized Chinese Christians in the villages of Xinghua, but actual bloodshed was minimal, and government forces were largely inactive. The conflict spread into the neighboring subprefecture of Yongchun, and several other rebel leaders emerged to lead attacks on local Christians and their property. There were rumors that the leader of the disturbances in Dehua, a man named Su Yi, had joined forces with Huang Lian, but a much-feared joint assault never materialized.[100]

Foreign authorities were outraged by what they perceived as the apathy of the Chinese government and the local military. The provincial government sent a deputy to Xinghua to negotiate with Huang Lian in early June, and some of the rebel leader's demands were met. Jiang Zubao, son of ex-censor Jiang Chunlin (former negotiator and rumored rebel sympathizer), was appointed magistrate of Xianyou county, but it was Huang's demand that he be appointed military commander over the 2,000 government troops now in Xianyou and Putian that really infuriated Fowler.[101] Soldiers were not sent from Fuzhou to Xinghua until mid-June; they succeeded in rescuing ten kidnapped Christians but did little else besides cut queues and collect

---

98. PRO, FO 228/2454, no. 95, enclosure in Werner to Alston, 11 June 1913; PRO, FO 228/2454, no. 85, enclosure in Alston to Foreign Office, 11 June 1913.

99. For Chinese and English versions of this proclamation, see USDS (1910–29), 893.00/1797, reel 12, enclosure 4 in no. 39, Fowler to Secy. of State, 27 June 1913. See also USDS (1910–29), 893.00/1795, reel 12, enclosure in no. 51, Fowler to Secy. of State, 21 June 1913.

100. USDS (1910–29), 893/1807, reel 12, Williams to Secy. of State, 9 July 1913; USDS (1910–29), 893.00/1941, reel 12, no. 61, Fowler to Secy. of State, 6 Aug. 1913.

101. A recent Chinese account asserts that although Jiang Zubao began his tenure in a praiseworthy fashion, he ended up promoting gambling and opium use for his own financial gain (Lin Zongtang, "Minguo shiqi Xianyou xianzhang qunxiang").

Fig. 8.3 This photograph of Huang Lian, his men, and a number of government negotiators in 1913 infuriated western diplomats who would have preferred military action against Huang rather than an apparently civil gathering such as this. U.S. consul Fowler apparently wrote the numbers on the photo for identification purposes. Huang Lian is number 6, seated on the far right and dressed in dark robes. To his left is Pan Mu (number 8), who served as magistrate when Huang and his rebels took Xianyou City. Standing directly behind Huang is a prominent local member of the Fujian for the Fujianese Society. Sitting to Huang's right (number 4) and sporting a western style hat, trousers, and cane, is Lin Zhizhao, provincial assemblyman. And immediately to Lin's right is the commander of local troops (courtesy U.S. State Department records at the National Archives, Gaithersburg, Maryland).

taxes.[102] Sun Daoren's repeated orders to the Xinghua troops to engage and capture the rebels were ignored, and the soldiers continued to antagonize the populace. One British missionary alleged that many of the disobedient Hunanese soldiers were angry because they were poorly paid and had not received much, if any, remuneration for their help in the revolution.[103] Jiang Chunlin proposed another compromise, but his plan to collect money for an indemnity from all local residents, including Christians, was greeted with anger by Fowler and the U.S. missionaries. The American legation insisted on action from Beijing, but Chinese authorities in Fuzhou and Beijing were occupied with problems outside Xinghua prefecture.[104]

The apparent inaction of the government troops in Xinghua coincided with the outbreak in Fujian of the so-called Second Revolution, a multi-province rebellion against Yuan Shikai. In July, to the horror of Fowler and

---

102. USDS (1910–29), 893.00/1807, reel 12, Williams to Secy. of State, 9 July 1913; USDS (1910–29), 893.00/1816, reel 12, no. 55, Fowler to Secy. of State, 9 July 1913.

103. CMS Fuhkien Mission, Original Incoming (1911), no. 253.

104. USDS (1910–29), 893.00/1797, reel 12, no. 53, Fowler to Secy. of State, 27 June 1913; USDS (1910–29), 893.00/1815, reel 12, no. 54, Fowler to Secy. of State, 8 July 1913; USDS (1910–29), 893.00/1830, reel 12, Williams to Secy. of State, 26 July 1913.

the Methodists, Xu Chongzhi recalled to Fuzhou the approximately 1,500 soldiers deployed in and around Xinghua. The revolution was short-lived, however, and by early August Xu had fled to Japan and Sun Daoren briefly regained control.[105] The situation in Xinghua undoubtedly was affected by these developments. Yuan Shikai initially may have preferred a conciliatory approach toward the rebels because he feared that harsh action on his part would cause them to join forces with the elements promoting the Second Revolution.[106] A telegram from Yuan Shikai's cabinet (Guowu yuan) to Sun Daoren specifically endorsed Sun's plan to combine persuasion and force in dealing with the rebels.[107]

A Rancorous Resolution

As far as the British government was concerned, the conflict concluded in August 1913, when the Chinese government compensated British missionaries and their converts for losses incurred in the uprising and its suppression.[108] Methodist converts had also drawn up a claim, but the foreign and Chinese leaders of the church objected to any resolution that allowed Huang Lian to go unpunished. From this point on, the revolt devolved into a diplomatic ping-pong match between the Chinese and American governments that outlasted the actual rebellion by nearly a year. American consul Fowler was adamantly opposed to any settlement that did not include the surrender and punishment of Huang Lian, conditions Chinese authorities feared would set off more popular protests.

The case then was taken up in earnest by E. T. Williams, the American chargé d'affaires in Beijing, who in October 1913 met with Sun Baoqi (1867–1931), China's minister of foreign affairs. The minister confidentially informed Williams that Minister of the Navy Liu Guanxiong would be arriving in Fuzhou with a sizable force for the stated purpose of inspecting the navy. Actually, Sun implied, Admiral Liu would oversee the disbanding of

---

105. USDS (1910–29), 893.00/1912, reel 12, enclosure in no. 62, Fowler to Secy. of State, 6 Aug. 1913; USDS (1910–29), 893.00/1803, reel 12, telegram from Fowler to Secy. of State, 4 Aug. 1913.
106. Copplestone, *Twentieth-Century Perspectives*, p. 714.
107. Zhongguo dier lishi dang'anguan, *Zhonghua minguoshi dang'an ziliao huibian*, pp. 935–36.
108. USDS (1910–29), 893.00/1941, reel 12, no. 61, Fowler to Secy. of State, 6 Aug. 1913. See also PRO, FO 228/1872, no. 46, Werner to Jordan, 27 Aug. 1913; "Kaoding yu buchong," p. 72.

Fujian's New Army, an action that would hopefully strengthen the chain of command from Beijing and produce results in Xinghua.[109] Beijing then ordered Sun Daoren in Fuzhou to capture and punish the bandit leaders. Yuan Shikai even issued a presidential mandate to that effect on 19 October 1913, although widespread posting of the order did not occur until January 1914, after numerous protests by Fowler. Yuan also ordered the dissolution of the Freedom Party throughout the province.[110]

The wrangling was occasionally taken to almost comic extremes. When Sun Daoren's deputy, Zheng Biming, traveled a second time to Xinghua for negotiations with Huang Lian, the rebel leader's wife informed the official that Huang had died several days earlier, on 30 October 1913. The authorities in Fuzhou called for an inquest but stalled. Several people informed officials that they had seen Huang Lian up and about after his alleged demise, but since the rebel's power had diminished considerably, Fuzhou seemed willing to suspend its disbelief and negotiate with a secondary rebel leader. Fowler, however, was implacable and demanded that the body be exhumed.[111] In the presence of two deputies from the Ministry of Foreign Affairs, the corpse was examined and immediately declared a fraud.[112]

Much of the blame for this incident fell on Provincial Assemblyman Lin Shizhao, who apparently had been one of the local leaders who had confirmed Huang's death to Sun Daoren. Lin had based his report on his observation of Huang's casket but never opened it. Several desperate telegrams from Lin and his friends to the provincial authorities pleaded his case by emphasizing Lin's upstanding character. One lengthy telegram from Lin not only asserted his innocence but strongly condemned the brutality of the government troops and sympathized with the supporters of the rebellion. He and his friends were particularly outraged by the seizing of Lin's elderly grandfather as a hostage until Lin turned himself in. The telegrams con-

---

109. USDS (1910–29), 893/2012, reel 13, no. 1063, Williams to Secy. of State, 20 Oct. 1913.

110. USDS (1910–29), 893.00/2020, reel 13, no. 1082, Williams to Secy. of State, 27 Oct. 1913; USDS (1910–29), 893.00/2022, reel 13, no. 79, Fowler to Secy. of State, 13 Oct. 1913; USDS (1910–29), 893.00/2073, reel 13, no. 99, Fowler to Secy. of State, 6 Jan. 1914.

111. PRO, FO 228/1872, no. 61, Werner to Jordan, 10 Dec. 1913; PRO, FO 228/1872, Werner to Jordan, December Quarter Intelligence Report (1913), 31 Dec. 1913.

112. Apparently the body was in a very advanced state of decomposition, indicating that death had occurred long before Huang's alleged passing. USDS (1910–29), 893.00/2065, reel 13, enclosures in no. 89, Fowler to Secy. of State, 25 Nov. 1913.

demned this action as cruel and arbitrary and clearly expressed elite dissatisfaction with the coercive methods of the new Republic.[113]

Sun Daoren accepted the report disavowing Huang's death but "pleaded the difficulty of dealing with [Huang] severely owing to [Huang's] influence in the district."[114] Sun's hesitation stemmed not only from frustration at Fowler's increasingly strident demands but also from the instability of the military and political situation in Fuzhou. Until Admiral Liu oversaw the disbanding of the Hunan troops, large-scale military action was too risky.[115] In fact, by late November, Sun Daoren himself had been replaced by Liu. Sun apparently was undone in part by his failure to resolve the Xinghua situation, as well as by accusations of embezzlement and Beijing's fear of his pro–Sun Yatsen leanings.[116]

By mid-December 1913, the disbanding and repatriating of the Hunanese troops had concluded without incident. They were replaced by soldiers primarily from Shandong and Zhili provinces, but the troops numbered only around 4,000, approximately half the province's previous military strength.[117] The new troops vigorously sought out rebel fugitives in Xinghua and fought those still active in Yongchun.[118]

The whole affair sputtered to a halt in June 1914, when the MEC accepted a cash indemnity from the local Chinese governments in Xinghua prefecture and Yongchun, but the uprising claimed casualties even after its formal termination.[119] Several bandits and cooperating gentry were executed,

---

113. Zhongguo dier lishi dang'anguan, *Zhonghua minguoshi dang'an ziliao huibian*, pp. 942–44.

114. PRO, FO 228/1872, Werner to Jordan, December Quarter Intelligence Report (1913), 31 Dec. 1913.

115. USDS (1910–29), 893.00/2065, reel 13, enclosure in no. 89, Fowler to Secy. of State, 26 Nov. 1913.

116. USDS (1910–29), 893.00/2060, reel 13, enclosure in no. 94, Fowler to Secy. of State, 10 Dec. 1913; USDS (1910–29), 893.00/2073, reel 13, enclosure in no. 99, Fowler to Secy. of State, 6 Jan. 1914; MAE/Paris, NS 53, no. 54, Danjou to Conty, 15 Dec. 1913.

117. MAE/Paris, NS 53, no. 22, Danjou to Conty, 3 Nov. 1913; MAE/Paris, NS 53, no. 47, Danjou to Conty, 22 Nov. 1913; MAE/Paris, NS 53, no. 30, Danjou to Paris, 16 Dec. 1913; USDS (1910–29), 893.00/2052, reel 13, enclosure in no. 87, Fowler to Secy. of State, 15 Nov. 1913; USDS (1910–29), 893.00/2060, reel 13, enclosure in no. 94, Fowler to Secy. of State, 10 Dec. 1913.

118. USDS (1910–29), 893.00/2062, reel 13, enclosure in no. 95, Fowler to Secy. of State, 18 Dec. 1913; USDS (1910–29), 893.00/2063, reel 13, enclosure in no. 97, Fowler to Secy. of State, 27 Dec. 1913.

119. The compensation totaled $36,000 (Mexican) (USDS [1910–29], 893.00/2168, reel 14, enclosure in no. 136, Fowler to Secy. of State, 3 July 1914).

including Su Yi, who led the disturbances in Dehua county, and Jiang Lu, the man who falsely reported Huang Lian's death. After decades of service, Fowler was removed from office for his intemperate behavior during the affair. Huang Lian himself disappeared, although it was rumored that he died from illness shortly after his second defeat at Xianyou City.[120] The Methodist church noted a dramatic rise in local interest in Christianity after the uprising, and the MEC even claimed that Huang and hundreds of his followers were received into the church in late 1913 or early 1914. This seems extremely unlikely, however, and was never mentioned in foreign diplomatic sources or Chinese accounts of the rebellion.[121]

As for the opium suppression campaign in Xinghua, it persisted until the death of Yuan Shikai and then collapsed, along with any semblance of political unity in the province. The official Anglo-Chinese joint inspection of Fujian in spring 1914 detected no significant poppy cultivation, but the inspectors did not even visit Xianyou. The Xianyou magistrate met them nearby and presented missionary-signed affidavits as proof that the county was free from significant poppy cultivation, again emphasizing the link between missionaries and the state in the context of opium suppression. In Xinghua, the inspectors ran into Chen Nengguang, then head of the Anti-Opium Bureau in southern Fujian, who had spent the past week clearing out most of the poppies in the region. The leader of the CMS in Xinghua confirmed that the region was poppy-free, thanks largely to proclamations and admonitions by the magistrate and the gentry.[122] But by 1918, the poppy was again being cultivated heavily in the vicinity of Xinghua City, "apparently wih the consent of the southern forces controlling the district."[123]

---

120. USDS (1910–29), 893.00/2276, reel 14, no. 36, Pontius to Secy. of State, 3 May 1915; USDS (1910–29), 893.00/2085, reel 13, no. 140, Reinsch to Secy. of State, 16 Feb. 1914; Yu Qiqiang, "Huang Lian qiyi," pp. 47-8; "Kaoding yu buchong," p. 64.

121. Oddly, Huang's conversion (he was called Ng-liang in this source) was mentioned only in passing by a Chinese church leader in the Xinghua area (MEC Archives, 73-43, 1183-6-2: 09; MEC *Annual Report*, 1913, p. 231).

122. PRO, FO 228/2458, no. 51, Turner in Little to Jordan, 2 Apr. 1914; USDS (1910–29), 893.114, reel 113, Amoy to Secy. of State, 22 Apr. 1914.

123. USDS (1910–29), 893.114, reel 113, no. 16, Foochow to Secy. of State, 12 Nov. 1918.

The Politics of Reform and Revolution

The escalation and lengthy duration of the hostilities associated with Huang Lian's Xinghua revolt were the result of Chinese social and political tensions, as well as heavy-handed diplomacy by foreign powers. The settlement of the affair illustrates the complexities involved in the implementation and enforcement of opium reform and reveals the real, but tenuous, hold of the fledgling Republican state on the province of Fujian in the face of enduring imperialist pressure.

Huang Lian's uprising originated in a variety of rural complaints that were typical of that period; thus, it was not the rebels' *choice* of targets that made this incident notable. Protests against levies on land, salt, and opium were among the most common forms of peasant resistance during the early Republic.[124] In Xinghua, these complaints were just part of a broader antigovernment sentiment, fueled by unmet and unrealistic expectations. Anger at the new regime for continuing to collect the taxes associated with the New Policies and for extending the anti-opium campaign into many previously undisturbed poppy fields sparked the violence. The rebels of Xinghua were not alone in their resentment. Disillusionment with the Republic erupted in waves of resistance throughout China as the masses quickly realized that revolution brought no relief from foreign influence and interference, intrusive reforms, and high taxes.[125]

To label Huang Lian's uprising an "opium rebellion"—in other words, a protest directed primarily at the Republic's continuation of the anti-opium campaign—denies the complexity of the incident and obscures the many ways in which opium policy had become entangled with local social tensions and the twists and turns of national and international politics.[126] Opium suppression was, however, one of the key arenas in which government policy—with its righteous, nationalistic tone and its paradoxical ties to imperialist demands—clashed with peasant survival strategies. Huang Lian's protection of poppy cultivation appealed to the people of Xinghua, as did his promise to permit no taxes on the illicit crop. Even otherwise supportive Chinese sources do not defend Huang's promotion of opium cultivation, but

---

124. Bianco, "Rural Tax Resistance."
125. Esherick, *Reform & Revolution in China*, pp. 250–52.
126. The label was first applied by Americans; see USDS (1910–29), 893.114, reel 113, enclosure in no. 57, Shanghai to Secy. of State, 15 Jan. 1912.

most accounts note that state opium and salt taxes imposed great financial hardships and drove local farmers to desperate measures.

The anti-Christian component of the rebellion was an especially incendiary issue for the new Republic. Labeling the uprising an "opium rebellion" was clearly to the advantage of a Chinese state trying to extricate itself from a diplomatic quagmire. This approach would, the government must have hoped, skirt the more complex and emotional issues involved in dealing with an anti-Christian outbreak. The forced uprooting of poppy fields demonstrated official concern and continuing commitment to the international opium suppression agreement, and provincial authorities could attempt negotiations with the rebels to defuse other local tensions. However, officials in Beijing and Fuzhou were constantly prodded by foreign diplomats and missionaries to reject negotiation in favor of military force, even though the Chinese authorities were struggling to stabilize the Chinese political situation.

Foreign missionaries also initially preferred to view the uprising as an opium rebellion despite persecution in the past. Rather than acknowledge any general anti-Christian sentiment among the populace of Xinghua, the missionaries chose to cast themselves and their converts as the victims of a gentry-bandit alliance opposed to the noble Christian stand against opium. In fact, the rebels' anti-Christian sentiment stemmed from anger at the MEC's open support for the new Republican state, which had failed to eliminate not only opium reform but also the influence of the Christian church and unpopular local officials. Methodists were persecuted throughout the revolt, probably because of their well-known support of opium reform, but the intensification of anti-Christian violence erupted in response to the depredations of government troops. Missionaries recognized that Christians were being blamed for summoning those troops and stressed that this strong and dangerous identification of the Methodist church with the unpopular policies of the Republican state entitled them and their converts to the protection of that state.[127] In short, the state's response to the violence altered the targets and objectives of the uprising.

Huang Lian's revolt raises important questions about the degree and depth of popular support for opium reform—a crucial gap in our understanding of why so little large-scale resistance to the campaign occurred in

---

127. MEC *Annual Report*, 1913, pp. 229–30, 235–36, 240–42; Copplestone, *Twentieth-Century Perspectives*, pp. 712–13; USDS (1910–29), 893.00/1589, reel 11, enclosure 3, Carson to Fowler, 12 Feb. 1913.

Fujian. This analysis suggests that resistance to the suppression campaign reflected a deep-seated resentment directed at authorities on both sides of the revolutionary divide. The Xinghua uprising indicates that in some rural locales compliance with the opium restrictions may have signified coerced obedience to a higher, more powerful authority rather than voluntary, genuine support for the campaign.[128] That authority often manifested itself by demanding taxes for ostensibly progressive reforms from those least able to afford the outlay or to enjoy the benefits.

Huang Lian's revolt incorporated elements of social, economic, and political protest, and support for the rebellion was not limited to the peasantry. Influential members of the local gentry sided with the rebels, at least until the central government began to crack down. Many of those elites professed strong provincial loyalties, and the only pre-existing organization that may have joined the rebels *en masse* was the militia raised by an anti-Hunan group during the Revolution of 1911. Local factional rivalries tied to national political trends clearly affected the course of the Xinghua rebellion. One theory holds that early Republican peasant resistance was grounded in opposition to the state rather than to social exploitation, but this incident indicates that the two factors were inextricably linked in the popular mind with the reforms begun in the late Qing.[129] Implicit in the Xinghua rebels' complaints about high taxes and opium reform was strong opposition to continuing state intrusion.[130]

The state had a strong interest in the successful conduct of the anti-opium campaign. For Yuan Shikai, abrogation or violation of the Anglo-Chinese opium agreement of 1911 could mean foreign military intervention or a resurgence of the Indian and domestic opium trade that would probably further the financial and political autonomy of the provinces. William Walker, in his book on opium and foreign policy, states: "Although Yuan Shih-k'ai's attempts to extend political centralization were resisted in many provinces, his leadership in the anti-opium struggle was accepted, however briefly, because it gave useful national expression to a common objective."[131]

---

128. I refer here to the state, at the provincial and national levels, but it is also possible that individual farmers planted poppies because they were ordered to do so by powerful clansmen or landlords. In any case, the objections of the farmers to the taxation and uprooting policies of the state remained the same.

129. Bianco, "Rural Tax Resistance," p. 36.

130. Duara, *Culture, Power, and the State.*

131. Walker, *Opium and Foreign Policy*, p. 24.

Walker is correct, for the most part, but I contend, however, that the conduct and resolution of the Xinghua revolt indicate that in Fujian, acceptance of Beijing's leadership in the campaign was a manifestation of Yuan's successful extension of state control by means of direct intervention and military might. This study indicates that the early Republic was still able to impose its will on the provinces when it had to, at least until the death of Yuan Shikai.

Fujian was, in some ways, a special case that demanded central government intervention. Fujian and Zhejiang shared a governor-general, but that official's military support and administrative apparatus were located in Fuzhou, and the central government was not especially involved in Zhejiang's affairs.[132] And unlike many other provinces, Fujian's New Army actively opposed Yuan Shikai in the Second Revolution. The importance of Fujian's strategic location as a buffer between the revolutionary province of Guangdong and the rest of China was also notable.[133] These factors may have meant that the central government had a large stake in maintaining or compelling Fujian's loyalty by taking an active role in its internal affairs.

American and British diplomats clearly felt that Beijing's apparent inability to control provincial authorities in Fuzhou reflected the weakness of the central government, but that analysis is simplistic and misleading. Juggling the interests of the local gentry, a restive and discontented peasantry, and rebellious provincial militarists without giving cause for imperialist intervention or further popular violence called for a compromise that relied less on the letter of the law than on a reasonable solution for a particular problem. As Ellsworth Carlson put it, the best resolution of a missionary case—for the Chinese government—was often no resolution at all, a "masterful passivity."[134] The strength of the Chinese government in the case of the Xinghua revolt should be measured not by how well it complied with the demands of a foreign power but by how well it was able to achieve its own goals.

The resolution of the Xinghua conflict may not have satisfied the American government, but peace in the countryside was restored, and opium cultivation seemed to be temporarily eliminated. Most significantly for Beijing and Fuzhou, poppy growing was eradicated long enough to enable the prov-

---

132. Rankin, *Elite Activism and Political Transformation in China*.
133. Falkenheim, "Provincial Administration in Fukien," pp. 33–34.
134. Carlson, *The Foochow Missionaries*, pp. 127–28, 137; Billingsley, "Bandits, Bosses, and Bare Sticks."

ince to pass the joint inspection in 1914.[135] Only a few token members of what American diplomats and missionaries termed "gentry abettors" were punished, and several of the military and civil officials dismissed for negligence during the revolt were simply reassigned. As for the indemnity, the Chinese government dropped its policy of assessing taxes on everyone in villages (including Christians) that had supplied the rebels with men or supplies but only after the MEC reduced its claim by more than half.[136] Sun Daoren felt that the hundreds of rebel casualties, which far outstripped the losses of Xinghua's Christian community, were punishment enough for the rebel rank-and-file.[137] This is not to say that there were no lapses in provincial or central government control during the uprising, particularly during the Second Revolution and its immediate aftermath. But when the rebellious troops from Hunan were replaced, Beijing and Fuzhou once again called the shots, literally and figuratively.

Finally, Huang Lian's revolt also sheds more light on the question of why opium reform thrived in the new public space for political activism in Fujian's cities but generated great hostility and violent resistance among many Xinghua residents. The proliferation of anti-opium societies and mass meetings in other parts of Fujian indicate that the campaign had strong popular support, but most of the choreographers of those activities were what historian Joseph Esherick has termed "urban reformist elites."[138] In cities like Fuzhou, the denizens of the public space could rely on the state for money, power, and legitimacy, whereas rural reformers were often drawn from the ranks of local officials, foreign missionaries, and Chinese Christians since many other prominent elites probably had close connections to the land on which the poppies were being cultivated. At the same time, the public spectacles that helped delineate the new public space in urban locales were not duplicated in the countryside to mark the uprooting or confiscation of carefully tended poppy fields. These actions destroyed livelihoods and generated far more fear and resentment than the ebullient urban processions that culminated in the destruction of smoking implements.

---

135. See Chap. 6, pp. 253–60.

136. USDS (1910–29), 893.00/2111, reel 13, enclosure in no. 119, Fowler to Secy. of State, 23 Mar. 1914.

137. USDS (1910–29), 893.00/1807, reel 12, Williams to Secy. of State, 9 July 1913; USDS (1910–29), 893.00/1978, reel 12, enclosures in no. 72, Fowler to Secy. of State, 8 Sept. 1913.

138. Esherick, *Reform & Revolution in China*, chap. 3.

The quelling of the revolt illustrates the need for the strength and oversight of the Republican state to accomplish opium suppression as well as the profound hostility of some Fujianese farmers toward the extractive nature of the anti-opium campaign. Ironically, it also marks the beginning of the end of effective state control over the campaign. Clearly, military force was necessary to quell the violence in Xinghua, but reforms dependent on military force seemed unlikely to persist once state attention and strength waned.

NINE

The Collapse of the Crusade, 1914–1927

Although references to Lin Zexu diminished with the tapering off of state enthusiasm for opium reform, his deeds still resonated with Chinese and international audiences as they observed the dramatic, formal conclusion of China's ten-year plan to eradicate opium. In January 1919, almost two years after the formal expiration of the agreement between the Chinese and the British, the Chinese government began burning over 1,200 chests of Indian opium left in the warehouses of Shanghai. The number of chests had increased steadily as more of China's provinces were closed to the drug, and their immolation was intended to serve as a clear indication to the world of China's resolve. After Chinese and foreign inspectors carefully inventoried and examined the opium to prevent fraud, the drugs were incinerated in special kilns and the ashes dissolved in the Yangzi River. The process took about a week, and the stirring public ceremonies recalled a similar scene 80 years earlier. "No such wholesale destruction of opium has taken place since the burning of 20,291 chests seized from foreign merchants by Commissioner Lin in 1839," claimed the senior British diplomat in China.[1]

But context makes all the difference, and this ceremony was a disturbing reminder of significant changes since the first Opium War. In many ways, the roles of the Chinese and the British were now reversed. The British reference to Lin was intended as praise for the Chinese government, and the ceremony represented the end of an era rather than a catalyst for military conflict. Chinese opium policy had also undergone major changes, and this ceremony was all the more significant because of the scandal that preceded

---

1. Great Britain, Foreign Office, *The Opium Trade*, vol. 4 (1917–21), Jordan to Curzon, 29 Jan. 1919, pt. XIII, pp. 20–21. The diplomat was misinformed; Commissioner Lin did not dispose of the contraband by burning.

it.[2] The question of the Shanghai opium stocks had been mired in warlord politics for several years, and more than once it had appeared likely that the drugs would find their way back into the Chinese opium economy with the implicit approval of the Chinese state. Public outrage, stirred by passionate editorials in Chinese newspapers and fueled by the disapproval of international and Chinese reform groups, ultimately forced President Xu Shichang (1855–1939) to adopt a more morally defensible strategy.

Once the stocks had been burned, the focus of international attention dissipated somewhat, and the Chinese political situation deteriorated. The Japanese replaced the British as the arch-villains of the Chinese opium trade, and the absence of any concrete guidelines for opium suppression transformed Chinese opium policy into a patchwork of ill-coordinated, largely ineffective provincial initiatives. Opium suppression remained an imperative of Chinese nationalism, but that lofty sentiment now paled in comparison with more concrete military and financial needs. Even the evil of opium smoking itself seemed less serious than the growing popularity of injectable morphine.[3]

When Yuan Shikai died in 1916, most of the ambitions and accomplishments of Fujian's opium suppression campaign dissolved along with the Republican state. The collapse of effective central authority, combined with a lack of British leverage, meant an end to national-level supervision and central leadership of opium reform. Fujian, along with most of the rest of China, fragmented into competing warlord regimes. Military commanders sought quick, easy, reliable sources of revenue to finance their forces and military campaigns and to maintain control over local populations. One such source was opium poppies. In some cases, military regimes ordered farmers to plant opium, but in most areas the new overlords simply levied such high land taxes that only a poppy harvest enabled farmers to comply. The exorbitant taxes or "fines" levied on opium consumption and sales allowed military commanders and local authorities to maintain the fiction of opposition to a vice that so recently had been the subject of a national suppression effort. In fact, the imposition of taxes on opium—as well as on prostitution and gambling—simply meant its legalization, just as it had in the aftermath of the *Arrow* War.

---

2. Scandal also followed the burning, as Chinese officials quarreled over whether some of the contraband had disappeared before the ceremony and the British press in Shanghai complained that the burning had consumed opium that could have been used medicinally (USDS [1910–29], 893.114, reel 114, doc. 2510, Shanghai to Peking, 18 Jan. 1919).

3. See Dikötter et al., "Narcotic Culture," for a discussion of this phenomenon.

For the members of the Anti-Opium Society, this deterioration must have been devastating. According to one source, the society "raised its voice in abhorrence, the media protested in an uproar, but the warlords remained indifferent."[4] The Chinese state remained the dominant influence in opium reform, but it was its absence that set the tone and content of national opium policy and contoured the public political space. Now the state was neither centralized nor committed to a nationalistic crusade to improve its image or the lot of its people. A strong central state was a memory, and authority rested in the hands of provincial military men who did not hesitate to exploit opium for the money they so desperately needed. Disheartened by the futility of its efforts, the Anti-Opium Society disbanded in 1921, its headquarters became the site of Fuzhou No. 4 Middle School until 1949, and the society itself "became nothing more than a name in history."[5] Other groups sought to take up its mantle, but none of them had the clout or cachet of the society in its late Qing prime.

What happened to unravel the accomplishments of reformers so rapidly? A strong central state was certainly the key to the conduct of the late Qing/early Republican suppression movement, but day-to-day enforcement of opium reform also hinged on the participation of activist officials and unofficial reform groups, particularly in urban areas. These groups had operated in a new and amorphous public political space distinct but not totally separate from the state. The new Republic initially had been able to absorb much of the power exercised in that vibrant space by offering official positions to many elite reformers and taking over many of the duties and sources of revenue of unofficial reform groups. After the collapse of the Republican state, the boundaries were redrawn again. Under a nominal central state, with provincial militarists hungry for revenue, territory, and political power, opium reformers operating in the public sphere became more vocal, more autonomous, and more openly oppositional even as their power was dramatically curtailed.

The late Qing/early Republican anti-opium campaign had created an environment in which the rhetoric of suppression had become an integral aspect of Chinese nationalism and remained a political necessity at the national and provincial levels. Despite that rhetoric, the unspoken goals of the Nationalists and the warlord regimes—to control and profit from the

---

4. Wu Jiaqiong and Lin Jiazhen, "Fujian jinyan yundong 'Qudu she,'" pp. 17–18.
5. Ibid., p. 18.

opium trade—stood in stark contrast to those of opium reformers. The reformers were reduced to monitoring the alarming situation and lobbying to get the attention of authorities inside and outside China. Popular mobilization in the form of mass meetings and public ceremonies was no longer feasible in many areas, and even where it was, the authorities were no longer willing to allow opium reformers to exercise police powers that might allow them to collect opium-related taxes or constrain the revived opium trade. Urban elites remained actively committed to opium suppression, but impermeable boundaries between society and a fragmented, militarized state now replaced the flexible state-supported framework in which they had amassed so much regulatory power.

Opium and China's New Reality

By 1914, the Sino-Indian opium trade was effectively ended, and the good-faith efforts of the Chinese, combined with pressure from the international anti-opium lobby and the distraction of World War I, worked to ensure that the British were eager to end their role in the opium trade and thus became less critical of the last stages of the suppression campaign. In 1915, the British intimated that once Guangdong, Jiangsu, and Jiangxi provinces were inspected and declared free of domestic poppies, China would be released from its obligation to admit Indian opium, even though five western provinces fairly inaccessible to the imported drug remained uncertified.[6]

Imperialist pressure continued to serve as an incentive for reform even as Chinese progress eroded. The ten-year agreement between the Chinese and the British was slated to expire in 1917, and although Great Britain continued to cooperate with the Chinese in conducting joint inspections of provinces still legally open to the foreign drug, the British balked at issuing a formal declaration terminating the agreement when the business of opium suppression clearly was unfinished. The matter of the Shanghai stocks was still to be determined at this point, and the reappearance of poppies all over China was a serious concern.[7] The British government vigorously and repeatedly protested what they termed violations of the 1911 agreement, in an attempt to maintain some leverage over the deteriorating situation, and served, with other foreign governments, as unofficial watchdogs of China's

---

6. Great Britain, FO, *The Opium Trade*, vol. 3 (1913–16), Caldecott to Grey, 4 Jan. 1915, pt. IX, pp. 1–3.

7. Ibid., vol. 4 (1917–21), Curzon to Jordan, 5 Apr. 1919, pt. XIII, pp. 21–22.

fading commitment to opium reform through the 1920s. This was not a new role for the British, but now their role was less morally ambiguous. As the British extracted themselves from the Sino-Indian opium trade, however, their influence waned. China's opium problem could no longer be blamed on British or British-Indian greed, and the onus for the revival of the opium economy rested with the Japanese and the Chinese themselves. Both the Chinese and the British knew that despite heated diplomatic threats, it was highly unlikely in the current political climate that Great Britain would sanction the resumption of the Sino-Indian opium trade.

As we have seen, opium reform never takes place in a vacuum. In the late Qing, the New Policy reforms, with their government-initiated mandate to rework the Chinese polity, combat imperialist aggression, and generate a new Chinese pride and nationalism, were the political media in which state-sanctioned opium reform flourished. During the warlord years, the intellectual ferment that galvanized the May Fourth–era activists also provided an important ideological context for the continuing battle against narcotics in China. The intense self-examination that characterized that era generated another politically charged milieu in which the nationalist rationale behind opium suppression coincided with the more concrete goal of socioeconomic stability. This movement was also led by progressive reformers who sought nothing less than the remolding of the Chinese character and the creation of a modern citizen of a new China. Modernity included strong physical as well as political components, as Henrietta Harrison's intriguing work clearly illustrates. A modern citizen rejected the torpor of both Confucian conservatism and the opium den.[8] But although the Chinese state continued to support the rhetoric of suppression—a political norm bequeathed by the previous anti-opium campaign—the central state was no longer able to impose a policy of opium prohibition on all the provinces, nor did it seek to do so.

Opium suppression remained an official goal of whatever entity claimed to represent the central Chinese state, but the agencies those authorities devised generally functioned more as mechanisms for collecting much needed opium-related taxes than for enforcing opium suppression. The most immediate and best-publicized legacy of China's ambitious late Qing / early Republican suppression campaign was the stockpile of Indian opium in Shanghai warehouses that accumulated as one province after another was closed to

---

8. Harrison, *The Making of the Republican Citizen*, chap. 2.

foreign opium imports. The scandal that preceded the triumphant public burning of these stocks clearly marked the decline of the Chinese state's commitment to suppression as well as a new role for reformers. Following the destruction of these stocks, reformist anger at the machinations of the Chinese government fueled the formation of several anti-opium organizations that epitomized the hardening of the boundaries between the weakened central state and a far more autonomous, oppositional public political space. The new organizations were vocal, but their power was based on their lobbying abilities and the general acceptance of anti-opium rhetoric established in the late Qing.

British missionaries and their colleagues from other western nations who had never hesitated to speak critically of Chinese or foreign involvement in the opium trade, took stock of the new political reality and threw their considerable energies into forming several prominent anti-opium organizations. A British missionary physician formed the International Anti-Opium Association (IAOA) in 1918 to agitate for global narcotics control and to push for Chinese action against poppy cultivation. The organization soon boasted twenty branch associations, including one founded in Fuzhou in November 1919. However, according to Edward Slack, the lack of a strong central state, the number and variety of warlord regimes, and the group's dissemination of English-language publications hobbled the IAOA's efforts.[9]

With foreign opium imports now officially forbidden, Chinese and international attention turned toward the growing problem of narcotics smuggling. The Japanese were roundly condemned for their leading role in smuggling morphine into China. Morphine imports had been prohibited in January 1909, and the manufacture and importation of cocaine, morphine, and instruments for their consumption were outlawed on 1 December 1910, but the subsequent tapering off of the opium trade provided a powerful incentive for Japanese merchants and Chinese consumers.[10] Morphine smuggling was especially difficult to halt in southern provinces like Fujian, since it was difficult to distinguish Chinese merchants from Taiwan carrying Japanese passports and harder to prosecute them. The public outcry led many European nations (including Great Britain) to stop selling morphine to the Japanese, but the

---

9. Slack, "The National Anti-Opium Association and the Guomindang State," pp. 249–50; USDS (1910–29), 893.114, reel 114, enclosure in no. 332, Foochow to Secy. of State, 15 Apr. 1921.

10. *China Medical Journal* 34, no. 3 (May 1920): 338–39.

Japanese began to manufacture the drug themselves in Japan and Taiwan. Japan also became one of the largest buyers of Indian opium, much of which was sold in Taiwan and in the Japanese colony of Qingdao.[11]

Opium in Fujian, 1914–1917

For Fujian, warlord rule actually began with the rise to power of Li Houji, the military man who dominated provincial politics until his removal in 1922. In the spring of 1914, Xu Shiying (1872–1964), a former Qing official and native of Anhui, became provincial governor and served in that position until the death of Yuan Shikai. Xu was then promoted out of Fujian entirely, becoming minister of interior under Duan Qirui (1865–1936) in Beijing. Into the vacuum stepped Li Houji, whose civil and military administrations set the tone for the ineffective attempts at opium prohibition for much of the warlord era.[12] His ascension came on the heels of the closing of the province to Indian opium, a development that ironically had hinged in large part on the military muscle provided by Li and his troops. Thus, the end of legal foreign opium imports into Fujian province in 1914 did not solve the opium problem; rather, it marked the end of effective British oversight and the enthusiasm of the Chinese state. That lack of motivation and the general deterioration of order in the countryside quickly allowed the resuscitation of the provincial opium economy and fueled a booming smuggling trade. Constant military conflict and frequent changes in local powerholders caused opium smoking, poppy cultivation, and banditry to flourish and documentation to shrink, at least until the Nationalist government was founded in Nanjing in 1927.[13] Since few comprehensive or reliable sources of information on the illicit revival of the provincial opium economy exist, much of the evidence that follows is uneven and gives us but a glimpse at the chaos in Fujian. Chinese Christians and foreign missionaries were vigilant observers and frequent correspondents on the topic of opium suppression, and their testimony forms the backbone of much of the available information for this turbulent period.

Within months of the closing of Fujian to Indian opium imports, the

---

11. Ibid., 33, no. 1 (Jan. 1919): 68–71.
12. Boorman, *Biographial Dictionary of Republican China*, 2: 141. For more on Li Houji and his subsequent domination of Fujian, see Li Guoqi, *Minguo shi lunji*, esp. chap. 3.
13. Accurate statistics on opium consumption, sales, etc., do not emerge again until the 1930s when the Nationalists asserted their determination to suppress the drug through a government-run opium monopoly.

provincial opium economy had begun to re-emerge, fueled by the persistence of demand, an increasingly lucrative smuggling trade, and general social disorder in the countryside. The growing power of Li Houji, the breakdown of Beijing's control over the provinces, and the absence of a British agreement that necessitated nationwide cooperation and coordination of suppression efforts ensured that enforcement was uneven at best and nonexistent in many areas. The approach of the provincial authorities seemed to veer between total apathy and brute force. The Anti-Opium Society and the provincial Opium Prohibition Bureau continued to exist, but their relationship was unclear and their role was generally confined to the larger cities.

As early as February 1915, a group of Chinese Christians in Ningde county in Funing prefecture complained to British authorities that strict enforcement of the opium restrictions had been loosened since the arrival of a new county magistrate named Zhu Ding. According to the document, Zhu viewed the opium restrictions as an avenue to wealth through bribery and extortion, and some of his victims were Christians. As proof of their claims, the Christians enclosed a poppy leaf in the letter. They complained that the poppy had appeared in at least five locations within Ningde and that the flowers could be seen only ten *li* (a little over three miles) from Ningde City.[14]

Monitoring the progress of opium reform in central Yanping prefecture became virtually impossible after March 1915, when banditry broke out in Youxi county. Provincial authorities sent to restore order approached their task with such vigor that several Chinese converts of the MEC were executed—presumably by mistake—in the process. Despite official military action, the problem continued for months, and some American diplomats believed that the troublemakers had been followers of Su Yi, a bandit leader who had taken advantage of Huang Lian's rebellion in Xinghua to stage his own uprising in nearby Yongchun subprefecture. Hostilities died down by June 1915.[15]

The provincial military was in great demand in Fujian, as anti-tax, anti-state uprisings began to crop up all over the countryside in the summer of 1915. In Xinghua, even after Huang Lian and much of the local poppy crop were eliminated, the basic problem persisted—without opium-related reve-

---

14. For Chinese and English versions of the petition, dated Feb. 1915, see PRO, FO 228/2461, no. 42.

15. Pontius to Reinsch, 22 Mar., 3 May, 6 May, and 19 June 1915, all in USDS (1910–29), reel 14.

nue, the authorities were forced to increase taxes. Once again, salt was one of the commodities they selected. When the salt tax was increased in May 1915 for the second time since the Revolution of 1911, Xinghua erupted. In June 1915, the provincial government was forced to send several hundred salt police to prevent violence there.[16]

The increase in salt taxes also caused some violence in nearby Yongchun that same summer. Rioters destroyed the salt depot and the salt yamen, but swift and severe punishment by local troops squelched the outbreak. In addition, scattered bands of rebels still operated in Dehua county, despite the execution of their leader, Su Yi, on 27 April 1915.[17]

In the summer and fall of 1915, scattered outbreaks of banditry throughout the province kept Fujian's civil and military authorities busy. Most of the incidents were quickly resolved by military force. In the southeast, however, rebel leaders Chen Zongyi and Lin Jiafeng and others gathered followers from Yongchun in the fall and moved into areas near the cities of Xiamen and Quanzhou. The insurgents again targeted salt offices, wrecking four in Quanzhou during their raids.[18] In general, the northern part of the province remained relatively calm at first, with the exception of extensive banditry in the counties of Youxi and Jiangle (both in Yanping prefecture), thanks in part to the strategic positioning of government troops. In some locations, such as Liangjiang and Yongan counties, the military helped local residents establish volunteer anti-bandit militias. But by early 1916, several northern counties, particularly Youxi, Sha, Yongan, and Guihua (Yanping and northern Tingzhou prefectures), were also besieged by bandits.[19]

In 1915, Yuan Shikai announced his intention to establish a new dynasty on 1 January 1916, and the reaction in Fujian was mixed but calm.[20] In 1916, in the neighboring province of Guangdong, a warlord named Chen Jiongming (1878–1933), whose political views were very much in line with those of Sun Yatsen (and who had opposed Yuan Shikai in the Second Revolution), rose up in protest and began to establish an anti-Yuan base in Guangdong and southern Fujian. These developments worsened the political turmoil in Fu-

---

16. Soldiers were also sent to Fuding county for the same purpose (USDS [1910–29], reel 14, no. 39, Pontius to Reinsch, 19 June 1915).
17. Ibid., no. 49, Pontius to MacMurray, 18 Aug. 1915.
18. Ibid., no. 54, Pontius to MacMurray, 4 Oct. 1915.
19. Ibid., no. 57, Pontius to Reinsch, 28 Oct. 1915; no. 63, 7 Dec. 1915; and no. 75, 15 Mar. 1916.
20. Ibid., no. 59, Pontius to Reinsch, 6 Nov. 1915, and no. 64, Fuzhou to Reinsch, 10 Dec. 1915.

jian and hastened the province's descent into warlordism. Not long after Yuan Shikai died in June 1916, the strategically situated province of Fujian began to fragment as the conflict between the north and south accelerated and the absence of effective central control encouraged countless groups of bandits to terrify the countryside.

Upon receiving the news of Yuan's death, mutinous soldiers in Pucheng county (Jianning prefecture) formed bandit gangs that attacked the salt customs houses and even forced the local magistrate to hand over a sum of money at gunpoint. Other bandits terrorized local families, especially the wealthy.[21] Many of these bandit gangs called themselves the Black Money Society (Heiqian hui), and they extorted cash through intimidation, kidnapping, and other forms of violence.[22] The depredations of this particular group extended as far north as Luoyuan, Ningde, and the port of Santu'ao.[23]

Even in areas where the situation was stable enough to enforce the opium prohibition, it was clear that the successes of the suppression campaign had faded. In northeastern Gutian county in Fuzhou prefecture, a British missionary did not seem to recognize the problematic aspect of what he saw as a victory against opium: "One of the signs of progress in China is that the Kutien [Gutian] magistrate is preparing to build an orphanage and a home for destitute old women with money taken in fines for opium, which is now a prohibited article and is only sold by stealth."[24] Although this official's altruistic motives appeared laudable and the statement concerning the stigma of clandestine opium sales was encouraging, the efficacy of opium prohibition was questionable if enough fines had been collected to enable construction of these institutions.

In the southeast, clandestine opium smuggling flourished, and poppy cultivation resumed, stimulated by the end of legal imports and the chaotic political situation. In 1915, the British consul at Xiamen noted that although no poppies had appeared in that area yet, "there is, however, extensive smuggling of opium, morphia and cocaine for surreptitious use."[25] "During the years 1915, 1916, and 1917 large quantities of the drug [opium] were brought in from Formosa [Taiwan] and elsewhere, the bulk of which was landed on the

---

21. *IWCD* 36, no. 364 (Nov. 1916): 174.
22. CMS Fuhkien Mission, Original Incoming, 1900–34, (1918), folder no. 56.
23. IMC, *Decennial Reports, Santuao, 1912–1921*, p. 127.
24. *IWCD* 36, no. 362 (Sept. 1916): 146.
25. PRO, FO 228/2462, no. 14, Little to Jordan, 19 Aug. 1915.

seaboard beyond the reach of the customs."[26] In November 1916, it was rumored that a large amount of poppy was being sown in Tongan county, an area notorious for flouting opium restrictions since the late Qing. Troops were to be sent to the scene.[27]

As the Sino-British agreement officially expired in 1917 and with it the official Chinese suppression campaign, the situation in Fujian was unsettled and unpromising. Provincial efforts were unorganized and uneven, and complaints by foreigners and Chinese seemed to produce little result. Unfortunately, the situation was about to become even worse.

Civil War, Unification, and Opium

From late 1917 to 1922, the people and authorities in Fujian had little time to focus on the niceties of opium reform. The domination of Li Houji and the outbreak of civil war made opium suppression a dead letter and a low priority for provincial authorities. The civil war erupted in late 1917, after a political crisis over China's entry into World War I resulted in yet another dissolution of the Chinese Parliament. A number of former members of Parliament traveled south to Guangzhou, where they elected Sun Yatsen, who had returned from Japan after Yuan Shikai's death, head of a military government. He sent troops north into Fujian and set off a string of military confrontations. The troops from Guangzhou, led by Chen Jiongming and Xu Chongzhi, were referred to as the "Southerners" and soldiers from Fujian became the "Northerners." Each army claimed to represent the legitimate authority of the state. Violent clashes shook the countryside, and the frontline shifted constantly. One of the most visible casualties of the war was the opium suppression campaign.

Getting rid of opium during the warlord era required addressing the problems of consumption, cultivation, and distribution, just as it had in the late Qing and early Republic, but a new campaign also would have to contend with the handicap of a weak and unresponsive state at the national and provincial levels. At the same time, China's narcotic scene had broadened to include injectable morphine, cocaine, and a new compound called heroin. The proximity of Taiwan exacerbated the problem of Japanese smuggling. Transported in small fishing boats by Chinese merchants protected by Japa-

---

26. IMC, *Decennial Reports, Amoy, 1912–1921*, p. 153.
27. PRO, FO 228/2463, doc. 69, Little to Jordan, 8 Nov. 1916.

nese extraterritoriality, morphine was readily available in the many Japanese pharmacies scattered throughout the province.[28]

As the situation in the countryside of Fujian deteriorated, control of various regions of the province shifted hands repeatedly, and in many instances, poppy planting was encouraged as a means of raising needed revenue for military expenses. In some areas, local authorities set quotas for the acreage that needed to be planted in poppies and left it to gentry to negotiate the distribution of the crop among local farmers.[29] Fujian became a battlefield on which the forces of the north and south clashed in a struggle for dominance. Most of the conflicts took place along the province's waterways, the primary arteries of commerce and travel.[30] The proliferation of bandits compounded the misery of the people and made opium suppression virtually impossible. The following patchwork of anecdotes from the four corners of Fujian reveals the rapidity with which the opium restrictions collapsed and the opium economy resurfaced from 1917 to 1927.

During the warlord era, most of Fujian's poppy crop was still located in the traditional trouble spots along the coast. According to Chinese accounts, because of the constant need for revenues to offset military expenses, farmers in those regions were encouraged and even compelled to cultivate opium poppies. For example, in Fu'an county (Funing prefecture), warlords apparently forced farmers to plant poppies instead of rice and wheat in 1922 even after a devastating flood had decimated local food stores.[31] Farmers in Zhangpu county (Zhangzhou prefecture) were said to have planted poppies to pay the high land taxes imposed by warlords.[32] Local authorities also allegedly set a quota for poppy production and forced farmers in Shunchang county (Yanping prefecture) to meet it.[33] The need for revenue undoubtedly was the primary impetus behind the resurgence of poppy cultivation in Fujian, but whether farmers planted poppies under duress remains uncertain. Most Chinese sources insist that heavy taxes made lucrative cash crops such

---

28. *China Medical Journal* 33, no. 1 (Jan. 1919): 69.

29. USDS (1910–29), 893.114, reel 114, enclosure in no. 228, Hanson to Tenney, 28 Feb. 1920.

30. Quale, "The Mission Compound in Modern China," pp. 125–27.

31. Miao Xiaoning, "Fu'an renmin fankang yapian," p. 55. The poppy first reappeared in 1919, "apparently with official sanction," but then was eradicated for at least another couple of years (IMC, *Decennial Reports, Santuao, 1912–1921*, p. 130).

32. Ya Ji, "Yapian dui Zhangpu renmin de duhai," p. 29.

33. Xia and Ye, "Yapian zai Shunchang de duhai yu jinyan," p. 203.

as opium a regrettable necessity for otherwise unwilling Fujianese peasants.

Not surprisingly, much of the conflict and much of the illegal opium cultivation centered in Xinghua prefecture, strategically situated along the coast between Xiamen and Fuzhou and already infamous for Huang Lian's revolt. The ever-shifting frontlines of the civil war made for a tense and dangerous existence. In July 1918, an American Methodist missionary despaired, "We live in an atmosphere of rumor. Some people move from the walled cities into the country for protection. Others flee from the country to the City. Killing, plundering, burning are of daily occurrence."[34]

One of the few certainties was the profit to be made from opium. Another U.S. missionary reported alarming news about the resurgence of poppy planting in Xinghua:

There are thousands of acres of poppy. Some fields are just reaching full bloom. Many have just been planted. There is more of it in territory under the control of the southerners and their bandit allies, than in territory under control of the northerners, but there is a great deal of it in territory under the control of the latter.

It seems to me that it does little good for the Allies to protest against the sale of opium in ports such as Shanghai, when vast areas of the country are being given over to the production of the drug. Absolutely nothing is being done by either the North or the South to prevent the growing of poppy here.[35]

In a scene that recalled the tensions that gave rise to the earlier trouble in Xinghua, an American missionary reported that local farmers grew very agitated when an officer from the U.S. military attaché's office photographed the poppy fields, because they assumed he was a missionary. A local Chinese preacher quickly corrected their mistake.[36]

Although the revived poppy crop initially was alleged to have flourished under southern influence, an American missionary noted that after an emergency trip to Fuzhou to consult with provincial authorities, the Putian magistrate who had vigorously led the fight against opium changed his tactics and levied a tax on the poppies. The tax revenue was to be divided among the magistrate, northern troops, and the provincial government, with the lion's share going to the province.[37] The magistrate claimed that without the

---

34. MEC Archives, 73-43, folder 1183-6-2: 08, Cole to North, Xinghua, 27 July 1918.
35. USDS (1910–29), 893.114, reel 113, no. 28, Foochow to Secy. of State, enclosure no. 32, Hollister to Hanson, 27 Dec. 1818.
36. Ibid., reel 114, no. 55, Hanson to Reinsch, 13 Feb. 1919.
37. Ibid., enclosure in no. 85, Foochow to Secy. of State, 19 May 1919.

money, the northern troops might become "unmanageable."[38] Subsequent U.S. reports indicated that the magistrate took a very personal approach to the problem, visiting opium fields to assess the quality and quantity of the crop for tax purposes. Local farmers apparently were relieved that the eradication had ceased, since an opium harvest was their only hope of paying off the various fines and taxes. By spring 1919, more than 100,000 *mu* of land in Putian were planted in poppies.[39] However, despite the large poppy crop in the Xinghua area, taxes were so high that most local farmers reaped no profits, and by late 1919 many had fled the province altogether to seek work abroad. Soldiers terrorized and impoverished those who remained, extorting and plundering at will.[40]

Opium smoking also reappeared, and about 50 opium dens sprung up to serve the approximately 35,000 residents of Xinghua City. Each den paid a monthly license fee to the municipal authorities.[41] In order to encourage opium smoking, proprietors of opium dens paid a tax to ensure military protection for their business. Various forms of gambling sprung up under similar circumstances.[42]

Near Xinghua, poppies also began to appear in Yongchun subprefecture, allegedly under the orders of the southern military, led in that region by longtime Sun Yatsen supporter Xu Chongzhi,[43] a revolutionary leader in Fujian's military in 1911 and the officer who led Fujian into the short-lived Second Revolution of 1913. Under Xu, the southern military's demands for money terrorized and devastated the local populations, who tried to comply for fear of their lives. According to one American missionary in Yongchun: "Some have sold their houses and lands or have mortgaged them. Others have sold their children. On failing to pay the assessments the people are beaten and their houses are burned. Have heard of men selling their wives. Scarcely a gold or silver ornament is to be seen in those regions as all have been turned into money."[44] Under such circumstances, many farmers turned to poppies. The local magistrate, Zhu Jiantai, was himself an opium smoker

---

38. Ibid., no. 62, Foochow to Secy. of State, 9 May 1919.
39. Ibid., no. 110, Hanson to Reinsch, 5 June 1919.
40. Ibid., no. 202, Hanson to Tenney, 15 Dec. 1919.
41. Ibid., enclosure in no. 85, Foochow to Secy. of State, 9 May 1919.
42. Ibid., no. 222, Hanson to Tenney, 18 Feb. 1920.
43. Ibid., reel 114, no. 55, Hanson to Reinsch, 13 Feb. 1919. For biographical information on Xu, see Boorman, *Biographical Dictionary of Republican China*, 2: 124–26.
44. MEC Archives, 73-43, folder 1183-6-2: 08, Cole to North, 18 Oct. 1918.

and apparently oversaw the distribution of poppy seeds to local farmers. The southerners were driven out in early 1919, but equally rapacious bandits or corrupt officials often replaced them.[45]

Similar scenes unfolded in the northwestern prefecture of Shaowu in late 1919, as southern troops forced farmers to purchase and plant poppy seeds.[46] A proclamation from the local authorities, clandestinely torn down and translated by an American missionary, warned that animals were to be strictly contained and prevented from grazing in carefully tended poppy fields.[47]

When hostilities first erupted between Fujian and Guangdong provinces at the end of 1917, some farmers in southeastern Fujian were among the earliest to take advantage of the chaos to plant poppies. Soldiers from Guangdong occupied much of southeastern Fujian in 1918, and according to foreign customs officials, "an opium tax, called 'field tax' was openly collected by the Fukien military officials who declined to enforce the opium prohibition order (issued by the Fukien Military and Civil Governors) under the pretext that it was beyond their power." The farmers were said to have reaped enormous profits.[48]

The traditional poppy-growing county of Tongan also experienced a revival of this notorious crop, and in Hui'an, the opium situation became increasingly serious by 1918. A British missionary commented on conditions in Hui'an that year:

I am going into the district where much opium is being grown this year, [and] one spot where I was a couple of weeks ago was as thick with the deadly thing as we used to see it in the old days before the thing was tackled. Raw opium has dropped to a third of its price last year which means that there has been an enormous increase in the supply.... There is only one gleam of comfort, a number of Japanese merchants who had bought heavily at high prices last year & were hoping to make bigger profits were losing very heavily.[49]

By 1919, so much poppy was being cultivated in southern Fujian that the price for the domestic drug was almost ten times cheaper than it had been only two years earlier. Opium from southern Fujian had driven the foreign

---

45. USDS (1910–29), 893.114, reel 114, no. 55, Hanson to Reinsch, 13 Feb. 1919.
46. Ibid., reel 114, enclosure in no. 205, Hanson to Tenney, 30 Dec. 1919.
47. Ibid., enclosure in no. 197, Foochow to Secy. of State, 10 Mar. 1920.
48. IMC, *Decennial Reports, Amoy, 1912–1921*, pp. 153, 158.
49. LMS/CWM, Box 12—Correspondence-China-Fukien, 1916–19, folder 4, Brown to Hawkins, 27 Feb. 1919.

drug completely out of the local market and was secretly being transported to Hongkong and Shanghai, where it also sold briskly.⁵⁰ According to foreign customs officials in Fuzhou, "At present the criminal code provides the heavier penalty for the smoker and the lighter for the grower, which would seemingly indicate that there is no intention on the part of the law to kill the goose that lays the golden eggs."⁵¹

One consequence of increased poppy cultivation in the south was Xiamen's emergence as the hub for a lucrative, well-organized, and apparently officially sanctioned opium smuggling operation. According to a U.S. report, the raw drug was ferried to Xiamen, transferred to armed sampans, and transported to nearby water police stations to be stamped and taxed. The liquid opium was then prepared in the city for smoking and exported by boat to Fuzhou, Shanghai, Hongkong, Singapore, the Philippines, and even San Francisco. The prepared drug was sold under a number of brandnames; many were designated by the picture of an animal or plant such as Stork, Deer, Cock, Fir Tree and Deer, Two Peaches, Banyan and Heron, and Unicorn or a Chinese character such as the Happiness (Fu) brand. Apparently, the Cock brand was especially popular because it was alleged to be pure opium rather than an adulterated compound. Xiamen customs officials reported seizing more than a ton of prepared opium from September 1920 to March 1921, but this did not seem to slow the trade.⁵² The smuggling operation, fueled by triple cropping in some areas, continued to thrive as late as 1926.⁵³

In the north, where very little cultivation occurred and opium was much harder to obtain, inexpensive morphine pills became the narcotic of choice for chair-bearers and other manual laborers. Morphine was the key ingredient in a number of patent medicines that flooded the market. Shanghai and Japan were believed to be the source of many of these pills. The U.S. consul at Fuzhou reported that a group of northern troops arriving in Yanping in January 1919 unsuccessfully tried to buy morphine from a local missionary hospital, and he noted, "Each had his own Japanese hypodermic syringe with him." What little opium was for sale in this part of the province was said to have been transported from Taiwan and Japan.⁵⁴

---

50. IMC, *Decennial Reports, Amoy, 1912–1921*, pp. 153–54.
51. IMC, *Decennial Reports, Foochow, 1912–1921*, p. 140.
52. USDS (1910–29), 893.114, reel 114, unnumbered dispatch, Carleton to Secy. of State, 30 Apr. 1921.
53. Ibid., reel 115, unnumbered dispatch, Webber to Secy. of State, 10 Feb. 1926.
54. Ibid., reel 114, no. 55, Hanson to Reinsch, 13 Feb. 1919.

No real effort at suppression could be undertaken without the express permission of the authorities. Even then, solutions were temporary, and the realities of Fujianese politics often derailed the best intentions. American diplomats reported that the authorities in Beijing had ordered Li Houji to suppress opium throughout Fujian, but the complex and often violent relationship between northerners, southerners, and local bandit gangs rendered those orders moot. Southern troops, for example, refused to allow northern soldiers to attack bandits in territory claimed by the south.[55]

In many areas, a brief respite from the violent civil war and coerced opium farming occurred in 1920 and 1921 when Sun Yatsen ordered Xu Chongzhi and Chen Jiongming and their troops out of Fujian and back to Guangdong province. In Xinghua, an energetic military officer forcibly destroyed poppy fields. However, a serious bandit problem in Xianyou county put suppression efforts on hold there, and Xianyou farmers conducted a lucrative overland opium trade with dealers in Fuzhou.[56] Further north, in Santu'ao, 1921 marked the arrival of an inspector sent by the provincial head of opium suppression (*jinyan dayuan*), who allowed local officials to shut down illegal opium shops that had been run by Chinese from Taiwan for years.[57] However, by 1922, the convoluted politics of the south forced Xu and his men back into Fujian, where he occupied Fuzhou in the fall of that year. Xu oversaw the ouster of Li Houji in January 1923, ending Li's domination of provincial politics.[58] After Li's departure, Fujian was run by a succession of military men, each of whom claimed to support the notion of opium suppression but did little more than issue a series of proclamations condemning the drug.

The years 1923–24 were rife with violence directly related to the demands of local militarists in the Fujian countryside. An IAOA investigation claimed that in some areas, "Predecessors of the present Generals had collected land taxes three years in advance, and the only means left for raising necessary funds by the present incumbents was either to collect one or two further years of land taxes, or impose one special tax which could only be raised by opium

---

55. Ibid., reel 113, no. 28, Foochow to Secy. of State, enclosure no. 32, Hollister to Hanson, 27 Dec. 1818.
56. Ibid., reel 113, no. 308, Hanson to Secy. of State, 28 Feb. 1921.
57. IMC, *Decennial Reports, Santuao, 1912–1921*, pp. 129–30.
58. Boorman, *Biographical Dictionary of Republican China*, 2: 125, 381.

cultivation."⁵⁹ Apparently, the decision to impose the opium levy resulted in widespread resistance, although a petition from one group of Chinese Christians in Hui'an county indicated that a number of "wicked people of Huian ... [were] in league with the military officers and the poppy tax collector" in forcing poppy cultivation and the payment of a very high "field tax."⁶⁰ Again from the IAOA: "Riots have been frequent and in several places numbers of peasants have been shot down and villages burnt." The situation became particularly volatile in Hui'an, where an initial victory by peasant forces prompted a brutal retaliation from soldiers, who torched and massacred an entire village. Despite protests from Chinese and foreign anti-opium organizations, the problem persisted. The plight of the farmers was exacerbated by a bumper harvest of opium that drove the price of the drug down and diminished anticipated profits.⁶¹ Local militarists in Yanping encouraged planting by posting proclamations that provided farmers with detailed instructions for sowing and nurturing poppy plants; the instructions were illustrated, so that even the illiterate had no excuse for noncompliance.⁶²

Monopolies had always been a controversial strategy in China's opium suppression movement because in dishonest hands, they were designed more to exploit the trade than to control it. Local warlords in Xiamen outraged opium reformers by establishing an open monopoly on the drug on 1 February 1924, the term "open" reflecting the very public nature of the arrangement.⁶³ Ostensibly, the Special Bureau, as the monopoly was called, was to deal with opium suppression and halt illicit sales.⁶⁴ All sales and cultivation of opium were regulated by the monopoly, and the profits were said to be enormous. Similar arrangements were reported in Guangzhou and Jiangxi province. As an IAOA member commented in the group's

---

59. USDS (1910–29), 893.114, reel 115, *Annual Report of the International Anti-Opium Association, Peking* 4, no. 1 (1924), and "Opium Cultivation and Traffic in China: An Investigation in 1923–4 by the International Anti-Opium Association, Peking," pp. 23–24.

60. Ibid., reel 115, enclosure in no. 274, Carleton to Beijing, 17 Jan. 1924.

61. Ibid., *Annual Report of the International Anti-Opium Association, Peking* 4, no. 1 (1924), and "Opium Cultivation and Traffic in China: An Investigation in 1923–4 by the International Anti-Opium Association, Peking," pp. 23–24.

62. Ibid., reel 115, enclosures in no. 128, Fuzhou to Beijing, 29 Dec. 1923.

63. Ibid., *Annual Report of the International Anti-Opium Association, Peking* 4, no. 1 (1924), and "Opium Cultivation and Traffic in China: An Investigation in 1923–4 by the International Anti-Opium Association, Peking," p. 24. See also Slack, *Opium, State, and Society*, pp. 68–69.

64. Ibid., reel 115, enclosure in no. 277, Carleton to Beijing, 31 Jan. 1924.

Annual Report, "If these open monopolies gave the slightest hint that restriction was intended much might be said in their favour but it is not so, their sole object is to more effectively secure the revenues and to centralize their possession."[65] That conclusion was borne out by later observations that the Special Bureau freely issued inexpensive licenses for opium dens, presumably to encourage smoking.[66]

By the end of 1926, the Northern Expedition had taken Fuzhou, ushering in a new central state that would face an opium problem as bad if not worse than that confronted by the deposed Qing dynasty. In 1927, the American consul in Fuzhou submitted a detailed report on the opium situation in north Fujian in which he stated that although cultivation was not as extensive as in the south, several areas produced significant poppy harvests. Not surprisingly, the most productive region was Xinghua, followed by Funing prefecture. Just as in the south, a high tax imposed on farmers prompted many to grow poppies, and in one instance that particularly outraged the missionary informant, local farmers were ordered to plant poppies and then fined for violating the ban on opium cultivation. Much of the revenue allegedly funded the provincial navy.[67] A U.S. missionary submitted further statistics gathered by his compatriots in north Fujian that revealed some poppies in all counties, extensive cultivation (estimated at more than 40 percent of "suitable" land) in five counties, and the spread of smoking to all strata of society. Local officials were said to encourage these developments, and the tax revenue apparently was considerable.[68]

Opium and the Public Sphere, 1914–1927

No movement can be carried through successfully unless backed by public opinion.[69]

One of the most startling phenomena in the early Republican era was the way in which the strengthening of the existing anti-opium discourse coincided with the dramatic deterioration of opium control.[70]

---

65. Ibid., *Annual Report of the International Anti-Opium Association, Peking* 4, no. 1 (1924), and "Opium Cultivation and Traffic in China: An Investigation in 1923-4 by the International Anti-Opium Association, Peking," p. 24.
66. Ibid., reel 115, no. 393, Webber to Secy. of State, 20 Aug. 1925.
67. Ibid., enclosure in no. 36, Fuzhou to Beijing, 10 May 1928.
68. Ibid., no. 36, Fuzhou to Beijing, 10 May 1928.
69. Excerpt from *North-China Daily News*, 3 Oct. 1919, reprinted in *China Medical Journal* 33, no. 6 (Nov. 1919): 584.

The depressing trajectory of Fujian's opium economy from 1914 to 1927 followed the twisted course of Chinese politics and was alleviated only in part by the emergence of Chinese and international organizations dedicated to narcotics control. Despite the discouraging situation, those organizations formed a vocal anti-opium lobby inside and outside China that continued to agitate for an end to the drug trade. Warlord-era opium reformers occupied a public political space in which they staged public meetings against opium and tried to generate anti-opium sentiment, much like their predecessors. However, instead of symbolizing the unity of officials and unofficial reformers, those gatherings, far more low-key than in the late Qing, now signified implicit or explicit public protests against the corruption or ineffectiveness of the state. Reformers now worked to spark a movement rather than to implement a campaign. The state, as represented by the authorities in Fuzhou and Beijing, verbally supported a policy of opium suppression and felt compelled by that policy to meet with and attempt to appease the reformers. In reality, military exigencies trumped nationalistic rhetoric. Unofficial reform groups continued to monitor the discouraging revival of Fujian's opium economy, but over time they no longer participated actively in the enforcement of opium suppression. Their regulatory role and the police powers that had come with it were absorbed by a militarized and fragmented state interested more in profiting from opium than in suppressing it.

The authorities' reluctance to allow groups like those involved in opium reform to exercise the police powers they had enjoyed in the past sprung in part from the volatility of the public political space, which had become a space in which debate and outright hostility toward the state was expressed. This was a time of great intellectual excitement in China, and the nationalistic sentiment that sparked the May Fourth movement and encompassed calls for opium suppression did not bypass Fujian. British missionaries reported that enraged students in Fuzhou planned a general strike in June 1919, but Li Houji thwarted their plans by closing government schools. Many shopkeepers closed their doors for two days in sympathy, and students from government and mission schools in the city staged demonstrations and boycotts to protest Japanese imperialism and formed a student league.[71] The strikes continued into 1920 and broadened to include members of the

---

70. Zhou Yongming, *Anti-Drug Crusades in Twentieth-Century China*, p. 40.

71. CMS Fuhkien Mission, Original Incoming 1900-1934, (1919) folder, no. 80, 18 June, and no. 139, 10 Oct.

YMCA, many of whom had been involved in opium reform. The YMCA group suffered casualties when they were attacked and beaten by Japanese subjects in response to one of the boycotts of Japanese goods. Li shut down the league headquarters and forbade publications by the group, but Fuzhou students, consumed by a "great spirit of unrest," protested.[72] Merchant organizations, such as the Support National Goods Society (Guohuo weichi hui) in Santu'ao, also supported a boycott of Japanese goods.[73] Although these protests were not tied directly to the suppression movement, opium reform was an integral part of twentieth-century nationalism, and the Japanese role in narcotics smuggling was well known.

The Fujian branch of the IAOA met for the first time in November 1919, and its mixed foreign and Chinese membership devoted their efforts to monitoring the alarming revival of the opium economy and lobbying for state action against it. The Fujian IAOA's first step was to assess the nature and dimensions of the province's opium problem. It collected and coordinated pieces of evidence such as photographs of poppy fields and local proclamations announcing poppy taxes and sent them to the provincial government. Although the Fujian IAOA did represent the endurance of anti-opium sentiment among progressive elites and Christians, its clout was limited. Li Houji and even authorities in Beijing felt it politically expedient to meet and negotiate with members and to offer a clear show of support, but Li either had no real intention of halting a profitable scheme or lacked the ability to do so. Apparently, the organization reached an impasse fairly early on because its Chinese members (many of whom worked for the provincial government) were loathe to challenge Li Houji. The reluctance of these reform-minded officials was a far cry from the supervisory role played by the official opium suppression bureaucracy in its heyday in the late Qing/early Republic. Although it continued to meet, it seemed to accomplish little.[74]

However, the IAOA did not represent all the Chinese voices protesting the opium economy. In south Fujian, the recall of southern troops in 1920 gave anti-opium activists there a chance to re-emerge and to form a group of their own, independent of the IAOA, despite the region's political instability.

---

72. Ibid., (1920) folder, no. 8 (n.d.); Dunch, *Fuzhou Protestants and the Making of a Modern China*, p. 188.

73. IMC, *Decennial Reports, Santuao, 1912–1921*, p. 128.

74. USDS (1910–29), 893.114, reel 114, enclosure in no. 255, Price to Secy. of State, 4 Nov. 1920.

In Xiamen, local progressive reformers established the Southern Fujian Poppy Prohibition Association (Minnan yanmiao jinzhong hui; SFPPA) in September of that year. According to one foreign customs official, however, "The efforts of this association were doomed to failure through lack of official support, and the poppy was again extensively grown." The following year saw a temporary reversal of this gloomy scenario when official-military cooperation brought the destruction of many of the region's poppy fields.[75]

The SFPPA did not shy from the considerable challenge, however, and the power of its leader's personality and pocketbook enabled the group unusual access to the provincial administration. The energetic and reform-minded president of the SFPPA, Chen Jiageng (1874–1961), was also the founder of Xiamen University and a man described as an "Amoy millionaire-philanthropist."[76] One of Chen's first actions after founding the SFPPA was to organize a meeting with Li Houji. Representatives of the Fujian IAOA and a foreign member of the YMCA accompanied Chen, and the delegation argued forcefully for action against the growing opium menace. In response, Li apparently not only promised the group that he would support their efforts by prohibiting the sowing of poppy seeds but also gave them permission to punish officials who disobeyed. Li subsequently issued twelve "Provisional Regulations Governing Prohibition of Poppy Cultivation," which spelled out his strategy for reform. However, U.S. diplomats noted that publicity and enforcement of the new regulations focused primarily on urban areas, where few poppies were planted. It is unlikely that regional military leaders would permit local reformers to exercise such powers. Li's office was to coordinate the campaign, which was to rely heavily on persuading farmers to submit written guarantees that they would not plant poppies. If local leaders, officials, and the cadre of inspectors appointed by Li found persuasion inadequate, then they were to request military assistance from whatever soldiers were in the area. Poppy fields were to be planted with edible grains, a measure that Li hoped would ward off famine such as that ravaging the northern provinces in the wake of a typhoon. Local circuit intendants, the commissioner of industry, and the Opium Prohibition Bureau were also involved in monitoring and enforcing the policy.[77]

---

75. IMC, *Decennial Reports, Amoy, 1912–1921*, pp. 153–54.
76. Chen was a member of the Tongmenghui during the Revolution of 1911.
77. USDS (1910–29), 893.114, reel 114, enclosure in no. 350, Peking to Secy. of State, 19 Nov. 1920, and no. 255, Price to Secy. of State, 4 Nov. 1920.

The Collapse of the Crusade, 1914–1927

The results of Li's new policy were less than impressive. The American consulate at Xiamen claimed, on the basis of reports from foreign missionaries, that the poppy crop was even larger in 1920 than in 1919.[78] However, those reports also indicated that public opinion was strongly against the drug. Chen Jiageng's SFPPA stoked and responded to that sentiment by sending telegrams of protest to Li Houji as well as to the Chinese president, Beijing newspapers, and the IAOA's Beijing headquarters.[79] Another meeting with Li Houji resulted in Li's admission that the problem continued despite his commands and produced yet another round of ineffectual orders and proclamations. One local military commander named Wu Wei took it upon himself to write to various foreign legations to complain that one of Li's generals posted to the Xinghua area had ordered the locals to sow poppy seeds and then, along with a number of "bad gentry," had collected a tax on those fields. American diplomats confirmed the scheme, but questioned Wu's motivations and the targets of his accusations.[80]

By 1920–21, Fujian's once-respected opium suppression campaign had become the target of pointed remarks by foreign observers. The official Opium Prohibition Bureau, whose employees were appointed and paid by the provincial government, was moribund. According to a U.S. diplomat, "In fact, many sinister stories have been current in Foochow tending to show that the Bureau used its nominal official status to extort squeeze from wealthy residents of Foochow on the threat of discovering opium on their premises."[81]

The decline of the venerable Fujian Anti-Opium Society also invited criticism. One foreign customs official remarked, "The Anti-Opium Society still exists, but if all one hears is true it would appear to be a case of *quis custodiat custodes*.[82] Certainly, the Society has fallen into disrepute of recent years, and it is rumoured that much blackmail is levied in its name."[83] The police were plagued by a similar trend. "The police system inaugurated in 1909 still continues, but the men are slipshod in appearance and spend more

---

78. Ibid., enclosure in no. 517, Peking to Secy. of State, 2 Dec. 1920. As additional evidence, he also cited an increase in the importation of beancake, a common fertilizer for opium.
79. Ibid.
80. Ibid., enclosure in no. 332, Foochow to Secy. of State, 15 Apr. 1921.
81. Ibid., enclosure in no. 255, Price to Secy. of State, 4 Nov. 1920.
82. "Who will guard the guardians themselves?" Thanks to the Union College classicists—Scott Scullion, Sarah Mace, and Christie Sorum—for their help with a quick and accurate translation and for correcting the misspelling of the original.
83. IMC, *Decennial Reports, Foochow, 1912–1921*, p. 140.

of their time sitting in shops than on their beat. At night few are to be seen."[84] The more reputable members of the progressive elite seemed to believe that their best chance of success lay in eschewing grassroots activism for higher-level lobbying. That choice was certainly less risky in the highly charged political climate.

Some reformers outside the big cities worked toward the goal of reform clandestinely for fear of military retribution. A secret organization in Nan'an county in Quanzhou prefecture petitioned the Fujian branch of the IAOA in mid-1921 for help in combating official corruption and the flagrant violation of anti-opium regulations. The petition alleged that despite the prominent posting of Li Houji's anti-cultivation proclamations, military officials "secretly ordered the villagers to sow the [poppy] seeds without delay, telling them that no matter whether the poppy is grown or not, the tax would have to be paid just the same." An intimidating delegation from the local Opium Tax office (established as a punitive organization), the Salt Gabelle, and several military men collected the tax. The petitioners complained of extortion, the shameful mistreatment of a local schoolmaster who attempted to intervene on behalf of a local clan, and recent attempts by local powerholders to force residents to open opium dens and engage in other forms of trafficking that could then be taxed heavily.[85] The identities of the organization's members are unknown, although their familiarity with the local administration and their particular outrage at the detention of a prominent local educator leads one to believe that they were gentry reformers. What is notable is not only their strong opposition to compulsory poppy cultivation and their implicit recognition of the authority of groups such as the Fujian IAOA and the SFPPA but also their inability to participate publicly in suppression activities ostensibly promoted by the provincial government.

The increasing autonomy and oppositional tone of the public political space during the warlord years was a profound departure from the late Qing/early Republican opium suppression campaigns, but when the state made occasional attempts to suppress the drug, it encountered some striking similarities with those earlier campaigns. The most obvious was the persistent link between salt and opium, a connection that has been noted at many points in this volume, particularly in the context of Huang Lian's revolt. The

---

84. Ibid., p. 144.
85. USDS (1910–29), 893.114, reel 114, no. 48, enclosure in Carleton to Secy. of State, 23 June 1921.

key problem that surfaced for the state was that salt taxes had to be raised to make up for the loss of revenue from the opium trade; the state then had to deal with the popular dissatisfaction that arose in response. The supreme irony is that Fujian's finances were now managed by none other than Lin Bingzhang, whose financial acumen now was deemed more valuable to the state than his genealogy and symbolic clout.

In 1916, Lin Bingzhang was appointed head of the Fujian Provincial Department of Finance (Fujian caizhengting) and the Fujian Water Conservancy Bureau (Fujian shuiliju); he served in those offices for several years until he took over the administration of the provincial maritime customs.[86] Lin, Chen Peikun—another leading opium reformer—and Liu Hongshou came to be known as the "three heroes of Fujian finance" (*Fujian licai sanjie*). Their work on opium suppression merits only passing mention in one volume of biographical sketches.[87]

However, Lin was not ignorant of or uninvolved with Fujian's opium problem, and on 29 January 1921, he was elected vice chair of the Fuzhou Branch of the IAOA. His name apparently did not carry the same influence internationally as it did among his fellow Fujianese, as evidenced by the election of Bishop J. D. D. Hind, head of the CMS in Fuzhou, as the association's chair. A letter from U.S. consul G. C. Hanson at Fuzhou noted that the foreign members of the Fuzhou IAOA were determined not to allow Lin to lead the group because Lin "could dominate the gathering and bring about the election of his friends, whom the missionaries distrusted." Hanson did not elaborate on the nature of their distrust. In stark contrast to the importance in foreign eyes of Lin's symbolic leadership of Fujian's Qing dynasty suppression campaign, Hanson referred to Lin only as "a prominent Chinese official," with no indication that the Lin name had any other significance. Unlike the flamboyant and very public ceremonies of years past, the annual meeting at which Lin was elected attracted only about a hundred people.[88]

On 20 March 1921, a more dramatic, spontaneous, and very public attempt to organize popular opinion and provincial policy against the drug unfolded in a crowded public garden in Fuzhou. There, Chen Aitao called for

---

86. Wu Jiaqiong, "Lin Bingzhang shengping gaishu," p. 102.
87. Liu Decheng and Zhou Xianying, *Fujian mingren cidian*, pp. 207, 212.
88. USDS (1910–29), 893.114, reel 114, no. 319, Hanson to Secy. of State, 19 Mar. 1921. The missionaries apparently urged Hanson himself to run for office, but he refused to be associated with the group because it might hamper his ability to negotiate with the provincial authorities.

the formation of the Fujian Self-Governing Anti-Opium Relief Society (Fujian zizhi jinyan xieji hui), a group that would carefully coordinate the rationing of government-grown opium to registered addicts. All other smoking and poppy cultivation would be forbidden. To demonstrate his own sincerity and commitment, Chen ended what U.S. consul Hanson termed his "harangue" by slicing his own finger. Chen was rumored to have petitioned Li Houji for permission to establish the society, but Hanson deemed the plan impractical in large part because of likely British objections to any legalized poppy cultivation and predicted that Li would not allow the society to organize.[89] Unfortunately, neither Chen's background nor the fate of his proposed reform group is known. However, his actions do emphasize the atmosphere of protest in the public political space.

Despite their inability to compel Li Houji to halt the resurgence of the provincial opium economy, Fujian's anti-opium organizations, in conjunction with diplomatic protests from Great Britain and the United States, apparently succeeded in pushing the Beijing government to take some action on occasion. In November 1921, a Quanzhou native named Wang Dazhen was appointed special high commissioner of the central government for the investigation of opium suppression in Fujian, Anhui, and Hubei and charged with bringing the situation under control. Wang met with the U.S. consulate in Xiamen, who viewed the new initiative hopefully, but with a skepticism born of past experience. Apparently, Wang's predecessor, his own elder brother, had embarked on a similar tour of south Fujian the previous year and had been able to file a positive report because his visit did not coincide with the poppy-growing season.[90] Wang Dazhen had a staff of several dozen assistants and inspectors, but his job was to monitor suppression efforts while the duties of enforcement and punishment remained with local authorities under the auspices of Li Houji.[91] The Fujian opium reform organizations and the British apparently had tried unsuccessfully to get the Chinese to agree to having a British observer accompany Wang on his rounds.[92] When Wang reported back to the U.S. consulate in February 1922

---

89. Ibid., no. 326, Hanson to Secy. of State, 4 Apr. 1921.

90. Chen Jiageng insisted that Wang and his brother, Wang Daheng, who had served in the same position the previous year and had distinguished himself for corruption, could not be trusted (ibid., no. 76, Carleton to Secy. of State, 3 Nov. 1921).

91. Ibid., no. 62, Carleton to Secy. of State, 10 Sept. 1921, no. 81, Carleton to Secy. of State, 16 Nov. 1921, and no. 431, Carleton to Secy. of State, 8 Nov. 1921.

92. Ibid., no. 405, Foochow to Secy. of State, 21 Sept. 1921.

after his tour of Fujian, he noted progress in the south and no poppies in the north. Foreign observers were dismayed at his upbeat assessment of the conditions in the north, and Wang admitted to the American consul that his commission dealt solely with poppy growing, which was not prevalent in the north, and not with the trafficking that plagued that region.[93]

From 1922 until the founding of the Nationalist government in 1927, the Fujian IAOA, other unofficial reform groups, and unaffiliated foreign missionaries and diplomats focused their energies on calling Chinese and international attention to a number of practices that arose as a result of Fujian's revived opium economy. First, they vehemently objected to any Chinese scheme that purported to control the opium trade through taxation and denounced this strategy as a façade for extortion or the establishment of a legal opium monopoly. They also continued to protest the levying of exorbitant land taxes and other more direct methods of forcing farmers to plant opium poppies.

Local revenue-raising schemes that might compel Chinese Christians to compromise their beliefs by planting poppies deeply disturbed foreigners and reform groups with a Christian affiliation.[94] American consular officials received dozens of desperate letters from missionaries and Chinese Christian congregations complaining that local military authorities did not respect Christian objections to opium. In Xinghua, Christians who attempted to sidestep the dilemma by promising to fulfill their tax quota while refusing to plant poppies were threatened with arrest. Military authorities apparently viewed Christian resistance as a dangerous precedent that might encourage other forms of dissent or compromise—not without reason, apparently. In Fuding county in Fuzhou prefecture, a Chinese preacher who negotiated a settlement between his flock and local troops was arrested when he was caught trying to convince non-Christians to defy the planting order.[95]

The IAOA and its branch in Fujian continued to be forceful voices for suppression, and the authorities in Beijing and Fuzhou frequently met with the representatives of the anti-opium group and responded to their protests with politeness and promises. In fall 1922, the Beijing government appointed another opium prohibition commissioner for Fujian and Anhui provinces.

---

93. Ibid., no. 9, Price to Secy. of State, 13 Mar. 1922.
94. This complaint was echoed in dozens of letters from missionaries and Chinese Christian congregations that were included in the correspondence between American consular officers in Fujian and the secretary of state in Washington, D.C.; see ibid., reel 115.
95. Ibid., enclosures in no. 128, Fuzhou to Beijing, 29 Dec. 1923.

The officer took up residence in Xiamen and issued a set of twelve instructions to govern the suppression policy. His approach relied on many methods that had been attempted previously—cooperation between local officials and reformers, threats of punishment for apathetic or corrupt officials, mutual responsibility systems for pressuring farmers to cease planting poppies—all of which were to be funded by fines collected on violators of the restrictions. The Fujian IAOA was responsible for publicizing the campaign by posting proclamations and delivering public lectures.[96]

Chinese reformers formed two national organizations—the Anti-Narcotics Commission (Judu weiyuanhui; ANC) and the National Anti-Opium Association (Zhonghua guomin judu hui; NAOA)—that sought to defend China's interests at international meetings on narcotics, collect accurate data on China's opium problem, and facilitate the dissemination of IAOA propaganda. Publicity was the primary function of the ANC, a Christian group founded on 4 June 1923 that was well equipped to handle the work of translation. The Chinese Christians and foreign missionaries who constituted the bulk of the ANC's membership also sought to compile additional reports and inspire public activism. The NAOA, established on 5 August 1924, worked closely with the ANC and the ANC's parent organization, the National Christian Council of China (NCC). Although many of the NAOA's and ANC's members were not Christians, both of these groups relied heavily on Christian activists and professed a strong nationalistic motivation.[97] These organizations were forced to construct their goals around the reality of a public space for political activism substantially different from that in which groups like the Fujian Anti-Opium Society had operated. Now, state support was nominal at best. However, even if provincial authorities in Fujian were sincere about their desire to combat the revived opium economy after the ouster of Li Houji, and that is a questionable assumption, local militarists often foiled their plans. In Xinghua, for example, outspoken Chinese reformers were silenced by a military ban in late 1923 on telegrams that mentioned opium.[98]

---

96. Ibid., no. 176, Carleton to Secy. of State, 23 Sept. 1922.
97. Slack, *Opium, State, and Society*, pp. 54–58. Slack (p. 251) also asserts that the NAOA "provided Chinese Christians with an important tributary into the mainstream of Chinese nationalism."
98. USDS (1910–29), 893.114, reel 115, enclosures in no. 128, Fuzhou to Beijing, 29 Dec. 1923.

Despite state discouragement, in October 1923, students from Fuzhou area colleges staged a large anti-opium demonstration (apparently not associated with the IAOA) that the IAOA *Annual Report* claimed "more by good luck than good management escaped conflict with the troops, although the students' office was fired on later in the day." The students apparently distributed tracts that linked the military to the revival of the opium economy in no uncertain terms, and the IAOA blamed their intemperate language for prompting local authorities to ban the visiting head of the NCC from addressing a public gathering.[99] The Fujian Provincial Assembly also continued to push for opium reform, but with little effect.[100]

International gatherings to discuss global narcotics issues provided more sympathetic forums in which to highlight the unwelcome revival of China's opium problem, as well as to discuss and design efforts to address that problem. These meetings also revealed the troubling extent of China's postrevolutionary opium economy and the degree to which the public political space for anti-opium activism had to exist in opposition to the state. The League of Nations organized the most significant such meeting during this time period; under its auspices, the Geneva Opium Conferences met from November 1924 to February 1925. The NAOA was organized in August 1924 specifically to provide a nongovernmental delegation to the Geneva Opium Conferences (the Chinese government sent a separate official delegation).[101]

As a prelude to that meeting, the U.S. consul at Xiamen reported in October 1924 that "a movement to stamp out the use of opium and other narcotics in this county has been started in Amoy by some of the responsible citizens and prominent organizations." The group had organized a public demonstration on 26 September and distributed anti-opium tracts that condemned the drug for damaging China's international reputation. The tracts further warned that if China proved unable to vanquish the perceived opium problem, "we will be called into account by the International Anti-Opium Association and we shall gain no recognition as a power in our international relations." In an attempt to elicit national attention and support for the crusade, the NAOA designated the last Sunday in September "Anti-Opium Day." A five-person committee consisting of the Chinese secretary for the

---

99. Ibid., *Annual Report of the IAOA* 4, no. 1 (1924), pp. 9, 14.
100. Ibid., Beijing to Fuzhou, 20 Nov. 1923.
101. Slack, *Opium, State, and Society*, p. 251.

local YMCA, a teacher, two Chinese Christian preachers, and a teacher/journalist led the organization.[102]

Even before the founding of the Nanjing regime, Nationalist Party leaders had professed strong support for the elimination of opium as part of their patriotic agenda. Sun Yatsen had revealed his virulent opposition to opium as early as 1889, and after the revolution, Sun's antipathy to the drug was manifested in several laws against smoking. He also agitated for the end of Indian opium imports. "Imitating Lin Zexu's letter to Queen Victoria, Sun's May 1912 correspondence to Whitehall titled 'A Letter to the People of England on the Sovereignty of Opium Prohibition' argued that all of China's prohibition work would be in vain unless Indian imports were simultaneously curtailed."[103] For the Nationalist Party, however, the most important statement of Sun's anti-opium sentiment was immortalized in a 1924 newspaper interview that came to be known as Sun's Anti-Opium Will (*judu yixun*). Through this document, Sun in many ways supplanted Lin Zexu as the symbol of China's commitment to opium suppression and the representative of the link between patriotism and opium suppression. However, "despite his commitment to an opium-free China, even Sun Yatsen could not ignore the fiscal realities of the times," and he presided over the establishment of an opium monopoly in Guangzhou in January 1924.[104] Not surprisingly, when the Nationalist Party established a government in Nanjing in 1927, Chiang Kaishek took up the mantle of Sun Yatsen and publicly committed himself to opium suppression. But he, too, fell victim to the need for revenue, and the Nationalist policy became what Edward Slack terms, "de jure prohibition and de facto monopoly."[105]

A decade after the implementation of the Sino-British opium agreement, the poppy was again extensively cultivated in Fujian. According to reports included in a survey ordered by the French government, more than 70,000 *mu* of poppies were planted in southern Fujian, 50,000 in Xinghua alone.[106] The French consul in Fuzhou reported that in 1927 the president of the Fujianese government named a committee to repress the cultivation of opium

---

102. USDS (1910–29), 893.114, reel 115, unnumbered dispatch from Xiamen, 3 Oct. 1924; Slack, *Opium, State, and Society*, pp. 61–62.
103. Slack, *Opium, State, and Society*, pp. 70–71.
104. Ibid., pp. 71–72.
105. Ibid., p. 87.
106. MAE/Nantes, Pekin no. 158, Soulange-Teissier to Cosme, 16 Oct. 1928.

and to close opium dens in the province. That committee consisted of provincial officials and other elite reformers who faced a task perhaps more daunting than that tackled by their predecessors in the late Qing. One of those men was a holdover from the earlier fight. Lin Yushi, a member of the Nationalist Party, was one of the two men elected to serve as head of the Fujian Anti-Opium Society after the Revolution of 1911.[107] The other leaders of Fujian's anti-opium campaign had disappeared. Chen Peikun was deeply involved in provincial administration. Chen Nengguang left the province for Shanghai not long after Fujian was closed to Indian opium imports and took a job there with the postal service.[108]

The war against opium was not over, but one stage of the battle had concluded. And as it tapered off, the public political space in which much of the fighting had taken place was transformed from a place in which reformist elites carefully choreographed public opinion in conjunction with state policy to a more tumultuous, more autonomous, and more dangerous forum for anti-state protest and what can only be termed an anti-opium movement. Many of the older elite reformers, some of whom retained official positions, continued their vocal opposition to opium from the relative safety of national and international reform organizations; this left the space open for students and other activists with less prestigious pedigrees and fewer, if any, ties to the state.

The Ignominious End of the Crusade

From the death of Yuan Shikai until the ascension of Chiang Kaishek and beyond, China's national and provincial authorities derived legitimacy from their military power, and revenues generated from taxes on poppy cultivation and opium sales helped sustain that power. The remnants of the old opium suppression campaign and the seeds of the new crusade now took place in a public sphere where state support was at best nominal and often nonexistent. Without state sanction, the police powers that had previously accrued to elite reformers disappeared, and their partnership with local officials grew tenuous or dissolved. Elite activists responded by joining anti-opium groups whose functions were confined to lobbying for the end of forced cultivation of opium under warlord rule (and later under the Japanese)

---

107. Ibid.
108. *Fuzhou Meiyimei nianhui shi*, p. 90.

and attempting to monitor the deteriorating situation within China. As China's opium economy revived, younger and less traditionally "respectable" opium reformers staked out a position for themselves in a space that was increasingly autonomous from the state and in opposition to it. The nature of imperialist involvement and the perception of that involvement also changed after the collapse of the new Republic. Chinese reformers and officials had chafed at the obstacles placed in China's path by the British in the early stages of the campaign, but once the terms of the agreement had been fulfilled and the British possessed no real leverage, the Chinese were free to deal with opium within their borders at their own pace and on their own terms. International opprobrium could—and did—greet any evidence of Chinese backsliding, but the British were no longer politically capable of wielding the threat of resuming Indian opium exports to China.

After 1917, conditions in Fujian degenerated rapidly. Civil war between the northern troops loyal to Beijing and southerners fighting for the Nationalist cause raged in Fujian's countryside from 1918 to 1922, and the depredations of local warlords exacerbated the already unstable situation. Opium prohibition, much like the central government, existed only as a façade. And in many locations in Fujian, local military leaders did not even bother with appearances. Foreign observers noted that "the healthy antiopium spirit which stirred up the Chinese a decade ago seems to have evaporated. The masses have fallen back into a state of indifference and no agitation of any force is apparent."[109] What still remains unclear is the extent of popular resentment in the countryside toward the loosening of opium restrictions in this chaotic, dangerous time. Many farmers clearly were coerced into growing poppies and impoverished by rapacious military men, but others may have found opium a rare means of supporting themselves.

The public space for political activism was still open to unofficial, elite-led reform groups that wished to tackle the revived opium problem, but that public space and the role of those groups had changed considerably. The Fujian branch of the IAOA did little more than raise another small voice against a problem of overwhelming dimensions, and two years after the IAOA was founded, the venerable Fujian Anti-Opium Society dissolved. Elite reformers in the large urban areas were given some leeway to criticize and publicize the ineffective policy of the provincial government, but unofficial reform groups

---

109. Excerpt from *North-China Daily News*, 3 Oct. 1919, reprinted in *China Medical Journal* 33, no. 6 (Nov. 1919): 584.

now had no means to force compliance with the longstanding restrictions on opium smoking, sales, and cultivation except through publicity in China and abroad. Well-meaning reformers who in the late Qing might have been used to help police the city streets were now relegated to the elevated yet powerless position of national conscience to a fractured nation. In the realm of opium suppression, the more autonomous reform groups were from the state, the less power they had to influence state policy.

Twenty years after Fujian's "ambitious interlude" began in September 1906, the stage was set for another incarnation of the Chinese state, this time headed by Chiang Kaishek's Nationalist Party, to begin its futile attempt to muzzle China's opium problem without totally sacrificing the revenue it generated. Anti-opium sentiment among progressive elites and ordinary Chinese endured, but in many cases harnessing public opinion became risky. The new state insisted that the campaign continued in the newly unified Chinese Republic, but most observers knew that the campaign was a pretense for extracting as much revenue from the ostensibly despised trade as possible.

And what of Lin Zexu's crusading descendant, the symbolic link between the righteous mission behind the Opium War and the noble late Qing/early Republican crusade? Lin Bingzhang outlived the Anti-Opium Society he had founded by only two years, dying in 1923 at the age of 48. Much of his later years were occupied in a number of official positions in his hometown of Fuzhou. His work in the Water Conservancy Bureau there put him in charge of a large-scale drainage project that resulted in the lovely West Lake Park, still an oasis among the concrete and asphalt that is Fuzhou at the dawn of a new millennium. In 1999, a large bronze statue of Lin Zexu stood in the middle of West Lake Park—the face determined and the torso draped in a cloak that appeared to be blown back slightly, giving the impression that he was striding forward or standing upright against brisk winds. Lin was dramatically positioned in front of the Provincial Museum as a symbol of provincial pride, but a few years later the museum was torn down and relocated. At the turn of the twenty-first century, Lin Zexu looks resolutely out at the park and at the city of Fuzhou with nothing behind him but rubble.

EPILOGUE

The Challenge of Narcotics Control in China

> What I contemplated in these Confessions was to emblazon the power of opium—not over bodily disease and pain, but over the grander and more shadowy world of dreams.
> —Thomas De Quincey

The dreams discussed in this volume were not the somnolent fantasies of writers like De Quincey but the patriotic dreams of officials and scholars like Lin Zexu and his great-grandson Lin Bingzhang. And the drug did indeed overpower those dreams. Both Lins sought independence from the bonds of imperialism and addiction, Lin Zexu through moral righteousness and military conflict and Lin Bingzhang by means of a nationwide anti-opium campaign and international treaties. Ultimately, however, it was less the addictive quality of the drug and more its financial potential that proved so difficult to combat.

Since at least the mid-nineteenth century, the widespread use of opium and its derivatives has been viewed with increasing alarm in East Asia and abroad. Law enforcement officials, policymakers, and social workers across the globe have devoted their efforts to contending with this perceived problem, and countless theories and rancorous debates have arisen over the nature and origins of that problem as well as possible solutions. The emphasis on controlling narcotics abuse and trafficking, however, has also tended to result in a very narrow scholarly approach to the topic of opium in East Asia. Until quite

---

EPIGRAPH: De Quincey, *Confessions*, p. 7.

recently, in fact, "narcotic history has been used in mechanistic ways to justify particular departures in policy or specific ways of looking at drugs."[1]

This is even true with regard to China, a country that became synonymous with opium in the early twentieth century. Despite its deep connections with China's social, economic, and political systems, the story of opium in China has long remained the bailiwick of diplomatic historians whose interests focused primarily on the emergence of regional and worldwide narcotics trafficking networks and the international efforts to control or dismantle them. This left an enormous gap in the literature between the Opium Wars and the emergence of the infamous narcotics underworld in the 1920s and 1930s. That gap obscured an important episode in the troubled history of China's encounter with opium—the opium suppression campaign that began in 1906. The campaign is significant not only because it achieved an unexpected degree of success at a time of great political chaos but also because it reveals several important historical trends, most important, the evolution of a public political space and the beginnings of oppositional politics. The public space in which opium reform unfolded was structured by a complex and dynamic combination of nationalism, state control, and elite mobilization strategies. This was the arena in which unofficial reformers originally empowered by the state eventually became coopted and then alienated from it. The campaign also illuminates the ambiguity of popular attitudes toward opium and opium suppression, due to the deep roots of China's opium economy.

The supply of and demand for opium in Fujian generated a multilayered and tenacious opium economy inextricably linked to the policies of the central Chinese state and the constraints imposed on the Chinese by foreign powers. Early prohibitions spawned a thriving smuggling network that expanded after the first Opium War. In 1858, the Treaty of Tianjin compelled de facto the legalization of foreign opium imports into China by mandating a fixed tariff rate. The opium trade grew rapidly over the next few decades, generating enormous profits for foreigners and lucrative transit tax revenues within China. The demand for opium inspired an upsurge of poppy cultivation among Chinese farmers. Around 1890, the Qing government overturned its own longstanding prohibition on poppy cultivation in an attempt to prevent the further erosion of the Chinese economy. This gambit contributed to the dramatic reduction of foreign imports but worsened the nation's social and economic dependence on the drug. In late 1906, spurred by

---

1. Berridge and Edwards, *Opium and the People*, p. xxvi.

the promise of international cooperation, the Qing government announced an internal crusade against opium. Shortly thereafter, China signed an agreement with the British to end Indian opium exports to China over the next ten years.

Most observers were highly skeptical that the seemingly decrepit Qing government could oversee a campaign of such importance and magnitude, particularly since it would alienate powerful local interests. On the national level, successful implementation of opium reform would free China from the specter of widespread addiction and social degradation, end domestic poppy cultivation, halt the influx of the foreign drug, and help to strengthen the moral authority of the state. However, opium-related revenues were an important source of funding for the cash-strapped Qing state, and those moneys also provided a crucial economic prop for many ailing provincial and county-level treasuries, not to mention impoverished farmers. Despite the risks, the central Chinese state had a strong interest in the successful conduct of the anti-opium campaign, since the ethical considerations embedded in late Qing/early Republican opium policy were also accompanied by serious pragmatic concerns. For Qing officials, and for Yuan Shikai and the new Republic, abrogation or violation of the Anglo-Chinese opium agreements of 1908 and 1911 could have meant a resurgence of the Indian and domestic opium trades that would have put the Chinese nation back on the road to social and economic disintegration and seriously undercut support for the Chinese state from nationalistic officials and reformist elites.

China's central state was the guiding force behind the late Qing/early Republican anti-opium movement in Fujian province, and its policies were responsible for the gradual hardening of boundaries between the state and the public political space in which unofficial reform groups worked to eliminate opium. The legal and chronological framework established by the Qing state in 1906 laid out the timetable for reform and broadly outlined the measures each province was to adopt. The framework specifically encouraged the participation of unofficial, elite-led reform groups and left limited room for provinces and localities to respond to local conditions. But the framework itself contributed to the erosion of state/elite cooperation. The agreements with the British made the success of the campaign attainable, but only if the Qing government ensured that the entire nation adhered to the terms of the agreement. Thus, the central Chinese state had even more incentive to retain control over provincial opium reform efforts. At the same time, the international agreements alienated many Chinese reformers because their terms allowed substantial foreign interference in the campaign (and favored the foreign drug) and were perceived as slowing the momentum and thoroughness of reform.

The scarcity of manpower and money to implement and enforce the measures mandated by the new suppression policy opened an avenue through which unofficial reform groups entered the nascent public political arena at the behest of the central state. Beijing may indeed have viewed this as "an extension of government capacity," much like traditional elite involvement in local social welfare and public works.[2] But the Fujian Anti-Opium Society did not fit the traditional mold of an elite-led philanthropic society, except that it was founded by prestigious members of local society whose pedigrees stemmed from family influence and their imperial degrees. Many well-meaning elites in Fujian joined or contributed to groups such as the Do Only Good Society (Weishan she), which listed among its many admirable goals the repair of roads, aid to the impoverished elderly, the purchase of coffins and burial services for the poor, the encouragement of reverence for chaste widows, and the veneration of printed works (xi zizhi).[3] In contrast, the officers and staff members of the Anti-Opium Society patrolled the streets for violators of the prohibition on opium smoking, licensed opium smokers and shops, conducted surprise raids on suspected opium dens, ran treatment facilities to cure drug addiction, staged public rallies exhorting the people to join the crusade, and published a journal dedicated to the cause.

Narcotics control appealed to Fujian's reformist elites, both as an outlet for budding nationalist sentiment *and* as an avenue for extending direct administrative control over local society. In this case, that control could not have been established without the legitimizing presence of the state and the permeability of the public political space. The extraordinary police powers acquired by the Anti-Opium Society were permissible only because the state had committed itself to opium reform. Permeability not only meant the ability of those in the public sphere to employ the symbolic as well as the actual resources of the state but also gave the state the ability to co-opt and control unofficial reformers when their goals converged. Actors in the public political space passed through its fluid boundaries into bureaucratic positions and

---

2. R. Bin Wong, "Opium and Modern Chinese State-Making," p. 196.
3. *Fuzhou weishan she zhengxin lu.*

vice versa, and a number of reformers kept one foot in the bureaucracy and the other in unofficial reform groups like the Anti-Opium Society. By late 1911, international pressures and domestic financial problems restricted the Qing state's ability to respond to the momentum for further and faster reform, and many members of the Anti-Opium Society chafed at the subordination of their nationalist goals to the treaty obligations of a dynasty seemingly cowed by the British. However, during the revolutionary transition (and even before), some of those who moved into official positions and became part of the new Republican state recognized the power and the volatility of the arena from whence they had come and intentionally moved to establish more direct state control over the Anti-Opium Society.

After the Revolution of 1911, the re-establishment of central control helped maintain the momentum of the campaign even as its focus and enforcement methods changed. The state absorbed many of the society's leaders, sources of funding, and powers just as the new agreement with the British compelled the Republic to put a high priority on the elimination of poppy cultivation. Unofficial reform groups had never played as important a role in reducing the supply of opium as they had in the elimination of demand for it, and this policy shift resulted in the further erosion of the vitality and scope of the public political space for opium reformers. At the same time, the inability of reformers to completely eliminate demand for the drug meant that any relaxation of state-sanctioned and state-driven enforcement could easily result in a provincial relapse. Indeed, when Fujian's poppies were hastily razed and the supply of opium from India cut off in 1914, the substantial demand for the drug (and the profits it generated) that still existed was a powerful incentive for smuggling. When the terms of the agreement were fulfilled, the state turned its attention to more pressing tensions that threatened to fragment the new Republic. When the Republic collapsed after Yuan Shikai's death, so did any semblance of a commitment to opium reform, and opium became the currency of warlord regimes. The Chinese central state fell victim to warlord politics, and meeting military expenses took priority over lofty nationalist goals. As the unofficial reformers in the public political space became autonomous, vocal opponents of the state, that opposition lost them much of their power. The anti-opium movement ultimately broke down because once the terms of the international agreement of 1911 were fulfilled, British leverage virtually evaporated, and there was less incentive for close scrutiny on the part of China's central state and not much of a state left to conduct that oversight.

In the end, the 1906–17 anti-opium campaign in Fujian province was undeniably ambitious, but all too brief.

State policies shaped the contours of the public political space, but the identity and roles of those who performed in that space were determined by their status and their goals. The leaders and most members of the Anti-Opium Society and other unofficial reform groups were progressive, educated elites, many of whom had acquired traditional degrees and all of whom sought to act in the national interest. Nationalism provided the foundation for elite activism in the opium suppression campaign, starting with (and probably even preceding) Lin Zexu and continuing to the time of Lin Bingzhang. From the emergence of the Fujian Anti-Opium Society as a nationalistic protest during the Anti-American boycott of 1905 to the vocal but ineffectual anti-opium groups of the warlord years, Fujian's reformist elites put the interests of the nation first. For the first few years of the campaign, national interests coincided with those of the Qing state, but as those two sets of goals began to diverge around 1911, many reformers began to see revolution as the only way to mold a truly modern China.

For many of Fujian's reformers, an essential part of the process of developing a modern nationalist sentiment was expanding the public political space to include ordinary Chinese. The Qing dynasty mobilized elite reformers—with the clear caveat that they not become involved in broader political discussions—but it was the elite reformers who then carefully mobilized the masses. Reformers realized that the involvement of the general population was the key to the success of opium reform because eradicating such a pervasive social vice required not only new regulations but also the inculcation of new values. Publicly supporting opium reform was a political act that stated one's desire to change China. Rejecting opium smoking was a key element in constructing the new Chinese character, a national persona uncowed by foreign aggression and clearly proud of its Chinese identity. Passivity in the face of imperialism and poverty was to be replaced by active participation in the process of modernization. The word "active" was to be taken quite literally, as opium smoking even clashed with aspirations for the appearance of modern Chinese. As Henrietta Harrison notes, the new Chinese man was, among other things, to assume an upright and forward-looking carriage.[4] Obviously, this stance rejected the languid, recumbent posture of the opium smoker.

---

4. Harrison, *The Making of the Republican Citizen*, pp. 79–83.

I have frequently referred to the late Qing/early Republican anti-opium policy as a campaign, a label that follows the lead of current Chinese historians rather than the terminology employed by the opium reformers themselves. Maoist-style mass campaigns sought to achieve a policy goal by educating and empowering the people even while those people were carefully guided by propaganda and party cadres. Most campaigns were marked by public demonstrations that commended those who complied and vilified those who resisted.[5] The late Qing/early Republican opium suppression campaign was not a Maoist-style mass campaign; the state did not explicitly call for mass mobilization because the political climate of the time was too volatile and those in power too conservative and wary to delegate that much control to the unpredictable masses. However, the campaign must certainly be considered an important historical precedent for that strategy of policy implementation.[6]

Opium reform was a state-led campaign only as far as that term can be applied in the late Qing/early Republic, but it came to resemble a movement during the 1920s. It is not a coincidence that this occurred just when the New Culture Movement burst on the scene. Opium suppression was one of many reforms Beijing was neglecting, and reform-minded individuals could no longer rely on state sanction for their political activism. The New Policies, which were instituted to forestall revolution but served as a template for the reform agenda of many late Qing/early Republican elites, had largely been abandoned as the country fragmented into warring regimes. The frustration of students, among others, generated public protests and the transformation of the public political space. Opium suppression must be included, then, within the broader process that marked the emergence of oppositional politics in China.

Elite reformers saw that mass involvement not only contributed to the formation of a broad sense of national community but also eased the task of enforcement by creating a more supportive social environment. It also elevated and cemented their own status as social leaders as they marched at the head of a procession or addressed an enormous crowd. At first, elite reformers needed and used the mantle of the state to acquire legitimacy and power. Officials were invited to address gatherings, and their presence added to the

---

5. Bennett, *Yundong*, p. 11–37.
6. See Zhou Yongming, *Anti-Drug Crusades in Twentieth-Century China*, esp. chap. 6, for a detailed analysis of the Communist-led anti-opium campaign that began in 1949.

weight of the crusade and implicitly endorsed the powers exercised by unofficial reform groups.

The mobilization strategy appeared fairly effective in the large urban centers of Fujian, where elite reformers and state oversight were more intensive. Mass demonstrations and dramatic pipe burnings sought to educate the audience and imbue observers with a sense of involvement in this pathbreaking crusade against harmful old habits. These ceremonies, intended by their elite organizers to demonstrate Chinese antipathy to opium and opium smoking, not only delineated the boundaries of the emergent public political space but also served as occasions for individuals and groups to categorize themselves as part of the new China. The early Republican state consisted largely of reformist elites, and the state more explicitly encouraged mass participation in the notable rituals and ceremonies of political life.[7] Officials now supervised mass meetings and demonstrations associated with the antiopium campaign, but the new focus on eliminating poppies meant fewer and often smaller parades.

The suppression campaign, and the public political space in which it unfolded, looked quite different in the countryside. The cities were more crowded, occupations more varied, and the population more anonymous, but in the rural poppy-growing regions elites and non-elites were more closely bound by the nature of the local economy and local power relationships. Opium smoking often was less the target of state intrusion than was poppy growing, and the destruction of plants, homes, and fields was not an occasion for public celebration. Elite reformers could and did monitor compliance with the restrictions on poppy planting, but the local magistrate and the troops at his disposal supervised or conducted the uprooting of illicit crops. The entrenched rural opium economy meant that agitation against the trade generally took place on a much smaller scale.

After 1914, the nature of the suppression campaign changed again as the Chinese state fragmented into warlord regimes bent on the acquisition of territory, power, and money, and the flow of legal Indian opium ceased. Mobilization became more risky, despite the supportive rhetoric of authorities at all levels of government. Opium became a mainstay of most military regimes, and serious attempts to eradicate it were not greeted warmly. Many ordinary Chinese were concerned more with survival than reform campaigns. Elite activism remained public but did not incorporate the masses to the

---

7. Harrison, *The Making of the Republican Citizen*.

same degree as they had during the late Qing heyday of opium reform. Unofficial reformers joined high-profile organizations that had little influence. The focus on the good of the nation as the goal of opium suppression remained, even as the campaign itself was battered by the unpredictable course of Chinese politics.

Another key component of late Qing / early Republican nationalism in the context of opium reform was opposition to imperialist aggression. Foreign imperialism played an important role in structuring the suppression campaign by sparking the growth of China's opium economy and more positively through the imposition of the two Sino-British agreements to end the opium trade. Foreign opium merchants and smugglers were the primary—and illicit—source of China's opium until the second half of the nineteenth century. The British worked with the central Chinese state in the late Qing to structure the prohibition campaign in a way that ensured continued profits for purveyors of Indian opium; these arrangements also exacerbated anti-Qing sentiment. The rejection of imperialist domination and greed was a key element of the anti-opium campaign, and anti-imperialism has served as the rhetorical cornerstone of every Chinese attempt to eliminate the drug within its borders from the Opium Wars to the present. However, the Qing state could not hope to enforce prohibitions on consumption and cultivation of the domestic drug if the flow of foreign imports was unchecked. The agreements with the British were a Faustian bargain for the Qing that allowed them to sign a treaty to end Indian opium imports but enabled the British to establish a number of stipulations that privileged the foreign drug at a time when the nationalistic zeal of reformers could—and did—very easily become revolutionary anger. At the same time, as a global consensus arose in opposition to the abuse and trafficking of narcotics, the British had to tread lightly if they did not wish to earn international opprobrium. The conduct of the anti-opium campaign implies that China's relationship with western imperialist powers entailed a complex balancing act on the part of both the Chinese and the British, in which each government held up the rhetoric of suppression against its more concrete financial and political imperatives.

At the same time, missionaries struggled to distinguish themselves from their opium-peddling compatriots and plunged into Fujian's crusade to eliminate opium. Despite the numerous instances in which foreign missionaries found their benevolent intentions questioned because of the indisputable link between foreigners and opium, missionaries managed (most likely through their work with opium addiction) to craft a new image of themselves as opium reformers in the popular Chinese mind. That image, however, sometimes proved just as detrimental to missionary goals as the actions of their imperialist home governments. Most notably, in Xinghua, Christians were attacked not as imperialists but as supporters of the Republican state and its unpopular taxes and reforms.

Nationalism was certainly a driving force behind opium reform and its limited successes, but by the early twentieth century Chinese and foreigners generally recognized that the Chinese were equally culpable for China's opium problem. The opium trade undeniably began in earnest with British smuggling of the drug, but the trade could not have grown without Chinese distributors and consumers. Likewise, the anti-opium campaign could not have achieved what most observers felt was considerable success without the support of many elite and ordinary Chinese. To analyze the evolution of China's well-documented relationship with opium accurately, we must first remove it from the moralistic and political rhetoric that has oversimplified the complex socioeconomic dynamics of its trade and use and obscured the fundamental ambivalence of many Chinese toward this much-maligned drug.

By the nineteenth century, the nature of the opium trade in China had become as problematic as opium smoking itself, because the rapid spread of addiction was intimately tied to imperialist aggression and a perceived decline of Qing authority. The early anti-opium crusaders, including Commissioner Lin, were often officials who recognized and openly deplored the corruption of the Chinese bureaucracy, the greed of Chinese and western merchants, and the weakness of individual smokers that enabled the illegal opium trade to flourish.[8] Accordingly, the Chinese government and nationalistic Chinese elites supported the elimination of opium imports from abroad and the eradication of domestic poppy cultivation and opium smoking at home.

After the Opium Wars, however, this stream of Chinese rhetoric fed into and was overwhelmed by a swelling chorus of international condemnation of the Sino-Indian opium trade and its socioeconomic consequences. The loudest voices now belonged to outraged Chinese elite activists and missionaries (most from the United States and Great Britain). These groups sought to end the opium trade by calling attention to British greed and to the physical and moral decay that accompanied opium addiction. Acknowledgment of

---

8. Polachek, *The Inner Opium War*, pp. 142–44.

widespread Chinese complicity in the opium trade or of popular objections to opium reform would have seriously undermined the righteous fervor of those involved in the suppression movement, since it would have shifted the blame away from Great Britain. Until recently, similar concerns about undermining the fundamental dichotomy between the righteous masses and the exploitative elite-official alliance that justified the Communist revolution generated similar biases in sources from the Chinese mainland.

In reality, anti-opium sentiment was common among the urban elite population before, during, and after the official anti-opium campaign. However, it remains difficult to say to what degree that outlook extended to the lower classes or rural dwellers. It is true that from the beginning of the illicit opium trade in Fujian in the 1820s to the coming to power of the Nationalist Party in 1927, some ordinary Chinese had expressed their hostility to opium and the opium trade in a variety of ways. Evidence of anti-opium sentiment among the masses of Fujian was manifested in occasional efforts to rid their villages of opium addiction, in the recollection of anti-opium folk songs decades after their composition, in the impressive size of audiences for urban anti-opium rallies, and in the popularity of heterodox sects that prohibited opium smoking. However, this cannot be taken as a groundswell of popular support for opium reform, given the depth and resilience of the provincial opium economy and documented incidents of resistance to the suppression campaign.

While many Fujianese were decrying the damage wrought by opium, many of their compatriots were deeply involved in sustaining the opium trade. The opium suppression campaign made considerable progress in a remarkably brief time, but the crusade was never completely successful, and the rapid resurgence of the opium economy in the warlord years could only have been possible in the absence of either a strong central state or broad-based, well-organized popular support for opium reform. Although violent resistance to even the most coercive suppression measures was minimal in Fujian, it did occur, and small-scale or passive resistance was endemic in the poppy-growing regions. The difficulties of enforcing the opium restrictions, as well as the ease with which Fujian's opium economy reappeared during the revolutionary transition and after the death of Yuan Shikai, point to the likelihood that the lower classes for the most part complied with the restrictions when enforcement was strict and resumed cultivating, selling, and smoking opium when it was not.

Fig. 10.1 Statue of Lin Zexu at his birthplace in Fuzhou (photograph by the author, July 1999).

This tendency was particularly evident in the opium-growing regions along the Fujian coast. The campaign reached into every district in the province, and the strategies adopted throughout Fujian were remarkably consistent. They reflected the widespread acceptance of the guidelines issued in Beijing and Fuzhou and often involved an important role for unofficial reform groups, specifically the branches of the Fujian Anti-Opium Society, in reducing opium smoking in more urban areas. In the poppy-growing regions, the degree to which the campaign was enforced before 1911 is unclear; if many areas were unaffected, this helps to explain the outburst of violence that accompanied the crackdown on cultivation after the Revolution. When effective state control broke down during the Revolution, almost every district in Fujian where opium had been cultivated during the late Qing—and even some where it had not—experienced an immediate resurgence of poppy planting. This reflected the farmers' appreciation for the coercive powers of the state (and their absence) and the lucrative nature of the crop. And it also implies that the relative lack of violent resistance before the Revolution had little to do with a strong sense of nationalism on the part of many farmers.

In other words, the thoroughness of enforcement was directly tied to the popularity of state-mandated reforms and the regulatory strength of the Chinese state at the national, provincial, and local levels. Although the crucial and visible role of the state in establishing and sanctioning Fujian's opium suppression campaign inspired nationalistic feelings among some Chinese, it also generated considerable ill-will among those targeted by government taxes and regulatory mechanisms. Just as popular hostility to opium and the opium trade was part of a larger anti-state, anti-imperialist sentiment that fueled Chinese nationalism among urban elites in the early twentieth century, resistance to opium suppression was encompassed within a broader opposition (especially in China's rural areas) to the intrusive, extractive nature of the New Policy reforms.

At the same time, nationalism did not always mean adhering to the priorities of the central state. Around 1911, activists in Fujian chafed under Qing orders to pace the provincial campaign to comply with the terms of the agreement with the British, convinced that provincial needs were compatible with their vision of a strong China. The desire of many Fujianese elites and officials to rid the province of Manchus, Hunan soldiers, and unwanted imperialist influence meshed nicely with the campaign to eradicate opium, because opium consumption represented Chinese weakness on many different levels.

China has yet to defeat the scourge of narcotics. In its most recent incarnation, China's ongoing problem with narcotics is again perceived as originating outside China, with the drugs flowing in from the infamous Golden Triangle (Burma, Laos, and Thailand). This time, drug abuse not only is condemned for taking its toll on individuals and the social body but also is blamed for introducing the terrible "foreign" disease called AIDS. Again, the public political space has served as the location of most of the state's anti-drug efforts. In 1999, for example, Lin Zexu's birthplace in Fuzhou was the showplace for a gruesome exhibit of photographs documenting the consequences of drug use on the bodies and lives of Chinese youth. Throughout China, the 1990s were punctuated by mass arrests, rallies, and executions of drug offenders in an attempt to reassert the will of the state and to reinject a sense of purpose in a Chinese population shaken by official corruption and the dismantling of central economic planning. Success will remain elusive as long as the state refuses to recognize how deeply the narcotic economy is intertwined with a whole range of other socioeconomic problems plaguing Chinese society.

Understanding the nature of China's relationship with opium and other drugs has never been an easy task, given the historiographical impediments to research, as well as changing perceptions of addiction. The often-passionate anti-opium rhetoric that has dominated much of the history of the drug in China obscures the reality of a Chinese population torn between lofty nationalism and financial gain. In a classic article on the Chinese opium problem, Jonathan Spence eloquently concludes: "The considerable success of the opium suppression campaigns between 1906 and 1915 points up the force of emergent Chinese nationalism and the recovery of a sense of social purpose, just as the fall back into massive addiction between 1915 and 1945 points to the premature frustration of that nationalism and sense of purpose."[9] Meribeth Cameron has forcefully asserted that "the most successful of all the Manchu reforms was the eradication of the cultivation and use of opium," and she, too, attributes that success to the popularity of the campaign and the ability of all Chinese to understand its goals.[10]

Nationalistic rhetoric was indeed an important aspect of the anti-opium campaign in Fujian and was a recurrent theme in edicts issued from Beijing, as well as in the language adopted by various unofficial reform groups. The normatization of the rhetoric of suppression as a nationalist imperative of the Chinese state is perhaps the most significant legacy of the late Qing / early Republican suppression campaign. However, this study reveals that although nationalism galvanized the Chinese state, the reformers who served that state, and even an unknown percentage of the general population, it was undercut by the lack of support for the campaign among many of Fujian's farmers and ordinary Chinese, in addition to officials and warlords who either engaged in the sale or smoking of opium or resented the intrusive nature of the campaign. The complex and multilayered opium economy that permeated the fabric of Fujianese society could not be dislodged by nationalism alone. In the end, it was the moral authority and regulatory presence of the Chinese state, shaped in large part by international pressures and the beginnings of Chinese political opposition, that determined the course of the campaign.[11] On the surface, it seems paradoxical to discuss the opium

---

9. Spence, "Opium Smoking in Ch'ing China," p. 173.
10. Cameron, *The Reform Movement in China*, pp. 136, 200.
11. Some mainland Chinese historians argue that the campaign was the state's response to a grassroots movement for opium suppression, but that does not seem to be true. In Fujian, just as in other provinces, such as Shandong, the campaign was a social movement dictated by

suppression campaign as a manifestation of state strength when the lack of money and manpower (as well as China's dependence on foreign goodwill) was largely responsible for encouraging the crucial involvement of unofficial reform groups. However, those groups needed state sanction to exercise the powers necessary to conduct opium suppression, and when the state fractured, so did the cohesion and fleeting success of the campaign. It was the presence or absence of the state that determined the course of opium reform from the 1820s to the 1920s. The revival of Fujian's opium economy was more about the lack of an effective state presence and the profit motive than a dearth of nationalism.

---

the central state until after 1916 (on Shandong, see Zhang Yufa, *Zhongguo xiandaihua de qucheng yanjiu*, pp. 774–83).

Reference Matter

Character List

NOTE: The entries are ordered alphabetically by syllable in the Hanyu pinyin romanization. That is, "Duzhi gongsuo" comes before "Duan Qirui" because the syllable "du" precedes the syllable "duan" alphabeticallly.

afurong 阿芙蓉
Anchashi si 按察使司
Anxi 安溪

baogao 報告
baojia 保甲
bendi jiang 本地醬

Caizheng ju 財政局
Cen Chunxuan 岑春暄
Changle 長樂
Changtai 長泰
Chen Aitao 陳愛濤
Chen Baochen 陳寶琛
Chen Bi 陳璧
Chen Bingzhang 陳秉璋
Chen Jiageng (Tan Ka-ki) 陳嘉庚
Chen Jiongming 陳炯明
Chen Maoding 陳懋鼎
Chen Nengguang 陳能光
Chen Peikun 陳培錕
Chen Qiao 陳樵
Chen Shuyi 陳淑頤
Chen Weilin 陳為霖

Chen Xipeng 陳錫朋
Chen Xiurong 陳秀榕
Chen Yi 陳儀
Chen Zongshu 陳宗書
Chen Zongyi 陳宗儀
chengcan 丞參
Chengxuan shizhengshi si 承宣市政使司
Chiang Kaishek (Jiang Jieshi) 蔣介石
Chongan 崇安
chu 處
Cixi 慈禧
Cui Zhaoxiang 崔兆祥

Dabai hui 大伯會
Datian 大田
dao 道
Daoguang 道光
daotai 道臺
Dehua 德化
difang guan 地方官
ding 丁
Ding Zhenduo 丁振鐸

Donglu guancha shi 東路觀察使
doufu 豆腐
dougun 鬥棍
dudu 都督
Duzhi bu 度支部
Duzhi gongsuo 度支公所
Duan Qirui 段祺瑞

fengshui 風水
Fu 福
Fu'an 福安
Fuding 福鼎
Fuji yanghang 福記洋行
Fujian 福建
Fujian caizhengting 福建財政廳
Fujian jinyan gongsuo suozhang
    福建禁煙公所所長
Fujian jinyan ju zongban 福建禁煙
    局總辦
Fujian junjing tongmenghui 福建
    軍警同盟會
Fujian licai sanjie 福建理財三傑
Fujian qudushe (zong)she jibao 福建
    去毒社(總)社季報
Fujian qudu zongshe 福建去毒
    總社
Fujian quansheng jingwuting
    tingzhang 福建全省
    警務廳廳長
Fujian shuiliju 福建水利局
Fujian zhenshoushi 福建
    鎮守使
Fujian zizhi jinyan xieji hui 福建
    自治禁煙協濟會
Funing 福寧
Fuqing 福清
fu yizhang 副議長
Fuzhou 福州
Fuzhou meiri huisheng bao 福州每日
    回聲報

Fuzhou yunjitang tushang 福州
    允濟堂土商

ganbu 干部
Gan Huangtao 甘黃濤
Gao Dengli 高登鯉
Gaojuan ju 膏捐局
Gelaohui 哥老會
gongfu 功夫
gongsheng 貢生
gongyi 公益
gongyi she 公益社
gongyisuo 工藝所
Gulangyu 鼓浪嶼
Gutian 古田
Guan'gao ju 官膏局
guanshen huanzhu 官紳歡祝
Guangze 光澤
Guangzhou (Canton) 廣州
Guihua 歸化
Guo Daozhi 郭道直
Guo Gongmu 郭公木
Guohuo weichi hui 國貨維持會
Guomindang 國民黨
Guowu yuan 國務院

Haicheng 海澄
Haifang ting 海方廳
Haiguan 海關
Hanjun 漢軍
Hanlin Academy 翰林院
Hanzu duli hui 漢族獨立會
He Chun 合春
Heihu zhongyi tang 黑虎忠義堂
Heiqian hui 黑錢會
Hong Xiuquan 洪秀全
Hubu 戶部
Hugong Mountain 壺工山
hujun shi 護軍使
Humin she 護民社

Huashui (zong)ju 華稅(總)局
Huang Lian 黃濂
Huang Naishang 黃乃裳
Huang Peisong 黃培崧
Huangpu (Whampoa) Anchorage 黃埔
Huang Tingyuan 黃廷元
Hui'an 惠安
Huiyi zhengwu chu 會議政務處

Jiaqing 嘉慶
Jian'an 建安
Jianning 建寧
Jiang Chunlin 江春霖
jiangjun 將軍
Jiangle 將樂
Jiang Lu 江露
Jiang Yujing 江畬經
Jiang Zubao 江祖苞
jiao 角
jiaoyu sizhang 教育司長
Jieyan huishe 戒煙會社
jieyan ju 戒煙局
jieyan pai 戒煙牌
jieyan suo 戒煙所
Jinjiang 晉江
jinshi 進士
jinyan dachen 禁煙大臣
jinyan dayuan 禁煙大員
jinyan diaocha ju 禁煙調查局
Jinyan ducha chu 禁煙督察處
jinyan gongsuo 禁煙公所
Jinyan ju 禁煙局
Jinyan zongju 禁煙總局
Jingwu bu 警務部
Jing Xing 景星
Jiulong River 九龍江
Judu weiyuanhui 拒毒委員會
judu yixun 拒毒遺訓
juren 舉人

Junji chu 軍機處
Kun Ji 坤記
kuping 庫平

Lao She 老舍
laobaixing 老百姓
li 里
Li Dihu 李迪瑚
Li Funan 李馥南
Li Houji 李厚基
lijin 釐金
lijin guan 釐金官
lijin weiyuan 釐金委員
lishi 歷史
Liancheng 連城
Lianjiang 連江
liang 兩
liang dao 糧道
Liang Guandeng 梁冠澄
Liao Shangqing 廖上清
Lin Binghua 林炳華
Lin Bingzhang 林炳章
Lin Jiafeng 林家風
Lin Lucun 林輅存
Lin Qigan 林其幹
Lin Shaonian 林紹年
Lin Shizhao 林師肇
Lin Yushi 林雨時
Lin Zexu 林則徐
Lin Zhixuan 林志烜
Lin Zikeng 林資鏗
Lingding (Lintin) Island 零丁
Liu Guanxiong 劉冠雄
Liu Hongshou 劉鴻壽
liumin 流民
Liu Xuexun 劉學詢
Longxi 龍溪
Longyan 龍巖
Lü Chenghan 呂承翰
Lu Chuhuang 盧初璜

Lujun bu 陸軍部
Lu Zhuanlin 鹿傳霖
lunshuo 論說
Luo Jincheng 羅金城
Luoyuan 羅源

Mahang 馬巷
Majiaxiang 馬家鄉
Mawei 馬尾
Meng Sipei 孟思培
Min county 閩縣
Minhou 閩候
Minnan jiuhuo hui 閩南救火會
Minnan yanmiao jinzhong hui 閩南煙苗禁種會
Minqing 閩清
Min River 閩江
Minxin ribao 閩心日報
Min-Zhe zongdu 閩浙總督
Minzheng bu 民政部
Min zhengfu waijiaosi 民政府外交司
minzheng zhang 民政長
Mingyu 明玉
mu 畝

Nan'an 南安
Nanjing 南靖
Nanping 南平
Nanri 南日
Nantai 南台
Nanxi 南溪
Neizhengbu, Jingzhengsi 內政部警政司
Ningbo 寧波
Ningde 寧德
Ninghua 寧化
Ningyang 寧陽

Pan Mu 潘木

Peng Shousong 彭壽松
Pinghai 平海
Pinghe 平和
Pingnan 屏南
pozi 破仔
Prince Gong (Puwei) 恭親王(溥偉)
Pucheng 浦城
Pushou 樸壽
Putian 莆田

qixiazi 旗下仔
qian 錢
Qiangdao hui 槍刀會
Qiaonan gongyi she 橋南公益社
Qing 清
Qudu she zongzhishe zong bu ke cai 去毒社總支社總不可裁
quandao yuan 勸導員
Quanzhou 泉州

Rilong gongsi 日龍公司

Sa-Iong (Xiyang) 西洋
Santu'ao 三都澳
Sha county 沙
Sha Han tuan 殺漢團
Shanchun 善純
Shantou (Swatow) 汕頭
Shanghang 上杭
Shangzheng ju 商政局
Shao Jiquan 邵繼全
Shaowu 邵武
Shao Zhicheng 邵質誠
sheyou 社友
sheyuan 社員
shendong 紳董
shenshang 紳商
shengyuan 生員
shi nong gong shang 士農工商
Shima 石馬

Shi Shiji 施士吉
Shouning 壽寧
Shuiji 水吉
Shuikou 水口
Shunchang 順昌
Shuobao she 說報社
si dao 司道
Songshou 松壽
Su Wukai 蘇吾楷
Su Yi 蘇益
Suishan 崇善
Sun Baoqi 孫寶琦
Sun Baorong 孫寶鎔
Sun Daoren 孫道仁
Sun Erzhun 孫爾準
Sun Yatsen (Sun Zhongshan) 孫逸仙 (中山)

Taizhou 台州
Tang Shaoyi 唐紹儀
tidiao 提調
Tixueshi si 提學使司
Tingzhou 汀州
Tongan 同安
Tongmenghui 同盟會
tongshui 統稅
Toubei 頭北
tufei 土匪
tugao dian 土膏店
tu jiang 土漿
Tuyao tongshui fenju 土藥統稅分局
Tuyao tongshui zongju 土藥統稅總局

Waijiao bu 外交部
Waijiao si 外交司
Waiwu bu 外務部
Wang Dazhen 王大貞
Wang Junwen 王君文

Wang Renkan 王仁堪
Wang Shengling 王聲玲
Wang Shouchang 王壽昌
Wang Ziyi 王子懿
Weishan she 惟善社
Wenkai (Wenjie) 文楷
wenshi ziliao 文史資料
wenzhang 文章
Wenzhou 溫州
Wu Hongbin 吳鴻賓
Wuping 武平
Wu Tingchang (Wu Guangchen) 吳庭棖 (吳光臣)
Wu Wei 吳威
Wu Wei'ao 吳微鼇
Wuyi shan (Bohea Hills) 武彝山
Wu Zeng 吳增
wuzhi xiang 無知鄉

xi zizhi 惜字紙
Xixiang 西鄉
Xiamao 夏茂
Xiamen (Amoy) 廈門
Xiapu 霞浦
xian 縣
Xianfa bianchaguan 憲法編查館
Xianfeng 咸豐
Xianyou 仙遊
xiaogui 小桂
Xiao jing 孝經
xiaoshuo 小說
xiao tu 小土
Xiaoxi 小溪
Xiehe (school) 協和書院
xieling 協領
Xinghua 興化
Xinzheng 新政
Xu Chongzhi 許崇智
Xu Peihua 徐培華

Xu Shichang 徐世昌
Xu Shiying 許世英
Xu Yingkui 許應騤

Yakou 衙口
Yama (Yanluo) 閻羅
yamen 衙門
yapian gui 鴉片鬼
yanfa dao 鹽法道
yanguan 煙館
yangui 煙鬼
Yanping 延平
yanyun shi 鹽運使
yang yao 洋藥
Yang Jingwen 楊景文
Yangmian 洋面
Yang Tinglun 楊廷綸
Yang Zhanyun 楊展雲
Ye Keliang 葉可樑
Ye Xindi 葉新第
Ye Yongyuan 葉永元
Yigu 貽穀
yishen 議紳
yishi huiyuan 議事會員
Yiteheng'e 依特恒額
Yi Tongfu 伊通甫
Yiwen she 益聞社
yizhang 議長
Yongan 永安
Yongchun 永春
Yongfu 永福
Yongzheng 雍正
Youxi 尤溪
Youzhuan bu 郵傳部
Yu Ji 玉記
Yu Maolong 裕茂隆
Yuqi 毓祺
Yu Wenzao 余文藻
yuan 圓
Yuan Shikai 袁世凱

yundong 運動
yujin yuzhen 寓禁於征

zazhi 雜誌
Zeng Fengyuan 曾逢源
Zhan Xianba 詹賢拔
Zhao'an 詔安
zhangcheng 章程
Zhangpu 漳浦
Zhang Yuanqi 張元奇
Zhang Zanting 張贊廷
Zhang Zengjue 張增爵
Zhang Zhidong 張之洞
Zhangzhou 漳州
Zhang Zuhan 張祖漢
Zhao'an 詔安
Zhejiang 浙江
Zhenkong jiao 真空教
Zheng Biming 鄭必明
Zheng Chenggong (Koxinga) 鄭成功
Zhenghe 政和
Zheng Shouxing 鄭守馨
Zhengwu chu 政務處
Zheng Zuyin 鄭祖蔭
zhishi 知事
zhiyuan 職員
Zhonghua guomin juduhui (NAOA) 中華國民拒毒會
Zhu Ding 朱鼎
Zhu Huanpo 祝煥坡
Zhu Jiantai 朱建泰
Zhuqi 竹崎
zihua 紫花
Ziyi ju 諮議局
Ziyou dang 自由黨
zizhi hui 自治會
zongban 總辦
zuoling 佐領
Zuo Zongtang 佐宗棠

Bibliography

Abrams, M. H. *The Milk of Paradise: The Effects of Opium Visions on the Works of De Quincey, Crabbe, Francis Thompson, and Coleridge.* Cambridge, Mass.: Harvard University Press, 1934.

Addams, Jane. *Twenty Years at Hull-House with Autobiographical Notes.* Urbana and Chicago: University of Illinois Press, 1990.

Adshead, S. A. M. "Opium in Szechwan, 1881–1911." *Journal of Southeast Asian History* 7, no. 2 (Sept. 1966): 93–99.

Annual Report of the Foochow Medical Missionary Hospital in Connection with the ABCFM Mission. Fuzhou: Foochow Printing Press, 1877.

Anti-Cobweb Club. *Fukien: A Study of a Province.* Shanghai: Presbyterian Mission Press, 1925.

Barclay, Wade Crawford. *Widening Horizons, 1845–95. The Methodist Episcopal Church, 1845–1939,* vol. 3. New York: Board of Missions, Methodist Church, 1957.

Barkan, Lenore. "Patterns of Power: Forty Years of Elite Politics in a Chinese County." In *Chinese Local Elites and Patterns of Dominance,* ed. Joseph Esherick and Mary B. Rankin, pp. 191–215. Berkeley: University of California Press, 1990.

Bates, M. Searle. "The Theology of American Missionaries in China, 1900–1950." In *The Missionary Enterprise in China and America,* ed. John King Fairbank, pp. 135–58. Cambridge, Mass.: Harvard University Press, 1974.

Baumler, Alan. "Opium Control Versus Opium Suppression: The Origins of the 1935 Six-Year Plan to Eliminate Opium and Drugs." In *Opium Regimes: China, Britain, and Japan, 1839–1952,* ed. Timothy Brook and Bob Tashashi Wakabayashi, pp. 270–91. Berkeley: University of California Press, 2000.

Baumler, Alan, ed. *Modern China and Opium: A Reader.* Ann Arbor: University of Michigan Press, 2001.

Beal, Edwin George, Jr. *The Origin of Likin, 1853–1864.* Chinese Economic and Political Studies. Cambridge, Mass.: Harvard University Press, 1958.

Beattie, Hilary J. "Protestant Missions and Opium in China." *Papers on China* 22A. Cambridge, Mass.: Center for East Asian Studies, 1969.

Beeching, Jack. *The Chinese Opium Wars*. San Diego: Harcourt Brace Jovanovich, 1975.

Benedict, Carol. "Bubonic Plague in Nineteenth-Century China." Ph.D. diss., Stanford University, 1992.

———. *Bubonic Plague in Nineteenth-Century China*. Stanford: Stanford University Press, 1996.

Bennett, Gordon. *Yundong: Mass Campaigns in Chinese Communist Leadership*. Center for Chinese Studies China Research Monograph, no. 12. Berkeley: University of California, 1976.

Berridge, Virginia, and Griffith Edwards. *Opium and the People: Opiate Use in Nineteenth-Century England*. London: Allen Lane; and New York: St. Martin's Press, 1981.

Bianco, Lucien. "Rural Tax Resistance in Early Republican China (1912–1937): The Variety of Tax Targets." *Proceedings of the Conference on Eighty Years History of the Republic of China, 1912–91*, 4: 21–38. Taibei: Xingzheng yuan, Xinwen ju, 1991.

Billingsley, Phil. "Bandits, Bosses, and Bare Sticks: Beneath the Surface of Local Control in Early Republican China." *Modern China* 7, no. 3 (July 1981): 235–88.

Bitton, Nelson. *The Regeneration of New China*. London: Church Missionary Society, 1914.

Blatt, Marilyn. "Problems of a China Missionary—Justus Doolittle." *Papers on China* 12 (1958): 28–50.

Boorman, Howard, ed. *Biographical Dictionary of Republican China*. 4 vols. New York: Columbia University Press, 1968.

Brook, Timothy, and B. Michael Frolic, eds. *Civil Society in China*. Armonk, N.Y.: M. E. Sharpe, 1997.

Brook, Timothy, and Bob Tadashi Wakabayashi, eds. *Opium Regimes: China, Britain, and Japan, 1839–1952*. Berkeley: University of California Press, 2000.

Brunnert, H. S., and V. V. Hagelstrom. *Present Day Political Organization of China*. 1911. Reprinted—Taibei: Ch'eng wen, 1978.

Buck, John Lossing. *Land Utilization in China*. Nanjing: University of Nanjing, 1937. Reprinted—New York: Paragon, 1968.

Cai Rujin 蔡如金. "Taiping jun zhuanzhan Zhangzhou" 太平軍轉戰漳州 (The Taiping army's battles in Zhangzhou). *Lishi jiaoxue* 8 (1983): 15–16.

Cai Shaoqing. "On the Origin of the Gelaohui." *Modern China* 10, no. 4 (Oct. 1984): 481–508.

Calhoun, Craig, ed. *Habermas and the Public Sphere*. Cambridge, Mass.: MIT Press, 1992.

Cameron, Meribeth E. *The Reform Movement in China, 1898–1912*. Stanford: Stanford University Press, 1931. Reprinted—New York: Octagon Books, 1963.

Cantlie, James, and C. Sheridan Jones. *Sun Yat Sen and the Awakening of China*. New York and Chicago: Fleming H. Revell, 1912.

Carlson, Ellsworth C. *The Foochow Missionaries, 1847–1880*. Cambridge, Mass.: East Asian Research Center, Harvard University, 1971.

Chang Hsin-pao. *Commissioner Lin and the Opium War*. Cambridge, Mass.: Harvard University Press, 1971.

Charles, Robert. "Olyphant and Opium: A Canton Merchant Who 'Just Said No.'" *International Bulletin of Missionary Research*, Apr. 1992: 66–69.

Chen Guansan 陳冠三 and Zou Xiutong 鄒修桐. "Yapian yandu zai Jianning de fanlan yu chajin" 鴉片煙毒在建寧的泛濫與查禁 (The spread and prohibition of opium in Jianning). *Jianning wenshi ziliao* 1986, no. 5 (Oct.): 43–46.

Chen Hanguang 陳漢光. "Fujian renkou jianjie" 福建人口簡介 (A brief introduction to the population of Fujian). *Fujian wenxian* 1969, no. 7 (Sept. 30): 9–15.

———. "Minguo yilai Fujian sheng difang xingzhengqu hua" 民國以來福建省地方行政區畫 (The drawing of local administrative boundaries in Fujian after the founding of the Republic). *Fujian wenxian* 1969, no. 5 (Mar.): 22–24.

Chen Jiming 陳基明. "Chen Zhencheng quanjie yapian yishi" 陳振成勸戒鴉軼事 (An anecdote about Chen Zhencheng urging the prohibition of opium). *Liancheng wenshi ziliao* 1991, no. 15 (Aug.): 169–71.

Chen Kan 陳侃. "Wusi qianhou de Xianyou shehui" 五四前后的仙游社會 (Xianyou society before and after May 4). *Xianyou wenshi ziliao* 1985, no. 3 (July): 73–82.

Chen Yongfa 陳永發. "Hong taiyang xia de yingsu hua: yapian maoyi yu Yan'an mushi" 紅太陽下的罌粟花：鴉片貿易與延安模式 (The blooming poppy under the red sun: The Yan'an way and the opium trade). *Xin shi xue* 1, no. 4 (Dec. 1990): 40–115.

Chen Zhangcheng 陳長城. "Xinhai qianxi Putian qunzhong zifa kangguan douzheng" 辛亥前夕莆田群眾自發抗官鬥爭 (Spontaneous mass struggles against officials in Putian on the eve of the 1911 Revolution). *Putian wenshi ziliao* 2 (1981): 106–16.

China Medical Journal (1900–1919). Housed at the National Library of Medicine, Bethesda, Maryland.

China Mission Year Book. Shanghai: Christian Literature Society for China, 1911–17.

China Year Book. Shanghai: North China Daily News & Herald, 1912–20.

Chinese Recorder. Shanghai: American Presbyterian Mission Press, 1906–23.

Clark, Hugh R. *Community, Trade, and Networks: Southern Fujian Province from the Third to the Thirteenth Century*. Cambridge, Eng.: Cambridge University Press, 1991.

CMS/CEZMS: Church Missionary Society / Church of England Zenana Missionary Society Archives. Housed at the University of Birmingham, England.

Coates, P. D. *The China Consuls: British Consular Officers, 1843–1943*. Hong Kong, Oxford, and New York: Oxford University Press, 1988.

Cochran, Sherman. "A Guide to Memoirs in Chinese Periodical Literature: A Review of a New Bibliography." *Republican China* 21, no. 2 (1996): 91–93.

Cohen, Paul A. *China and Christianity: The Missionary Movement and the Growth of Chinese Anti-foreignism, 1860–1870*. Harvard University Press, 1963.

Collis, Maurice. *Foreign Mud: The Opium Imbroglio at Canton in the 1830s and the Anglo-Chinese War*. New York: W. W. Norton, 1946.

Copplestone, J. Tremayne. *Twentieth-Century Perspectives (The Methodist Episcopal Church, 1896–1939). The Methodist Episcopal Church, 1845–1939*, vol. 4. New York: Board of Missions of the Methodist Church, 1957.

Courtwright, David T. *Dark Paradise: Opiate Addiction in America Before 1940*. Cambridge, Mass.: Harvard University Press, 1982.

Crafts, Wilbur F.; Mary Leitch; and Margaret W. Leitch. *Protection of Native Races Against Intoxicants & Opium: Based on Testimony of One Hundred Missionaries and Travelers*. Chicago: Fleming H. Revell, 1900.

Cressey, George. *China's Geographic Foundations: A Survey of the Land and Its Peoples*. New York: McGraw-Hill, 1934.

Crossley, Pamela Kyle. *Orphan Warriors: Three Manchu Generations and the End of the Qing World*. Princeton: Princeton University Press, 1990.

———. "Thinking About Ethnicity in Early Modern China." *Late Imperial China* 1 (June 1990): 1–34.

Darley, Mary E. *The Light of the Morning: The Story of C.E.Z.M.S. Work in the Kienning Prefecture of the Fuh-kien Province, China*. London: Church of England Zenana Missionary Society and Marshall Brothers, 1903.

Deming, Philander. *The Best Adirondack Stories of Philander Deming*. Syracuse, N.Y.: Syracuse University Press, 1997.

De Quincey, Thomas. *Confessions of an English Opium-Eater*. London: J. M. Dent, 1907.

Des Forges, Alexander. "Opium/Leisure/Shanghai: Urban Economies of Consumption." Brook and Wakabayashi, ed., In *Opium Regimes: China, Britain, and Japan, 1839–1952*, ed. Timothy Brook and Bob Tadashi Wakabayashi, pp. 167–88. Berkeley: University of California Press, 2000.

Des Forges, Roger. *Hsi-liang and the Chinese National Revolution*. New Haven: Yale University Press, 1973.

Dierci Fujian ziyi ju yi shi suji lu 第二次福建諮議局議事速記錄 (Minutes of the second session of the Fujian Provincial Assembly). N.p., 1910. In the Fujian Provincial Library, Fuzhou, China.

Dikötter, Frank; Lars Laamann; and Zhou Xun. "Narcotic Culture: A Social History of Drug Consumption in China." *British Journal of Criminology* 42, no. 2 (Spring 2002): 317–36.

Doolittle, Justus. *Social Life of the Chinese*. 2 vols. New York: Harper & Brothers, 1895. Reprinted—Singapore: Graham Brash, 1986.

Duara, Prasenjit. *Culture, Power, and the State: Rural North China, 1900–1942*. Stanford: Stanford University Press, 1988.

Dudgeon, John. *Review of the Customs Opium Smoking Returns*. Shanghai: American Presbyterian Mission Press, 1882.

Dunch, Ryan. *Fuzhou Protestants and the Making of a Modern China, 1857–1927*. New Haven: Yale University Press, 2001.

———. "Piety, Patriotism, Progress: Chinese Protestants in Fuzhou Society and the Making of a Modern China, 1850–1927." Ph.D. diss., Yale University, 1996.

Dyer, Alfred S., ed. *Word-Pictures of Chinese Life*. London: All Nations Missionary Union, 1905.

Eisenlohr, L. E. S. *International Narcotics Control*. New York: Arno Press, 1981.

Elliot, Mark. "Bannermen and Townsmen: Ethnic Tension in Nineteenth-Century Jiangnan." *Late Imperial China* 11, no. 1 (June 1990): 36–74.

Esherick, Joseph W. *The Origins of the Boxer Uprising*. Berkeley: University of California Press, 1987.

———. *Reform & Revolution in China: The 1911 Revolution in Hunan and Hubei*. Berkeley: University of California Press, 1976.

Esherick, Joseph W., and Mary Backus Rankin, eds. *Chinese Local Elites and Patterns of Dominance*. Berkeley: University of California Press, 1990.

Fairbank, John King. "The Legalization of the Opium Trade Before the Treaties of 1858." *Chinese Social and Political Science Review* 17, no. 2 (July 1933): 215–63.

Faithfull-Davies, Margaret E. *The Banyan City*. London: Church of England Zenana Missionary Society, 1910.

Falkenheim, Victor Carl. "Provincial Administration in Fukien: 1949–1966." Ph.D. diss., Columbia University, 1974.

Fan nietai lilin Qudu zongshe kai huiyi an 潘臬臺蒞臨去毒總社開會議案 (A meeting of the headquarters of the Anti-Opium Society honored by the attendance of Provincial Judge Fan). Fuzhou: n.p., 1909. In the Fujian Provincial Library, Fuzhou, China.

Fay, Peter Ward. *The Opium War, 1840–1842*. Chapel Hill: University of North Carolina Press, 1975.

Fewsmith, Joseph. *Party, State, and Local Elites in Republican China: Merchant Organizations and Politics in Shanghai, 1890–1930*. Honolulu: University of Hawaii Press, 1985.

Fitzgerald, John. *Awakening China: Politics, Culture, and Class in the Nationalist Revolution.* Stanford: Stanford University Press, 1996.

FMMH: *Report of the Foochow Medical Missionary Hospital in Connection with the ABCFM Mission.* Fuzhou: Foochow Printing Press, 1872–89. Becomes the *Annual Report,* Ponasang Missionary Hospital, 1891–1909; and then the *Annual Report,* Foochow Missionary Hospital, 1910–22. In the National Library of Medicine, Bethesda, Maryland.

The Foochow Messenger. Published by the ABCFM Mission, 1903–30.

The Friend of China. Organ of the Society for the Suppression of the Opium Trade. London: P. S. King & Son, 1901–16.

Frolic, B. Michael. "The Emergence of Civil Society in China." *East Asia Policy Papers* (Toronto: University of Toronto–York University Joint Centre for Asia Pacific Studies), no. 14 (1996).

FRUS: U.S. Department of State. *Papers Relating to the Foreign Relations of the United States.* Washington, D.C.: GPO, 1906.

Fu Lo-shu. *A Documentary Chronicle of Sino-Western Relations (1644–1820).* 2 vols. Tucson: Association of Asian Studies and University of Arizona Press, 1966.

Fujian jinyan jishu 福建禁煙記述 (An objective report on opium prohibition in Fujian). N.p., n.d. (probably 1912/1913). In the Fuzhou Provincial Library, Fuzhou, China.

Fujian xianding jinyan xinzhang 福建憲定禁煙新章 (New regulations for opium prohibition set by the Fujian government). Handwritten date of 1911. In the Fujian Provincial Library, Fuzhou, China.

Fujian ziyi ju diyi jie quanti yiyuan yilan biao 福建諮議局第一全體議員一覽表 (Comprehensive list of representatives to the first session of the Fujian Provincial Assembly). N.p., handwritten date of 1910. In the Fujian Provincial Library, Fuzhou, China.

Fujian ziyi ju diyi jie yi an zhaiyao 福建諮議局第一屆議案摘要 (Summary of resolutions at the first session of the Fujian Provincial Assembly). N.p., handwritten date of 1909. In the Fujian Provincial Library, Fuzhou, China.

Fuzhou Meiyimei nianhui shi 福州美以美年會史 (Methodist Episcopal Church annual history). Fuzhou: Methodist Publishing House, n.d.

Fuzhou shuobao she zhangcheng 福州説報社章程 (Regulations of the Fuzhou Speak the News Society). N.p., n.d. In the Fujian Provincial Library, Fuzhou, China.

Fuzhou weishanshe zhengxin lu. 福州惟善社征信社 (A record of the mission of the Fuzhou Do-Only-Good Society). Fuzhou: Fuzhou weishanshe bian, 1911. In the Fujian Provincial Library, Fuzhou, China.

Gantt, T. Fulton [aka ZOR]. *Breaking the Chains: A Story of the Present Industrial Struggle.* In *The Knights in Fiction: Two Labor Novels of the 1880s,* ed. Mary C. Grimes. Urbana and Chicago: University of Illinois Press, 1986.

Gardella, Robert P., Jr. "Fukien's Tea Industry and Trade in Ch'ing and Republican China: The Developmental Consequences of a Traditional Commodity Export." Ph.D. diss., University of Washington, 1976.

———. *Harvesting Mountains: Fujian and the China Tea Trade, 1757–1939*. Berkeley: University of California Press, 1994.

Gewurtz, Margo S. "Do Numbers Count? A Report on a Preliminary Study of the Christian Converts of the North Henan Mission, 1890–1925." *Republican China* 10, no. 3 (1985): 18–26.

Goodman, Bryna. *Native Place, City, and Nation: Regional Networks and Identities in Shanghai, 1853–1937*. Berkeley: University of California Press, 1995.

Gray, Arthur R., and Arthur M. Sherman. *The Story of the Church in China*. New York: Domestic and Foreign Missionary Society, 1913.

Great Britain. Foreign Office. *The Opium Trade, 1910–1941*. Facsimile reproduction of the Foreign Office Collection (FO 415) in the Public Record Office, London. 6 vols. Wilmington, Del.: Scholarly Resources, 1974.

Great Britain. Parliamentary Papers. *China No. 1 (1908). Correspondence Respecting the Opium Question in China*. London: Wyman and Sons, 1908.

———. *China No. 3 (1909). Despatches from His Majesty's Minister at Peking, Forwarding Reports Respecting the Opium Question in China*. 1910.

Great Britain. Royal Commission on Opium. Vol. 1, *First Report of the Royal Commission on Opium with Minutes of Evidence and Appendices*. Vols. 2–4, *Minutes of Evidence Taken Before the Royal Commission on Opium from 29 January to 22 February 1894 with Appendices*. Vol. 5, *Appendices Together with Correspondence on the Subject of Opium with the Straits Settlement and China, etc*. Vol. 6, *Final Report of the Royal Commission on Opium*. Vol. 7, *Supplement to the Report*. London: Eyre and Spottiswoode, 1894–95.

Guo Gongmu 郭公木. "Xinhai Fuzhou guangfu jige wenti de diaocha yanjiu" 新亥福州光復几各問題的調查研究 (An investigation into several issues concerning the recovery of Fuzhou in 1911). *Fuzhou wenshi ziliao xuanji* 1981, no. 1 (Sept.): 90–93.

———. "Xinhai geming Fuzhou chuli baqi guanbing jingguo" 新亥革命福州處理八旗官兵經過 (The experiences of the Banner soldiers and officers in Fuzhou during the 1911 Revolution). *Fuzhou wenshi ziliao xuanji* 1981, no. 1 (Sept.): 50–57.

Gurr, Ted. *Why Men Rebel*. Princeton: Princeton University Press, 1970.

Habermas, Jürgen. *The Structural Transformation of the Public Sphere*. Trans. Thomas Burger with Frederick Lawrence. Cambridge, Mass.: MIT Press, 1989.

Harding, Geoffrey. *Opiate Addiction, Morality and Medicine: From Moral Illness to Pathological Disease*. New York: St. Martin's Press, 1988.

Harmon, Nolan B., gen. ed. *The Encyclopedia of World Methodism*. 2 vols. Nashville: United Methodist Publishing House, 1974.

Harrison, Henrietta. *The Making of the Republican Citizen: Political Ceremonies and Symbols in China, 1911–1929*. Oxford: Oxford University Press, 2000.

Hayter, Alethea. *Opium and the Romantic Imagination: Addiction and Creativity in De Quincey, Coleridge, Baudelaire, and Others*. New York: Sterling, 1988.

Ho Ping-ti. "In Defense of Sinicization: A Rebuttal of Evelyn Rawski's 'Reenvisioning the Qing.'" *Journal of Asian Studies* 57, no. 1 (Feb. 1998): 123–55.

———. *Studies on the Population of China, 1368–1953*. Cambridge, Mass.: Harvard University Press, 1959.

Howard, Paul. "Ministers of Health: Medical Missionaries and the Effort to Cure Opium Addiction in Late Nineteenth-Century China." Paper presented at the Association for Asian Studies Conference, Mar. 24–27, 1994.

Hsieh, Winston. "Triads, Salt Smugglers, and Local Uprisings: Observations on the Social and Economic Background of the Waichow Revolution of 1911." In *Popular Movements and Secret Societies in China, 1840–1950*, ed. Jean Chesneaux, pp. 145–64. Stanford University Press, 1972.

Huang, Philip. "'Public Sphere' / 'Civil Society' in China? The Third Realm Between State and Society." *Modern China* 19, no. 2 (Apr. 1993): 216–40.

Huang Shangyuan 黃裳元. "Ershi nian huo Xian zhi yanmiao" 二十年禍仙之煙苗 (Twenty years of disaster—opium in Xianyou). *Xianyou wenshi ziliao* 1983, no. 1 (Jan.): 41.

———. "Nongmin douzheng shihuo si ze" 農民斗爭史活四則 (Four incidents in the history of the peasants' struggle). *Xianyou wenshi ziliao* 1983, no. 1 (Jan.): 31–41.

Huang Yunqing 黃允清. "Minguo shiqi de Shouning jin yapian qingkuang xushu" 民國時期的壽寧禁鴉片情況敘述 (Recounting the circumstances of opium prohibition in Shouning during the Republican era). *Shouning wenshi ziliao* 1990, no. 5 (May): 27–38.

Hung, Chang-tai. *War and Popular Culture: Resistance in Modern China, 1937–45*. Berkeley: University of California Press, 1994.

Hurlbut, Floy. *The Fukienese: A Study in Human Geography*. Ph.D. diss., University of Nebraska published by the author, 1939.

Husain, Akhtar, and J. R. Sharma. *The Opium Poppy*. Lucknow, India: Central Institute of Medicinal & Aromatic Plants, 1983.

Im, Kaye Soon. "The Rise and Decline of the Eight Banner Garrisons in the Ch'ing Period (1644–1911): A Study of the Kuang-Chou, Hang-Chou, and Ching-Chou Garrisons." Ph.D. diss., University of Illinois, 1981.

IMC (Imperial Maritime Customs). *Reports and Special Series*. Shanghai: Kelly & Walsh.

———. *China Opium Trade, 1889–1894.*
———. *Decennial Reports, Amoy, 1882–1891, 1892–1901, 1902–1911, 1912–1921.*
———. *Decennial Reports, Foochow, 1882–1891, 1892–1901, 1902–1911, 1912–1921.*
———. *Decennial Reports, Santuao, 1892–1901, 1902–1911, 1912–1921.*
———. *Decennial Reports, Wenchow, 1882–1891.*
———. SS No 9 (Special Series No. 9, *Native Opium*). 1887.
———. SS No. 10 (Special Series No. 10, *Opium: Crude and Prepared*). 1888.
———. SS No. 14 (Special Series No. 14, *Opium Trade, March Quarter*). 1889.
IOC (International Opium Commission). *Report of the International Opium Commission, Shanghai, China, February 1 to February 26, 1909.* 2 vols. London: P. S. King and Son, 1909.
IWCD: *India's Women and China's Daughters.* CEZMS: 1895–1918. In the University of Birmingham, England.
Jiang Qiuming 蔣秋明 and Shi Qingbao 失慶葆. *Zhongguo jindu licheng* 中國禁毒歷程 (The course of narcotic prohibition in China). Tianjin: Tianjin jiaoyu chubanshe, 1996.
Jiaowu jiao'an dang 教務教案檔 (Anti-missionary cases), vols. 6–7. Taibei: Modern History Institute, Academia Sinica, 1980, 1981.
Jieyan diaocha zhangcheng 戒煙調查章程 (Regulations on the cessation and investigation of opium). Fuzhou: Fujian shizhengshisi (Office of Civil Administration), 1908. In the Fujian Provincial Library, Fuzhou, China.
Kane, Harry H. *Opium Smoking in America & China.* New York: Arno Press, 1976.
"Kaoding yu buchong" 考訂與補充 (Corrections and supplementary materials). *Xianyou wenshi ziliao* 1983, no. 1 (Jan.): 62–72.
Kennedy, Thomas L. "Mausers and the Opium Trade: The Hupeh Arsenal, 1895–1911." In *Perspectives on a Changing China*, ed. Joshua A. Fogel and William T. Rowe, pp. 118–23. Boulder, Colo.: Westview Press, 1979.
King, Paul. *In the Chinese Customs Service: A Personal Record of Forty-Seven Years.* London: T. F. Unwin, 1924. Reprinted—New York: Garland, 1980.
Kuo, Pin-chia. *A Critical Study of the First Anglo-Chinese War, with Documents.* Shanghai: Commercial Press, 1935. Reprinted—Connecticut: Hyperion Press, 1973.
Lamley, Harry J. "Lineage and Surname Feuds in Southern Fukien and Eastern Kwangtung Under the Ch'ing." In *Orthodoxy in Late Imperial China*, ed. Kwang-ching Liu, pp. 255–78. Berkeley: University of California Press, 1990.
———. "Lineage Feuding in Southern Fujian and Eastern Guangdong Under Qing Rule." In *Violence in China: Essays in Culture and Counterculture*, ed. Jonathan N. Lipman and Stevan Harrell, pp. 27–64. Albany, N.Y.: SUNY Press, 1990.
Lan Hanmin 藍漢民. "Yapian wei hai Shanghang suoji" 鴉片危害上杭瑣記 (Notes on the damage done to Shanghang by opium). *Shanghang wenshi ziliao* 1984, no. 3 (Dec.): 19–21.

Lao She. *Cat Country: A Satirical Novel of China in the 1930's.* Trans. William A. Lyell, Jr. Columbus: Ohio State University Press, 1970.

Latourette, Kenneth Scott. *A History of Christian Missions in China.* New York: Russell & Russell, 1929.

Layton, Thomas L. *The Voyage of the 'Frolic': New England Merchants and the Opium Trade.* Stanford: Stanford University Press, 1997.

Lefebure, Molly. *Samuel Tayler Coleridge, Opium, and Kubla Khan.* New York: Octagon Books, 1975.

Li Guoqi [Li Kuo-ch'i] 李國祁. *Minguo shi lunji* 民國史論集 (Discussions of Republican history). Taibei: Nantian shuju, 1990.

———. "Qingmo Minchu Min-Zhe diqu renkou liudong yu dushihua de yanjin, 1866–1916" 清末民初閩浙地區人口流動與都市化的演進 (Developments in population flows and urbanization in the area of Fujian and Zhejiang, 1866–1916). *Lishi xuebao,* no. 5 (April 1977): 489–522.

———. *Zhongguo xiandaihua de quyu yanjiu: Min-Zhe-Tai diqu, 1860–1916* 中國現代化的區域研究：閩浙臺地區 (Regional research on China's modernization: the Fujian-Zhejiang-Taiwan region, 1860–1916). Taibei: Zhongyang yanjiuyuan, 1982.

Li Hanzhou 李漢洲. "Longyan jinyan shihua" 龍岩禁煙史話 (History of opium prohibition in Longyan). *Longyan wenshi ziliao* 1991, no. 19: 101–4.

Li Shengping 李盛平. *Zhongguo jinxiandai renming dacidian* 中國近現代人名大辭典 (A dictionary of modern and contemporary Chinese notables). Beijing: Zhongguo guoji guangbo chubanshe, 1989.

"Lieming kenqing Min-Zhe zongdu Song yuanzhao xinyue jinyun yangyao jin Fujian kou chengwen" 列名懇請閩浙總督松援照新約禁運洋藥進福建口呈文 (Signed petition begging Governor-General Song to prohibit the importation of foreign opium into Fujian in accordance with the new treaty). N.d. (1911?). In the Fujian Provincial Library, Fuzhou, China.

Lin Honghuan 林鴻煥. "'Qudu she' shimo" 去毒社始末 (The beginning and end of the Society to Eliminate the Poison). *Taijiang wenshi* 1986, no. 2 (Oct.): 48–49.

Lin Man-houng 林滿紅. "Integrating or Disintegrating the National Economy? The Opium Market Within China, 1820s–1906." Paper presented at the Conference on Opium in East Asian History, 1830–1945. University of Toronto, Canada, May 9–10, 1997.

———. "Qingmo benguo yapian zhi tidai jinkou yapian" 清末本國鴉片之替代進口鴉片 (The substitution of native opium for imported opium in the late Qing). *Jindaishi yanjiusuo jikan* 8 (1980): 385–432.

———. "Qingmo shehui liuxing xishi yapian yanjiu—gongjimian zhi fenxi (1773–1906)" 清末社會流行吸食鴉片研究—供給面之分析 (1733–1906) (A study on the spread of opium smoking in late Qing society—a supply-side analysis, 1773-1906). Ph.D. diss., Taiwan National University, 1985.

———. "Wan Qing de yapian shui" 晚清的鴉片稅 (The opium tax in the late Qing). *Si yu yan* 16, no. 5 (Jan. 1979): 11-59.

Lin Renchuan 林仁川. "Qingdai Fujian de yapian maoyi" 清代福建的鴉片貿易 (The opium trade in Qing dynasty Fujian). *Zhongguo shehui jingji yanjiu* (Xiamen: Fujian xinwen) 1985, no. 1: 62-71.

Lin Wenhui 林文慧. *Qingji Fujian jiao'an zhi yanjiu* 清季福建教案之研究 (A study of anti-missionary cases in late Qing Fujian). Taibei: Taiwan shangwu yinshuguan, 1989.

Lin Wenji 林文吉. "Jiefang qian de Shima 'san hai'" 解放前的石馬三害 (The "three evils" of pre-liberation Shima). *Longhai wenshi ziliao* 1988, no. 10 (Dec.): 60-62.

Lin Zhiping 林治平. "Jidujiao chuanjiaoshi yu Zhongguo jinyan yundong" 基督教傳教士與中國禁煙運動 (Christian missionaries and China's anti-opium movement). In *Jindai Zhongguo yi jidujiao lunwen ji* 近代中國亦基督教論文集 (Collected essays on contemporary China and Christianity), ed. Lin Zhiping, pp. 307-25. Taibei: Yuchou guang chubanshe, 1981.

Lin Zongtang 林宗湯. "Minguo shiqi Xianyou xianzhang qunxiang" 民國時期仙游縣長群像 (A group portrait of Xianyou magistrates during the Republic). *Xianyou wenshi ziliao* 1985, no. 3 (July): 42-60.

Liu Decheng 林德城 and Zhou Xianying 周羨穎, eds. *Fujian mingren cidian* 福建名人詞典 (Dictionary of famous Fujianese). Fuzhou: Fujian renmin chubanshe, 1995.

Liu Shoulin 劉壽林, ed. *Xinhai yihou shiqinian zhiguan nianbiao* 辛亥以後十七年職官年表 (A roster of gentry and officials in the seventeen years following 1911). Beijing: Zhonghuo shuju, 1966.

Liu Wanhang 劉萬航. "Yan yu yanju" 煙與煙具 (Opium and smoking tools). *Gugong wenwu yuekan* 2, no. 12 (1985): 75-77.

Lodwick, Kathleen L. "Chinese, Missionary, and International Efforts to End the Use of Opium in China, 1890-1916." Ph.D. diss., University of Arizona, 1976.

———. *Crusaders Against Opium: Protestant Missionaries in China, 1874-1917*. Lexington: University Press of Kentucky, 1996.

LMS/CWM: Archives of the Council for World Mission, incorporating the London Missionary Society. In the School of Oriental and African Studies (SOAS), University of London, England.

Lubbock, Alfred B. *The Opium Clippers*. Glasgow: Brown, Son & Ferguson, 1933.

Luo Ergang 羅爾綱. "Fujian qiyi de Xiaodaohui lingxiu shi shei?" 福建起義的小刀會領袖是誰 (Who were the leaders of the Small Knife Society uprising in Fujian?). *Lishi jiaoxue* 1981, no. 4: 18-20.

Luo Yudong 羅玉東. *Zhongguo lijin shi* 中國釐金史 (The history of the transit tax in China). 2 vols. Shanghai: Shangwu yinshuguan, 1936.

"Luoyuan yanhai yu jinyan jishi" 羅源煙害與禁煙記實 (The true story of opium's damage and prohibition in Luoyuan). *Luoyuan wenshi ziliao* 1990, no. 4 (Dec.): 19–24.

Ma Guanwu 馬冠武. "Qiantan Taiping tianguo de jinyan zhengce" 淺談太平天國的禁煙政策 (A brief discussion of the Taipings' anti-opium policy). *Guangxi shiyuan xuebao* 1981, no. 1: 45–52.

MacGillivray, Donald, ed. *A Century of Protestant Missions in China (1807–1907)*. Shanghai: American Presbyterian Mission Press, 1907.

Macgowan, John. *Sidelights on Chinese Life*. London: Kegan Paul, Trench, Trubner & Co., 1907.

Madancy, Joyce A. "Ambitious Interlude: The Anti-Opium Campaign in China's Fujian Province, 1906–17." Ph.D. diss., University of Michigan, 1996.

———. "Revolution, Religion, and the Poppy: Opium and the Rebellion of the 'Sixteenth Emperor' in Early Republican Fujian." *Republican China* 21, no. 1 (Nov. 1995): 1–41.

———. "Unearthing Popular Attitudes Toward the Opium Trade and Opium Suppression in Late Qing and Early Republican Fujian." *Modern China* 27, no. 4 (Oct. 2001): 436–83.

MAE/Nantes: Archives de Ministère des Affaires Etrangères, Consular file for Foutcheou [Fuzhou] (1871–1946). Nantes, France.

MAE/Paris: Archives de Ministère des Affaires Etrangères. Nouvelle séries [NS]/Chine/Questions sociales, Opium (1896–1917), vols. 584–94; and NS/Chine/Politique intérieure/Dossier général (1897–1917), vols. 1–66. Paris.

Mann, Susan. *Local Merchants and the Chinese Bureaucracy, 1750–1950*. Stanford: Stanford University Press, 1987.

Marx, Karl. *Marx on China, 1853–1860: Articles from the "New York Daily Tribune."* With an Introduction and notes by Dona Torr. London: Lawrence & Wishart, 1951.

McMahon, Keith. *The Fall of the God of Money: Opium Smoking in Nineteenth-Century China*. Lanham, Md., and Oxford: Rowman & Littlefield, 2002.

MEC: (Methodist Episcopal Mission). Archives of the United Methodist Church. At the General Commission on Archives and History, Drew University, Madison, N.J.

MEC *Annual Report* (1906–14). In the Archives of the United Methodist Church. At the General Commission on Archives and History, Drew University, Madison, N.J.

Mercy and Truth. Published by the Medical Department of the Church Missionary Society. 1906–17. At the University of Birmingham, England.

Miao Xiaoning 缪小宁. "Fu'an renmin fankang yapian juan douzheng jishi" 福安人民反抗鸦片捐斗争記實 (A record of the struggle of the people of Fu'an against opium). *Fujian dangshi yuekan* 1988, no. 2: 54–59.

Michael, Franz. *The Taiping Rebellion: History and Documents.* 3 vols. Seattle: University of Washington Press, 1966.

Milligan, Barry. *Pleasures and Pains: Opium and the Orient in Nineteenth-Century British Culture.* Charlottesville: University Press of Virginia, 1995.

Min dudufu Minzhengsi Jinyan gongsuo yuebao 閩都督府民政司禁煙公所月報 (Monthly reports of the Opium Prohibition Office of the Ministry of Internal Affairs, Office of the Military Governor of Fujian). Fuzhou, 1912. In the Fujian Provincial Library, Fuzhou, China.

Min Tu-ki. *National Polity and Local Power: The Transformation of Late Imperial China.* Ed. Philip A. Kuhn and Timothy Brook. Cambridge, Mass.: Council on East Asian Studies, Harvard University, and Harvard-Yenching Institute, 1999.

Minxian xiangtuzhi 閩縣鄉土志 (Min county gazetteer). Fuzhou: 1906. In the Fujian Provincial Library, Fuzhou, China.

Morse, Hosea Ballou. *International Relations of the Chinese Empire.* 3 vols. Shanghai and London: Longmans, Green, and Co., 1910–18.

———. *The Trade and Administration of the Chinese Empire.* Shanghai: Kelly & Walsh, 1907. Reprinted—Taibei: Ch'eng-wen, 1966.

Murray, Dian, in collaboration with Qin Baoqi. *The Origins of the Tiandihui: The Chinese Triads in Legend and History.* Stanford: Stanford University Press, 1994.

New Catholic Encyclopedia. 19 vols. Washington, D.C.: Catholic University, 1967.

Newell, G. Papers. Foochow, China, American Board Mission. At Burke Library, Union Theological Seminary, New York City.

Newman, R. K. "Opium Smoking in Late Imperial China: A Reconsideration." *Modern Asian Studies* 29, no. 4 (1995): 765–94.

No. 1 Ming/Qing Archives, Beijing, China; particularly the records of the Jinyan zongju 禁煙總局 (Anti-Opium Commission).

OSOL: *Our Sisters in Other Lands.* Presbyterian Church of England, Foreign Missions Committee. 1881–27. At the School of Oriental and African Studies (SOAS), University of London, England.

Owen, David Edward. *British Opium Policy in China and India.* New Haven: Yale University Press, 1934.

Ownby, David, and Mary Somers Heidues, eds. *"Secret Societies" Reconsidered: Perspectives on the Social History of Modern South China and Southeast Asia.* Armonk, N.Y.: M. E. Sharpe, 1993.

Pan Youlian 潘友廉. "'Zhenkong jiao' liuxing zai Youxi"眞空教流行在尤溪 (The popularity of the Zhengkong Sect in Youxi). *Youxi wenshi ziliao* 1989, no. 8 (Feb.): 51–53.

Park, William Hector, ed. *Opinions of Over 100 Physicians on the Use of Opium in China.* Shanghai: American Presbyterian Mission Press, 1899.

Parssinen, Terry M. *Secret Passions, Secret Remedies: Narcotic Drugs in British Society, 1820–1930.* Philadelphia: Institute for the Study of Human Issues, 1983.

PCE: Presbyterian Church of England Foreign Missions Archives. At School of Oriental and African Studies (SOAS), University of London, England.

Pitcher, Philip W. *In and About Amoy.* Shanghai and Fuzhou: Methodist Publishing House in China, 1909.

Polachek, James M. *The Inner Opium War.* Cambridge, Mass.: Harvard University, Council on East Asian Studies, 1992.

Pomeranz, Kenneth. *The Making of a Hinterland: State, Society, and Economy in Inland North China, 1853–1937.* Berkeley: University of California Press, 1993.

Prazniak, Roxann. *Of Camel Kings and Other Things: Rural Rebels Against Modernity in Late Imperial China.* Rowman & Littlefield, 1999.

———. "Tax protest at Laiyang, Shandong, 1910: Commoner Organization Versus the County Political Elite." *Modern China* 6, no. 1 (Jan. 1980): 41–71.

———. "Weavers and Sorceresses of Chuansha." *Modern China* 12, no. 2 (Apr. 1986): 202–29.

PRO, FO: Public Record Office, Foreign Office, Great Britain. FO 228: China: Embassy and Consular Archives. At Kew Gardens, Richmond, England.

Pruitt, Ida. *Daughter of Han: The Autobiography of a Chinese Working Woman.* New Haven: Yale University Press, 1945. Reprinted—Stanford: Stanford University Press, 1967.

Qi Sihe 齊思和, ed. *Huang Juezi zhoushu, Xu Naiji zouyi hekan* 黃爵滋奏疏, 許乃濟奏議合刊 (Joint compilation of the memorials of Huang Jiezi and Xu Naiji). Beijing: Zhonghua shuju, 1959.

Qi Sihe 齊思和, Lin Shuhui 林樹惠, and Shou Jiyu 壽紀瑜, eds. *Yapian zhanzheng* 鴉片戰爭 (The Opium War). 6 vols. Shanghai: Shanghai renmin chubanshe, 1957.

Qian Shifu 錢實甫, ed. *Qingji xinshe zhiguan nianbiao* 清季新設職官年表 (Roster of newly established offices in the late Qing). Beijing: Zhonghua shuju, 1961.

Qiaonan gongyi she zhengxin lu, 1908–1909 橋南公益社徵信錄 (Financial records of the South of the Bridge Public Welfare Society, 1908–9). Fuzhou: Qiming, 1909.

Quale, G. Robina. "The Mission Compound in Modern China: The Role of the United States Protestant Mission as an Asylum in the Civil and International Strife of China, 1900–1941." Ph.D. diss., University of Michigan, 1957.

Quarterly: Fujian qudu zongshe jibao 福建去毒總社季報 (Fujian Anti-Opium Society quarterly). At the Fujian Provincial Library, Fuzhou, China.

Rankin, Mary Backus. *Elite Activism and Political Transformation in China: Zhejiang Province, 1865–1911.* Stanford: Stanford University Press, 1986.

———. "The Ku-t'ien Incident (1895): Christians Versus the Ts'ai-hui." *Papers on China* (Harvard University) 15 (Dec. 1961): 30–61.

———. "Some Observations on a Chinese Public Sphere." *Modern China* 19, no. 2 (Apr. 1993): 158–82.

Rawski, Evelyn Sakakida. *Agricultural Change and the Peasant Economy of South China.* Cambridge, Mass.: Harvard University Press, 1972.

———. "Reenvisioning the Qing: The Significance of the Qing Period in Chinese History." *Journal of Asian Studies* 55, no. 4 (1996): 829–50.

Reins, Thomas D. "China and the International Politics of Opium, 1900–1937: The Impact of Reform, Revenue and the Unequal Treaties." Ph.D. diss., Claremont Graduate School, 1981.

———. "Reform, Nationalism and Internationalism: The Opium Suppression Movement in China and the Anglo-American Influence, 1900–1908." *Modern Asian Studies* 25, no. 1 (1991): 101–42.

Remer, C. F., with the assistance of William B. Palmer. *A Study of Chinese Boycotts with Special Reference to Their Economic Effectiveness.* Baltimore: Johns Hopkins Press, 1933. Reprinted—New York: Arno Press, 1979.

Republican Advocate. Shanghai. 1912–13.

Reynolds, Douglas R. *China, 1898–1912: The Xinzheng Revolution and Japan.* Cambridge, Mass.: Council on East Asian Studies, Harvard University, 1993.

Rhoads, Edward J. M. *Manchus & Han: Ethnic Relations and Political Power in Late Qing and Early Republican China, 1861–1928.* Seattle: University of Washington Press, 2000.

Richards, John F. "The Indian Empire and Peasant Production of Opium in the Nineteenth Century." *Modern Asian Studies* 15, no. 1 (1981): 59–82.

———. "Opium and the British Empire: The Royal Commission of 1895." *Modern Asian Studies* 36, no. 2 (2002): 375–420.

RIOCS: International Opium Commission. *Report of the International Opium Commission, Shanghai, China, February 1 to February 26, 1909.* Vol. 1, *Report of the Proceedings.* Vol. 2, *Reports of the Delegations.* Shanghai: North China Daily News and Herald, 1909.

Rowe, William T. *Hankow: Commerce and Society in a Chinese City, 1796–1889.* Stanford: Stanford University Press, 1984.

———. *Hankow: Conflict and Community in a Chinese City, 1796–1895.* Stanford: Stanford University Press, 1989.

———. "The Problem of 'Civil Society' in Late Imperial China." *Modern China* 19, no. 2 (Apr. 1993): 139–57.

———. "The Public Sphere in Modern China." *Modern China* 16, no. 3 (July 1990): 309–29.

Rush, James R. "Opium in Java: A Sinister Fiend." *Journal of Asian Studies* 44, no. 3 (May 1985): 549–60.

———. *Opium to Java: Revenue Farming and Chinese Enterprise in Colonial Indonesia, 1860–1910*. Ithaca, N.Y.: Cornell University Press, 1990.

Schneider, Elisabeth W. *Coleridge, Opium, and Kubla Khan*. New York: Octagon Books, 1975.

Schoppa, R. Keith. *Chinese Elites and Political Change: Zhejiang Province in the Early Twentieth Century*. Cambridge, Mass.: Harvard University Press, 1982.

Shen Laiqiu 沈來秋. "Xinhai qianhou de Peng Shousong" 辛亥前后的彭壽松 (Peng Shousong before and after the Revolution of 1911). *Fuzhou wenshi xuanji* 1981, no. 1 (Sept.): 38–43.

Shih, Vincent Y. C. *The Taiping Ideology: Its Sources, Interpretations, and Influences*. Seattle: University of Washington Press, 1967.

Shue, Vivienne. *The Reach of the State: Sketches of the Chinese Body Politic*. Stanford: Stanford University Press, 1988.

Skinner, G. William. "Presidential Address: The Structure of Chinese History." *Journal of Asian Studies* 44, no. 2 (Feb. 1985): 271–92.

Skocpol, Theda. *States & Social Revolutions: A Comparative Analysis of France, Russia, & China*. Cambridge, Eng.: Cambridge University Press, 1979.

Slack, Edward R., Jr. "The National Anti-Opium Association and the Guomindang State, 1924–1937." In *Opium Regimes: China, Britain, and Japan, 1839–1952*, ed. Timothy Brook and Bob Tadashi Wakabayashi, pp. 248–69. Berkeley: University of California Press, 2000.

———. *Opium, State, and Society: China's Narco-Economy and the Guomindang, 1924–1937*. Honolulu: University of Hawaii Press, 2001.

Spence, Jonathan D. "Opium Smoking in Ch'ing China." In *Conflict and Control in Late Imperial China*, ed. Frederic Wakeman, Jr., and Carolyn Grant, pp. 143–73. Berkeley: University of California Press, 1975.

———. *The Search for Modern China*. New York and London: W. W. Norton, 1990.

Stapleton, Kristen. "The Rule of Avoidance Reaffirmed: County Administration in Late-Qing Sichuan." Draft prepared for the Annual Meeting of the Association for Asian Studies, March 24-28, 1994.

Stauffer, Milton T., ed. *The Christian Occupation of China: A General Survey of the Numerical Strength and Geographical Distribution of the Christian Forces in China Made by the Special Committee on Survey and Occupation, China Continuation Committee, 1918–21*. Shanghai: China Continuation Committee, 1922.

Strand, David. *Rickshaw Beijing: City People and Politics in the 1920s*. Berkeley: University of California Press, 1989.

Su Tong. "Opium Family." In idem, *Raise the Red Lantern: Three Novellas*. Trans. Michael S. Duke. Harmondsworth, Eng.: Penguin Books, 1993.

Su Zhiliang 蘇智良. *Zhongguo dupin shi* 中國毒品史 (The history of narcotics in China). Shanghai: Shanghai renmin chubanshe, 1997.

Tahara Tennan 田原天南, ed. *Shinmatsu minsho Chūgoku kanshin jimmeiroku* 清末民初中國官紳人民錄 (Biographies of Chinese officials and gentry in the late Qing / early Republic). Dalian: Chūgoku kenkyūkai, 1918.

Tan Zongying 談宗英 and Zhou Linmei 周林妹, eds. *Zhongguo jindaishi cidian* 中國近代史詞典 (A dictionary of modern Chinese history). Shanghai: Shanghai cishu chubanshe, 1982.

Taylor, Arnold H. *American Diplomacy and the Narcotics Traffic, 1900–1939: A Study in International Humanitarian Reform*. Durham, N.C.: Duke University Press, 1969.

Thaxton, Ralph. "State Making and State Terror." *Theory and Society* 19 (1990): 335–76.

Thompson, Roger. *China's Local Councils in the Age of Constitutional Reform, 1898–1911*. Cambridge, Mass.: Council on East Asian Studies, Harvard University, 1995.

———. "Statecraft and Self-Government: Competing Visions of Community and State in Late Imperial China." *Modern China* 14, no. 2 (Apr. 1988): 188–221.

Trocki, Carl. *Opium and Empire: Chinese Society in Colonial Singapore, 1800–1910*. Ithaca, N.Y.: Cornell University Press, 1990.

———. *Opium, Empire and the Global Political Economy: A Study of the Asian Opium Trade, 1750–1950*. London and New York: Routledge, 1999.

———. "The Rise and Fall of the Ngee Heng Kongsi in Singapore." In *"Secret Societies" Reconsidered: Perspectives on the Social History of Modern South China and Southeast Asia*, ed. David Ownby and Mary Somers Heidues, pp. 89–119. Armonk, N.Y.: M. E. Sharpe, 1993.

Tsin, Michael. *Nation, Governance, and Modernity in China: Canton, 1900–1927*. Stanford: Stanford University Press, 1999.

Turner, F. S. *British Opium Policy and Its Results to India and China*. London: Sampson Low, Marston, Searle, & Rivington, 1876.

USDS: United States. Department of State Archives. National Archives, College Park, Md.

——— (1844–1906). Despatches from the United States Consuls in Amoy, China. Microfilm.

——— (1849–1906). Despatches from the United States Consuls in Foochow, China. Microfilm.

——— (1906–1910). Records of the United States Department of State Relating to the Internal Affairs of China (The Numerical File). Microfilm.

——— (1910–1929). Records of the United States Department of State Relating to the Internal Affairs of China (The Decimal File). Microfilm.

U.S. War Department. Bureau of Insular Affairs. *Report of the Committee Appointed by the Philippine Commission to Investigate the Use of Opium and the Traffic Therein and* the Rules, Ordinances and Laws Regulating Such Use and Traffic in Japan, Formosa, Shanghai, Hongkong, Saigon, Burmah, Java and the Philippine Islands. Washington, D.C.: GPO, 1905.

Wagner, Rudolf G. "The Canonization of May Fourth." In *The Appropriation of Cultural Capital: China's May Fourth Project*, ed. Milena Doleželová-Velingerová and Oldřich Král, pp. 66–120. Cambridge, Mass.: Harvard University Asia Center, 2001.

Wakeman, Frederic, Jr. "The Civil Society and Public Sphere Debate." *Modern China* 19, no. 2 (Apr. 1993): 108–38.

———. "Models of Historical Change: The Chinese State and Society, 1839–89." In *Perspectives on Modern China: Four Anniversaries*, ed. Kenneth Lieberthal et al., pp. 68–102. Armonk, N.Y.: M. E. Sharpe, 1991.

———. *Policing Shanghai 1927–37*. Berkeley: University of California Press, 1995.

———. *Strangers at the Gate: Social Disorder in South China, 1839–1861*. Berkeley: University of California Press, 1966.

Waley, Arthur. *The Opium War Through Chinese Eyes*. London: Allen & Unwin, 1958.

Walker, William O., III. *Opium and Foreign Policy: The Anglo-American Search for Order in Asia, 1912–1954*. Chapel Hill: University of North Carolina Press, 1991.

Wang Hongbin 王宏斌. *Jindu shijian* 禁毒史鑒 (A historical examination of narcotics prohibition). Hubei: Yuelu shushe, 1997.

Wang Jinxiang 王金香. "Qingdai dierci jinyan yundong tanlüe" 清代第二次禁煙運動探略 (A brief exploration of the second anti-opium movement during the Qing dynasty). *Shixue yuekan* 1990, no. 2: 62–66.

Wang Shiqing 王世慶. "Riju chuqi Taiwan zhi Jiangbihui yu jieyan yundong" 日據初期台灣之降筆會與戒煙運動 (The Divine Writing Society and the anti-opium movement during the Japanese occupation of Taiwan). *Taiwan wenxian* 37, no. 4 (1986): 111–51.

Wang Shuhuai 王樹槐. "Yapian duhai: Guangxu ershisan nian wenjuan diaocha fenxi" 鴉片毒害：光緒二十三年文卷調查分析 (Opium damage: an analysis of the 1897 questionnaire). *Jindaishi yanjiusuo suo jikan* 1980, no. 9 (July): 183–200.

Wang Yiwei 王義遺. "Xianyou dashi jiyao" 仙游大實記要 (Record of important events in Xianyou). *Xianyou wenshi ziliao* 1985, no. 3 (July): 6–29.

Waung, W. S. K. "Introduction of Opium Cultivation to China." *Xianggang zhengzhixue xuebao* 1 (1979): 208–21.

Wei Hongyuan 魏鴻源. "Kaifang 'san jin' gei Jianyang renmin dailai de huohai" 開放三禁給建陽人民帶來的禍害 (Lifting the ban on the "three prohibitions" brought a scourge to the people of Jianyang). *Jianyang wenshi ziliao* 1985, no. 5 (Dec.): 51–54.

Wen Gongzhi 文公直. *Zuijin sanshinian Zhongguo junshi shi* 最近三十年中國軍事史 (A history of the past thirty years of Chinese military history). Shanghai: Taiping yang shuju, 1930.

Whitaker, Ben. *The Global Connection: The Crisis of Drug Addiction*. London: Jonathan Cape, 1987.

White, Gordon; Jude Howell; and Shang Xiaoyuan. *In Search of Civil Society: Market Reform and Social Change in Contemporary China*. Oxford: Clarendon Press, 1996.

Wolf, Margery. "Women and Suicide in China." In *Women in Chinese Society*, ed. Margery Wolf and Roxane Witke, pp. 111–41. Stanford: Stanford University Press, 1975.

Wolferstan, Bertram. *The Catholic Church in China from 1860 to 1907*. London and Edinburgh: Sands & Co., 1909.

Wong, J. Y. *Deadly Dreams: Opium, Imperialism, and the Arrow War (1856–1860) in China*. Cambridge, Eng.: Cambridge University Press, 1998.

Wong, R. Bin. "Great Expectations: The 'Public Sphere' and the Search for Modern Times in Chinese History." *Studies in Chinese History* 3 (Oct. 1993): 7–49.

———. "Opium and Modern Chinese State-Making." In *Opium Regimes: China, Britain, and Japan, 1839–1952*, ed. Timothy Brook and Bob Tadashi Wakabayashi, pp. 189–227. Berkeley: University of California Press, 2000.

Wright, Mary C., ed. *China in Revolution: The First Phase 1900–1913*. New Haven: Yale University Press, 1968.

Wu Jiaqiong 吳家瓊. "Lin Bingzhang shengping gaishu" 林炳章生平概述 (Brief biography of Lin Bingzhang). *Fujian wenshi ziliao* 1988, no. 19: 98–104.

Wu Jiayu 吳家瑜 and Lin Jiazhen 林家臻. "Fujian jinyan yundong 'Qudu she'" 福建禁煙運動去毒社 (The Fujian anti-opium movement's Anti-Opium Society). *Fuzhou wenshi ziliao xuanji* 1983, no. 2 (Dec.): 15–18.

Wu Tianchang 吳天昌. "Wu Tingcheng xiansheng chuangban Qudu she" 吳庭根先生創辦去毒社 (Mr. Wu Tingchang establishes the Anti-Opium Society). *Lianjiang wenshi ziliao* 1981, no. 3 (July): 27–28.

Wyman, Judith. "The Ambiguities of Chinese Antiforeignism: Chongqing, 1870–1900." *Late Imperial China* 18, no. 2 (Dec. 1997): 86–122.

———. "Opium and the State in Late-Qing Sichuan." In *Opium Regimes: China, Britain, and Japan, 1839–1952*, ed. Timothy Brook and Bob Tadashi Wakabayashi, pp. 212–27. Berkeley: University of California Press, 2000.

———. "Opium and the State in Sichuan Province During the Late Qing." Paper presented at the 46th Annual Meeting of the Association for Asian Studies, Boston, Mar. 24–27, 1994.

———. "Social Change, Anti-Foreignism and Revolution in China: Chongqing Prefecture, 1870s to 1911." Ph.D. diss., University of Michigan, 1993.

Xia Weijian 夏維堅 and Ye Xiangrong 葉向榮. "Yapian zai Shunchang de duhai yu jinyan" 鴉片在順昌的毒害與禁煙 (The damage caused by opium in Shunchang and its prohibition). *Shunchang wenshi ziliao* 1987, no. 5 (Oct.): 203–4.

Xian dang'anguan 縣檔案館 (County archives). "Minguo shiqi Xianyou liren xianzhang renqi jiankuang" 民國時期仙游歷任縣長任期簡況 (Abbreviated chart of magistrates serving successively in Xianyou in the Republican era). *Xianyou wenshi ziliao* 1985, no. 3 (July): 58–60.

Xiao Qinglun 肖慶倫, Zheng Xuezhang 鄭學長, and Shu Yin 舒因, comps. and adaptors. "Jin yapian ge" 禁鴉片歌 (Anti-opium song). *Sha xian wenshi ziliao* 1987, no. 6 (Dec. 1): 142–43.

Xu Liangxiao 許良曉. "Pujiang jindu ji" 普江禁毒記 (A record of opium prohibition in Pujiang). *Pujiang wenshi ziliao* 1993, no. 14: 137–41.

Xu Youchun 徐友春. *Minguo renwu da cidian* 民國人物大辭典 (A dictionary of Republican notables). Hubei: Hubei renmin chubanshe, 1991.

Ya Ji 亞季. "Yapian dui Zhangpu renmin de duhai" 鴉片對漳浦人民的毒害 (The harm done by opium to the people of Zhangpu). *Zhangpu wenshi ziliao* 1986, no. 6 (Oct.): 28–30.

"Yapian dui Changtai renmin de huohai: jiantan Changtai de yapian juan" 鴉片對長泰人民的禍害: 兼談長泰的鴉片捐 (The damage wrought by opium on the people of Changtai and a discussion of opium taxes in Changtai). *Changtai wenshi ziliao* 1988, no. 11 (Oct.): 97–103.

Yi Tongfu 伊通甫. "Xinhai geming qianhou Fuzhou Manzu qiying neiqing shilu" 辛亥革命前后福州滿族旗營內情實錄 (The true inside information regarding the Revolution of 1911 in Fuzhou's Manchu quarter). *Fujian wenshi ziliao* 1991, no. 27: 1–38.

Young, Ernest P. "Politics in the Aftermath of Revolution: The Era of Yuan Shih-k'ai, 1912–16." In *The Cambridge History of China*, vol. 12, pt. I, ed. John K. Fairbank, pp. 208–55. Cambridge, Eng.: Cambridge University Press, 1983.

Yu Ende 于恩德. *Zhongguo jinyan faling bianqian shi* 中國禁煙法令變遷史 (History of the changes in China's anti-opium laws). Shanghai: Zhonghua shuju, 1934.

Yu Qiqiang 余啟鏘. "Huang Lian qiyi yu Xianyou cheng" 黄濂起義與仙游城 (Huang Lian's uprising and Xianyou City). *Xianyou wenshi ziliao* 1983, no. 1 (Jan.): 45–49.

Yu Zuliu 余祖柳. "Gutian lishishang de jinyan yundong" 古田歷史上的禁煙運動 (The anti-opium movement in Gutian's history). *Gutian wenshi ziliao* 1990, no. 10: 81–85.

Zhang Jianhui 張建輝. "Qingdai yapian zhengce jianshu" 清代鴉片政策簡述 (A brief sketch of Qing opium policy). *Zhongguo jindai shi* 1991, no. 3: 15–16.

Zhang Xingsheng 張興生. "'Jinyan' zaji" 禁煙雜技 (Miscellaneous notes on "opium prohibition"). *Pucheng wenshi ziliao*, Sept. 1987, 31–32.

Zhang Yufa 張玉法. *Zhongguo xiandaihua de quncheng yanjiu, Shandong sheng, 1860–1916* 中國現代化的區域研究，山東省 (Studies on Chinese modernization, Shandong province, 1860–1916). Taibei: Zhongyang yanjiusuo, 1983.

Zhao Erxun 趙爾巽. *Qingshi gao* 清史稿 (A draft history of the Qing dynasty). Beijing: Zhonghua shuju, 1976.

Zheng Bangning 鄭邦宁. "Minchu xianling Su Shouqiao" 民初賢令的蘇壽橋 (Su Shouqiao—a virtuous man of the early Republic). *Guangze wenshi ziliao* 8 (July 1989): 60–63.

Zheng, Yangwen. "The Social Life of Opium in China, 1483–1999." *Modern Asian Studies* 37, no. 1 (2003): 1–39.

Zheng Zuyin 鄭祖陰 et al., eds. *Fujian xinhai guangfu shiliao* 福建辛亥光復史料 (Historical materials on the Revolution of 1911 in Fujian). Fuzhou: Jianguo chubanshe, 1940.

Zhongguo dier lishi dang'anguan 中國第二歷史檔案管. *Zhonghua minguoshi dang'an ziliao huibian* 中國第二歷史檔案資料匯編 (Collection of materials from the Chinese Republican Archives). Nanjing: Jiangsu guji chubanshe, 1991.

Zhou Ruiguang 周瑞光. "Qing Huanghua daoren 'jieyan shi' qianshi" 清黃花道人戒煙詩淺釋 (A simple explanation of "an anti-opium poem" by the Chrysanthemum Daoist of the Qing). *Fuding wenshi ziliao* 1984, no. 3 (Oct.): 161–69.

Zhou Yongming. *Anti-Drug Crusades in Twentieth-Century China: Nationalism, History, and State Building*. Lanham, Md., and Oxford: Rowman & Littlefield, 1999.

Zou Lu 鄒魯. "Fujian guangfu" 福建光復 (Fujian recovered). In *Xinhai geming* 辛亥革命 (The Revolution of 1911). 7 vols. Shanghai: Shanghai renmin chubanshe, 1962.

ZZGB: *Zhengzhi guanbao* 政治官報 (The government gazette). Beijing, 1907–10.

Index

addiction: as metaphor, 82; as disease, 274, 288
Additional Article to the Chefoo Convention, 58–59, 70, 109
AIDS, 385
Alcock, Rutherford, 266
Alexander, Joseph, 293
American Board of Commissioners for Foreign Missions (ABCFM), 84, 271, 273
American Methodist Episcopal Church (MEC), 170, 266, 271, 287, 292, 295, 297, 346; Alden Speare Memorial Hospital, 153; and Huang Lian's uprising, 324, 331, 337; anti-opium society, 293; in Xinghua, 305–6, 311, 313, 317–18
Anglo-Chinese opium agreements, see Great Britain
Anhai, 258
Anti-American boycott, 99, 378
Anti-Narcotics Commission (Judu weiyuanhui, ANC), 366
Anti-Opium Commission, see Opium Prohibition Commission
Anti-Opium Day, 367
Anxi, 51, 66, 244, 246–47, 258
Arrow War, 6, 48, 54–55, 268
Augustine Heard and Company, 269

Ball, J. Dyer, 298

Banner people, *see* Fuzhou Banner garrison
Barckhardt, Frederick, 266
Bashford, James Whitford, 317, 321
Beijing Convention, 54
Bianco, Lucien, 180
Black Money Society, 348
Black Tiger Righteousness Society, 316–17, 323
Blackburn, A. D., 253–56, 259–60
Bohea Hills (Wuyi shan): and Fujian tea cultivation, 68
Boxer Indemnity, 309
Boxer Rebellion, 104
boycotts: anti-American, 99, 378; of against Japanese goods, 359
Brewster, William N.: and Huang Lian's uprising, 319–21
British East India Company, 49–50, 52
Brother-in-Law Society (Dabai hui), 154

Cameron, Meribeth, 386
Canton System, 42, 266
Carlson, Ellsworth, 336
Carson, Stanley F., 323
Cen Chunxuan, 223, 319–20
chandu, 30
Changle, 242, 271
Changtai, 173, 244, 257
Chen Aitao, 363–64

Chen Baochen, 99–100, 122, 127
Chen Bingzhang, 169
Chen Jiageng, 360–61
Chen Jiongming, 349, 355
Chen Maoding, 99–100
Chen Nengguang, 114–15, 201, 221, 228–29, 233–39, 252–54, 258, 295, 322, 369
Chen Peikun, 115, 152, 169, 221, 227–29, 249, 253, 255, 257–58, 363, 369
Chen Qiao, 312
Chen Weilin, 158–63, 232
Chen Xipeng, 138
Chen Xiurong, 228
Chen Yi, 173–74
Chen Zongshu, 232
Chen Zongyi, 347
Chiang Kaishek, 19, 368–69, 371
China Medical Missionary Association, 293
Chinese Christians: and opium suppression, 126, 181, 337; and Huang Lian's uprising, 314, 319
Chinese Communist Party (CCP), 4, 14, 21
Chinese Recorder, 294
Chongan, 153
Christianity: and popular hostility to opium, 91; Church Missionary Society (CMS), 151–52, 156, 157, 270–71, 284, 286, 291–92, 306, 363; hospitals, 216, 241, 243; and Chinese nationalism, 267; and opium suppression in Xinghua, 310–11, 332
Church of England Zenana Missionary Society (CEZMS), 163, 270–71, 296, 306
Cixi (Empress Dowager), 122
Classic of Filial Piety (Xiao jing), 80
cocaine, 107, 209, 344, 348–49
codeine, 29–30
Coleridge, Samuel Taylor, 31
Collins, Wilkie, 278
consolidated opium tax (*tongshui*), 76–78

Crossley, Pamela, 186
Cui Zhaoxiang, 125

Daoguang emperor, 5
Datian, 250–51
Dehua, 250, 327, 347
Deming, Philander, 279
De Quincey, Thomas, 28, 31, 34, 373
Dickens, Charles, 278
Ding Zhenduo, 105
Doolittle, Justus, 269
Do Only Good Society (Weishan she), 376
Douglas, Carstairs, 269
Doyle, Arthur Conan, 278
Duan Qirui, 345
Dudgeon, John, 290

Eight Banner System, 184, 186
Eight Trigrams Society, 244
Elles & Co., 167
Elliott, Mark, 186
Emptiness sect (Zhenkong jiao), 89–90
Esherick, Joseph, 337

Fairbank, John King, 268
Fowler, John, 314, 327–32
Freedom Party, 308–9, 320, 330
Friend of China, 293, 298
Fu'an: poppy cultivation in, 67, 72, 164; opium suppression in, 82, 164, 243, 256; substitution of cotton for poppies, 130; Anti-Opium Society branch, 164; compulsory poppy cultivation in, 350
Fuding, 72, 75, 242, 271
Fujian: poppy cultivation, 4, 23, 25, 44–48, 59, 63–64, 72–73, 93–94, 96, 129, 178, 180, 238, 296; opium smuggling, 4–6, 23, 38–39, 44, 48, 50–52, 93–94; legalization of opium imports, 7; opium trade, 17, 22, 27, 59–60; opium smoking, 23, 25, 49, 60, 80–85, 102, 121–22, 125, 178, 231, 242, 259;

taxation of opium, 23, 70–71, 79, 94; closure to Indian opium imports, 26, 261–63, 345; geography and topography, 44; Ming/Qing trade restrictions, 47; tea trade, 48, 68–69; anti-Qing sentiment in, 48, 143, 210; gender and opium smoking, 83–84; opium suppression campaign in navy, 191, 193; Revolution of 1911, 199–200, 220; Tongmenghui in, 200; anti-Manchu sentiment in, 202; Prepared Opium Tax Bureau, 208; post-Revolutionary unrest, 224; warlordism in, 265, 345, 349–70; civil war, 340, 349–57; banditry in, 345, 347, 350, 355
—northeast region: Qing opium suppression in, 154–64; Republican opium suppression in, 242–44, 259
—northwest region: opium and popular sentiment in, 19–23, 86–89, 91; Qing opium suppression in, 149–54; Republican opium suppression in, 240–42
—opium economy, 4, 7, 44, 48, 51, 71, 79, 84, 86, 92–94, 102–3, 120, 178, 180, 189, 259, 297, 345–46, 350, 358–59, 364, 374, 380, 383, 386–87; construction of, 6, 23, 28; and tea trade, 7, 92; Chinese complicity in, 19–20; tenacity of, 23, 110, 252; revival of, 25, 240, 264–65, 365, 367, 370; and Opium Wars, 37; and role of Chinese state, 43, 92, 95; and legalization of poppy cultivation, 70; and interprovincial opium trade, 74; impact of Chinese laws, 78; and *lijin* taxes, 92; and provincial topography/climate, 92, 190; fears of resurgence, 209
—opium suppression campaign, 6, 17, 129, 147, 178–81, 198, 200, 260, 365, 375, 378, 381; in Qing, 1–2, 23–25, 97–98, 102–3, 110–33, 135–43, 146, 166, 177, 183, 208–9, 375, 377–78; state-elite cooperation in Qing, 4, 10, 23–24, 40, 110, 112, 118–19, 123, 127, 139–42, 183; state-elite cooperation in Republic, 4, 10, 230, 237, 254, 256, 264–65; elite activism in, 6, 24, 26, 110, 141; and role of Qing state, 6, 25, 103, 110, 126, 128, 131–32, 137, 139, 207; in Republic, 6, 25–26, 220–25, 230–33, 238–40, 252, 254–55, 257, 259–60, 263, 265; and the public political space, 14, 142; resistance to suppression, 20, 27, 156, 180–81, 199, 206, 222, 224, 238, 265; popular sentiment toward, 22, 26, 263; and missionaries, 26; and role of Republican state, 25, 233, 235, 255, 264; and the image of Lin Zexu, 96–97, 100; and police, 98, 110–12, 117, 206, 210, 223, 311–12; mass meetings, 98, 141–42, 238; regional deadlines set, 139; and Chinese nationalism, 205, 262; provincial and national interests in, 205–6, 264; changes in tax collection, 208; Qing vs. Republican strategies, 260, 265
—southeast region: Qing opium suppression in, 164–71, 178; Republican opium suppression in, 246–52
—southwest region: Qing opium suppression in, 171–77; Republican opium suppression in, 244–45
Fujian Anti-Opium Bureau, *see* Fujian Opium Prohibition Bureau
Fujian Anti-Opium Society, 12–13, 22, 127–28, 133, 144–45, 147, 154–55, 202, 208, 210, 223, 244, 249, 253, 264, 341, 346, 366, 369, 371, 376–78, 384; mass demonstrations, 1–2, 15, 103, 116, 125; and Lin Zexu, 5, 101, 116; activities and powers of, 9–10, 98–99, 102–3, 110, 112, 116–18, 120, 122, 125, 128, 141–42, 237; and poppy cultivation, 24–25, 102, 128; and Provincial Assem-

bly, 98, 134–39, 143, 264; and Chinese nationalism, 99, 102–3; leadership, 99–101, 227; treatment for opium addiction, 103, 120–21, 124, 231; branches of, 112–13, 117, 120, 177, 179, 254, 295; membership, 112–17; and Chinese Christians, 113–14; and role of Qing state, 120, 127, 140–41, 183, 200, 208; enemies of, 121; state subsidy for, 138, 147; revolutionary sentiment among members, 201; petition to end foreign opium imports, 205–6; and Opium Prohibition Bureau, 206, 229; diminished influence in Republic, 221, 226–27, 229, 239–40; and role of Republican state, 227, 229–30, 236, 238; celebration of closing of Fujian, 261; declining reputation of, 361; dissolution of, 370

Fujian Anti-Opium Society Quarterly, 22, 113, 116–18, 296

Fujian New Army, 25, 186, 189, 324, 330–31; revolutionary sentiment in, 190, 199, 219; and Yuan Shikai, 225; and Second Revolution, 336

Fujian Opium Prohibition Bureau, 112, 140, 208, 210, 228–29, 234, 237–38, 239–40, 243, 253; and Anti-Opium Society, 206, 208, 221; and Republican opium suppression, 230–33, 236–37; conflict with Japan, 237

Fujian Protection Society (Humin she), 224, 324

Fujian Provincial Assembly, 143, 152, 156, 161, 164, 171, 176, 179, 217, 309; and opium suppression, 24, 133–40, 142–43, 148–49, 200–201, 221, 232, 367; and Anti-Opium Society, 98, 134–39, 143, 264; and Revolution of 1911, 199, 211; and New Policy Reforms, 133–35; roster, 135–36; petition for end of foreign opium imports, 205–6; and Freedom Party, 308

Fujian Self-Governing Anti-Opium Relief Society (Fujian zizhi jinyan xieji hui), 364

Funing, 67, 72, 75, 82, 130, 163–64, 178, 243, 271, 350

Fuzhou, 1, 148n, 164–65, 177, 285, 292–93; suppression campaign, 1–2, 23, 97, 122–24, 126, 128, 144–45, 149, 167, 170, 175, 178–82, 187, 210, 217, 232; opium smoking in, 25, 84, 185, 187, 189–90, 195–96; opium suppression campaign in, 25, 182, 185–86, 191–98, 218–19; and Fujian's opium economy, 48; *lijin* rates, 56; opium taxation in, 56, 62; opium imports to, 56–57, 59–60, 232; price of domestic opium in, 73; imports of domestic opium, 74–75; opium problem in, 82, 85, 148; police, 111–12, 122, 189; Anti-Opium Society branch, 114, 135, 155, 160, 168–69, 174, 176–77, 179, 208, 259, 295; poppy cultivation in, 128, 146n, 190; anti-Manchu sentiment in, 187, 190; Fuzhou Banner garrison, 187, 216; Tongmenghui branch, 199; and New Policy Reforms, 211; New Army, 211, 219; and Revolution of 1911, 211–13; Revolution of 1911, 211–17; ethnic tensions after Revolution, 217; Opium Prohibition Bureau, 257–58; celebration of closing of Fujian, 261–62; missionaries in, 271; modern campaign against drugs, 385; women and the opium problem, 197

Fuzhou Chamber of Commerce: and Peng Shousong, 224

Fuzhou Medical Missionary Hospital, 84

Fuzhou Opium Asylum, 84, 290

Gan Huangtao, 232
Gantt, T. Fulton, 274, 278
Gao Dengli, 135, 138, 139, 227
Gelaohui, 199, 305, 308
Geneva Opium Conferences, 367
Golden Triangle, 385
Gong, Prince, 266
Great Britain: end of Indian exports to China, 3, 7, 253; and Chinese opium suppression, 4, 103, 108–10, 119, 128, 131, 180–81, 183, 202, 233, 235, 342, 345, 364, 375, 377; 1911 opium agreement with China, 6, 16, 25, 27, 203–8, 221–22, 234, 248, 264–65, 305, 335; and Chinese opium trade, 19, 92, 109, 368, 382–83; anti-opium movement in, 108; opium consumption in, 35, 275–79; 1908 opium agreement with China, 108–10, 149, 152–53, 202–3; diminished influence in China, 260, 263; opium agreements with China, 120, 141, 143, 147, 184, 205, 300, 342, 349, 368, 375–77, 385. *See also* joint inspections
Guangdong, 6, 38–39, 90, 342
Guangxi, 38, 136
Guangzhou, 6, 38, 50, 269, 349, 356
Guihua, 174–76, 239n, 347
Guizhou, 63, 78
Gulangyu, 72
Guo Daozhi, 169
Guo Gongmu, 186, 215–16
Gutian, 73, 158–63, 180, 242–43, 271, 287, 297, 348

Habermas, Jürgen, 10, 12
Haicheng, 244–45
Han Independence Union (Hanzu duli hui), 202
Harrison, Henrietta, 142, 343, 378
He Chun, 236
Heard and Co., *see* Augustine Heard and Company
Heilongjiang, 130

heroin, 29, 349
Hind, J. D. D., 363
Hong Kong, 7, 40, 269, 354
Hong Xiuquan, 80, 90
Huang Lian, 302–3, 305, 310, 314–16; uprising, 302, 304, 307–9, 313–38, 346, 351, 362; resistance to opium suppression, 303, 319, 325; anti-Christian sentiment, 303, 323, 334; popular support for, 313, 322–23, 325; opposition to taxes, 319, 322, 335; meeting with government negotiators, 328; death hoax and disappearance of, 330, 332; rumors of Christian conversion, 332
Huang Naishang, 138
Huang Peisong, 233, 324–25
Huang, Philip, 12
Huang Tingyuan, 169
Hubei Arsenal, 107
Hui'an, 148n, 165–67, 246–47, 257–58, 271, 352, 356
Hunan troops: in Fujian New Army, 190, 199, 223; and Second Revolution, 225; disbanding and repatriation of, 225, 331, 337; Fujianese hostility toward, 305, 308, 324, 335, 385

India: opium trade with China, 3, 50, 109, 147, 202–3, 209, 268, 300, 342–43, 345, 368, 380–82; opium consumption and preparation in, 29, 31; types of opium, 49; poppy cultivation in, 49, 380
India's Women and China's Daughters (IWCD), 294
International Anti-Opium Association (IAOA), 344, 355–57, 359, 362–63, 365–67, 370
International Opium Commission (IOC), 293
International Reform Bureau (IRB), 293

Japan; and Taiwan opium monopoly, 137, 232, 275; and opium smuggling, 209, 269, 349–50; and narcotics smuggling in Fujian, 237, 359; and morphine smuggling, 251–52, 345, 350; obstacle to opium suppression in Republican Fujian, 252, 343
Japanese Dragon Company (Rilong gongsi), 237
Jardine Matheson & Company, 50, 232
Java, 31
Jian'an, 199
Jiang Lu, 332
Jiang Chunlin, 319, 327–28
Jiang Yujing, 233, 326
Jiang Zubao, 327
Jiangle, 347
Jiangsu, 342
Jiangxi, 75, 342, 356
Jianning, 74, 85, 146n, 148n, 149–52, 154, 240–41, 271, 286, 292, 348
Jiaqing emperor, 37
Jing Xing, 105
Jinjiang, 168, 244
John, Griffith, 273
joint inspections, 26, 252–60, 297, 332, 337
Jordan, John, 235

Kill Han Regiment (Sha Han tuan), 212, 214n, 216
King, Charles W., 274
Kun Ji, 234

Lao She, 33–35
laudanum, 277
League of Nations, 367
Li Dihu, 135, 152
Li Funan, 99, 135
Li Houji, 225, 345, 355, 358–62, 364, 366
Li Jiang, 235
Liancheng, 175, 245
Liang Guandeng, 310
Lianjiang, 155–57, 180, 242, 256, 289, 347

Liao Shangqing, 232
lijin (transit) tax, 55–58, 92
Lin Jiafeng, 347
Lin Binghua, 243
Lin Bingzhang, 5, 6, 99–102, 115, 121–22, 127–28, 160, 168–69, 221, 224, 227–28, 296, 363, 371, 373
Lin Lucun, 136, 169
Lin Man-houng, 129
Lin Qigan, 324
Lin Shaonian, 99–100
Lin Shizhao, 315, 323, 326, 330
Lin Yushi, 227, 369
Lin Zexu, 6, 16, 37–40, 42, 52–53, 92, 116, 156, 243, 253, 274, 339, 368, 371, 373, 378, 382, 385; meanings of his image, 5, 40, 96, 97, 100–101, 261, 265
Lin Zhixuan, 99
Lin Zhizhao, 308, 328
Lin Zikeng, 135, 169
Liu Guanxiong, 225, 329, 331
Liu Hongshou, 363
Liu Xuexun, 99
London Missionary Society (LMS), 167, 174, 271
Longxi, 173, 244, 257
Longyan, 74, 148n, 173–74, 245
Lu Chenghan, 206, 208, 210
Lu Chuhuang, 138
Lu Zhuanlin, 105
Luo Jincheng, 99
Luoyuan, 157–58, 242–43, 348

Macgowan, John, 28, 266
Mahang, 257–58, 260
Majiaxiang, 247
Manchus, 317, 385. *See also* Fuzhou Banner garrison
Mao Zedong, 4
Marx, Karl, 54
Marxism–Leninism–Mao Zedong Thought: and opium suppression, 18

Matheson, James, 50
Mawei, 191
May Fourth era, 13, 343
May Fourth Movement, 14, 358
McMahon, Keith, 36
MEC, see American Methodist Episcopal Church
Mehta case, 235–36
Meng Sipei, 135, 152
Mercy and Truth, 294
Ming Yu, 215
Minhou, 242
Minqing, 242
missionaries: and Chinese opium consumption, 4–5, 21–22, 277–85; and treatment for addiction, 26, 61, 91, 289–93; and the opium trade, 26, 91, 266–69, 273–75, 344, 358; and Chinese opium suppression, 26, 155, 181, 267–68, 306, 321, 332, 334, 336–37; and opium suicides, 36; and imperialism, 54, 268–69; and British anti-opium movement, 108; students and opium suppression, 123, 126–27; and the Fujian joint inspections, 253; Roman Catholic, 267; association with opium trade, 268–69, 280, 286; Protestant groups in Fujian, 270–71; Chinese hostility toward, 272–73, 292; addicted to opium, 287–88; and Huang Lian's uprising, 314–15, 322, 324, 326, 329
Moncrieff, Hope, 272
Morpheus, 30
morphine, 29–30, 61, 107, 244, 251–52, 276, 290–91, 310, 340, 344–45, 348–50, 354
Morrison, Robert, 269

Nan'an, 51, 247–48, 258, 362
Nanjing (county), 244
Nanjing regime, 16
Nanjing Treaty, 48, 54
Nanping City, 148n

Nanri Island, 269
Nantai, 1, 51, 126, 191, 366–68
National Anti-Opium Association (NAOA), 366
National Christian Council of China (NCC), 366
Nationalist Party, 7, 13, 19, 383; opium policy of, 368, 371
New Army, see Fujian New Army
New Culture Movement, 379
Newman, R. K., 21–22
New Policy Reforms, 2, 11, 97–98, 111, 113, 141, 171, 179, 183–84, 190, 201, 211, 343, 379, 385; popular hostility toward, 27, 102, 133, 200, 210, 218, 303, 312, 333, 335
Ningbo, 56
Ningde, 72, 82, 243, 253, 256, 348
Ninghua, 245
Ningyang, 245
Northern Expedition, 357

Olyphant & Company, 274
opium: and popular sentiment, 1–2, 370–71, 382–83, 385–86; as metaphor, 2, 3, 29, 86, 93; legalization of poppy cultivation, 3, 69–71, 79, 93, 374; and alcohol, 3, 85, 273, 279; and Chinese nationalism, 5–6, 41, 86, 93, 267, 302, 333, 339–43, 358, 368, 374–76, 378–79, 381–82, 385, 387; rhetoric of suppression, 6, 93, 343–44, 355, 358–59, 381; cultivation of, 7, 18, 29, 43, 45, 55, 78, 80, 92–93, 177, 181, 296–300, 313–14, 319, 340, 345, 354, 365–66, 370, 374–75, 380, 382, 384, 386; taxation of, 7, 43, 59, 69, 71–72, 74, 93–94, 133, 167–68, 208, 340–43, 350–52, 355–57, 362–63, 365, 370, 374–75; historiography of, 7–8, 17–22; effects of, 28, 30–34; and social stigma in China, 29, 79–82, 86; smoking, 29–30, 32, 34, 44, 60–61, 79–80, 277–80, 282, 288, 340, 357,

371, 382–84; addiction, 30, 375, 382, 386; as medicine, 30–31, 37, 210, 275–77, 280; consumption of, 30–32, 34, 36, 49, 56, 81–82, 274, 345, 352, 385; in Europe and China, 32; Chinese restrictions on, 32, 36–39, 53, 63, 67, 274, 354, 374; and Chinese identity, 33; as poison, 35, 276, 282–83; suicides, 35–36, 151, 283–84, 287, 290; and sexuality, 36; varied meanings of, 36; legalization of imports, 38, 48, 52, 63, 78–79, 93, 267, 300; and the Qing, 42, 382; smuggling, 43–44, 49, 52–53, 56–57, 209, 269, 291, 345–46, 348, 354–55; domestic vs. imported, 49; price of, 61, 93, 232, 352, 356; and tobacco smoking, 79–80; and missionaries, 91; and Qing finances, 93; popular sentiment against, 103, 358–59; dens, 151, 277, 343, 352, 357, 362, 369, 376; monopolies, 226, 356, 365; resistance to suppression, 268, 300, 302, 310, 312–14, 318–22, 333–35, 337–38, 383–85; and the Chinese diaspora, 277–79; in Great Britain and U.S., 277–81; and gender, 279–80, 282–85, 288; treatment for addiction, 285–87, 289–93, 295, 299, 311, 376; forcible uprooting, 303; and salt taxes, 303, 313–14, 334, 362–63; revival of poppy cultivation, 346, 348, 350, 357, 360, 368; opposition to taxation, 356; compulsory cultivation, 356, 361–62, 369–70; restrictions on, 360, 371; global opposition to, 366–67, 381; and nationalism, 367, 384, 386. *See also* Great Britain

—suppression, 1–2, 144–45, 177, 179, 181, 266–67, 274–75, 288–302, 339–41, 373–77, 381–86; in Qing, 1–3, 9, 37, 42, 44, 78–79, 81, 93, 96–98, 101, 104–7, 119, 166–67, 183, 198, 200, 209, 288, 303, 311, 314, 339–41, 343–44, 359, 362–63, 371, 377–87; role of Chinese state, 1–4, 8–9, 16–18, 96–97, 104, 108, 141, 177, 226, 302, 314, 335, 339, 340–41, 343–44, 355, 358, 364–67, 369, 371, 375, 384–87; and elite activism, 2, 4, 8–9, 13–14, 16, 97, 105, 107, 302, 374, 386–87; and Chinese nationalism, 2, 4, 14, 16, 18, 26–27, 97–98, 101, 107, 119, 141, 143, 184, 199, 207, 218; and warlords, 3, 7, 9, 16, 339–41, 343–46, 348–50, 352, 355–62, 364–67, 369–70, 377–80, 386; in Republic, 3, 9, 204, 226, 234, 313–14, 319–22, 326, 332–36, 338–41, 359, 362, 370–71, 377–80, 386; in Qing and Republic, 4, 8, 12, 14, 16, 18, 20, 28–29, 41; and police, 9, 226, 311–12; campaign vs. movement, 14–15; and popular sentiment, 15, 18–19, 41, 107, 302–4, 334–35; in People's Republic of China, 18–19; state-elite cooperation, 12, 15, 40–41, 107–8, 159; and anti-Qing sentiment, 108, 218–19; and missionaries, 266–68, 273–75, 287–301, 344–45, 366, 381–82; and Chinese Christians, 294–95, 299, 346, 356, 365–66; and Nationalists, 341, 345, 368–69, 371; and Chinese character, 378

opium economy, 37–38, 43, 106, 289, 297, 340, 345–46, 350, 352, 358–59, 364–65, 367, 370, 374, 380–81, 383, 386–87

opium trade, 4, 6, 16, 27, 33, 37–38, 42–44, 55–56, 59, 61–62, 305, 313, 344, 335, 374; and imperialism, 2, 33, 40, 92, 104; legalization of, 3, 43, 54–55; and Qing economy, 3, 96; Chinese complicity in, 18, 42, 50–51; early Qing attempts to control, 38, 44, 50, 52; and popular sentiment, 43, 86; and development of Fujian treaty ports, 48; and Fujian tea regions, 50; and Qing authority, 79, 103–4; Brit-

ish opposition to, 108; global opposition to, 275
Opium Prohibition Bureau, 286, 332, 346, 360–61
Opium Prohibition Commission, 105–6, 111, 125, 137, 192
opium prohibition commissioners, 105
Opium Prohibition Office, 226
Opium Prohibition Supervisory Department, 226
Opium Tax office, 362
Opium Wars, 5, 7, 17, 37, 40, 47–48, 53–54, 63, 86–87, 92, 109, 261, 266, 268, 288, 339, 371, 374, 381–82

Pan Mu, 309, 328
Peng Shousong, 200–201, 211, 223–24, 228
Petigura case, 234–35, 254–55, 263
Philippines, 275
Pinghe, 199
Pingnan, 242
Poisons and Pharmacy Act, 276
Polachek, James M., 38–39
police, 171, 228, 231, 361–62, 371
Prazniak, Roxann, 303
Presbyterian Church of England (PCE), 166, 251, 271, 306
Price, Horace Mc. E., 253–54
Prince Gong, 105
public political space, 113, 225, 300, 337, 341–42, 358, 364, 366–67, 369–70, 374–80, 385; and opium suppression, 2, 4, 8, 12–14, 23–24, 26–27, 97, 117, 125–27, 140, 142–43, 209, 221–22, 226, 229–30, 237–38; public sphere debate, 10–12; after the Revolution of 1911, 16–17; and New Policy Reforms, 98, 219; and Revolution of 1911, 217–18
Pucheng, 51, 73, 148n, 152, 240–41, 348
Pushou, 187, 189, 217; opium suppression strategies, 110, 182, 185, 189–90, 193–98, 201; and Revolution of 1911, 182, 211–14; death of, 182, 214–16; allegations of opium addiction, 194
Putian, 199, 311–12, 351–52

Qianlong emperor, 42
Qing dynasty: contemporary criticism of, 19; collapse of, 25; and Chinese nationalism, 183–84
Qingdao, 245
Quanzhou, 148n, 170, 269, 347; poppy cultivation in, 48, 73, 128, 146n, 164–66, 190, 246; and early opium smuggling, 51; imports of domestic opium, 75; spirit writing societies in, 90; opium suppression campaign, 164, 168, 247–48, 257–58; Tongmenghui branch, 199; missionaries in, 271
Quarterly, The, see Fujian Anti-Opium Society Quarterly

Rawski, Evelyn, 186
(Dutch) Reformed Church of America (RCA), 271
Reins, Thomas, 59
Republic: popular sentiment toward, 303, 308; popular hostility toward, 325, 331, 333, 335
Resolution Society, 154, 294–95
Revolution of 1911, 3, 8, 16, 24, 26, 102, 170, 173–74, 176, 181–83, 187, 204, 296, 304–5, 308, 347, 369, 377, 384; and opium suppression, 9, 211, 217–8; in Fuzhou, 210–17, 219; and breakdown of opium suppression in Fujian, 220; and Huang Lian's uprising, 316–17
Rights Recovery Movement, 104
Royal Commission on Opium, 275

Salt Gabelle, 362
salt taxes: popular hostility toward, 224, 313–14, 347–48; and opium suppression, 133

Santu'ao, 348, 355
Schoppa, Keith, 11, 146
Second Revolution, 224–25, 236, 265, 308, 328, 336–37, 347
Second Revolutionary Party, *see* Fujian Protection Society
Sha (county), 206, 347
Shanchun, 195
Shanghai, 36, 54, 56, 290–91, 354; opium stocks, 7, 339–40, 342–44
Shantou, 56, 60
Shanxi, 130
Shanyang, 206
Shao Jiquan, 257
Shao Zhicheng, 99
Shaowu, 146n, 149, 154, 223, 240–42, 271
Shi Shiji, 169
Shima, 85, 173
Shouning, 256, 259
Shuiji, 148n
Shuishan, 192
Shunchang, 350
Sichuan, 44, 63, 73, 75, 78, 93, 130
Skinner, G. William, 24, 146, 148
Skinner, James E., 154
Slack, Edward, 344, 368
Society for the Suppression of the Opium Trade (SSOT), 293
Society to Benefit the Hearer (Yiwen she), 114, 190, 201
Songshou, 81–82, 120, 128–29, 146n, 161–62, 164, 187–88, 190, 217, 312; and opium suppression in Fujian, 110–11, 122–25, 127–33, 139–40, 192, 198, 205, 207; allegations of opium addiction, 194; and Revolution of 1911, 211; suicide of, 183, 213–14
Southern Fujian Poppy Prohibition Association (Minnan yanmiao jinzhong hui, SFPPA), 360–61
South of the Bridge Public Welfare Society (Qiaonan gongyi she), 126, 202, 224

Spanish Dominicans, 306
Speak the News Society (Shuobao she), 113, 201
Special Bureau, 356–57
Spence, Jonathan D., 83, 386
Su Yi, 327, 332, 346–47
Sun Yatsen, 199
Sun Baoqi, 329
Sun Baorong, 318–19, 323
Sun Daoren, 215, 223–24, 308, 317–18, 331; and Fujian New Army, 199; and Revolution of 1911, 211, 213–14; and Fuzhou Manchus, 216–17; and Second Revolution, 224–25, 329; dismissed, 225; and Republican opium suppression, 231, 235–36; and Huang Lian's uprising, 318, 322, 324, 326, 330–31, 337
Sun Erzhun, 48, 65
Sun Yatsen, 221, 225, 296, 308, 347, 349, 352, 355, 368
Support National Goods Society (Guohuo weichi hui), 359

Taiping Rebellion, 11, 186, 199; and Fujian opium trade, 53, 91; and *lijin* taxes, 55–56, 91; and opium smoking, 80, 90
Tait & Company, 167
Taiwan, 269; and opium suppression, 44, 252; Japanese occupation of, and Fujian's tea trade, 68; spirit writing societies in, 90; opium monopoly, 137, 232; and opium smuggling, 209, 344, 348–49; and morphine smuggling, 344–45
Taizhou, 75
Tang Shaoyi, 109
tea trade: and Fujian's opium economy, 61, 68–69, 78, 92
Tianjin Treaty, *see* Treaty of Tianjin
Tingzhou, 146n, 148n, 171, 174–77, 180, 216n, 245, 271, 292

Tongan, 67, 83, 258; and women in opium production, 65–66; poppy cultivation in, 65–67, 72, 129, 165–66, 246, 349, 352; missionaries in, 166, 271; resistance to suppression, 166, 246–48, 257, 349
Tongmenghui, 191, 201, 308, 315
Treaty of Nanjing, 48, 54
Treaty of Tianjin, 54, 57, 109, 268, 374
tribute system, 42
Tsin, Michael, 15
Turner, W. P., 253, 256–60

United States, 275, 364

Walker, Ronald, 322
Walker, William, 335–36
Wang Dazhen, 364, 365
Wang Hongbin, 226
Wang Junwen, 262
Wang Shengling, 326
Wang Shouchang, 236
Wang Ziyi, 138
Wenkai, 212, 216
Wenzhou, 56, 75
Werner, E. T. C., 207, 230, 233–37, 314, 316, 320, 326
White, W. C., 291
Whitney, Henry T., 84
Wilkinson, F. E., 234, 253, 255, 263
Wilkinson, G., 291
Williams, E. T., 329
World War I, 27, 234, 349
Worley, James H., 297
Wu Hongbin, 312
Wu Tingchang, 156–57
Wu Tingfang (Wu Guangchen), 135
Wu Wei, 361
Wu Wei'ao, 228
Wu Zeng, 88
Wuping, 175

Xiamao, 88

Xiamen, 148n, 174, 271, 347; and Fujian's opium economy, 48, 248–49; taxation of opium in, 54, 56, 62, 71, 167–70; *lijin* tax, 56, 69; opium imports to, 56–57, 60–61, 75, 209; morphine imports, 61, 290–91; poppy cultivation in, 67, 129; opium consumption in, 85, 148, 168; cocaine imports, 107; Police Department, 112; Anti-Opium Society branch, 136, 168–70, 249–50; opium suppression in, 146, 164–65, 167–68, 170, 178, 250, 366–67; merchant culture in, 167; Chamber of Commerce, 167–68; Tongmenghui branch in, 199; Opium Prohibition Bureau scandal, 250; opium smuggling, 348, 354; formation of SFPPA, 360
Xiamen University, 360
Xianyou, 148n, 309–10, 325
Xiaoxi, 271
Xiapu, 243
Xinghua, 51, 148n, 269, 292, 295, 304–5, 314, 326; Huang Lian's uprising, 27, 224–25, 252, 333, 346–47; poppy cultivation in, 131, 146n, 164, 246, 297, 300, 305, 313, 319–21, 332, 351–52, 357, 368; anti-Christian sentiment, 246, 302, 306–7, 309, 323–27, 334; resistance to opium suppression, 246, 310, 313–14, 366, 382; missionaries in, 271, 306, 309, 311, 313, 317, 321; opium suppression in, 305, 310–12, 326–27; Opium Prohibition Bureau, 310; anti-tax sentiment, 309, 326; anti-Republican sentiment, 318, 326; anti-military sentiment, 326; resistance to compulsory cultivation, 365
Xinzheng reforms, *see* New Policy Reforms
Xixiang, 176
Xu Chongzhi, 199, 211, 223–25, 308, 329, 349, 352, 355

Xu Shichang, 340
Xu Shiying, 345
Xuantong emperor, 184, 316

Yang Jingwen, 169
Yang Tinglun, 115
Yang Zhanyun, 227
Yang Zhengqun, 230
Yanping, 149, 153–54, 241, 271, 294, 346–47, 350, 356
Ye Keliang, 255
Ye Xindi, 125
Ye Yongyuan, 53
Yi Tongfu, 186
Yigu, 197
Yiteheng'e, 195
YMCA, 262, 359, 368
Yongan, 347
Yongchun, 51, 164, 170–71, 246, 250–51, 271–72, 285, 327, 347, 352
Yongfu, 73, 242, 271
Yongzheng emperor, 37
Youxi, 82, 90, 347
Yu Ji, 234
Yu Maolong, 234
Yu Wenzao, 309
Yuan Shikai, 7, 9, 14–16, 19, 27, 204, 220–21, 223–26, 264–65, 296, 308, 315–16, 318–19, 326, 328–30, 332, 335–36, 340, 345, 347–48, 369, 375, 377, 383
Yunjitang Merchants Association, 236
Yunnan, 44, 63, 67, 73, 75, 78, 93, 130

Zaifeng, 184
Zhang Yuanqi, 321, 324
Zhang Zanting, 99
Zhang Zengjue, 257
Zhang Zhidong, 76, 107
Zhang Zhijun, 242
Zhang Zuhan, 241, 242
Zhangpu, 244–45, 271, 350
Zhangzhou, 49, 51, 75, 85, 128, 146n, 148n, 170–71, 173, 190, 244, 257, 260, 271, 350
Zhao'an, 51, 244–45, 257
Zhejiang, 6, 39
Zheng Biming, 330
Zheng Chenggong, 47
Zheng Shouxing, 255
Zheng Yangwen, 32, 84
Zheng Zuyin, 138–39, 190, 214–15
Zhenghe, 73, 87, 148n
Zhili, 130
Zhu Ding, 346
Zhu Jiantai, 352
Zuo Zongtang, 199, 308

Harvard East Asian Monographs
(* out-of-print)

*1. Liang Fang-chung, *The Single-Whip Method of Taxation in China*
*2. Harold C. Hinton, *The Grain Tribute System of China, 1845–1911*
3. Ellsworth C. Carlson, *The Kaiping Mines, 1877–1912*
*4. Chao Kuo-chün, *Agrarian Policies of Mainland China: A Documentary Study, 1949–1956*
*5. Edgar Snow, *Random Notes on Red China, 1936–1945*
*6. Edwin George Beal, Jr., *The Origin of Likin, 1835–1864*
7. Chao Kuo-chün, *Economic Planning and Organization in Mainland China: A Documentary Study, 1949–1957*
*8. John K. Fairbank, *Ching Documents: An Introductory Syllabus*
*9. Helen Yin and Yi-chang Yin, *Economic Statistics of Mainland China, 1949–1957*
*10. Wolfgang Franke, *The Reform and Abolition of the Traditional Chinese Examination System*
11. Albert Feuerwerker and S. Cheng, *Chinese Communist Studies of Modern Chinese History*
12. C. John Stanley, *Late Ching Finance: Hu Kuang-yung as an Innovator*
13. S. M. Meng, *The Tsungli Yamen: Its Organization and Functions*
*14. Ssu-yü Teng, *Historiography of the Taiping Rebellion*
15. Chun-Jo Liu, *Controversies in Modern Chinese Intellectual History: An Analytic Bibliography of Periodical Articles, Mainly of the May Fourth and Post-May Fourth Era*
*16. Edward J. M. Rhoads, *The Chinese Red Army, 1927–1963: An Annotated Bibliography*
17. Andrew J. Nathan, *A History of the China International Famine Relief Commission*
*18. Frank H. H. King (ed.) and Prescott Clarke, *A Research Guide to China-Coast Newspapers, 1822–1911*
19. Ellis Joffe, *Party and Army: Professionalism and Political Control in the Chinese Officer Corps, 1949–1964*
*20. Toshio G. Tsukahira, *Feudal Control in Tokugawa Japan: The Sankin Kōtai System*
21. Kwang-Ching Liu, ed., *American Missionaries in China: Papers from Harvard Seminars*
22. George Moseley, *A Sino-Soviet Cultural Frontier: The Ili Kazakh Autonomous Chou*

Harvard East Asian Monographs

23. Carl F. Nathan, *Plague Prevention and Politics in Manchuria, 1910–1931*
*24. Adrian Arthur Bennett, *John Fryer: The Introduction of Western Science and Technology into Nineteenth-Century China*
25. Donald J. Friedman, *The Road from Isolation: The Campaign of the American Committee for Non-Participation in Japanese Aggression, 1938–1941*
*26. Edward LeFevour, *Western Enterprise in Late Ching China: A Selective Survey of Jardine, Matheson and Company's Operations, 1842–1895*
27. Charles Neuhauser, *Third World Politics: China and the Afro-Asian People's Solidarity Organization, 1957–1967*
28. Kungtu C. Sun, assisted by Ralph W. Huenemann, *The Economic Development of Manchuria in the First Half of the Twentieth Century*
*29. Shahid Javed Burki, *A Study of Chinese Communes, 1965*
30. John Carter Vincent, *The Extraterritorial System in China: Final Phase*
31. Madeleine Chi, *China Diplomacy, 1914–1918*
*32. Clifton Jackson Phillips, *Protestant America and the Pagan World: The First Half Century of the American Board of Commissioners for Foreign Missions, 1810–1860*
33. James Pusey, *Wu Han: Attacking the Present Through the Past*
34. Ying-wan Cheng, *Postal Communication in China and Its Modernization, 1860–1896*
35. Tuvia Blumenthal, *Saving in Postwar Japan*
36. Peter Frost, *The Bakumatsu Currency Crisis*
37. Stephen C. Lockwood, *Augustine Heard and Company, 1858–1862*
38. Robert R. Campbell, *James Duncan Campbell: A Memoir by His Son*
39. Jerome Alan Cohen, ed., *The Dynamics of China's Foreign Relations*
40. V. V. Vishnyakova-Akimova, *Two Years in Revolutionary China, 1925–1927*, tr. Steven L. Levine
*41. Meron Medzini, *French Policy in Japan During the Closing Years of the Tokugawa Regime*
42. Ezra Vogel, Margie Sargent, Vivienne B. Shue, Thomas Jay Mathews, and Deborah S. Davis, *The Cultural Revolution in the Provinces*
*43. Sidney A. Forsythe, *An American Missionary Community in China, 1895–1905*
*44. Benjamin I. Schwartz, ed., *Reflections on the May Fourth Movement.: A Symposium*
*45. Ching Young Choe, *The Rule of the Taewŏngun, 1864–1873: Restoration in Yi Korea*
46. W. P. J. Hall, *A Bibliographical Guide to Japanese Research on the Chinese Economy, 1958–1970*
47. Jack J. Gerson, *Horatio Nelson Lay and Sino-British Relations, 1854–1864*
48. Paul Richard Bohr, *Famine and the Missionary: Timothy Richard as Relief Administrator and Advocate of National Reform*
49. Endymion Wilkinson, *The History of Imperial China: A Research Guide*
50. Britten Dean, *China and Great Britain: The Diplomacy of Commercial Relations, 1860–1864*

Harvard East Asian Monographs

51. Ellsworth C. Carlson, *The Foochow Missionaries, 1847–1880*
52. Yeh-chien Wang, *An Estimate of the Land-Tax Collection in China, 1753 and 1908*
53. Richard M. Pfeffer, *Understanding Business Contracts in China, 1949–1963*
54. Han-sheng Chuan and Richard Kraus, *Mid-Ching Rice Markets and Trade: An Essay in Price History*
55. Ranbir Vohra, *Lao She and the Chinese Revolution*
56. Liang-lin Hsiao, *China's Foreign Trade Statistics, 1864–1949*
*57. Lee-hsia Hsu Ting, *Government Control of the Press in Modern China, 1900–1949*
58. Edward W. Wagner, *The Literati Purges: Political Conflict in Early Yi Korea*
*59. Joungwon A. Kim, *Divided Korea: The Politics of Development, 1945–1972*
*60. Noriko Kamachi, John K. Fairbank, and Chūzō Ichiko, *Japanese Studies of Modern China Since 1953: A Bibliographical Guide to Historical and Social-Science Research on the Nineteenth and Twentieth Centuries, Supplementary Volume for 1953–1969*
61. Donald A. Gibbs and Yun-chen Li, *A Bibliography of Studies and Translations of Modern Chinese Literature, 1918–1942*
62. Robert H. Silin, *Leadership and Values: The Organization of Large-Scale Taiwanese Enterprises*
63. David Pong, *A Critical Guide to the Kwangtung Provincial Archives Deposited at the Public Record Office of London*
*64. Fred W. Drake, *China Charts the World: Hsu Chi-yü and His Geography of 1848*
*65. William A. Brown and Urgrunge Onon, translators and annotators, *History of the Mongolian People's Republic*
66. Edward L. Farmer, *Early Ming Government: The Evolution of Dual Capitals*
*67. Ralph C. Croizier, *Koxinga and Chinese Nationalism: History, Myth, and the Hero*
*68. William J. Tyler, tr., *The Psychological World of Natsume Sōseki*, by Doi Takeo
69. Eric Widmer, *The Russian Ecclesiastical Mission in Peking During the Eighteenth Century*
*70. Charlton M. Lewis, *Prologue to the Chinese Revolution: The Transformation of Ideas and Institutions in Hunan Province, 1891–1907*
71. Preston Torbert, *The Ching Imperial Household Department: A Study of Its Organization and Principal Functions, 1662–1796*
72. Paul A. Cohen and John E. Schrecker, eds., *Reform in Nineteenth-Century China*
73. Jon Sigurdson, *Rural Industrialism in China*
74. Kang Chao, *The Development of Cotton Textile Production in China*
75. Valentin Rabe, *The Home Base of American China Missions, 1880–1920*
*76. Sarasin Viraphol, *Tribute and Profit: Sino-Siamese Trade, 1652–1853*
77. Ch'i-ch'ing Hsiao, *The Military Establishment of the Yuan Dynasty*
78. Meishi Tsai, *Contemporary Chinese Novels and Short Stories, 1949–1974: An Annotated Bibliography*

Harvard East Asian Monographs

*79. Wellington K. K. Chan, *Merchants, Mandarins and Modern Enterprise in Late Ching China*

80. Endymion Wilkinson, *Landlord and Labor in Late Imperial China: Case Studies from Shandong by Jing Su and Luo Lun*

*81. Barry Keenan, *The Dewey Experiment in China: Educational Reform and Political Power in the Early Republic*

*82. George A. Hayden, *Crime and Punishment in Medieval Chinese Drama: Three Judge Pao Plays*

*83. Sang-Chul Suh, *Growth and Structural Changes in the Korean Economy, 1910–1940*

84. J. W. Dower, *Empire and Aftermath: Yoshida Shigeru and the Japanese Experience, 1878–1954*

85. Martin Collcutt, *Five Mountains: The Rinzai Zen Monastic Institution in Medieval Japan*

86. Kwang Suk Kim and Michael Roemer, *Growth and Structural Transformation*

87. Anne O. Krueger, *The Developmental Role of the Foreign Sector and Aid*

*88. Edwin S. Mills and Byung-Nak Song, *Urbanization and Urban Problems*

89. Sung Hwan Ban, Pal Yong Moon, and Dwight H. Perkins, *Rural Development*

*90. Noel F. McGinn, Donald R. Snodgrass, Yung Bong Kim, Shin-Bok Kim, and Quee-Young Kim, *Education and Development in Korea*

91. Leroy P. Jones and Il SaKong, *Government, Business, and Entrepreneurship in Economic Development: The Korean Case*

92. Edward S. Mason, Dwight H. Perkins, Kwang Suk Kim, David C. Cole, Mahn Je Kim et al., *The Economic and Social Modernization of the Republic of Korea*

93. Robert Repetto, Tai Hwan Kwon, Son-Ung Kim, Dae Young Kim, John E. Sloboda, and Peter J. Donaldson, *Economic Development, Population Policy, and Demographic Transition in the Republic of Korea*

94. Parks M. Coble, Jr., *The Shanghai Capitalists and the Nationalist Government, 1927–1937*

95. Noriko Kamachi, *Reform in China: Huang Tsun-hsien and the Japanese Model*

96. Richard Wich, *Sino-Soviet Crisis Politics: A Study of Political Change and Communication*

97. Lillian M. Li, *China's Silk Trade: Traditional Industry in the Modern World, 1842–1937*

98. R. David Arkush, *Fei Xiaotong and Sociology in Revolutionary China*

*99. Kenneth Alan Grossberg, *Japan's Renaissance: The Politics of the Muromachi Bakufu*

100. James Reeve Pusey, *China and Charles Darwin*

101. Hoyt Cleveland Tillman, *Utilitarian Confucianism: Chen Liang's Challenge to Chu Hsi*

102. Thomas A. Stanley, *Ōsugi Sakae, Anarchist in Taishō Japan: The Creativity of the Ego*

103. Jonathan K. Ocko, *Bureaucratic Reform in Provincial China: Ting Jih-ch'ang in Restoration Kiangsu, 1867–1870*

104. James Reed, *The Missionary Mind and American East Asia Policy, 1911–1915*

105. Neil L. Waters, *Japan's Local Pragmatists: The Transition from Bakumatsu to Meiji in the Kawasaki Region*

Harvard East Asian Monographs

106. David C. Cole and Yung Chul Park, *Financial Development in Korea, 1945–1978*
107. Roy Bahl, Chuk Kyo Kim, and Chong Kee Park, *Public Finances During the Korean Modernization Process*
108. William D. Wray, *Mitsubishi and the N.Y.K, 1870–1914: Business Strategy in the Japanese Shipping Industry*
109. Ralph William Huenemann, *The Dragon and the Iron Horse: The Economics of Railroads in China, 1876–1937*
110. Benjamin A. Elman, *From Philosophy to Philology: Intellectual and Social Aspects of Change in Late Imperial China*
111. Jane Kate Leonard, *Wei Yüan and China's Rediscovery of the Maritime World*
112. Luke S. K. Kwong, *A Mosaic of the Hundred Days:. Personalities, Politics, and Ideas of 1898*
113. John E. Wills, Jr., *Embassies and Illusions: Dutch and Portuguese Envoys to K'ang-hsi, 1666–1687*
114. Joshua A. Fogel, *Politics and Sinology: The Case of Naitō Konan (1866–1934)*
*115. Jeffrey C. Kinkley, ed., *After Mao: Chinese Literature and Society, 1978–1981*
116. C. Andrew Gerstle, *Circles of Fantasy: Convention in the Plays of Chikamatsu*
117. Andrew Gordon, *The Evolution of Labor Relations in Japan: Heavy Industry, 1853–1955*
*118. Daniel K. Gardner, *Chu Hsi and the "Ta Hsueh": Neo-Confucian Reflection on the Confucian Canon*
119. Christine Guth Kanda, *Shinzō: Hachiman Imagery and Its Development*
*120. Robert Borgen, *Sugawara no Michizane and the Early Heian Court*
121. Chang-tai Hung, *Going to the People: Chinese Intellectual and Folk Literature, 1918–1937*
* 122. Michael A. Cusumano, *The Japanese Automobile Industry: Technology and Management at Nissan and Toyota*
123. Richard von Glahn, *The Country of Streams and Grottoes: Expansion, Settlement, and the Civilizing of the Sichuan Frontier in Song Times*
124. Steven D. Carter, *The Road to Komatsubara: A Classical Reading of the Renga Hyakuin*
125. Katherine F. Bruner, John K. Fairbank, and Richard T. Smith, *Entering China's Service: Robert Hart's Journals, 1854–1863*
126. Bob Tadashi Wakabayashi, *Anti-Foreignism and Western Learning in Early-Modern Japan: The "New Theses" of 1825*
127. Atsuko Hirai, *Individualism and Socialism: The Life and Thought of Kawai Eijirō (1891–1944)*
128. Ellen Widmer, *The Margins of Utopia: "Shui-hu hou-chuan" and the Literature of Ming Loyalism*
129. R. Kent Guy, *The Emperor's Four Treasuries: Scholars and the State in the Late Chien-lung Era*
130. Peter C. Perdue, *Exhausting the Earth: State and Peasant in Hunan, 1500–1850*
131. Susan Chan Egan, *A Latterday Confucian: Reminiscences of William Hung (1893–1980)*

Harvard East Asian Monographs

132. James T. C. Liu, *China Turning Inward: Intellectual-Political Changes in the Early Twelfth Century*
133. Paul A. Cohen, *Between Tradition and Modernity: Wang T'ao and Reform in Late Ching China*
134. Kate Wildman Nakai, *Shogunal Politics: Arai Hakuseki and the Premises of Tokugawa Rule*
135. Parks M. Coble, *Facing Japan: Chinese Politics and Japanese Imperialism, 1931–1937*
136. Jon L. Saari, *Legacies of Childhood: Growing Up Chinese in a Time of Crisis, 1890–1920*
137. Susan Downing Videen, *Tales of Heichū*
138. Heinz Morioka and Miyoko Sasaki, *Rakugo: The Popular Narrative Art of Japan*
139. Joshua A. Fogel, *Nakae Ushikichi in China: The Mourning of Spirit*
140. Alexander Barton Woodside, *Vietnam and the Chinese Model: A Comparative Study of Vietnamese and Chinese Government in the First Half of the Nineteenth Century*
141. George Elision, *Deus Destroyed: The Image of Christianity in Early Modern Japan*
142. William D. Wray, ed., *Managing Industrial Enterprise: Cases from Japan's Prewar Experience*
143. T'ung-tsu Ch'ü, *Local Government in China Under the Ching*
144. Marie Anchordoguy, *Computers, Inc.: Japan's Challenge to IBM*
145. Barbara Molony, *Technology and Investment: The Prewar Japanese Chemical Industry*
146. Mary Elizabeth Berry, *Hideyoshi*
147. Laura E. Hein, *Fueling Growth: The Energy Revolution and Economic Policy in Postwar Japan*
148. Wen-hsin Yeh, *The Alienated Academy: Culture and Politics in Republican China, 1919–1937*
149. Dru C. Gladney, *Muslim Chinese: Ethnic Nationalism in the People's Republic*
150. Merle Goldman and Paul A. Cohen, eds., *Ideas Across Cultures: Essays on Chinese Thought in Honor of Benjamin L Schwartz*
151. James M. Polachek, *The Inner Opium War*
152. Gail Lee Bernstein, *Japanese Marxist: A Portrait of Kawakami Hajime, 1879–1946*
153. Lloyd E. Eastman, *The Abortive Revolution: China Under Nationalist Rule, 1927–1937*
154. Mark Mason, *American Multinationals and Japan: The Political Economy of Japanese Capital Controls, 1899–1980*
155. Richard J. Smith, John K. Fairbank, and Katherine F. Bruner, *Robert Hart and China's Early Modernization: His Journals, 1863–1866*
156. George J. Tanabe, Jr., *Myōe the Dreamkeeper: Fantasy and Knowledge in Kamakura Buddhism*
157. William Wayne Farris, *Heavenly Warriors: The Evolution of Japan's Military, 500–1300*
158. Yu-ming Shaw, *An American Missionary in China: John Leighton Stuart and Chinese-American Relations*
159. James B. Palais, *Politics and Policy in Traditional Korea*
160. Douglas Reynolds, *China, 1898–1912: The Xinzheng Revolution and Japan*

Harvard East Asian Monographs

161. Roger R. Thompson, *China's Local Councils in the Age of Constitutional Reform, 1898–1911*
162. William Johnston, *The Modern Epidemic: History of Tuberculosis in Japan*
163. Constantine Nomikos Vaporis, *Breaking Barriers: Travel and the State in Early Modern Japan*
164. Irmela Hijiya-Kirschnereit, *Rituals of Self-Revelation: Shishōsetsu as Literary Genre and Socio-Cultural Phenomenon*
165. James C. Baxter, *The Meiji Unification Through the Lens of Ishikawa Prefecture*
166. Thomas R. H. Havens, *Architects of Affluence: The Tsutsumi Family and the Seibu-Saison Enterprises in Twentieth-Century Japan*
167. Anthony Hood Chambers, *The Secret Window: Ideal Worlds in Tanizaki's Fiction*
168. Steven J. Ericson, *The Sound of the Whistle: Railroads and the State in Meiji Japan*
169. Andrew Edmund Goble, *Kenmu: Go-Daigo's Revolution*
170. Denise Potrzeba Lett, *In Pursuit of Status: The Making of South Korea's "New" Urban Middle Class*
171. Mimi Hall Yiengpruksawan, *Hiraizumi: Buddhist Art and Regional Politics in Twelfth-Century Japan*
172. Charles Shirō Inouye, *The Similitude of Blossoms: A Critical Biography of Izumi Kyōka (1873–1939), Japanese Novelist and Playwright*
173. Aviad E. Raz, *Riding the Black Ship: Japan and Tokyo Disneyland*
174. Deborah J. Milly, *Poverty, Equality, and Growth: The Politics of Economic Need in Postwar Japan*
175. See Heng Teow, *Japan's Cultural Policy Toward China, 1918–1931: A Comparative Perspective*
176. Michael A. Fuller, *An Introduction to Literary Chinese*
177. Frederick R. Dickinson, *War and National Reinvention: Japan in the Great War, 1914–1919*
178. John Solt, *Shredding the Tapestry of Meaning: The Poetry and Poetics of Kitasono Katue (1902–1978)*
179. Edward Pratt, *Japan's Protoindustrial Elite: The Economic Foundations of the Gōnō*
180. Atsuko Sakaki, *Recontextualizing Texts: Narrative Performance in Modern Japanese Fiction*
181. Soon-Won Park, *Colonial Industrialization and Labor in Korea: The Onoda Cement Factory*
182. JaHyun Kim Haboush and Martina Deuchler, *Culture and the State in Late Chosŏn Korea*
183. John W. Chaffee, *Branches of Heaven: A History of the Imperial Clan of Sung China*
184. Gi-Wook Shin and Michael Robinson, eds., *Colonial Modernity in Korea*
185. Nam-lin Hur, *Prayer and Play in Late Tokugawa Japan: Asakusa Sensōji and Edo Society*
186. Kristin Stapleton, *Civilizing Chengdu: Chinese Urban Reform, 1895–1937*
187. Hyung Il Pai, *Constructing "Korean" Origins: A Critical Review of Archaeology, Historiography, and Racial Myth in Korean State-Formation Theories*

Harvard East Asian Monographs

188. Brian D. Ruppert, *Jewel in the Ashes: Buddha Relics and Power in Early Medieval Japan*
189. Susan Daruvala, *Zhou Zuoren and an Alternative Chinese Response to Modernity*
190. James Z. Lee, *The Political Economy of a Frontier: Southwest China, 1250–1850*
191. Kerry Smith, *A Time of Crisis: Japan, the Great Depression, and Rural Revitalization*
192. Michael Lewis, *Becoming Apart: National Power and Local Politics in Toyama, 1868–1945*
193. William C. Kirby, Man-houng Lin, James Chin Shih, and David A. Pietz, eds., *State and Economy in Republican China: A Handbook for Scholars*
194. Timothy S. George, *Minamata: Pollution and the Struggle for Democracy in Postwar Japan*
195. Billy K. L. So, *Prosperity, Region, and Institutions in Maritime China: The South Fukien Pattern, 946–1368*
196. Yoshihisa Tak Matsusaka, *The Making of Japanese Manchuria, 1904–1932*
197. Maram Epstein, *Competing Discourses: Orthodoxy, Authenticity, and Engendered Meanings in Late Imperial Chinese Fiction*
198. Curtis J. Milhaupt, J. Mark Ramseyer, and Michael K. Young, eds. and comps., *Japanese Law in Context: Readings in Society, the Economy, and Politics*
199. Haruo Iguchi, *Unfinished Business: Ayukawa Yoshisuke and U.S.-Japan Relations, 1937–1952*
200. Scott Pearce, Audrey Spiro, and Patricia Ebrey, *Culture and Power in the Reconstitution of the Chinese Realm, 200–600*
201. Terry Kawashima, *Writing Margins: The Textual Construction of Gender in Heian and Kamakura Japan*
202. Martin W. Huang, *Desire and Fictional Narrative in Late Imperial China*
203. Robert S. Ross and Jiang Changbin, eds., *Re-examining the Cold War: U.S.-China Diplomacy, 1954–1973*
204. Guanhua Wang, *In Search of Justice: The 1905–1906 Chinese Anti-American Boycott*
205. David Schaberg, *A Patterned Past: Form and Thought in Early Chinese Historiography*
206. Christine Yano, *Tears of Longing: Nostalgia and the Nation in Japanese Popular Song*
207. Milena Doleželová-Velingerová and Oldřich Král, with Graham Sanders, eds., *The Appropriation of Cultural Capital: China's May Fourth Project*
208. Robert N. Huey, *The Making of 'Shinkokinshū'*
209. Lee Butler, *Emperor and Aristocracy in Japan, 1467–1680: Resilience and Renewal*
210. Suzanne Ogden, *Inklings of Democracy in China*
211. Kenneth J. Ruoff, *The People's Emperor: Democracy and the Japanese Monarchy, 1945–1995*
212. Haun Saussy, *Great Walls of Discourse and Other Adventures in Cultural China*
213. Aviad E. Raz, *Emotions at Work: Normative Control, Organizations, and Culture in Japan and America*
214. Rebecca E. Karl and Peter Zarrow, eds., *Rethinking the 1898 Reform Period: Political and Cultural Change in Late Qing China*
215. Kevin O'Rourke, *The Book of Korean Shijo*

Harvard East Asian Monographs

216. Ezra F. Vogel, ed., *The Golden Age of the U.S.-China-Japan Triangle, 1972–1989*
217. Thomas A Wilson, ed., *On Sacred Grounds: Culture, Society, Politics, and the Formation of the Cult of Confucius*
218. Donald S. Sutton, *Steps of Perfection: Exorcistic Performers and Chinese Religion in Twentieth-Century Taiwan*
219. Daqing Yang, *Technology of Empire: Telecommunications and Japanese Imperialism, 1930–1945*
220. Qianshen Bai, *Fu Shan's World: The Transformation of Chinese Calligraphy in the Seventeenth Century*
221. Paul Jakov Smith and Richard von Glahn, eds., *The Song-Yuan-Ming Transition in Chinese History*
222. Rania Huntington, *Alien Kind: Foxes and Late Imperial Chinese Narrative*
223. Jordan Sand, *House and Home in Modern Japan: Architecture, Domestic Space, and Bourgeois Culture, 1880–1930*
224. Karl Gerth, *China Made: Consumer Culture and the Creation of the Nation*
225. Xiaoshan Yang, *Metamorphosis of the Private Sphere: Gardens and Objects in Tang-Song Poetry*
226. Barbara Mittler, *A Newspaper for China? Power, Identity, and Change in Shanghai's News Media, 1872–1912*
227. Joyce A. Madancy, *The Troublesome Legacy of Commissioner Lin: The Opium Trade and Opium Suppression in Fujian Province, 1820s to 1920s*

UNIVERSITY OF ST. THOMAS LIBRARIES

HV 5840 .C62 M33 2003
Madancy, Joyce A.
The troublesome legacy of
Commissioner Lin

WITHDRAWN
UST
Libraries